THE COOKBOOK
THAT BECAME A CLASSIC

This is America's bestselling basic cookbook of all-time—the one indispensable cookbook that includes a complete range of recipes in every category: everyday, classic, foreign, and de luxe. Everything needed for the success of a recipe is clearly explained and illustrated, and recipes within a recipe are cross-referenced at the point of use by volume and/or page number. For example, in this volume a recipe to be found in Volume 2, Page 194 will be cross-referenced as (II, 194).

JOY OF COOKING, now being published in two convenient-to-use volumes, has added over 1,200 new recipes, new menus, and new chapters on ingredients and entertaining to the trusted, well-loved material that has made it first among the basic cookbooks for more than a quarter of a century.

JOY OF COOKING
The encyclopedia of cooking know-how

"A masterpiece of clarity."

—*Craig Claiborne*, author,
NEW YORK TIMES COOKBOOK

"As essential as the kitchen range."

—*Clementine Paddleford*,
THIS WEEK Food Editor

Other SIGNET Books of Special Interest

VOLUME I
MAIN COURSE DISHES

JOY OF COOKING

IRMA S. ROMBAUER
MARION ROMBAUER BECKER

ILLUSTRATED BY
Ginnie Hoffmann
AND
Beverly Warner

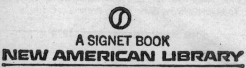

A SIGNET BOOK
NEW AMERICAN LIBRARY
TIMES MIRROR

Published by arrangement with the Bobbs-Merrill Company, Inc.

Ⓞ

SIGNET TRADEMARK REG. U.S. PAT. OFF. AND FOREIGN COUNTRIES
REGISTERED TRADEMARK—MARCA REGISTRADA
HECHO EN CHICAGO, U.S.A.

SIGNET, SIGNET CLASSICS, MENTOR, PLUME, MERIDIAN AND NAL
BOOKS *are published by The New American Library, Inc.,*
1633 Broadway, New York, New York 10019

First Signet Printing, May, 1974

12   13   14   15   16   17   18   19   20

PRINTED IN THE UNITED STATES OF AMERICA

CONTENTS

	PAGE
DEDICATION	vi
Foreword and Guide	vii
The Foods We Eat	1
Beverages	14
Salads	29
The Foods We Heat	72
Soups	106
Cereals and Pastas	153
Eggs, Soufflés and Timbales	183
Brunch, Lunch and Supper Dishes	208
Vegetables	249
Salad Dressings, Sauces, Gravies, Marinades, Glazes and Seasoned Butters	340
Fish	392
Shellfish	421
Meat	449
Game	554
Stuffings, Dressings, Farces or Forcemeat	560
Poultry and Game Birds	567
Index	601

DEDICATION

In revising and reorganizing "The Joy of Cooking" we have missed the help of my mother, Irma S. Rombauer. How grateful I am for her buoyant example, for the strong feeling of roots she gave me, for her conviction that, well-grounded, you can make the most of life, no matter what it brings! In an earlier away-from-home kitchen I acted as tester and production manager for the privately printed first edition of "The Joy." Working with Mother on its development has been for my husband, John, and for me the culmination of a very happy personal relationship. John has always contributed verve to this undertaking, but during the past ten years he has, through his constant support and crisp creative editing, become an integral part of the book. We look forward to a time when our two boys—and their wives—will continue to keep "The Joy" a family affair, as well as an enterprise in which the authors owe no obligation to anyone but themselves—and you.

MARION ROMBAUER BECKER

*"That which thy fathers have bequeathed to thee,
earn it anew if thou wouldst possess it."*

GOETHE: *Faust*

FOREWORD AND GUIDE

"The cook," said Saki, "was a good cook, as cooks go; and as cooks go, she went." Indeed she did go, leaving us, whether in charge of established or of fledgling families, to fend for ourselves. We are confident that after you have used this book steadily for a few months, paying due attention to our symbols ✻, ▲, ( ), ◉, 人, 目, ★, and especially to our "pointers to success" ♦—as identified at the end of the Foreword—you will master the skills the cook walked off with. What is more, we believe that you will go on to unexpected triumphs, based on the sound principles which underlie our recipes, and actually revel in a sense of new-found freedom. You will eat at the hour of your choice. The food will be cooked and seasoned to your discriminating taste. And you will regain the priceless private joy of family living, dining and sharing.

For a number of years, manuscript in hand, I have lunched with friends to whom the preparation and presentation of food is a major interest. At these meetings this text, as it grew, came in for lively critical evaluation. I wish you could have been part of the proceedings, as the chefs, food chemists, processors and artists piled in on the problems which arose, searching for the simplest, the most practical and the most comprehensive approaches to this fresh version of "The Joy," and pored over our new illustrations.

The nucleus of this group included Chef James E. Gregory, American-trained and French-finished, with his flair for making food as appetizing to look at as it is delicious, and Chef Pierre Adrian, at whose restaurant we gathered. Pierre grew up in the Vosges, and has a down-to-earth understanding of food as it comes from the land, coupled with a mastery of the *haute cuisine*.

Other "regulars" were Lolita Harper who, as chief home economist for Cincinnati's utility company, has made a career of rescuing frantic housewives from one dilemma after another; and Luella Schierland, a well-traveled, knowledgeable and skilled hostess. Always present through their handiwork, and sometimes in person, were Ginnie Hofmann and Beverly Warner, whose sensitive response to our layouts resulted in the spirited drawings which make our cooking techniques come alive.

What fun we have had talking out and resolving culinary questions—which I brought back for further scrutiny to the staff at home: to Jane Brueggeman who headed it, and whose unerring common sense and devotion have been invaluable; to Dorothy Wartenberg, our consultant for the English edition; and to Odessa Whitehead, who kept the stove warm and the kitchen bright.

As you can guess, we are also indebted to uncounted friends and "fans" of "The Joy," and to any number of technical consultants, both private and governmental, who have given generously of their time, experience and special competence. Of course, any expression of indebtedness does not discharge us from responsibility for the entire contents of the book—a responsibility which rests with Mother and me as its sole authors.

We have assumed that in buying this book you intend to use it daily. For this reason every effort has been made, space permitting, to provide information at the point of use. Whenever emphasis is needed, when an important principle is involved, we have inserted a "pointer." "Pointers" are vital, friendly reminders which guide you through more exacting processes—beating egg whites, heating delicate food over—not in—hot water, the proper temperatures for holding and storage.

There are also the seven other graphic symbols mentioned in the first paragraph. Among these we have retained from the previous edition the parentheses to indicate that an ingredient is optional: its use may enhance, but its omission will not prejudice, the success of a recipe.

You will notice too that we have attached to certain words, phrases and categories special meanings. For example, any meat, fish, or cereal, unless otherwise specified, is *raw*, not cooked. Again, eggs are the 2-ounce size; milk means fresh whole milk; butter means sweet, unsalted butter; chocolate means bitter baking chocolate; flour denotes the all-purpose variety; spices are ground, not whole; condensed canned soup or milk is to be used undiluted. Recipes which have the word "BLENDER" in their title are only successful when an electric blender is used. Many dishes made with cooked, canned and frozen cooked food are grouped in the chapter BRUNCH, LUNCH AND SUPPER DISHES.

Also, for greater clarity, we define culinary terms for which there are no generally accepted meanings: see the Index for "parboil," "simmer," and "casserole." Finally, in response to many requests from users of "The Joy" who ask "What are your favorites?", we have added to some of our recipes the word "Cockaigne," which signified in medieval times "a mythical land of peace and plenty," and also happens to be the name of our country home.

There are two other parts of the book with which we hope you will quickly acquaint yourself: KNOW YOUR INGREDIENTS, and THE FOODS WE HEAT. Both are brand new. INGREDIENTS will tell you in detail about the properties of the materials you commonly combine in cooking, how and why they react as they do and, when feasible, how to substitute for them. To us, the chapter on HEAT is one of the most important. When you become familiar with its contents you will understand why we assign a high priority to it. And do read the ABOUTS for special information.

We have tried to correlate the entire text so that you can readily find your way around in it. But, as in the past, we have kept in mind the tremendous importance of a detailed Index. Not the least of its virtues is the stimulus it gives to the cook's aspiring eye.

New, too, in this edition is a far more conscious emphasis on interpreting the classic cuisine—those dishes whose circulation is worldwide, and whose traditional language, like that of love and diplomacy, is French. We propose clearing up once and for all the distinctions between terms like *printanière, bonne femme, bordelaise, allemande,* and *polonaise,* while giving at the same time authentic descriptions of such national culinary enthusiasms as *couscous,* Devonshire cream, *strudel, zabaglione* and *rijsttafel.* Actually, the experienced cook will recognize many of these exotics as intimates whom she has known for years in her own kitchen under other names.

Ever since the last revision, a decade ago, we have been refashioning "The Joy" into a handbook which will more faithfully and flexibly meet your needs. How do we know these needs? From the hundreds and hundreds of heart-warming letters which have set out in detail your own experiences with our book, and reflected new tastes and trends in American living. Many of your messages reflected not only the revolution in transport which has made available distant and previously unobtainable foods, but showed a reawakened interest in the cookery of far-off lands.

Most important to us are all of you, both at home and abroad, who are preoccupied every day with that old yet ever-new question, "What shall we have for dinner?" This revision, we hope, is the inclusive and effective answer.

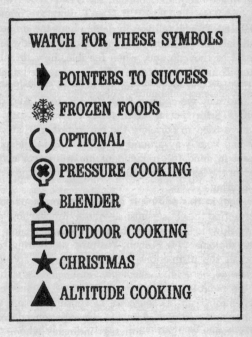

WATCH FOR THESE SYMBOLS

- POINTERS TO SUCCESS
- FROZEN FOODS
- ( ) OPTIONAL
- PRESSURE COOKING
- BLENDER
- OUTDOOR COOKING
- ★ CHRISTMAS
- ▲ ALTITUDE COOKING

THE FOODS WE EAT

We enjoy the cynical story of the old-fashioned doctor who insisted first on going straight to the kitchen of the afflicted household. Not until he had effusively thanked the cook for giving him a new patient did he dash upstairs to see how he could relieve the cook's victim. The fact is that everyone who runs a kitchen can, in the choice and preparation of food, decisively influence family health and happiness.

Nutrition is concerned not with food as such but with the substances that food contains. To present these essential nutrients in the very best state for the body's absorption is the cook's first and foremost job. Usually taste, flavor and color, at their best, reflect a job well done. Read The Foods We Heat, and follow our pointers ▶ for effective ways to preserve nutrients during cooking.

To live we must eat. To live in health we must eat intelligently. By whose intelligence? How directed? The intuitions and impulses of the present generation seem, alas, not to be the kind that led our forebears to search for greens each spring. The sensational press releases which follow the discovery of fascinating fresh bits and pieces about human nutrition confuse the layman. And the oversimplified and frequently ill-founded dicta of food faddists can lure us into downright harm.

On the positive, scientific side we may turn to the helpful information contained in the United States Handbook on the Composition of Foods. For further guidance we print later in this book the daily allowances recommended by the Food and Nutrition Board of the National Research Council as well as calorie values based on the edible portion of common foods. All three are extremely helpful in alerting us to the source-material of a sound dietary. But no one chart or group of charts is the definitive answer for most of us, who are simply not equipped to evaluate the complex relationships of these elements, or to adapt them to the practicalities of daily living. Such studies are built up as averages, and thus have greater value in presenting an overall picture than in solving the nutrition problem of the individual.

Nevertheless, by applying plain common sense to available mass data, we, as well as the experts, are inclined to agree that most Americans are privileged to enjoy superabundance ▶ and that our nutritional difficulties have to do generally not with under- but overeating. Statistics on consumption also bear out other trends: first, that we eat too much of certain kinds of food; and, second, that many of us overconsume drugs as well as foods. Medication, often a lifesaver, may, when used habitually, induce an adverse effect on the body's ability to profit fully from even the best dietary intake.

We must consider, too, that while great strides have been made in the keeping of foods (II, 527), many of today's additives and preserving processes have a devitalizing effect on them. ⟩ If fresh foods are available, and in their prime, start with fresh foods every time. For the relative nutritive values in frozen, canned and dried vegetables, see page 251.

ABOUT CALORIES

With these thoughts in mind, let's review other changing attitudes that underlie today's thinking about nutrition. A too naive theory used to prevail for explaining regeneration through food. The human system was thought of as an engine, and you kept it stoked with foods to produce energy. Food can be and still is measured in units of heat, or calories, a Calorie being the amount of heat needed to raise one kilogram of water one degree Centigrade. Thus translated into food values, each gram of protein—egg, milk, meat, fish—is worth four calories; each gram of carbohydrate —starches and sugars—four calories; and each gram of fat— butters, vegetable oils, drippings, etc.—about nine. The mere stoking of the body's engine with energy-producing foods may keep life going in emergencies. But food, to maintain health, must also have, besides its energy values, the proper proportions of biologic values. Proteins, vitamins, enzymes, hormones, minerals and their regulatory functions are still too complicated to be fully understood. But fortunately for us the body is able to respond to them intuitively and instantly.

What we really possess, then, is not just a simple stoking mechanism, but a computing setup far more elaborate and knowledgeable than anything that man has been able to devise. The body sorts and routes nutrients on their way as soon as they are ingested. Our job is to help it along as much as possible neither stinting it nor overloading it. Depending on age, weight and activity the following is a rough guide to the favorable division of daily caloric intake: about 15% for proteins, under 25% for fats and about 60% for carbohydrates.

ABOUT PROTEINS

A greater and greater emphasis has been placed in recent years on the need for protein at all ages—for proteins contain a great many of the essential elements the body must have to rebuild itself. Proteins are complexly constructed of amino acids, some of which the body can and some of which it cannot manufacture from other substances. So to make food really useful to the body we must include in every meal or snack some of those protein foods that have the non-manufacturable amino acids already built into them. These are present in the most favorable proportions in eggs, milk, meat and fish. They are also present in nuts, seeds, whole grains and legumes. But in such vegetable foods some of the essential aminos are either lacking entirely or are not available in satisfactory proportions. This is why pork is often served with beans, and why pastas are reenforced with cheese, meat or fish—to provide those essential aminos in which the vegetable content of the dish is deficient. Again, complete reliance on grain protein combinations is not nearly as satisfactory as one based on eggs, milk, meat and fish; partly because such large quantities of the grain must be consumed to amass enough proteins whose biologic values approach animal-derived proteins in strength. Climate and age also change protein requirements. The colder the climate the greater the need. ▶ And no matter what the climate, growing children, pregnant women and nursing mothers need a larger proportion of protein than the average adult.

The need in everyone, from birth to death, to establish a kind of "endless chain" of protein intake persists. ▶ Since the vegetable proteins are incomplete, it is wise to draw two-thirds of the daily protein intake from animal sources. Meats should preferably be fresh, not pickled, salted or highly processed. Protein foods should also be very carefully cooked at not too high heat, so that their values are not impaired. Familiar danger signals are curdling in milk, "stringiness" in cheese, dryness in meat and fish.

ABOUT FATS

While fats have fallen into disrepute of late, we must not forget how essential they are. As parts of our body fabric ▶ they act as fuel and insulation against cold, as cushioning for the internal organs, and as lubricants. Without fats there is no way to utilize fat-soluble vitamins. Furthermore the fats we eat which are of vegetable origin contain unsaturated fatty acids which harbor necessary growth factors, and help with the digestion of other fats. For more about the character of fats and their use, see (II, 170).

▶ We suggest, again, the consumption of a variety of fats from animal and vegetable sources; but remind you that the fat consumption of the United States has climbed in twenty years from the recommended minimum of 20 per cent to over 40 per cent today. Check your diet for the percentage you are getting, taking into account that ▶ there are hidden fats in food—as discussed in greater detail on (II, 170).

All fats are sensitive to high temperatures, light and air. For best nutritive values store them carefully; and when cooking with them be sure that you do not let them reach the smoking point. If properly handled they have no adverse effect on normal digestion. Favorable temperatures are indicated in individual recipes. Fats are popular for their flavor, and for the fact that, being slow to leave the stomach, they give a feeling of satiety.

ABOUT CARBOHYDRATES

Vegetables and fruits are included in the carbohydrate category, as well as flour, cereals and sugars. The caloric value of fruits and vegetables is frequently lower than that of cereals; while that of all concentrated sweets is high. It is possible for children and athletes to consume larger amounts of sugars and starches with less harm than more inactive people; but most of us tend to eat a greater amount of carbohydrates than we can handle. Our consumption of sweet and starchy foods, to say nothing of highly sweetened beverages, is frequently excessive. The imbalance that results is acknowledged to be one of the major causes of malnutrition, for the demands excess carbohydrates make on the system may cause a deficiency in its supply of the vitamin B complex.

ABOUT ACCESSORY FACTORS IN FOOD

There are some forty-odd important known minerals, vitamins, enzymes, hormones and other accessory factors which the body needs from the diet. A few it can store; but many must constantly be replaced. These latter, like vitamin C, often occur in those fragile food constituents that are lost through indifferent handling, excessive processing, and poor cooking. To retain as many of them as possible please follow the cooking suggestions given in the chapters on vegetables, meats, fish, eggs and cereals.

While we have printed below the average daily caloric needs, and we have discussed their approximate distribution, we have still to assure ourselves a practical way of including optimal amounts of accessory factors. If you check prime sources of minerals and vitamins you will find that foods rich in one vitamin or mineral may also be rich in others. It happens too that some foods heavily weighted with biologic values yield the best quality proteins. Many of the foods rich in accessory values also have bulk, a factor to be considered in planning the daily intake so as to include more high- than low-residue foods. A few accessory factors the body can store—such as the fat soluble vitamins A, D, E and K. Some, like the water-soluble C and B-complex, must be replenished constantly.

Here is a shopping guide for accessory factors. ♦ Fill your market basket so that it holds a minimum of 2 fruits and 3 vegetables daily. Concentrate on salad materials, especially the lively green ones, and on green and yellow vegetables. Cultivate the cabbage family, root vegetables, potatoes and especially sweet potatoes, tomatoes, peppers and avocados. Include in the fruits apricots, peaches and melons, as well as plenty of citrus types. Be on your guard in distinguishing genuine fruit juices from the so-called "juice drinks," for many of the latter are higher in carbohydrate values than anything else, and their C-vitamin values are frequently low. Prime choices in the protein budget are milk, cheese and eggs, fish and fish roe, organ meats such as liver, kidneys, heart and brains, lean-muscle cuts of beef, pork and lamb, dried peas and beans, especially soybeans and peanuts. See triple-rich Cornell Flour Formula (II, 243). Include also 1 tablespoon daily of butter or fortified fat or oil, and 1 pint of milk or equivalent milk products. Bake with whole grains and flavor with brown sugar, molasses, wheat germ and butter. Don't forget the cheapest of all accessory factors, outdoor exercise, to whet your appetite, tone your muscles and get you out where you absorb the sunlight vitamin D.

Other incidentals to bear in mind are to drink seven or eight glasses of fluid a day, see About Water (II, 147), and to use iodized salt, see About Salt (II, 195), if you live in ⅃ region that calls for it.

The schedule outlined above is not necessarily a costly one. It is nearly always possible to substitute cheaper but equally nutritious items from the same food groups. Vegetables of similar accessory value, for example, may be differently priced. Seasonal foods, which automatically give us menu variations, are usually higher in food value and lower in cost. Whole-grain cereals are no more costly than highly processed ones. Fresh fruits are frequently less expensive than canned fruits loaded with sugar.

If you are willing to cut down on refined starch and sugar items, especially fancy baked goods, bottled drinks and candies, a higher percentage of the diet dollar will be released for dairy products, vegetables and fruits. Do not buy more perishable foods than you can properly store. Use leftovers cold, preferably. To reheat them with minimal loss, see page 98.

Summing up, our fundamental effort always must be to provide this highly versatile body of ours with those elements it needs for efficient functioning, and to provide them in such proportions as to subject it to the least possible strain.

Well-grown minimally processed foods are usually our best sources for complete nourishment; and a well-considered choice of them should in most cases meet our needs without the use of synthetic vitamin preparations.

You will find in this book, along with the classic recipes, a number which remain interesting and palatable although they lack some usual ingredient, like eggs, flour or fat, and which may be used by those who may be allergic. But we do not prescribe corrective diets, feeling that such situations demand special procedures in consultation with one's physician. As to the all-too-prevalent condition of overweight, it is now generally recognized that the on and off use of crash reducing diets is dangerous, and that re-education in moderate eating habits is the only safe and permanent solution to this problem.

We stress again that the housewife who has the responsibility for supplying her family with food will do well to keep alert to advances in the field of nutrition and to the individual needs of herself and her family.

CALORIE VALUES

"Personal size and mental sorrow have certainly no necessary proportions. A large, bulky figure has as good a right to be in deep affliction as the most graceful set of limbs in the world. But, fair or not fair, there are unbecoming conjunctions, which reason will patronize in vain—which taste cannot tolerate—which ridicule will seize."
—Jane Austen.

The following calorie list is given hopefully to offset those "unbecoming conjunctions." We have tried, from data furnished by the U.S. Department of Agriculture and other authoritative sources, to give you as accurate a calorie count as possible for an average individual serving of food as it comes to you at table. In each instance, the number of calories is based on the total edible portion. These are not diet portions. Smaller servings of the foods mentioned will mean a proportionate reduction in their calorie count. Our soup figures are for canned soups diluted with the same amount of water—or whole milk, in the case of cream soups—unless we specify them as home-made. A cup is the standard 8 oz. measure, and a tablespoon or teaspoon is always a level one. Since we do not expect you to weigh your food at table, this chart should give you a fairly accurate guide for normal servings to a healthy adult. Remember, however, that two martinis before dinner count as much as a generous slice of pie for dessert and, if you are trying to keep your weight constant, second thoughts are better than second helpings. In addition,

"Let your contours be your guide."

Food	Calories
Almonds, 12 to 14 shelled	100
Apple, 1 medium-sized, baked with 2 tablespoons sugar	200
Apple, 1 large fresh, 3″ diam.	117
Apple butter, 1 tablespoon	37
Apple dumpling, 1 medium-sized	235
Apple juice, 1 cup	126
Apple pie, ⅙ of 9″ pie	377
Applesauce, sweetened, ½ cup	92
Applesauce, unsweetened, ½ cup	50
Apricots, canned, sweetened, 4 halves, 2 tablespoons juice	80
Apricots, dried, stewed, sweetened, 4 halves, 2 tablespoons juice	123
Apricots, 3 whole fresh	60
Artichoke, globe, 1 large, cooked	51
Artichoke, Jerusalem, 4 small	70
Asparagus, 8 stalks	25
Asparagus soup, cream of, 1 cup	160
Avocado, ½ medium-sized	275
Bacon, 1 crisp 6″ strip	48
Banana, 1 medium-sized	130
Banana cream pie, ⅙ of 9″ pie	300
Batter cakes, 2	150
Beans, baked, canned, ½ cup	162
Beans, green or snap, ½ cup cooked	13
Beans, kidney, ½ cup cooked	115
Beans, Lima, ½ cup cooked or canned	80
Beans, navy pea, ½ cup cooked	118
Bean soup, 1 cup, homemade	260
Bean sprouts, Mung, ½ cup cooked	13

Food	Calories
Bean sprouts, ½ cup raw	10
Beef, corned, 3 oz., 3 slices 3″ x 2½″ x ¼″	216
Beef, corned, hash, ½ cup	145
Beef, dried, 2 thin slices 4″ x 5″	61
Beef, 1 filet mignon, 4 oz.	400
Beef, hamburger, 1 large patty	300
Beef heart, 3 oz.	118
Beef loaf, 1 slice 2½″ x 2¼″ x ⅝″	115
Beef, rib roast, 3″ x 2½″ x ¼″ slice	96
Beef soup, 1 cup	113
Beefsteak, sirloin, 3 oz.	300
Beef stew, 1 cup	260
Beef tongue, 3 slices, 3″ x 2″ x ⅛″	160
Beer, 12 oz. can or bottle	173
Beer, 1 glass, 8 oz.	115
Beet greens, ½ cup cooked	30
Beets, ½ cup	40
Berry pies, ⅙ of 9″ pie, average	365
Biscuit, baking powder, 2½″ diam.	130
Blackberries, fresh, ¾ cup	62
Blueberries, fresh, ¾ cup	64
Bologna sausage, 1 slice, 4½″ diam. x ⅛″	66
Bouillon, 1 cup	32
Bouillon cube, 1	2
Brazil nut, 1 shelled	50
Bread, commercial, rye, 1 slice, ½″ thick	55
Bread, commercial, white, 1 slice, ½″ thick	60–65
Bread, commercial, whole wheat, 1 slice, ½″ thick	55
Bread, gluten, 1 slice, 4″ x 4″ x ⅜″	64
Bread pudding, ½ cup	200
Broccoli, 1 large stalk or ⅔ cup, cooked	29
Brown Betty, ½ cup	254
Brussels sprouts, ½ cup, approx. 5	30
Butter, 1 square, ¼″ thick	50
Butter, 1 tablespoon	100
Buttermilk, 1 glass, 8 oz.	85

Food	Calories	Food	Calories
Cabbage, ½ cup chopped, raw	10	Chicken, fried, ½ breast	232
Cabbage, ½ cup, cooked	20	Chicken, fried, drumstick	64
Cake, angel, plain, 3″ slice	150	Chicken livers, 1 medium-large liver	74
Cake, cheese, 2″ wedge	250	Chicken pie, 1 individual pie 3¾″ diameter	460
Cake, chocolate layer, 2″ square	356	Chicken, roasted,	
Cake, coffee, 1 piece 3″ x 2½″ x 2″	133	Chicken, roasted, 4″ x 4″ x ¾″ slice, dark meat	170
Cake, cup, 1 medium-sized, frosted	229	Chicken, roasted, 4″ x 4″ x ¾″ slice, light meat	166
Cake, fruit, dark, 1 small slice ½″ thick	142	Chicken salad, ½ cup	200
Cake, sponge, 2″ slice	145	Chicory, or Curly Endive, 15 to 20 inner leaves	10
Cantaloupe, ½ of a 4½″ melon	30	Chocolate, 1 cup made with milk	277
Caramels, 1 medium	42	Chocolate bar, milk, 1 oz.	154
Carbonated water	0	Chocolate creams, 1 small	51
Carrots, ½ cup cooked	30	Chocolate éclair, custard filling, 1 average-size	316
Carrot, 1 whole raw, small	20		
Cashew nuts, 6 to 8	88	Chocolate fudge, 1″ square	100
Catsup, 1 tablespoon	17	Chocolate ice cream, ½ cup	180
Cauliflower, cooked, 1 cup	30		
Caviar, granular sturgeon, 1 tablespoon	66	Chocolate malted milk, made with 8 oz. milk	502
Celeriac, 1 medium-sized	40	Chocolate milk shake, made with 8 oz. milk	421
Celery, raw, 3 small inner stalks	9	Chocolate soda	255
Charlotte Russe, 1 serving	265	Cinnamon bun, 1 average	200
Cheese, American, 1″ cube	79	Clam chowder, Manhattan, 1 cup	87
Cheese, Camembert, 2″ wedge	220	Cocoa, made with milk and water, 1 cup	150
Cheese, cottage, ½ cup	100	Cocoa, made with whole milk, 1 cup	232
Cheese, cream, ½ 3 oz. cake	159	Coconut, shredded, dried, 2 tablespoons	83
Cheese, Edam, 1″ cube	51		
Cheese, Liederkranz, 1 oz.	85	Coconut custard pie, ⅛ of 9″ pie	311
Cheese, Parmesan, grated 1 tablespoon	20	Codfish, creamed, ½ cup	200
Cheese, Roquefort, 1″ cube	39	Codfish balls, 2 of 2″ diameter	200
Cheese, Swiss, 1 oz.	105	Cod liver oil, 1 tablespoon	100
Cheese soufflé, 1 cup	238	Coffee, clear, 1 cup	0
Cheese straws, 3	100	Coffee, with 1 tablespoon cream, 1 cup	30
Chef salad without dressing, ¾ cup	90		
Cherries, canned, sweetened, ½ cup	100	Coffee with 1 lump sugar, 1 cup	27
Cherries, fresh, sweet, 15 large	61	Cola beverages, 1 glass, 8 oz.	105
Chicken, broiler, ½ medium	125	Consommé, canned, 1 cup	35
Chicken, canned, ½ cup boned meat	200	Cookies, sugar, 1 3″ diameter	64

Food	Calories	Food	Calories
Corn bread, 1 square 2" x 2" x 1"	139	Egg, 1 whole, boiled or poached	75
Corn, canned, ½ cup drained solids	70	Eggnog, ½ cup	196
Corn flakes, ¾ cup	62	Eggplant, 2 slices ½" thick, breaded and fried	210
Corn meal, cooked, ⅔ cup	80	Egg yolk, 1 raw	61
Corn on cob, 1 medium	92		
Corn sirup, 1 tablespoon	57	Farina, ¾ cup cooked	100
Corn soup, cream, ½ cup	100	Fig, 1 large dried	55
Cornstarch blancmange, ½ cup	152	Figs, 3 small fresh	79
Crab meat, canned, ½ cup	91	Flounder, baked, average serving	204
Crab meat fresh, ½ cup	54	Frankfurters, 1	125
Cracker, graham, 1 2½" square	14	French dressing, commercial, 1 tablespoon	59
Crackers, oyster, 12 1"	50	French dressing, home-made, no sugar, 1 tablespoon	86
Cracker, saltine, 1 2" square	17	French toast, 1 piece	170
Cracker, soda, 1 #2 ½" square	24	Frog legs, 2 large, fried	140
Cracker, butter, 1	16	Fruit cocktail, fresh, ½ cup	50
Cranberry jelly, 2 tablespoons	47	Fruit cocktail, canned, drained, ½ cup	50
Cream, coffee, 18.5% fat, 2 tablespoons	60	Fruit cocktail, fresh, with 1 tablespoon dressing	150
Cream, cultured, sour, 1 tablespoon	45		
Cream soups, canned	250		
Cream, whipping, 36%–40% fat, 2 tablespoons	98	Gelatin, dry, 1 tablespoon	34
Cream of wheat, cooked ¾ cup	100	Gelatin dessert, ½ cup	103
		Gin, 1 oz.	70
Cream sauce, white, ¼ cup	180	Ginger ale, 1 cup	80
Cucumber, 12 slices	10	Gingerbread, 1 2" square	200
Custard, ½ cup	164	Ginger snap, 1	20
Custard pie, ⅙ of 9" pie	266	Goose, roast, 3½ oz. serving	354
		Gooseberries, cooked, sweetened, ½ cup	100
Daiquiri cocktail, 3 oz.	130	Grapefruit, ½ medium	70
Dates, 3 or 4	85	Grapefruit juice, unsweetened, 1 cup	92
Divinity, 1½" cube	102	Grape juice, 1 glass, 8 oz.	178
Doughnut, cake type, plain, 1	135	Grapes, green seedless, 60	66
Doughnut, sugared, 1	151	Grapes, Malaga or Tokay, 22	66
Doughnut, yeast, plain, 1	121	Gravy, thick, 3 tablespoons	180
Duck, roast, 1 medium piece	300	Green pepper, 1 whole	20
Dumpling, 1 small	100	Griddle cakes, 2 of 4" diam.	150
		Grits, hominy, cooked, ¾ cup	90
Egg, 1 fried with 1 teaspoon butter	105	Guavas, 1 medium	70
Egg, 1 scrambled with 2 tablespoons milk and 1 teaspoon butter	130	Gum drop, 1 large	35

Food	Calories
Haddock, 1 fillet 3″ x 3″ x ½″, fried	214
Halibut steak, 3″ x ½″ x 1″, sautéed	125
Ham, baked, medium fat, 4¼″ x 4″ x ½″ slice	400
Ham, boiled, 4¼″ x 4″ x ¼″ slice	200
Hamburger—see Beef	
Hard Sauce, 1 tablespoon	50
Herring, fresh, 3 oz.	128
Herring, pickled Bismarck, 3½″ x 1½″ x 1¼″	218
Herring, smoked, 3 oz.	200
Hickory nuts, about 12	100
Hollandaise sauce, 1 tablespoon	65
Honey, 1 tablespoon	62
Honeydew melon, ¼ medium-sized	32
Horseradish, grated, 1 tablespoon	12
Ice cream, commercial, plain, ½ cup	100–150
Jam or jelly, 1 tablespoon	60
Kale, 1 cup, cooked	50
Kidneys, beef, braised, 3 ½ oz.	159
Kohlrabi, ½ cup, cooked	23
Kumquats, 3	35
Lady fingers, 1	37
Lamb, roast leg, 2 slices 3″ x 3¼″ x ⅛″	206
Lamb chop, broiled, 1 ¾″ thick	175
Lamb stew with vegetables, 1 cup	250
Lard, 1 tablespoon	126
Leek, 1	10
Lemon, 1 medium-sized	30
Lemonade, 1 cup	100
Lemon gelatin, ½ cup	100
Lemon ice, ½ cup	116
Lemon juice, 1 tablespoon	4
Lemon meringue pie, ⅛ of 9″ pie	280
Lentil soup, 1 cup, home-made	606

Food	Calories
Lettuce, iceberg, ¼ large head	18
Lettuce, 6 large leaves	18
Lime juice, 1 tablespoon	4
Liver, beef, fried, 2 slices 3″ x 2¼″ x ⅜″	175
Liver, calf, fried, 2 slices 3″ x 2¼″ x ⅜″	147
Liverwurst or liver sausage, 2 slices 3″ diam. x ¼″	160
Lobster, canned, 1 cup	108
Lobster, fresh, 1 cup	105
Lobster, whole, small, baked or broiled with 2 tablespoons butter	308
Loganberries, canned, ½ cup	55
Macaroni, cooked, plain, ½ cup	110
Macaroni and cheese, ½ cup	300
Mackerel, broiled, 3 oz.	200
Malted milk, 8 oz.	270
Mangoes, tropical, 1 large	85
Manhattan cocktail, 3 oz.	160
Maple sirup, 1 tablespoon	50
Margarine, 1 tablespoon	100
Marmalade, 2 tablespoons	120
Marshmallows, 5	125
Martini cocktail, 3 oz. 3:1	145
Mayonnaise, 1 tablespoon	109
Meat loaf, beef and pork, 1 slice 4″ x 3″ x ⅜″	264
Melba toast, 1 slice 4″ x 4″	39
Milk, condensed, sweetened, ½ cup	490
Milk, evaporated, ½ cup	173
Milk, half and half, ½ cup	165
Milk, powdered, skim, 1 tablespoon	28
Milk, powdered, whole, 1 tablespoon	40
Milk, skimmed, 1 cup	88
Milk, whole fresh, 1 cup	166
Mincemeat pie, ⅛ of 9″ pie	398
Mints, chocolate cream, 3 small	100
Molasses, 1 tablespoon	55
Muffin, 2″ diameter	120
Muffin, English, 1 large	280
Mushrooms, canned, ½ cup	14
Mushrooms, fresh, 10 small	16

Food	Calories	Food	Calories
Mushrooms, sautéed, 7 small	78	Pepper, green, 1 medium-sized	25
Mustard greens, cooked, 1 cup	60	Perch, breaded and fried, 3 oz.	195
Mutton—see Lamb		Persimmons, 1 medium-sized	78
Nectarine, 1	40	Pickles, cucumber, 1 large dill	15
Noodles, egg, cooked, ½ cup	100	Pickles, cucumber, 1 sweet-sour	20
		Pigs' feet, pickled, ½ foot	125
Oatmeal, cooked, ½ cup	75	Pineapple, canned, 1 slice with juice	78
Okra, 10 pods	38	Pineapple, fresh, ½ cup sliced	52
Old-fashioned cocktail, 1 glass	185	Pineapple ice, ½ cup	120
Olive oil, 1 tablespoon	124	Pineapple juice, 1 cup	120
Olives, green, 2 small or 1 large	20	Plums, fresh, 3 or 4	100
Olives, ripe, 2 small or 1 large	25	Plums, canned, 3 or 4 with juice	150
Onion soup, 1 cup	100	Pimiento, canned, 1 medium	10
Onions, 4 small	100	Popcorn, 1½ cups, no butter	100
Onions, creamed, ⅓ cup	100	Popover, 1	100
Onions, raw green, 5 medium	23	Pork chop, rib, broiled, 3" x 5" x 1"	290
Orange, 1 average-sized	75	Pork roast, 4 oz.	450
Orange ice, ½ cup	110	Pork tenderloin, 2 oz.	200
Orange juice, 1 cup	110	Potato, baked, 1 medium-sized	90
Oxtail soup, 1 cup	100	Potato, boiled, 1 medium-sized	90
Oysters, raw, 6 medium	75	Potato chips, 8 to 10 large	100
Oyster stew, with milk, 1 cup	275	Potato salad, ½ cup	167
		Potato, sweet, baked, 1 medium-sized	155
Pancake, 1 4" dia.	75	Potatoes, French-fried, 10 pieces	155
Papaya, ½ medium	72	Potatoes, mashed, 1 cup, milk and butter added	230
Parsley, chopped, 2 tablespoons	2	Praline, 1	300
Parsnips, cooked, ½ cup	65	Preserves, 1 tablespoon	75
Peaches, canned, 2 halves with 2 tablespoons juice	85	Pretzels, 5 small sticks	20
Peach, fresh, 1 large	50	Prune juice, 1 cup	170
Peanut butter, 2 tablespoons	180	Prunes, dried, 1 large	25
Peanuts, 20 to 24 nuts	100	Prunes, stewed, 4 medium with 2 tablespoons juice	120
Pears, canned, 2 halves with 2 tablespoons juice	85	Pumpkin, 1 cup	76
Pear, fresh, 1 medium-sized	60	Pumpkin pie, ⅛ of 9" pie	300
Peas, canned, ½ cup	73		
Peas, dried, cooked, ½ cup	103	Rabbit, baked, 3½ oz.	177
Peas, fresh, cooked, ½ cup	56	Radishes, 5 medium	10
Pea soup, cream, 1 cup	270		
Pecans, 6 halves or 2 tablespoons chopped	52		

Food	Calories	Food	Calories
Raisins, seedless, ¼ cup	107	Sole, Dover, steamed, 3½ oz.	84
Raspberries, red, fresh, ½ cup	42	Sole, fillet—see Flounder	
Raspberries, red, frozen, sweetened, ½ cup	120	Soybeans, dried, cooked, ½ cup	120
Red snapper, baked, 3" x ½" x 4"	183	Spaghetti, plain, cooked, 1 cup	218
Rhubarb, fresh, 1 cup diced	20	Spareribs, meat from 6 average-sized ribs	246
Rhubarb, stewed, sweetened, ½ cup	137	Spinach, cooked and chopped, ½ cup	23
Rice, brown, cooked, ½ cup	100	Spinach soup, cream, 1 cup	240
Rice, white, cooked, ½ cup	100	Split pea soup, 1 cup	268
Rice, wild, cooked, ⅔ cup	103	Squab, 1 whole, unstuffed, 2½ oz. meat	149
Roll, hard, white, 1 average-sized	95	Squash, Hubbard or winter, cooked, ½ cup	50
Roll, Parker House, 1	81	Squash, summer, cooked, ½ cup	19
Rum, 1 oz.	73		
Rutabagas, cooked, ½ cup	25	Starch, cornstarch, etc., 1 tablespoon	29
		Strawberries, fresh, ½ cup	30
Salmon, canned, ½ cup	206	Strawberries, frozen, sweetened, ½ cup	120
Salmon, fresh, poached, 3½ oz.	200	Strawberry shortcake with cream, average serving	350
Sardines, canned, 4 large	100	Succotash, canned, ½ cup	85
Sauerkraut, ⅔ cup	27	Sugar, brown, 1 tablespoon	50
Sauerkraut juice, ½ cup	4	Sugar, confectioners', 1 tablespoon	42
Sausage, pork link, 3" x ½"	94	Sugar, granulated, 1 tablespoon	50
Scallops, fried, 5 to 6 medium-sized pieces	427	Sweetbreads, broiled, ½ pair medium	185
Shad roe, sautéed, average serving	175	Swordfish, average serving	180
Sherbets, ½ cup	135	Tangerine, 1	35
Sherry, dry, 3 oz.	110	Tangerine juice, ½ cup	50
Sherry, sweet, 3 oz.	150	Tapioca pudding, ½ cup	133
Shortcake with ½ cup berries and cream, 1 medium-sized biscuit	350	Tartar sauce, 1 tablespoon	100
		Tea, clear, unsweetened, 1 cup	0
Shredded wheat biscuit, 1 large	100	Tomatoes, canned, 1 cup	50
Shrimp, boiled, 5 large	70	Tomato catsup, 1 tablespoon	17
Shrimp, fried, 4 large	259	Tomato, fresh, 1 medium-sized	25
Shrimp cocktail with sauce, ½ cup	100	Tomato juice, 1 cup	50
Sirup, corn, 1 tablespoon	57	Tomato purée, 1 tablespoon	6
Smelts, baked or broiled, 4 or 5 medium-sized	91		
Smelts, fried, 4 to 5 medium-sized	448		
Snow pudding, ⅔ cup	114		
Sole, Dover, fried, 3½ oz.	241	Tomato soup, clear, 1 cup	100

Food	Calories	Food	Calories
Tomato soup, cream, home-made, 1 cup	250	Venison, baked, 3 slices 3½″ x 2½″ x ¼″	200
Tripe, cooked in milk, average serving	150	Waffles, 1, 5½″ diameter	232
Trout, brook, broiled, 3 oz.	216	Waldorf salad, average serving	137
Trout, lake, broiled, 3 oz.	290	Walnuts, English, 4 to 8 halves	50
Tuna fish, canned, water packed, ½ cup	165	Water cress, 1 bunch	20
Tuna fish, canned in oil, ½ cup	300	Watermelon, 1 slice, ¾″ thick, 6″ diameter	90
Turkey, roast, dark meat, 4″ x 4″ x ¾″	205	Welsh rarebit, 4 tablespoons on 1 slice toast	200
Turkey, roast, light meat, 4″ x 4″ x ¾″	183	Whisky, bourbon, 1 oz.	83
Turnip greens, cooked, 1 cup	45	Whisky, Scotch, 1 oz.	73
Turnips, cooked, 1 cup	40	Whitefish, average serving	100
		White sauce, ¼ cup	106
Veal chop, loin, fried, 1 medium-sized	186	Wines, dry, 3 oz.	65–95
Veal cutlet, breaded, average serving	217	Wines, sweet or fortified, 3 oz.	120–160
Veal roast, 2 slices 3″ x 2″ x ⅛″	186	Yams—see Potatoes, sweet	
Veal stew, 1 cup	242	Yeast, brewers, 2 teaspoons	18
Vegetable cooking fats, 1 tablespoon	110	Yeast, compressed, 1 cake	10
Vegetable juice, 1 cup	48	Yogurt, whole milk, ½ cup	83
Vegetable soup, 1 cup	100	Zucchini, cooked, 1 cup	40
		Zwieback, 1 slice	35

RECOMMENDED DAILY DIETARY ALLOWANCES (ABRIDGED)[1]

[DESIGNED FOR THE MAINTENANCE OF GOOD NUTRITION OF HEALTHY PERSONS IN THE U.S.A.]

Persons	Age in years From up to	Weight in pounds	Height in inches	Food energy Calories	Protein Grams	Calcium Grams	Iron Milligrams	Vitamin A International units	Thiamin Milligrams	Riboflavin Milligrams	Niacin equivalent[2] Milligrams	Ascorbic acid Milligrams
Infants	0–⅙	9	22	lb. x 54.5	lb. x 1.0	0.4	6	1,500	0.2	0.4	5	30
	⅙–½	15	25	lb. x 54.0	lb. x .9	0.5	10	1,500	0.4	0.5	7	35
	½–1	20	28	lb. x 45.5	lb. x .8	0.6	15	1,500	0.5	0.6	8	35
Children	1–2	26	32	1,100	25	0.7	15	2,000	0.6	0.6	8	40
	2–3	31	36	1,250	25	0.8	15	2,000	0.6	0.7	8	40
	3–4	35	39	1,400	30	0.8	10	2,500	0.7	0.8	9	40
	4–6	42	43	1,600	30	0.8	10	2,500	0.8	0.9	11	40
	6–8	51	48	2,000	35	0.9	10	3,500	1.0	1.1	13	40
	8–10	62	52	2,200	40	1.0	10	3,500	1.1	1.2	15	40
Boys	10–12	77	55	2,500	45	1.2	10	4,500	1.3	1.3	17	40
	12–14	95	59	2,700	50	1.4	18	5,000	1.4	1.4	18	45
	14–18	130	67	3,000	60	1.4	18	5,000	1.5	1.5	20	55
Men	18–22	147	69	2,800	60	0.8	10	5,000	1.4	1.6	18	60
	22–35	154	69	2,800	65	0.8	10	5,000	1.4	1.7	18	60
	35–55	154	68	2,600	65	0.8	10	5,000	1.3	1.7	17	60
	55–75+	154	67	2,400	65	0.8	10	5,000	1.2	1.7	14	60
Girls	10–12	77	56	2,250	50	1.2	18	4,500	1.1	1.3	15	40
	12–14	97	61	2,300	50	1.3	18	5,000	1.2	1.4	15	45
	14–16	114	62	2,400	55	1.3	18	5,000	1.2	1.4	16	50
	16–18	119	63	2,300	55	1.3	18	5,000	1.2	1.5	15	50
Women	18–22	128	64	2,000	55	0.8	18	5,000	1.0	1.5	13	55
	22–35	128	64	1,900	55	0.8	18	5,000	1.0	1.5	13	55
	35–55	128	63	1,850	55	0.8	18	5,000	1.0	1.5	13	55
	55–75+	128	62	1,700	55	0.8	18	6,000	1.0	1.5	13	55
Pregnant				+200	65	+0.4	18	6,000	+0.1	1.8	15	60
Lactating				+1,000	75	+0.5	18	8,000	+0.5	2.0	20	60

1 Source: Adapted from Recommended Dietary Allowances, Seventh Edition 1968. Publication 1694, 169 pages. Published by National Academy of Sciences—National Research Council, Washington D.C. 20418. Also available in libraries. This publication includes discussion of allowances, eight additional nutrients, and adjustments needed for age, body size, and physical activity.

2 Niacin equivalents include dietary sources of the vitamin itself plus 1 milligram equivalent for each 60 milligrams of dietary tryptophan.

3 Entries for age range 22 to 35 years represent the reference man and woman at age 22. All other entries represent allowances for the midpoint of the specified age group.

NOTE.—The Recommended Daily Dietary Allowances should not be confused with Minimum Daily Requirements. The Recommended Dietary Allowances are amounts of nutrients recommended by the Food and Nutrition Board of National Research Council as considered adequate for maintenance of good nutrition in healthy persons in the United States. The allowances are revised from time to time in accordance with newer knowledge of nutritional needs.

The Minimum Daily Requirements are the amounts of selected nutrients that have been established by the Food and Drug Administration as standards for labeling purposes of foods and pharmaceutical preparations for special dietary uses. These are the amounts regarded as necessary in the diet for the prevention of deficiency diseases and generally are less than the Recommended Dietary Allowances.

BEVERAGES

As our friend, Edgar Anderson, points out in his stimulating book, "Plants, Man and Life," primitive man located the only sources of caffeine known to this day: in tea, coffee, cola, cocoa and yerba maté and its relatives. Other less brisk brews have been made from leaves, roots, bark, blossoms and seeds. In France, for example, the tisane mentioned so lovingly by Colette is frequently served as a comforting after-dinner drink, page 20. If you don't grow and dry your own herbs, the drugstore will do very well as a source.

The recipes in this chapter, except for a few variations under Coffee and Tea, are nonalcoholic. For alcoholic liquors of all kinds, their preparation and use, see Drinks (II, 25). Remember that, in any beverage you may brew, the quality of the water greatly affects results.

ABOUT COFFEE

Coffee has always thrived on adversity—just as people in adversity have thrived on it. When this beverage began its highly successful career, the Mohammedan priesthood identified it with wine—a new kind of wine which was all the more offensive to Koranic teaching because it did not merely loosen men's tongues, but sharpened their critical faculties.

Thanks especially to vacuum-packed cans, making good coffee at home has become a surefire delight. Of the several ways of preparing this beverage, we prefer the drip method. Vacuum preparation and the percolator have their advocates, too; but we regard them as, respectively, more troublesome and less apt to produce fresh flavor. The steeped-coffee recipe which follows is suggested for campers or others who happen to lack any equipment more specialized than a saucepan. Illustrated are two devices for making filtered coffee: the first employs a metal filter, the second, which is made of chemical glass, uses a paper filter folded into conical shape.

The latter gives a pure essence, with no sediment—which a coffee connoisseur demands in a perfect brew. Also sketched is the proper equipment for Caffè Espresso and Turkish coffee.

Whatever device you choose ◗ follow the directions of its manufacturer carefully, especially as to the grind recommended—regular, drip or fine. In each case, to assure a full-bodied brew, ◗ use not less than 2 level tablespoons of coffee to each ¾ cup of freshly drawn water. Other things to remember are: use soft, not softened or hard, water; when brewing coffee keep the coffeemaker almost full; time your method consistently; keep the coffeemaker scrupulously clean, rinsing it with water in which a few teaspoons of baking soda have been dissolved and always scalding it before re-use. If cloth filters are required, do not allow them to become dry, but keep them immersed in cold water. ◗ Never boil coffee, since boiling brings out the tannic acid in the bean and makes for a bitter as well as a cloudy brew. Remember that any moisture activates coffee and that water between 200°–205° is ideal for extracting flavor without drawing acids. Never, of course, re-use coffee grounds.

If coffee is ground in the household, it should be done in small quantities, in a meticulously clean grinder. Open only one can at a time. Store ground coffee in a tightly closed jar in the refrigerator.

For those who love coffee but are highly sensitive to caffeine or in whom it induces insomnia, we suggest the use of a decaffeinized product rather than a coffee substitute. It may be helpful to remember also, that certain varieties of coffee—such as those grown in Puerto Rico—have a substantially lower caffeine content than the typical Brazilian or Colombian bean.

For those who hanker after coffee such as the kind their German grandmother used to make or a brew which reminds them of that little brasserie on the Left Bank, the answer may be to add an ounce of ground chicory to a cup of ground coffee before brewing. ◗ When cream is used in coffee, allow it to reach room temperature beforehand, so as to cool the drink as little as possible. For coffee-chocolate combinations, see About Chocolate, page 20, and Brazilian Chocolate, page 21.

DRIP COFFEE OR CAFÉ FILTRÉ

Place finely ground coffee in drip filter.
Allow:

> 2 tablespoons coffee for
> each ¾ to 1 cup water

Pour freshly boiled water over the coffee. When the dripping process is complete, serve coffee at once. Dripping coffee more than once, contrary to popular belief, does not strengthen the brew.
Serve with a:

> Twist of lemon peel

VACUUM-METHOD COFFEE

Allow:

> 2 tablespoons regular or
> fine-ground coffee for
> every
> ¾ to 1 cup water

Measure water into lower bowl. Place on heat. Place a wet filter in upper bowl and add the ground coffee. Insert upper bowl into lower one with a light twist to insure a tight seal. Insert it at this time or not, depending on your equipment. If your equipment has a vented stem, you may place it on the heat already assembled. If it does not have this small hole on the side of the tube above the hot-water line, wait until the water is actively boiling before putting the upper bowl in place. When nearly all the water has risen into the upper bowl—some of it will always remain below—stir the water and coffee thoroughly. In 1 to 3 minutes, the shorter time for the finer grinds, remove from heat.

PERCOLATED COFFEE

Place in the percolator:
> ¾ to 1 cup cold water for every 2 tablespoons coffee you have measured into the percolator basket

When water boils, remove percolator from heat. Put in the basket. Cover percolator, return to heat and allow to percolate slowly 6 to 8 minutes. Remove the coffee basket and serve.
◗ Over-percolating does not make coffee stronger. It impairs its flavor.

STEEPED COFFEE

Place in a pot:
> 2 tablespoons regular or fine grind coffee to each ¾ to 1 cup freshly boiling water

Stir the coffee for at least ½ minute. Let it stand covered in a pan of boiling water from 5 to 10 minutes, depending on the grind and the strength of brew desired. Pour the coffee off the grounds through a strainer; or, if preferred, settle the grounds by stirring into the pot before draining:
> (1 slightly beaten egg)

The egg merely serves to clarify the coffee. If anything, it detracts from rather than adds to its flavor.

COFFEE IN QUANTITY   [40 to 50]

Put in a cheesecloth bag large enough to allow for double expansion:
> 1 lb. medium-grind coffee

Shortly before serving, have ready a kettle holding:
> 5 to 7 quarts water

Bring the water to a boil. Place the coffee-filled bag in it. Permit to stand in a warm place from 7 to 10 minutes. Agitate the bag several times during this period. Remove bag, cover kettle, serve at once.

INSTANT COFFEE

The polls are against us, but we really can't yet regard the jiffy product as in any way comparable to the one that takes a few minutes longer to prepare. If you insist, use for each serving:
> 1 teaspoon instant coffee 5½ oz. boiling water

For 6 servings:
> 6 teaspoons instant coffee 1 quart boiling water

Add the water to the instant coffee to avoid foaming. A better flavor is obtained by simmering gently for about 2 minutes.

ESPRESSO COFFEE

This Italian specialty, which, of course, is called Caffè Espresso on its home grounds, must be carefully distinguished from any brew made by filtering, no matter how concentrated. The Espresso machine works by an entirely different "steam pressure" principle, uses a very dark, very powdery grind identified as "Espresso" on the package and delivers a powerful drink with the consistency of light cream. Use the recipe for Espresso which comes with your equipment and serve it after dinner, in a demitasse or Espresso glass, with or without lemon peel. Vary the brew with a dash of Tía Maria or a dash of Strega and a dollop of whipped cream.

COFFEE CAPUCCINO

Combine equal parts of:
> Espresso Coffee
> Hot Milk
> Dash of Cinnamon or
> Grating of Nutmeg

TURKISH COFFEE

As Turkish coffee settles very rapidly, it is made at the table, over an alcohol lamp. The average content of the long-handled metal pot is about 10 ounces of liquid, and it should never be filled to more than ⅔ capacity. The pot is narrowed before it flares at the top, to allow the swishing and swinging of its contents between "frothings"— a procedure which keeps the very finely divided grains in suspension, until the liquid is sipped from tiny stemmed cups holding about a tablespoon of fluid. In the Near East it is not considered polite to drink more than three of these—although more may be served in the United States. The glass of ice water and the Rahat Loukoum candy (II, 519) served on the side for "non-habitués" are often welcome additions. The connoisseur adds no sweetening to the brew itself. Serve the coffee so that a little of the lighter frothy top goes into each cup first and is followed on the next round by some of the heavier liquid on the bottom. No commercial grind available in America proves fine enough for Turkish coffee; so take the finest you can get and pulverize it further in an electric blender. For each serving, bring to a boil in a Turkish coffeemaker:

⅓ cup water
1 teaspoon to 1 tablespoon
  finely pulverized coffee
  (2 teaspoons sugar)
Place the pot over heat and allow the coffee to rise. Remove pot from heat, momentarily. Repeat this process a second and third time. ◗ Never allow the coffee to boil. Serve it at once, as described above.

CAFÉ AU LAIT

The famous milk coffee of France.
Combine equal parts of:
> Strong coffee
> Hot milk
> (Sugar to taste)

CAFÉ BRÛLOT,   [8]
DIABLE OR ROYAL

This festive coffee bowl requires a darkened room. Prepare:
1 small orange
by studding it with:
20 whole cloves
Place in a deep silver bowl the thinly sliced:
> Peel of 1 orange
> Peel of 1 lemon and
> 2 sticks cinnamon
> 10 small cubes sugar
Heat ◗ do not boil, and pour over these ingredients:
¾ cup brandy or ¼ cup
  Cointreau
Place bowl on a tray and bring bowl, orange and a ladle to the table. Ignite the brandy and ladle the mixture repeatedly over the spices until the sugar melts. Pour into the bowl:
4 cups freshly made coffee
Now fill the ladle with:
¼ cup warm brandy or
  ¼ cup Cointreau
Tip the orange carefully into it, ignite liquid, and lower the flaming ladle into the bowl, floating the orange. Ladle the café brûlot into demitasse cups. Here are 2 easier versions:
For individual servings put a

small cube of sugar in a coffee spoon, saturate it with brandy, ignite. When sugar is melted, lower spoon into a partially filled demitasse of hot coffee. Add a lemon twist, 1 or 2 cloves and stir mixture with a cinnamon stick. Also, you may simply stir a teaspoonful of warmed light rum or whisky into a small cup of hot coffee—adding a twist of lemon peel and sweetening to taste.

IRISH COFFEE

[Individual Serving]
Some people hold that Irish coffee can only be made "proper" with Demarara sugar (II, 166). It does make a difference. Try it sometime.
Heat ♦ but do not boil and place in a prewarmed 7-ounce goblet or coffee cup:

1 jigger Irish whisky
1 or 2 teaspoons sugar

Fill to within ½ inch of top with:

Freshly made hot coffee

Stir until sugar is dissolved. Float on top of liquid:

Chilled whipped cream

ICED COFFEE

Prepare any way you wish, using:

2½ to 3 tablespoons to ¾ cup water, Coffee, page 15

Chill it or pour it hot over cubed ice in tall glasses. You may sweeten the drink with:

(Sugar or Sugar Sirup to taste)

Stir in:

(Cream)

or top with:

(Whipped Cream or Vanilla Ice Cream)

ICED COFFEE VIENNOISE

[Individual Serving]
Prepare:

Iced Coffee

in a tall glass. Add:

1 small jigger light rum

Top with:

Whipped cream

⅄ BLENDER FROZEN COFFEE

Place in electric blender for each drink:

¼ cup coffee

prepared as for Iced Coffee, above.

1 tablespoon sugar
1⁄16 teaspoon ground cloves
(1 small jigger medium rum)

Add not less than:

2 cups crushed ice

Blend thoroughly and serve in chilled, tall glasses.

ABOUT TEA

In one of Lin Yutang's books, he tells of the infinite care with which a certain sage living in the second or Classical period of Chinese teamaking procured from a famous spring, in just the proper sort of earthen pot, sufficient water for a brew with which he intended regaling an honored guest; how, on a clear, calm evening, taking pains to keep the water undisturbed, he sailed with it cautiously across an arm of the sea to his home; and how, before steeping the choice leaves, he brought the water to precisely the critical boil. There were other refinements, too, most of them equally unthinkable in our less leisurely age.

However, no matter how we abridge the teamaking ritual today, it is well to keep in mind the importance of the water we use and its temperature. It should be freshly drawn, soft—not softened and not hard—and heated, if possible, in a glass or enameled vessel. When the leaves are dropped into it, the water should only just have arrived at a brisk rolling boil—so the tea will not have a flat flavor and the leaves will describe a deep wheel-like movement, each one opening up for fullest infusion. If you doubt the effectiveness of this step, test it for yourself, adding tea leaves to underboiled, just boiling and overboiled water. Then watch the difference.

Tea brewers who do not wish to trouble with a strainer and are willing to compromise may use a tea ball. In any case ⯈ stirring the brew just before serving in a scalded, preheated pot is imperative, since it circulates through the liquid the essential oils which contribute so much to tea's characteristic flavor.

There is only one tea plant; but there are many commercial varieties of tea, depending upon soil, locality, age of leaf, manufacture, grading, blending and the addition of blossoms, zests or spices. The two chief basic types are green and black. The former is dried immediately after plucking, the latter—by all odds the more favored—is allowed to ferment before further processing. Oolong, a semi-fermented leaf, is in a class by itself.

Chinese teas which, less than a century ago, dominated the world market, have now largely yielded to the more robustly aromatic varieties of India, Ceylon and Southeastern Asia. Unfortunately, tea producers have not yet followed the example of coffee manufacturers, by putting up tea in vacuum packages. Therefore, when it reaches your kitchen, we suggest you place it at once into a tightly sealed jar.

TEA

Place tea leaves in a preheated pot. Allow:

  1 teaspoon tea leaves

for each:

  5 to 6 oz. water

Proceed as indicated above, permitting the leaves to steep not less than 3 and not more than 5 minutes. Serve the tea promptly, stirring and straining. Sugar or lemon? Yes, if you wish—the earliest teamakers, curiously enough, added salt! On a chilly afternoon we sometimes like to put a small decanter of rum or brandy on the tea tray for the cup that cheers. But we draw the line at tea bags and cream. The bag container or the fat in the cream will adulterate the flavor of this subtle beverage. Milk, of course, is frequently added in England. Never steep tea leaves more than once.

SPICED TEA   [8]

Prepare an infusion by bringing to a boil:

  ½ cup water
  ¾ cup sugar

Remove from heat and add:

  ¼ cup strained orange juice
  ½ cup strained lemon juice
  6 cloves
  1 stick cinnamon

Meanwhile, prepare:

  Tea, above

Use, in all, 10 teaspoons tea and 5 cups water—in a regular measuring cup. Put the hot, spiced infusion in a heavy crystal bowl.

Pour the steeped tea over the mixture and serve at once in punch or tea cups.

ICED TEA

We swell with patriotic pride when we recall that this beverage originated in our native town, St. Louis—even though the inventor was actually an Englishman who arrived at the concoction as an act of desperation. The year was 1904; the place, the St. Louis World's Fair; the provocation, the indifference of the general public, in the sweltering midwestern heat, to Richard Blechynden's tea concession. In brewing iced tea, avoid China teas—they lack the requisite "body." Hard water produces murky iced tea due to a precipitate.

Prepare:

> Tea, page 19

Use twice the quantity of leaves indicated for making the hot beverage. Stir, strain and pour over cubed ice. Serve with:

> Lemon slices
> (Sprigs of mint)
> (Sugar to taste)

FLAVORINGS FOR ICED TEA

I. Pour hot, steeped tea over:

> Bruised mint leaves
> Lemon rind

Chill the tea. Remove leaves and rind. Pour the tea into tall glasses. Add ice cubes and:

> (Sprigs of mint)
> Sugar to taste

II. Add to each serving of iced tea:

> 1 teaspoon rum

Garnish the glasses with:

> Slices of lemon or lime
> (Sprigs of lemon thyme)

ABOUT TISANES AND OTHER INFUSIONS

From time immemorial various plants, less stimulating than tea or coffee, have been used the world over as restoratives. They range all the way from such homely makings as rose hips and sassafras bark to that Paraguayan tea shrub, maté, the leaves of which are still commercially obtainable in some North American localities.

Some of the homegrown herbs which, singly or in combination, may become interesting beverages are the fresh or dried leaves of alfalfa, angelica, bergamot, hyssop, lemon verbena, mints, sages, thymes; the blossoms of camomile, clover, linden, orange, lemon, wintergreen and elderberry; also, the seeds of anise and fennel. There is a good general rule for quantity per cup of water in preparing these infusions.

For strong herbs, allow:

> ½ to 1 tablespoon fresh
> material
> ¼ to ½ teaspoon dried
> material

For mild herbs, allow:

> Twice the above amounts

◆ Never use a metal pot. Steep for 3 to 10 minutes in water brought to a rolling boil before straining and serving. Serve with:

> (Honey or lemon)

Habitués say "never use cream." Try one of the following dried herbs, allowing for each cup:

> 1 star anise cluster
> 6 camomile flowers
> ⅛ teaspoon powdered mint
> ¼ teaspoon powdered
> fennel
> ½ teaspoon linden blossom
> ½ teaspoon verbena

Steep for 5 minutes before serving.

ABOUT CHOCOLATE AND COCOA BEVERAGES

Chocolate, an Aztec drink, comes to us via Spain with the addition of sugar and spice. ◆ It really pains us to speak evil of so distinctively delicious a drink. But chocolate, with its high fat and sugar content, if habitually substituted for milk, may create an imbalance in the diet. In some places, unless you ask for French chocolate, the base will be water and the drink garnished with whipped cream. In France, you can count on a milk base and cream incorporated into the drink. In Vienna, they add a generous topping of whipped cream. In America, you may have to face a marshmallow or a piece of cinnamon-stick candy; in Russia and Brazil, coffee is added; and in modern Mexico, we find in it cinnamon and even orange rind and sherry. For more information about chocolates and cocoas, see (II, 191).

Cocoa does not always combine easily with liquid. To remove any lumps before cooking, combine it with the sugar or mix it in the blender with a small quantity of the water called for in the recipe. You may want to keep on hand homemade cocoa or chocolate sirups, see page 22. ◗ Both coco.. and chocolate scorch easily, so brew them over hot water as suggested below. In Mexico, a special wooden stirrer or whipper called molinillo is used to fluff chocolate drinks just before serving. This also inhibits the formation of the cream "skin" which often forms on top. If you want this aerated effect, try a wire whisk or a rotary beater. Serve the hot beverage in a deep narrow chocolate cup so as to retain the heat.

COCOA
[About 4 Servings]

Combine, stir and boil for 2 minutes—in the top of a double boiler over direct but low heat:

    1 cup boiling water
    ¼ cup cocoa
    ⅛ teaspoon salt
    2 to 4 tablespoons sugar
Then add:
    ½ teaspoon cinnamon
    1/16 teaspoon cloves and/or
        nutmeg
Place the top of the boiler ◗ over boiling water. Add:
    3 cups scalded milk
Stir and heat the cocoa. Cover and keep over hot water for 10 more minutes. Beat with a wire whisk before serving.

CHOCOLATE
[About 4 Servings]

Melt ◗ in the top of a double boiler:
    1½ to 2 oz. chocolate
with:
    1 cup boiling water
Now, over direct heat, bring this mixture in the top of the double boiler to the point where it begins to foam up. Quickly lift it from the heat. Let the liquid recede, then repeat the foaming and receding process 3 or 4 times in all. Scald:
    3 cups milk
with:
    1 vanilla bean
Dissolve in the hot milk:
    ¼ cup sugar
    ⅛ teaspoon salt
Remove the vanilla bean. Pour these ingredients while hot over the smooth chocolate mixture and beat well with a wire whisk. In each cup, place:
    (A stick of whole
        cinnamon)
Before serving, fold into the mixture or top it with:
    (¼ cup whipped cream at
        room temperature)

BRAZILIAN CHOCOLATE
[About 4 Servings]

Melt in a double boiler ◗ over hot water:

1 oz. chocolate
¼ cup sugar
⅛ teaspoon salt
Add and stir in:
1 cup boiling water
Continue to heat 3 to 5 minutes.
Add:
½ cup hot milk
½ cup hot cream
1½ cups freshly made hot
coffee
Beat mixture well and add:
1 teaspoon vanilla
(A gráting of cinnamon)

ICED CHOCOLATE

Prepare and then chill:
Chocolate, or
Brazilian Chocolate,
above
Serve over crushed ice. Top
with:
Whipped cream or coffee
ice cream
Garnish with:
Grated sweet chocolate

CHOCOLATE OR [20]
CHOCOLATE MALT
SHAKE SIRUP

First, make the following sirup
which you may keep on hand
in the refrigerator about 10
days.
Melt in the top of a double
boiler over hot water:
7 oz. chocolate
Stir slowly into the melted
chocolate:
15 oz. sweetened condensed
milk
1 cup boiling water
Stir in, until dissolved:
½ cup sugar
Cool the sirup.
To make up an individual shake,
use:
2 tablespoons chocolate
sirup
1 cup chilled milk
Beat the mixture well or blend
it. For increased food value,
add:

(½ cup milk solids or malt)
(2 teaspoons debittered
brewers' yeast)
Serve at once blended with:
A dip of vanilla,
chocolate, or mint
ice cream
or over:
Cracked ice

COCOA SHAKE SIRUP

[About 8 Servings]
In the top of a double boiler
make a lumpless paste of:
1 cup sugar
½ cup cocoa
¼ cup cold water
(½ cup malt)
Bring this mixture just to a boil
over low direct heat, stirring
constantly. Then continue to
heat over hot water from 3 to 5
minutes. Cool mixture. You may
store it covered and refrigerated
for 2 to 3 weeks.

HANDY HOT CHOCOLATE
OR COCOA

[About 1 Serving]
Prepare:
Chocolate Shake Sirup or
Cocoa Shake Sirup,
above
For each 8 oz. cup of cocoa desired, use:
2 tablespoons sirup
Stir in slowly:
¾ cup scalding milk
and heat thoroughly without
boiling before serving.

MILK AND EGG
BEVERAGES

Some of the formulas given in
this section are nutritious enough
to serve as complete meals for
dieters or invalids.

MILK EGGNOG [4]

Combine in a shaker:
4 cups chilled milk
4 eggs

4 tablespoons confectioners'
sugar or honey
1 teaspoon vanilla, grated
orange or lemon rind
(½ cup orange juice)
½ cup cracked ice

Shake the eggnog well. Sprinkle
the top with:

Freshly grated nutmeg .

Of course, it will do no harm to
add a jigger or two of whisky,
cognac or rum.

FRUIT MILK SHAKE [4]

Combine in a shaker or blender:
1⅓ cups chilled sweetened
apricot, prune,
strawberry or raspberry
juice
2⅔ cups cold milk
Serve over cracked ice.

ABOUT JUICES AND
FRUIT BEVERAGES

Fresh herbs and fruits, when
available, make attractive garnishes for cold fruit beverages.
Try a sprig of common mint or
velvety, frosty-looking apple
mint. A few leaves of borage or
its bright, starry blossoms are
pretty additions or the wheel-
like foliage of sweet woodruff
—the German Waldmeister, see
(II, 215). Use also garnishes of
lemon balm, lemon thyme, pineapple sage and scented ger-
anium.

Charming decorations for beverages are strawberries and cherries. So are pineapple slices or
citrus fruits, cut into attractive
shapes. For winter concoctions,
put a few cloves into the citrus
slices and use them to garnish
the glasses, adding one or two
thin twisted citrus rind shavings
to the drink itself. Another way
to heighten the charm of cold
beverages is to spruce them up
with decorative ice cubes. Fill a
refrigerator tray with water.
Place in each section one of the
following: a maraschino cherry,

a preserved strawberry, a piece
of lemon or pineapple, a sprig of
mint, etc.

You may flavor the cubes, before freezing, with sherry or
whisky—using not more than 2
tablespoons per tray. The short
recipes which immediately follow are designed mainly to whet
the appetite. They are dedicated
to two kinds of people—those
who cannot take cocktails because of their alcoholic content
and those who like to appear
convivial but who are convinced
that a stiff alcoholic drink before dinner blunts the flavor of
good food. Their basic liquid ingredients may, of course, be
served without our suggested
modifiers.

To make rich vegetable juices,
blend vegetables, but be sure to
cook first any fibrous ones such
as celery. Don't forget the convenience of frozen concentrates,
especially for strongly flavored,
quick-chilling drinks.

FRESH TOMATO JUICE [4]

Simmer for ½ hour:
12 medium-sized, raw, ripe
tomatoes
with:
½ cup water
1 slice onion
2 ribs celery with leaves
½ bay leaf
3 sprigs parsley
Strain these ingredients. Season
with:
1 teaspoon salt
¼ teaspoon paprika
¼ teaspoon sugar
Serve thoroughly chilled.

CANNED TOMATO [4]
JUICE

Combine in shaker:
2½ cups tomato juice
½ teaspoon grated onion
1 teaspoon grated celery
½ teaspoon horseradish

1½ tablespoons lemon juice
A dash of Worcestershire
or hot pepper sauce
⅛ teaspoon paprika
¾ teaspoon salt
¼ teaspoon sugar

This juice may be served hot or chilled. Curry powder, a few cloves, a stick of cinnamon, tarragon, parsley or some other herb may be steeped in the cocktail and strained out before it is served.

CHILLED TOMATO [4]
CREAM

Combine in a shaker:
1½ cups chilled tomato juice
¾ cup chilled cream
1 teaspoon grated onion
⅛ teaspoon salt
⅛ teaspoon celery salt
A few drops hot pepper
sauce
A few grains cayenne
¼ cup finely cracked ice

TOMATO AND [4]
CUCUMBER JUICE

Combine in a shaker:
2 cups tomato juice
2 tablespoons salad oil
1 tablespoon vinegar
½ teaspoon salt
⅛ teaspoon paprika
(¼ teaspoon basil)
Peel, seed, grate and add:
1 cucumber
½ cup cracked ice

ORANGE AND [4]
TOMATO JUICE

Combine in a shaker:
1½ cups tomato juice
1 cup orange juice
1 teaspoon sugar
1 tablespoon lemon or
lime juice
½ teaspoon salt
½ cup crushed ice

SAUERKRAUT JUICE [4]

This is also called Lumpensuppe

and is recommended by some people for a hangover.
I. Combine:
1 teaspoon lemon juice
⅛ teaspoon paprika
2 cups sauerkraut juice

II. Chill, then combine:
1 cup sauerkraut juice
1 cup tomato juice
(½ teaspoon prepared
horseradish)

CLAM JUICE [4]

Combine:
2 tablespoons lemon juice
1½ tablespoons tomato
catsup
2 cups clam juice
A drop hot pepper sauce
Salt if needed
(½ teaspoon grated onion)
¼ teaspoon celery salt
Chill these ingredients. Strain before serving. This is a good combination, but there are many others. Horseradish may be added, so may Worcestershire sauce. The cocktail may be part clam juice and part tomato juice. Serve sprinkled with:
Freshly ground pepper

ORANGE AND LIME [4]
JUICE

Combine in a shaker:
2 cups orange juice
1 tablespoon lime juice or
2 tablespoons lemon juice
⅛ teaspoon salt
½ cup cracked ice

FRESH PINEAPPLE JUICE

[About 1½ Cups of Juice]
A very refreshing drink.
Peel a:
Pineapple
Cut it into cubes. Extract the juice by putting the pineapple through a food grinder or a ⅄ blender. There will be very little pulp. Strain the juice and serve it iced with:
Sprigs of mint

PINEAPPLE AND TOMATO JUICE [4]

Combine in a shaker:
> 1 cup pineapple juice
> 1 cup tomato juice
> ¼ teaspoon salt
> ½ cup crushed ice

PINEAPPLE AND GRAPEFRUIT JUICE [4]

Boil for 3 minutes:
> ⅓ cup sugar
> ⅓ cup water
Chill the sirup. Add:
> 1¼ cups grapefruit juice
> ⅔ cup pineapple juice
> ¼ cup lemon juice
Serve chilled.

FRUIT SHRUBS OR VINEGARS

These are most refreshing in hot weather. Try adding rum in the winter.
Prepare:
> Fruit juice
Depending on the sweetness of the juice, simmer until the sugar is dissolved:
> 1 cup juice
> 1 to 1½ cups sugar
For every cup of juice, add:
> ¼ cup white wine vinegar
Bottle in sterile jars. Serve the shrub over shaved ice.

CITRUS-FRUIT JUICE MEDLEY [4]

Combine in a shaker:
> ¾ cup grapefruit juice
> ¼ cup lemon juice
> ½ cup orange juice
> ⅓ to ½ cup sugar
> 1 cup cracked ice
Pour into glasses and serve garnished with:
> Sprigs of mint

★ HOT OR MULLED CIDER

Good on a cold night, with canapés or sandwiches. Heat well, but do not boil:

> Apple cider
> A few cloves
> A stick of cinnamon

CRANBERRY JUICE [4]

Cook until skins pop open, about 5 minutes:
> 1 pint cranberries
> 2 cups water
Strain through cheesecloth. Bring the juice to a boil and add:
> ¼ to ⅓ cup sugar
> (3 cloves)
Cook for 2 minutes. Cool. Add:
> ¼ cup orange juice or
> 1 tablespoon lemon juice
Serve thoroughly chilled. Garnish with:
> A slice of lime

FRUIT JUICE TWOSOMES

Good combinations are equal parts of:
> Orange juice and pineapple juice

or:
> Loganberry juice and pineapple juice

or:
> White grape juice and orange juice

or:
> Cranberry juice and sweetened lime juice

or:
> Grapefruit juice and cranberry juice

★ HOT CRANBERRY JUICE

Heat well, but do not boil:
> Cranberry juice
> A thinly sliced lemon
> A few cloves
> A cracked nutmeg
> (Honey to taste)
Serve in mugs, with cinnamon stick stirrers.

⅄ ABOUT BLENDED JUICES

The blender transforms many kinds of fruit and vegetables

into rich and delicious liquid food. The only trouble in using it is that the enthusiast often gets drunk with power and whirls up more and more weird and intricate combinations— some of them quite undrinkable. Resist the temptation to become a sorcerer's apprentice.

Sometimes too, a gray color results. If so, gradually stir in lemon juice, a little at a time. Serve immediately after adding the lemon juice, as the clear color may not last long. A few suggestions follow. Each recipe yields about 3 cups.

I. Combine in blender:
    1½ cups chilled, seeded
        orange pulp
    1 cup chilled melon meat
        (cantaloupe or
        honeydew)
    2 tablespoons lemon juice
    ⅛ teaspoon salt
    ½ cup finely crushed ice

II. This is almost like a sherbet. Combine in blender:
    1½ cups chilled apricot or
        peach pulp
    ½ cup milk
    ½ cup cream
    2 tablespoons sugar
    ½ cup finely crushed ice
    (1 tablespoon lemon juice)

III. Combine in blender:
    1 cup chilled, unsweetened
        pineapple juice
    1 cup peeled, seeded,
        chilled cucumber
    ½ cup water cress
    2 sprigs parsley
    ½ cup finely crushed ice

IV. Combine in a blender:
    1½ cups chilled, unsweetened
        pineapple juice
    1 ripe banana
    2 teaspoons honey
        Juice of ½ lime
    ½ cup finely crushed ice
    (4 maraschino cherries)

Garnish with:
    (Sprigs of mint)

PINEAPPLE OR ORANGE EGGNOG [4]

Combine in a shaker or blender:
    2 cups chilled pineapple or
        orange juice
    1 tablespoon confectioners'
        sugar or honey
    1½ tablespoons lemon juice
    1 egg or 2 egg yolks
        A pinch of salt
    ¼ cup cracked ice
Shake or blend well.

ABOUT PARTY BEVERAGES

As with Party Drinks, each of the following recipes, unless otherwise indicated, will yield about 5 quarts and accommodate approximately 20 people. For "ice-bowl" containers and other suggestions for attractively serving large groups of people, see Party Drinks (II, 43).

GALA TOMATO PUNCH

For a summer brunch in a shady corner of the veranda. Combine:
    4 quarts tomato juice
        (II, 537)
    1 quart canned beef
        consommé
Season to taste with:
    Garlic salt
    (A chiffonade of herbs)
Chill, pour into bowl and decorate with:
    Decorative ice ring
        (II, 43)
in which has been set:
    An herb bouquet

LEMONADE

For each cup of water, add:
    1½ tablespoons lemon juice
    3 to 4 tablespoons sugar
    ⅛ teaspoon salt
The sugar and water need not be boiled, but the quality of the lemonade is improved if they

are. Boil the sugar and water for 2 minutes. Chill the sirup and add the lemon juice. Orange, pineapple, raspberry, loganberry, white grape juice and other fruit juices may be combined with lemonade. Chilled tea, added to these fruit combinations, about ⅓ cup for every cup of juice, gives lemonades an invigorating lift.

LEMONADE FOR 100 PEOPLE

Boil for 10 minutes:
 4 cups water
 8 cups sugar
Cool the sirup. Add:
 7½ cups lemon juice
Stir in the contents of:
 2 No. 2½ cans crushed pineapple or 6 to 8 cans frozen juice concentrate
Add:
 8 sliced seeded oranges
 4 gallons water
Chill. Serve over ice.

LEMONADE SIRUP

[About 4½ cups]
I. Boil for 5 minutes:
 2 cups sugar
 1 cup water
 Rind of 2 lemons, cut into thin strips
 ⅛ teaspoon salt
Cool and add:
 Juices of 6 lemons
Strain the sirup. Store in a covered jar.
Add:
 2 tablespoons sirup
to:
 1 glass ice water or carbonated water
II. Add:
 1 tablespoon sirup

 2 tablespoons orange, apricot or pineapple juice
to:
 1 glass ice water or carbonated water

ORANGEADE

Serve undiluted:
 Orange juice
over:
 Crushed ice
or add to the orange juice, to taste:
 (Water, lemon juice and sugar)

PINEAPPLE PUNCH

Place in a large bowl:
 2 cups strong tea
Add and stir well:
 ¾ cup lemon juice
 2 cups orange juice
 2 tablespoons lime juice
 1 cup sugar
 Leaves from 12 sprigs mint
Place these ingredients on ice for 2 hours. Shortly before serving, strain the punch and add:
 8 slices pineapple and juice from can
 5 pints chilled ginger ale
 4 pints chilled carbonated water
 Crushed ice

FRUIT PUNCH

Boil for 10 minutes:
 1¼ cups sugar
 1¼ cups water
Add:
 2½ cups strong, hot tea
Cool the mixture. Add:
 1 cup crushed pineapple
 2½ cups strawberry juice or other fruit juice

Juice of 6 lemons
Juice of 7 oranges

Chill these ingredients for 1 hour. Add sufficient water to make 4 quarts of liquid. Immediately before serving, add:

1 cup maraschino cherries
1 quart carbonated water

Pour over large pieces of ice in punch bowl.

FRUIT PUNCH FOR 50 PEOPLE

Make a sirup, by boiling for 10 minutes:

1¼ cups water
2½ cups sugar

Reserve ½ cup of this. Add to the remainder, stir, cover and permit to stand for 30 minutes or more:

1 cup lemon juice
2 cups orange juice
1 cup strong tea
2 cups white grape juice, grapefruit juice, pineapple juice or crushed pineapple
1 cup maraschino cherries with juice
2 cups fruit sirup

The fruit sirup, we find, is the main ingredient. Your punch is apt to be just as good as this touch. Strawberry jam may be diluted, canned raspberry or loganberry juice may be sweetened and boiled until heavy. Strain these ingredients. Add ice water to make about 1½ gallons of liquid.

Add at the last minute:

1 quart carbonated water

If you find the punch lacking in sugar, add part or all of the reserved sugar sirup.

STRAWBERRY FRUIT PUNCH

Boil for 5 minutes:

4 cups water
4 cups sugar

Cool the sirup. Combine:

2 quarts hulled strawberries
1 cup sliced canned or fresh pineapple
1 cup mixed fruit juice— pineapple, apricot, raspberry, etc.
Juice of 5 large oranges
Juice of 5 large lemons
(3 sliced bananas)

Add the chilled sirup or as much of it as is palatable. Chill these ingredients. Immediately before serving, add:

2 quarts carbonated water
3 cups or more crushed ice

This is a strong punch. It is purposely prepared this way, as the ice will thin it. Water also may be added if desired.

MOCHA PUNCH

Prepare, then chill well:

7 cups freshly made coffee

Whip until stiff:

2 cups whipping cream

You may whip an additional ½ cup heavy cream and then reserve about a cup to garnish the tops. Have in readiness:

2 quarts chocolate ice cream

Pour the chilled coffee into a large chilled bowl. Add ½ the ice cream. Beat until the cream is partly melted. Add:

¼ cup rum or 1 teaspoon almond extract
¼ teaspoon salt

Fold in the remainder of the ice cream and all but a cup of the whipped cream. Pour the punch into tall glasses. Garnish the tops with the reserved cream. Sprinkle with:

Freshly grated nutmeg or grated sweet chocolate

SALADS

We remember the final scene of a Maeterlinck play. The stage is strewn with personages dead and dying. The sweet young heroine whimpers, "I am not happy here." Then the head of the house—or what remains of it—an ancient noble, asks quaveringly, "Will there be a salad for supper?"

The primal craving for fresh greens can urge you out, seasonally, trowel in hand, to dig along the roadside and in the wild; or, like Willa Cather's Archbishop —no matter how torrid the climate, how dry the soil—to tend carefully a small patch of succulent leafage or herbs.

There is an ever-increasing demand for salads of all kinds, and a greater and greater appreciation of their contribution to our gastronomical enjoyment and our improved health. Salads figure prominently in reducing diets, too, for they are low in calories. But to achieve your goal, be sure to serve them with only a sprinkling of lemon juice, a touch of spiced vinegar or a low-calorie dressing, page 345.

When to serve the salad? It used to appear almost invariably after the main entrée but has taken, these days, to gadding about. In California, where people have a habit of doing things their own way, you may expect it on the table ready to eat when you sit down. In restaurants, if the service is leisurely, this priority is a lifesaver. At informal luncheons, salads often accompany the entrée or may even be the main dish. Don't neglect the possibility of using salads like Celeri-Rave Remoulade, page 43, as an hors d'oeuvre and, vice versa, appetizers like Vegetables à la Grecque, page 257, as a salad.

Originally, salads were the edible parts of various herbs or plants dressed only with salt—from which the word salad comes. But they now include a wide variety of ingredients, cooked and uncooked. Aside from fruits, vegetables and herbs, all kinds of meat, cheese and fish abound in salads—all served with some sort of moist dressing. The danger in this embarrassment of richness is that, in some carelessly planned meals, the salad tends to outshine the main entrée and plays the part of a "satisfier," rather than that of a stimulator.

♦ Keep the rest of the menu well in mind when preparing your salad and its dressing. A rich, heavy entrée demands a tart green salad. Slaws go well with casual meals, cookouts and impromptu suppers—at which hearty, uncomplicated foods are served. Elaborate salads, beautifully arranged and garnished, brilliant aspics and decorative chaud-froids, all look well on formal buffet tables or at special summer luncheons. In some cases, these are made as individual servings rather than as a grand "pièce de résistance."

♦ Always use your common sense and good taste in the matter of dressings. We have suggested suitable dressings for the individual salads in this chapter and want you to try some of the variations listed. Don't go overboard, however, in experimenting: a heavy dressing, undiluted, will make any lettuce, except iceberg, collapse just when you want to keep it crisp. Your dressing should enhance the salad by summoning forth its special flavor and texture and adding a delicate piquency.

ABOUT CULTIVATED SALAD GREENS

▶ Do experiment with some of the greens sketched on the next page. On successive rows reading left to right are on the bottom row: Bibb lettuce, escarole, corn salad or mâche and oak leaf lettuce; on the second row: Boston and water cress; on the top row, iceberg and Chinese or celery cabbage, Belgian, French or Witloof endive, romaine or Cos and curly endive.

ICEBERG OR CRISP HEAD LETTUCE:

Large, firm head, with crisp, brittle, tightly packed leaves. The outer leaves are medium green and fringed, the inner ones are pale green and tightly folded. Can be torn, shredded or sliced like cabbage for a salad. Adds "crunch" to it and does not wilt.

ROMAINE OR COS LETTUCE:

Elongated head, with long stiff leaves which are usually medium dark to dark green on the outside and become greenish-white near the center. Its more pungent flavor adds a tang to tossed salad.

BOSTON OR BUTTERHEAD LETTUCE:

Smaller, softer head than iceberg. Delicate leaves, of which the outer are green, the inner light yellow with a buttery feeling.

BIBB LETTUCE:

The aristocrat of all lettuce. Dark, succulent green leaves, loosely held together; tender and mild.

LEAF LETTUCE:

Crisp and, unless very young, a somewhat tough, non-heading type. The loose leaves branch from a single stalk and are light or dark green. Frequently used as an undergarnish for molded salads, aspic or arrangements of salad vegetables and fruits.

OAKLEAF LETTUCE:

A type of leaf lettuce resembling its name. There are two types: one green, one bronze.

LAMB'S LETTUCE, MACHE, OR FIELD OR CORN SALAD:

Although found wild here, lamb's lettuce or mâche is cultivated extensively and in a number of varieties in France and Italy. It is an excellent winter salad and can be grown outside without protection. Small smooth green leaves, loosely formed into a head. Good for tossed salad and sometimes used as cooked greens.

CURLY ENDIVE OR CHICORY:

Curly fringed tendrils, coming from a yellow-white stem. It adds a bitter flavor and rather prickly texture to a tossed salad. Also used as a garnish.

ESCAROLE OR CHICORY ESCAROLE:

Also known as Batavian endive. The leaves are broader and less curly than endive, also a paler green. The taste is less bitter.

BELGIAN OR FRENCH ENDIVE OR WITLOOF:

These 6- to 8-inch, elongated, crisp yellow-white leaves look like a young unshucked corncob. The bitter flavor complements blander lettuces in a tossed salad or a bland filling for an hors d'oeuvre.

CHINESE OR CELERY CABBAGE:

About the size of a bunch of celery, its closely packed, whitish-green leaves are crisp and firm and, as the name implies, the flavor is between that of cabbage and celery.

WHITE MUSTARD:

A European annual, with small tender green leaves, usually cut about a week after the seeds have been sown and used with garden cress in salads or for garnish.

GARDEN CRESS:

Do not confuse with water cress. Has very tiny leaves, picked 14 days after sowing. It is frequently combined in sandwiches, hors d'oeuvre, etc., with mustard greens.

WATER CRESS:

Dime-size dark green glossy leaves, on sprigged stems. The leaves and tender part of stems are spicy and peppery additions to the tossed salad.

Water cress in France is the invariable accompaniment to a roast chicken. In America, it is one of our most interesting greens, frequently available in the wild. Its consumption, however, is often discouraged by the fact that it may be growing in ▶ polluted water. To settle any doubts you may have, soak the cress first in 2 quarts of water in which 1 tablet of water purifier has been dissolved. Then rinse the cress in clear water. Dry and chill before serving.

▶ To keep water cress, cut off ½ inch of the stems. Loosen the tie and set in a container which does not press it on the sides or top. Fill the container with 1 inch of cold water, cover and set in the refrigerator. Wash thoroughly when ready to use. Cut off the tough ends before tossing.

SEA KALE:

A native of most seacoasts of Western Europe, sea kale is cultivated for its leafstalks, but the curly leaves can be used uncooked in salad, either alone or with lettuce.

CELERY AND SPINACH:

Both these stables lend color variation to salads.

ABOUT WILD GREENS

These can add a different flavor and texture to your mixed green salads. Be absolutely sure, however, that you know the ones you are using and wash them very carefully. Here are some of the more common edible varieties, which can be identified fairly easily:

DANDELION, TARAXACUM OFFICINALE:

Abundant in lawns, fields, meadows and roadsides. It is easiest to handle and wash if it is cut off at the root crown, so that the cluster of leaves holds together. Its slightly acrid taste goes well with beetroot. After flowering, the plants become tough and rather bitter.

SORREL, RUMEX ACETOSELLA OR RUMEX ACETOSA:

There are many edible varieties of sorrel. Both grow in cultivated and recently filled soil, neglected fields and old grasslands. The leaves have a sour or acid taste and are best for salads when gathered young and small. Cooked and puréed sorrel is good with fish.

WINTER CRESS OR BARBAREA VULGARIS:

This cress has dark-green, smooth, shiny leaves and yellow flowers. It is common in waste and cultivated ground, fields, roadsides and streams. Use the rosette of root leaves for salad and gather the early spring growth and the new growth in late fall and early winter.

ABOUT TOSSED SALADS

We hesitate to admit how often we follow the injunction, "Serve with a tossed salad." A tossed salad arouses the appetite, complements a rich entrée and, incidentally, provides us with valuable vitamins and minerals.

The resigned acceptance of ready-made salad dressing has deprived many of us of a treasured prerogative—the making of French dressing at table. Presiding over cruets, seasonings and greens was, not so long ago, a ceremonial privilege of host or hostess. If the host officiated, it was apt to have a markedly meticulous and conversational quality. Methods of mixing the dressing varied with individual taste, but there was no question of the importance of the moment or of its dignity.

♦ Salad ingredients prepared long in advance suffer a loss of nutritive value, and arrive at the table looking discouragingly limp. To serve one of the choicest treats of the table, take care ♦ to have salad ingredients fresh. ♦ In washing greens, be sure not to bruise them. ♦ Be sure, too, that they are well chilled, crisp and, especially, dry.

♦ To prepare lettuce, separate the leaves and wash them thoroughly. With iceberg lettuce this is difficult unless you core the solid part of the stem, either by using a sharp knife or pounding the bottom of the head quite hard on a wooden board, when the core will simply fall out. Hold the head upside down under running water. Water pressure pushes the leaves apart without bruising them. Boston and field lettuces must be inspected carefully for grit and sand. Try some of the wild as well as the cultivated salad greens previously listed, for their texture and flavors distinctively differ.

◗ Dry greens by letting them drip in a colander, wrapping them lightly in a soft absorbent towel until dry and chilling in the refrigerator until crisp and ready to use. Whirling greens in a wire salad basket is often recommended, but a Breton friend, observes that, at home, this kind of treatment is contemptuously referred to as "a ride in the jail wagon," because it manhandles the occupants. If you like to whirl, try doing it in a tea towel. To dry lettuces such as Bibb, that may be cleaned while still in head form, invert to drain, then place in the refrigerator on a turkish towel, cover with another plain towel and chill for several hours. Gravity and capillary action make them dry and crisp.

ABOUT MAKING A TOSSED SALAD

It is usual to tear rather than cut greens, except iceberg lettuce, which, if you desire smaller pieces, can be sliced or shredded. Place them in an ample bowl and give them a preliminary light coating of oil. About 1 tablespoon of salad oil will suffice for a medium-sized head of lettuce. Toss repeatedly by lifting the leaves gently with a large fork and spoon until each leaf is completely coated. This improves the salad from the standpoint of nutrition as well as that of gastronomy. Follow up with more oil, vinegar, and further tossing. If the salad is mixed on this principle, it will stay crisp, although it is usually eaten too rapidly to prove it.

Since vinegar and salt release juices and impair vitamin content, add them as close to serving time as possible. A good way to "toss" salad for a picnic is to have prepared, washed and drained greens in a large plastic bag. Take the dressing along in a separate container. Just before serving, pour the dressing into the bag and gently work it until the salad greens are coated. Serve from the bag or turn out into a large bowl.

The choice of salad oil is important. First in order of excellence is virgin-press olive oil, light in color and with a faint aroma. French and Italian groceries sell a very acceptable blend of olive, peanut and cotton seed oils which is more economical and has a greater degree of polyunsaturated fats (II, 170). You will also encounter an occasional gourmet who uses nothing but sesame oil or a cholesterol-conscious person who will eat only oil of safflower. An economical and effective substitute for straight safflower oil is a mixture of 20% safflower and 80% of another poly-unsaturated oil. If you find the taste of olive oil too strong, try combining it with one of the bland, more highly-polyunsaturated salad oils. Your

choice of a sour ingredient will
depend on your own taste, but
a good wine vinegar or lemon
juice is the usual accompaniment to oil. Various kinds of
herb vinegars are frequently
chosen, but you may prefer to
add these herbs separately later
when you add the other seasonings. For a discussion of vinegars, see (II, 150). Remember
the old admonition: "Be a spendthrift with oil, and a miser with
vinegar." The classic proportions
are 3 to 1.

Additional dressings, condiments and trimmings may be
added after oil and vinegar to
produce that infinite variety of
flavor which is one of the chief
charms of a tossed salad. Garlic
is perhaps the most essential.
There are two ways of giving to
a salad a delicate touch of this
pungent herb. Split a clove of
garlic and rub the inside of the
salad bowl with it, or rub a
rather dry crust of bread on all
sides with a split clove of garlic.
This is called a "chapon." Place
the bread in the bowl with the
salad ingredients. Add the dressing and toss the salad lightly to
distribute the flavor. Remove the
chapon and serve the salad at
once. If you wish to have a
slightly stronger flavor of garlic,
you may mash it at the bottom
of your salad bowl with other
seasonings before adding oil and
vinegar. This seems to modify
its heavy pungency. ♦ Never
leave a whole clove of garlic in
any food brought to the table.
Withhold salt until all other ingredients have been incorporated. Salting your salad may be
unnecessary. If, after a cautious
taste-test, you decide that it will
improve your mix, sprinkle it on
very sparingly and give the salad
a final thorough tossing.

♦ Additions to tossed salads
may include sliced hard-cooked
eggs, radishes, chopped olives,
nut meats, pimiento or green
peppers, sardines, anchovy, slivered cheese, julienned ham,
chicken, tongue, grated carrots,
cubed celery, onions—pickled,
grated or as juice—and horseradish. Even a bit of cream or
catsup may transfigure an otherwise lackluster mayonnaise,
French or boiled dressing. ♦ In
particular, the use of fresh herbs
(II, 204) may make a salad the
high point of a meal.

♦ It is unwise to add cut-up
tomatoes to a tossed salad, as
their juices thin the dressing.
Dress them separately and use
them for garnishing the salad
bowl. The French cut tomatoes
in vertical slices, see page 49,
since they bleed less this way.
Another nice last-minute addition is small, hot Croutons, page
390, sprinkled over a tossed
salad just before serving.

Well-seasoned wooden salad
bowls have acquired a sort of
sacred untouchability with some
gourmets—which we think is
misplaced. If the surface of a
wooden salad bowl is protected
by a varnish, as many are nowadays, the flavors of the oil,
vinegar and herbs will not penetrate it, and you might just as
well wash it in the usual way.
An untreated wooden surface
will certainly absorb some of the
dressing used, but the residue
left after wiping the bowl tends
to become rancid, since we house
our utensils in quarters warmer
than they are abroad. This rancidity can noticeably affect the
flavor of the salad. We prefer a
bowl made of glass, of pottery
with a glazed surface or of hard,
dense, grease-proof plastic.

DRESSINGS FOR TOSSED
SALADS

French Dressing, page 341
French Dressing with
Cream Cheese

Roquefort or Bleu French
Dressing, page 343
Water Cress Dressing,
page 343
Blender Cress Dressing,
page 343
Chiffonade Dressing,
page 344
Half and Half Dressing,
page 350
Lorenzo Dressing, page
342
Thousand Island
Dressing, page 349
Anchovy Dressing, page
342
Anchovy and Beet
Dressing, page 342
Low Calorie Dressing,
page 345

CAESAR SALAD [4]

For this famous recipe from California, leave:
1 clove garlic, peeled and
sliced
in:
½ cup olive oil: none other
for 24 hours. Sauté:
1 cup cubed French bread
in 2 tablespoons of the garlic oil,
above. Break up into 2-inch
lengths:
2 heads romaine
Wash and dry well. Place the
romaine in a salad bowl. Sprinkle
over it:
1½ teaspoons salt
¼ teaspoon dry mustard
A generous grating of
black pepper
(5 fillets of anchovy, cut up
small or mashed to a
paste, see (II, 218)
(A few drops of
Worcestershire sauce)
Add:
3 tablespoons wine vinegar
and the remaining 6 tablespoons
garlic oil. Cook gently in simmering water for 1 to 1½ minutes, or use raw:
1 egg
Drop the egg from the shell onto

the ingredients in the bowl.
Squeeze over the egg:
The juice of 1 lemon
Add the croutons, and:
2 to 3 tablespoons
Parmesan cheese
Toss the salad well. Serve it at
once.

WESTERN SALAD [4]

Prepare:
Caesar Salad, above
omitting the anchovies and adding:
2 tablespoons crumbled
Blue cheese

WILTED GREENS [4]

Sauté until crisp:
4 or 5 slices bacon
Remove from the pan, drain on
absorbent paper and cut or
crumble in small pieces. Heat:
2 tablespoons melted
butter, bacon drippings
or oil
Add:
¼ cup mild vinegar
(1 teaspoon chopped fresh
herbs (II, 204))
Add the bacon and also, at this
time, if you choose:
(1 teaspoon grated onion)
(1 teaspoon sugar)
Pour the dressing, while hot,
over:
1 head lettuce, separated,
shredded cabbage,
dandelion, young spinach
leaves or other greens
Serve it at once from a warm
bowl onto warm plates, garnished with:
Hard-cooked sliced eggs

CHICORY AND
BEETROOT SALAD [4]

This is a favorite winter salad
in France. Cut in ½-inch slices,
into a salad bowl:
6 heads Belgian or French
endive

Add:
>   2 cups sliced canned or
>   cooked beets

Toss in:
>   French Dressing, page
>   341, or Water Cress
>   Dressing, page 343

ORIENTAL BEAN SPROUT SALAD [6]

Place in a salad bowl:
>   4 cups crisp salad greens
>   1 cup drained bean sprouts
>   ½ cup thinly sliced water
>   chestnuts
>   ¼ cup toasted, slivered
>   almonds

Toss, just before serving, in:
>   ¼ to ⅓ cup Oriental Dip
>   (II, 84)

thinned with:
>   2 tablespoons cream

COLE SLAW [6]

Red cabbage may be used. Very finely shredded red and white cabbage may also be combined with good effect. Pared and diced pineapple or apple may be added.

Remove the outer leaves and the core from:
>   A small head of cabbage

Shred or chop the remainder, cutting only as much as is needed for immediate use. Formerly, the chopped cabbage was soaked in ice water for 1 hour. If soaked, drain well, dry between towels and chill. Immediately before serving, moisten with:
>   French Dressing, page
>   341, or Boiled Dressing,
>   page 350, Sour Cream
>   Dressing, page 351, or
>   equal parts mayonnaise
>   and chili sauce, or
>   thick cream, sweet
>   or cultured sour

If you choose the cream, be sure to use a little vinegar, salt and sugar. You may add to any of these dressings:
>   (Chopped anchovies)
>   (Dill, caraway or celery
>   seed)
>   (Chopped parsley, chives
>   or other herbs)

COLE SLAW DE LUXE [8]

Shortly before serving time, remove the core of:
>   A small head of cabbage

Cut into the thinnest shreds possible. Place in a deep bowl. Add:
>   1 to 2 tablespoons lemon
>   juice
>   (Fresh herbs: chopped
>   parsley, chives, etc.)

Beat until stiff:
>   ¾ cup whipping cream

Fold in:
>   ½ teaspoon celery seed
>   ½ teaspoon sugar
>   ¾ teaspoon salt
>   ¼ teaspoon freshly ground
>   white pepper
>   1 cup seedless green grapes
>   ½ cup finely shredded
>   blanched almonds

Pour it over the cabbage. Toss quickly until well coated. Serve at once with:
>   Tomatoes or in an Aspic
>   Ring, page 58

ROQUEFORT COLE SLAW [4]

This is based on a recipe from Herman Smith. His splendid books, "Stina" and "Kitchens Near and Far," should appeal to all lovers of good eating and reading.

Shred finely:
>   1½ cups red or green young
>   cabbage

Peel and cut into long, narrow strips:
>   1 cup apples

In order to keep them from discoloring, sprinkle them with:
>   Lemon juice

Toss salad lightly with:
>   Roquefort Sour Cream

Dressing
Serve at once, garnished with:
Parsley

▤ COLE SLAW FOR [6] BARBECUE

The tangy dressing in this slaw
goes well with meat broiled or
barbecued outdoors. If you are
cooking farther from home than
your own backyard or patio, try
the plastic bag method of "tossing" the slaw, described on page
33.
Combine.

1 cup mayonnaise, page
345
4 chopped scallions
1 tablespoon tomato catsup
2 teaspoons vinegar
⅛ teaspoon Worcestershire
sauce
¼ teaspoon salt
⅛ teaspoon pepper
¼ teaspoon sugar

Add this mixture to:

3 cups shredded cabbage
3 cups salad greens
1 thinly-sliced carrot
½ green pepper, cut in
strips

Toss salad lightly and serve.

HOT SLAW WITH [6] APPLE

Place in a skillet:

½ lb. finely diced salt pork

Render it slowly, then remove
the crisp, browned pieces, drain
them on absorbent paper and reserve. Add to the rendered fat
in the skillet:

3 tablespoons vinegar
2 tablespoons water
1 tablespoon sugar
1 teaspoon caraway or
celery seed
1 teaspoon salt

Cook and stir these ingredients
over quick heat until they boil.
◗ Reduce the heat to a simmer.
Stir in:

3 cups shredded cabbage

1 large peeled, grated
apple

Simmer the slaw for about one
minute longer and serve garnished with the tiny browned
cubes of salt pork. You may also
use the recipe for Wilted Greens,
page 35, using the crumbled
bacon as a garnish instead of
hard-cooked eggs.

⅄ BLENDER SLAW [4]

This can only be made satisfactorily in a 2-speed blender
with a chopping action.
Quarter and core:

1 small head of cabbage

Core, seed and remove membrane of:

½ green pepper

Peel:

½ medium onion
1 carrot

Chop these vegetables coarsely
into the blender container, until
it is half filled. Add to within 1
inch of the top:

Cold water

◗ Cover and blend for 2 seconds,
no longer, using the chopping
speed. Empty the vegetables
into a sieve to drain and repeat
the process until all the vegetables are shredded. Place them in
a salad bowl and sprinkle with:

(1 teaspoon caraway seeds)

Toss lightly in:

Mayonnaise, page 345, or
Sour Cream Dressing,
page 351

thinned with:

2 tablespoons lemon juice

GINGHAM SALAD [4] WITH COTTAGE CHEESE

Place in a mixing bowl and toss:

1½ cups coarsely chopped
young spinach leaves
2 cups shredded red
cabbage
⅓ teaspoon salt
¼ teaspoon celery seed
3 tablespoons chopped
olives or chives

1 cup cottage cheese
Place these ingredients on:
4 large lettuce leaves
Serve the salad with:
>Mayonnaise, page 345,
>Sour Cream Dressing,
>page 351, or Green
>Mayonnaise, page 348

ABOUT TOSSED COMBINATION SALADS

Serve combination salads as a luncheon main dish, accompanied by Toasted Cheese Rolls, (II, 59) or savory sandwiches, page 240. Practically every restaurant serves some kind of combination salad, often named after its own inventive chef, but each has the chief distinction of containing some form of protein such as meat, chicken or cheese, in addition to the greens and vegetables. Here are variations:

COMBINATION SALADS

I. Rub a salad bowl with:
>Garlic
Place in it:
>Lettuce or spinach leaves
>Cut-up anchovies
>Chopped, pitted, ripe olives
>Sliced radishes
>Sliced hard-cooked eggs
>Shredded Swiss cheese
Toss the salad with:
>French Dressing,
>page 341
Garnish it with:
>Peeled and quartered tomatoes

II. Combine:
>Lettuce
>Endive
>Romaine

Water cress
Cut into narrow strips:
>Salami
>Sautéed bacon
>Anchovies
>Swiss cheese
Dice and add:
>Raw cauliflower
>Cooked string beans
Marinate these ingredients for ½ hour in:
>French Dressing,
>page 341
Serve the salad half wilted.

GARNISHES FOR SALADS

To garnish salads, use the following:
>Tomato slices, dipped in finely chopped parsley or chives
>Parsley or water cress in bunches or chopped
>Lettuce leaves, cress, endive, romaine, etc.
>Heads of lettuce, cut into slices or wedges
>Lemon slices with pinked edges, dipped in chopped parsley
>Shredded olives or sliced stuffed olives
>Cooked beets, cut into shapes or sticks
>Carrots, cut into shapes
>Pearl onions
>Pickles
>Capers
>Pomegranate seeds
>Fennel slices
>Cucumbers or Cucumber Slices, page 43
>Green and red peppers, shredded
>Pepper slices
>Mayonnaise or soft cream cheese, forced through a tube

Aspic jellies in small molds or chopped aspic
Eggs—hard-cooked, sliced, riced or stuffed
Dwarf tomatoes, stuffed with cottage cheese
Cherry tomatoes
Fresh herbs, sprigs or chopped
Mint leaves
Nasturtium leaves
Nut meats
Chopped truffles
Shaped truffles

ABOUT CUTTING VEGETABLE GARNISHES AND CASES

Use vegetables as cases for piquant sauces, as sketched below. A pepper hollowed out, which can be lidded with its handsomely fat stem portion; an onion sliced to produce rings which will hold vinaigretted asparagus upright on an hors d'oeuvre tray; onion cups made from raw or slightly blanched onions; a cucumber slashed and hollowed to hold olives or gherkins and a simpler scored cucumber cup. Citrus rind rings or green or red pepper rings can be used in the same manner to hold food upright.

Try your hand at carving vegetables and see what fun you can have and how attractive your trays can look with a little effort. Don't force effects. Use them sparingly. See illustration for some very simple suggestions. Begin on the left with carrots cut in scrolls, etc., radishes made into roses and pickles into fans. Make geometric accents with hors d'oeuvre cutters and scoops, shown at center and at the top on the right. Shape flowers and borders of olives, as shown on the lower right, also twists of cucumber. Make an ingenuous turnip or egg white and carrot daisy, gay for spinach dishes, or small daffodil blooms of carrots shown above. These can have chive stems and leaves if you like. Try for some asymmetric drawing-like effects, such as shrimps suggested by thin lines of red pepper. One of the loveliest decorations we ever saw were 2 small lobsters, cut in a modern feeling from red peppers and placed casually on the side and the top of a cream-covered mousse. Seaweed was indicated by fennel leaves and partially crowned the top. See also (II, 101), for varied lemon garnishes.

ABOUT VEGETABLES FOR SALADS

A welcome summertime alternative to the crisp green salads or slaws is a vegetable salad, attractively arranged and dressed. Try cooked and chilled vegetables, served with a vinaigrette or chiffonade dressing or use Vegetables à la Grecque, page 257, including podded peas, as occasion pieces, as well as in a whole salad. Your vegetables should have some "bite" to them and we prefer fresh, cooked or canned vegetables to frozen ones, which lose their crispness and tend to have tough skins when cooked.

COOKED VEGETABLE
SALAD PLATTER

Cook separately a variety of:
> Vegetables—cauliflower,
> carrots, snap beans, Lima
> beans, beets, soy beans,
> bean sprouts, etc.
Marinate them in separate bowls for several hours with:
> French Dressing
> page 341
Use about ¼ cup of dressing to 2 cups of vegetables. Drain well. Arrange in some attractive way on a large platter. For example, place the cauliflower or the beets in the center and alternate the other vegetables according to color in mounds, about them, on:
> Lettuce leaves
Garnish the platter with:
> Curled celery, radishes,
> sliced or riced hard-
> cooked eggs or deviled
> eggs
or, place in the center of a platter, chilled:
> Snap Bean Salad, page 42
Surround it with overlapping slices of skinned:
> Tomatoes or cherry
> tomatoes filled with
> cottage cheese
Garnish the platter with:
> Shredded lettuce or
> watercress
> Deviled eggs or sardines

RUSSIAN SALAD [6]

This recipe is quickly made with canned vegetables, although it is not quite as good. If you wish, you may marinate your vegetables for 1 hour in French dressing, then drain and toss in the mayonnaise. Prepare and dice in ¼-inch cubes:
> 1 cup cooked carrots
> 1 cup cooked waxy potatoes
> 1 cup cooked beets
> ½ cup cooked green beans
Add:
> ½ cup cooked peas
Toss the vegetables in:
> Mayonnaise, page 345
with:
> (A few capers)
> (Julienned strips of ham)
Serve in mounds, on lettuce leaves.

ITALIAN SALAD [6]

Prepare and dice:
> 1 cup cooked beets
> 1 cup cooked carrots
These proportions may be varied. Chill the vegetables. Combine them with:
> 1 cup chopped celery
> ½ cup cooked or canned
> green peas
> (½ cup pared, seeded and
> diced cucumbers)
Moisten the vegetables with:
> Boiled Salad Dressing,
> page 350, mayonnaise
> thinned with cream, or
> Sour Cream Dressing,
> page 351
Serve the salad in a bowl garnished with:
> Lettuce
For more elegant occasions, mold the salad into a fish shape and cover with thin, overlapping slices of cucumber for scales.

STUFFED ARTICHOKE
SALADS

I. With Sea Food
Cook:
> Artichokes, page 259

Chill, and remove the inedible choke. Marinate:

> Shrimp, crab meat,
> oysters or bay scallops

with:

> French Dressing,
> page 341

Fill the artichokes with sea food and serve with:

> Mayonnaise

on a bed of:

> Shredded lettuce

II. With Caviar

Fill the artichokes with:

> Cultured sour cream
> Caviar

III. With Meat

Fill with:

> Ham, veal, tuna or
> chicken salad or
> liver pâté, page 525

ARTICHOKE HEARTS SALAD

Cooked or canned, these are delicious in salad. They may be cut up and added to green salads or aspics or they may be used as a basis on which to build up an attractive individual salad plate.

ASPARAGUS SALAD

Cook:

> Asparagus, page 260

Drain and chill. Cover the tips with:

> Mayonnaise or Boiled
> Salad
> Dressing, page 350

Thin the dressing with a little:

> Cultured sour cream

Add:

> (Chopped tarragon)

If that is not available, add:

> (chopped parsley or
> chives)

or serve asparagus salad with:

> Vinaigrette Dressing,
> page 341

ASPARAGUS TIP SALAD

Drain the contents of a can of:

> Asparagus tips

Place around 4 or 5 tips a ring of:

> Red or green pepper or
> pimiento

Place the asparagus in the ring on:

> Shredded lettuce

Serve the salad with:

> French Dressing, page
> 341 or mayonnaise

ASPARAGUS AND EGG SALAD [6]

Chill in a dish:

> 2 cups cooked, well-drained
> asparagus, cut in pieces
> 3 sliced hard-cooked eggs
> 6 sliced stuffed olives

Wash, drain and place in refrigerator to crisp:

> 1 bunch water cress
> 1 small head lettuce

When ready to serve, combine:

> ½ cup cultured sour cream
> 2 teaspoons grated onion or
> chopped chives
> 2 tablespoons lemon juice,
> caper liquor or vinegar
> 1 teaspoon salt
> ¼ teaspoon paprika
> $\frac{1}{16}$ teaspoon curry powder
> (2 tablespoons capers)

Line a serving dish with the larger lettuce leaves. Break the rest into pieces. Add these to the asparagus mixture. Chop and add the water cress. Pour the dressing over these ingredients. Toss them lightly. Place them in the serving dish. Serve the salad at once, garnished with:

> Parsley

DRIED BEAN SALAD [4 to 6]

Lentils, kidney, navy, Lima or miniature green soy beans, cooked or canned, are the basis of these "stick-to-the-ribs" salads. Drain well and chill:

> 2½ cups canned or cooked
> kidney or Lima beans

Combine with:
 ¼ cup French Dressing,
  page 341
  (A pinch of curry powder
  or ¼ cup chopped
  gherkins or pearl onions)
Serve on:
 Lettuce leaves
Sprinkle with:
 Chopped parsley
 Chopped chives or grated
  onion

SNAP BEAN SALAD [4 to 6]

This is a fine picnic salad.
Prepare:
 3 cups cooked Snap Beans,
  page 262
Drain well and toss, while warm,
in:
 French Dressing, page
  341, or Lorenzo Dressing,
  page 342
Chill thoroughly, then add:
 Chopped or grated onion,
  chives or pearl onions
Serve on:
 Lettuce leaves

HOT SNAP BEAN   [6]
SALAD

Prepare:
 3 cups cooked Snap Beans,
  page 262
Drain them. Combine them with
the dressing for:
 Wilted Greens, page 35
Season as desired or with:
 (Summer savory)
Serve from a warm bowl onto
warm plates.

COLD BEET CUPS

Pressure cook:
 Large Beets, page 270
and chill. Fill the beets with:
 Marinated Cucumbers
  with cultured sour cream
  or Russian Salad, page 40
 Cole Slaw, page 36 or
 Deviled Eggs, page 195

Garnish with:
 Curly Endive

PICKLED BEET SALAD

Drain:
 2½ cups cooked or canned
  beets
Reserve the juice. Slice the
beets. Place them in a fruit jar.
Boil:
 ½ cup sharp vinegar
 ½ cup beet juice
Add and heat to boiling:
 2 tablespoons sugar
 2 cloves
 ½ teaspoon salt
 3 peppercorns
 ¼ bay leaf
 (1 sliced green pepper)
 (1 small sliced onion)
 (½ teaspoon horseradish)
Pour these ingredients over the
beets. Cover the jar. Serve the
beets very cold.

CARROT SALAD WITH   [4]
RAISINS AND NUTS

Scrape well:
 4 large carrots
Place them on ice for 1 hour.
Grate them coarsely into a bowl.
Add and mix lightly:
 ½ cup seedless raisins
 ½ cup coarsely chopped
  pecans or peanuts
 ¾ teaspoon salt
  Freshly ground black
  pepper
 2 teaspoons grated lemon
  peel
 1 tablespoon lemon juice
Place the salad in a bowl. Pour
over it:
 1 cup or more cultured sour
  cream
Toss the salad if you wish.

CELERY CABBAGE SALAD

Use celery cabbage in any recipe
for hot or cold slaw, page 35,
or in the colorful recipe below:
Wash well, then crisp:
 1 stalk celery cabbage

Cut it crosswise into shreds. Serve it very cold with:

    French Dressing,
    page 341

This cabbage combines superbly with:

    Water cress

Use any convenient proportion. Garnish the salad with:

    Pickled Beets, page 42

COOKED CELERY OR ENDIVE SALAD

I. Prepare:

    Braised Celery or Endive,
    page 282

and serve cold on:

    Lettuce leaves

II. Simmer until tender:

    Trimmed, halved dwarf
    celery or endive heads

in a quantity of:

    Veal or chicken stock

Drain. Reserve the juices for soup or sauces. Marinate the vegetable in:

    French Dressing,
    page 341

to which you may add:

    1 teaspoon anchovy paste

Chill and serve on:

    Lettuce

CELERIAC OR CELERY ROOT SALAD

Prepare:

    Celeriac, page 283

Chill it. Toss it in:

    Mayonnaise, well
    seasoned with mustard

or, best of all, in:

    French Dressing,
    page 341

to which you may add:

    Minced shallots or chives

Serve it on:

    Endive or water cress

CELERIAC OR   [5 to 6] CELERI-RAVE REMOULADE

One of the more classic ways is

as follows: Blanch for 1 to 2 minutes and chill:

    ½ lb. celeriac

Steep it in:

    Cold Mustard Sauce I,
    page 344

for 2 to 3 hours. Serve chilled.

CUCUMBER SALAD

Be sure to select firm, hard, green cucumbers. The slightly flabby or yellowing ones are old and often pithy and the skin seems to toughen. Some people who are allergic to cucumber find they can eat it if the skin is left on. It should have a slight sheen, but if highly polished it is probably waxed and in such case the skin should not be used. If you wish to make the cucumbers more decorative, leave unpared and score with a fork, as sketched, before slicing.

Chill, pare and slice:

    Cucumbers

Combine them with:

    French Dressing, page
    341, or Sour Cream
    Dressing, page 351

to which you may add:

    Finely minced parsley

Serve at once.

WILTED CUCUMBERS

Although nutrients are undoubtedly lost in soaking, this process gives cucumbers a quality that is cherished by many. It rids the cucumber of a slightly acrid taste and produces an appetizing texture. So, on occasion, try soaking them.

I.

Peel and slice very thin:
> Cucumbers

A potato peeler does a fine job. Dispose them in layers in a bowl. Salt each layer and place a weight over the cucumbers. A plate with a heavy weight over all will do. Cover and refrigerate 3 to 6 hours. Drain and toss in:
> Cultured sour cream

Garnish with:
> Chopped dill, basil or
> tarragon

Serve chilled at once.

II. [3]

Slice, leaving the skins on, if very young and unwaxed:
> 1½ to 2 cups cucumbers

Salt and weight as above. Refrigerate 2 hours. Rinse in cold water, drain and dry. Place the cucumbers in a bowl and toss in:
> ¼ cup vinegar

also:
> 1 tablespoon sugar

dissolved in:
> 1 tablespoon water
> Correct the seasoning

Chill 1 to 2 hours and serve garnished with:
> Chopped dill or burnet
> or very thinly sliced
> Bermuda onion rings

COLD STUFFED CUCUMBERS

Good for a luncheon plate or as hors d'oeuvre.
Chill:
> Small, shapely cucumbers

Pare them. Cut them in halves lengthwise or cut off a slice lengthwise and remove the seeds. The cucumber boats may be wrapped in waxed paper and chilled. Fill them with:

> Chicken Salad, page 51
> or a Fish Salad, pages
> 50–51

or anything suitable that you can think of, such as:
> Celery, nut meats, green
> grapes, olives, etc.

These ingredients may be moistened with or served with:
> Mayonnaise, Beet and
> Anchovy Dressing, page
> 342, Chutney Dressing,
> page 344, etc.

Serve the cucumbers on:
> Shredded lettuce or water
> cress

LOTUS ROOT SALAD

Peel and slice thin, crosswise:
> 1 lb. lotus root

Soak for 10 minutes in:
> Acidulated Water
> (II, 148)

Drain and dip slices in:
> Fresh, boiling, acidulated
> water

Plunge quickly in:
> Cold water

and drain again. Heat and mix:
> 2 tablespoons sesame oil
> 1 to 2 drops hot pepper
> sauce
> 1½ tablespoons sugar
> 2 tablespoons soy sauce

Pour this sauce over the drained lotus root and allow to stand about 1 hour. Serve chilled in the sauce.

OKRA SALAD

A fine hot-weather salad. The marinated pods are slightly reminiscent of oysters.
Prepare:
> Stewed Okra, page 300

Place the drained okra in a dish and cover with:
> Well-seasoned French
> Dressing, page 341
> Horseradish Dressing,
> page 343, Mayonnaise,
> page 345

Chill. Serve very cold on:
> Lettuce

HEARTS OF PALM SALAD

I. Cut into lengthwise strips:
> Chilled canned hearts of
> palm

Serve on:
> Romaine

garnished with:
> Stuffed olive slices
> Green pepper rings

Sprinkle with:
> Chopped parsley
> Paprika

Serve with:
> French Dressing, page
> 341, or Mayonnaise,
> page 345

II. If you live in Florida, you
can have fresh:
> Hearts of palm

But be sure to eat them as soon
as peeled, for they discolor
quickly. Cut into dice, sprinkle
with:
> Lemon juice

and serve with:
> French Dressing, page
> 341, made with lime juice

Another way to serve is to treat
the hearts as for Cole Slaw, page
36.

PEPPER SLICES WITH FILLINGS

[8 to 10 slices]

These slices are highly decorative. They make a pretty salad
and are good as canapés, on
toast or crackers.

> 2 medium-size red or green
> peppers

Cut a piece from stem end and
remove the seeds and mem-
branes. Stuff the peppers with a
Cream Cheese Spread (II, 58)
or Ham Salad, page 52, and chill
for 12 hours. Slice them with a
sharp hot knife and replace
them on ice. Serve the slices on:
> Lettuce

with:
> French Dressing, page
> 341, or Mayonnaise,
> page 345

★ FILLED PIMIENTOS [6] OR CHRISTMAS SALAD

A decorative and delicious salad,
but do not expect the peppers
to look like fresh ones. They are
simply a casing for the soft
filling:

Drain:
> 6 large canned pimientos

Dice:
> 2½ cups drained canned
> pineapple

Add to it:
> 1½ cups diced celery
> 1 tablespoon tiny pickled
> pearl onions

Whip until stiff:
> ¼ cup whipping cream

Combine it with:
> 1 cup mayonnaise

Fold into these ingredients the
pineapple, celery and onions.
Stuff the pimientos with the
mixture. Chill. Bed on a nest of:
> Shredded lettuce

Roll into small balls:
> 6 oz. soft cream cheese

Roll the balls in:
> Chopped parsley

Place them around the pimientos
or, if they are served individually, beside them.

POTATO SALAD

Potato salad is best made from
potatoes cooked in their jackets
and peeled and marinated while
still warm. The small red waxy
potatoes hold their shape and
don't crumble when sliced or
diced; furthermore, they do not
absorb an excessive amount of
dressing or become mushy. Do
not try to make potato salad
with yesterday's cold boiled potatoes—it is not good. For hot
weather picnics, use an eggless
dressing to avoid dangerous
spoilage.

I.   **[4]**
Prepare as above:
> 2 cups sliced, boiled, waxy
> potatoes

Marinate them in:
> ½ cup heated French
> Dressing, page 341

Mix in gently with a wooden
spoon, just before serving:
> 1 tablespoon chopped
> parsley
> 1 tablespoon chopped
> chives or 1 tablespoon
> finely grated onion
> (1 cup sliced cooked
> scallops)

Serve tepid.

II.   [4]

Marinate the potatoes well with:
> ½ cup French Dressing,
> page 341, soup stock or
> canned bouillon

Chop or slice and add discreetly
a mixture of any of the following:
> Hard-cooked eggs,
> onions, olives, pickles,
> celery with leaves,
> cucumbers, capers
> 1 tablespoon salt
> Paprika
> A few grains cayenne
> (2 teaspoons horseradish)

After one hour or more of refrigeration, add:
> Mayonnaise, Boiled Salad
> Dressing, page 350, or
> cultured sour cream

Refrigerate about 1 hour longer.
Shortly before serving, you may
toss in:
> (Coarsely chopped water
> cress)

POTATO AND HERRING [6]
SALAD

Place in a large bowl and toss
gently:
> 2 cups diced boiled
> potatoes
> 1¼ cups diced marinated or
> pickled herring fillets
> ¾ cup chopped celery with
> leaves
> 1 tablespoon minced
> parsley
> 1 tablespoon minced chives

> 6 tablespoons cultured sour
> cream
> 1½ tablespoons lemon juice
> ¾ teaspoon paprika

Serve the salad chilled in:
> Lettuce cups

GERMAN HOT   [6]
POTATO SALAD

Cook in their jackets, in a covered saucepan, until tender:
> 6 medium-size waxy
> potatoes

Peel and slice while they are hot.
Heat in a skillet:
> 4 strips minced bacon or 2
> tablespoons bacon
> drippings

Add and sauté until brown:
> ¼ cup chopped onion
> ¼ cup chopped celery
> 1 chopped dill pickle

Heat to the boiling point:
> ¼ cup water or stock
> ½ cup vinegar
> ½ teaspoon sugar
> ½ teaspoon salt
> ⅛ teaspoon paprika
> (¼ teaspoon dry mustard)

Pour these ingredients into the
skillet. Combine them with the
potatoes and serve at once with
chopped parsley or chives.

POTATO SALAD   [12]
NIÇOISE

Cook:
> 3 cups new potatoes

in water to which a clove of
garlic has been added. Peel and
slice and, while still warm,
sprinkle with:
> ½ cup heated white wine or
> ¼ cup wine vinegar and ¼
> cup stock

Let stand at 70° for 1 hour.
Have ready:
> 3 cups chilled cooked
> green beans
> 6 peeled quartered
> tomatoes

which have been marinating in:
> French Dressing,
> page 341

To serve, mound the potatoes in a volcano in the center of a platter garnished with:

>Salad greens

Garnish the potatoes with:

>Capers
>Small pitted black olives
>1 dozen anchovy fillets

Alternate the tomato quarters and small heaps of the green beans around the potatoes. See the following Salad Niçoise for a version of this salad without potatoes, from the south of France.

SALAD NIÇOISE

Rub your salad bowl with garlic then place in it:

>2 peeled and quartered tomatoes
>1 peeled and finely cut cucumber
>6 coarsely chopped fillets of anchovy
>12 coarsely chopped pitted black olives
>1 cup Bibb lettuce
>1 cup romaine

Toss in:

>French Dressing, page 341

RICE SALAD   [4]

Prepare:

>2 cups steamed rice

The grains must be dry and fluffy for the success of this salad. While the rice is warm, mix in:

>¼ cup French Dressing, page 341
>preferably made with tarragon vinegar and olive oil
>A pinch of grated nutmeg
>¼ cup coarsely chopped green pepper
>¼ cup finely chopped celery
>10 black olives, pitted and halved

Garnish with:

>Peeled, quartered tomatoes

in a bowl lined with:

>Leaf lettuce

This goes well with cold chicken or cold smoked tongue. Serve the salad tepid.

ABOUT TOMATOES FOR SALAD

Good flavor and texture are particularly important in tomatoes for salad. If you can get vine-ripened tomatoes, they are infinitely superior to those picked green and allowed to ripen on their way to the supermarket. The latter often become mealy and almost tasteless in spite of their deceptively ruddy complexion. Use them for Stuffed Tomatoes, page 48, where they can be spiced up with a peppy filling.

Always cut out the stem-end core. It is tough and often tastes bitter. If you are going to stuff the tomato in one of the ways suggested later in this chapter, turn it upside down so that the cored rest ends on the plate. If you wish, you can fake a stem and leaves by making a tiny hole in the lid and inserting a sprig of mint, parsley or some other fresh herb. Keep your eyes open at market for the topepo, a hybrid between a tomato and red pepper which makes a good substitute for tomato.

FRENCH TOMATO SALAD

Cut into very thin vertical slices, page 49:

>6 medium unpeeled tomatoes

Place them so that they overlap around a cold platter or across it. Pour over them a dressing made of:

>French dressing
>¼ cup minced parsley
>2 minced shallots or green onions

CANNED TOMATO SALAD

Chill·the contents of a can of:
> Whole tomatoes

or use the firm part of any canned tomatoes. Place them in individual dishes. Sprinkle them with:

> Celery salt
> Salt
> Lemon juice
> Brown sugar

or anything you like. The main thing is to serve them very cold.

ABOUT COLD STUFFED TOMATOES

A bit of tomato skin was once as much out of place at a dinner table as a bowie knife. The discovery that tomato skins contain highly valued vitamins makes them "salon-fähig"—so whether to serve tomatoes skinned or unskinned rests with the hostess' sense of delicacy or her desire for health.

♦ To skin tomatoes, first wash them and then use one of the following methods: stroke the skin with the dull edge of a knife blade until the skin wrinkles and can be lifted off; or, dip the tomato in boiling water for 1 minute and then immediately in cold water, drain and skin; or, pierce the tomato with a fork and rotate it over a burner until the skin is tight and shiny, plunge into cold water and peel.

♦ To prepare tomato cases, first skin the tomatoes as described above, then hollow them. Invert the tomatoes to drain for 20 minutes. Chill them and fill the hollows with one of the fillings suggested below.

Tomatoes can be cut and filled in a variety of attractive ways and they provide a gay splash of color for buffet salads. If you do not wish to serve large portions, cut the tomatoes in halves or in slices. Place on each slice a ring of green pepper ½ inch or more thick. Fill the ring.

You can also cut them crosswise in zigzag fashion, fill them sandwich style and top with a mint leaf. Or slash into 6 sections, nearly to the base, and fill the center. Garnish with a stuffed olive.

Slice horizontally into quarters and fill as a club sandwich. Garnish with a slice of black olive or pimiento star or cover with a pepper lid as sketched.

FILLINGS

I. Pineapple and Nut Meats
Combine equal parts of:
> Chopped celery
> Fresh shredded pineapple
> A few walnut meats
> Mayonnaise

II. Eggs and Anchovies
Combine:
> Chopped hard-cooked eggs
> Chopped anchovies or anchovy paste
> Onion juice or grated onion
> Chopped parsley or other herb
> Mayonnaise or thick cultured sour cream
> Paprika and salt

III. Eggs and Ham
Combine:
> 2 chopped hard-cooked eggs

1 cup ground or minced
ham
½ cup chopped celery
12 sliced olives
Fresh or dried savory
2 chopped sweet pickles
Sour Cream Dressing,
page 351 or mayonnaise

IV. Deviled Eggs
Place in each tomato hollow:
½ Deviled Egg, page 195
Serve on:
Lettuce
with:
Anchovy Dressing,
page 342

V. Aspic
For about 6 tomato cases prepare:
1½ cups aspic
This may be an Aspic Salad,
page 58, to which chopped meat
or fish and vegetables, etc., may
be added. When the aspic is
about to set, fill the tomato
cases. Chill until firm. Garnish
with:
Olives, parsley, etc.
and serve with:
Mayonnaise

VI. Some other good fillings are:
Wilted Cucumbers I,
page 44
Crab Meat Salad, page
50, or A Fish Salad,
pages 50–51
Chicken Salad, page 51
Guacamole I (II, 61)
Cole Slaw, page 36
Avocado chunks
Shrimp with mayonnaise
Cottage cheese or soft
cream cheese mixed
with mayonnaise and
chopped chives

**TOMATO AND ONION
OR CUCUMBER SALAD**

Skin and chill:
Medium-size tomatoes
Cut 5 or 6 crosswise gashes in
the tomatoes, equal distances

apart. Place in each gash, as
shown below, a thin slice of:
Bermuda onion or
cucumber
Serve the tomatoes on:
Lettuce or water cress
with:
French Dressing, page
341, or Sour Cream
Dressing, page 351, etc.

**MOLDED EGG AND
CAVIAR SALAD**

Also good as hors d'oeuvre.
Crush with a fork:
8 hard-cooked eggs
Stir into them:
3 tablespoons soft butter
⅓ teaspoon dry mustard
2 oz. caviar
3 tablespoons lemon juice
1 tablespoon
Worcestershire sauce
Pack these ingredients into a tall,
oiled glass. Chill. Unmold and
cut into ½- to 1-inch slices.
Serve on:
Thick tomato slices
or use to decorate a salad platter.
Cover with a dab of:
Mayonnaise
(A rolled anchovy)

STUFFED LETTUCE ROLLS

Beat until smooth:
Cottage cheese
Add all or some of the following:
A sprinkling of chives or
grated onion
Chopped boiled ham
Seedless raisins
Chopped celery

Chopped green peppers
Chopped nut meats
Spread a thick layer of the
cheese mixture on:

Large lettuce leaves

Roll the leaves and secure with
toothpicks. Chill. Allow 2 or 3
rolls to a person and serve with:

Mayonnaise or French
Dressing, page 345

You may also use a fancy cut
vegetable garnish, as sketched
on page 39.

MACARONI OR   [5]
SPAGHETTI SALAD
OR CALICO SALAD

Exact proportions are unimportant.
Prepare:

1 cup cooked elbow
macaroni, page 170

Drain it. Beat well:

1½ tablespoons lemon juice
or 2 tablespoons vinegar
1 tablespoon salad oil

Toss this into the cooked macaroni. There should be about 2
cups of it. Chill the salad for
several hours. Toss into it:

1 teaspoon grated onion or
2 tablespoons chopped
chives
1 cup diced celery with
leaves
1 cup minced parsley
½ cup chopped stuffed
olives
¾ teaspoon salt
Freshly ground black
pepper
3 tablespoons cultured sour
cream
2 tablespoons chopped
pimiento

Serve on:

Lettuce

This makes an attractive filling
for a tomato aspic ring.

CRAB MEAT OR
LOBSTER SALAD

Combine:

1 cup crab meat or lobster

1 cup pared shredded
apples
½ cup mayonnaise

CRAB LOUIS   [4]

This salad is a product of the
West Coast, where the magnificent Pacific crab is frequently
served in this way. Arrange
around the inside of a bowl:

Lettuce leaves

Place on the bottom:

¾ cup shredded lettuce
leaves

Heap on these:

2 cups crab meat

Pour over the crab:

1 cup Pink Mayonnaise or
Sauce Louis, page 350

Sometimes eggs are added to the
salad. Slice:

(2 hard-cooked eggs)

Place them on top of the crab.
Sprinkle over them:

Chopped chives

★ HERRING SALAD

[About 20 Servings]

Herring is a traditional dish for
our family at Christmastime. Its
rich color, thanks to the red
beets, and elaborate garnishing
make this dish an imposing
sight.
Soak in water for 12 hours.

6 milter herring

Skin them, remove the milt and
the bones. Rub the milt through
a colander with:

1 cup dry red wine or
vinegar

Cut into ¼-inch cubes the herring and:

1½ cups cold cooked veal
2 hard-cooked eggs
1½ cups Pickled Beet Salad,
page 42
½ cup onions
½ cup pickles
2 stalks celery
½ cup cold boiled potatoes

Prepare and add:

3 cups diced apples

Blanch, shred and add:
    1 cup almonds
Combine the milt mixture with:
    1 cup sugar
    2 tablespoons horseradish
    2 tablespoons chopped
        parsley
Pour this over the other ingredients. Mix well. Shape the salad
into a mound or place it in a
bowl. Garnish it with:
    Riced hard-cooked eggs
    Pickles and olives
    Sardelles and parsley

LOBSTER SALAD [4]

Dice:
    1 cup canned or cooked
        lobster meat
Add:
    (Grated onion)
Marinate with:
    ¼ cup French dressing
Chill for 1 hour. Combine with:
    1 cup chopped celery
Place on:
    Lettuce
Cover or combine with:
    ½ cup mayonnaise
to which you may add:
    (2 tablespoons dry sherry)
Garnish with:
    Lobster claws
    Olives and radishes
    Hard-cooked eggs
    Capers and pickles
or prepare:
    Tomato Aspic, page 65
Place it in a ring or in individual
molds. Invert the aspic on:
    Lettuce
Fill the ring or surround the
molds with lobster salad.

SHRIMP OR LOBSTER [4]
MOLD

This makes a lovely center for
an hors d'oeuvre tray. Grind together:
    1 lb. cooked shrimp or
        lobster
    1 tablespoon capers
    ⅓ of a small onion

Add and mix well:
    ⅓ cup softened butter
    3 tablespoons heavy cream
    2 tablespoons Pernod
    A dash of hot pepper
        sauce
    1 teaspoon salt
    1 teaspoon fresh tarragon
Pack into a mold. Refrigerate for
3 to 4 hours before serving. For
a special occasion, mold the mixture flat in either individual
molds or one large mold. Cover
with a thin icing of:
    Whipped cream
Cut large crescents from pieces
of:
    Red peppers
to suggest the tails, claws and
feelers of lobster or shrimp.
Apply them in these patterns.
For an added touch of realism,
garnish with seaweed made of:
    Wisps of finocchio leaf
and a few:
    Seedless green grapes

TUNA FISH, SHRIMP [4]
OR SHAD ROE SALAD

Have ready:
    1 cup canned fish
Flake it with a fork. Add:
    ½ to 1 cup diced celery or
        cucumber
Make a French dressing using:
    2 tablespoons olive oil
    2 tablespoons lemon juice
or use ¼ cup mayonnaise. Add:
    (1 tablespoon chopped
        chives)
    (1 tablespoon chopped
        parsley)
Serve very cold on:
    Lettuce

CHICKEN SALAD [8]

A traditional "party" dish,
chicken salad should taste of
chicken, the other ingredients
being present only to add variety of texture and to enhance
the flavor. So always keep the
proportions of at least twice as
much chicken as the total of

your other ingredients. Since it is usually combined with mayonnaise, be careful to ♦ refrigerate it, particularly if you make it in advance.

Dice:

> 2 cups cooked chicken
> 1 cup celery
> (¼ cup salted almonds)

Chill these ingredients. They may be marinated lightly with:

> French Dressing,
> page 341

When ready to serve, combine with:

> 1 cup mayonnaise

Season the salad, as required, with:

> Salt and paprika

Serve it on:

> Lettuce

Garnish with:

> Pimiento and olives
> (Sliced hard-cooked eggs and capers)

Quantity note: Generous main dish servings for 50 will require:

> 1 gal. cooked cubed chicken

To obtain this amount, you need about 17 lbs. ready to cook chicken. If you substitute turkey, you need only a 12-pounder.

CHICKEN SALAD VARIATIONS

Follow the preceding recipe. You may substitute cooked duck, turkey or veal for the chicken, remembering to keep the proportions of 2 of meat or fowl to 1 of the other ingredients.

> Chicken, celery and hard-cooked eggs
> Chicken, bean sprouts and water chestnuts
> Chicken, cucumber and English walnut meats
> Chicken, Boiled Chestnuts, page 283, and celery—pimiento may be added
> Chicken and parboiled oysters

> Chicken and fruit such as seedless grapes, fresh chopped pineapple and pomegranate seeds

You may add to the mayonnaise:

> (Strained chili sauce)

See also Chicken Mousse, page 60.

HOT CHICKEN SALAD [4]

Preheat oven to 350°.

Combine:

> 2 cups cubed cooked chicken
> 1 cup finely diced celery
> ½ teaspoon salt
> ½ teaspoon monosodium glutamate
> ¼ teaspoon tarragon
> ½ cup toasted almonds
> 1 tablespoon chopped chives
> 2 tablespoons lemon juice
> ½ cup mayonnaise
> ½ cup Béchamel Sauce, page 359

Bake in very shallow individual bakers for 10 to 15 minutes or until heated. Garnish with:

> Parsley or small sprigs of lemon thyme

HAM, CORNED BEEF, VEAL OR BEEF SALAD

Let this be a matter of inspiration.

Dice:

> Cooked ham, corned beef, veal or beef
> Hard-cooked eggs
> Celery with leaves
> (Green peppers or pickles)

Combine these ingredients with:

> Tart mayonnaise or French Dressing, page 341

Garnish with:

> Chopped chives, parsley or other herbs

Surround the meat with tomatoes, sliced or whole.

ABOUT FRUIT SALADS

The purist frowns on fruit salads except for dessert and we ourselves have shuddered at the omnipresent peach half with cottage cheese and a blob of mayonnaise. Nevertheless, such a wide variety of fruit is available to us throughout the year, including many tropical ones, that we often delight in their color and taste in salad before or with the main entrée. Fruit salads offer great scope for the artist. A large arranged platter can substitute for flowers as a centerpiece on a buffet. With protein, such as chicken, meat, cheese, or fish, fruits make wonderful summer luncheon dishes. As a general rule, keep the dressings for pre-dessert fruit salads fairly tart, so that the appetite is not dulled. As a change from the usual base of salad greens, serve fruit salads, where suitable, in baskets, cups or cases made from fruit, as described on (II, 104). In preparing fruit salad in advance, ♦ store bananas, peaches and other easily discolored fruit covered with the acid dressing you plan on using, to avoid discoloration.

APPLE, PEAR, OR PEACH SALAD

Try this with an omelet, French bread and coffee.
Pare, core, slice and sprinkle with lemon juice to keep them from discoloring:

> Well-flavored apples,
> pears, or peaches

Serve them on:

> Lettuce

with:

> Lemon and Sherry
> Dressing, page 352, or
> French Dressing

Garnish the salad with:

> Cream cheese and nut
> balls or Roquefort
> cheese balls

The apples may be cut into rings and the cheese balls placed in the center.

WALDORF SALAD   [6]

Prepare:

> 1 cup diced celery
> 1 cup diced apples
> (1 cup Tokay grapes,
> halved and seeded)

Combine with:

> ½ cup walnut or pecan
> meats
> ¾ cup mayonnaise or Boiled
> Salad Dressing, page 350

ABOUT AVOCADO SALADS

Please read About Avocados (II, 96). To prepare avocado cups, cut the fruit in half lengthwise, place between the palms of the hands and gently twist the halves apart. Tap the large seed with the edge of a knife and lift or pry it out. ♦ To prevent the fruit from darkening after cutting, sprinkle with lemon juice. ♦ To store, spread with mayonnaise, soft butter or cream, allow the seed to remain in it and cover well with wax paper or plastic. Avocado has a soft, buttery texture and taste which combines best with citrus fruits or tomatoes and a sharp or tangy dressing. It also has an unexpected affinity with shrimp, crab or lobster. All of these combinations offer a pleasing contrast of color, as well as texture and taste—the hallmark of a delectable salad.

AVOCADO SLICES

These may be used as a garnish for meats and fish.
Chill:

> Avocados

Pare and slice them. Marinate for about 5 minutes in chilled, highly seasoned:

French Dressing, page 341

You may also add:
(Hot pepper sauce, chili sauce, catsup, etc.)

Sprinkle with:
Chopped parsley or chopped mint

Try these avocado slices in:
(Tomato Aspic, page 65)

AVOCADO AND FRUIT SALAD

Pare:
Avocados
Slice them lengthwise and arrange them with skinned sections of:
Orange and grapefruit or pineapple slices
in wheel shape, on:
Lettuce
or, make a rounded salad by alternating the fruit with the green slices into an approximate half globe on the lettuce. Serve with:
French Dressing, page 341, or Lemon or Sherry Dressing, page 352
Prepare the dressing with lime juice in preference to lemon juice or vinegar.

AVOCADO SALAD CUPS

Cut into halves and remove the seeds from:
Chilled avocados
You may then fill the hollows with:
I. Chili sauce seasoned with horseradish

II. Marinated seedless grapes
Garnish with:
A sprig of parsley, mint or water cress

III. Dress up:
Crabmeat, chicken or fruit salad
with:
Mayonnaise
thinned with a little:
Lemon or lime juice
and fill the avocado cup.

IV. Fill with a Tomato Ice which can be made like:
Fruit Ice (II, 493)
only substitute tomato juice for the fruit juice.

V. Scoop the pulp out of the skin, instead of paring the avocado. Turn it into:
Guacamole (II, 61)
Put the mixture back in the half shell and garnish with:
A slice of stuffed olive

BANANA AND NUT SALAD

For each serving, peel and split lengthwise:
1 banana
Spread on the cut sides a thin coating of:
Peanut butter
Sprinkle with:
Chopped peanuts or chopped English walnuts
Serve on:
Lettuce
Garnish with:
Orange sections or red currant jelly
or sprinkle with:
Honey Dressing, page 352

CHERRY AND HAZELNUT SALAD

Drain and pit:
Canned white cherries
Insert in each cherry:
A hazelnut meat
Serve very cold with:
Cottage cheese
Mayonnaise

ABOUT GRAPE SALADS

Grapes are not only delicious as part of fruit and vegetable aspics but are superlative when served alone. Ever peel a grape? Well, it takes time, but what is more luxurious than a lovely mound of peeled, seeded grapes, lightly tossed in a mild olive oil and vinegar dressing, served in lettuce cups or as the center for a gelatin ring mold! You may also toss a few peeled, seeded grapes in a salad of tender lettuce. To make a baroque grape finish on a gelatin top, see (II, 185). See also Seedless Grape and Asparagus Aspic, page 64, or mix seedless grapes with cultured sour cream or yogurt as a fruit salad garnish.

GRAPE AND COTTAGE CHEESE SALAD

Place in an oiled ring mold or in individual ring molds:
> Cottage cheese

Chill and invert onto:
> Lettuce

Dust with:
> Paprika

Serve filled with:
> Seedless grapes

marinated in:
> French Dressing, page 341

GRAPEFRUIT SALAD

Prepare:
> Grapefruit segments (II, 100)

Serve them with:
> French Dressing, page 341

Use grapefruit juice in place of vinegar and add a little:
> Confectioners' sugar

MELON SALAD

Prepare:
> Melon Baskets (II, 104), or Melon Rounds

Fill the baskets with:
> Hulled berries
> Diced pineapple or seedless grapes

Moisten with chilled:
> French Dressing, page 341, or cultured sour cream

ORANGE AND ONION SALAD

Arrange:
> Skinned orange sections

or peeled, sliced oranges
> Thin slices of Bermuda onion
> (Pink grapefruit sections)

on:
> Lettuce leaves, endive or escarole

Serve with:
> French Dressing, page 341

An Italian version of this salad adds:
> Pitted black olives

ORANGE AND GRAPEFRUIT SALAD

Prepare as directed (II, 100, 102):
> Orange and grapefruit segments

Place them on individual plates on:
> Lettuce or water cress

You may place between alternate segments of the fruit:
> Long slivers of green pepper and pimiento

Serve with:
> French Dressing, page 341

BLACK-EYED SUSAN SALAD

Skin unbroken whole or half sections of:
> Orange or grapefruit

Arrange them on:
> Lettuce

around a center of:
> Chopped dates and nuts

Serve with:
> French Dressing, page 341

ORANGE SALAD   [4]
FCR GAME

Peel and separate the skin from the sections of:
> 4 oranges

Arrange them on:
> Water cress

Combine and pour over them:
> 2 tablespoons brandy
> 2 tablespoons olive oil

1 teaspoon sugar
¼ teaspoon salt
A few grains cayenne
Sprinkle the tops with:
Chopped tarragon

FRESH PEACH AND [6]
CHEESE SALAD

Cut into 6 parts:
3 oz. cream cheese
Roll the cheese into balls, then
in:
Chopped nut meats
Pare, cut into halves and pit:
6 peaches
Place a ball of cheese between
2 peach halves. Press the peach
into shape. Roll it in lemon juice.
If the peaches are not to be
served at once, chill them in
closed containers. Serve the
peaches on:
Water cress
with:
French Dressing,
page 341
A bit of cress, a stem and several
leaves may be placed in the stem
end of each peach. Decorative—
though it may affront a horticulturist.

PEAR SALAD

Chill and pare:
Fresh pears or drained
canned pears
Follow the preceding recipe for
Peach Salad. Brush the side of
each pear with:
Red coloring or paprika
Place in the blossom ends:
A clove
and in the stem ends:
A bit of water cress
Serve with:
French dressing
Garnish with:
Nut Creams (II, 73), or
large black cherries,
seeded and stuffed with
cottage cheese
Or fill the hollows with cream
cheese combined with chopped
ginger.

PEAR AND GRAPE SALAD

Pare:
Fresh pears
or drain:
Canned pears
Place half a pear, cut side down,
on a plate. Thin to spreading
consistency:
Cream cheese
with:
Cream
Cover each pear half with a
coating of cheese. Press into the
cheese, close together to look
like a bunch of grapes:
Stemmed seedless grapes
Add a leaf of some kind, preferably grape, but an ivy leaf and
a bit of stem is a good substitute. Serve with:
Mayonnaise or French
Dressing, pages 345, 341

JAPANESE PERSIMMON
SALAD

This is an attractive-looking
salad. If you wish to skin the
fruit, rub it first with the blunt
side of a knife and peel with the
sharp edge.
Chill:
Ripe Japanese
persimmons
Serve them whole or cut lengthwise almost to the base and insert in the slashes:
Slices of peeled orange,
grapefruit and avocado
and serve with:
Boiled Salad Dressing III,
page 350

PINEAPPLE SALAD

Drain:
Slices of canned
pineapple
Serve them on:
Lettuce with French
Dressing, page 341
Add to the French dressing:
A little confectioners'
sugar
Or cover the slices with:
Riced soft cream cheese

Topped with:

A spoonful currant jelly
Serve the salad with:

French Dressing, page
341 or mayonnaise

ABOUT MOLDED SALADS

Any clever person can take a few desolate-looking refrigerator leftovers and glorify them into a tempting molded aspic salad or mousse. For utilizing leftovers, an aspic is second only to a soufflé. Well-combined scraps result in a dish that is sometimes as good as one composed of delicacies and with a further advantage to the busy housewife as it can be prepared a day in advance and chilled in the refrigerator until ready to serve. ♦ Do not freeze. Each of these salads depends on gelatin to hold its shape, so please read About Gelatin (II, 183). Molds may be filled when dry; but a jellied mixture is more readily removed when a mold has been moistened with water. If the mixture lightly brush the mold with oil. i. not a clarified one, you may Be sure to taste your salad before molding and correct the seasoning. ♦ Undersalt if it is to be held 24 hours.

Many of the recipes that follow can be made either in a large mold or in individual small ones. Ring molds can be used if you wish to fill the centers with some other kind of salad, such as chicken, Vegetables à la Grecque, page 257, fruit or cream cheese, dressed and garnished to your fancy. Fish-shaped molds can make a sea food aspic appear very professional. For large groups, you can even use small paper drinking cups for molding individual salads and tear off the cup when the salad is jellied and ready to serve. Or use large No. 2½ size cans and cut around the bottom of the can when ready to serve the salad. Push the salad out of the bottom of the can, slice and serve the rounds on lettuce.

♦ Aspics and other molded salads with a clear "body" lend themselves to highly decorative treatment, although their preparation can be time-consuming (II, 185). However, certain ingredients naturally come to rest either at the top or bottom of a jelling salad and you can achieve interesting layered effects by using "floaters" and "sinkers." See, on (II, 185), the list of ingredients which can be incorporated in your salad simultaneously.

ABOUT ASPICS

Nothing gives a cooler, lovelier effect on a hot summer night and nothing is easier to prepare than a brilliantly clear aspic. The problem, of course, is to keep the aspic properly chilled when serving. For small groups, chilled plates, individually served, will do, if you can control the timing. For large groups, if you want to use a quivery aspic, serve it molded in a crystal clear glass bowl set in another larger glass bowl with crushed ice between them or on a handsome, well-chilled platter, set on ice.

The most delicious aspics of all are reduced chicken and veal stocks, cooked down from the clarified gelatinous portions of these animals, page 58. Clarified strong meat, fish and fowl stocks with added gelatin are next in favor—but the average housewife seldom clarifies her own. She depends largely on canned bases for her jellies. ♦ Canned consommés, if over a year old, tend to lose some of their jelling power, so it is wise to refrigerate the can before using to test for texture. The consommé is still good to eat if it fails to jell just

out of the can, but when used
for aspic it will need about 1
teaspoon of gelatin per cup of
consommé to firm it. To add
gelatin, see (II, 184). If you
save vegetable stocks (II, 138),
you can add them to meat or
fish stocks to modify and enrich
the otherwise easily identifiable
canned flavors. It is wise to
choose a stock that has the same
general base as the food to be
molded: fish stock for fish, meat
stock for meat.

♦ To make aspics, allow 1
tablespoon gelatin to 1¾ to 2
cups liquid. Use the lesser
amount of liquid if the solids to
be incorporated are juicy or
watery. ♦ Never reduce aspic
made with added gelatin, with
the idea of thickening it. It only
wastes your good stock and
never thickens. If you run into
trouble, start the gelatin process
over again, judging the amount
of fresh gelatin you should add.

♦ The addition of wine or
liqueur to your aspics can make
them something rather special.
Don't add too much ♦ one or
two tablespoons per cup of liquid is sufficient to heighten the
flavor significantly. Substitute
the wine for part of the liquid
called for in the recipe ♦ and
add it when the gelatin has been
dissolved and is beginning to
cool. Dry white wine or a dry
sherry go well with savory aspics
such as chicken and veal.
Sweeter wines, such as sauterne,
cognac or fruit-flavored liqueurs,
are good for molded fruit salads.

Aspic should be clarified unless you want to serve up something that resembles a molded
London fog. If you decide to
skip this process, be sure to plan
to mask your mold, see Mayonnaise Collée, page 387, or Sauce
Chaud-froid, page 388.

♦ To clarify, see (II, 140).
♦ To make decorative molds, see
(II, 185). Clear aspic jelly can

make an attractive garnish for
a meat or chicken aspic. Chill
it in a refrigerator tray ♦ but do
not freeze and, when ready to
serve, cut in squares or fancy
shapes or chop it rather fine and
arrange it around the mold.

Many salads can become full-
fledged luncheon dishes with the
addition of various types of
chopped meat, chicken or flaked
fish. For other recipes including
meat, fish and shellfish and
Chicken Mousses see pages 60,
61.

A choice or a combination of
the following ingredients may be
included in a molded salad:

> Cooked diced meat or
>   poultry
> Cooked flaked fish
> Hard-cooked eggs
> Cooked sweetbreads
> Shredded cabbage
> Diced celery
> Diced cucumbers
> Cooked celeriac
> Sliced green peppers
> Raw or cooked carrots
> Cooked beets
> Canned asparagus
> Halved cranberries
> Seedless grapes
> Skinned grapefruit
>   sections
> Stuffed ripe or green
>   olives
> Pickles
> Nut meats
> Chopped parsley, chives
>   or other herbs

BASIC ASPIC OR   [5]
GELATIN SALAD

Please read About Gelatin (II,
183).
Soak:
    1 tablespoon gelatin
in:
    ¼ cup cold water
Dissolve it in:
    ¼ cup boiling stock
Add this to:
    1½ cups cold stock or 1¼

cups stock plus ¼ cup
tomato juice
2 tablespoons vinegar or
1½ tablespoons lemon
juice
Salt and paprika
Celery salt
(1 tablespoon grated onion)

If the aspic is to cover unseasoned food, make the gelatin mixture "peppy." Chill it and when about to set combine it with:

1½ to 2 cups solid ingredients

Pour the aspic into a wet mold and chill until firm. Unmold. Surround with:

Lettuce leaves

Serve with or without:

Mayonnaise, Sour Cream
Horseradish Dressing,
page 351, etc.

ASPIC GARNISH

Prepare:

Basic Aspic Salad, above

When firm and just before serving, chop the aspic so the light catches its many facets, and use it to garnish salads or meats.

LUNCHEON ASPIC SALAD [8]

▶ Please read About Gelatin (II, 183).
Drain, reserving the juices:

2½ cups canned grapefruit
sections
¼ cup green or white
cooked asparagus
1 cup canned or cooked
crab meat or shrimp

Cut the asparagus into pieces. Pick over the crab meat or remove the intestinal vein from the shrimp. Add to the juices, to make 2¾ cups of liquid:

Chicken broth, Stock,
page 490, canned
consommé or dissolved
chicken bouillon cubes

Soak:

1½ tablespoons gelatin

in ½ cup of this liquid.
Dissolve it in 1 cup hot liquid. Combine the gelatin and the remaining liquid. Season well with:

Juice of 1 or more lemons
or with ¼ cup dry white
wine

Add, if needed:

Salt

Add:

(3 or more tablespoons
capers)

Chill the gelatin until it begins to thicken. Have ready a mold which has been rinsed in cold water. Pour part of the gelatin into it, sprinkle some grapefruit, crabmeat and asparagus over it, then alternate layers of gelatin and of the other ingredients. Wind up with gelatin on top. Chill the aspic until it is very cold. Serve on:

Lettuce

with:

Green Mayonnaise,
page 348

JELLIED VEAL STOCK [4 to 6]

Sometimes it is fun to make an aspic without added gelatin.
Place in a soup kettle:

A knuckle of veal
¼ cup cut-up onion
½ carrot
6 ribs celery with leaves
1 teaspoon salt
¼ teaspoon pepper

Cover the veal with:

Boiling water

Simmer the meat until it is tender. Strain the liquid. Reserve it. Remove the veal. When cold, cut the meat into small cubes. Remove the fat from the stock. Heat the stock. Add the veal or reserve it for other dishes and use the stock after clarifying it (II, 140) to mold other ingredients.

Correct the seasoning

add:
    (1 teaspoon dried herb—
        basil, tarragon, etc.)
Rinse out a mold in cold water.
Pour in the veal mixture. Cover
and keep in a cold place to set.
Unmold and slice.

CHICKEN ASPIC   [6 to 8]

Soak:
    1 tablespoon gelatin
in:
    ¼ cup cold water
Dissolve it in:
    2 cups boiling chicken
        broth or stock
Add:
    Seasoning, if needed
Chill and when the gelatin begins to set, rinse a mold in cold
water and fill it with:
    ½ inch of the jelly
Build up layers of:
    3 cups cooked, diced
        chicken
and the jelly. Ornament the
layers with:
    1 cup canned mushroom
        caps
    2 hard-cooked eggs
    12 sliced stuffed olives
Chill the jelly until firm. Unmold
it and serve with or without:
    Mayonnaise

JELLIED CHICKEN OR VEAL MOUSSE

I.   [10]
Use the recipe for Jellied Ham
Mousse, below. Use chicken
stock. Substitute cooked ground
chicken or veal for the ham or
use part chicken and part ham.

II.   [8]
Soak:
    1½ tablespoons gelatin
in:
    ¼ cup Chicken Stock
        (II, 142)
Dissolve it in:
    ½ cup hot stock
Beat:
    3 egg yolks

Add:
    1½ cups milk
Cook these ingredients in a
double boiler until they are
smooth and fairly thick. Stir in
the dissolved gelatin. When the
mixture is cool, add:
    2 cups cooked minced or
        ground chicken or veal
    (½ cup diced seeded
        cucumber)
Season it with:
    Salt, white pepper and
        paprika
Chill the jelly and when it is
about to set fold in:
    1 cup whipping cream
Place the mousse in a wet mold
and chill it until it is firm. Unmold it.

JELLIED HAM   [10]
MOUSSE

Soak:
    1 tablespoon gelatin
in:
    ¼ cup cold water
Dissolve it in:
    1½ cups boiling Stock
        (II, 141)
Chill the jelly. When it is nearly
set, combine it with:
    3 cups cooked ground or
        chopped ham
    ¼ cup chopped celery
    1 tablespoon grated onion
    ½ cup mayonnaise
    ¼ cup sour or sweet-sour
        chopped pickles
Add, if required:
    Worcestershire sauce
    Seasoning
Seasonal variation: Omit onion,
olives and pickles and add:
    (1 cup seedless green
        grapes)
Moisten a mold with cold water.
If desired, decorate the sides
and bottom with:
    Stuffed olives and sliced
        hard-cooked eggs
Add the other ingredients. Chill
the mousse until it is firm.

JELLIED CLAM [8]
JUICE RING

♦ Please read About Gelatin
(II, 183).
Dilute:

Clam juice or minced
clams

with:

Water or vegetable juices
to make a palatable mixture.
There should be 4 cups of liquid.
Season this with:

Lemon juice and paprika
A few drops
Worcestershire sauce

Soak:

2 tablespoons gelatin

in ½ cup of the liquid.
Heat ♦ just to the boiling point
1 cup of the liquid. Dissolve
the soaked gelatin in it. Return
it to the remaining liquid with
the minced clams if they were
used. Pour in a wet 9-inch ring
mold. Chill until firm. Invert the
jelly onto a plate. Fill the center
with:

Cottage cheese

Surround it with:

Tomato and cucumber
slices

Serve with:

Mayonnaise

MADRILÈNE RING
WITH SHAD ROE

A fine summer dish.
Fill a ring mold with:

Canned Madrilène
aspic or well-seasoned
meat stock aspic

Chill. Invert on:

Shredded lettuce

Place in the center:

Chilled canned shad roe

Garnish with:

Mayonnaise
Lemon wedges or parsley

If the Madrilène is of a wobbly
type, serve it from a small dish,
surrounded by pieces of roe on
lettuce.

MOUSSELINE OF [6]
SHELLFISH

Line a 1½-quart fish mold with
half-set:

Fish or Chicken Aspic,
page 60

Refrigerate it. Prepare:

2 cups Fish Velouté, page
362

to which has been added:

1 tablespoon gelatin

soaked in:

¼ cup cold stock or water

Combine the cooled sauce with:

1 lb. cooked chopped
shellfish meat

Add:

½ cup partially whipped
cream
Correct the seasoning

and pour into the fish mold over
the aspic. Chill before unmolding onto a cold serving platter.

JELLIED SEAFOOD [6]
RING OR MOLD

♦ Please read About Gelatin
(II, 183).
Prepare:

Basic Aspic Jelly, page 58

using a fish fumet or light meat
stock. Dice.

Celery

Pare, seed and dice:

Cucumbers or green
peppers

Drain and flake:

Salmon, crab or tuna fish:
1½ cups fish and
vegetables in all

Add:

(2 chopped hard-cooked
eggs)
(Sliced stuffed olives)

When the jelly is nearly set,
combine it with the solid ingredients. Pour it into a wet
mold and chill until firm. Unmold and serve on:

Lettuce

with:

Mayonnaise or boiled
dressing

MOLDED CREAMED FISH [6]

◗ Please read About Gelatin (II, 183).
Soak:
    ¾ tablespoon gelatin
in:
    2 tablespoons water
Combine in a double boiler, then stir constantly ◗ over—not in—boiling water until thickened:
    2 egg yolks
    1½ tablespoons soft butter
    ½ tablespoon flour
    1½ teaspoons salt
    2 teaspoons sugar
    1 teaspoon Worcestershire sauce, ¾ teaspoon curry or 1 teaspoon dry mustard
    1 teaspoon grated onion
    A few grains red pepper
    ¼ cup lemon juice
    ¾ cup milk or tomato juice
Add gelatin and stir until it is dissolved. Refrigerate. Prepare:
    1½ cups seafood: cooked or canned shrimp, salmon, etc.
Or use part fish and part chopped celery. When the gelatin is nearly set, place part of it in the bottom of an oiled ring mold, add part of the fish, then more gelatin. Repeat this until all ingredients have been used, finishing with gelatin on top. Chill the salad until it is firm. Serve it on:
    Water cress
Fill the ring with:
    Marinated cucumbers
Surround it with:
    Sliced tomatoes

SEAFOOD MOUSSE [6]

◗ Please read About Gelatin (II, 183).
Soak:
    2 teaspoons gelatin
in:
    ¼ cup cold water

Dissolve it in:
    ¼ cup boiling water
Add it to:
    ¾ cup mayonnaise
Combine it with:
    1 cup flaked crab meat or flaked tuna fish
    ½ cup chopped celery or carrots
    2 tablespoons chopped parsley
    ½ cup chopped cucumber
    2 tablespoons chopped stuffed olives
    1 tablespoon or more lemon juice
    Correct the seasoning
and place these ingredients in a wet mold. Chill them until they are firm. Unmold them on:
    Cress or shredded lettuce
Serve with:
    Cucumbers in Sour Cream
If you want a mousse based on whipped cream, see Lobster Mousse.

LOBSTER MOUSSE [6]

◗ Please read About Gelatin (II, 183).
This is an attractive salad, made in a 9-inch ring mold.
Soak:
    1 tablespoon gelatin
in:
    ¼ cup water
Dissolve it over boiling water.
Combine:
    ¾ cup minced celery
    1½ cups canned or cooked lobster meat
    (⅔ cup minced apple)
Season these ingredients with:
    Salt and paprika
Stir the gelatin into:
    ¾ cup mayonnaise
    3 tablespoons lemon juice
    (1 teaspoon dry mustard)
    (½ clove pressed garlic)
    (A few drops hot pepper sauce)
Whip until stiff, then fold in:
    ⅓ cup whipping cream

Fold this mixture into the other ingredients. Place the mousse in a wet mold. Chill it thoroughly. Unmold it on a platter, garnished with:

> Water cress
> Marinated cucumbers

Serve it, if you like, filled with the following sauce. Simmer:

> 1 cup tomatoes

When reduced to ½ cup, chill the tomatoes. Add to them:

> ½ cup olive oil
> ½ teaspoon sugar
> ½ teaspoon salt
> 1 tablespoon chopped parsley
> Freshly grated pepper
> ½ teaspoon Worcestershire sauce

EGGS IN ASPIC OR OEUFS EN GELÉE

Make one of the above:

> Stock aspics, flavored with port and cognac

Have ready:

> Poached eggs, page 184

Swish cold water in individual molds until they are cold and wet. Drain but do not dry. Coat the interior with the jelling aspic so that it adheres to the sides. Chill until congealed. Place an egg in the center of each mold and fill with more aspic. Chill. Serve masked with:

> Mayonnaise Collée, page 387, or cold mayonnaise

EGGS IN ASPIC COCKAIGNE

Molded with one half egg this makes a pleasant hors d'oeuvre. With three halves, it makes enough for a luncheon salad. Prepare:

> Eggs in Aspic, above

using rich chicken stock for the aspic base and replacing the poached eggs with:

> Deviled Eggs, page 195

Place the molds on a bed of:

> Water cress

Mask the eggs with a coating of:

> Cultured sour cream

Garnish with:

> Finely chopped chives, basil and chervil
> Red caviar and tomato slices

MOLDED VEGETABLE GELATIN SALAD   [6]

Dissolve the contents of:

> 1 package lime- or lemon-flavored gelatin

in:

> 2 cups hot water

Prepare and add, when the jelly is about to set:

> 1½ cups finely diced vegetables:
> cucumber, carrot, celery, unpeeled radishes, olive, pimiento
> ½ diced green pepper
> 2 teaspoons grated onion
> ¾ teaspoon salt
> ¼ teaspoon paprika

Place the salad in well-oiled individual ring molds. Chill thoroughly. Unmold on:

> Lettuce or water cress

Fill the centers with:

> Mayonnaise or Boiled Salad Dressing II, page 350

GOLDEN GLOW GELATIN SALAD   [8 to 10]

Good in flavor and lovely in color.

Grate or grind:

> 2 cups raw carrots

Drain, reserving the juice:

> 1 cup canned crushed pineapple

Heat to the boiling point:

> ⅞ cup pineapple juice
> ⅞ cup water
> ½ teaspoon salt

Dissolve in the hot liquid:

> 1 package lemon-flavored gelatin

Chill and when the jelly is about to set, combine it with the carrots, the pineapple and:

(½ cup chopped pecans)
Place in a wet mold. Chill until
firm. Unmold on:
> Lettuce
Serve with:
> Mayonnaise

SEEDLESS GRAPE   [10]
AND ASPARAGUS ASPIC

♦ Please read About Gelatin
(II, 183).
A refreshing summer salad.
Drain the contents of:
> 2 cups canned asparagus
> tips

Reserve the liquor. The tips may
be cut in two or they may be
used whole as a garnish around
the edges of the mold. Soak:
> 1 tablespoon gelatin

in:
> 3 tablespoons asparagus
> liquor

Heat the remaining asparagus
liquor and dissolve the gelatin
in it. Add to it to make 2 cups
of liquor in all:
> Chicken bouillon or
> canned bouillon

Season these ingredients with:
> Salt and paprika

Chill them. When they are
nearly set, combine them with:
> 2 cups seedless grapes
> 1 cup chopped celery

and the cut asparagus tips.
Chill the salad until firm. Unmold and serve with:
> Mayonnaise

BEET GELATIN SALAD   [8]

Wash well, then boil:
> 8 medium-size beets or use
> canned beets

Drain them. Reserve the beet
juice. Peel the beets and dice
them. There should be about 1
cup. Prepare:
> ¾ cup diced celery

Dissolve the contents of:
> 1 package lemon-flavored
> gelatin

in:
> 1 cup boiling water

Add to it:
> ¾ cup beet juice
> 3 tablespoons vinegar
> ½ teaspoon salt
> 2 teaspoons grated onion
> 1 tablespoon prepared
> horseradish

Chill these ingredients until they
are about to set. Fold in the
beets and the celery. Place the
salad in a wet mold. Chill until
firm. Unmold on:
> Lettuce or endive

Serve with:
> Mayonnaise, Boiled Salad
> Dressing, page 350, or
> cultured sour cream

CUCUMBER GELATIN   [8]
ON TOMATO SLICES

♦ Please read About Gelatin
(II, 183).
Fine for a meat platter or a ring
mold.
Pare and seed:
> Cucumbers

Grate them. There should be 4
cups of pulp and juice. Soak:
> 2 tablespoons gelatin

in:
> ½ cup cold water or chicken
> stock

Dissolve it in:
> ¾ cup boiling water or
> chicken stock

Add:
> 6 tablespoons lemon juice
> 2 teaspoons grated onion

Add the gelatin mixture to the
cucumber pulp with:
> 1 teaspoon sugar
> Salt, as needed
> ¼ teaspoon paprika

Strain the jelly. Place it in small
wet molds. When firm invert
onto:
> Thick slices skinned
> tomatoes

Garnish the slices with:
> Water cress

Serve the salad with:
> Mayonnaise

or, place in a 9-inch wet ring
mold. Chill the jelly. When firm,

invert onto a platter. Fill the center with:

> Marinated shrimp

Garnish the edge with alternating:

> Tomato slices
> Cucumber slices

Serve the ring with:

> Green Mayonnaise, page 348, or Water Cress Dressing, page 343

CUCUMBER MOUSSE [6]

▶ Please read About Gelatin (II, 183).
Soak:

> 2 teaspoons gelatin

in:

> 3 tablespoons cold water

Dissolve these ingredients over heat. Add:

> 2 teaspoons vinegar or lemon juice
> 1 teaspoon grated onion
> ¾ teaspoon salt
> ¼ teaspoon paprika

Chill until about to set. Drain well:

> 1 cup pared, seeded, chopped cucumbers

Whip until stiff:

> 1 cup whipping cream

Beat the gelatin mixture gradually into the cream. Fold in the cucumbers. Oil individual molds. Fill them with the mousse. When they are thoroughly chilled, invert the mousse onto a garnished platter.

CUCUMBER AND SOUR [6] CREAM MOUSSE

Dissolve:

> 1 package lime-flavored gelatin

in:

> ¾ cup hot water

Add:

> ¼ cup lemon juice
> 1 tablespoon grated onion

Chill until about to set, then stir in:

> 1 cup cultured sour cream
> 1 cup finely chopped

unpared cucumber

Pour into 6 small oiled molds and chill until firm.

TOMATO ASPIC

[8 Servings, without the addition of solid ingredients]

▶ Please read About Gelatin (II, 183).

I. Simmer, for 30 minutes, then strain:

> 3½ cups tomatoes
> 1 teaspoon salt
> ½ teaspoon paprika
> 1½ teaspoons sugar
> 2 tablespoons lemon juice
> 3 tablespoons chopped onion
> 1 bay leaf
> 4 ribs celery with leaves
> (1 teaspoon dried basil or tarragon)

Soak:

> 2 tablespoons gelatin

in:

> ½ cup cold water

Dissolve it in the strained hot juice. Add water to make 4 cups of liquid. Chill the aspic. When it is about to set add 1 or 2 cups of solid ingredients—a choice or a combination of:

> Sliced olives
> Chopped celery
> Chopped green peppers
> Grated or chopped carrots
> Chopped meat
> Flaked fish
> Well-drained oysters
> Sliced avocados, etc.

Chill the aspic until firm. Unmold and serve with:

> Mayonnaise or Boiled Salad Dressing, page 350

II. If you prefer a ring, keep the aspic simple and fill the center with:

> Cole slaw, marinated cucumbers or avocados, chicken or shrimp salad or cottage cheese and chives

Serve with a suitable dressing.

TOMATO ASPIC WITH [8]
TASTY CENTERS

I. Prepare:
> Tomato Aspic, page 65

When it is about to set, pour into wet individual molds or ice cube molds and fill them to ⅓ of their capacity. Combine and roll into balls:

> 1 package of soft cream
>   cheese: 3 oz.
> 1 tablespoon anchovy paste
> 2 drops Worcestershire
>   sauce

Drop a ball into each mold and cover it with aspic. Chill the aspic until firm. Unmold on lettuce leaves. Serve with:

> Mayonnaise

II. Use for the filling:

> Any small pieces of
>   cooked meat, fowl or fish

CANNED TOMATO OR [8]
VEGETABLE JUICE ASPIC

◗ Please read About Gelatin (II, 183).
Soak:

> 2 tablespoons gelatin

in:

> ½ cup cold canned tomato
>   juice

Dissolve it in:

> 3½ cups hot tomato juice or
>   canned tomato and
>   vegetable juice

Tomato juice varies. It is wise to taste the aspic to see whether additional seasoning is required. Lemon juice is good, so is a teaspoon of chopped or dried herbs (II, 203), preferably basil. Add, if desired, 1 or 2 cups of solid ingredients. See Tomato Aspic, page 65. Mold, chill, unmold and serve the aspic as directed.

BASIC GELATIN FOR [6]
FRUIT SALADS

◗ Please read About Gelatin (II, 183). It is well to know that fresh pineapple cannot be added to a gelatin salad without ruining it. This also applies to frozen pineapple juice, alone or combined with other frozen juices such as orange or grapefruit. The pineapple must be brought to ◗ a boil. Canned pineapple complies with this rule and may be used as is. The frozen juice is usable if boiled.
Soak:

> 1 tablespoon gelatin

in:

> ½ cup cold water

Dissolve it in:

> 1 cup boiling water or
>   fruit juice

Add:

> 4 to 6 tablespoons sugar,
>   less if sweetened fruit
>   juice is used
> ⅛ teaspoon salt
> ¼ cup lemon juice

Chill the aspic and when it is about to set, combine it with:

> 1½ cups prepared drained
>   fruit

Place it in a wet mold and chill until firm. Serve with:

> Cream Mayonnaise, page
> 348

MINT GELATIN FOR
FRUIT SALADS

Pour:

> 1 cup boiling water

over:

> ¼ cup crushed mint leaves

Allow to steep for 5 minutes. Drain this infusion. Add:

> A few drops of green
>   vegetable coloring

Prepare, by the recipe above:

> Basic Fruit Salad Gelatin

substituting the mint infusion for the boiling water.

MOLDED AVOCADO [3 to 4]
SALAD

Soak:

> 1 tablespoon gelatin

in:

> 2 tablespoons water

Dissolve it in:
>   1 cup boiling water
Add:
>   ¼ cup lemon juice
>   1 cup mashed avocado
>   ¼ teaspoon celery salt
>   1 teaspoon salt
>   ½ teaspoon Worcestershire
>   sauce
>   A few grains cayenne
>   ¼ cup chopped pimiento
Mold and serve.

BLACK CHERRY AND   [6]
ALMOND ASPIC

Prepare:
>   Basic Fruit Salad
>   Gelatin, above
Substitute for part of the boiling
water:
>   Fruit juice
Cool the gelatin mixture. When
it is about to set add:
>   1¼ cups pitted black cherries
>   ⅓ cup blanched shredded
>   almonds
These proportions may be
varied. Place the aspic in a wet
mold. Chill until firm. Unmold
and serve with:
>   Mayonnaise

MOLDED CRAN-   [6 to 8]
BERRY SALAD

◆ Please read About Gelatin
(II, 183).
Soak:
>   1 tablespoon gelatin
in:
>   3 tablespoons water
Cook until the skins pop:
>   2 cups cranberries
in:
>   1 cup boiling water or
>   fruit juice
Use the cranberries strained or
unstrained. If the former, strain
them at this time. Add and cook
5 minutes:
>   ½ cup sugar
>   ¼ teaspoon salt
Add the soaked gelatin. Chill the
jelly. When it is about to set,
fold in:

>   ⅔ cup diced celery
>   (½ cup chopped nut meats)
>   (1 cup canned, drained
>   crushed pineapple)
Place in a wet mold and chill
until firm. Serve with:
>   Mayonnaise

MOLDED CRAN-   [8 to 10]
BERRY AND APPLE SALAD

◆ Please read About Gelatin
(II, 183).
Put through a food grinder:
>   1 lb. cranberries
Add:
>   The grated rind of 1
>   orange
>   ½ cup orange juice
>   3½ tablespoons lemon juice
>   1½ cups sugar
Refrigerate overnight. Soak:
>   1 tablespoon gelatin
in:
>   3 tablespoons cold water
Dissolve:
>   1 package lemon-flavored
>   gelatin: 3¼ oz.
in:
>   1 cup boiling water
Add the soaked gelatin. Stir
until dissolved. Combine these
ingredients with the cranberry
mixture. Pare, then chop and
add:
>   3 tart apples
Place the salad in a greased
mold. When firm, unmold and
serve on:
>   Water cress
with:
>   Cream Mayonnaise,
>   page 348

GINGER ALE SALAD   [10]

◆ Please read About Gelatin
(II, 183).
This is about the best molded
fruit salad given.
Soak:
>   2 tablespoons gelatin
in:
>   ¼ cup cold water
Dissolve it in:
>   ½ cup boiling fruit juice

Add:

    ½ cup sugar
    ⅛ teaspoon salt
    2 cups ginger ale
    Juice of 1 lemon

Chill these ingredients until the jelly is nearly set. Combine with:

    ½ lb. skinned, seeded Tokay grapes
    1 skinned, sliced orange
    1 grapefruit in skinned sections
    6 slices canned pineapple, cut in pieces
    3 teaspoons chopped preserved ginger

Place the salad in a wet mold. Chill and unmold on:

    Lettuce

Serve with:

    Cream Mayonnaise, page 348

GRAPEFRUIT JELLY WITH SHERRY [10]

♦ Please read About Gelatin (II, 183).

Soak:

    2½ tablespoons gelatin

in:

    ½ cup cold water

Stir over heat until the sugar is dissolved:

    ½ cup water
    1 cup sugar

Dissolve the gelatin in the hot sirup. Cool. Add:

    2 cups and 6 tablespoons fresh grapefruit juice
    3 tablespoons lemon juice
    ½ cup dry sherry
    ¼ teaspoon salt

Pour these ingredients into a well-oiled 9-inch ring mold. Chill the jelly until firm. Turn it out on a platter. Fill the center with:

    Soft cream cheese balls, rolled in chopped nuts

Garnish the outer edge of the platter with:

    Avocado slices

alternating with skinned:

    Grapefruit or orange sections

on:

    Water cress or shredded lettuce

Sprinkle with:

    Pomegranate seeds

Serve the salad with:

    Mayonnaise or French Dressing, pages 345, 342

MOLDED PEAR SALAD [6]

♦ Please read About Gelatin (II, 183).

Drain and reserve the juice from:

    3½ cups canned Bartlett pears

Soak:

    1 tablespoon gelatin

in:

    ¼ cup cold water

Add to the pear juice enough water to make 1¾ cups of liquid. Heat part of the liquid to the boiling point. Dissolve the soaked gelatin in it. Combine it with the rest of the liquid. Add:

    3 tablespoons lemon juice
    ¼ teaspoon salt

Cool these ingredients. Moisten:

    1 package of soft cream cheese or pimiento cheese

with a very little:

    Cream

Use just enough to soften it. Add to the cheese:

    ¼ cup chopped nut meats
    (¼ teaspoon salt)

Form the cheese into balls. Place one in the center of a half pear and cover with another half pear. If the pears are large, do not cover them. Place the stuffed pears in a ring mold or in cups. Pour the gelatin mixture over them. Add, if desired:

    1 cup or more seedless grapes

Chill the gelatin until firm. Unmold on:

    Crisp lettuce

SALADS   69

Serve with:
    Mayonnaise
This recipe may also be made
with:
    1 package lime or lemon
        gelatin
    1 cup boiling water
    1 cup pear juice
    1½ tablespoons lemon juice
    ⅛ teaspoon ginger
    ¼ teaspoon salt
Substitute this for the gelatin
mixture given in the recipe.

MOLDED STUFFED [8]
FRUITS

▶ Please read About Gelatin
(II, 183).
Soak:
    2½ tablespoons gelatin
in:
    ½ cup water
Drain and reserve the juice
from:
    3½ cups canned peaches,
        apricots or pears
Combine and boil:
    2 cups of the juice
    1½ cups sugar
Dissolve the gelatin in it. Add
these ingredients to the remaining juice with:
    ¾ cup lemon juice
    3 tablespoons lime juice
    ¼ teaspoon ginger
Add water or other fruit juice
to make up 4 cups of liquid in
all. Chill the gelatin until it is
about to set. Soften:
    Cream cheese
with a little:
    Mayonnaise
Roll it into balls. Roll the balls
in:
    Chopped nut meats
Stuff a cheese ball in each fruit,
then place each fruit in an oiled
individual mold. Chill well and
invert onto:
    Water cress
Serve with:
    Mayonnaise

MOLDED PINEAPPLE [8]
RING

▶ Please read About Gelatin
(II, 183).
Soak:
    2 tablespoons gelatin
in:
    ½ cup cold water
Strain and reserve the juice of:
    2½ cups canned crushed
        pineapple
Add to the juice:
    ½ cup hot water
Bring these ingredients to the
boiling point. Stir in the soaked
gelatin until dissolved. Add:
    ⅝ cup sugar: ½ cup, plus
        2 tablespoons
Cool the mixture. Add the pine-
apple and:
    (2 cups grated cabbage)
    The grated rind of 1
        orange or lemon
    ¾ cup orange juice
    5 tablespoons lemon juice
Pour these ingredients into a
wet 9-inch ring mold. Chill the
gelatin. Unmold on a bed of:
    Lettuce or water cress
Fill the center with:
    Cottage cheese, soft
    cream cheese balls
    rolled in chopped nut
    meats, chicken salad,
    etc.
Serve with or without:
    Mayonnaise

SEEDLESS GRAPE [8 to 10]
AND CELERY RING

Prepare:
    Lemon Jelly or Orange
    Jelly, or Basic Fruit
    Gelatin, page 66
When it is about to set, add to
it:
    3 cups seedless grapes and
        diced celery, combined
        in any proportion
Place the jelly in a wet 9-inch
mold and chill. Unmold on:
    Lettuce

Fill the center with:
>   Cream Mayonnaise,
>   page 348

FROSTED MELON OR PAPAYA SALAD [6]

You may use this as salad or dessert.
Pare:
>   1 large melon or papaya

leaving it whole. Cut off enough from one end so you can scrape out the seeds. Fill the cavity with water, pour it into a measuring cup; this is to guide you for the amount of gelatin you have to prepare. Stand the melon upside down to drain. Then fill, depending on the color of the melon flesh, with:
>   Fruit-flavored gelatin
>   (Diced or small fruits)

Try a combination of:
>   Orange-flavored gelatin,
>   canned crushed pine-
>   apple, canned mandarin
>   oranges or sliced bananas

or try:
>   Raspberry gelatin with
>   fresh raspberries

After the center is set, you may coat the melon with:
>   8 oz. cream cheese

softened with:
>   A little milk

and whipped until fluffy. Chill until ready to serve. Cut crosswise in 1-inch slices and serve on:
>   Lettuce

with:
>   French Dressing,
>   page 341

SOUFFLÉ FRUIT SALAD [4]

Dissolve:
>   1 package lime gelatin

in:
>   1 cup hot water

Add:
>   ½ cup cold water
>   ½ cup mayonnaise

>   2 tablespoons lemon juice
>   ¼ teaspoon salt

Whip with a rotary beater until well blended. Pour into a refrigerator tray and chill until firm at the edge but still soft in the center. Turn into a bowl and whip in the same manner until fluffy. Fold in:
>   1 cup peeled and diced
>   apples
>   ¼ cup chopped pecans
>   ¾ cup seeded Tokay grapes

Pour into a mold and refrigerate until firm.

STRAWBERRY AND RHUBARB SALAD MOLDS [8 to 10]

Dissolve:
>   3 packages strawberry
>   gelatin

in:
>   3 cups hot water

Drop in:
>   2 packages frozen rhubarb

Stir to separate the rhubarb. When the jelly begins to set, add:
>   1 quart sliced fresh
>   strawberries

Pour into individual wet molds and chill until set. Unmold on:
>   Water cress

Garnish each with:
>   A fresh whole strawberry

Serve with:
>   Cream Mayonnaise, page
>   348, or Fruit Salad
>   Mayonnaise, page 348

TWENTY-FOUR-HOUR FRUIT SALAD WITH CREAM [12 to 14]

Cook in a double boiler until thickened:
>   2 egg yolks
>   ¼ cup sugar
>   ¼ cup cream
>   Juice of 2 lemons
>   ⅛ teaspoon salt

Stir these ingredients constantly. Chill them and add:

6 diced slices canned
pineapple
2 cups pitted Queen Anne
cherries
1 cup blanched, shredded
almonds
½ lb. marshmallows, cut in
pieces
1 cup heavy cream,
whipped

(½ lb. peeled, seeded
grapes)
Chill the salad for 24 hours.
Serve on:
Lettuce
with:
Mayonnaise
or as a dessert, garnished with:
Whipped cream

THE FOODS WE HEAT

What do you think of when you think of cooking? Our own minds rush at once, with confidence, to a vision of food deliciously prepared, perfectly seasoned, beautifully presented —to, in short, the final product. But somewhere along the line, in perhaps ninety-nine out of a hundred kitchen sequences, heat has been applied—and its application is of crucial importance. From Charles Lamb's legendary Bobo—you will remember him from your high school English classes as the boy who couldn't make roast pig without burning down the house—to the bride of the moment, described by her maid of honor as incapable of boiling an egg, heating food has often turned into a frustrating, sometimes even a disastrous, experience.

It needn't be. We have tried throughout our book, but especially in this chapter, to identify and explain the various types of cooking heat; to tell you simply and clearly how these heats are initiated, controlled and arrested to ensure best flavor, nutritive value, texture and color. We have tried to indicate what processes, when followed, will bring cooked food to the table in that ideal state of readiness the French call "à point."

Asking a cook why he heats food at all is, of course, like asking an architect why men do not live in caves. The obvious answer is that it usually tastes better that way. There are other reasons, too. Some are prosaic. Cooking destroys unwanted and sometimes unfavorable microorganisms. Contrary to some remarkably persistent notions, it makes many categories of food more digestible and of more nutritive value and less—to toss in a stylish term—allergenic.

Cooking, again, can seal up in food most of those natural juices which nourish and delight us, instead of squandering them away on pan or oven. For some kinds of preparation—Stocks (II, 138), and soups are examples—the objective is just the reverse. It is true, also, that certain salted and variety meats, as well as a good many vegetables, profit by a precooking or blanching, page 88, which modifies texture or releases disagreeable odor and off-flavors.

Many cooks, like the rest of humankind, are born innovators, too. And they often introduce stimulating refinements in the heating of food, some of which —it must be said—emphasize taste at the expense of nutritional integrity.

▲ Cooking in mountainous country is an art all in itself. If high altitudes are new to you, watch for the high altitude cooking symbol ▲ which will give you formulas for adjusted ingredients or temperatures. Roasting procedure does not differ materially from that at sea level. But high altitudes do affect boiling considerably. In the following chart, we plot the difference in the boiling temperatures of water at sea level and at graduated elevations. Any process involving liquid will be proportionately lengthened **as** altitude increases.

	F.	C.
Sea level	212°	100°
2,000 ft.	208°	98°
5,000 ft.	203°	95°
7,500 ft.	198°	92°
10,000 ft.	194°	90°
15,000 ft.	185°	85°
30,000 ft.	158°	70°

Adjustments required in using sea-level baking recipes at high altitudes are indicated where necessary for each baking category. Basic cake recipes for high altitudes and their baking temperatures, marked ▲, may be found on (II, 381–385).

If these hints are not sufficiently specialized for your area, write the Home Economics Department of your State College or call your County Home Demonstration Agent for more information. And if you are doing any pressure cooking, the accuracy of the gauge is vital. These agencies can also tell you where to have gauges tested.

ABOUT HEATS

Let us consider first how heats are transferred to food, whether in air or in moisture, in fat or through a pan. Results in each case will be quite astonishingly different. Cooking heats are generally known as ◗ dry or moist. In the text following, we shall list types of each separately. Then, if a specific type of dry or moist heat involves more than one kind of food, a detailed description of it will follow. On the other hand, should the heat-process apply only to a single food category, like meat, you will find it elsewhere, under the cooking instructions for that particular food.

ABOUT DRY HEATS

◗ Truly dry heats are achieved in a number of ways. Grilling over coals is one, broiling or roasting in a ventilated oven another. When we say "barbecue," we may be referring to Pit-Cooking, page 90, in which case we refer to a moist heat process. Or we may mean skewer-cooking with its variants —spit, brochette or rotisserie— which is a dry one and itself a form of grilling. Parenthetically, the word "barbecue" has been traced back by some philologists to the Spanish "barbacoa," a raised platform for cooking; but we like to think of it, with other authorities, as originating among the French settlers in Florida, who roasted the native goats whole, "de barbe en queue"— from beard to tail. Some further remarks on barbecuing will be found farther along in this chapter, see Outdoor Cooking, page 89.

Baking is a dry heat process, too. In addition to the reflected and radiant heat of the oven, heat is transferred from the pan to the food and may be further diffused by the use of paper liners, temporary covers of foil or a dusting of flour between food and pan-bottom. Since, in baking, moisture is released from the food itself and, as warm vapor, continues to circulate in the closed oven chamber, this process is less dry than those previously mentioned.

Oddly enough, deep-fat frying is still another kind of dry heat cooking. Here the heat is not only transferred by the oil or grease used as a cooking medium, but by the moisture in the food itself—some of the steam from the food juices being forced into the fat and then out into the atmosphere. Among dry heat pan-processes, sautéing, page 253, uses the least fat. Pan-broiling and pan-frying are successive steps beyond sautéing and away from the driest heat.

In pan-broiling and pan-frying, the food develops a greater amount of rendered fat than in sautéing and it absorbs a larger share of it. In doing so, it gives up proportionately more of its juices. To keep both pan-frying and pan-broiling at their best, excess fat should be poured off during cooking.

While reducing—or concentrating—food through heat usually involves liquids, it also counts technically as a dry heat process since no additional moisture is introduced in accomplishing it.

Among dry heat processes which may be described as "partial" are planking and flambéing—or flaming. Either way, the food is heated beforehand and through them is given only its final finishing touch.

BROILING

The principle of broiling, whether on a grill or in a range, is identical. The heat is a radiant glow; and the process differs from roasting or baking in that only one side of the food at a time is exposed to the heating source.

However, all three of these types of dry heat depend, for their effectiveness, on proper ventilation. In the great majority of modern ranges, either gas or electric, you are given no selectivity in broiling temperatures. And individual variations in wattage—coil or burner area —and venting capacity make it necessary that you become familiar with the special requirements of your own equipment. Some ranges, for example, must be preheated before broiling can begin; in others, broiler heat is almost instantaneous. Likewise, in some electric ranges, broiling takes place with the oven door ajar; in others, the

door may, or even must, be kept closed.

When the heat indicator on a household range is turned to a ◗ broil position, the temperature is normally 550° or slightly above. If you wonder why you cannot always match the results you admire in some restaurant meat and fish cookery, remember that commercial installations deliver temperatures up to between 700° and 1000° and that these are quite beyond the reach of home equipment.

Under the limitations of the household range ◗ as much temperature control in broiling is exerted by the placement of the oven rack as by any other means. It is usually adjusted so that there is a 3-inch space between the source of heat and the top of the food. ◗ To lower the broiling heat for browning fragile sauces or delicate dishes like sweetbreads or for cooking very thick meats—where the heat must have time to penetrate deeply without charring— lower the broiling rack to make a 4- to 6-inch interval between food and broiler. Place food on a cold rack to prevent sticking. If the rack is hot, grease it—or grease the food. For details of broiling Steaks, etc., see page 455, Fowl, page 575; Fish, page 399; Vegetables, page 254.

SKEWER COOKING

From a marshmallow impaled on a stick to the most delicate bay scallops, this type of grilled food never seems to lose its charm for young or old. A most important first step is to ◗ choose items that will cook at the same rate of speed or to make the proper adjustment if they do not. When the meat or fish selected is a quick-cooking one, see that the onions, peppers or other more resistant vegetables which alternate with it are blanched in advance, so they will all be done at the same time. Should the meat need relatively longer cooking, skewer delicate alternates like tomatoes and mushrooms separately and mingle meat and vegetables in serving. Protect delicate meats —sweetbreads, liver, etc.—with breading or a wrapping of thinly sliced bacon. Choose skewers, whether metal or wood, that are either square or oval in section, so that, as the food softens in cooking, it will not slip while revolving.

If using a grill, grease it and cook the skewered food over medium heat. Turn the skewers often. Food grilled in this way may take anywhere from 6 to 12 minutes.

If cooking in a range, broil on a greased grill about 3 inches from the source of heat or adjusted on a pan, as shown on the illustration above. You may, of course, prefer to use the skewer element on your rotisserie. For more details about rotisserie or spit-cooking, see pages 93–94. Should you decide to precook any sort of skewered food, you may do so on the skewers themselves in a skillet, provided, of course, the skewers are no longer than the pan bottom. Sometimes partially precooked, skewered foods are coated with a sauce or with a bound breading and then cooked to completion in deep fat. When handled in this way, they are called atteraux. In flambéing

skewered foods, page 80, provide some protection for your hand.

Attractive combinations for skewers or brochettes include the following: scallops, shrimps, or oysters with or wrapped in bacon, and firm miniature tomatoes; chicken livers or pieces of calf liver or kidney alternating with cocktail sausages and mushrooms; diced eggplant or squash, blanched small onions, firm small tomatoes and bacon; shrimp or diced lobster, diced cucumber and stuffed olives; pieces of fish, sections of blanched celery and bacon; pieces of sausage and pickled onions; bacon and pieces of unpeeled apple; scallops, bacon and blanched pieces of onion. In this sketch are some of the foods we have just mentioned as suitable for skewering and a decorative way to impale cocktail skewers in a potato or grapefruit, after they have had their turn at the grill.

DEEP-FAT FRYING

Deep-fat frying, like a number of other accomplishments in cooking, is an art in itself—an art in which experience is the best teacher. Even a novice, however, who follows our instructions to the letter, can succeed in turning out delicious dishes in this ever-popular category—and, what's more, food fried without excess fat absorption. A serving of French fried potatoes properly cooked may have a lower calorie count than a baked potato served with butter. Remember, too, that fat-absorption increases with the length of cooking time and with the amount of surface exposed to the fat.

We simply do not believe, as a cynic has remarked, at least in deep-fat frying, that "foresight is the last gift of the gods to man." While our directions may, at first glance, seem complicated, read them calmly and carefully and you will be rewarded with crisp, golden-brown fried foods every time.

◆ First, equipment need not be elaborate, for equally good French fried potatoes can come out of a black iron kettle as from the latest model electric fryer. This is not to underestimate the value of the fryer, which offers the convenience of a built-in thermostat and furnishes also a storage space for the fat—after straining—between fryings. Proper fat storage is of considerable importance, as fat must be kept covered and in a cool place if it is to remain in good condition for repeated use.

Any deep kettle or saucepan, preferably a heavy one, serves nicely for deep frying. Use in a 3- or 4-quart kettle about 3 pounds of fat. It isn't wise to try to skimp on the amount, for there must always be enough to cover the food and to permit it to move freely in the kettle. ◆ There must also be room in the kettle for the quick bubbling up of the fat which occurs naturally in frying potatoes, onions and other wet items. ◆ Never fill any container more than half full of fat. ◆ Remember, too, to heat the fat gradually, so that any moisture in it will have evaporated by the time it reaches the required temperature.

The kettle should have a flat bottom, so that it will set firmly on the burner. One without a long handle is desirable, to avoid the danger of accidentally overturning the hot fat and causing a small conflagration. In case fat should ever catch on fire, have a metal lid handy to drop over the kettle. You may also smother the flame with salt. ◆ Never, under any circumstances, use water, as this will only spread the fire.

For frying certain types of food such as doughnuts and fritters where bubbling is not a problem, a heavy skillet or electric fry-pan rather than a deep kettle is sometimes preferred, because of its wider surface, which permits frying more pieces at one time.

A wire basket is practically a necessity for successful results in frying any quantity of material such as potatoes, oysters, onions, eggplant, etc. The food is then raised and lowered more easily, and even browning is assured.

Helpful, too, in deep frying, is a slotted metal spoon and long-handled metal tongs. A supply of absorbent paper for draining the fried food is important for the final disposal of excess fat.

For judging the temperature of the fat, use a frying thermometer, no other. Have the thermometer ready in a bowl of hot water to lessen the chance of breakage; but ◆ never plunge it into the fat without wiping it very dry. Nothing is more important in frying than proper temperatures. As that wise old gourmet, Alexander Dumas, so aptly put it, the food must be "surprised" by the hot fat, to give it the crusty, golden coating so characteristic and so desirable. And the easiest way to assure this is by using a thermometer.

When no thermometer is

available, a simple test for temperature can be made with a small cube of bread about 1-inch square. When you think the fat is hot enough, drop in the bread cube and count slowly to sixty or use a timer for sixty seconds. If the cube browns in this time, the fat will be around 375°, satisfactory for frying most foods. A few—Soufflé Potatoes for instance, page 316—may require higher or lower temperatures, but these will always be noted in the specific recipes.

Above all, do not wait for the fat to smoke before adding the food. This is not only hard on the fat, since smoke indicates that it is breaking down and may be spoiled for re-use, but the crust that forms on the food is likely to be overbrowned before the product is cooked through; and the result will be burned on the surface and raw inside. On the other hand, food introduced into fat that isn't hot enough to crust immediately will tend to be grease-soaked.

Once the proper temperature is established, you are ready to add the food. ♦ Do not try to fry too much at a time. This will lower the temperature unduly and may also cause the fat to bubble up too fast and go over the top of the kettle. Naturally, the colder the food when

added to the fat, the more the fat temperature will be reduced.

♦ Whenever possible, foods should be at room temperature when introduced into the kettle. ♦ Always immerse gently with long-handled tongs or a slotted spoon or in a frying basket. ♦ Always dip these utensils into the hot fat first, so that the food will release quickly from them without sticking. And have a pan ready in which to rest the utensils when they come dripping from the fat.

After frying one batch ♦ let the temperature come up again to the required heat, so that you may continue to "surprise" each additional one. ♦ Skim out bits of food or crumbs frequently—as they collect in the fat during frying. If allowed to remain, they induce foaming, discolor the fat and affect the flavor of the food.

At the end of frying, and after the fat has cooled somewhat, strain it to remove all leftover particles. Return it to the container and store for re-use. Adding some fresh fat for each new frying materially increases its length of life. When the fat becomes dark and thickish-looking, it will no longer be satisfactory for frying. At this stage, the smoking point has dropped too low; the flavor that it contributes to the food will be unpleasant and absorption high. Discard it.

▸ The household cooking fat known as "all-purpose" or sometimes simply as "shortenings" are American favorites. These include the solid fats such as lard, the plastic and hydrogenated fats and the liquid oils, among which corn, cottonseed and peanut are most commonly available for household use. Except for lard, which has a characteristic odor and flavor, these fats are bland and very similar in appearance and composition. Most of them are 100% vegetable in origin. The oils, in particular, are so much alike that unless one knows the source or examines the label, it is practically impossible to tell which is made from peanuts and which from corn or cottonseed. They all have smoking points well above those needed for deep frying.

Butter and margarines, valuable as they are for other purposes, are not considered suitable for deep frying, because of their low smoking points. As has been mentioned earlier, smoking of fat during frying should not be tolerated. It is hard on the food, hard on the fat itself and unpleasant when wafted through the house.

Various other fats are sometimes used for deep frying. Olive oil is popular where it is locally produced and soybean, safflower, rape and sesame oils are widely used where they are commonly grown and processed.

For special purposes and in certain circumstances chicken and goose fat are rendered in the home for frying, as are also veal, pork, suet and beef kidney fats. These are inclined to have low smoking points, but when handled with care they can be used to produce acceptable fried foods. If it seems desirable, the smoking point of these animal fats can be brought up to the required limit by blending them with any one of the cooking oils.

▸ The best way to render animal fats in the home is to cut them into small pieces—after removing bits of membrane, skin, etc.—and heat in a double boiler until melted. This process can be hastened by pressing down on the fatty pieces occasionally with a fork or spoon. Strain through cheese cloth to remove solid particles and store the rendered fat in a covered container in a cool place. ▸ Do not use drippings or fats skimmed from soups or gravies.

▸ For good results, the food to be fried must be properly prepared. Pieces should be uniform in size, preferably not thicker than 2 inches, so that they will all cook in the same length of time. Small pieces, obviously, will cook through faster than large ones. It is difficult here to give advice about length of cooking. When in doubt, it is wise to remove one piece and try for doneness.

Raw foods, ▸ especially wet ones, should be patted between towels or absorbent paper before cooking to remove excess surface moisture. This not only helps to keep the fat temperature from dropping too low, but it reduces the amount of bubbling when the food is introduced. In adding a batch of raw potatoes—French fries or chips—always lower the basket gradually so that you can observe the amount of bubbling and be ready to lift it up if it looks as though the fat might be going over the top. Until you have developed that "sixth sense," do not try to put too many pieces in the basket—rather fry several small batches than one large one. The cooked food may be kept hot on a paper-lined pan in the oven, set at very low heat.

Certain types of food need special coating for proper browning and crust formation —croquettes, eggplant, fish, etc. For Breading, see (II, 160). The coating may be simply flour, cornmeal or finely crushed dry cereal. Or it may be a Fritter Batter (II, 125), an egg and crumb mixture or even a pastry envelope. Whatever it is, it should cover the surface evenly.

Foods to be coated with batter—shrimp, for instance, or pineapple slices—should be surface-dried before applying the batter. Doughnuts, fritters and other batter-foods need no extra coating, as the egg-starch mixture browns nicely by itself when lowered into the hot fat. Many cooks do not realize that the richer a dough or batter mixture, the more fat it will absorb during frying. By adding even a little too much shortening or sugar to the mix, a doughnut may become so rich that it will end up by being grease-soaked. Or a fritter may simply disintegrate in the hot fat or the batter may slide off onion rings altogether.

✳ Frozen foods designed for deep frying are usually completely prepared. All that remains to be done is defrosting, which is better accomplished outside the package. Otherwise moisture may form on the surface and interfere with proper browning and crusting. Frozen foods that have to be coated should be defrosted, dried on the surface, if necessary, and the coating applied as usual.

In deep-fat frying ▲ at high altitudes, you will find that the lower boiling point of the water inside moist foods will require lower fat temperatures. For instance, French fries, which call for 375° in their final frying period, might need only a 365° fat temperature at high altitudes.

SAUTÉING

"Sauter" literally means "to jump," and this is just what happens to the food you cook by this method. The cooking is done in an ▶ open pan, which is kept in motion. The process is rapid, the food usually thin or minced and the ▶ heat must be kept up from the moment cooking starts until the food is tender. Any reduction in heat will draw juices. There are other requirements. The ▶ small quantity of fat used must be hot enough, when the food is added, to sear it at once—again to prevent the loss of juices. ▶ This can only be accomplished if the food is 70° or more, cut to a uniform thickness and size and dry on the surface. If it is too cold it will lower the heat, and if it is wet it will not brown properly. Worst of all, steam will form and break the seal holding the juices. To ensure a dry surface, food is frequently floured or breaded, see (II, 160). ▶ Steam will also form if the pan is crowded. There must be space between the pieces of food you are sautéing.

For the best sauté, use a Clarified Butter, page 383, or a combination of 3 parts butter and 4 parts oil. When these fats reach the point of fragrance, the 70° food is added, but not so much at a time as to reduce the heat in the pan. To keep the food, which should be heated to at least 340°, from too quick browning agitate the pan constantly. Too much turning of the food delays the quickness of heating. But food with a Bound Breading (II, 160), especially if the coating has not been dried long enough before cooking, may steam. In this case, turning will help to release some of that steam more rapidly. Usually sautéed meat is browned or cooked on one side until the blood comes up to the surface of the exposed side, then turned and browned on the other side.

To serve sautéed food with a sauce, remove the food from the pan and keep it warm on a hot serving dish. Quickly deglaze the delicious brown residue in the sauté pan—unless you have been cooking a strongly flavored fish—with stock or wine. Reduce the sauce and pour it over the sautéed food. If you heat sautéed food in sauce, you steam it too much.

PAN-FRYING

Dredge the food with seasoned breading, flour, cornmeal or a Bound Breading, see (II, 160). Melt a small amount of fat in a heavy pan over moderate heat. For meat, use fat from the meat you are cooking. Brown the meat on one side. When juice begins to appear on the upper surface, turn the meat with tongs and brown it on the other side. Drain and serve at once. Proceed in the same way for fish; but the cooking time is apt to be less. Cook on one side until golden brown before turning. Drain on paper towels and serve at once.

REDUCING LIQUIDS

This process is used mainly to intensify flavor: a wine, a broth or a sauce is evaporated and condensed over lively heat. A so-called "double consommé" is made in this way, the final product being half the original in volume. Naturally, reducing applies only to sauces without egg. And those which have a flour base must be watched carefully and stirred often to avoid scorching.

PLANKING

Why bother about planking? One reason is the attractive appearance of a planked meat, surrounded with a decorative band of Duchess Potatoes, page 319, beautifully browned on their fluted edges and garnished with colorful vegetables, after it emerges from the oven. Another reason is the delicious flavor an oak slab can give to meat. Planks are of 1-inch-thick kiln-dried oak. An 18-inch oval usually serves four to six. They often have a tree design cut down their length to drain juices into a shallow depression toward one end.

If all the cooking is done on the plank, it will char rapidly. Usually steaks are broiled on an oven grille fully on one side and partially on the other before being planked. To season a new plank ♦ brush it with cooking oil and heat in a 225° oven for at least one hour before using. To protect it when cooking, oil well any exposed part or cover, as suggested above, with a decoration of mashed potatoes or other puréed vegetables.

FLAMBÉING

Flaming always comes at a dramatic moment in the meal, sometimes a tragi-comical one if you manage to get only a mere flicker. To avoid anticlimax, remember that ♦ food to be flamed should be warm and that the brandy or liqueur used in flambéing should also be warm —but well under the boiling point. For meat, do not attempt this process with less than one ounce of liquor per serving. For nonsweet food served from a chafing dish or electric skillet, pour the warmed liquor over the surface of the food and ignite by touching the edge of the pan with the flame of a match or taper. For hot desserts in similar appliances, sprinkle the top surface with granulated sugar, add the warm liqueur and ignite as above.

ABOUT MOIST HEATS

What a number of processes can be assigned to the moist heat category! There are complete ones like boiling, pressure cooking, scalding, simmering, poaching, stewing, fricasseeing, braising, casseroling, cooking in wraps, double boiler cookery and steaming. Also, just as with dry heats, there are partial moist heat processes, like those in blanching and fireless cookery. We may as well mention here and now—although not on the side of simplification—that certain classic terms for kinds of moist heat cookery are broadly interpreted, even by the most knowledgeable cooks. Also a number are neither moist nor dry, but a combination of both. Some stews, for example, may be begun in a pan by browning, while others, like the Irish variety, never see the inside of a skillet. Similarly, a braise, a fricassee and a "smother" may all, like a browned stew, have their origin in dry heat sautéing and then are finished by cooking in a little stock.

BOILING

Discussing this process tempts us to mention stews again, in connection with the old adage "A stew boiled is a stew spoiled." And we may point out that the same sentiment can be applied to almost every other kind of food. While recipes often call for foods to be brought to the boiling point or to be plunged into boiling water, they hardly ever demand boiling for a protracted period. Even "boiled" eggs, so-called, should be simmered.

Quick evaporation—seldom advisable—is one of the few justifications for keeping a food at boiling point. When evaporating, never boil covered, as steam condenses on the lid and falls back into the pot, reducing the amount of liquid very little, if at all.

Adding foods to boiling water will lower the boiling point, unless the quantity of water is at least three times as much as will cover the food—to offset its lower temperature. Such compensation is recommended in Blanching, page 88, and in the cooking of cereals and pasta. When the pores of food are to be sealed, it may be plunged into rapidly boiling liquid, after which the temperature is usually reduced to a simmer.

✪ PRESSURE COOKING

A sound approach to pressure cooking involves an appreciation of its advantages and a knowledge of its limitations.

No matter how high the heat source, boiling in water in the presence of air can never produce a temperature over 212°. But, because in pressure cooking the air in the pan is withdrawn first, heat as high as 250° can be maintained at 15 lbs. gauge-reading. Some home cookers are geared to a range of from 3¾ to 20 pounds, although 15 pounds is commonly used. Cooking time at 15 pounds pressure takes only about ⅓ the total time—from the lidding of the pressure cooker through the capping of the vent and the release of pressure—that it takes to cook food in conventional ways at boiling temperatures. In pressure cooking vegetables over short periods at these higher temperatures, more than time is saved. Nutrients and flavor are also well conserved, see Steam Pressuring of Vegetables, page 252.

♦ In the pressure cooking of meats and soups, however, the higher heats involved tend both to toughen the protein and affect flavor adversely. Therefore, we recommend this method only when time is more important to you than choice results.

♦ In the canning of all nonacid foods, the higher heat of pressure cooking is essential to kill unwanted organisms, see (II, 538).

♦ Pressure cooking of beans and cereals and dried or puréed fruits, which may sputter and clog the vent, is not recommended because of this danger.

A pressure cooker may be used also for sterilizing baby bottles. Allow 10 minutes at 10 lbs. pressure.

It is essential in any pressure cooking to know your equipment well. ♦ Follow manufacturer's directions to the letter, observing these general principles. ♦ Never fill a pressure cooker with more food than ½ its capacity if there is much liquid or ⅔ if the contents are mainly solids. ♦ Be sure the required amount of liquid has been put in the cooker. ♦ Season lightly, as there is less liquid to dilute the flavor than in more traditional types of cooking. Solid foods may be placed at once over high heat. If soup or foods requiring more than the usual amount of water are to be cooked, the heat is brought up slowly. ♦ Always be sure to exhaust the air in the cooker before capping the vent, as trapped air will cause cold pockets and uneven cooking. Allow the steam to come out in a solid column before capping. When the ♦ indicator shows that the desired degree of pressure

has been reached or when the gauge or weight jiggles reduce the heat to just maintain desired pressures. ♦ Time from the moment of capping the vent. The pressure pan should show a mild form of activity by hissing occasionally during the cooking period.

If you have a stop clock, use it; if not, watch the time carefully as overcooking results very quickly. ♦ As soon as the time is up, to arrest further cooking and reduce the pressure in your cooker instantly, place it in cool water or let cool water run over the sides. Exceptions are steam puddings, preserves and soups, which should be allowed to cool gradually. When the temperature is brought down, exhaust the steam fully by removing the gauge.

♦ The cover must not be removed until all the steam is out of the pressure cooker. Here again, handle your particular type of appliance exactly as you are instructed. ♦ When the cover is difficult to remove, do not force it; there is still steam in the container which will be exhausted if you wait a few minutes.

If the amount of food to be cooked is increased, also increase the amount of liquid unless the units of the food are very small, when little or no additional liquid is necessary. But do not increase the amount of cooking time.

When cooking foods that require different periods of cooking, begin with the ingredient that requires the longest time. Always reduce the pressure, as directed in the manufacturer's booklet, before opening the lid to add the ingredient that requires the shorter period of cooking. Readjust the cover, place the cooker again over high heat and proceed as before.

When the desired degree of pressure has been reached, reduce the heat and begin to count the rest of the cooking time.

Or, when cooking together vegetables that require an unequal period of cooking, equalize them by cutting into small dice those that require the longer period: potatoes, turnips, etc.

▲ A general rule for pressure cooking at high altitudes, whether you are cooking at 10, 15 or 20 pounds pressure, is to ◗ maintain the same timing as at sea level, but to increase the pressure by ½ lb. for every rise of 1,000 feet.

For additional details about High Altitude pressure cooking, see Vegetables, page 254, Meat, page 457, Canning, page 748. To use a pressure cooker as a steamer, see Steam Puddings, page 703.

SCALDING

As the term is used in this book, scalding means cook at a temperature of about 185° or just below boiling. You will find this process discussed in relation to Milk (II, 137), the food for which it is most frequently used.

SIMMERING

This ranks as one of the most important moist heats. The temperatures range from about 135° to 160°. Simmering protects fragile foods and tenderizes tough ones. The French verb for it is "mijoter" and they engagingly refer to low simmers—between 130° and 135°—as "making the pot smile." When food is simmering, bubbles come gently to the surface and barely seem to break. It is the heat best used in cooking, uncovered, for soups and, covered, for stews, braises, pot-roasts, poêles, étouffés, page 493, and fricassees, page 577.

POACHING

This kind of moist heat cooking is one that most people associate only with eggs, but its range is much wider. The principle of poaching never varies. The heat source is a liquid just under the boiling point and a distinguishing feature of the process is the basting or self-basting which is constant during the cooking period.

◗ When an egg is properly poached, it is floated on simmering water and then either basted with this simmering liquid or covered with a lid, so that steam accumulates to perform a self-basting action. Because the egg cooks in just a few minutes, the lid does not allow the formation of excess steam. In poaching meat or fish, where the cooking period is lengthened, entrapped steam may become too heavy. For these and delicate foods, therefore, a lid is not recommended. Instead, substitute a poaching paper, see sketch.

A poaching paper permits excess steam to escape through its small top vent and around the sides. The narrow vent also maintains better color in the food than when air is excluded altogether—as in other more tightly confined moist heat processes, such as casseroling. ◗ To make a poaching paper, take a piece of square parchment, the sides of which are a little larger than the diameter of the pan you wish to cover. Fold it in fourths and roll it diagonally: begin at the folded corner, as sketched. Hold it over the pan to determine the radius. Then snip off the part that projects beyond the edge of the pan. Cut a tiny tip off the pointed end to form a vent. When you unfold the paper you will have a circle just the area of your pan, with a perforation at its center. Place it over the food to form a self-baster. If the cooking process is a short one or if the food to be cooked is in small units, the liquid may be at simmering point when the food is added. If the food is chunky, like a whole chicken, the water it put on cold, the food added and the water brought to a simmer ◗ uncovered. The liquid may then be skimmed and the poaching paper applied. Should the liquid become too much reduced during the cooking process, it must be replenished. ◗ This type of poaching is often miscalled boiling or stewing.

CASSEROLING

The term casserole has been bandied about so carelessly that it is time we took stock of its meaning—or, rather, meanings. In correct parlance, a "casserole" is both a utensil—usually a lidded one—and the process used for cooking a raw food in that utensil. But it has also come to mean a favorite type of self-serve dish which graces so many American buffets, but is not in the least the real McCoy. This mock casserole is a mixture of several foods, one of which may be a pasta or rice in a sauce. The mixture is often precooked or consists of a combination of precooked and quick-cooking food; and it is served in the baker in which it was heated. ◗ Mock casseroles, if cooked covered, will develop too much steam and the sauce they are served in will break down. They often have a gratinéed top, page 389, to protect the food and absorb excess grease. ◗ It is wise to wipe "prefabricated" casserole dishes well before heating, so they will not show any browned spilled-over areas on the outside surface when served. Often, for large groups, a rather shallow dish is used, both to ensure its heating through quickly and the presence of plenty of gratinéed top for each serving. If topping with biscuit or corn pone, heat in a 375° to 400° oven.

Let's go back to the casserole as a utensil. The unglazed clay ware used in Europe today has not changed shape since very ancient times. It is squat, with bulging sides, easily grasped round handles and a slightly arched lid. ◗ To season unglazed casseroles and to prevent an "earthy" taste or the subsequent retention of unwanted flavors, rub them well, inside and out, with cut cloves of garlic. Then fill with water, add onion skins, celery and leek tops, put in a low oven, let the water come to a boil and simmer about 2 hours. Finally, discard the water, wash the dish and lid, after which the casserole is ready for use. ◗ To avoid cracking, never set clay casseroles on heating elements unless they have previously had butter, oil or other food put in them; and if your burner is not thermostatically controlled, it is wise to use an asbestos pad or wire trivet.

Today the word casserole is applied to any deepish pot in which cooking actually goes on, or even to pots more rightly called sauteuses or deep skillets. ◗ In true casseroling, as distinguished from "mock" casseroling, a tight lid is integral to the process. The very slow cooking goes on in about a 300° oven and develops a bare simmer. There is a continuous self-basting action, as steam condenses on the lid and falls back on the food. Inasmuch as only a small quantity of water has been used to begin with, the long, slow cooking condenses this and the food juices into a delicious residue. After the food is removed, the residue when degreased, if necessary, and then deglazed, forms the sauce for the dish. This form of closed cooking with only the barest escape of steam is also called cooking "à l'étouffée." Pot roasting of chicken or veal is sometimes carried on in a partially lidded casserole. This variant, because of greater evaporation, needs basting, and the meats should not be overcooked.

WRAP COOKERY

Food commonly needs heat; but we are forever inventing ways to protect it from drying out while cooking. Lids, as well as double boilers, are familiar to us all; but sometimes more interesting flavors and textures can be developed by other means. One of the most mouth-watering sights we ever saw was a movie of an Indonesian tribe on the march. When mealtime came, oldster to tot began devising cases for cooking their food in the coals: intricately folded leaves, large stoppered sections of bamboo, reed baskets. You knew at once that the cases all had enough moisture to withstand the heat of the coals they were buried in and that they would give special flavor and succulence to the food. Cooking in wraps may take other forms, too, and in less primitive company—from the clay enclosed meat pies of English kiln-workers to the "en croûte" cookery so esteemed in France, see page 458.

LEAF-WRAPPINGS

These make wonderful food cases. Choose only very fresh, unblemished green leaves. How to use them depends on the kind chosen.

◗ To prepare cabbage leaves: cut the stem from a head of cabbage deep enough to start a separation of the very outer leaves from the core. Dip the head in boiling water. This will loosen 3 or 4 leaves. Dip again and continue to remove the loosened leaves. Blanch, page 82, the leaves for 2 minutes, drain and plunge into cold water. To wrap meat in the leaves, see the illustration on the next page. Either tie the leaf-packet as shown or place it, if it is left untied, seam-side down. ◗ Cook the leaf-packets as follows.

I. Melt in casserole:
    2 tablespoons butter

Add:

**2 cups boiling water or
stock**

Put food in a single layer on bottom of casserole. Place a plate on top to give weight during cooking. If filling is uncooked, bake or simmer the packets, covered, 35 to 40 minutes—longer for pork. If filling is precooked, 10 minutes is enough to heat the food through.

II. If packets are tied, they may be dropped into simmering broth and cooked gently until done. See timing under I.

II. Or, as in Tamales, page 287, packets, see right above, may be steamed in a vegetable steamer. See timing under I.

♦ To prepare lettuce leaves: soak them very briefly in boiling water. Drain, dry and fill. Wrap as for cabbage leaves and cook as for I or III. They are not strong enough to cook as for II.

♦ To prepare fresh grape leaves for Dolmas, page 522, drop young pale-green leaves into boiling water and blanch till color darkens—about 4 to 5 minutes. Remove leaves. Drain them on a skimmer. Should you have to use large leaves, remove the tough part of the central rib. Place shiny side down on a board. Roll the filling in ¾-inch balls. If the filling is of rice, use not more than 2 teaspoons, as the rice will swell. Set one ball near the broad end of a leaf,

fold over the left and right segments, as sketched. Then roll the leaf from beyond the filling ball toward its tip, just as though you were rolling a cigarette. Place it, loose end down, and cook as directed above.

♦ To prepare and separate canned grape leaves, place them briefly in hot water.

♦ To prepare papaya leaves, cover them with cold water. Bring ♦ just to the boiling point —uncovered. Drain. This will remove any bitterness. Plunge into boiling water to cover and ♦ simmer, uncovered, until tender.

♦ To prepare corn husks place them in boiling water, remove from heat and allow to stand 5 minutes before draining. To roll food in them, overlap two or three corn husks. Place the filling in an oblong shape centered on the leaves. Fold the leaves first from the sides and then from the ends, as shown, so they can be tied with one string.

FOIL COOKERY

Aluminum foil solves many kitchen problems, but if you cook food wrapped in foil, please consider the following. The foil is impervious to air and moisture from the outside. Therefore, it traps within its case all the moisture released from the food during the cooking period. So, even if the heat source is dry, like that of an oven, the result will always be a steamed food, never a roasted one. Since the foil also has high insulating qualities, foil-wrapped food will require longer cooking at 75° higher heat. You may be willing to pay for both the foil and the extra heat needed to have the convenience of an effortless Pot Roast, see page 498. If you are cooking out of doors, see Campfire Vegetables and the comments in Outdoor Cooking, pages 89–90.

COOKING EN PAPILLOTE

This is a delightful way to prepare delicate, quick-cooking, partially cooked or sauced foods. The dish, served in the parchment paper in which it was heated, retains the aromas until ready to be eaten. As the food cooks, some of the unwanted steam it generates evaporates through the paper. Just the same, the paper rises and puffs as heating progresses, putting considerable strain on the folded seam. So, note the following directions and sketches carefully.

To make a papillote: fold a parchment of appropriate size in half, crosswise. Cut from the folded edge to the open edge, a half heart shape, so that when the paper is opened, as shown, the full heart shape materializes.

Be generous in cutting—allowing almost twice again as much paper as the size of the object to be enclosed. Place the food near the fold—not too close to the seam. Turn the filled paper with the folded edge toward you. Holding the edges of the paper together, make a fold in a small section of the rim. Crease it with your fingers and fold it over again. Hold down this double fold with the fingers of one hand and with the other start a slightly overlapping and

again another double overlapping fold. Each double fold overlaps the previous one. Repeat this folding, creasing and folding around the entire rim, finishing off at the point end of the heart with a tight twist of the parchment—locking the whole in place. Now butter the paper well. Place it in a buttered ovenproof dish in a 400° preheated oven for 5 to 6 minutes or until the paper puffs. In serving, snip about ¾ of the paper on the curved edge just next to the fold to reveal the lovely food and release the aroma.

DOUBLE BOILER COOKING

For those foods which are quickly ruined beyond hope of resurrection if overheated, even for a short period—especially egg, cream or chocolate dishes—we recommend the use of a double boiler. It is a peaceful way to cook delicate sauces, particularly if you are obliged to make them at a time when preparing other dishes which need close surveillance.

Sometimes food is started over direct heat in the top of a double boiler and is finished ♦ over—not in—hot water. For sauces, we like a double boiler that is rather wide. Deep and narrow vessels tend to overheat the sauce at the bottom even when it is stirred—if it is held for any time at all. ♦ The material of which the upper portion of the double boiler is made is very important. When the material is too thin, it transmits heat too fast. If it is too thick, it absorbs and retains too much heat. For years, we made magnificent Hollandaise in a stoneware bowl that fit the base of an aluminum double boiler. It was a completely effortless procedure. Then the bowl broke and the magic fled. We found stainless steel and aluminum too quick. A deluxe saucière of stoneware, deep set in a copper base, was too reluctant and, when it finally heated, too retentive of heat. A flame-resistant glass double boiler, for all the irritation of using a protective trivet at the heat source, has been a reliable substitute for our favorite old makeshift and does allow us to keep track easily of the ♦ over—not in—hot water factor.

STEAMING

For cooking vegetables, steaming is an excellent process to use. On page 252, we describe two methods for this purpose: direct steaming over boiling water and pressure steaming at greater temperatures. Direct steaming is also a good way to plump raisins, to release salt from smoked birds and, more importantly, to cook fish, page 398.

BLANCHING AND PARBOILING

These terms are among the most carelessly used in a cook's vocabulary. To introduce some order into traditional confusion we describe and differentiate between four different types of blanching. Which type is required will, we believe, be clear from the context of our individual descriptions.

♦ BLANCHING I

This means pouring boiling water over food to remove outer coverings, as in loosening the brown hulls of almonds or making the skins of peaches and tomatoes easier to peel off. This process is also used to soften herbs and vegetables for more flexible and longer-lived decoration.

♦ BLANCHING II OR
PARBLANCHING

This involves placing food to be blanched into ♦ a large quantity of cold water ♦ bringing it slowly to a boil ♦ uncovered, and continuing to ♦ simmer it for the length of time specified. Following this hot bath, the food is drained, plunged quickly into cold water to firm it and to arrest further hot water cooking and then finished, as directed in the recipe. This is the process used to leach excess salt from tongue, cured ham or salt pork and to remove excess blood or strong flavors from variety meats. The cold water plunge after blanching effectively firms the more fragile variety meats, like brains and sweetbreads.

♦ BLANCHING III OR
PARBOILING

This means that food is plunged into ♦ a large quantity of rapidly boiling water a little at a time so as not to disturb the boiling and then cooked for the period indicated in the recipe. The purpose of this particular kind of blanching or parboiling may be to set color or—by partial dehydration—to help preserve nutrients and firm the tissues of vegetables. If further cooking follows immediately, the blanched food need not be chilled as above, but merely drained. Should an interval elapse before cooking and serving, use the cold water plunge, drain and store the food refrigerated. Blanching vegetables in this way preparatory to canning or freezing is described in greater detail on (II, 556). Small amounts of the vegetable are plunged into ▶ boiling water just long enough to retard enzymatic action and to shrink the product for more economical packaging. Then the vegetables are ▶ drained and quickly plunged into ▶ ice water, so that the cooking process is arrested at once.

▶ BLANCHING IV, STEAM
BLANCHING OR PARSTEAMING

An alternate method for freezing and canning is also described on (II, 556).

FIRELESS COOKING

If fuel is scarce, and for food needing a long heating period, there is a possible advantage in using a fireless cooker. This appliance is enclosed on all sides by material that is a nonconductor of heat and is preheated to a desired temperature by an electric coil or by hot stones. Hot food set in it continues to cook without the addition of further heat.

OUTDOOR COOKING

Cooking out-of-doors may put to use all kinds of heat; but its enthusiasts do best when they stick to simple methods. As soon as cookouts get complicated, the whole party—in our perhaps jaundiced opinion—will do well to move back into the kitchen, where equipment is handy, controls positive and effects less problematical. We never attend a patio barbecue featuring paper chef's hats, aprons with printed wise-cracks, striped asbestos gloves, an infra-red broiler on white-walled wheels and yards and yards of extension cord and culinary red tape, without anticipating a deservedly heavy thunderstorm.

For campers, al fresco cooking is a necessity—rather than a pleasant indulgence. On long trips or in emergencies, very primitive heat sources will do a surprisingly good job. This is true especially if the camper's cooking utensils can be largely confined to kettle, coffeepot and skillet. The illustration on page 89 foreground shows perhaps the easiest of all outdoor cooking set-ups. It is called ◗ a hunter's fire. Two fairly chunky green logs are set directly on the ground, open-V fashion, and oriented so that the prevailing wind enters at the wide end of the V. If big logs are not available, build the V of rocks. When the fire, which has been built inside, burns to embers, kettle, skillet and coffeepot can span the logs, as shown. ◗ Before bringing any sort of cooking container in close contact with a wood fire, remember to cover its under-surfaces with a film of soap or detergent. This precaution will greatly facilitate the removal of soot later, when the pan is cleaned.

Speaking of easy outdoor cooking devices, we once went on a picnic with some friends in a beech woods. Our host, toward supper-time, made criss-cross fires, just big enough for each individual steak. First, he set up

log-cabin-like cribs about four layers high, with twigs approximately 1-inch thick. In these, he laid a handful of dry leaves and fine brush. On top of the cribs, he continued to build for about three inches an additional structure of pencil-like material. When, after firing, the wood had been reduced to a rectangular framework of glowing rods, he unlimbered some thin steaks from a hamper and, to our consternation, laid them calmly and directly on the embers. In a few moments he removed them with tongs, shook off whatever coals had adhered, turned the steaks over and repeated the process on the other side. They were delicious.

Another device for rough-and-ready outdoor cookery involves the principle of the crane. Two versions are illustrated, both for kettle cookery and both largely self-explanatory. A ring of rocks around a campfire will keep the flames from spreading and reflect the heat back into the cooking circle.

Pit-cooking is perhaps the most glamorous of all primitive types—glamorous because it is so largely associated with picturesque places, hearty group effort and holiday spirit. Pits may be small holes, of just sufficient depth and width to take a bean pot, a three-legged kettle or a true braizing pot with a depression on top for coals, as sketched; or they may be big enough to accommodate a king-size luau, replete with suckling pigs. Sometimes hardwood embers are left in the pit. Then steel rods are put across it—held a few inches above the fire on the rocks or logs set around its periphery. The rods, in turn, support a wire mesh grid on which the food is cooked. A switch from direct pit-firing to fireless pit-cooking and a completely different range of culinary effects can be achieved by a variant of this procedure.

Fairly large scale cookery of the latter type will require digging a pit, to begin with, not less than 2 feet deep, 3 feet across, and 4 feet long. If pit-cooking is more than occasional and the locale does not vary, you may find it more convenient to build a pit in reverse, by constructing a hollow rectangle of concrete blocks, about the same height as a true pit is deep.

The next step is to line the bottom and sides of the pit with medium-size flat rocks ♦ never with shale, which may explode when heated. Toss in enough additional rock to approximate the area of the pit. Now spread over the rocks a substantial bonfire of hardwood deadfall or driftwood. Hickory, beech, maple or ironwood are prime for this purpose. And grape-vine cuttings lend grilled food special distinction. The French, incidentally, regard food broiled over grape-wood, or "sarments de vigne," as extraordinarily choice. When the fire has completely burned down—this should take not less than 2 hours—rake out the red embers and the top rocks. Now, sprinkle a quart or so of water over the hot rock bed remaining and add a two-inch layer of green leaves —grape, beech, pawpaw, sas-

safras, cornhusks or seaweed. If you have remembered to bring along some handfuls of aromatic herbs, add them too. ♦ Work quickly at this point, so that the rocks do not lose their stored heat. On the bed of packed foliage arrange the elements of your meal: fish, cuts of meat, green peppers, onions, corn in its husks, unpeeled potatoes, acorn squash. Pile over them a second layer of green leafage, then a second grouping of food and, finally, a third layer of green leafage. Cap the stratification off with the remaining hot rocks, a tarpaulin or canvas cover and four inches of earth or sand to weight things down and to keep heat and steam at work inside—cooking your meal. How long this will take depends, of course, on what's cooking—maximum time will probably be required for a small pig; it should test 190° when done and takes about 20 minutes per pound.

For shore dinners, with seaweed as filler, wire mesh is often placed over at least one layer to better support small crustaceans, clams and oysters. For details of a Clam Bake, see page 428. Such tidbits may also be steamed in closed kettles—we have used a clean refuse can with a tight-fitting lid ♦ but be careful not to let such containers rest directly on the hot rocks or to cook any food that is very acid directly in them. Allow one live lobster or three softshell crabs per person.

In Hawaii, and in the East Indies generally, food cooked in pits is frequently wrapped in papaya leaves which not only protect but tenderize, see page 522. In the West Indies, petate mats are used for this purpose. ♦ Wrapping food before introducing it into direct heat is almost as old as cooking itself.

Primitive societies to this day surround pieces of food with a leaf and then with clay, to protect them from burning.

In France the technique has given rise to a branch of food preparation called "en croûte" cookery, page 458, in which the encasement is dough. Its principle is increasingly exploited in ◗ papillote, page 87. Both in the pastry and paper casings some steam escapes. But, in cookouts today, if ◗ wrapping the food in heavy duty aluminum foil, page 87, it must be remembered that the imperviousness of the foil makes for a truly steamed product and that texture and flavor are far removed from that of food typically cooked by direct heat. Indeed this is true of the closed-in type of pit-cookery, as described above, in general, but there the flavor of the charcoal and seaweed or leaves adds a delicious touch.

The whole pit-cookery operation, whether it is carried out on the beach or in the woods, has a distinctly adventurous character. And periodic tests for doneness performed on the foods closest to the edge of the pit are an essential part of the process.

In lifting the tarp and in removing it altogether when you are ready to serve, be extremely careful not to get food fouled up with sand or earth.

There are several ways to rig up simple stoves for camp cooking. One is made from a tin can of fairly large capacity—from a gallon on up, see the sketch at right, above. Its features are basic to stoves of any sort. The cylinder, or body, of the can shelters the fire from draft and supports the cooking pan; the fire below is kept supplied with oxygen by the bottom opening. The upper opening can be regulated to sustain the flow of heat and allows the release of smoke and hot gases. The holes punched in the top of the can steadily bring up a supply of heat to the pan. This can be fueled with canned heat or a small twig fire. ◗ You can cut a cooking utensil from a second can, but be sure to handle it with gloves!

Probably the most effective do-it-yourself device for smoking food is merely a modification of the tin-can stove—a can-on-can affair, with two hollow cylinders closely fitted together, as sketched. The fuel here is sawdust from nut or fruitwood, which is piled up to one-fourth the height of the lower can and which smolders

rather than burns, giving off, in so doing, the required abundance of smoke. The can should be preheated before the food is added. For smoking ham, meat, fowl or fish see (II, 543–546). The food to be treated is hung from a crossbar or bars inserted across the upper cylinder. ◗ To retain as much smoke as possible in the curing area, the upper can has only a single vent at the tops of the cans, some side-perforations at the bottom, and a 4-inch square base-vent.

By projecting the device just described further, the Chinese, centuries ago, perfected a wholly distinctive type of food preparation, which is gaining popularity in this country today: smoke-cookery. A section through a typical smoke oven is L-shaped. The horizontal leg of the L contains the firebox; the vertical portion is fitted with horizontal bars or wire racks on which the food is placed. After igniting the fuel—generally fruitwood spiced with dried herbs—the box is closed and firing continued until the temperature of the stack reaches 400° to 500°, at which time the food to be smoke-cooked is introduced.

To return to the camper for a final word: There is no law, of course, against his availing himself of ready-made cooking gear; and as much of it as the traffic will bear. A gasoline or propane-fired stove is a great convenience and,

if he expects to do any baking, a reflector oven a downright necessity. Shown on page 89 is a folding oven. If that is not available, use as a substitute a camp skillet, as sketched, braced either by a forked stick or rocks. There are even available, for the Davy Crocketts of the New Frontier, various solar heat cookers; but it is suggested that they be given home-side tryouts in advance.

We have described—at least briefly—the elements of camp and pit cookery. The disadvantages of the latter, as we have indicated, are several. The greatest, perhaps, is its relative inconvenience. That is one reason why the above-ground cookout —as distinguished from the subterranean type—is far and away the more popular. There, again, we most enjoy the simpler techniques and procedures: those which involve direct heat from reduced charcoal. Among them, we prefer, also, portable rather than built-in cookers; and here we seem to be following a definite trend. The rather formidable backyard fireplace is less and less favored. It had metal components which were hard to clean and rusted in the weather. These built-in features offered unintended hospitality to spiders, wasps and field-mice. And its homely architecture can hardly be said to have graced its surroundings. Now, the most popular cookout stove is the portable brazier-type, of which the hibachi is the Far-Eastern representative. To accommodate a main dish for groups of four or more, only the larger Westernized brazier offers an adequate cooking surface. A hibachi-type broiler or two will supplement this larger grill in the preparation of side dishes, such as hors d'oeuvre and vegetables. The circular grill (page 94) boasts some improvements over the original prototype. It has, of course, fairly good-size wheels for easy transport, as well as a hood or collar to protect the grill surface against wind. The grill itself may be twirled, to expose food to the most active area of the heat and is equipped with a screw device which raises and lowers it for varied exposures. We also show another model with a bellows, which compensates for the small lower draft-port found on the hibachi. This

enables the cook to bring up quick high heat for searing and rewarming. Some braziers with horizontal grills have superim-

posed over them a spit, in which case they are commonly protected from wind by three bent metal walls and a metal roof, rather than a simple hood. Without an electrical connection or making use of a cumbersome counter-weight system, the only practical way to turn a spit is by hand; and this—make no mistake—is a real chore. On the whole, should you go in extensively for spit-cooking, we should advise either precooking the meat in the kitchen till nearly done or investing in an electric rotisserie. Remember that in all spit cooking, the weight losses due to shrinkage are great.

If you do cook out of doors electrically, you may want to make use of a vertical, rather than a horizontal, broiler which, in theory at least, exposes a maximum of food surface to the heat source. Newer still are infrared broilers. But these, for what they are worth, we regard as strictly indoor appliances. Whatever equipment you use, pay close attention to the directions furnished with it by its manufacturer. Such brochures have become more and more informative and presently cover not only how to use the appliance itself, but how to cook a large number of typically outdoor dishes with it.

For cookout accessories, assuming a full scale operation, the following are recommended: a kettle for boiling water; a black iron pot for burgoos, stews or beans; a skillet or two; hinged wire basket grills with long handles—especially desirable for broiling fish and hamburgers; some sharp knives; a metal fork with an insulated handle; a spatula; tongs; a long pastry brush for glazing; a chopping block; skewers—these must be nonrusting ♦ square or oval, not round, in section and sharp-pointed; a roll of double-strength aluminum foil; a supply of potholders or a couple of pairs of asbestos mitts; individual serving trays; a pail of water and, with it, a flare-up quencher. For this last, an extra baster will do—or a water pistol. If you plan to roast a fowl or a joint, you will need, in addition, a baster, shown on page 457, and a meat thermometer.

♦ To prepare a brazier fire with charcoal, be sure that you build a big enough bed of coals to last out the cooking operation. We find prepared hardwood briquets most uniform and convenient. They should be put into the brazier approximately two deep—preferably over a layer of gravel—enough to level the bed out to the edge of the bowl.

A circle of aluminum foil, cut to size and put down over the gravel, will keep it from getting greasy and act as a heat reflector. Ignition may be helped along by pouring over the briquets a small amount of commercial lighter fluid ♦ before, not after, applying the match. Never use any strong-smelling substance as starter. To ready fuel for an extended firing period, arrange an extra circle of briquets around the edge of the brazier. As the center of your fire burns to embers, these may be pushed inward.

To ignite charcoal is often frustrating, especially if it is old and has been exposed to air—for it absorbs moisture so easily. A good way to avoid irritation is to keep a few briquettes soaking in lighter fluid ♦ in a tightly lidded metal container. You will find 1 or 2 of these saturated blocks is a great help.

Confect for yourself a 12- or 15-inch length of lightweight stove pipe, cut at the base every two inches with a tin snips to the depth of about 2½ inches to make a fluted edge—or punch holes in it about 1 inch up. Place it in the grill, put some paper near one of the fluted openings, place one or two of the saturated briquettes on the paper and then the other briquettes you are going to use on top. Light the paper. In about 5 to 10 minutes the briquettes will have become well ignited. Gently pull up the chimney with tongs and the briquettes will spread out so you can arrange them in whatever grilling pattern you plan to use—in one layer on one-half of the fire box of your circular twirl grill, as shown on page 94, or spaced at 1- to 2-inch intervals over the whole surface of the firebed or in a double ring around the edge for a spitted bird.

If you use any kind of smoked or flavored chips, soak them in water for several hours beforehand and then wait until a few minutes before the charcoal is completely reduced, which should take anywhere from a half hour to 45 minutes, before placing them on the coals. ♦ When the charcoal is covered with a fine white ash, you are ready to begin cooking. Flick off the ash, which acts as insulation.

Judging the heat of a brazier fire is strictly a matter of manual training. Hold your hand above the grill at about the same distance from the coals that the food will be while cooking, think of the name of a four-syllable state—"Massachusetts" or "Mississippi" will do nicely. If you can pronounce it once before snatching your hand away, your coals are delivering high heat; twice, medium heat; if three times, low heat.

Remember always that a number of factors influence the degree of heat transferred to food cooked on outdoor braziers; some of these being charcoals; their depth; distance between coals and grill; temperature of ingredients, which, if possible should be about 70°. You may also considerably influence heat transfer by your arrangement of coals: deepening them for concentration, spreading them apart for diffusion, etc. If you have the kind of brazier grill which twirls, heaping hot coals up on one side of the fire pot will make instantly available both very high and very moderate heat.

What food should be cooked out of doors? Just as we recommend simple cooking equipment in the open, so we now urge simple outdoor menus. The truth is that refined or fancy effects are—in the nature of things—all but impossible not to say inappropriate. Again, certain kinds of food respond unfavorably or indifferently to outdoor cooking techniques: yeast breads are a conspicuous example; some vegetables are another; and among the meats, veal and pork, except, of course, pork sausages and—just because they are so delicious on a sparkling autumn afternoon—spareribs. But spareribs should be at least parboiled beforehand, page 88, and only finished off and rebasted on spit or grill out of doors.

Build your cookout meal around one basic delicious grilled or roasted meat course, complemented by crisp bread and a crisp salad. Let side dishes be strictly side-issues. The dessert should be correspondingly uncomplicated and, if baked, prepared beforehand in the kitchen. ◗ Remember with Picnic Food (II, 23) to protect it always against insects.

Throughout this book you will find recipes which we regard as suitable for outdoor cookery marked with this grill-like symbol ⊟. While, obviously, panbroiled and pan-cooked food may be prepared over a brazier out of doors, you will not find such recipes singled out by the distinctive outdoor cookery symbol. We have in large part, selected those in which the flavor is actually improved by the outdoor cooking medium.

Steaks and chops are extraordinarily well suited to flatbroiling on a brazier. ◗ Choose well-marbled meat—in other words, meat that is rather fatty in texture, page 450. But, by this, we definitely do not mean meat which has a rim or collar of fat. On the contrary, it is important ◗ to trim off all excess fat before broiling, to reduce the risk of flare-up. Also, cut through encircling sinew—being careful not to slice into the meat itself —so that the meat does not curl up under the high heat which initiates its cooking. ◗ Avoid excessively thick cuts: an inch and a half should be the limit for individual servings. Grease the grill first with some of the meat fat or with a vegetable oil. ◗ To sear the meat and seal in its juices, lower the grill close to the coals before laying the meat on it or use the bellows attachment if it is equipped with one.

Searing to seal is even more essential in flat-broil grilling than in pan or oven broiling, because the meat juices, once lost, are irrecoverable. After searing, raise the grill to about three inches from the fire and broil the meat until done. No specific time schedule for doneness can be set up because so much depends not only on the degree of heat itself, but on the age of the animal, how long the meat has been hung, the nature of the cut and, of course, individual preference.

Here are a few things to keep in mind: First, just as in indoor Timing, page 458, large cuts do not take weight for weight proportionately more cooking time. Second, to secure rareness in meat, turn it—but best practice is to turn as infrequently as possible. Third, if the cut is large, testing for doneness with a thermometer is safer than testing with a knife or fork. We would like to spare you the ordeal of an old friend of ours, whose enthusiasm for outdoor grilling is repeatedly dampened by his wife's low-voiced but grim injunction: "Remember, Orville, medium-burnt, not well-burnt."

◗ If you flat-broil chicken or other fowl, restrict the weight of the bird to two pounds or under. Split it in half, grease both sides with cooking oil, set the halves on the grill, cavity side down. The bony structure of the bird will transmit heat to the flesh above and at the same time provide insulation. Finish the cooking on the fleshy side; but ◗ to keep the skin from sticking, make sure to lower the heat before doing so.

Spit and rotisserie cooking are best for very small or large fowl; for joints, like leg of lamb, and for other chunky cuts of meat. Here again, consult the directions which come with your equipment to determine maximum weight, which will probably be in the neighborhood of ten pounds for roast meat and up to 15 for fowl. Smaller birds should be strung transversely on the spit, larger ones head to tail along the spit's axis, as illustrated.

For spareribs, get your butcher to cut them in half crosswise, forming two long strips; prebake or parboil them in the kitchen and then string them, in turn—like an accordion—on your outdoor spit, as shown. Fowl and certain other types of meat must be trussed before spitting. Especially if they are heavy or of irregular shape, it is necessary, while adjusting them to the skewer, to determine their approximate center of gravity.

Fowl on a spit should be carefully coated in advance with melted butter or cooking oil. You may baste with butter or oil during the cooking period but ◗ do not apply any barbecue sauce until the last 15 to 20 minutes of cooking. For Barbecue Sauces, see page 374.

▤ ◗ For cooking Vegetables, see page 253.

▤ ◗ For Cooking on Skewers, see pages 75 and above.

TIMING IN COOKING

How long to heat food? There are many answers. They lie in the interaction of the heat source, the equipment and the cooking medium, air, liquid or fat.

Consider the following rates of heat transferral. A dough that either bakes at 400° or steams at 212° for 20 minutes will cook in deep fat heated to 400° in 3 minutes. A hard-cooked egg will cool off in five minutes if plunged into ice water, but will need 20 minutes to cool in 32° air. A vegetable that will cook in 20 minutes in water at 212° will need only 2 minutes steaming under 15 lbs. pressure at 250°.

A great deal in timing depends on the freshness of food—this is especially true of vegetables—on the aging and fat content of meat and on the size of the food unit. Large, thick objects like roasts need lower heat and a longer cooking period than cutlets, to allow heat penetration to the deep center. The amount of surface exposed is also a factor, as you know from experience with whole as against diced vegetables.

Still another determinant is the reflective and absorptive quality of the pan. Recent tests have shown that a whole hour can be cut from the roasting time of a ten- or twelve-pound turkey if it is cooked in one of those dark enamel pans which absorb heat rather than in a shiny metal one that reflects it. And we have discussed elsewhere, page 86, the insulative qualities of foil when used in wrap-cooking. Personal preference affects timing, of course, as well as the idiosyncrasies of equipment. Even placement in an oven, page 100, makes a difference and, last but not least, the temperature of food at the onset of heating. For all these reasons it is with some trepidation that we have indicated cooking periods in our individual recipes. And with some reluctance we have discarded the simple, safe admonition "cook until done." We know from our fan mail that cooking times are among the most worrisome of all problems for the beginning cook. Therefore, if our timing does not correspond to yours, we beg you to look for solutions in the facts we have set down above, before you take pen in hand.

HOLDING FOOD AT SERVING TEMPERATURES AND REHEATING FOOD

Everyone knows that food which is held hot or reheated is not as tasty or nutritious as that served immediately after preparation. Unfortunately, laggards and leftovers are a cook's frequent fate. Here are a few hints on the best procedures.

◆ There are 2 ways to reheat dishes which are apt to curdle when subjected to high, direct temperatures. These include au gratin, egg or creamed dishes or any other dish rich in fat. One way is to put them in the oven in a container of hot water—allowing the water to come up about two thirds of the way on the cooking pan. The other way is to place under the pan a cookie tin, with the shiny side down—so that the heat is deflected. The latter suggestion is particularly handy in reheating pies or cakes to avoid overbrowning.

◆ Reheat other cream and egg-sauced foods in a double boiler ◆ over—not in—hot water.

◆ To retain color in vegetables which are reheated in a double boiler, use a vented lid.

◆ If reheating whole roasts, bring them to room temperature and then heat through in a moderate oven.

◆ If reheating roasted meat, slice it paper thin and put it on hot plates just before pouring over it ◆ boiling hot gravy. Any other method of reheating will toughen it and make it taste second-hand.

◆ To reheat deep-fat fried foods, which tend to go limp if steam develops, spread them on racks ◆ uncovered, in a 250° oven.

◆ To hold pancakes, place them on and between cloth towels in a 200° oven.

♦ To reheat casseroles, bring to 70° then place in a 325° preheated oven.

♦ To hold delicate sauces, use a wide-mouthed vacuum bottle.

♦ To reheat creamed or clear soups or sauces, heat to boiling point and serve immediately.

Devices which also hold foods for short periods are electrically controlled trays, individual retractable infra-red lamps, the age-old chafing dish and the bain-marie or steam table. None of these should be used for a protracted period, however, if you hope to preserve real flavor. Holding temperatures should be at about 140°.

ABOUT COOKING EQUIPMENT

Certain cooking effects we have admired away from home and would like to bring back with us seem to defy domestication. Part of the difficulty may have to do with the way food is grown elsewhere or to the fact that it is sometimes impossible to buy ingredients of comparable freshness. But, just as often, the loss in translation may be traced to special techniques which simply cannot be duplicated in the average kitchen. This is true of the following: the quick, intense, short-lived fires and the huge pans which are essential to Chinese stir-frying; the very low, long-retained heat of the "étuve" in old French kitchens—so ideal for drying out meringues or for simmering foods in covered pots; and, for that matter, the open-air charcoal grilling in our own country, which imparts its distinctive aroma to a steak, or the seaweed-smother which gives that authentic touch to lobsters pit-cooked at the shore.

Conditions like these may be approximated in cooking on modern ranges, but never completely reproduced.

If you grew up using gas for cooking heat, you appreciate its dynamic flexibility of control. If your experience has been with electric ranges, you value the evenness of their broiling heat and the stored warmth of their surface units. The relatively new infra-red cooking appliances—including infra-red attachments for the conventional electric range—have attracted favorable attention because of their ability to reduce heating time to a fraction of its former length. Should you decide to invest in this type of equipment, be sure to read the manufacturer's booklet with care, making some mental reservations about the feasibility of "plate dinner" cooking.

Indeed, whatever your source of cooking heat, learn the characteristics of your range, thoroughly. Find out if the broiling elements need a preheating period; if broiling in the oven requires an open or a closed door; whether, when you turn the switch to "Bake," you do better leaving the top oven element in or taking it out.

In purchasing, consider the safety value of controls which are located along the front of a range instead of at the rear, where they may be obstructed by tall pans or cause injuries by bringing the hand and clothing into too near proximity to the burners. Pay particular attention, also, to the quality of oven insulation in the range you plan buying and to its venting characteristics.

In loading ovens, we make the following suggestions. ♦ Place oven racks where you want them before heating, not after. For soufflés, arrange racks to bring the dish below center, as on page 100. Often, in modern ovens, slight heat is provided by a top element, enough to harden the surface of a soufflé if set too close—keeping it from expanding. For cake-baking, the best position for the pan is just above center, as shown. Commercial ovens often feature devices for introducing moisture into an oven, as needed. In the home range, a practical substitute—should the recipe require it—consists of a shallow pan partially filled with water, as sketched on the right, below.

♦ Make sure that the pans or sheets you are using will fit the oven shelf comfortably and at the same time leave at least a 2-inch margin between them and all four walls of the oven. Overcrowding of pans must also be avoided, with none touching. If space for air circulation is not provided for, your baking will burn at the bottom. Never use 2 shelves if you can avoid doing so; but if you must, stagger the pans, as shown below. For a discussion of heat and pan-size relationships, see (II, 336).

In baking, set the oven control for the temperature indicated and ♦ preheat for not less than 5 minutes—in some cases, where noted, longer—before inserting the pans as quickly as possible. Try not to peek until the time is up; but if you have any doubts, wait until almost the end of the baking period.

If you use a thermostatically controlled gas or electric oven, don't think you are speeding things up by setting the thermostat higher than the recipe indicates. You will get better results at the stated temperature. And don't, incidentally, press a thermostatically controlled oven into service as a kitchen heater. This will throw the thermostat out of gear. Ovens vary, however, and thermostats, even under normal use, need frequent adjustment—at least once every 12 or 14 months.

Keep in mind always that a clean oven will maintain temperature and reflect heat more accurately than an untidy one.

As to the range top, here again, as with its interior, familiarity breeds assurance. Questions about its use are, almost without exception, answered fully in the booklet which comes with the equipment. But, if you are confronted with a range for which printed instructions are lacking or if special problems arise, call your local utility company. They maintain a staff of the most obliging and well-trained consultants, prepared to give you advice, free of charge. A most important discovery to make in electric ranges is whether your surface heating units—one or several—are thermostatically controlled to level off disconcertingly when you most need sustained heat for a sauté. Also, learn if they are so differentiated as to provide all the potentials of an electric skillet.

In using gas burners, watch not only the dial, if you have

a dial set, but the relation of flame to pan. ◗ The flame should never extend farther than ½ inch inside the outer edge of the pan-bottom.

ABOUT UTENSILS

The material of which pots and pans are made, as well as their size and shape, can often spell success or failure. So, often in this book we not only caution about too high heat, but especially warn against the combination of high heat and thin cooking pans. We do so because when our mail brings distress signals—which are few—they are run up, as often as not, by users of "The Joy" who have neglected this warning. In addition to their other disadvantages, too-thin pans develop hot-spots, to which food will invariably stick. ◗ Choose a pan, then, of fairly heavy gauge, the bottom of which will diffuse heat evenly.

HEAVY ALUMINUM

This has good diffusion but it will pit—no matter how expensive. And it will tend not only to discolor but will affect the color of some foods adversely. Don't clean aluminum with harsh soaps, alkalis or abrasives. To remove discoloration, boil in aluminum pans a solution of 2 teaspoons cream of tartar to 1 quart of water for 5 to 10 minutes.

COPPER

This is best in heavier gauges. It gives a quick, even heat distribution if kept clean. But, unless well tinned, or lined with stainless steel on surfaces contacting the food—it is affected by acids and can prove poisonous.

STAINLESS STEEL

Of course, this is the easiest material of all to keep clean. Its poor heat-conductivity is usually offset by thinning down the gauge, so that hot spots develop and food cooked in it is apt to burn easily.

IRON

This also has low conductivity, rusts easily and discolors acid foods. To treat new iron skillets or Dutch ovens, grease well and place in a 450° oven for 30 minutes. Scour with steel wool before using.

TEMPERED GLASS AND PORCELAIN ENAMEL

Both are poor heat conductors. The glass is apt to crack and the enamel chips. Unless of best quality and treated to resist acid foods, the glaze of enamel ware is quickly affected by them. It also is marked by metal spoons and beaters, so only wooden utensils should be used with it.

EARTHENWARE

While a poor conductor of heat, glazed or unglazed earthenware holds heat well and doesn't discolor foods. But it is heavy and breaks easily with sudden temperature changes. To treat an earthenware casserole, see page 84.

TINWARE

This has good conductivity, but it is apt to mar and then it rusts quickly. It turns dark after use and is affected by acid foods.

GREASELESS PANS

These are a delight to people suddenly put on fat-free diets, for cooking in such utensils resembles pan frying. The soapstone griddle is the ancestor of greaseless pans. And then there are skillets with nonsticking silicone and fluoro-carbon resin surfaces. These need care in handling. Use a wooden paddle for turning or a wooden spoon for stirring—to avoid marring the surface which will melt off at 450°. Eggs, breaded fish and meat will need added water.

If you are on a fat-free diet and get tired of broiling or using greaseless utensils, remember that poaching in skim milk, fruit juice, stock or wine can flavor food without the addition of fat.

PLASTICS

There are plastics which can stand high heat. But many storage containers, funnels and other kitchen utensils cannot be washed in water over 140°. Others are ruined by oil and grease. The surfaces of all plastic utensils retain grease, so don't try to get egg whites to whip in a plastic bowl (II, 181).

You will wonder after reading these pros and cons what pan materials to choose. Fortunately there are on the market today a number of ◆ brands of cooking ware with good flat bottoms that combine metals to take advantage of the good diffusion of aluminum, the quick conductivity of copper and the noncorrosiveness of stainless steel. But while we are speaking of combinations of metal, let us say that ◆ copper, even when tin-lined, and iron pots must not be covered with aluminum foil if the food to be cooked is very acid, as the foil can be dissolved into it. In fact, it is usually best to avoid dissimilar metal pots and lids when cooking any very acid foods. In the final analysis, you may still prefer a heavy iron Dutch oven

for stews, an earthenware casserole for fondues, a flameproof glass vessel for sauce-making. ◆ Don't invest in large pan sets of a single material, until you know what your preference really is.

When you cook, choose a pan that fits the size of the burner. This correlation gives better cooking results and is more economical of fuel. Be sure that the lid is tight-fitting if the process calls for one. In vegetable cookery, see that the pan is filled ½ to ⅔ full if you are using a small amount of water, so enough steam can develop to cook quickly. ◆ Be sure the cooking pan is appropriate in size to its contents. Especially in braising and baking is this vital, see pages 492 and (II, 337). Round pans will give you more even browning when baking. Square pans tend to brown too heavily at the corners. ◆ Note, too, that shiny metal baking pans deflect heat and that dark enamel or glass ones both catch and hold the heat more. Therefore, food cooked in glass or enameled pans needs at least a 25° reduction in the oven temperatures given in our recipes. While vitreous or dark metal materials may brown cookies too rapidly, they will insure better browning for pies and puff pastes. If cooking fuel is scarce, a great saving can be effected by the use of these heat-retaining pans.

In pan broiling or when using a griddle, utensils should be brought up slowly to cooking temperature. ◆ Do not make a habit of placing an unfilled pan on high heat unless it has grease or liquid in it.

◆ And should you scorch food by some unlucky chance, plunge the pan first into cold water before transferring the food to a clean container. This way the scorched taste is greatly lessened.

♦ To clean scorched pots, soak overnight with some detergent in the water. If that isn't enough, bring to boil with 1 teaspoon washing soda or cream of tartar for each quart of water.

♦ There is a certain pace in food preparation that an experienced cook learns to accept. This doesn't mean she scorns short cuts, but she comes to know when she has to take the long way 'round to get proper results. She senses, in short, not only the demands of her equipment but the reactions of her ingredients (II, 129).

A man once summed up his wife's life with the epitaph, "She died of things." It might have happened to any of us. We are constantly encouraged to buy the latest gadget that will absolutely and positively make kitchen life sublime. No kitchen can ever have enough space at convenient levels to take care of even a normal array of equipment. So think hard before you buy so much as an extra skewer.

♦ Get pans that nest well. And if you can't resist a bulky mold, see that it hangs on an out-of-the-way pegboard panel or make it a decorative feature for an odd, unused nook. Buy square rather than round canisters for economical storage—see (II, 337) for area comparisons. Keep them and your spices in alphabetical arrangement for quick identification. ♦ And place these close to the areas where you will be using them most.

Most kitchens today are fairly scientifically laid out. Everyone is aware that the big kitchen is a time and energy waster; and that ♦ the U-shape or a triangular relationship of sink, stove and refrigerator—with their accompanying work spaces—are step-savers. But it pays occa-

sionally to think about your work habits. See if you can make them more efficient.

♦ Nonrusting well-designed hand tools save your towels and your temper. The following is a basic, reasonably comprehensive equipment list.

HOUSEHOLD NEEDS

FOR COOKING

2 saucepans with lids
2 frying pans—large and small —with lids
1 large stewing or soup kettle
1 Dutch oven
1 double boiler
1 mold for steaming
1 dessert mold
1 deep-fat fryer
3 strainers
1 steamer
1 colander
1 bean pot
Coffee maker
Tea kettle
China teapot
Candy thermometer
Deep fat frying thermometer

FOR THE OVEN

1 open roasting pan with rack
3 round 9-inch cake pans
2 square 9-inch cake pans
2 loaf or bread pans
2 cake racks for cooling
1 muffin tin
2 pie pans—tin or glass
2 cookie sheets
1 large casserole
6 custard cups
1 9-inch tube pan
1 shallow 9 x 12-inch pan
1 8-inch soufflé baker ♦
Meat thermometer

FOR PREPARATION

1 set of mixing bowls
1 8-oz. dry measuring cup
1 8-oz. liquid measuring cup
1 set of measuring spoons
Serving spoons

1 wooden slotted spoon for cake
    mixing
3 wooden spoons
1 large fork
1 small fork
2 paring knives
1 bread knife and 1 meat knife
1 French chopping knife
Grapefruit knife
Cutting board
Spatula
1 egg beater and mixer
Ladle
A 4-sided and a rotary grater
1 meat grinder
1 sugar or flour scoop
Funnel
Tongs
Flour sifter
Potato ricer or food mill
Potato masher
Wooden chopping bowl and
    chopper
Salad bowl
Doughnut cutter
Biscuit cutter
Pastry blender
Pastry board
Pastry brush
Vegetable brush
Rolling pin
Pastry cloth and cover for roll-
    ing pin
Pancake turner
Apple corer
Vegetable slicer or parer
Rubber scraper
Weighing spoon or scales
Ice-cream freezer
Griddle
Citrus fruit juicer
Food mill or ricer
Electric mixer
Blender
Pressure cooker
Toaster
Waffle iron

KITCHEN ACCESSORIES

4 canisters
1 bread box and 1 cake carrier
1 dish drainer
1 garbage can
1 waste basket

1 vegetable bin
1 or more trays
Bottle opener
Corkscrew
Can opener
Pot holders
1 bucket
Kitchen shears
Toothpicks for testing cake
Nutcracker
Salt and pepper shakers
Knife sharpener
Set of refrigerator containers
Waxed paper
Plastic storage bags
Aluminum foil
Paper towels
Dishpan
Whisk broom
1 broom
1 dust mop
1 scrubbing brush
Dust pan and brush
12 dish towels
4 dish cloths
2 dust cloths
Plastic detergent dispenser with
    brush
Plastic sponges
Asbestos pad

ABOUT BURNS AND BURNING

In the foregoing pages we have
supplied, among other information, enough facts to keep our
readers from ever burning the
food they heat. Now for a few
safeguards against burning the
cook—and what to do should
such an emergency occur.

▶ Never throw water on a
grease fire. Use salt, soda or, if
the area is a small one, a metal
lid.

▶ Choose a range, if you can
find one, on which the burners
are level with the surrounding
platform area, so pots cannot tip.

▶ Use flat-bottomed, well-bal-
anced pans that are steady when
empty. Be sure handles are not
too heavy for the pot so they
will tip; or so long that they can

be knocked against or catch a sleeve.

◗ When deep-fat frying, please note the precautions given on pages 75–79.

◗ Put boiling liquid to the back of the stove, out of reach of small children.

◗ In pan-frying, keep a colander handy to place over the pan should the fat begin to sputter.

◗ In pouring hot liquids into glass, be sure to put a metal spoon in the glass to absorb excess heat.

◗ Watch that your hands or the cloths you are using are not damp in touching or wiping electrical equipment.

◗ Have polarized attachments put on your electrical appliances to avoid shock.

◗ Should you receive extensive or painful burns, call a doctor, lie down until skilled help comes and keep quiet and warm to avoid subsequent shock. If someone is with you, let her remove any loose clothing near the burned area, but do not let her touch any material that is sticking to the burned flesh. If you are burned over a limited area, cover the burn with a sterile petrolatum salve and sterile gauze. Never use cotton on a burned area. If the burn is more extensive but light, apply strips of sterile bandage that have been dipped in a solution of 3 tablespoons soda or Epsom salts to 1 quart clear water. A new therapy for the treatment of small burns about the hands is to plunge the burned area into cold water as quickly as possible.

SOUPS

In the good old days, when a soup "bunch" cost a nickel and bones were lagniappe, pounds and pounds of meat trimmings and greenstuff were used in the household to concoct wonderful essences for everyday consumption. The best soups are still based on homemade stocks. ♦ Please read About Stocks (II, 138), and all the suggestions offered for the long slow cooking of meat stocks or the rapid cooking of fish fumets and vegetable stocks, which apply to soup making. Fish and vegetable stocks are especially important in "au maigre" or meatless cooking.

To minimize cooking time, use your ⅄ blender as a preliminary step for the processing of raw vegetables, your ♥ pressure cooker for suitable meat scraps, fresh or leftover. See Quick Household Stock (II, 142). Because not everyone wants to bother with the painstaking methods often required to extract soup stock, and because soups are such an interesting addition to or base for meals, we suggest toward the end of this chapter a large number of time-saving prepared soup combinations. Have on hand a supply of canned, dried or frozen bases to bring quick and revivifying soups into the range of even the most casual cook. No one can afford to be without a varied store of these consistently good, and often excellent products. However, just because they are so convenient and constantly served, even as our spoons stir

up their aroma, our palates weary of these prepared soup flavors.

Learn to use herbs and seasonings (II, 202–222). Keep your own economical stockpot (II, 138) to dilute concentrated soups, and to enrich them with added minerals and vitamins. Astound your friends with effortlessly made and unusually flavored soup sensations!

No matter by what method made, soup should complement or contrast with what is to follow; and however enticing its name, it will fit into one of the categories below:

Bouillon—concentrated
  brown stock ......page 111
Consommé—clarified
  double-strength
  brown stock ......page 109
Broths—clear liquors
  from fish, meat, fowl
  and vegetables
                (II, 143–145)
Jellied Soups—made
  from gelatinous
  knuckle bones, clarified
  and used as they
  are or with added
  gelatin .... page 113
Vegetable Soups—all
  vegetable or prepared
  with meat or fish stocks
  in which the vegetables
  predominate .. pages 116–117
Purée of Vegetables
  and Legumes—with
  or without
  cream added
            page 117 and page 118
Cream Soups—cream,
  butter, cereal or

egg-thickened soups,
often on a vegetable
base ....page 125
Bisques—shellfish based
cream soups ......page 133
Chowders—thick fish,
meat and vegetable
soups, to which salt
pork, milk, diced
vegetables, even bread
and crackers may
be added ....pages 136–138

Some of the above are served
hot, some cold, some either way,
like bouillons, borsch and vichyssoise. ♦ To serve soups piping
hot—use tureens, lidded bowls
or well-heated cups. Especially
if drinks and hors d'oeuvre have
been offered before, a hot soup
helps to recondition the palate.

♦ Cold soups should be very
well chilled, and served in
chilled dishes—especially jellied
soups, which tend to break
down more rapidly because they
are relatively light in gelatin.
Cold soups, when not jellied,
may be prepared quickly by
using a ⅄ blender and chilling
in the freezer. On informal occasions, they may be chilled in
a tall jug and served directly
from it into chilled cups or
bowls.

You should be able to count
on about 6 servings from a quart
of soup, unless it is being used
as the mainstay for a lunch—as
is so frequently the case with a
potage, or a soup rich in solids.
♦ The quantities noted under the
titles of individual recipes are
consistently given in standard
8-ounce cups.

There are some classic dishes
—Petite Marmite, New Eng-
land Boiled Dinner or Goulash—
that occupy middle ground between soups and stews.

▲ Above 2500 feet, soups
need longer cooking periods
than called for in the regular

recipes, as the liquids boil at a
a lower temperature.

ABOUT SEASONING SOUP

Soup is as flavorful as the stock
on which it is based. See (II,
138), and the comments on seasoning (II, 140).

The addition of wine to soup
frequently enhances its flavor,
but ♦ do not oversalt soups to
which wine is added, as the
wine intensifies saltiness. Wines
that blend well with bland soups,
such as those made with chicken
or veal, are a not too dry sherry
or Madeira. Don't use more than
¼ cup wine to 1 quart soup.
A strongly flavored soup, prepared with beef or oxtail, is improved by the addition of some
dry red table wine—½ cup wine
to 1 quart soup. A dry white
table wine adds zest to a fish,
crab or lobster bisque or chowder. Use ⅛ to ¼ cup wine to 1
quart soup. Wines should be
added to the hot soup shortly
before it is served. ♦ Do not boil
the soup after adding the wine.

Beer adds a tang to bean, cabbage and vegetable soups. Use
1 cup for every 3 cups soup.
Add the beer just before serving.
Reheat the soup well, but ♦ do
not boil.

ABOUT COLORING SOUP

If soups have been cooked with
browned onions or onion skins,
and if the amount of meat used
has been substantial, they should
have a good, rich color. Tomato
skins also lend color interest.
Caramelized Sugar II (II, 169)
may be added if necessary. We
prefer it to commercial soup
coloring, which is apt to over-
whelm a delicately flavored
soup with its own pervasive and
telltale aroma. About Vegetables
for Soup, see (II, 144).

ABOUT CEREALS FOR THICKENING SOUPS

Precooked cereal garnishes, such as rice, noodles and dumplings, give an effect of body to a clear soup, but a very different one from the more integral raw thickeners suggested below. These make for intriguing texture and elegance of flavor.

To add any of the following, bring the soup to a boil and reduce the heat again to a simmer as soon as the addition has been made. Stir ♦ raw cereals into soup for the last hour of cooking. For a light thickening, allow to the original amount of water approximately:

1 teaspoon barley to 1 cup water
1 teaspoon green kern to 1 cup water
1 teaspoon rice to 1 cup water
1 teaspoon oatmeal to 1 cup water
2 tablespoons wheat germ flour to 1 cup water
2 tablespoons peanut flour to 1 cup water
2 tablespoons soya flour to 1 cup water
½ teaspoon quick-cooking tapioca to 1 cup water

If you wish to thicken cooked soup with flour, allow:

1½ teaspoons flour to 1 cup soup

Make a paste of the flour with about:

Twice as much cold stock, milk or water

Pour the paste slowly into the boiling soup, while stirring. Simmer and stir for 5 to 10 minutes. Or, as in cream sauce, make a Roux, see page 355, of:

1½ teaspoons butter
1½ teaspoons flour

Pour the soup over this mixture, stirring constantly until smooth and boiling. Or add:

Flour and butter

to cooled soup in a 人 blender—then reheat the soup. Bring to a boil, lower heat and simmer for 5 minutes.

Additional thickenings for soup are dry, crustless French bread or Panades, page 123. Also, thick cream or a cream or Béchamel sauce, page 359, may be used.

ABOUT OTHER THICKENINGS FOR SOUPS

Egg yolks are one of the richest and best soup thickeners—but they must be added just before serving. ♦ Care must be taken, when this is done, that the soup is not too hot.

Allow for each cup of soup:

1 egg yolk, beaten with 1 tablespoon cream or sherry

To avoid curdling, it is wise to add to this beaten mixture a small quantity of the hot soup before incorporating it into the soup pot. ♦ When using egg or cream-based thickeners, it is always essential that the soup, after their addition, be kept below the boiling point. You may prefer riced hard-cooked eggs. Allow:

2 yolks for each cup of soup

Add at the last minute and, of course, do not allow the soup to boil.

A good soup thickener, for those whose diet does not include flour, consists of:

3 tablespoons grated raw potato

for each cup of soup. Grate the potato directly into the soup about 15 minutes before it has finished cooking. Then simmer until the potato is tender, when it will form a thickener.

Soups cooked with starchy vegetables, such as dried beans, peas or lentils, will separate and must be bound. To do this, allow:

    1 tablespoon melted butter
    1 tablespoon flour

Well blended with a small amount of:

    Cold water, stock or milk

Stir this mixture into about:

    3 cups strained boiling
      soup

and simmer at least 5 minutes before serving.

ABOUT REMOVING GREASE FROM SOUP

I. Chill the soup. The grease rises at once and will solidify when cold. It is then a simple matter to remove it.

II. Float a paper towel on the surface of the soup and when it has absorbed as much grease as it will hold discard it; or roll a paper towel and use one end to skim over the soup surface to remove the fat. When the ends become coated with grease, cut off the used part with scissors and repeat the process.

III. Use your meat baster with bulb as a suction device.

ABOUT SOUP MEAT

Any meat that is ♦ immersed in cold water and simmered for a long period is bound to give its best flavor to the cooking liquor. But some food values remain in the meat and it may be heightened in flavor by serving it, when removed from the soup, with one of the sauces below:

    Horseradish Sauce, page 362
    Mustard Sauce page 363
    Tomato Sauce, page 376
    Brown Onion Sauce, page 366

ABOUT CLEAR SOUPS

Because so much valuable material and expert time goes into the making of clear soups and because they taste so delicious, most of us assume that they have high nutritive value. It disappoints us to have to tell you that, while they are ♦ unsurpassed as appetite stimulators, the experts give them an indifferent rating as foods. If you have the time, do create these delicious broths by degreasing, clarifying and correcting the seasonings of stocks.

I. For chicken broth use:
    Chicken Stock (II, 142)

II. For game broth use:
    Fowl, Rabbit or Game Stock (II, 143)

III. For fish broth use:
    Fumet or Fish Stock (II, 143)

IV. For vegetable broth use:
    Vegetable Stock (II, 145)
♦ Be sure to see Garnishes for Soups, page 144.

CONSOMMÉ

Prep re:
    Brown Stock I (II, 141)
and clarify it by the quick method (II, 140). This will give you a clear, thin consommé. For double strength, clarify the stock by the second method.

CONSOMMÉ BRUNOISE

[3 Cups]
Make a mixture of the following finely diced vegetables:

1 rib of celery
1 small carrot
½ small turnip
½ small onion
Sauté them gently in:
    1 tablespoon heated butter
Enough time should be allowed
to let the vegetables absorb the
grease but ♦ do not let them
brown. Add:
    1 cup consommé
and continue cooking, covered,
until the vegetables are tender.
Pour into:
    2 cups hot consommé
Degrease and
    Correct the seasoning
Just before serving, add:
    1 tablespoon finely
        chopped chervil
    1 tablespoon cooked peas
    1 tablespoon finely diced
        cooked green beans

CONSOMMÉ MADRILÈNE

[About 5 Cups]
Heat to the boiling point and
strain:
    2 cups tomato juice
    ½ teaspoon grated onion
    2 cups Chicken Stock,
        page 109
    A piece of lemon rind
    Salt and pepper
Flavor with:
    Lemon juice, dry sherry
        or Worcestershire sauce
Or garnish with:
    Cultured sour cream
dotted with:
    Red caviar

CHICKEN OR TURKEY BROTH

♦ See the many cream soups,
page 125, and egg garnished
soups, page 145, based on this
simple broth.
Prepare:
    Fowl, Rabbit or Game
        Stock (II, 143)
or use canned stock.
When it is boiling, remove from

heat. You may add for each 4
cups:
    ½ cup cream
Reheat but ♦ do not boil. Serve
with a chiffonade of herbs, page
151, with dumplings, page 146.

CHICKEN BROTH OR BOUILLON WITH EGG

[Individual Serving]
A good dish for an invalid, but
not to be scorned by those in
good health.
Degrease, clarify, and heat:
    Chicken Broth, above
    Correct the seasoning
For every cup added:
    (1 teaspoon lemon juice)
    (1 tablespoon chopped
        parsley)
When the soup is hot add:
    An egg drop, page 145
allowing 1 egg per serving. Serve
at once.

POT-AU-FEU, POULE-AU-POT OR PETITE MARMITE

[About 6 Cups Broth]
A marmite is an earthenware
lidded pot, higher than it is
wide. Its material accounts in
part for the flavor of the soup.
In pot-au-feu, another name for
petite marmite, the major meat
is beef, with an addition of
chicken wings and gizzards. In
making poule-au-pot, the beef is
cooked with a juicy hen—the
hen which Henry IV wanted for
every pot. Marrow bones are
usually included, tied in cheesecloth. The vegetables may be
seasonally varied. Blanched cabbage is often added.
Put in a marmite:
    2½ quarts cold water
    2 lbs. shank or chuck beef,
        cut in chunks
Tie in cheesecloth and add:
    (1 knucklebone)
Bring this mixture ♦ slowly to a
boil and ♦ skim well. Cut Parisienne style, page 251, and add:
    2 carrots

1 small turnip
3 leeks: white parts only
1 whole onion stuck with
1 clove
1 teaspoon salt
1 Bouquet Garni II (II,
220)

Bring these ingredients to a boil.
♦ Skim again. ♦ Cover and cook
slowly for about 3 hours in a
350° oven. The bouillon should
be clear and amber in color.
To serve, either start with the
clear soup and offer the meat
and vegetables on the side or
reserve them for a second meal.
Crusty thin slices of bread,
which may be spread with Parmesan cheese, are delightful accompaniments to a pot-au-feu.

BOUILLON

Bouillon is an unsalted strong
beef stock, not as sweet as con-
sommé.
Clarify and reduce by ⅓:
　　Brown Soup Stock I or
　　II (II, 141)
　　Correct the seasoning
Serve with:
　　A Garnish for Clear
　　Soups, page 144

TOMATO BOUILLON

[About 3 Cups]
Bring to the boiling point and
simmer for about 5 minutes:
3 cups strained tomato
juice
½ small bay leaf
¼ cup cut up celery, with
leaves
2 tablespoons chopped
fennel
2 whole cloves
1 tablespoon fresh basil
(1 small skinned, chopped
and sautéed onion)

Strain, and degrease if necessary.
　　Correct the seasoning
Serve hot or cold in cups,
topped with a teaspoon of:
　　Whipped cream or
　　cultured sour cream

BEEF TEA

[About ¾ Cup]
Grind twice:
1 lb. lean round steak or
neck bone meat
Place in a quart mason jar and
add:
1 cup cold water
½ teaspoon salt

Cover the jar lightly. Place the
jar on a cloth in a pan containing as much cold water as possible without upsetting the jar.
Bring the water slowly to a
gentle boil and continue for
about 1 hour. Remove the jar.
Place on a cake rack to cool as
rapidly as possible. Strain the
juice. Store it in a covered container in the refrigerator until
ready to heat and serve.

KREPLACH SOUP

[About 4 Cups]
Prepare:
　　Noodle Dough II, page
　　149

This will make about 20 pastries.
Do not allow the dough to dry,
however, before cutting it into
3-inch squares. Put about 1½
tablespoons of one of the following fillings in the center of each
square.

I. Sauté in:
1 tablespoon cooking oil
½ cup minced onions
½ lb. ground beef
Add:
¾ teaspoon salt
¼ teaspoon pepper

II. Or combine:
1½ cups minced cooked
chicken
¼ cup minced sautéed
onion
1 egg yolk
¾ teaspoon salt
1 tablespoon chopped
parsley

Fold the dough over into a triangular shape. Press the open
edges carefully with a fork to

seal them completely. Before
cooking ◗ allow the kreplach to
dry on a flour-dusted towel for
30 minutes on each side. Then
drop them into:

>About 1 gallon rapidly
>boiling broth or salted
>water

and ◗ simmer gently for 7 to
10 minutes. Drain well and
serve in:

>3 cups strong broth

WON TON SOUP
[About 4 Cups]
Prepare:

>Noodle Dough II, page
>149

The fillings may be:

>Cooked pork, chicken,
>shrimp, crabmeat or
>Chicken Farce, page 564

Combine:

>½ lb. cooked pork or veal,
>etc.
>2 finely chopped green
>onions, white parts only
>1 cup chopped spinach
>1 beaten egg

There are many fancy wrappings for won ton, which in most
cases produce a high proportion
of paste to meat. If truly Chinese, won tons emerge with a
rather loose shape and a fluttery
outline. Cook by putting all the
won ton at once into:

>About 1 gallon rapidly
>boiling water

Lower the heat at once to medium. When the water again
comes to a boil, add:

>2 cups cold water

to temper the dough. About 10
minutes should elapse from the
time the won tons are first added
to the boiling water until they
are ready to serve. Put 5 won
tons for each serving into a soup
bowl. Sprinkle them with:

>(Soy sauce)

Have ready and pour over them:

>3 cups hot, seasoned, clear
>chicken broth or bouillon

A few prettily cut Chinese vegetables or partially cooked spinach leaves with midstems removed, usually garnish the
broth. Grated cheese is often
served separately.

VEGETABLE BROTH
[About 3½ Cups]
Quickly made and very good.
Serve strained or unstrained, hot
or chilled.
Chop:

>3 cups or more Vegetables
>for Soup (II, 145)

Sauté them gently and slowly
for 5 minutes in:

>3 tablespoons butter

◗ Do not let them brown. Add:

>4 cups boiling water or
>part water and tomatoes
>or tomato juice

Simmer the soup, partially covered, for about 1 hour. Season
and add:

>(1 bouillon cube)

MUSHROOM BROTH
I. [About 6 Cups]
Prepare:

>¾ lb. diced mature
>mushrooms
>2 ribs celery, diced
>½ skinned and diced carrot
>¼ skinned and diced onion

Cover these vegetables with:

>3 cups water

◗ Simmer partially covered for
45 minutes. Strain the broth.
Add, to make 6 cups of liquid:

>Chicken Stock (II, 142)
>or Beef Consommé,
>page 109

Add, if needed:

>Salt and paprika

Serve very hot. Add to each
cup:

>1 tablespoon dry sherry

II. Blend or chop until fine:

>¾ lb. mature mushrooms

Add them to:

>6 cups Chicken Stock (II,
>142), or consommé

Simmer, partially covered, for
about 15 minutes or only 5 if

you use the ⅄ blender. Strain if
you like or thicken, page 108.
Serve as for I, above.

ONION SOUP

[6 Cups]
Onion soup, with vegetable sub-
stituted for meat stock, is used
for meals "au maigre," also see
Fish Stock (II, 143).
Sauté until well browned, but
not burned:
    1½ cups thinly sliced onions
in:
    3 tablespoons butter
Add:
    6 cups beef or chicken
        broth
    ¼ teaspoon freshly ground
        black pepper
Cover and cook over low heat or
in a 275° oven for 30 minutes.
Either way, the soup is now put
into a casserole, covered with:
    6 slices toasted French
        bread
Sprinkle over the toast:
    1 cup grated Parmesan
        cheese
Heat in the oven for about 10
minutes or until the cheese is
melted. Add:
    (A dash of cognac or
        dry sherry)

CLEAR WATER CRESS SOUP

[About 5 Cups]
Simmer together:
    5 cups hot chicken broth
    1½ cups chopped water cress
for 4 to 6 minutes or until watercress is just dark green—not an
olive green. Serve at once.

COLD TOMATO SOUP OR GAZPACHO

[About 6 Cups]
A summer delight—chilled veg-
etable soup with fresh herbs.
Peel and seed:
    2 large ripe tomatoes
Seed and remove membrane
from:

    1 large sweet pepper
Peel:
    1 clove garlic
Wash:
    ½ cup or more fresh mixed
        herbs: chives, parsley,
        basil, chervil, tarragon
Place all ingredients in a wooden
chopping bowl. Chop them. Stir
in, gradually:
    ½ cup olive oil
    3 tablespoons lemon or
        lime juice
    3 cups chilled water or
        light stock
Add:
    1 peeled, thinly sliced
        sweet Spanish onion
    1 cup peeled, seeded, diced
        or grated cucumber
    1½ teaspoons salt or more,
        if needed
    ½ teaspoon paprika
Some cooks prefer to use their
⅄ blender for the above vegetables. Chill the soup for 4 hours
or more before serving.
To serve, place in each bowl:
    2 ice cubes
    1 tablespoon chopped
        parsley
Add the soup and sprinkle the
tops with:
    ½ cup crumbled stale bread

JELLIED CLEAR SOUPS

These delicious warm weather
soups may be more highly seasoned than hot soups, but ◗
watch their salt content. If you
prepare them in advance, their
saltiness is intensified.
Serve with:
    A lemon and parsley
        garnish
You may add to the soup before
jelling:
    A few drops of
        Worcestershire sauce
Or allow per cup:
    1 tablespoon sherry or
    1 teaspoon lemon juice
If you add more lemon juice, be
sure you have allowed sufficient

gelatin. Stock made from veal knuckle and beef bone may jell enough naturally to be served without added gelatin. We have learned that if canned consommé is from a new pack, it, too, has enough gelatin in it to respond favorably to mere chilling. If the pack is as old as two years, it must be treated as though it had no gelatin. ◗ Do not freeze it, but try it out by refrigerating for at least 4 hours, to see how much additional thickening it will need. Keep in mind that, if too stiff, soup jellies are not very attractive. Allow, if necessary:

> 1½ teaspoons gelatin

to each:

> 2 cups consommé or broth

For rapid chilling, you may place clear soups in a bowl over cracked ice or give them a start by leaving them in the freezer for a few minutes ◗ but not longer, as intense cold, if continued, destroys the texture.

JELLIED TOMATO BOUILLON

[About 5 Cups]
Soak for 5 minutes:

> 2 tablespoons gelatin

in:

> ½ cup cold water

Heat to the boiling point and strain:

> 2 cups tomato juice
> ½ teaspoon grated onion
> 2 cups Light Soup Stock (II, 142)
> A piece of lemon rind
> Salt and pepper

Dissolve the gelatin in the hot stock. Cool. Flavor with:

> Lemon juice, dry sherry or Worcestershire sauce

Pour stock into a wet mold. Chill. The bouillon may be beaten slightly before serving and garnished with:

> Lemon slices, chopped chives, mint, small nasturtium leaves,

> chopped olives,
> hard-cooked riced eggs,
> relish, horseradish,
> parsley or watercress

JELLIED BEET CONSOMMÉ   [4]

Combine and heat:

> 1 cup beet juice
> 1 cup consommé

Add:

> 1 tablespoon gelatin dissolved over hot water (II, 184)
> Correct the seasoning

When about to jell add:

> (1 tablespoon lemon juice)
> 1 cup minced cooked beets

Pour gelatin mixture into cups. In serving, garnish each cup with:

> 1 teaspoon caviar
> A slice of lemon decorated with minced fresh tarragon or basil, or a dab of cultured sour cream

BROTH ON THE ROCKS

For the guest who shuns an alcoholic drink, offer a clear broth, such as:

> Chicken broth or bouillon

combined with:

> (Tomato and orange juice)

poured over ice cubes. ◗ Be sure the broth is not too rich in gelatin, for it may suddenly congeal.

FRUIT SOUPS

[4 Cups]
In Scandinavia, fruit soups are served as a dessert, but in Germany, they constitute a summertime chilled prelude to the entrée. Either dried or fresh fruits, cooked until they can be puréed easily, may be used. Cherries are the most popular. Prepare:

> 1 lb. stoned cherries

Place in an enamel pan and cover with:

> 2 cups water
> 1 cup red wine

Add:

> ¼ cup sugar
> ½ teaspoon grated orange rind

Cook until the fruit is soft, about 10 minutes. Blend or sieve the fruit and thicken the juice with:

> 1 teaspoon arrowroot

mixed with a little of the cooled sirup. Return the mixture to the soup and cook about 2 minutes. Serve hot or cold. Garnish with:

> Unsweetened whipped cream or croutons or dumplings, page 146

ABOUT THICK SOUPS

Purée, cream, bisque, velouté, potage—to the connoisseur each of these is a quite distinctive embodiment of the indispensable thick soup.

If you like to attach a label to your creations, know that a purée is a soup which gets its major thickening from the vegetable or other food put through a sieve and has butter swirled into it at the very last moment. By omitting the butter or lessening the amount of it and adding cream and sometimes egg yolk, you get—guess what?—a cream soup! If that soup is on a shell fish base—and only if it is—you may call it a bisque. If you add both eggs and cream and a velouté sauce, see page 362, to a purée base, you achieve a velouté soup.

Potages, the most variable of soups, are likely to have the phrase "du jour" added, meaning that they are both the specialty of the day and, from the cook's point of view, seasonal and convenient to compose. Potages, which tend to be hefty, taste best when their vegetables are first braised in butter. For ways to thicken soups, see page 108.

Here are a few practical hints that will help you make the most of thickened soups. First, be sure to scrape the purée off the bottom of the strainer. ◗ If you use a ⅄ blender, first parblanch or cook any vegetables with strings, like celery, or hulls, like peas. After butter, cream or eggs are added ◗ never allow the soup to reach a boil. If you are not serving at once, heat it in a double boiler. To avoid a slight granular separation in legume soups, see page 108. Thick soups should not be served as the first course of a heavy meal. The wonderful thing about them is that they are nearly a meal by themselves. Balanced by a green salad or fruit, they make a complete luncheon.

BARLEY SOUP

I.

[About 9 to 10 Cups]

A favorite of French farmers. For the best flavor use stock from country cured hams, but not aged ones like Smithfield, Kentucky or Virginia.

Melt in a skillet:

> 2 tablespoons salt pork

Cook, until translucent, in the above:

> 3 tablespoons shallots or onions

Add:

> ½ cup barley

Agitate the pan to coat the barley well in the hot fat. After about 5 minutes, add:

> 1 quart hot stock from country cured ham

Cook the mixture, covered, until the barley is tender, about 30 minutes. Bind or not as you like, depending on how rich and thick you want the soup, with:

> 3 well-beaten egg yolks
> 1 cup cream

◗ Heat, but do not boil after adding the eggs and cream. Before serving, add as a garnish:

2 tablespoons finely chopped parsley
1 cup sautéed, coarsely chopped mushrooms

To keep the mushrooms white, add:

½ tablespoon lemon juice

II. Scotch Broth
[About 10 to 12 Cups]
Soak for 12 hours:

½ cup pearl barley

in:

2 cups water

If you use other barley, soak it for 1 hour. Add this to:

3 lbs. mutton or lamb with bones
10 cups water

Simmer, covered, for 2 hours or until the meat is tender. Add for the last ½ hour of cooking:

2 cups browned vegetables for soup (II, 145)
(A dash of curry)

Remove the meat from the soup. Dice it, return it to the soup. You may use a flour or egg thickener, page 108, to bind the soup.

Correct the seasoning

Serve garnished with:

Chopped parsley

GREEN KERN SOUP

[About 9 Cups]

If you are English, corn means wheat, if you are Scottish it means oats, but if you come from "down under" or are American, you know corn grows on a cob. Kern sounds as though it too might be somebody's word for corn, but it isn't. It's dried green wheat and makes a favorite European soup.

Soak for ½ hour:

½ to 1 cup green kern

in:

4 cups water

Drain, then cook, as for Barley

II, above, replacing the lamb with beef.

VEGETABLE SOUP OR SOUP PAYSANNE

[5 Cups]

Place in a large kettle or pressure cooker:

2 tablespoons bacon fat or butter

Sauté briefly in the fat:

¼ cup diced carrots
½ cup diced onion
½ cup diced celery

Add:

3 cups hot water or stock
1 cup canned tomatoes
(½ cup peeled, diced potatoes)
(½ cup peeled, diced turnips)
1 tablespoon chopped parsley
½ teaspoon salt
⅛ teaspoon pepper

Cover and cook for about 35 minutes; then add:

(½ cup chopped cabbage, spinach or lettuce)

If using a ✪ pressure cooker, cook at 15 pounds pressure for 3 minutes. Remove from heat and let stand for 5 minutes, then reduce pressure instantly.

Correct seasoning

and serve with:

Melba Cheese Rounds, page 152

VEGETABLE CHOWDER

[About 6 Cups]

Cut the stems from:

1 quart okra

Slice the okra. Prepare:

2 cups diced celery

Seed and dice:

1 green pepper

Skin and chop:

1 small onion

Sauté the vegetables for 5 minutes in:

¼ cup butter or bacon drippings

Skin, chop and add:

2 large ripe tomatoes or 1
cup canned tomatoes
1 teaspoon brown sugar
¼ teaspoon paprika
4 cups boiling water

Stew the vegetables gently until
they are tender, for about 1
hour. Add, if required:

Salt and paprika

Cooked chicken, meat, fish or
crisp bacon may be diced and
added to the chowder. Serve
with:

Boiled Rice, page 158

⅄ BLENDER VEGETABLE SOUP

[About 4 Cups]
Blend in:
¼ cup stock
2 cups mixed, coarsely cut
vegetables

If cucumbers, celery, asparagus
or onions are used, blanch them
first to soften seeds or fibers and
to make the onion flavor more
agreeable. Heat the blended
vegetables until tender in:

3 cups boiling stock

Serve at once.

BEET SOUP OR BORSCH

[About 5 Cups]
There are probably as many versions of borsch as there are Rus-
sians. For good, quick versions,
see page 140.
Peel and chop until very fine:
½ cup carrots
1 cup onions
2 cup beets

Barely cover these ingredients
with boiling water. Simmer
gently, covered, for about 20
minutes. Add and simmer for 15
minutes more:
1 tablespoon butter
2 cups beef or other stock
1 cup very finely shredded
cabbage
1 tablespoon vinegar

Place the soup in bowls. Add to
each serving:

1 tablespoon cultured sour
cream
mixed with:
Grated cucumber
Correct the seasoning
and serve hot or cold with:
Pumpernickel bread
Serve beer rather than wine with
this dish.

CABBAGE SOUP

[About 6 Cups]
This superb cabbage soup, quick
and inexpensive, is from Herman
Smith's book, "Kitchens Near
and Far." You will find it, as
well as his incomparable "Stina,"
most rewarding.
Sauté gently in a saucepan until
tender and yellow:
1 large minced onion
1½ tablespoons butter
Grate or shred and add:
1 small head green
cabbage: about ¾ lb.
Bring to a boil:
4 cups Brown Stock I
(II, 141)
Add the stock to the vegetables.
Season as needed with:
Salt and pepper
Simmer the soup for about 10
minutes. If you wish, use this
delicious topping:
½ cup cultured sour cream
1 tablespoon minced
parsley
(½ teaspoon caraway seeds)
Place a spoonful of the sour
cream mixture on each plate of
soup.

CHICKEN CURRY OR SENEGALESE SOUP

[About 2 Cups]
Melt:
1 tablespoon butter
Add to it:
¾ to 1 teaspoon curry
powder
Stir in, until blended:
¾ tablespoon flour
Stir in slowly:
1½ cups chicken broth

When the soup is boiling, season
it with:

Paprika

Reduce the heat. Beat:

1 egg yolk
¼ cup rich milk or cream

When the soup is no longer boiling, stir these ingredients into
it. Stir over low heat until the
egg has thickened slightly ◗ but
do not boil. Add also, still not
allowing the soup to boil:

¼ cup slivers of cooked
white chicken meat
(2 tablespoons chutney)

Serve, hot or chilled, garnished
with:

Chopped chives

CHICKEN GUMBO

[About 12 Cups]

Cut into pieces and dredge with
flour:

1 stewing chicken

Brown it in:

¼ cup bacon grease

Pour over it:

4 cups boiling water

Simmer, uncovered, until the
meat falls from the bones. Drain
the stock and chop the meat.
Place in the soup kettle and
simmer, uncovered, until the
vegetables are tender:

2 cups skinned tomatoes
½ cup green corn
1 cup sliced okra
(1 large green or
2 small red peppers)
½ teaspoon salt
¼ diced onion
¼ cup rice
5 cups water

Combine these ingredients with
the chicken meat and stock.

Correct the seasoning

Add:

(1 to 2 teaspoons filé
powder, moistened with
a little water)

After adding the filé ◗ do not
boil the soup, as it will become
stringy.

BEEF GUMBO

[About 10 Cups]

Melt in a skillet:

2 tablespoons butter

Add and sauté until dark brown:

A soup bone with meat:
3 lbs.

Pour in:

12 cups water: 3 quarts

Simmer these ingredients, covered, for 2 hours. Add and simmer, covered, until the meat falls
from the bone:

¼ cup chopped celery
¼ cup shredded parsley
¼ cup chopped onion
½ teaspoon salt
¼ teaspoon paprika

Strain, cool and skim the stock.
Melt:

2 tablespoons butter

Add and sauté for 3 minutes:

½ cup chopped onion
½ cup fresh or canned
sliced okra
1 cup chopped celery with
leaves

Add:

2½ cups tomatoes
2 tablespoons quick-
cooking tapioca
1 tablespoon sugar
The soup stock

Simmer the soup, covered, for
1 hour longer.

Correct the seasoning,
and serve.

ABOUT LEGUME SOUPS
Lentils, Beans, Peas

Some packaged, dried legumes
do not require soaking. Follow
directions on the label. Soak if
required, using ham stock, other
stock, a broken-up turkey or
chicken carcass, to which you
may add ½ cup tomato juice or
purée, making in all about 10
cups of liquid. Add flavor with
bacon or scraps of ham or fresh
pork fat. Try them out (II, 174),
then brown an onion in the
fat. Reserve the cracklings to
garnish the soup, or cook them

in it. For vegetables and seasonings, see the following recipes.

For easy removal of fat, chill the soup, see page 109. Legume soups may be served unstrained, although they are usually more digestible if strained. They may be thinned with stock, tomato juice or milk. Navy bean soup always calls for milk.

Legume soups, whether made of fresh or dried materials, should be bound. To do this, melt 1 tablespoon butter, blend in 1 tablespoon flour and add a small amount of cold water, stock or milk. Stir this mixture into about 3 cups strained boiling soup and simmer at least 5 minutes before serving.

✪ We do not recommend the use of a pressure cooker for legume soups.

DRIED BEAN SOUP

[4 Cups]
If you use marrow beans and add the optional mashed potato, you will have come close to reproducing the famous United States Senate Bean Soup.
Soak, see above:

>½ cup dried navy, kidney, Lima or marrow beans

Add:

>A small piece of ham, a ham bone or ⅛ lb. salt pork
>4 cups boiling water
>½ bay leaf
>3 or 4 peppercorns
>3 whole cloves

Cook the soup slowly until the beans are soft, for about 2½ to 3 hours. For the last 30 minutes, add:

>1 diced carrot
>3 ribs celery with leaves, chopped
>½ sliced onion
>(1 minced clove garlic)
>(⅛ teaspoon saffron)
>(½ cup freshly cooked mashed potatoes)

>(½ cup chopped sorrel)

Remove and mince the meat. Put the soup through a food mill, ⅄ blender or sieve. Thin the soup, if required, with boiling water or milk.

Correct the seasoning
Serve with the meat and:

>Croutons, page 151
>Chopped chives or parsley

BLACK BEAN SOUP

[About 9 or 10 Cups]
Follow the recipe for Split Pea Soup, page 120.
Substitute for the peas:

>2 cups black beans

As this soup is drier, add:

>3, instead of 2, tablespoons butter

Serve garnished with:

>2 teaspoons deviled or Smithfield ham for each cup
>Thin slices of lemon
>Thin slices of hard-cooked eggs
>(1 tablespoon dry sherry for each cup)

BEAN SOUP WITH VEGETABLES OR GARBURE

[About 10 Cups]
A highly variable soup. Perhaps the most famous version comes from Béarn. It includes preserved goose and is cooked in a glazed casserole. Exotic? It is made in season with freshly hulled haricot beans. Soak overnight:

>1 cup dried haricot or navy or fava beans

You may blanch, page 88, or not, depending on its maturity:

>2 lbs. green or white cabbage

Shred the cabbage finely the length of the leaf. Peel and slice:

>1½ cups potatoes
>1 cup carrots
>1 cup white turnips

¼ cup leeks, using white
   portion only
½ cup onion
1 sprig thyme
   (A ham bone)

Place all the above ingredients
in a heavy pan and cover with:
      Liquid
Use water if you plan to add salt
pork; game stock (II, 143),
with game.
Add:
      1 lb. diced salt pork or
         boneless game or veal
▶ Simmer, partially covered, for
2½ hours or until the meat is
tender.
      Correct the seasoning
and serve the meat on the side.
Pour the soup over:
      Garlic buttered croutons,
         page 151

MINESTRONE

[About 8 Cups]
An Italian soup made with many
kinds of vegetables, even zucchini blossoms. Sometimes elbow
macaroni or other pasta and
sometimes rice is added instead
of dried beans. Sweet sausages
and smoked spareribs may also
be put in at the end. Simmer
for about ¾ hour in a large
soup kettle:
      2 quarts stock
      4 oz. diced fatty ham
      1 cup chopped celery
      ½ cup fresh kidney beans
      ¾ cup fresh peas
Heat:
      3 tablespoons olive oil
Sauté in it:
      1 cup chopped spinach
      1 small chopped vegetable
         marrow
      ¼ cup minced onion
      1 diced carrot
      1 cup chopped Savoy
         cabbage
      1 cup diced tomatoes
      1 diced leek
Pour the sautéed vegetables into
the stock mixture and simmer

about 25 minutes longer. Add:
      1 tablespoon chopped
         parsley
      1 tablespoon minced fresh
         sage
      1 pressed garlic clove
Cook for 5 minutes more and
      Correct the seasoning
Add:
      ½ cup Parmesan cheese
and serve with:
      Italian Bread

LENTIL SOUP

[About 8 Cups]
Wash well and drain:
      2 cups lentils
Add:
      10 cups boiling water
      ¼ lb. salt pork or a piece
         of ham or a ham bone
▶ Simmer for about 4 hours.
During the last hour, add:
      1 large minced onion
which has been sautéed in:
      3 tablespoons butter
      Correct the seasoning
and serve puréed or not, as you
prefer.

SPLIT PEA OR LENTIL
SOUP

[About 8 Cups]
Try this on a cold winter day.
Wash and soak, page 118.
      2 cups split peas
Drain the peas, reserving the
liquid. Add enough water to the
reserved liquid to make 10 cups.
Adding peas again, cook cov-
ered, for about 2½ to 3 hours
with:
      A turkey carcass, a ham
         bone or a 2-inch cube
         salt pork
Add and simmer, covered, for ½
hour longer until tender:
      ½ cup chopped onions
      1 cup chopped celery with
         leaves
      ½ cup chopped carrots
Add:
      (1 clove garlic)

(1 bay leaf)
(1 teaspoon sugar)
    (A dash of cayenne or a
    pod of red pepper)
(¼ teaspoon thyme)

Remove bones, carcass or salt
pork. Put the soup through a
sieve. Chill. Remove grease.
Melt:

    2 tablespoons butter or
        soup fat

Stir in it until blended:

    2 tablespoons flour

Add a little of the soup mixture, slowly. Cook and stir until
it boils, then stir it into the rest
of the reheated soup.

    Correct the seasoning

Serve with:

    Croutons, or sour black
    bread and Pickled Pigs'
    Feet

⅄ BLENDER SPLIT PEA SOUP

[About 1 Quart]

Simmer about 45 minutes or
until tender:

    ½ cup split peas

in:

    2½ cups water

When slightly cooled, pour into
a blender and add:

    1 cup chopped pork
        luncheon sausage
    1 small sliced onion
    1 diced stalk celery with
        leaves
    1 clove garlic
    1 teaspoon salt
    2 teaspoons Worcestershire
        sauce
    A pinch of rosemary
    ⅛ teaspoon pepper

Blend until smooth. Return the
soup to saucepan to heat. Rinse
the blender with:

    1 cup water

Add this to the soup and simmer
for about 10 minutes. Garnish
with:

    Pieces of crisp bacon
    Cultured sour cream

SPLIT PEA SOUP AU MAIGRE

Use the recipe for Spit Pea Soup
to make either a thick or thin
soup. During the last 20 minutes
of cooking, substitute for the
fowl or ham bone any clean
fish scraps—such as heads, tails
and fins.

GREEN PEA SOUP OR POTAGE ST. GERMAIN

[About 6 Cups]

Do not attempt to make this
soup with canned or frozen peas.
▶ If you do not have fresh peas,
it is better to try the good Quick
Pea Soup.
Hull:

    3 lbs. green peas

There should be about 3 cups
hulled peas. Shred:

    1 head Boston lettuce
    1 peeled onion
    ½ cup or more celery with
        leaves
    2 sprigs parsley

Sauté the vegetables gently,
until tender, in:

    2 tablespoons butter

Add:

    2½ cups chicken stock
    2 cups of the hulled peas
    10 or 12 pea pods
    (⅓ bay leaf)

Simmer these ingredients, covered, until the peas are very
soft. Put the soup through a
food mill or a potato ricer.
Simmer until tender:

    1 cup of the hulled peas

in:

    1½ cups chicken stock

Add them to the strained soup.
To bind the soup, see About
Legume Soups, page 118.

    Correct the seasoning

You may color the soup with a
drop or two of:

    Green vegetable coloring

and serve it with:

    Butter Dumplings, or
    Sponge Dumplings
    (2 teaspoons chopped mint)

BOULA-BOULA [6]

◗ Simmer in boiling water until tender:

    2 cups green peas

Purée them through a fine sieve. Reheat and add:

    2 tablespoons sweet butter
    Correct the seasoning

Add:

    2 cups canned green turtle soup
    1 cup dry sherry

Heat ◗ but do not boil the soup. Spoon soup into heated cups. Top each with:

    2 tablespoons whipped cream

Place briefly under broiler. Serve at once.

MULLIGATAWNY SOUP

[About 4 Cups]

Sauté lightly, but do not brown:

    ½ cup diced onion
    1 diced carrot
    2 stalks celery, diced

in:

    ¼ cup butter or olive oil

Stir in:

    1½ tablespoons flour
    2 teaspoons curry powder

Stir and cook these ingredients for about 3 minutes. Pour in and simmer for 30 minutes:

    4 cups chicken broth

Add and simmer for 15 minutes longer:

    ¼ cup diced tart apples
    ½ cup boiled rice
    ½ cup diced cooked chicken
    1 teaspoon salt
    ¼ teaspoon pepper
    ⅛ teaspoon thyme

Immediately before serving, stir in:

    ½ cup hot cream

OXTAIL SOUP

I. [About 7 Cups]

Brown:

    1 disjointed oxtail or 2 veal tails: about 2 lbs.

    ½ cup sliced onions

in:

    2 tablespoons butter or fat

Add to the above and ◗ simmer, uncovered, for about 4½ hours:

    8 cups water
    1½ teaspoons salt
    4 peppercorns

Add and simmer ½ hour longer or until the vegetables are tender:

    ¼ cup shredded parsley
    ½ cup diced carrots
    1 cup diced celery
    ½ bay leaf
    ¼ cup barley
    ½ cup tomato pulp
    1 teaspoon dried thyme, marjoram or basil

Strain, chill, degrease and reheat the stock. The meat and vegetables may be diced or blended and added to the soup later. Brown in a skillet:

    1 tablespoon flour

Add and stir until blended:

    2 tablespoons butter

Add the stock slowly and

    Correct the seasoning

Shortly before serving you may pour in:

    (¼ cup dry sherry or Madeira or ½ cup red wine)

Serve the soup with:

    Fritter Garnish, or slices of lemon

II. ⊗ [About 3 Cups]

Sear in a pressure cooker:

    1 oxtail, joints separated
    1 small diced onion

in:

    3 tablespoons fat

Add:

    4 cups hot water or ½ water, ½ tomato juice
    1 teaspoon salt
    2 peppercorns

Adjust cover. Cook at 15 pounds pressure for 15 minutes. Reduce pressure quickly. Remove the cover. Remove ox joints. Add to liquid in cooker:

    1 diced carrot

4 ribs celery, diced

Readjust cover. Pressure cook the soup for 5 minutes longer. Degrease the soup after chilling it. Reheat and:

Correct the seasoning

You may add:

(2 tablespoons dry sherry
or tomato catsup)

Separate meat from the joints. Add to soup. Serve with:

Chopped parsley

PANADES

[About 4 Cups]

These bread-thickened vegetable soups are practical and filling. They are a good way of utilizing leftover bread. Panades combine well with leeks, celery and sorrel; but watercress, spinach, lettuce, etc., may be substituted. Use:

1 cup finely chopped celery,
leeks or onions

Cook the vegetables slowly until soft, but not brown, in:

1 tablespoon butter

Cover with a lid. If a leafy vegetable is used, add it to the butter, cover and cook slowly until wilted and reduced to about one fourth. Add:

2 cups hot water or milk
½ teaspoon salt
3 cups diced fresh or stale
bread

Stir well and permit the mixture to boil. Simmer for ½ hour. Beat well until smooth with a wire whisk or in a ⅄ blender. Combine:

1 cup rich milk
1 large egg

Stir this slowly into the hot soup. Heat but ◗ do not permit the soup to boil. Serve it with:

Chopped parsley
Freshly grated nutmeg

PEPPER POT

[About 5 Cups]

Cut into small pieces and sauté in a heavy saucepan until clear:

4 slices of bacon

Add and simmer for about 5 minutes:

⅓ cup minced onion
½ cup minced celery
2 seeded, minced green
peppers
(1 teaspoon marjoram or
summer savory)

Wash and cut into fine shreds:

¾ lb. cooked honeycomb
Tripe, page 548

Put into the saucepan with:

8 cups Brown Stock (II,
141)
1 bay leaf
½ teaspoon freshly ground
pepper

Bring these ingredients to the boiling point. Add:

1 cup raw, peeled and
diced potatoes

Gently simmer the soup, uncovered, until the potatoes are tender. Melt:

2 tablespoons butter

Stir in, until blended:

2 tablespoons flour

Add a little of the soup. Bring these ingredients to the boiling point, then pour them into the rest of the soup.

Correct the seasoning

Shortly before serving add:

½ cup warm cream

COCK-A-LEEKIE

[5 to 6 Cups]

Old recipes for this leek, chicken and cream soup start with a fowl or cock simmered in strong stock, and wind up with the addition of prunes. The following version is delicious, if not traditional.

Remove the dark green part of the tops and the roots from:

6 leeks

Wash them carefully—they may be sandy. Cut them in half lengthwise, then crosswise in ⅛-inch slices. There should be about 4 cups. Place in a pan with:

>3 cups boiling water
>1½ teaspoons salt

Simmer from 5 to 7 minutes or until tender but not mushy. Add and heat to a boil:

>2 tablespoons chicken fat or butter
>1½ cups well-seasoned strong chicken broth

Scald and stir in:

>½ cup cream
>Correct the seasoning

SAUERKRAUT SOUP

[About 7 Cups]
Sauté until golden brown:

>½ cup chopped onion

in:

>3 tablespoons bacon fat

Add:

>½ clove minced garlic
>½ lb. diced lean pork

Cover and cook over low heat for about 20 minutes. Add:

>1 lb. chopped sauerkraut
>6 cups stock

Cook until soft, about 45 minutes. Melt:

>1½ tablespoons butter

Stir in:

>1½ tablespoons flour

Stir in slowly a little of the hot soup, blend and return the mixture to kettle. Add:

>(1 teaspoon sugar)
>Correct the seasoning

and garnish with:

>Diced salami or ham

SPINACH SOUP

[About 6½ Cups]
Pick over, wash, drain thoroughly, then chop fine or blend:

>2 lbs. tender young spinach

You may use instead 4 cups cooked or two 14-ounce packages of frozen spinach, defrosted.
Melt in a saucepan:

>¼ cup butter

Sauté in it until golden brown:

>¼ cup minced onion

Add the spinach. Stir to coat it well with the butter. Cover, and cook gently till the spinach is just tender. ⅃ Blend or put the spinach through a food mill or sieve. Return to pan and add:

>4 cups chicken stock
>A grating of nutmeg
>Salt or paprika

Bring the soup slowly to a boil and serve; or you may serve it cold, garnished with:

>Diced, seeded cucumbers or chives and cultured sour cream

GREEN TURTLE SOUP

[About 8 Cups]
It is a timesaver to buy canned or frozen turtle meat. But if you can turn turtles, feel energetic and want to prepare your own, see page 447.
Place in a saucepan and bring to the boiling point:

>1 lb. green turtle or terrapin meat cut into pieces
>3 cups water
>3 cups Brown Stock (II, 141)
>1 bay leaf
>1 sprig fresh thyme
>2 cloves
>¼ teaspoon ground allspice
>Juice and thinly sliced peel of ½ lemon
>A few grains cayenne
>¼ teaspoon freshly ground black pepper
>½ teaspoon salt
>4 whole corianders

These pods will rise to the top by the end of the cooking period and can be skimmed out before serving.
Heat:

>2 tablespoons cooking oil

Sauté in this for 2 minutes:

>2 medium-sized chopped onions

Stir in:

>1 tablespoon flour

Add:

    1½ cups fresh skinned seeded tomatoes

Permit these ingredients to cook for 10 minutes. Combine them with the turtle mixture and:

    1 tablespoon chopped parsley

    2 cloves minced garlic

Simmer the soup until the meat is tender, at least 2 hours. You may add a few drops of caramel coloring. Add to each serving:

    1 tablespoon dry sherry

Garnish the soup with:

    2 chopped hard-cooked eggs
    Lemon slices

MOCK TURTLE SOUP

[About 12 Cups]

This full-bodied, nourishing soup, served with crusty rolls, can be the main dish for any meal.

Cover:

    5 lbs. veal bones

with:

    14 cups water

Bring to the boiling point. Add and simmer for about 4 hours:

    6 chopped celery ribs with leaves
    5 coarsely cut carrots
    1 cup chopped onion
    2 cups canned tomatoes
    1 small can Italian tomato paste
    6 crushed peppercorns
    1 tablespoon salt
    2 teaspoons monosodium glutamate
    6 whole cloves
    2 bay leaves
    ½ teaspoon dried thyme

Degrease. Sauté for about 5 minutes in a greased skillet:

    2 cloves minced garlic
    2 lbs. ground beef
    2 teaspoons salt

Add to the stock, with:

    ¼ teaspoon Worcestershire sauce
    4 teaspoons sugar

Blend:

    6 tablespoons browned flour (II, 153)
    1 cup cooled stock

Stir this paste into the simmering soup. Permit it to simmer for 20 minutes more. Add:

    2 thinly sliced lemons
    1 set chopped, parboiled calf brains, page 540

Garnish the soup with:

    3 sliced hard-cooked eggs

NEW YEAR'S SOUPS

Suggested below are traditional New Year's soups, served just before parties break up. They are also known as hangover soups, or Lumpensuppe, and are sometimes helpful for the morning after.

I. Onion Soup, page 113, with the addition of:

    1 cup red wine

II. Lentil Soup with sour cream and sausage.

ABOUT CREAM SOUPS

These favored luncheon soups are also sometimes served at dinner. In this latter role, they satisfy what is, as often as not, a mechanical rather than a nutritional need. Like hors d'oeuvre, they act as a stabilizer for the cocktails which have just been drunk or as a buffer against the wines which are about to come.

For the richest of cream soups —the veloutés—first, sauté the vegetables in butter, purée them and combine the purée in equal parts with Velouté Sauce, page 362. Bind with egg yolk, allowing 2 to 4 yolks for each pint of soup. Simpler cream soups may be made on a Béchamel sauce base, page 359, or on this quick Béchamel: use 2 tablespoons butter to 1½ tablespoons flour, plus 2 cups cream and ¾ to 1 cup vegetable purée. Should you wish to thin these ingredients, use a little well-flavored stock.

For everyday cream soups, we find we can purée the tender vegetables raw or cook the more mature, fibrous ones and process them in a ⅃ blender. The soup is served without straining. ◗ If seafood or fowl is blended, it tends to be unpleasantly stringy and the entire soup will need straining before serving.

◗ All cream soups, whether bound with egg or not, are ruined by boiling, so be sure to heat just to the boiling point or cook them in the top of a double boiler ◗ over, not in, hot water. Reheat them this same way.

CREAM OF ASPARAGUS SOUP

[About 6 Cups]
Wash and remove the tips from:
> 1 lb. fresh green asparagus
Simmer the tips, covered, until they are tender in a small amount of:
> Milk or water
Cut the stalks into pieces and place them in a saucepan. Add:
> 6 cups Veal or Chicken Stock (II, 142)
> ¼ cup chopped onion
> ½ cup chopped celery
Simmer these ingredients, covered, for about ½ hour. Rub them through a sieve. Melt:
> 3 tablespoons butter
Stir in, until blended:
> 3 tablespoons flour
Stir in slowly:
> ½ cup cream
Add the asparagus stock. Heat the soup well in a double boiler. Add the asparagus tips. Season the soup immediately before serving with:
> Salt, paprika and white pepper
Garnish with:
> A diced hard-cooked egg

CREAM OF CAULIFLOWER SOUP

[About 6 Cups]
Prepare:
> 1 large cauliflower, page 281
Drain it, reserving the water and about ⅓ of the florets. Put the remainder through a food mill, blender or sieve. Melt:
> ¼ cup butter
Sauté in it, until tender:
> 2 tablespoons chopped onion
> 3 celery ribs, minced
Stir in:
> ¼ cup flour
Stir in slowly and bring to the boiling point:
> 4 cups Veal or Chicken Stock (II, 142) and the reserved cauliflower water
Add the strained cauliflower and:
> 2 cups scalded rich milk or cream
Add the florets and:
> A grating of nutmeg
> Salt and paprika
Garnish with:
> (Grated cheese)

CREAM OF CELERY SOUP

[About 4 Cups]
Melt:
> 1 tablespoon butter
Add and sauté for 2 minutes:
> 1 cup or more chopped celery with leaves
> (⅓ cup sliced onion)
Pour in and simmer for about 10 minutes:
> 2 cups Veal or Chicken Stock
Strain the soup. Add and bring to the boiling point:
> 1½ cups milk
Dissolve:
> 1½ tablespoons cornstarch
in:
> ½ cup milk
Stir these ingredients gradually into the hot soup. Bring to the

boiling point. Stir and cook for about 1 minute. You may add:

A grating of nutmeg

Serve with:

(2 tablespoons chopped parsley)

CHESTNUT SOUP

[About 3 Cups]

Prepare:

1 lb. chestnuts

Mash and beat them until smooth in:

2 cups milk

Melt:

¼ cup butter

Add and simmer until soft and golden:

1 minced onion

Sprinkle with:

1 tablespoon flour
1 teaspoon salt
⅛ teaspoon each nutmeg and pepper
½ cup chopped celery leaves

Stir and slowly add the chestnut and milk mixture. ◖ Simmer for about 10 minutes. Pour in:

1 cup cream

Heat ◖ but do not boil and serve immediately garnished with:

Parsley
Croutons, page 151

CREAM OF CHICKEN SOUP

[About 4½ Cups]

Simmer:

3 cups Chicken Stock (II, 142)
½ cup finely chopped celery

When the celery is tender, add and cook for 5 minutes:

½ cup cooked Rice, page 158

Add:

½ cup hot cream
1 tablespoon chopped parsley
Salt and paprika

◖ Do not boil the soup after adding the cream.

CREAM OF CORN SOUP

[About 5 Cups]

Put through a food mill or coarse sieve:

2½ cups cream style canned corn or 2½ cups corn, cut from the ear, simmered until tender in 1 cup milk

Melt:

3 tablespoons butter

Simmer in it until soft:

½ medium-sized sliced onion

Stir in:

3 tablespoons flour
1½ teaspoons salt
A few grains freshly ground pepper
(A grating of nutmeg)

Stir in the corn and:

3 cups milk or 2½ cups milk and ½ cup cream

Serve the soup sprinkled with:

3 tablespoons chopped parsley or chives

CORN CHOWDER

[About 6 Cups]

Sauté slowly until lightly browned:

½ cup chopped salt pork

Add and sauté until golden brown:

3 tablespoons chopped onion
½ cup chopped celery
3 tablespoons chopped green pepper

Add and simmer:

1 cup raw, peeled, diced potatoes
2 cups water
½ teaspoon salt
¼ teaspoon paprika
½ bay leaf

When the potatoes are tender, in about 45 minutes, combine until blended, bring to the boiling point, and add to the above:

3 tablespoons flour
½ cup milk

Add:

1½ cups hot milk
2 cups whole kernel corn

Heat but do not boil the soup.
Serve it sprinkled with:
    Chopped parsley

COLD BULGARIAN CUCUMBER SOUP

[About 3 Cups]
"Nazdrave" as the Bulgarians
say for "Bon appétit."
Two to 6 hours before serving,
refrigerate, covered:
    1½ cups peeled, diced
        cucumbers
marinated in a mixture of:
    1 teaspoon salt
    ¼ teaspoon pepper
    ¼ to 1 cup chopped walnuts
    2 tablespoons olive oil
    1 clove minced garlic
    2 tablespoons chopped
        fresh dill
◗ The fresh dill is the essential
touch. When ready to serve,
add:
    1 to 1½ cups thick yogurt
        or 1 cup cultured sour
        cream
Place 1 or 2 ice cubes in each
soup bowl. Pour in the mixture.
It should have the consistency
of chilled borsch. If not thin
enough, it can be thinned with
a small amount of light stock.
Serve at once.

CHILLED CREAM OF CUCUMBER HERB SOUP

[6 Cups]
Pare, seed and slice:
    2 medium-sized cucumbers
Add to them:
    1 cup water
    2 slices onion
    ¼ teaspoon salt
    ⅛ teaspoon white pepper
Cook the cucumbers, covered,
until very soft. Put them through
a fine strainer or an ⅃ electric
blender. Stir until smooth:
    ¼ cup flour
    ½ cup chicken stock
Stir into this flour paste:
    1½ cups chicken stock
Add the cucumber purée and:

    ¼ bay leaf or 2 cloves
Stir the soup over low heat.
Simmer for 2 minutes. Strain
and chill in a covered jar. Stir
into these ingredients:
    ¾ cup chilled cream or
        cultured sour cream or
        yogurt
    1 tablespoon finely
        chopped dill, chives or
        other herb or grated
        lemon rind
    Correct the seasoning
Serve the soup very cold.

CREAM OF MUSHROOM SOUP

[About 4½ Cups]
The flavor of mushrooms is more
pronounced if they have begun
to color. Prepare for cooking:
    ½ lb. mature mushrooms
        with stems
Sauté lightly in:
    2 tablespoons butter
Add them to:
    2 cups chicken stock or
        water
    ½ cup chopped tender
        celery
    ¼ cup sliced onion
    ⅛ cup shredded parsley
Simmer, covered, for 20 minutes.
Drain the vegetables, reserving
the stock. ⅃ Blend them or put
them through a food chopper.
Prepare:
    Cream Sauce I, page 359
Pour the liquid slowly into the
cream sauce, cook and stir until
the soup just reaches a boil. Add
the ground vegetables. Heat ◗
but do not boil. Season the soup
with:
    1¼ teaspoons salt
    ⅛ teaspoon paprika
    (⅛ teaspoon nutmeg)
    (3 tablespoons dry white
        wine)
Serve, topped with:
    (Whipped cream)
Garnish with:
    Paprika

Sprigs of parsley or
chopped chives

CREAM OF NETTLE SOUP

[About 4 Cups]
Using rubber gloves, remove the
central stem from:
> 1 quart young nettle tops

Have boiling:
> 5 cups stock

Blend in:
> 2 tablespoons cooked rice
>   or oatmeal

Add the nettles and simmer for
about 15 minutes.
> Correct the seasoning

and serve.

CREAM OF ONION SOUP OR ONION VELOUTÉ

[About 4 Cups]
Melt:
> 3 tablespoons butter

Add and sauté till a golden
brown:
> 1½ cups thinly sliced onions

Stir in:
> 1 tablespoon flour
> ½ teaspoon salt

Add:
> 4 cups milk or cream and
>   Stock (II, 141)

Simmer, covered, until the onions are very tender. Add:
> 4 beaten egg yolks

Heat but ♦ do not boil. Season
with:
> Salt and paprika
> Freshly grated nutmeg or
>   (Worcestershire sauce)

Place in each cup:
> 1 teaspoon chopped parsley

Pour the hot soup over it.

POTATO SOUP

[About 3 Cups]
Peel and slice:
> 2 medium-sized potatoes

Skin and chop:
> 2 medium-sized onions
> 4 ribs celery

Sauté these ingredients in:
> 1½ tablespoons butter

Add:
> Boiling water to cover
> ½ teaspoon salt
> (½ bay leaf)

Boil the vegetables until the
potatoes are tender or ✪ pressure cook them for 3 minutes
at 15 pounds pressure. Put them
through a ricer or ⅄ blender.
Beat into them:
> 2 tablespoons butter

Thin the soup to the desired
consistency with:
> Rich milk and/or
> Chicken Stock (II, 142)

Add if required:
> Salt and paprika
> A dash Worcestershire
>   sauce

Serve with:
> Chopped parsley, chives
>   or watercress
> 1 cup sliced frankfurters,
>   chopped, cooked shrimp
>   or diced ham

POTATO SOUP WITH TOMATOES

[About 10–12 Cups]
A more sophisticated version of
the previous recipe.
Prepare:
> 2 cups sliced onions

Sauté very gently until translucent in:
> ¼ cup butter

Add the onions to:
> 2 cups sliced potatoes
> 6 cups boiling water

Simmer for about ½ hour. Add
and simmer, covered, for about
20 minutes:
> 5 cups sliced tomatoes or
>   3 cups canned tomatoes
> 2 teaspoons sugar
> 1 teaspoon salt
> ⅛ teaspoon paprika
> A pinch of chervil

Put the soup through a fine
strainer or ⅄ blender. Reheat
and
> Correct the seasoning

Scald and stir in:
> 1 cup cream

Heat ◗ but do not boil. Serve
at once.

VICHYSSOISE OR LEEK POTATO SOUP

This leek soup may be served
hot or very cold. Yes, the last
"s" is pronounced. Most Americans shun it, in a "genteel" way,
as though it were virtuous to
ignore it. Be sure to serve the
soup reduced to a velvety
smoothness.

I. [About 6 Cups]
Mince the white part of:
  3 medium-sized leeks
  1 medium-sized onion
Stir and sauté them for 3 minutes in:
  2 tablespoons butter
Peel, slice very fine and add:
  4 medium-sized potatoes
Add:
  4 cups clarified Chicken
    Stock (II, 142)
Simmer the vegetables, covered,
for 15 minutes or until tender.
Put them through a very fine
sieve, food mill or ⅄ blender.
Add:
  1 to 2 cups cream
  (¼ teaspoon mace)
  Salt and white pepper
  Chopped watercress or
    chives

II. [About 2½ Cups]
Superlative! Less rich and made
in about 20 minutes by using a
⅄ blender and ✿ pressure
cooker. Serve it hot or chill it
quickly by placing it in a refrigerator tray or deep freeze.
Prepare as above:
  Vichyssoise
using ½ the amount of ingredients given. After adding the
potatoes and stock, pressure
cook the soup for 3 minutes at
15 pound pressure. Cool. Add:
  1 cup peeled, seeded and
    diced cucumbers
Blend covered until smooth,

about 1 minute. Place the soup
in a jar. Chill it thoroughly.
You may add the cream, but
you will probably like the result
just as well without it. Hot or
cold, sprinkle the top with:
  Chopped chives

PUMPKIN SOUP

[About 4 Cups]
Place:
  3 cups canned or 2 lbs.
    cooked fresh pumpkin
in:
  3 cups scalded milk
Add:
  1 tablespoon butter
  1 tablespoon sugar or 2
    tablespoons brown sugar
  Salt and pepper
  (Nutmeg and cinnamon)
  A very small pinch
    saffron
  ½ cup finely julienned ham
Heat ◗ but do not boil. Serve
at once.

CREAM OF SORREL SOUP

[About 5 to 6 Cups]
Also known as **Potage Germiny**
and a favorite combination with
veal and fish dishes. Because of
the oxalic acid in sorrel ◗ use a
stainless steel or enamel pan.
Clean, shred from the mid rib
and chop:
  2 cups sorrel leaves
Sauté them, until wilted, in:
  1 to 2 tablespoons butter
When they are sufficiently
wilted, there will be only about
3 tablespoons of leaves. Add:
  5 cups Chicken Stock
    (II, 142)
  (1 tablespoon fresh pea
    purée)
Simmer for about 2 minutes.
Remove from the heat and add:
  ½ cup cream
  3 beaten egg yolks
Heat until the soup thickens
slightly ◗ but do not boil. Serve
garnished with:
  Chopped chervil

CREAM OF SPINACH OR LETTUCE SOUP

[About 5 Cups]

Pick over and wash:

1 lb. spinach or 1 lb. leaf
lettuce

Or you may use:

1 cup frozen spinach

Place it, while moist or frozen,
in a covered saucepan. Cook for
about 6 minutes. Drain. Put
through a strainer or ⅄ blender.
Melt in a saucepan:

2 tablespoons butter

Add and sauté for 3 minutes:

1 tablespoon grated onion
or 1 slice of onion which
can be removed easily

Stir in and cook until blended:

2 tablespoons flour

Stir in gradually:

4 cups milk and/or stock

Season with:

¾ teaspoon or more salt
¼ teaspoon paprika
(A grating of nutmeg)

Add the spinach or lettuce. Heat
the soup well. Serve sprinkled
with:

(Grated Parmesan cheese
or sieved egg yolk)

CREAM OF TOMATO SOUP

[About 5½ Cups]

Simmer, covered, for about 15
minutes:

2 cups canned or fresh,
cut-up tomatoes
½ cup chopped celery
¼ cup chopped onion
2 teaspoons white or brown
sugar

Prepare:

4 cups Cream Sauce I,
page 359

Strain into this the tomato and
vegetable stock.

Correct the seasoning

and serve with:

Croutons, page 151
Chopped parsley, burnet
or basil

If served chilled, garnish with:

Chopped chives or
whipped cream and
paprika

CREAM OF WATER CRESS OR PURSLANE SOUP

I. [About 4 Cups]

Sauté:

1 cup chopped cress or
purslane

in:

1 tablespoon butter

Add.

Salt, white pepper and
paprika
½ cup white wine
4 cups cream

Heat but do not boil. Serve at
once:

II. [About 5 Cups]

To:

5 cups hot Cream of
Chicken Soup, page 127

Add:

1½ cups chopped or ⅄
blended water cress

Or, if you wish to try Gandhi's
favorite vegetable, use an equal
amount of:

(Purslane)

Simmer the soup about 5 minutes. Add and stir a small quantity of the soup into:

2 well-beaten eggs

Add this to the rest of the soup,
stirring it in slowly. Heat the
soup ▶ but do not boil. Serve
at once.

An interesting taste variation results by adding:

2 slices fresh ginger

which have been lightly sautéed
in:

Butter
Salt

Remove ginger after reheating
but before serving the soup.

MILK TOAST OR SOUP

[Individual Service]

While not exactly a soup, this
dish can bring something like
the same cozy comfort to the
young or the ailing.

Toast lightly on both sides:
>   A slice of bread, ¾ inch
>   thick
Spread it lightly with:
>   Butter
Sprinkle it with:
>   (Salt)
Place it in a bowl and pour over
it:
>   1 cup hot milk

ABOUT FISH SOUPS

Making a good broth or fumet
of fish is like making a stock of
any kind of meat in that the
process toughens the meat. It
differs in that it takes a good
deal less time. Extraction is
limited to a ◗ 20 to 30 minute
period ◗ over relatively high
heat, instead of the slow simmering recommended for warm-
blooded meat. ◗ As a conse-
quence, most fish soups are
quick soups. When fisherman's
stews are served, the meat is
often presented on the side;
and in the preparation of delicate bisques based on shellfish, the shrimp or lobsters are
often poached separately, then
pounded in a mortar or minced
before incorporation in a separate stock, cream and egg base.
The original stock may be
used as a court bouillon for
cooking other fish or reduced for
use in "au maigre" or meatless
sauces. Bisques, as well as oyster,
clam and mussel soups and
stews, need so little heat that
the stock bases are warmed first
and the shellfish then just heated
through in them, preferably in a
double boiler ◗ over, not in, hot
water. Serve fish soups at once.
If you must hold or reheat, be
sure to do so again ◗ over, not
in, hot water.

CLAM BROTH OR SOUP

[About 4 Cups]
Clams are of various types, see
About Clams, page 427. The
broth is delicious when fresh,
but may be frozen until mushy
and served in small glasses or
on the shells with wedges of
lemon. The meat of the clams
themselves may be used in various sea-food dishes, see pages
229–234.
Wash and scrub well with a
brush, then place in a kettle:
>   2 quarts clams in shells
Add:
>   1¾ cups water
>   3 cut up ribs celery with
>   leaves
>   A pinch of cayenne
◗ Cover the kettle closely. You
may double the quantity of this
soup, even though the clam
flavor will be lessened, by adding about 4 cups of water and
minced vegetables which are
suitable for soup, see Court
Bouillon (II, 146). ◗ Steam the
clams until the shells open, page
430. Strain the liquor through
wet double cheesecloth to remove any sand. It may be heated
and diluted with warm cream or
rich milk. Add:
>   1 teaspoon butter
>   Correct the seasoning
and serve.

COQUINA BROTH

If you are lucky enough to be
on a beach in Florida, collect in
a sieve at ebb tide:
>   Coquinas
the little native periwinkle clams,
in rainbow-hued shells.
Rinse them clean of sand, then
barely cover with:
>   Water
Bring slowly to a boil and ◗ simmer for about 10 minutes. Pour
the broth through a fine sieve.
When you imbibe it, remember
the advice of an old German
who said, when serving a fine
vintage, "Don't gullop it, zipp
it!"

CRAWFISH BISQUE

[About 6 Cups]
Wash and scrub with a brush
under running water:
    3 dozen crawfish
Soak for 30 minutes in salted
water, 1 tablespoon salt to 4
cups of water. Rinse thoroughly.
Place the crawfish in a saucepan with:
    6 cups boiling water
    A few grains of cayenne
    ½ teaspoon salt
Bring to a boil, then ◗ simmer
for 15 minutes. Drain, reserving
the stock. Remove the heads and
reserve 18 of them to be stuffed
as a garnish for the bisque. Remove the meat from the heads.
Devein the tails. Return all remaining shells to the stock.
Bring to a boil. Add:
    4 ribs chopped celery
    2 tablespoons chopped
        parsley
    ½ diced carrot
    ⅛ teaspoon thyme or a
        sprig of fresh thyme
Simmer for 30 minutes. Strain.
Meanwhile, prepare the stuffing
for the heads. Mince the crawfish meat. Sauté until golden:
    2 tablespoons minced onion
in:
    2 tablespoons butter
Add and cook for 3 minutes:
    2 tablespoons finely minced
        celery
    1 tablespoon finely minced
        parsley
Remove from heat and add ½
the crawfish meat and:
    ½ cup bread crumbs
Beat and add:
    1 egg
    Salt and paprika as
        required
Stir lightly with a fork. Stuff the
heads with this mixture. Place
them on a greased shallow pan.
Dot each head with butter. For
10 minutes, before serving the
soup, bake the heads in a preheated 425° oven. Melt:

    2 tablespoons butter
Sauté in it until delicately
browned:
    ¼ cup minced onion
Add and stir until lightly
browned:
    2 tablespoons flour
Add the fish stock slowly, stirring until smooth. Add the remaining crawfish meat and
    Correct the seasoning
◗ Simmer the bisque for about
5 minutes, stirring it often. To
serve, place the heated heads in
hot soup plates, then pour the
bisque over them.

LOBSTER BISQUE

[About 6 Cups]
Remove the meat from:
    2 medium-sized boiled
        lobsters
Dice the body meat and mince
the tail and claw meat. Reserve
it. Crush the shells. Add to them
the tough end of the claws and:
    2½ cups Chicken Stock
        (II, 142) or Fumet
        (II, 143)
    1 sliced onion
    4 ribs celery with leaves
    2 whole cloves
    1 bay leaf
    6 peppercorns
Simmer these ingredients for ½
hour. Strain the stock. If there
is coral roe, force it through a
fine sieve, combine it with the
butter in a mortar or bowl, add
the flour and when well blended
pour the heated milk slowly on
it, stirring until the mixture is
smooth.
Otherwise, melt:
    ¼ cup butter
Stir in:
    ¼ cup flour
Add gradually:
    3 cups milk
    ¼ teaspoon nutmeg
    Correct the seasoning
When the sauce is smooth and
boiling, add the lobster and the
stock. ◗ Simmer the bisque,

covered, for 5 minutes. Turn off the heat. Stir in:

> 1 cup ◆ hot but not boiling cream

Serve at once with:

> Minced parsley
> Paprika
> Dry sherry

MUSHROOM AND CLAM BISQUE

[About 3 Cups]
Sauté:

> ½ lb. chopped mushrooms

in:

> 2 tablespoons butter

Stir in:

> 2 tablespoons flour

Stir in slowly:

> 2½ cups clam broth

Simmer for 5 minutes. Remove from the heat. Heat ◆ but do not boil:

> ¾ cup cream

Add to the other ingredients.

> Correct the seasoning

and serve with:

> Chopped parsley or chives

SHRIMP BISQUE

[About 5 Cups]
Remove shells and intestines from:

> 1½ lbs. Poached Shrimp, page 442

Put the shrimp through a meat grinder or ⋏ blender. Cook, covered, in the top of a double boiler ◆ over, not in, hot water for 5 minutes:

> 6 tablespoons butter
> 2 tablespoons grated onion

Add the ground shrimp and:

> 3 cups warm milk

Cook for 2 minutes. Stir in slowly, heat ◆ but do not boil:

> 1 cup cream

Add:

> Salt, if needed, and paprika or freshly ground white pepper
> A grating of nutmeg
> 3 tablespoons sherry

> 2 tablespoons parsley or chives

Serve at once.

OYSTER STEWS AND BISQUES

Here are 2 good recipes which differ in nutritive value and effort of preparation. The first calls for milk and is unthickened; the second, a bisque, calls for milk, cream and egg yolks. To clean oysters, see page 422.

I. [About 4 Cups]

Our instructions are foolproof, as the use of a double boiler prevents overcooking of the oysters. Combine in the top of a double boiler over, not in, hot water:

> 2 to 4 tablespoons butter
> ½ teaspoon or more grated onion or leek, a sliver of garlic or ½ cup stewed celery

Sauté lightly and add:

> 1 to 1½ pints oysters with liquor
> 1½ cups milk
> ½ cup cream
> ½ teaspoon salt
> ⅛ teaspoon white pepper or paprika

Place the pan ◆ over, not in, boiling water. When the milk is hot and the oysters float, add:

> 2 tablespoons chopped parsley

II. [About 4 Cups]

This is a true oyster bisque.
Prepare:

> Oyster Stew I, above

Before adding the parsley, remove the soup from the heat and pour a small quantity over:

> 2 beaten egg yolks

After mixing, add them slowly to the hot bisque. Heat slowly for 1 minute but ◆ do not allow to boil; or hold over hot water in a double boiler until ready to serve.

MUSSEL STEW

Clean the mussels and remove the beard, page 426. Steam, strain and reserve the liquor. Use either recipe for Oyster Stew, above, substituting mussels for oysters.

LOBSTER STEW

[About 5 Cups]
Sauté for 3 or 4 minutes:
  1 cup diced fresh lobster
    meat
in:
  3 tablespoons butter
Add slowly:
  4 cups scalded milk
  2 teaspoons onion juice
A Maine correspondent writes that this stew is much improved by the addition, at this time, of ½ to 1 cup clam broth.
    Correct the seasoning
and serve.

SHRIMP, CRAB AND OYSTER GUMBO

[About 8 Cups]
Melt:
  1 tablespoon butter.
Stir in and cook until golden:
  ¼ cup chopped onion
Stir in until blended:
  2 tablespoons flour
Add and stir until smooth:
  1½ cups strained tomatoes
    4 cups Stock (II, 141)
    or Fumet (II, 143)
  1 quart thinly sliced okra
Break into small pieces and add:
  ½ lb. raw, shelled, cleaned
    shrimp
  ½ lb. raw crab meat
♦ Simmer these ingredients until the okra is tender. Add:
  16 shelled oysters
    Correct the seasoning
and serve the gumbo as soon as the oysters are plump. Sprinkle with:
    Chopped parsley

ABOUT BOUILLABAISSE AND OTHER FISHERMAN'S STEWS

Necessity is the mother of invention; and convenience gave birth to the can and the frozen package. Use frozen or canned fish, if you must, for fisherman's stews; but remember that ♦ their fragrant, distinctive and elusive charm can only be captured if the fish which go into them are themselves freshly caught. Curnonsky reminds us of the legend that bouillabaisse, the most celebrated of fisherman's stews, was first brought by angels to the Three Marys, when they were shipwrecked on the bleak shores of the Camargue.

Divinely inspired or not, it is true that bouillabaisse can only be approximated in this country, even if its ingredients are just off the hook. For its unique flavor depends on the use of fish which are native to the Mediterranean alone: a regional rock fish, high in gelatin content, for example, which gives a slightly cloudy but still thin texture to the soup, and numberless finny tidbits, too small for market. We offer a free translation of bouillabaisse into American—realizing fully that we have succeeded only in changing poetry to rich prose.

A similar accommodation has been made for matelote or freshwater fish stew, in which eel, carp, bream, tench and perch are combined with wine. A certain amount of freewheeling must be the rule, too, in concocting chowders and stews of both sea and fresh fish, which are milk-based and often have potatoes added. Whatever fish you use, see that it is as ♦ fresh as possible and experiment with combinations of those that are most quickly available.

BOUILLABAISSE

[8 Cups]
Have ready:

    ¼ cup finely chopped onion
    4 finely julienned leeks:
        use the white portions
        only

Skin and squeeze the pulp out
of and then dice:

    4 medium-sized tomatoes

Combine:

    5 cloves minced garlic
    1 tablespoon finely chopped
        fresh fennel
    ½ to 1 teaspoon saffron
    2 pulverized bay leaves
    1 teaspoon grated orange
        rind
    2 tablespoons tomato paste
    ⅛ teaspoon celery seed
    3 tablespoons chopped
        parsley
    1 teaspoon freshly ground
        pepper
    2 tablespoons salt

Heat in a large casserole:

    ¼ to ½ cup olive oil

When the oil is hot, add the
prepared ingredients above and
cook until the vegetables are
transparent. Meanwhile, cut into
1-inch dice and then add:

    4 lbs. very fresh fish in
        combination: red
        snapper, halibut,
        pompano, sea perch,
        scallops; also 1-inch
        pieces of well-scrubbed
        lobster, whole shrimp,
        clams and mussels—
        all in the shell

You may prefer to leave the fish
in 2-inch-thick slices and use
some of the smaller fish whole.
If so, add the thinner pieces or
small scrubbed shellfish to the
pot slightly later than the
thicker ones ◗ but do not disturb the boiling. Cover the fish
with:

    2½ cups hot Fumet (II,
        143) or water

◗ Keep the heat high and force
the boiling, which should con-

tinue rapid for 15 to 20 minutes.
Correct the seasoning
To serve, have ready to arrange
in the bottom of 8 hot bowls:

    ¾-inch slices of French
        bread

Dry the bread in the oven and
brush with:

    Garlic butter

When the bouillabaisse is ready,
arrange attractively some of
each kind of fish on and around
the bread. You may remove the
lobsters from the shell and remove the upper shells from the
clams and mussels. Then pour
the hot broth into the bowls and
serve at once. Or, you may strain
the broth onto the bread and
serve the sea food on a separate
platter. Plan the meal with a
beverage other than wine.

MATELOTE

[8 Cups]
Depending upon the amount of
wine used, this dish can be
either a soup or a stew.
Cook separately and have ready
to add as a garnish, just before
serving the matelote:

    12 small cooked onions,
        page 301
    ½ lb. sautéed mushrooms,
        page 296
    ½ lb. cooked shrimp,
        page 442

Now, clean and cut into 1-inch
slices:

    3 lbs. freshwater fish: eel,
        carp, tench, bream or
        perch

Cover first the fish that need the
longest cooking with a combination of ½:

    Good red wine

and ½:

    Fish fumet or meat stock

Take note of the approximate
amount needed, for this should
be reduced by about one half
later on. Add:

    2 teaspoons chopped
        parsley

½ cup chopped celery
1 small bay leaf
2 cloves garlic
¼ teaspoon thyme
1 teaspoon salt

Bring the mixture to a boil, remove from heat and float on the surface:

2 tablespoons warm cognac

Ignite the cognac, and when the flame dies down, return the mixture to heat, add the remaining fish, cover the pan and simmer the soup for about 15 minutes. Now, remove the fish to a serving dish and strain the liquid into another pan. Thicken the soup with a beurre manié of:

3 tablespoons butter
2½ tablespoons flour

Add it a little at a time to the hot soup. Bring the soup just to a boil, stirring constantly. It should be creamy in texture, but will go thin if boiled.

Correct the seasoning

To serve, put the fish into soup bowls, cover first with the onions and mushrooms, then with the sauce; garnish the whole with the shrimp; and serve with:

Soup Croutons, page 151

MANHATTAN CLAM CHOWDER

[About 8 Cups]
Prepare:

1 quart quahog clams, page 428

Wash them in:

3 cups water

Drain through cheesecloth. Reserve liquid. Cut the hard part of the clams from the soft part. Chop finely:

The hard part of the clams
A 2-inch cube of salt pork or
3 slices of bacon
1 large onion

Sauté the salt pork very slowly. Remove and reserve the scraps. Add the minced onions and hard

part of the clams to the grease. Stir and cook slowly for about 5 minutes. Sift over them and stir until blended:

3 tablespoons flour

Heat and stir in the reserved liquid. Peel, prepare and add:

2 cups raw diced potatoes
3 cups cooked or canned tomatoes
(½ cup diced green pepper)
(½ bay leaf)
(¼ cup catsup)

Cover the pan and simmer the chowder until the potatoes are done, but still firm. Add the pork scraps, the soft part of the clams and:

3 tablespoons butter

Simmer for 3 minutes more. Place the chowder in a hot tureen.

Correct the seasoning

Serve with:

Oyster crackers

You may substitute for the fresh clams:

2½ cups canned minced clams

Strain the juice. Add water to make 3 cups of liquid. Use this liquid in place of the water measurement given above. Chowder should be allowed to ripen; it is always better the following day.

NEW ENGLAND CLAM CHOWDER

[About 8 Cups]
Most New Englanders consider the above recipe an illegitimate child. They omit the tomatoes, green peppers and catsup, but pour in:

4 cups hot ♦ not boiling, milk

after the pork scraps have been added. ♦ Do not let the mixture boil. Serve with large crackers.

CONCH CHOWDER

Prepare:

Manhattan Clam Chowder, above

using conch meat to replace the fish. ◗ To prepare conch in the shell, cover:

2 to 15 conchs or large whelks

with cold water and ◗ simmer 20 to 30 minutes. Remove from shell and beat the white body meat in a canvas bag until it begins to disintegrate. Marinate 2 hours in:

¼ cup lime juice

After adding the conch meat to the chowder, simmer about 3 to 5 minutes longer than directed for Manhattan Clam Chowder.

ABOUT QUICK SOUPS

When we were very young, we were more appalled than edified by "Struwwelpeter," a book of rhymed fables for children, which had been written in Germany by a Korpsbruder of our great grandfather. We remember the story of Suppenkaspar, a little boy who resolutely refused to eat his soup, wasted away for his stubbornness and was buried with a tureen as his headstone. Looking back and taking note of our wonderful present-day battery of canned, frozen and dried soups, we can see that Kaspar was born a century too soon and would, in this generation, have chosen, beyond a doubt, to live.

Know the comfort and reassurance of a larder well-stocked with processed soups. With them, you may in a jiffy lay the foundation of a good, square meal. If the unexpected guest prefers a clear soup, use a canned consommé or chicken broth with any one of several quickly confected egg-drops, page 145. If he fancies a more filling dish, serve ⋏ Blender Borsch, page 140, or Quick Cucumber Soup Cockaigne, page 140.

Very special effects may be achieved in your canned and frozen soup repertory by mixing with them the meat and vegetable stocks which are the by-product of daily cooking (II, 138). Put these regularly by, along with meat glazes, for just this purpose. Occasionally, too, a bouillon cube will add interest. Please read About Soup Stock and Stock Substitutes (II, 138). If you have a plot or some pots of fresh herbs, now is the time to commandeer a clipping all 'round.

◗ One word of caution. Normally, we dilute ready-prepared soups considerably less than their manufacturers recommend, whether we use home-cooked stocks, milk or—less desirably— just plain water. But we find that the more concentrated the soup the more likely it is to taste oversalted. Test your mix and correct this tendency.

For very sturdy potages, casseroles, etc., see suggestions in Brunch, Lunch and Supper Dishes, page 208. There is also the possibility that you are harboring some refrigerator scraps which will respond in a constructive way to ⋏ blender treatment. Before processing, add to them a few mushrooms or a few leaves of spinach, lettuce or cress and a small amount of milk and cream. Be sure, though, if you blend uncooked vegetables, that they are tender and will not spoil the texture of your soup with stringy fibers or bits of hull.

If you have on hand some leftover bones, lean fowl or meat trimmings and have a little extra time, put your ⊘ pressure cooker to work, too, at building a soup base. Remember, in this connection, that most fish soups are quick soups, even when you start with raw materials. ◗ Please read About Fish Soups, page 132.

QUICK CANNED CONSOMMÉ VARIATIONS

A clear soup is supposed to be as bracing as a clear conscience.

Add to each serving of consommé, hot or cold:

> A slice of lemon or 1 tablespoon sherry or Madeira or diced avocado
> A dollop of sour cream

Or add to hot consommé:

> Egg Drops, page 145, Marrow Balls, page 150, or Noodles, page 149

QUICK TROPICAL CONSOMMÉ

[About 3 Cups]

Combine and heat the contents of:

> 1 can condensed consommé
> 1 can condensed madrilène

Stir in:

> The juice of 1 large orange

Serve chilled "on the rocks."

⅄ BLENDER GAZPACHO

[About 1 Cup]

Blend together for 2 or 3 minutes:

> ¼ cup skinned, seeded cucumbers
> ¾ cup skinned, seeded tomatoes
> ¼ cup consommé or water
> ½ teaspoon red pimiento

Add and blend for a shorter time:

> 1 teaspoon to 1 tablespoon olive oil

Add, but do not blend, as the flavor would be too strong:

> 1 teaspoon chopped chives
> Correct the seasoning

and serve by pouring the broth over 2 ice cubes. A good garnish is:

> Garlic croutons

QUICK VEGETABLE SOUP

[About 2½ Cups]

Utilize the water in which vegetables have been cooked.

Melt:

> 2 tablespoons butter

Add and stir until blended:

> 1⅓ tablespoons flour

Add and stir until smooth:

> 1½ cups vegetable water

Bring to a boil and cook for 2 minutes. Lower the heat and add:

> ½ cup cream or Stock (II, 141)

Add:

> ½ cup cooked, diced or strained vegetables
> 2 tablespoons chopped parsley
> (A dash of celery salt)
> Correct the seasoning

Heat thoroughly ♦ but do not boil if you have chosen to add the cream.

⅄ BLENDER CREAM OF VEGETABLE SOUP

Blend:

> 1 can condensed cream of vegetable soup
> 1 can condensed chicken rice soup
> 1 cup canned or strong asparagus stock
> (¼ cup cream)

Heat ♦ but do not boil and serve at once.

QUICK CREAM OF ASPARAGUS SOUP

[4 to 5 Cups]

Combine:

> 1 can condensed cream of asparagus soup
> 1 can condensed chicken broth
> (1 can condensed cream of mushroom soup)
> 1 cup milk

Heat, stirring until smooth.

QUICK CHILLED CREAM OF AVOCADO SOUP

[3 Cups]
Stir until smooth and at the boiling point:

2 cups condensed cream of chicken soup

Remove from heat. Chill and add:

½ cup puréed avocado

When ready to serve, stir in:

½ cup chilled cream
⅛ teaspoon white pepper

Serve in cups, sprinkled with:

1 teaspoon chopped chives or chervil

⚹ BLENDER BORSCH

I. [About 4 Cups]
Combine in a blender:

1 can condensed consommé
1 can condensed cream of chicken soup
1 can beets: No. 2½
(1 clove minced garlic)

Half of the liquid from the beets may be drained if a thick soup is desired. Blend until smooth and chill. Serve with a garnish of:

Cultured sour cream and Fines Herbes (II, 220)

II. [About 4 Cups]
Combine in a blender:

2 cups tomato juice
2 cups canned beets
3 dill pickles
3 tablespoons finely grated onion
1 drop hot pepper sauce
(1 clove minced garlic)

Chill the soup and serve garnished with:

4 thinly sliced hard-boiled eggs
Cultured sour cream
Fresh chopped dill or fennel

QUICK PEA SOUP

[About 6 Cups]

Combine and bring to the boiling point:

1 can condensed consommé
1 can clear chicken soup
1 can condensed pea soup

Add:

1⅓ cups water or stock
¼ cup finely diced cooked ham
(4 oz. fine noodles)
(1 tablespoon Worcestershire sauce)
(1 tablespoon chili sauce)

Simmer, covered, until hot or the noodles are done.

QUICK CREAM OF CHICKEN SOUP

Easy to make and very good.
Heat in a double boiler ♦ over, not in, hot water:

Chicken bouillon
Cream—about ¼ the amount of the bouillon

Add, if you wish:

A dash of nutmeg
Chopped parsley

Add, if you want to be really luxurious:

Ground blanched almonds—use about 2 tablespoons to 1 cup soup

QUICK CUCUMBER SOUP COCKAIGNE

[About 5 Cups]
Bring to a boil:

2 cups strong chicken broth

Drop in about:

1½ cups peeled, seeded and diced cucumbers

Simmer until translucent, about 15 minutes. Add:

1 can condensed cream of chicken soup

blended with:

½ cup chicken broth

Again bring to a boil. Now add:

½ cup canned crab meat, shrimp or minced clams
1 teaspoon fresh parsley or chervil

Heat ◗ but do not boil, and serve at once.

QUICK COLD CUCUMBER SOUP

[About 5 Cups]
Combine in a saucepan:
    1 can frozen condensed cream of potato soup
    An equal amount of milk
    1 chicken bouillon cube
    1⅓ cups finely chopped cucumber

Heat slowly, stirring until very hot and until the cucumber is partially cooked, about 10 minutes. ⅃ Blend or put through a food mill and refrigerate, covered, until chilled. Shortly before serving, stir in:
    1 cup light cream
    ½ cup minced cucumber

QUICK CREAM OF CAULIFLOWER SOUP

[About 3½ Cups]
Heat:
    2 tablespoons butter
Cook in the butter for 4 minutes:
    ¼ cup sliced onion
    2 minced small ribs celery with leaves
Add:
    1½ cups chicken broth
    1 cup cooked cauliflower, riced or mashed
Heat to the boiling point. Heat and add:
    1 cup rich milk
◗ Do not let the soup boil after adding the milk.
    Correct the seasoning and serve with:
    1 tablespoon chopped parsley
    A light grating of nutmeg

QUICK CHEESE SOUP

[About 4 Cups]
Combine and stir over low heat:
    1 can condensed celery soup
    1 can condensed consommé
    1¼ cups water or milk
    ½ cup grated cheddar or pimiento cheese
Add:
    (1 tablespoon chopped onion)
    (¼ teaspoon Worcestershire sauce)
Stir over low heat until the cheese is melted. ◗ Do not let the soup boil. Serve with:
    Chopped parsley

QUICK TOMATO CORN CHOWDER

[3 Cups]
Combine and heat, but ◗ do not boil:
    1 can condensed tomato soup
    An equal amount of milk
    ½ cup cream style corn
    1 teaspoon sugar
    (¼ teaspoon curry powder)
    Correct the seasoning and serve.

QUICK MUSHROOM SOUP

I. [About 4 Cups]
Combine, stir and heat:
    1 can condensed mushroom soup
    1 cup condensed beef or chicken bouillon or consommé
    1¼ cups water or milk

II. [4 Cups]
Soak for 30 minutes:
    Dried mushrooms
in:
    2 cans condensed consommé
Add:
    1 can condensed mushroom soup
Heat and serve.

QUICK ONION SOUP

[About 2 Cups]
Heat:
    1 can condensed onion soup

Add:
>   2 teaspoons lemon juice
>   A grating of lemon rind
>   ½ clove pressed garlic
>   ⅛ teaspoon nutmeg
>   (¼ cup sherry)
>   Correct the seasoning

Top each serving with:
>   Melba Cheese Rounds

QUICK OXTAIL SOUP WITH WINE

[About 2½ Cups]
Pare thinly in several strips:
>   The rind of 1 lemon

Add to it:
>   1 cup water
>   1 can condensed oxtail soup
>   1 teaspoon grated onion

◗ Simmer these ingredients for 5 minutes. Remove the lemon rind and
>   Correct the seasoning

Reduce the heat. Stir in:
>   ½ cup claret or ¼ cup very dry sherry
>   1 tablespoon minced parsley

Serve at once with:
>   Toasted crackers

QUICK SPINACH SOUP

[About 2 Cups]
Combine:
>   ½ cup cooked spinach
>   1 can condensed cream of chicken soup

If the spinach has already been creamed, use instead:
>   (1 can chicken broth)

You may thin the soup with:
>   Spinach water, stock or milk
>   Correct the seasoning

heat and serve.

QUICK TOMATO SOUP

[About 4 Cups]
◗ Simmer, covered, for 15 minutes or steam for 2 minutes in a ✪ pressure cooker, then strain:
>   2½ cups canned tomatoes

>   ¼ cup sliced onion
>   ½ cup chopped celery with leaves

Melt:
>   2 tablespoons butter

Add and stir until blended:
>   2 tablespoons flour

Add, cook and stir until smooth and boiling:
>   2 cups Stock (II, 141) or canned bouillon
>   ½ teaspoon sugar
>   ⅛ teaspoon paprika
>   The strained tomato stock
>   Correct the seasoning

and add, just before serving:
>   (1 tablespoon chopped fresh basil or ¾ teaspoon anchovy paste or whipped cream)

QUICK CHILLED FRESH TOMATO CREAM SOUP

⅄ I. [About 3 Cups]
One way to use surplus garden tomatoes. Peel, seed and chop coarsely:
>   2½ cups fresh, very ripe tomatoes

Blend briefly with:
>   1 cup cream
>   1 tablespoon parsley
>   1 tablespoon basil
>   Correct the seasoning

Chill and serve with:
>   Lemon slices

II. [About 3 Cups]
Combine in a cocktail shaker:
>   2 cups chilled tomato juice
>   1 cup chilled cream
>   4 or more ribs raw celery, grated
>   1 teaspoon grated onion
>   A few drops hot pepper sauce
>   A few grains cayenne
>   Correct the seasoning

and add:
>   ¼ cup chopped ice

Or, you may omit the onion and use:
>   (¼ teaspoon dry ginger)
>   (⅛ teaspoon allspice)

Shake well.

QUICK CLAM AND CHICKEN BROTH

Combine equal parts of:
    Clam broth
    Chicken stock
If the clam broth is very salty, you may have to use more chicken stock or water. You may use both clam and chicken stock canned or one fresh and the other canned. Season lightly with:
    White pepper
When the soup reaches a boil, remove from heat and place in hot cups. Add to each cup:
    1 tablespoon heavy cream or top it with 1 tablespoon whipped cream
Have the cream at room temperature. Sprinkle the top, for color, with:
    Paprika or chopped chives or parsley
Serve at once.

QUICK CRAB OR LOBSTER MONGOLE

[About 4 Cups]
Sprinkle:
    3 tablespoons dry white wine or 1 teaspoon Worcestershire sauce
over:
    1 cup flaked canned crab or lobster
Combine and heat to the boiling point:
    1 can condensed cream of tomato soup
    1 can condensed cream of green pea soup
Stir in slowly:
    1¼ cups rich hot milk or part cream and part bouillon
Add the crab. Heat the soup ◗ but do not let it boil.

QUICK LOBSTER SUPREME

[About 5 Cups]
Combine:
    1 can condensed asparagus soup
    1 can condensed mushroom soup
Add:
    2 cups light cream
Pick over and add:
    6 to 8 oz. canned lobster meat
Heat this soup but do not let it boil. Add:
    3 tablespoons dry sherry

QUICK LOBSTER CHOWDER

[About 6 Cups]
An easy-to-get soup meal.
Sauté in a saucepan for about 5 minutes:
    ¼ cup finely diced onion
    ½ cup finely diced celery
in:
    2 tablespoons butter
Add:
    1½ cups water
    1 small bay leaf
    1 package frozen mixed vegetables, defrosted
◗ Cover and bring to a boil. Cook the vegetables until they are barely tender, about 5 to 10 minutes. Remove the bay leaf. Drain, but reserve the liquor from:
    1 can chopped broiled mushrooms: 3 oz.
Stir into the liquor until smooth:
    1 tablespoon cornstarch
Add this to the mixture in the saucepan, stirring constantly until it thickens. Add the drained mushrooms and:
    1 cup tomato sauce
    2 cups milk
    1 cup canned rock lobster
    Correct the seasoning
and heat slowly ◗ but do not boil. Serve with an assortment of:
    Cheese
or, as they do in France, with:
    Crusty bread and sweet butter

QUICK SEAFOOD TUREEN

[About 6 Cups]

Melt in a saucepan:
    ¼ cup butter
Add:
    2 cups flounder fillets, cut
        in pieces
    1½ cups dry white wine
♦ Cover and simmer about 10
minutes. Add:
    1 cup cooked shrimp
    1 cup cooked lobster meat
    1 small can sliced
        mushrooms
    1½ cups condensed cream of
        mushroom soup
    2 tablespoons chopped
        pimientos
    1 clove crushed garlic
    ⅛ teaspoon saffron
Simmer about 5 minutes longer.
Add:
    (½ cup dry sherry)
    Correct the seasoning
and serve in a tureen with:
    Buttered toast or French
    bread

ABOUT GARNISHES FOR SOUP

Changing from marrow balls to
a chiffonade of cress in the same
clear soup can change the temper of a meal. Scan the parade
of breads and garnishes below
to determine your pace-setter du
jour. If serving an informal buffet, arrange a group of garnishes
around a tureen to give your
guests a choice between rich,
green or lean. Whip up some
satisfying dumplings for hungry
children or pass a rice ring, flavored with nutmeg. Tempt a
finicky appetite with an egg
drop. ♦ Be sure none of the garnishes is chilled, unless the soup
is an iced one.

FOR CLEAR SOUPS

Drop into the soup:
    Thin slices of lemon or
    orange
    Minced parsley, chives,
    watercress, onion, mint,
    basil, chervil. For some

classic flavor combina-
tions, see Seasonings
(II, 216)
Podded peas
Cucumber balls
Croutons, see many
varieties, page 151
and 390
Vegetables Brunoise,
page 109
Noodles, page 149
Gnocchi, page 156
Won Ton, page 112
Dumplings, page 146
Marrow balls, page 150
Quenelles, page 180
Thin slices of lemon-
drenched avocado
Thin slices of cooked
root: parsley, chervil or
celeriac
Small choux paste puffs
(II, 305), farci or plain
Spaetzle, page 179

FOR CREAM SOUPS

Garnish with:
    Salted whipped cream
    or sour cream and a
    dusting of mixed, finely
    chopped herbs
    Toasted cubed stuffing
    Chiffonade
    Blanched, shredded,
    toasted almonds or
    cashews
    Flavored popcorn or
    puffed cereals

FOR THICK SOUPS

Use:
    Thin slices of orange,
    lemon or lime
    Sliced small sausages or
    thin slices of hard
    sausages
    Sliced hard-cooked eggs
    Croutons, page 151
    Sour cream
    Julienne strips of ham,
    tongue, chicken or bits
    of sea food
    Grated cheeses or Pesto,
    (II, 218)

And see Thickenings for Soups, page 108.

BREADS TO SERVE WITH SOUPS

Fancy shapes in toasted
white, rye or wholewheat
Melba toast
Toasted rye sticks
Plain or toasted garlic
bread or other herbed
breads
Crackers, hot and plain
or spread with herb
butters, cheese spreads or
fish pastes
Cheese crackers and
straws
Pastry Snails (II, 55)
Hush Puppies (II, 279)
Corn Dodgers (II, 278)
or Zephyrs (II, 278)
Croutons, page 151

ABOUT EGG-GARNISHED SOUPS

If your travels have led you to the Mediterranean or China, you probably know the trick of turning a cup of broth into a bracing midmorning pickup or a light nourishing lunch. Our friend Cecily Brownstone gave us these infallible directions.

I.   [2]

Heat in a quart pan, until boiling vigorously:

2 cups chicken broth or
beef stock

Reduce the heat, so the broth ▶ simmers. This means that the bubbles form slowly and collapse below the surface of the liquid. Break into a cup:

1 egg, which has
reached 75°

▶ Beat it with a fork, just long enough to combine yolk and white. When the egg is lifted high, it should run off the tines of the fork in a watery stream. Now, with the broth ▶ simmering, hold the cup with one hand, 5 inches above the rim of the

saucepan. Pour a little of the beaten egg slowly in a fine stream into the broth. With a fork in the other hand, describe wide circles on the surface of the broth to catch the egg as it strikes and draw it out into long filmy threads. Rather than pour the egg in one fell swoop, break its fall 3 or 4 times, so as not to disturb the simmering broth. If you have a helper, he can pour the egg through a strainer instead of from a cup. Simmer for about 1 minute.

Add to taste:

Salt
(A squeeze of lemon)

Serve at once in hot cups.

II.   [6]

For a quick way to make a Mediterranean egg drop that does not "flower" so profusely, heat to a rolling boil:

3 cups chicken broth
¾ cup cooked rice or fine
noodles

Beat in a large bowl, just long enough to combine and be uniform in color:

2 eggs
2 tablespoons lemon juice
or wine

From on high ▶ gradually, so as not to curdle the eggs but to allow them to shred, pour the hot soup over them, stirring constantly. Serve at once in hot cups.

III.   [8]

A still stauncher mix is made in Germany and is called **Baum-wollsuppe**.

◗ Simmer:

    4 cups strong brown stock

Mix together:

    2 eggs
    1 tablespoon flour
    ¼ cup cream
    (1 tablespoon butter)
    (Pinch of nutmeg)

Mix and cook as described in **I**. Serve in hot cups.

IV.   [4]

In Italy a ragged fluffy drop is made by beating until well combined:

    1 egg
    1½ teaspoons grated
        Parmesan cheese
    1 tablespoon grated dry
        bread crumbs
    (½ clove pressed garlic)

Stir this mixture rapidly into:

    3 cups ◗ simmering
        consommé

Continue to simmer and stir until egg is set. Serve at once.

SOUP CUSTARD OR ROYALE

Preheat Oven to 325°.

These tender drops are used in clear soups. Bake them as for Cup Custard (II, 437). They may be poured initially to ½-inch thickness into a well-buttered 9-inch pie pan. Because of their fragile consistency, they must always be ◗ well cooled in a mold before handling. Any slight crusting may be trimmed. Beat well:

    ½ cup milk or stock
    ⅛ teaspoon each salt,
        paprika, and nutmeg
    1 egg
    (1 egg yolk)

Bake about 25 minutes, then ◗ cool, before cutting into dice or fancy shapes. Simmer the soup and drop the royales into it, just long enough to heat them through. Serve at once, allowing 3 or 4 small drops to each cup of broth.

HARD-COOKED EGG DROPS

Crush with a fork:

    2 hard-cooked egg yolks

Add to them and blend well:

    1 tablespoon soft butter
    1 raw egg yolk
        A few grains of cayenne
        A light grating of nutmeg
    ⅛ teaspoon salt

Form these ingredients into ½-inch balls. Roll them in:

    Flour

Cook the drops in ◗ simmering consommé for about 1 minute.

ABOUT DUMPLINGS

The secret of making light dumplings is to keep them steaming on top of ◗ simmering liquid. And be sure the temperature of the stock, gravy or water in which you are cooking them never goes higher than a simmer. Most dumplings are bound together by egg, and the protein in the egg must not be allowed to toughen. ◗ Use ample liquid in a wide-topped cooking vessel, giving each ball or drop a chance to expand. ◗ Never crowd the pan. The minute the batter is floating in the liquid ◗ cover the pot, so the steam can begin functioning. ◗ Do not lift the lid until the dumpling is done. This is not as hard to do as it sounds if you cover the pan with a tight-fitting heat-resistant glass pie pan or lid, so you can watch the swelling of the batter. When the dumplings look fluffy ◗ test them for doneness, as you would a cake, by inserting a toothpick. If it comes out clean, the dumplings are done. Once you are expert at timing, try simmering dumplings in a ✪ pressure pan. Proceed to cook as above, but instead of the glass cover use the pressure pan lid. ◗ Keep the vent off the entire time. Some good additions to dumpling dough are parsley or other herbs, cheese or grated onion. We have given ◗ dumpling amounts in cups, for some people like large dumplings, others small. A cup of dough will usually yield about eighteen to twenty 1-inch balls, but marrow, liver and meat balls do not expand as do those high in cereal and egg. ◗ For other dumplings more suitable for luncheon dishes or as an accompaniment to meat dishes, see pages 178–180.

SOUP OR STEW NOCKERLN

[About 1 Cup]
Beat until creamy:
    ¼ cup soft butter
    1 egg
Stir in:
    1 cup all-purpose flour
    ⅛ teaspoon salt
Add gradually, until a firm batter is formed, about:
    6 tablespoons milk
Cut out the batter with a teaspoon to form small balls. Drop them into boiling water or directly into the clear soup in which they will be served. Reduce the liquid to a ◗ simmer and continue to simmer, covered, for about 10 minutes. For a stew, cook nockerln in water, drain, and drop them into the meat mixture just before serving.

MATZO OR CRACKER MEAL DUMPLINGS

[About 2 Cups]
These light Passover soup drops are made with the finely crushed crumbs of special unleavened crackers.
Beat until thick and well blended:
    2 egg yolks
    3 tablespoons soft chicken fat
Pour over them and beat well:
    ½ cup hot stock
Stir in gently a mixture of:
    ¾ cup matzo meal or cracker meal
    ½ teaspoon salt
    (⅛ teaspoon ginger)
    (⅛ teaspoon nutmeg)
    (1 tablespoon finely chopped parsley)
    (1 tablespoon finely grated onion)
Beat until ◗ stiff, but not dry:
    2 egg whites
Fold the egg whites into the cracker mixture and chill, covered, for ½ to 1 hour. About ½ hour before you are ready to serve, form this dough lightly into small balls. If you wet your hands with cold water, the job will be easier. Drop them into:
    6 cups boiling stock
Reduce heat at once to a ◗ simmer and cook, covered, for about 15 minutes.

FARINA BALLS COCKAIGNE

[About 3 Cups]
Serve these stout but light

dumplings with a soup-and-salad meal.

Have ready at about 75°:
    2 eggs
Heat to the boiling point:
    2 cups milk
Add, stir and cook until thick:
    ½ cup farina
    1 tablespoon butter
    ½ teaspoon salt
    ⅛ teaspoon paprika
    (⅛ teaspoon nutmeg)
Remove the batter from the heat and beat in the eggs vigorously ♦ one at a time. The heat of the mixture will thicken the eggs. Drop the batter, a generous teaspoon at a time, into ♦ simmering soup stock. Cook, covered, for about 2 minutes and serve.

LIVER DUMPLINGS OR LEBERKLOESSE

[About 3 Cups]
Being the descendants of South Germans, we cannot well compile a cookbook without including a recipe that is typical of that neck of the woods—not exactly a handsome dish, but it has qualities.
Skin and remove the fiber from:
    1 lb. calf liver or chicken livers
Grind or chop until very fine. Slightly frozen liver is easy to grind. Soak in water for 3 minutes, then wring the water from:
    2 slices white bread: 1 cup
Beat, then stir into liver and bread:
    2 egg yolks
    ¼ cup soft butter
    2 teaspoons chopped onion
    2 tablespoons chopped parsley
    1½ teaspoons salt
    ½ teaspoon pepper
    2 tablespoons flour
Beat until stiff:
    2 egg whites
Fold them into the other ingredients. Shape this mixture into 1½-inch balls. Drop them into

gently boiling:
    Soup Stock (II, 141)
Cook them for 5 or 6 minutes. Serve them with the soup; or drop them into boiling water, drain them and serve with:
    Sautéed Onions,
    page 302

CHOUX PASTE GARNISH

[About 1½ Cups]
You may add:
    (4 to 6 tablespoons grated Parmesan cheese)
to the dough, for either of these garnishes.

I. Use a pastry bag with a ¼-inch-diameter tube. Fill with:
    Unsweetened or cheese-flavored Choux Paste (II, 306)
Squeeze onto a greased baking tin pea-sized bits of dough. Bake in a preheated 400° oven for about 10 minutes. Add these to the soup the instant before serving.

II. Fill a pastry bag with:
    Unsweetened Choux Paste (II, 306)
Make 1-inch rounds. Flatten carefully with a moistened finger any points remaining after the bag is lifted off. Glaze with:
    French Egg Wash (II, 433)
Bake in a preheated 400° oven for about 10 minutes. Be sure the puffs are well dried out before removing them from the oven. ♦ Fill them, the last minute before serving, with a farce that combines well with the soup. ♦ Place in soup the instant before serving to avoid sogginess.

FRITTER GARNISH

[About ¾ Cup]
Preheat Deep Fryer to 360°
Beat until light:
    1 egg

Add:

    ¼ teaspoon salt
    ⅛ teaspoon paprika
    ½ cup flour
    2 tablespoons milk

When the fat is ready, page 177, allow the batter to drop into it through a colander. Fry until the garnish is brown. Drain on paper. Place in the soup just before serving.

MEAT PASTRIES FOR SOUPS

Some pastry wrapped meats are used in soup itself, others as accompaniments, but with all of them the aim is the same—to make a covering of dough which is tender, yet strong enough to hold the filling. Chinese Won Ton, page 112, are frequently served in soup. They are very much like ravioli and can also be served with a sauce as an entrée or sautéed in butter and coated with cheese. If made in small sizes, they also make interesting cocktail snacks. Other soup accompaniments of this type are rissoles, turnovers or Piroshki, page 210.

BUTTER DUMPLINGS OR BUTTERKLOESSE

[About ¾ Cup]
Beat until soft:

    2 tablespoons butter

Beat and add:

    2 eggs

Stir in:

    6 tablespoons flour
    ¼ teaspoon salt

Drop the batter from a spoon into ♦ simmering soup and simmer the dumplings, covered, for about 8 minutes. You may also simmer them in the soup for about 4 minutes in a ✪ pressure cooker on which you keep the vent open the entire time.

WHITE OR GREEN NOODLE DOUGH OR FETTUCCINI

[About ½ Lb. Dry or 4 Cups Cooked Noodles]
♦ If you are a beginner, do not try to make noodles in damp weather.

I. On a large pastry board or marble table top make a well (II, 52) of:

    ⅔ cup all-purpose flour

Drop into it:

    1 egg

barely combined with:

    1 tablespoon water
    ½ teaspoon salt
    1 teaspoon oil

Work the mixture with your hands, folding the flour over the egg until the dough can be rolled in a ball and comes clean from the hands. If you want to make green noodles, at this point, add:

    (2 to 4 tablespoons very
        well pressed and dried,
        finely chopped cooked
        spinach)

Knead the dough as for bread (II, 240), about 10 minutes. Then let it stand, covered, for about 1 hour. Now roll the dough, pulling it as you wrap it around the rolling pin, stretching it a little more each time. Continue to sprinkle it with flour between each rolling and stretching to keep the dough from sticking to the pin or board or developing holes. Repeat this procedure about 10 times or until the dough is paper-thin and translucent. Let it dry for about 30 minutes. You can hang it as the Neapolitans do—like laundry on a line—over a piece of foil or plastic. Before it is brittle, roll it up like a scroll and cut it on the bias into strips of any width you prefer: ⅛ inch for soup or 1 inch for lasagna. Allow about 3 tablespoons uncooked noodles for each quart of soup. Cook the noodles in ♦ rapidly boiling salted water for about 10 minutes. Drain and quickly add them to the soup. If stored for future use, keep them, dry and uncooked, in a closed jar.

II. In making casing for Won Ton, Ravioli, etc., proceed as for above, but ♦ do not allow the dough to dry before cutting. Cut into 3-inch squares, fill and use at once.

SPATZEN FOR SOUP

[About 1½ Cups]
Prepare:
> Spatzen or Spaetzle,
> page 179

making these delicious dumplings in a smaller size. Drop the batter as directed into ♦ simmering soup, instead of water.

MEAT BALLS FOR SOUP

A superb main dish may be had by adding these to vegetable soup. Make up ½ the recipe for:
> German Meat Balls,
> page 518

You may use more bread, if desired. Mix the ingredients lightly with a fork. Shape them without pressure into 1-inch balls and drop into boiling soup or stock.

♦ Simmer them until done for about 10 minutes.

QUENELLES FOR SOUP

Prepare:
> Quenelles, page 180

As with all protein-based foods, these delicately poached drops should be added to ♦ simmering soup and cooked only until they are heated through thoroughly.

MARROW BALLS

[About ¾ Cup]
These delicate drops may be prepared several hours in advance and refrigerated.
Combine and beat until creamy:
> ¼ cup fresh marrow
> 2 tablespoons butter

Add:
> 3 egg yolks
> ¼ teaspoon salt
> ⅛ teaspoon paprika
> 2 tablespoons chopped
> parsley
> Cracker crumbs

Use just enough cracker crumbs, at least ½ cup, to make the mixture of the right consistency to shape into balls. Now, fold in:
> 3 stiffly beaten egg whites

Cook the balls in ♦ simmering soup for about 15 minutes or until they rise to the surface.

LIVER SAUSAGE DUMPLINGS

[About 1 Cup]
Combine and work with a fork:
> ¼ lb. liver sausage
> ½ egg or 1 egg white or
> yolk
> ½ cup cracker crumbs
> 1 tablespoon chopped
> parsley or chives
> (1 tablespoon catsup)

Shape the mixture into 1-inch balls. ♦ Simmer gently for about 2 minutes in soup stock.

SAUSAGE BALLS FOR SOUP

[About 1½ Cups]
Good in pea, bean or lentil soup.
Combine:

- ½ lb. raw sausage meat
- 1 egg white
- 2 teaspoons chopped parsley
- ½ teaspoon fresh basil
- ¼ teaspoon fresh rosemary
- 3 tablespoons toasted bread crumbs

Roll this mixture into 1-inch balls. Drop them into boiling stock. Reduce the heat at once and ♦ simmer the soup until the balls are done, for about 30 minutes.

CHEESE BALLS FOR SOUP

[About 1½ Cups]
Combine:

- 2 beaten egg yolks
- 2 tablespoons grated cheese: preferably Parmesan
- 2 tablespoons dry bread crumbs
- ⅛ teaspoon paprika
- ½ teaspoon dried herbs, fresh chives or parsley

Beat until stiff ♦ but not dry, then fold in:

- 2 egg whites
- ⅛ teaspoon salt

Drop the batter from a spoon into ♦ simmering soup. Simmer for only 1 or 2 minutes.

CHIFFONADE OF HERBS FOR SOUPS

To prepare a chiffonade, always use the freshest and most tender of greens ♦ being sure to remove stems and coarse mid ribs —lettuce, sorrel or parsley, alone or in combination with whatever fresh herbs you have on hand that are compatible with the flavor of your soup. Allow:

- 1 or 2 tablespoons fresh herbs or greens

to:

- 1 pint broth

Add the herbs to a small quantity of broth and chop in a ⅄ blender until fine. Combine the blended herbs with the remaining broth. If you have no blender, mince a combination of herbs very, very fine.

ABOUT FANCY BREADS AND CRACKERS FOR SOUP

We suggest in the following recipes a number of quick fancy breads, wafers and crackers, but ask that you consider also Bread Sticks and toasted Cheese Bread (II, 244), and look at things to do with Ready Baked Bread (II, 288).

✳ PUFFED BREAD BLOCKS

[About Thirty 1½-Inch Blocks]
These may be prepared in advance. Keep at room temperature until soft, then blend well:

- ½ lb. cheddar cheese
- ¼ lb. butter: 1 stick

Season palatably with:

- Mustard
- Curry powder
- Caraway or celery seed
- Salt and pepper or paprika

Cut bread into 1½ x ¾ x ¾-inch blocks. Cover them with the cheese spread. Keep them chilled until ready for use. Pop them into a 375° oven. They should brown lightly and puff.

SOUP CROUTONS

For other Croutons, see page 390.
To retain the crispness of these ever-popular diced toasts, serve them in individual dishes and let the guests add them to the soup as they are ready for them. Or,

use them diced small, so they are much like buttered toasted crumbs to garnish spinach, noodles or game. They may be flavored by sautéing in:

> Butter and olive oil

or dusting them with:

> Grated cheese

while still hot.

CHEESE OR BUTTER BREAD CUBES

Preheat Oven to 375°.

I. Beat together:

> 1 egg
> 1½ tablespoons melted butter

Cut into cubes or blocks of any size:

> Fresh bread

Roll the cubes in the egg mixture, then in:

> Finely grated American cheese
> Salt and cayenne or paprika

Toast the cubes on a buttered sheet until the cheese is melted. Serve them hot as appetizers. Good with soup or salads.

II. Spread bread cubes with a paste made of:

> Butter
> Grated Parmesan cheese
> Caraway or celery seed
> Salt and a few grains cayenne
> (Mustard)

Toast and serve, as above.

SEEDED CRACKERS

Brush:

> Small crisp salt crackers

with:

> Melted butter or partially beaten egg white

Sprinkle lightly with:

> Caraway, celery or sesame seeds

Toast and serve.

REFRIGERATOR CHEESE WAFERS OR STRAWS

These keep for weeks in a refrigerator or freezer and are quickly sliced and baked for the unexpected guest. Or just after mixing put the dough in a pastry tube to make straws. Or use the 1½-inch ribbon disk on a cookie press to make ribbons. Cut into 2 inch lengths.

I. [4 Dozen]
Preheat oven to 475°.
Grate or grind:

> ½ lb. aged cheddar cheese

Combine with:

> 3 tablespoons soft butter
> ¾ cup all-purpose flour
> (1 teaspoon Worcestershire sauce)
> ½ teaspoon salt
> Dash of hot pepper sauce

Form the dough into 1-inch rolls. Wrap in foil and refrigerate or freeze till cold enough to slice as thin as possible, under a quarter of an inch. Bake for about 10 minutes.

II.
Preheat oven to 475°.
Cream:

> ¼ cup butter

and mix it well with:

> ¾ cup all-purpose flour
> ¼ lb. grated aged cheddar cheese
> ⅛ teaspoon salt
> A dash of white pepper

Shape and bake as above.

MELBA CHEESE ROUNDS

Spread:

> Melba rounds

lightly with:

> Butter

Sprinkle generously with:

> Parmesan cheese

Just before using, run them under a broiler until toasted. Serve at once, floating one or two on:

> Onion or other soup

CEREALS AND PASTAS

ABOUT CEREALS

On a train trip from Palermo to Syracuse, a stranger leaned toward us to say in the most casual tone that this was the field where Pluto abducted Persephone and rushed her to his dark abode. This brought to mind the lamentations of her mother Ceres and a speculation as to how much greater those lamentations would have been had she known what today's processing was to do to the grains that bear her name. Until a century ago the entire kernel, including the germ, could be ground between cool millstones without risking rancidity. Today, the heat of steel grinding necessitates removal of the germ.

In spite of the incomplete protein makeup of cereals, they form almost a fourth of the average diet. So let's look at their values more closely. Especially, note that grain mixtures—when served with milk, cheese, egg or even small quantities of meat and fish—have a greatly increased nutritive protein content. If you buy ready-to-eat cereals, the grains have been highly processed. They are either exploded into puffs, under high steam, or malted, sugared and shattered into flakes under rollers; or mixed into pastes and formed. You pay as much for the processing, and the expensive packaging to keep these cereals crisp, as you pay for the cereal itself. You may have to give more time to the proper cooking of whole-grains but there is no question of nutritive and monetary savings. For further details about Whole-Grains, see About Flours (II, 152).

Partially precooked cereals in which the heat has been great enough to destroy the enzymes —which cause rancidity—keep better than raw cereals. They should be finish-cooked according to the directions on the label. ♦ All cereals should be stored covered against insect infestation and moisture absorption. Raw cereals will further profit by storage in a cool place, as even mild heat induces more rapid development of rancidity.

ABOUT COOKING CEREALS

Scientists tell us that cereals are edible as soon as the starch granules swell to their fullest capacity in hot liquid. This state they speak of glibly as gelatinization, although it remains something of a chemical mystery. To cooks, this phenomenon is evident in the thickening of cereals and sauces. While the technical-minded insist that the starch and protein in cereals are adequately cooked in a short period of time, many cooks claim that the results are not so nutty and sweet as when the older, slow-heat methods are used. Whether you back the cook or the scientist, on these points they agree: cereals must be added ♦ slowly to ♦ very rapidly boiling water and ♦ stirred in, so that each individual grain is surrounded and quickly penetrated by the hot liquid.

The boiling point of the water ♦ 212°, must be maintained throughout as the cereal is added.

With cereals that tend to gumminess, this slow addition to the boiling water allows the outer starch layers to stabilize and keeps the grains separated after swelling. Coarsely ground cereals may be added dry. Granular fine cereals may be moistened with part of the measured cold water to form a loose mush and may be poured so slowly into the boiling water that they do not disturb the boiling point. They are then cooked 2 to 3 minutes over direct heat and 5 to 20 minutes more in a double boiler. If you want to cook any of these cereals longer, start out as directed above and, if necessary, add more milk or water during the cooking period. If you cook cereals or starches in an acid liquid like fruit juices with sugar, the thickening power is lowered.

The cereal is done when it looks translucent. The grains should still be separated, retaining their individual shape even though they are soft. Serve at once.

Cereals increase in bulk depending on the amount of water they absorb. You may count 4 to 6 servings for each cup of uncooked cereal. If you cook cereal in advance of serving ♦ cover it at once while it is still hot from the first cooking—so no crust forms on the top. If you plan to use it more than an hour after the first cooking, refrigerate it. ♦ To avoid lumps on reheating, place the cereal over hot water and allow the cereal to become hot all the way through before stirring.

To make a gruel for the baby, cook the cereal with 3 times the called for amount of water or milk and cook twice as long. Strain and serve.

FINELY MILLED CEREALS

[About 4 to 6 Servings]

♦ Please read About Cooking Cereals, page 153. To prepare the fine granular cereals listed below, have water heated in the bottom of a double boiler. In the top of the boiler, over direct heat, bring to a rolling boil, 212°:

4 to 6 cups water or milk
1 teaspoon salt

Very slowly ♦ without disturbing the boiling point, dribble into the water:

1 cup dry corn meal, farina or hominy grits

Continue to cook over direct heat for 2 to 3 minutes, then cook covered over, not in, hot water 5 to 20 minutes. To avoid gumminess ♦ do not stir. To avoid serve at once see About Cooking Cereals, opposite, for reheating or storing. During the last few minutes of cooking, you may fold in lightly:

3 tablespoons dry skim-milk solids
2 teaspoons debittered yeast powder

for each cup dry cereal. These ingredients make no noticeable change in taste and are a great addition in food value. You may at that time also add:

Dates, figs, raisins and cooked dried fruits

Or serve with:

Cold or hot sliced canned or fresh fruits
A cinnamon-sugar mixture
Sugar and cream
Maple sirup
Jams and preserves

COARSELY MILLED CEREALS

[About 4 to 6 Servings]

These coarsely ground or cracked

grains have many different names, but all are cooked the same way. The wheats, whole-grain and cracked, also include bulghur—a parched cracked wheat—and couscous. Groats may be cracked wheat, buckwheat or oats. Coarsely ground buckwheat barley or millet is also called kasha. Cracked corn is called samp. Coarse oats come in a number of forms, steel cut or rolled. Prepare any of these as for the finely milled cereals above. Because they are coarser in grind, you need to use in all:

    2 to 4 cups water, milk or
      fruit juice
    1 teaspoon salt
for every:
    1 cup dry cereal
Cook about one hour as directed above.

ABOUT WHOLE CEREALS

Whole cereals like rice or barley may be cooked on two principles —the one described above for coarsely ground cereals or by the so-called fried method, in which the cereal is sautéed in oil or clarified butter before the liquid is added. For a detailed description of this method, see Risotto, page 166. For other ways to cook rice, see page 158, and the Index.

ABOUT HOMINY

Hominy is corn with the hull and germ removed. In an attempt to give it calcium values, it is sometimes also soaked in wood ash lye. It has recently gained favor as an antistrontium absorbent. Hominy grits are the broken grains.

HOMINY

I. [Yield 1 Quart]
Shell and wash:
    1 quart of dried corn

Put it in an enamel or stainless steel pan. Cover with:
    2 quarts water
Add:
    2 tablespoons baking soda
Cover the pan and let this mixture set 12 hours. Then bring it to a boil in the liquid in which it has soaked. Simmer about 3 hours or until the hulls loosen. If necessary, add water. Drain. Rub corn until hulls are removed. Bring to a boil in:
    2 quarts cold water
Drain. Repeat this boiling process again in fresh water, adding:
    1 teaspoon salt
Drain once more and serve. Season with:
    Melted butter

II. [6]
Preheat oven to 400°.
Combine and place in a greased baking dish:
    2 cups drained, cooked
      hominy, above
    1 cup Cheese Sauce,
      page 364
    ½ cup minced green pepper
Cover the top with:
    Strips of bacon
Bake the dish for about 20 minutes.

HOMINY CAKES [5]

These cakes are a variation on potatoes.
Drain:
    2½ cups cooked or canned
      hominy
Combine it with:
    2 tablespoons flour
    1 egg
    Salt and pepper
Form these ingredients into flat cakes.
Sauté them until they are brown in:
    Butter or drippings
Serve them hot—plain or with:
    Honey or sirup

SCALLOPED HOMINY   [4]
AND HAM

Preheat oven to 375°.
Combine:
> ½ cup water
> 1 can condensed tomato
> soup or 2 cups Cream
> Sauce I, page 359

Add:
> 1 cup diced cooked ham
> ½ teaspoon salt
> ½ teaspoon sugar
> ⅛ teaspoon paprika or
> pepper

Drain and add:
> 2½ cups cooked or canned
> hominy

Heat these ingredients. Combine:
> 1 cup soft bread crumbs
> 1 cup grated cheese
> ⅛ teaspoon paprika
> ¼ teaspoon salt

Place ½ the hominy mixture in
a greased baking dish, cover it
with ½ the bread mixture. Dot
the top with:
> 1 tablespoon butter

Repeat the process. Bake the
dish until the top is brown,
about 12 minutes.

CORN MEAL MUSH   [4]

Combine and stir:
> 1 cup water-ground corn
> meal
> 1 cup cold water
> 1 teaspoon salt

Place in the top of a double
boiler:
> 4 cups boiling water

Stir corn meal mixture in gradually. Cook and stir the mush
over quick heat from 2 to 3
minutes. Steam it, covered, over,
not in, hot water about 15 minutes. Stir it frequently. Serve
with:
> Maple sirup, honey or
> molasses

POLENTA

Just as our greatest architectural
surprise in Italy was to find St.
Francis' first church a log cabin,
so were we amazed to discover
that the Italians do even more
delicious and interesting things
with corn meal than you can
find in the deep South.
Cheese is sometimes cooked
with it, and sometimes it is
served sprinkled over it. Tomato
sauce, meat or a combination of
both is another favorite accompaniment.

I. Prepare:
> Corn Meal Mush,
> opposite

Add to it for the last 15 minutes
of cooking:
> ⅛ teaspoon paprika
> A few grains red pepper
> (½ cup grated cheese)

II. Prepare as above and sauté
it in:
> Olive oil or butter

BUCKWHEAT GROATS   [4]
OR KASHA

I.
Preheat oven to 350°.
Have ready:
> 1 cup kasha

Brown it in hot skillet with:
> 2 tablespoons hot chicken
> fat or butter

Stir with fork until each grain
is coated. Add:
> 3½ cups boiling water

Cover and cook for about 15
minutes, then transfer to greased
casserole and bake for about one
hour.

II. As a luncheon dish, add:
> Sautéed onions
> Salt and pepper
> Some almonds

and proceed as above.

GNOCCHI WITH   [4]
FLOUR

Serve as a separate course in
place of potatoes or as a soup
garnish.

Scald:
> 1 cup milk

Melt in a skillet:
> 2 tablespoons butter

Stir and blend in until smooth:
> 2 tablespoons flour
> 2 tablespoons cornstarch
> ½ teaspoon salt

Stir in the scalded milk. Reduce the heat and add:
> 1 egg yolk
> (½ cup grated cheese)

Beat the batter until the egg has thickened and the cheese has melted. Pour it onto a shallow greased platter or pan.
Preheat oven to 375°.
When the batter is cool, cut it into strips 2 inches long. Place the strips in a pan and pour over them:
> Melted butter

Sprinkle them with:
> (Grated cheese)

Heat them in the oven. We prefer poaching the batter after it has been cut into strips. Poach in gently boiling water or stock for 1 or 2 minutes. Drain the strips and serve them with melted butter.

GNOCCHI WITH FARINA [4]

Scald:
> 2 cups milk

Stir in, all at once:
> ¾ cup farina

Stir the mush over low heat until thick. Remove from heat and beat in until smooth:
> 1 tablespoon butter
> 1 egg yolk
> ¼ teaspoon salt

You may spread the mixture evenly in an 8 x 8-inch pan lined with foil to make handling easier. Chill for about 3 hours. Preheat oven to 425°.
Cut the farina mixture into 1½-inch squares. Place the squares in a well-greased ovenproof dish, letting them overlap slightly. Dot with:

> 2 tablespoons butter

Pour over them slowly:
> 1 cup Hunter's Sauce, page 366 or Aurore Sauce, page 362

Sprinkle the top with:
> 6 tablespoons grated Parmesan cheese

Bake for about 10 minutes.

GNOCCHI WITH POTATOES [6]

♦ The potatoes must be freshly cooked and used at once. Boil, then put through a ricer:
> 2 medium-sized potatoes

Heat to the boiling point:
> ½ cup milk
> 5 tablespoons butter

Stir in, until the dough forms a ball:
> 1 cup flour

Remove from heat. Beat in:
> 2 eggs
> 1 teaspoon salt

> ¼ teaspoon paprika
> (3 tablespoons grated cheese)

and the potatoes. Sprinkle the dough with flour. Roll it into sticks ½ inch thick. Cut it into 1-inch lengths. Drop the gnocchi into simmering salted water. Or force the gnocchi dough through a pastry bag. Cut into desired lengths as shown above before letting the gnocchi fall into the water. Simmer uncovered for 3 to 5 minutes. Drain. Place them on a greased pan in a hot oven for about 3 minutes. The baking is optional. Serve the gnocchi dressed with melted butter and grated cheese.

ABOUT RICE

"May your rice never burn," is the New Year's greeting of the Chinese. "May it never be gummy," is ours. So many people complain to us about the variability of their results in rice cookery. Like flour, it may have more or less moisture in its makeup when you start to use it. In Japan they have a standard ratio, allowing 8 cups of water to 8 cups of rice for the first six weeks after harvest. The amount of water then rises steadily. And when the rice is 11 months old, 8 cups of rice need 10 cups of water.

Not only is there moisture variability in rice, but the type must also be reckoned with. Brown rice, which retains its bran coat and germ, is much slower to tenderize—although more valuable nutritionally—than highly polished white rice.

There are also differences in the grain hybrids. Use short grain types—which cook up tender and moist—in recipes calling for sauces. Long grain types are best for soups, molding or stuffing. Also on the market are preprocessed rices, for which you must follow the directions on the label. Some of these which are parboiled before milling have greater nutritive value than polished white rice. Wild rice is not a true rice. The seed comes from a strictly American plant and needs its own recipes, see page 159.

◗ To keep rice white when cooking in hard water, add 1 teaspoon lemon juice or 1 tablespoon vinegar to the cooking water.

◗ One cup raw rice equals

3½ cups when cooked. If using preprocessed rice, the volume will be less. This is also true for recipes in which rice is browned in a skillet—with or without fat —prior to cooking it with moisture. But this browning helps to keep the granules separate and does contribute to good flavor.

BOILED RICE   [6 to 7]

I. Bring to a ◗ rolling boil:
    1¾ to 2½ cups water or
       stock
Add:
    ¾ teaspoon salt
You may add:
    (1 tablespoon melted butter)
to the rice before cooking, to keep it from sticking to the pot. Stir slowly into the water, so as not to disturb the boiling:
    1 cup white or brown rice
Cover and cook over slow heat. White rice will take from 20 to 30 minutes, brown from 40 to 50. If the rice becomes too dry, add ¼ cup or more ◗ boiling water. When the grains have swelled to capacity, uncover the pot for about the last 5 minutes of cooking. Continue to cook the rice over ◗ very low heat, shaking the pot from time to time until the grains have separated. Or fluff the cooked rice with a fork.

                              [3]

II. A moist Oriental-type rice. Wash and drain:
    ½ cup rice
Place in a deep, heavy kettle with:
    1½ cups cold water
Boil for 5 minutes until most of the surface water is gone and air bubbles can be seen on the surface of the rice. ◗ Reduce the heat and continue to cook ◗ uncovered, for about 20 minutes longer. Remove from heat and let the rice stand covered for about 20 minutes more. It is then ready to serve.

BAKED RICE [6 to 7]

Preheat oven to 375°.
Sauté:

> ½ chopped onion

in:

> ¼ cup butter

until translucent. Add, and stir until well coated:

> 1 cup long-grain rice

Add:

> 2 cups boiling chicken broth or boiling salted water

Cover and bake for about 18 minutes. Gently mix with the rice:

> 2 tablespoons melted butter

Serve the rice at once.

BAKED GREEN RICE [3]

Outstanding alone or as a stuffing for a veal breast. This amount will fill a 7-inch ring mold.
Preheat oven to 325°.
Beat:

> 1 egg

Add and mix well:

> 1 cup milk
> ½ cup finely chopped parsley
> 1 finely chopped clove garlic
> 1 small minced onion
> 2 cups cooked rice
> ½ cup sharp grated cheese or 2 tablespoons butter
> ⅛ teaspoon curry
> Salt to taste

Place these ingredients in a baking dish, in which has been poured:

> 2 tablespoons olive oil

Bake for 30 to 40 minutes.

RICE COOKED IN CHICKEN STOCK [3]

Melt in a saucepan:

> 2 tablespoons butter

Add and stir until golden brown:

> ½ chopped onion

Add and shake until the grains are coated:

> 1 cup rice

Add:

> 2 cups hot chicken stock

Cover the pot and simmer the rice, or bake it in a 375° oven until the liquid is absorbed.
Add:

> 2 tablespoons melted butter

Toss the rice with a fork to distribute it.

CURRIED RICE [3]

An unusual and delicious rice dish. Its popularity is undoubtedly due to the restraint with which the spice is used.
Pour:

> 2 cups hot water

over:

> ½ cup rice

Place the rice where it will remain hot, but will not cook, for about 45 minutes.
Preheat oven to 350°.
Add to the rice:

> ½ cup tomatoes
> ¾ teaspoon salt
> ¼ cup finely sliced onion
> ¼ cup sliced green peppers
> 2 tablespoons melted butter
> ¾ teaspoon curry powder

Bake these ingredients in a baking dish for 1½ hours or until done. Stir them from time to time. At first, there will be a great preponderance of liquid, but gradually the rice will absorb it. Remove the dish from the oven while the rice is still moist. Good served with beer.

ABOUT WILD RICE

Wild rice is a seed from a grass growing wild in the northern United States and remains a luxury because of the difficulty of harvesting it. For economy, combine cooked wild rice with cooked white or brown rice.
One cup of wild rice equals 3 to 3½ cups of cooked wild rice. Add 1 teaspoon salt to each cup uncooked rice.

WILD RICE [4]

Wash well in several waters,
pouring off the foreign particles
from the top:
> 1 cup wild rice

Drain it. Stir it slowly into:
> 4 cups boiling water
> 1 teaspoon salt

Cook it without stirring until
tender, for about 40 minutes.

WILD RICE RING [4]

Preheat oven to 350°.
Prepare as above:
> 1 cup wild rice

You may add:
> 1 sliced clove garlic

Cook the rice as above. Add:
> ¼ cup butter
> ½ teaspoon poultry
>   seasoning or freshly
>   grated nutmeg
> (1 cup sautéed onions and
>   mushrooms)
> (¼ cup dry sherry)

Place it in a well-greased 7-inch
ring mold. Set the mold in a pan
of hot water and bake for about
20 minutes. Loosen the edges
with a knife, invert the contents
onto a platter and fill the center
with:
> Creamed Mushrooms,
>   page 296
> Chicken Livers
>   Lyonnaise, page 534,
>   or Sautéed Onions,
>   page 302

CHINESE FRIED RICE [6]

The rice for this recipe must be
cooked, fluffy and at least one
day old. Heat in a heavy skillet:
> ¼ cup cooking oil

Toss in it:
> 3 cups Boiled Rice,
>   page 158

until hot and golden. Add:
> 4 minced scallions
> ¾ teaspoon salt
> (½ cup cooked julienned
>   roast pork or ham or

> 1 cup cooked diced
>   shrimp)

When these ingredients are well
mixed, hollow a center in the
rice. Break:
> 3 eggs

into the hollow and scramble
until semi-cooked—then stir
them into the rice mixture.
Sprinkle with:
> 1½ tablespoons soy sauce
> (¼ cup minced Chinese
>   parsley leaves)

and serve with:
> Podded Peas, page 307

CHEESE RICE [6 to 7]

This is a good dish to serve with
a cold supper.
Boil, page 158:
> 1 cup rice

When the water is nearly absorbed, add:
> ½ to ¾ cup or more
>   grated cheese
> ¼ teaspoon paprika
> A few grains cayenne

Add:
> 1 can condensed tomato or
>   mushroom soup: 10½ oz.

Stir the rice over low heat until
the cheese is melted.

SPANISH RICE [3 to 4]

Sauté until brown:
> 3 slices minced bacon

Remove the bacon. Stir and
cook in the drippings until
brown:
> ½ cup rice

Add and cook until brown:
> ½ cup thinly sliced onions

Add the bacon and:
> 1¼ cups canned tomatoes
> ½ teaspoon salt
> 1 teaspoon paprika
> 1 seeded and minced
>   green pepper
> (1 clove garlic)

Steam the rice in a double
boiler for about 1 hour. Stir it
frequently. Add water or stock

if the rice becomes too dry. It may be served with:

Cheese Sauce, page 364

RICE LOAF OR CASSEROLE

I. [5]

Boil, page 158:

⅔ cup rice

Line a buttered mold with it. Reserve ½ cup for the top. Preheat oven to 375°. Cook:

1 cup Cream Sauce II, page 359

Stir in and thicken over low heat:

1 egg yolk

Add:

1 cup diced canned salmon, cooked fish or meat
½ cup bread crumbs
1 tablespoon chopped parsley
1 tablespoon chopped onion
½ cup chopped celery
1 teaspoon lemon juice or 1 teaspoon Worcestershire sauce
Salt, paprika, nutmeg

Fill the mold and place the reserved rice over the top. Cover this with a piece of buttered paper. Set the mold in a pan of hot water and bake or steam it until it is set, for about 30 minutes. Invert the loaf onto a platter. Garnish it with:

Sprigs of parsley

Serve it with:

Tomato Sauce, page 376, or Mushroom Sauce, page 367, etc.

II. [6]

Preheat oven to 400°.
The proportions of rice and fish in this dish may be varied. Use about ½ as much cream sauce as you do of the other main ingredients combined. Boil, page 158:

⅔ cup rice

There should be about 2 cups cooked rice. Drain:

1 cup tuna fish

Break the tuna into pieces with a fork. Cook:

2 cups Cream Sauce II, page 359

Add:

½ teaspoon salt—more if rice is unsalted
½ teaspoon paprika
A few grains red pepper

Reduce the heat to low. Stir in until melted:

2 cups grated cheese

Place in a baking dish alternate layers of rice, fish and sauce. Dot the top with:

Au Gratin II, page 389

Bake the dish until the crumbs are brown. If preferred, bake the ingredients in a ring, invert and serve it with the center filled with Sautéed Mushrooms, page 296.

NUT LOAF [4]

Serve with broccoli or any green leafy vegetable.
Preheat oven to 375°.
Melt:

3 tablespoons butter

Sauté in it until soft:

1 minced onion
1 seeded chopped green pepper

Add:

1 cup cooked rice
⅓ cup bread crumbs
1 cup chopped tomatoes
1 cup chopped or ground walnut or other nut meats
1 beaten egg
2 tablespoons chopped parsley
¾ teaspoon salt
¼ teaspoon paprika
(1 teaspoon grated lemon peel)

Place these ingredients in a greased baking dish. Bake them for about 30 minutes. Cover the top with:

Mashed potatoes

Dot them generously with:

Butter

Brown them under a broiler. Serve the loaf with:

Tomato Sauce, page 376

RICE RING OR MOLD

A molded rice ring is a handsome way to enclose your main course. For color, include chopped parsley with the cooked rice, or try some of the following recipes.

I.   [6]
Preheat oven to 350°.
Boil, page 158:
1 cup rice
Season it with:
½ teaspoon grated nutmeg
Place it in a well-greased 7-inch ring mold. Melt and pour over it:
¼ cup butter
You may add:
(¾ cup blanched, coarsely chopped almonds)
Set the mold in a pan of hot water. Bake the rice for about 20 minutes. Loosen the edges, invert the contents of the mold onto a platter.
Fill the center with:

Creamed Chicken, page 226, Creamed Mushrooms, page 296, or a creamed or buttered vegetable

II. This works fine for any recipe not using egg to bind it. Otherwise use I, above. We have had success packing the hot cooked rice firmly into a well-buttered ring mold. Rest it 3 or 4 minutes and then turn it out onto the serving platter to be filled with the hot entrée.

CHEESE RICE RING   [3]

Preheat oven to 350°.
Boil:
½ cup Rice, page 158
Add:
1 beaten egg

2 tablespoons olive oil or melted butter
¼ cup milk
⅓ cup grated cheese
¼ tablespoon grated onion
1 teaspoon Worcestershire sauce
¼ teaspoon salt
3 tablespoons chopped parsley

Grease a 7-inch ring mold. Fill it with the rice mixture. Bake it, set in a pan of hot water, for about 45 minutes.

MUSHROOM RICE RING [6]

No need to bake this mold.
Boil, page 158:
1 cup rice
Grind, chop fine or ⅄ blend:
½ to 1 lb. mushrooms
Sauté them for 2 or 3 minutes in:
2 tablespoons butter
Add:
¼ cup hot stock or water
Combine the mushrooms and rice. Add:
(¾ cup blanched coarsely chopped almonds)
Correct the seasoning
Press the rice firmly in a greased 7-inch ring mold and let stand for 3 or 4 minutes. Invert the rice onto a platter. Fill the center with a buttered vegetable, creamed fish, etc.

RICE AND HAM RING   [6]

Preheat oven to 375°.
Combine:
2 cups cooked rice
1 cup diced cooked ham
Combine and beat:
1 egg
⅔ cup condensed mushroom soup
½ cup milk
¼ teaspoon salt
(½ teaspoon dried basil)
Grease a 9-inch ring mold. Place in it layers of rice and ham. Pour the liquid ingredients over them. Sprinkle the top with:

1 cup crushed potato chips
or bread crumbs

Bake the ring in 1 inch of hot water, for about ½ hour. Invert it onto a platter. Fill the center with:

A cooked vegetable,
carrots and peas, snap
beans, etc.

RICE AND ONION CASSEROLE [3 to 4]

Heat in a skillet:
2 tablespoons butter
Sauté in it, until lightly browned:
½ cup uncooked rice
½ cup sliced fresh or
canned mushrooms
Stir in:
1 package dried onion soup
1 cup water
Cover and cook over low heat, about 25 minutes, until the rice is tender.

RICE WITH SPINACH AND CHESTNUTS [6 to 8]

Preheat oven to 350°.
Combine:
1 cup cooked rice
1 cup cooked chopped
spinach
1 cup cooked chestnuts
½ to 1 cup grated cheese
Cover with:
Au Gratin II, page 389
Bake about 35 minutes or until thoroughly heated. Garnish with:
Sprigs of water cress and
ribbons of pimiento
before serving.

BACON AND RICE CUSTARD [4]

Preheat oven to 325°.
Cook until partly done:
8 slices bacon
Use 4 muffin tins. Line each one with 2 slices of bacon. Fill them with the following mixture. Combine:
2 cups cooked rice

1 beaten egg
2 tablespoons cream
1 tablespoon melted butter
1 tablespoon grated onion
1 tablespoon chopped
parsley
⅛ teaspoon salt
⅛ teaspoon paprika
Bake the custard until firm, for about ½ hour. Serve with:
Tomato or other sauce

BAKED PINEAPPLE RICE [6]

This good dish may be served with baked ham or fried chicken or as a dessert with cream.
Preheat oven to 350°.
Boil, page 158:
1 cup rice
Drain, then cut into pieces:
3½ cups cubed pineapple
Place in a buttered baking dish ⅓ the rice. Cover with ½ the pineapple. Repeat the layer of rice and pineapple. Place the last ⅓ of the rice on top. Dot each layer with:
1½ tablespoons butter
¼ cup brown sugar
Use in all 5½ tablespoons butter and ¾ cup sugar. Pour over all:
¾ cup pineapple juice
Bake the rice, covered, for about 1 hour.

ROMBAUER RICE DISH [4]

Freely varied each time it is made, but in such demand that we shall try to write a general rule for it.
Prepare:
½ cup Boiled Rice,
page 158
Prepare:
Veal stew: 1½ lbs. meat
Pare, slice and add for the last 20 minutes of cooking:
½ parsnip
2 carrots
2 onions
6 sliced ribs celery
3 sprigs parsley
Drain the stew. To make the

gravy, see page 358. There should be about 3 cups of stock. If there is not enough, add chicken bouillon, a bouillon or vegetable cube and water, rice water or sweet or sour cream to make up the difference. If there is not enough fat, add butter. The better the gravy, the better the dish. Combine the rice, meat, vegetable cube and water, rice them. Garnish with:

> Parsley

You may add a dash of curry powder and some herbs— thyme, basil, etc. (II, 204). You may use leftover meat, gravy and vegetables. You may serve the stew in a baking dish, au gratin or in individual bakers.

A de luxe dish is this recipe made with rice, chicken, sauce —with cream and chicken gravy —and blanched slivered almonds. An everyday dish is this recipe made with corned beef and some canned soup to substitute for gravy.

VEGETABLE RICE OR JAMBALAYA [4]

Ideal for a picnic supper.
Steam:

> ⅔ cup rice

Sauté lightly in butter:

> ¾ to 1 lb. mushrooms

Chop and add:

> 2 medium-sized green peppers, seeds and membrane removed
> 1 medium-sized onion
> 1 stalk of celery
> 2 canned pimientos
> 1¼ cups cooked or canned tomatoes

Season these ingredients with:

> ¾ teaspoon salt
> A few grains cayenne
> ½ teaspoon paprika

Add:

> ¼ lb. melted butter

These proportions may be varied.
Preheat oven to 300°.
Combine the rice and other in-

gredients. Place in a greased baking dish. Bake ◗ covered for about 1 hour. The sautéed mushroom caps and the pimientos may be used to garnish the top of the dish. They are highly decorative with a bunch of parsley in the center.

JAMBALAYA WITH MEAT OR FISH [6 to 8]

Sauté lightly in a saucepan:

> 2 slices diced bacon

Add and sauté until golden:

> ¼ cup chopped onion

Stir in:

> 1 tablespoon flour

Add:

> 1 cup tomato pulp
> ⅓ cup water

Bring these ingredients to the boiling point. Stir in:

> 3 cups cooked rice
> 2 cups coarsely diced cooked ham, chicken, sausage, tongue or shrimp, crab, etc., alone or in combination

Season these ingredients with:

> ¼ teaspoon thyme (Worcestershire sauce)
> Correct the seasoning

Stir over very low heat for about 10 minutes or heat over boiling water for about ½ hour. Serve sprinkled with:

> Chopped parsley

CHICKEN JAMBALAYA [4 to 6]

Cut into pieces:

> A young chicken

Sauté for about 5 minutes in:

> ¼ cup cooking oil or butter

Remove meat from pan. Sauté in the grease, also for about 3 minutes:

> ⅓ cup minced onion
> ½ cup skinned seeded and chopped tomato

Stir in:

> 1 diced green pepper, seeds and membrane removed

½ cup diced celery
1 cup rice

When the rice is well coated with grease, stir in the sautéed chicken. Cover these ingredients well with:

Boiling water

Add:

1 bay leaf
¼ teaspoon thyme
¼ cup chopped parsley
1 teaspoon salt
¼ teaspoon pepper

Simmer these ingredients until the chicken is tender and the rice almost done. Add:

½ lb. finely diced cooked ham

Correct the seasoning

Dry out the jambalaya by placing it for about 5 or 10 minutes in a 350° oven.

ITALIAN RICE OR [8 to 10] RISOTTO À LA MILANÈSE

This dish needs fairly constant watching for about 20 minutes and ◗ must be served at once to prevent gumminess. Melt in a heavy pan:

¼ cup Clarified Butter, page 383

Sauté in it, until golden:

1 small minced onion

Add and stir well with a wooden spoon until all the butter is absorbed:

2 cups rice

Have ready:

8 to 10 cups hot beef or chicken stock

After the rice is well coated with the fat, add 1 cup of the stock. Continue to stir, adding about ⅔ of the hot stock over a 10 minute period. Dissolve in a little of the stock:

(A tiny pinch of saffron)

Or add:

(½ teaspoon fennel seed)

Continue to stir and add stock for about 5 to 8 minutes longer, by which time the rice should

have absorbed all of the liquid. ◗ Do not let it dry out.

Correct the seasoning

Place the rice in a hot serving dish. Pour over it and mix:

¼ cup melted butter
(Sautéed chicken livers and giblets)

Sprinkle over it:

1 cup grated Parmesan cheese

PAELLA [8]

Preheat oven to 350°.

If you do not own a paellero, the vessel which gives this dish its name, you will need a generous lidded casserole in which to cook and serve it.

Have ready:

2 cups cooked chicken, cut in about 1- to 1½-inch pieces
4 cups hot chicken stock

Heat briefly in the casserole:

¼ cup olive oil
2 cloves garlic

Remove the garlic. Over moderate heat add, stirring until lightly browned:

2 cups rice

Add the hot stock, in which has been dissolved a small quantity of:

Saffron—or up to 2 teaspoons if you are Spanish

Add:

1 cup peas
2 sliced sweet red peppers
(6 artichoke hearts)
8 thin slices chorizo or hard Spanish sausage

Correct the seasoning

Also put in the chicken, arranging it toward the top of the mixture. Cover and bake in a 350° oven for about 15 minutes. Add, arranging them attractively on the top:

8 raw shrimp
16 well-scrubbed clams in their shells

Cover and steam about 10 minutes longer. Serve at once.

PILAF   [4]

A rice dish combined with shrimp or chicken livers, etc. It has many variations.
Boil, page 158:

    ⅔ cup long grained rice

Sauté until golden:

    3 tablespoons chopped
        onion

in:

    1 to 2 tablespoons butter

Add to the rice. Simmer until thick:

    2½ cups tomatoes
    ½ bay leaf
    3 ribs of celery with leaves
    ⅓ teaspoon salt
    ¼ teaspoon paprika
    ½ teaspoon brown sugar

Strain these ingredients.
Add:

    1 cup cooked shrimp,
        lobster meat, crab meat or
        sautéed or boiled chicken
        livers

Combine these ingredients with the rice.

    Correct the seasoning

Place the rice in a greased baking dish.
Sprinkle with:

    ¼ cup grated cheese and
        bread crumbs

Run under a heated broiler to brown.

FRUIT, NUT AND   [10]
RICE CASSEROLE

Cover with water and soak for ½ hour:

    2 cups dried apricots
    1 cup white raisins

Boil, page 158:

    2 cups rice

Preheat oven to 375°.
In a skillet, melt:

    ½ cup butter

Sauté:

    1 cup minced onion
    ½ cup chopped green
        pepper

    (½ teaspoon curry powder)

Add:

    (1 cup toasted almonds)

and the drained, chopped apricots and raisins and the cooked rice.

    Correct the seasoning

and put into a greased baking dish to bake for about 30 minutes.

RICE TABLE OR   [8]
RIJSTTAFEL

As this Javanese dish is very filling, it is ideal for suppers. Serve it with ice cold beer, followed by salad. It may be made as elaborate or as simple as you wish. If you object to coconut or if you do not like the flavor of curry, do not discard this dish. Instead, carry out the idea of the rijsttafel by substituting creamed chicken, ragoût fin or a lamb curry you do like, followed by vegetable and condiments served in some attractive way.
Grate:

    A fresh coconut or use
        about 2 cups canned
        coconut

Heat but do not scald:

    4 cups milk or coconut
        milk

Add the coconut. Permit these ingredients to stand for 2 hours in a cool place. Melt:

    1 tablespoon butter

Sauté in it, until light brown:

    ½ cup finely chopped onion

Add:

    Chopped gingerroot, a
        2-inch length
    1 chopped clove garlic
    1½ tablespoons curry powder

Strain and add the coconut. Add to the cooled, strained milk:

    1 cup milk or Chicken
        Stock (II, 142)

Mix with 3 tablespoons of the above liquid:

    1 tablespoon flour
    1 tablespoon cornstarch

Heat the remaining liquid and

stir the starch paste into it. Cook
and stir the sauce until it is hot
and thickened.

Correct the seasoning

Place ½ of the sauce in the top
of a double boiler. Add the
coconut mixture and:

> 3 cups cooked diced
> chicken, shrimp, fish,
> veal, sweetbreads,
> mushrooms, etc., either
> alone or in combination

Heat rest of sauce in another
double boiler.

Have ready:

> 2 cups steamed rice, page
> 158

Have it rather dry and flaky.
The ceremony of serving this
dish is part of its charm. In Java
one refers to it by the separate
dishes, as a "One boy curry" or
a "Twenty-two boy curry," each
boy representing one dish. Pass
the rice first. Spread it generously over your plate, forming a
base or "table." Pass the food
in the sauce next. Follow this
with:

> Onion Rings
> Sieved hard-cooked eggs
> Grated peanuts or toasted
> almonds
> Grated coconut, if there
> is none in the sauce
> Relish
> Chutney, raisins, pre-
> served ginger or kumquats
> Halved fried bananas
> Mixed pickles

Now pass the extra heated
sauce.

To simplify matters, the last 4
or 5 dishes may be served from
one large condiment dish. Servings from these various dishes
are placed upon the rice table.
Cut through the layers and proceed to feast.

"LONG RICE" OR HARUSAME

This is not a rice at all, but an
oriental pasta made of soy bean

powder. It is best described, we
feel, as threadlike cellophane
noodles, but we infinitely prefer
its native name of "Spring Rain."
To prepare, pour:

> Boiling water

over:

> Harusame

Let stand 15 minutes or until it
is limp. Cut into desired lengths.
Add as a garnish for soup, meat
or vegetables. It should then
♦ simmer during the last 15
minutes of the cooking of these
foods.

ABOUT SPAGHETTI, MACARONI AND NOODLES

So popular are these hearty
fillers that there are over 500
kinds and shapes to choose from.
Do we ever graduate from lov-
ing the alphabets or sea shells
and those large macaronis that
can be stuffed? When freshly
cooked and tossed in or served
with a meat, fish or cheese
sauce, pastas need only a salad
to make a nutritious, inexpensive and quick meal.

♦ If pastas must be cooked in
advance, moisten them with
butter, milk, bouillon, tomato
juice or a sauce to keep them
from drying out. Rarely are any
of the pasta types—except
Noodles, page 149—made in the
home. This is partly because
they require unavailable hard-
wheat flours.

◗ Always use a pot large enough to hold, without boiling over, water 3 times the volume of the pasta to be cooked. For ½ lb. pasta, use not less than 2 qts. water, seasoned with 2 teaspoons salt. Bring water to a ◗ rolling boil. You may put ◗ a tablespoon of fat in the water to help keep the pasta from clumping. It is said this will also deter the water from boiling over, but our experience does not validate this theory. Watch the pot to keep the boil active during the cooking period. The pasta should be ◗ added to the water so gradually that the brisk boiling is not disturbed. To cook long macaroni or spaghetti, hold it as on page 167 and, as it softens, push it into the boiling water.

◗ Do not overcook. Italians usually prefer pasta "al dente," a state in which it still offers some resistance to the teeth. If pastas are freshly made, like homemade noodles, they may require as little as 5 minutes' cooking. If they have been on a shelf a long time, 8 to 10 minutes is long enough for thin types. If thick, they may need all of 15 minutes. Try pastas "al burro," simply tossed in butter with a freshly grated Parmesan cheese topping.

BOILED SPAGHETTI

[4 Cups]
About 2 cups or ½ lb. uncooked spaghetti yields 4 cups cooked. In a large pan, have boiling:

 2 quarts water
seasoned with:
 2 teaspoons salt
Slowly add, so as not to disturb boiling:
 ½ lb. or about 2 cups
 spaghetti
Cook until tender—about 10 minutes more or less—to your own taste satisfaction. Drain it. Keep it hot. Heat a salad or

large bowl. Rub it with a cut:
 Clove of garlic
Place in it:
 ¼ teaspoon salt
 ¼ teaspoon paprika
 ¼ cup hot oil or melted
 butter
 1 cup grated cheese
Toss the spaghetti in the above dressing like a salad and serve at once.

BAKED SPAGHETTI

Preheat oven to 375°.
Prepare:
 Boiled Spaghetti, above
Alternate in a greased baking dish layers of spaghetti and:
 1 cup grated cheese
Pour over all:
 Tomato Sauce, page 376
Dot with:
 Butter
and bake about 15 minutes.

ITALIAN SPAGHETTI WITH SAUCE

[About 6 Servings]
In Italy spaghetti is served in one dish, the sauce in another and grated cheese in a third. The sauce may be poured over the spaghetti, which is tossed until the two are well blended.
Prepare:
 A Pasta Sauce, page 377
Cook:
 1 lb. unbroken spaghetti
When well drained, pour over it:
 ¼ cup melted butter
Put the spaghetti in a bowl. Pour the sauce over it and toss until well coated.

SPAGHETTI WITH   [4 to 6]
EGG AND CHEESE

Not the usual cheese sauce, but an Italian version.
Cook in boiling salted water for 8 to 10 minutes:
 1 lb. spaghetti

In the meantime, cook in a small skillet:

2 tablespoons olive oil
6 slices finely cut bacon

until the bacon is crisp. Add:

⅓ cup dry white wine

and reduce until the wine has evaporated. Beat together:

3 eggs
⅔ cup mixed Parmesan and Romano grated cheese

Drain the spaghetti and return it to the hot saucepan. Add the egg and cheese mixture and the hot bacon fat and bits, stirring it in quickly. The heat of the spaghetti will cook the egg mixture.

Correct the seasoning

Serve immediately.

QUICK SPAGHETTI   [4]
WITH TUNA FISH, SALMON OR BEEF

Drain and reserve the oil from:

1 can tuna fish or salmon

Sauté in the oil:

⅓ cup chopped onion

Or use the onion and:

½ lb. ground beef

Sauté in:

¼ cup drippings

Add to the onion the contents of:

1 can condensed tomato soup: 10½ oz.
2½ cups canned spaghetti

Fold in the flaked fish. Season with:

½ teaspoon sugar
A few grains cayenne
Salt and paprika

Cook it until it is thoroughly heated. You may rub a bowl with:

(A cut clove garlic)

Add the spaghetti. Garnish it with:

2 tablespoons chopped parsley

This dish may be served in an ovenproof baking dish, au gratin. Use a hot oven—400° —or a broiler to melt the cheese.

QUICK SPAGHETTI   [4]
MEAT PIE

Preheat oven to 375°.
Sauté lightly:

2 cups cooked cubed meat
2 teaspoons grated onion

in:

2 tablespoons butter

Add:

¼ cup cream

Season it with:

Salt and pepper
(½ teaspoon basil)

Place in a greased dish the contents of:

1 can spaghetti: 24 oz.

Make a depression in the center. Place the meat in it. Sprinkle the top with:

Au Gratin II, page 389

Bake for about 25 minutes.

QUICK SPAGHETTI   [4]
WITH SOUP AND BACON

Preheat oven to 375°.
Sauté until nearly crisp:

8 slices bacon or 1 cup chopped tongue, ham or potted meat

Cut them into large pieces. Combine the contents of:

1 can condensed mock turtle or pepper pot soup: 10½ oz.
2½ cups canned spaghetti

If preferred, cook and substitute 1¼ cups spaghetti or use 2½ cups cooked spaghetti. Add:

¼ cup hot water

Place alternate layers of this mixture and the bacon in a greased ovenproof dish. Cover the top with:

Buttered crumbs

Bake the dish for about 20 minutes, until it is thoroughly heated. If you wish, omit the soup and season the spaghetti with:

1 teaspoon prepared mustard
1 teaspoon grated onion

CHICKEN OR [8 to 10] TURKEY TETRAZZINI

A fan writes that she prefers using ¼ lb. macaroni and 1 lb. mushrooms. A bit more extravagant but very good.
Cut the meat from the bones of:
    A boiled chicken
There should be 2 to 3 cups of shredded meat. Cook:
    ½ lb. macaroni or spaghetti
Add to this:
    ½ to ¾ lb. Sautéed
        Mushrooms, page 296
    (½ cup blanched, slivered
        almonds)
Make a sauce of:
    3 tablespoons butter or
        chicken fat
    2 tablespoons flour
    2 cups chicken broth
        Seasoning
Remove from heat. Stir in:
    1 cup heated whipping
        cream
    3 tablespoons dry white
        wine
Preheat oven to 375°.
Add ½ the sauce to the chicken and ½ to the macaroni and mushrooms. Place the macaroni in a greased baking dish. Make a hole in the center. Place the chicken in it. Sprinkle the top with:
    Grated Parmesan cheese
Bake the dish until it is lightly browned.

SEAFOOD TETRAZZINI [8]

Preheat broiler.
Boil:
    ½ lb. spaghetti
Sauté until golden:
    6 tablespoons chopped
        onion
in:
    2 tablespoons olive oil
Add:
    2 cans cream of mushroom
        soup: 10½ oz.
    1⅓ cups water
    ¼ cup grated Romano
        cheese

Stir in and heat thoroughly:
    2 cups flaked, drained
        tuna, shrimp, or clams,
        etc.
    ⅔ cup sliced pitted ripe
        olives
Add:
    2 tablespoons chopped
        parsley
    2 teaspoons lemon juice
    ⅛ teaspoon dried thyme
        and marjoram
In a buttered casserole, mix the sauces and the drained spaghetti. Top with:
    ¼ cup grated Romano
        cheese
Heat under the broiler until golden brown.

BOILED MACARONI [6] WITH CHEESE

In a large pan have boiling:
    2 quarts water
seasoned with:
    2 teaspoons salt
Slowly add so as not to disturb boiling:
    ½ lb. or about 2 cups
        macaroni
Cook until tender, about 10 to 12 minutes. Drain. Return to the saucepan. Stir and reheat over slow heat with:
    ½ cup cream or rich milk
Place it in a dish and sprinkle it with:
    ½ cup or more grated
        cheese
Serve it with any of the Pasta Sauces on page 379, or with the Tomato Sauces on page 376.

BAKED MACARONI [4]

I.
Preheat oven to 350°.
Cook:
    4 oz. macaroni: 1 cup
Drain it. Place layers of macaroni in a buttered baking dish. Sprinkle the layers with:
    1 cup grated cheese
Beat until blended:
    1 or 2 eggs

⅔ cup milk
¼ teaspoon salt
⅛ teaspoon paprika
A few grains cayenne
Pour this mixture over the macaroni. Sprinkle the top with:
Au Gratin III, page 389
Bake the macaroni about 40 to 50 minutes.

II. Alternate layers of:
Macaroni, as in I, above
and:
¼ lb. sliced dried beef

III. Follow the above recipe. Substitute for the milk:
½ cup tomato juice
¼ cup cream
Add:
½ teaspoon sugar
(1 tablespoon chopped parsley or 1 teaspoon dried basil or thyme)

IV. One cup well-seasoned Cream Sauce I, page 359, may be substituted for the egg and milk mixture. Bake at 400° about 30 minutes.

MACARONI BAKED WITH SOUR CREAM [4]

Preheat oven to 400°.
Cook:
1½ cups macaroni
Drain it well. Toss it in:
3 tablespoons melted butter
Place it in a greased oven-proof dish. Make a hollow in the center into which pour:
1 cup cultured sour cream
You may sprinkle this with:
½ cup grated cheese
Bake the macaroni until the top is brown.

MACARONI LOAF [5]

Preheat oven to 350°.
This delectable dish is very attractive in appearance. It makes a fine ring dish.
Boil:
5 cups water

1½ teaspoons salt
Add:
¾ cup macaroni or spaghetti
Boil for about 10 minutes. Drain in a colander. Place in a bowl.
Scald:
½ cup milk or cream
Beat into it:
2 or 3 eggs
Melt and add:
3 tablespoons butter
Pour this over the macaroni. Add:
½ cup soft bread crumbs, without crusts
½ cup grated cheese
1½ sliced pimientos
¼ cup chopped green peppers or 2 tablespoons chopped parsley
1 tablespoon grated onion
¼ teaspoon salt
⅛ teaspoon paprika
A few grains cayenne
Place these ingredients in a buttered baking dish. Bake them for about 1 hour. Serve with:
Mushroom Sauce, page 367, or
Quick Tomato Sauce, page 376
It makes a somewhat lighter dish if you add only the egg yolks to the scalded milk. The whites, beaten until stiff, are then folded into the other ingredients at the last moment.

MACARONI WITH TOMATOES, LIVERS, MUSHROOMS AND CHEESE

[About 2 Quarts]
Preheat oven to 400°.
Cook, page 167:
½ lb. macaroni
Drain. Place in a deep casserole.
Sauté:
½ lb. Mushrooms, page 296
Sauté or boil until tender:
½ cup chicken livers or calf liver
Chop the mushrooms and the liver.

Simmer until fairly thick:
    4 cups canned tomatoes
Strain them. Season with:
    ¾ tablespoon salt
    1 teaspoon brown sugar
    A few grains cayenne
    (1 teaspoon dried basil)
Sauté:
    1 minced onion
    (½ minced clove garlic)
in:
    2 tablespoons butter
Combine these with the other
ingredients and pour them over
the macaroni. Mix them well
with 2 forks. Sprinkle the top
with:
    Grated cheese
Bake the macaroni until the
cheese is golden.

MACARONI WITH   [4]
SHELLFISH

Preheat oven to 350°.
Cook, page 167:
    1½ cups macaroni
Drain it. Sauté:
    1 tablespoon minced onion
in:
    3 tablespoons butter
Stir in until blended:
    1½ tablespoons flour
Stir in until smooth:
    1½ cups milk
    ¾ cup grated cheese
    1 teaspoon Worcestershire
    sauce
    ½ teaspoon lemon juice
    1 teaspoon salt
    ¼ teaspoon paprika
    A few grains cayenne
Have ready:
    1½ to 2 cups cleaned shrimp,
    oysters or clams, etc.
Place layers of macaroni and fish
in a baking dish. Pour the sauce
over them. Cover the top with:
    Au Gratin III, page 389
Bake the dish for about 45 min-
utes.

MOSTACCIOLI   [5]

Melt:
    1 tablespoon butter

Stir and brown in it:
    ¾ to 1 lb. ground round
    steak
    1 large chopped onion
    1 clove garlic cut into
    halves
Cover these ingredients with
boiling water. Add:
    ¾ teaspoon salt
    ⅛ teaspoon pepper
Simmer covered until almost
dry. Fish out the garlic. Add:
    2 cups canned tomatoes
Continue to simmer, stirring frequently. Cook until the sauce is
thick, from 1 to 1½ hours. Add
mushrooms when the sauce is
partly done. Wash well in warm
water, then drain:
    ¼ lb. dried reconstituted
    mushrooms (II, 221)
When the sauce is almost done
add:
    ¼ cup olive oil
Cook until tender, page 167:
    ½ lb. mostaccioli: about 2
    cups
Serve the mostaccioli on a hot
platter. First a layer of the pasta,
then a layer of sauce, then a
layer of the pasta and again a
layer of sauce. Sprinkle each
meat sauce layer generously
with:
    Grated Parmesan cheese
    Freshly grated black
    pepper

BOILED NOODLES   [5]

Drop:
    2 cups Noodles, page 149
into:
    3 quarts boiling, salted
    water—½ teaspoon salt
    to the quart—or chicken
    stock, consommé, etc.
Boil for about 8 to 10 minutes,
depending on size and your taste
preference. Drain in a colander
and immediately put back in
cooking pot, set over very low
heat and moisten them generously with:
    Melted butter or cream

(Chicken Stock (II, 142)

Serve with:

Au Gratin II, or III, page 382

Additions may be:

Chopped hard-cooked eggs

Chopped chives

2 tablespoons poppy seeds

(¾ cup cultured sour cream)

or:

½ cup blanched chopped almonds

sautéed in:

1 tablespoon butter

Boiled noodles may be arranged in a ring on a platter and the center filled with a creamed meat, vegetable or a hash.

BUTTERED [4 to 6] NOODLES OR FETTUCCINI AL BURRO

Alfredo II came to Cincinnati to demonstrate the making of those noodles which brought both him and his father fame. He carried along from Italy the hard special flour needed for the dough and the hard Parmesan cheese and sweet butter for tossing. Yet when the noodles were presented, he wished he had brought with him the Roman water in which to cook them.

Cook:

2 cups noodles

In:

3 quarts boiling salted water

for 6 to 8 minutes or until "al dente." Drain. Put on a hot platter:

½ cup butter

Cover with drained noodles. Toss until the noodles are coated with the butter. Have ready:

¾ cup grated Parmesan cheese

to pass at table.

FRIED NOODLES

To be served in the place of a starchy vegetable or as a garnish on vegetables or other dishes, notably Chinese mixtures. Boil in water for about 5 minutes:

Thin noodles

Place them in a colander and rinse them with cold water to rid of surface starch. Drain, separate and dry well.

Preheat deep fryer to 390°.

Fry them, a small amount at a time, until they are a delicate brown. Drain them on absorbent paper. Sprinkle them lightly with:

Salt

Keep them hot or reheat in a 400° oven.

NOODLE BASKETS

Preheat deep fryer to 390°.

For these you need a tea strainer about 3 inches in diameter and a second strainer about ⅜ inch smaller that fits into it but leaves space for the swelling of the noodles. Prepare:

Noodle Dough, page 149

Before the dough is dry fold it over and cut it into ¼-inch strips. Dip the strainers in hot fat to keep the noodles from sticking. Line the larger strainer with 3 layers of noodles, giving them a crisscross effect. Snip off the ragged edges. Place the smaller strainer over the noodle basket. Fry the noodle basket in deep fat, page 75, until lightly browned. Remove it carefully from the strainers and fry the next one. You may fill the fried baskets at once with creamed food, etc., or you may cool them and reheat them later by dipping them briefly in hot fat without the strainers.

Drain them on absorbent paper.

BAKED NOODLE [4] RING

Preheat oven to 350°.

I. Cook:

1½ cups Noodles, page 149

Drain them. Beat:

>2 egg yolks
>½ cup milk
>¾ tablespoon melted butter
>¼ teaspoon salt
>⅛ teaspoon paprika
>(½ cup grated cheese)
>(⅛ teaspoon nutmeg)

Combine this mixture with the noodles. Beat until stiff but not dry:

>2 egg whites

Fold them lightly into the noodles. Butter a 7-inch ring mold or individual ring molds. Fill them with the noodle mixture and bake them set in a pan of hot water in the oven until done, about 45 minutes for a large mold or 30 minutes for the small ones. Invert the contents of the molds on hot plates and fill the centers with:

>Creamed spinach, peas, mushrooms, hash, stewed tomatoes, Chicken à la King, etc.

II. Made with cheese this is our favorite. Follow the above recipe. Use in all:

>¾ cup milk

Add to the noodle mixture before folding in the egg whites:

>1½ teaspoons Worcestershire sauce
>½ tablespoon catsup
>¾ cup grated cheese

Also good made with:

>Cottage cheese

NOODLE RING WITH WHIPPED CREAM   [10]

Preheat oven to 350°.
Use a 9-inch ring. For 5 servings take half the recipe and use a 7-inch ring. Cook:

>2 cups fine Noodles, page 149

Drain. Beat and pour over the noodles:

>4 egg yolks
>¼ teaspoon paprika
>¾ cup melted butter

Whip until stiff:

>4 egg whites
>¼ teaspoon salt

Beat until stiff:

>1 cup whipping cream or use 1 cup cultured sour cream

Fold the egg whites and the cream lightly into the noodle mixture. Fill a well-greased ring. Place it in a pan of hot water. Bake it until firm, for about 1 hour or more. Invert the ring and fill it with:

>Green peas or creamed food, sweetbreads, fish, etc.

NOODLES, STEWED PRUNES AND CROUTONS

This is a traditional Good Friday dish in a number of European countries. It is a reminder of how good simple food may be in a tempting combination. Prepare:

>Boiled Noodles, page 149
>Dried Prunes (II, 108)
>Croutons, page 390

Serve the noodles hot with the croutons poured over them. Serve the prunes from a separate bowl.

HAM NOODLES   [8]

Preheat oven to 350°.
This recipe is capable of a wide interpretation and its proportions may be varied. Cook:

>1½ cups Noodles, page 149

Grease a baking dish. Place in it layers of noodles sprinkled with:

>¾ cup cooked diced or ground ham
>(½ cup grated cheese)
>(½ cup shredded green pepper and celery)

Combine:

>1½ cups milk
>1 or 2 eggs
>¼ teaspoon paprika
>¼ to ½ teaspoon salt—omit if the ham is very salty

Pour this over the noodles. The top may be covered with:

Bread or cracker crumbs

Bake the dish for about 45 minutes.

LEFTOVER NOODLE DISH

Follow the previous recipe. Substitute for the ham:

Diced cooked roast, chicken, crab, shrimp, chipped beef, mushrooms and other vegetables

Part gravy may be substituted for milk or you may like to try a ham and chicken combination in a Cream Sauce, page 359.

NOODLE RAREBIT

Prepare:

Cheese Rarebit I, page 237

When blended and hot stir in:

1 to 2 cups diced ham or smoked tongue

8 oz. cooked noodles

ROMANIAN NOODLE   [8]
AND PORK CASSEROLE

Preheat oven to 350°.

Cook until slightly underdone:

1 lb. fine noodles

Combine:

1 lb. ground cooked pork
1 slice bread which has been soaked in milk and wrung out
1 minced leek
½ to 1 teaspoon fennel seeds
¼ cup chopped parsley
1 teaspoon salt
½ teaspoon pepper

In a shallow large baking pan, arrange alternate layers of noodles and pork mixture, ending with noodles. Beat together:

4 eggs
⅔ cup cream
¼ cup grated cheese

Pour this mixture over the noodles and dot with:

¼ cup butter

Bake for about 45 minutes.

QUANTITY NOODLE   [18]
AND CHEESE LOAF

Preheat oven to 325°.

Cook:

5 cups Noodles, page 149

and drain them. Have ready:

1 lb. grated sharp cheese
1½ cups dry bread crumbs

Mix together half the cheese and one cup of the crumbs with:

¼ cup melted butter

Mix the rest of the crumbs and the cheese and the noodles with:

7 beaten eggs
1¾ cups milk
3 tablespoons grated onion
⅓ cup chopped pimiento
⅓ cup chopped green peppers, seeds and membranes removed
1 teaspoon salt
½ teaspoon white pepper
(1 cup finely chopped celery)
(½ cup sliced stuffed olives)

Divide the mixture in two parts and place in two 9 x 9 inch baking pans. Cover with the cheese, butter and crumb mixture. Bake for about 25 minutes or until the custard sets and the top is golden brown.

To test the custard for doneness, see (II, 436).

Serve with:

Mushroom Sauce, page 367
Tomato Sauce, page 376
Creole Sauce, page 376

TUNA, NOODLE AND
MUSHROOM SOUP
CASSEROLE

[4 Large Servings]

Preheat oven to 450°.

An excellent emergency dish.

Cook until tender:

2 cups Noodles, page 149

Drain them in a colander.
Drain:

> 1 cup canned tuna fish

Separate it with a fork into
large flakes. Do not mince it.
Grease an ovenproof dish. Arrange a layer of noodles, then
sprinkle it with fish and so on.
Have noodles on top. Pour over
this mixture:

> 1 can condensed mushroom
> soup: 10½ oz.

Season the soup with:

> Worcestershire sauce,
> curry powder, dry
> sherry, etc.

Cover the top with:

> Buttered cornflakes or
> cracker crumbs

Bake the dish until the top is
brown.

LASAGNE   [16]

The sauce may be made the day
before. Combine in a large
saucepan:

> 2 cans Italian-style peeled
> tomatoes: No. 2½
> 4 cans tomato sauce: 8 oz.
> each
> 2 teaspoons salt
> 3 teaspoons dried orégano
> (2 teaspoons onion salt)

Start simmering these ingredients uncovered. Sauté until
golden:

> 2 cups minced onions
> 2 minced cloves garlic

in:

> ⅓ cup olive oil

Add:

> 2 lbs. ground chuck roast
> or round
> 2 teaspoons salt

and cook until meat loses its
red color. Add to the tomato
sauce above. Simmer about 2½
hours longer. Prepare:

> ¾ lb. lasagne noodles

according to package directions
—usually in generous quantities
of water—and cook for about
25 minutes. Add to the water:

> 2 tablespoons cooking or
> olive oil

Stir occasionally. Drain and separate noodles.
Preheat oven to 350°.
Now let's build the lasagne! Put
into the bottoms of two 13 x 9 x
2½-inch baking dishes a thin
layer of sauce, then a criss-cross
layer of the lasagne noodles and
a layer of cheese.
In all, use:

> ¾ lb. Ricotta cheese
> ⅓ lb. thinly sliced or
> crumbled Mozzarella
> cheese
> ½ lb. grated Parmesan
> cheese

Repeat twice with sauce, noodles and cheese. The final
cheese layer is covered once
more with sauce and a dusting
of Parmesan.
Bake for about 40 minutes. Remove and let stand for 10 minutes. The lasagne can then be
cut for serving.

CANNELONI OR
MANICOTTI

[Ten 4 x 6 Inch Rolled
Squares]
Wrapped around fillings and
served with a sauce, the charm
of these "channels" or "little
muffs" lies in the freshness of
the dough; although the wrappings may be made in advance
and held between wax papers
in the refrigerator for several
hours. Have ready a filling made
by mixing together until well
blended:

> 1 cup grated Parmesan
> cheese
> ½ cup Mozzarella cheese
> 1¾ cups Ricotta cheese
> ⅛ teaspoon nutmeg
> 1 beaten egg
> ¼ cup Béchamel Sauce,
> page 359, or Cream
> Sauce IV, page 360

You may use instead of the

above filling a good chicken or sausage farce, page 564.

Correct the seasoning

Make a well and mix as described (II, 301).

2 cups flour
¾ teaspoon salt
2 eggs
2 to 4 tablespoons water

Knead for about 10 minutes or until the dough is smooth. Rest the dough ▶ covered under a cloth about 10 minutes. Divide the dough in half and roll each part paper thin. Cut into 4 x 6 inch squares. Have ready in a large pan:

8 quarts boiling water

Cook 5 squares at a time by dropping them into the boiling water ▶ reducing the heat at once and simmering about 5 minutes. Remove with a skimmer, and when drained place between the moist towels until all the dough is cooked and ready to fill.

Preheat oven to 400°.

Divide the filling into 10 oval parts. Place on the center of the squares, fold over the two edges and put seam-side down in a greased ovenproof dish, or in individual bakers allowing 2 per person.

Cover generously with:
A tomato sauce or butter and a sprinkling of fresh basil

Bake about 10 minutes.

Serve with:
Grated Parmesan cheese

RAVIOLI

If you are fond of this Italian savory pastry buy a mold for mass-producing it.

Prepare:
Noodle Dough II,
page 150

Cover it with a cloth and permit it to stand for 10 minutes. Roll the dough until it is very thin. Cut it into 2 sheets. On one sheet put a teaspoon of one of the ravioli fillings, in little mounds 2 inches apart. Cover them with the second sheet which may be brushed lightly with water. Press the top sheet gently around the ravioli mounds. Press the edges. Cut the dough into squares with a mound in each center. Use a pie jagger. Dry the ravioli for about 2 hours. Drop them into boiling, salted water or into chicken broth. Simmer them for about 10 minutes. Remove them from the liquid with a skimmer onto a hot platter. Sprinkle them with:

Grated Parmesan cheese

Serve with:
A tomato sauce, page 376

RAVIOLI FILLING

This is usually a spinach and meat mixture very finely chopped or put through a purée strainer. Grated cheese and light seasoning may be added. Sometimes the filling is thickened slightly with bread crumbs or egg. There can be much leeway in the composition of the filling and you may use any combination of meat and vegetables you like. For other fillings, see Farces, page 564.

I.

Combine:
¼ cup cooked puréed spinach
¼ cup chopped cooked meat
1 egg
2 tablespoons toasted bread crumbs
2 tablespoons grated cheese
Stock, cream or gravy to form a stiff paste
½ teaspoon dried basil
(½ clove minced garlic)

II.
Combine:
>   ½ cup cooked drained
>   spinach
>   ½ cup cooked minced
>   chicken
>   2 tablespoons grated
>   cheese
>   Salt and pepper
>   ½ teaspoon dried basil or
>   ⅛ teaspoon nutmeg
>   (½ clove minced garlic)

DUMPLINGS   [4]

◆ Please read About Dumplings,
page 146, where you will find
other recipes suitable for use
with meats.
Measure, then sift 3 times:
>   1 cup cake flour
>   2 teaspoons double-acting
>   baking powder
>   ½ teaspoon salt

Break into a measuring cup:
>   1 egg

Add until the cup is half full:
>   Milk

Beat well and stir the liquid
slowly into the sifted ingredients. Add more milk if necessary
but keep the batter as stiff as
possible. Add:
>   (¼ cup finely chopped
>   parsley or
>   1 tablespoon fresh chopped
>   herbs) or
>   (½ teaspoon grated onion
>   and 3 tablespoons minced
>   green peppers)

Thicken:
>   2 or 3 cups stock

with:
>   Flour—allow 1½
>   tablespoons flour to 1 cup
>   stock

Heat the stock in a 9-inch saucepan. To drop dumpling batter
from a spoon easily, dip the
spoon in water first. Then dip
the spoon in the batter, fill it
and drop the batter into the
stock. Continue doing this until
the dumplings are barely touching. Then cover them and sim-

mer for 5 minutes, turn them,
cook them 5 minutes longer.
They should be served at once.
If using a ⊙ pressure cooker,
drop the batter from a spoon
into at least 3 cups hot stock or
water. Adjust cover, steam over
low heat, vent open, for 5 minutes.

CHEESE DUMPLINGS

To the above recipe for:
>   Dumplings

Add:
>   2 tablespoons grated
>   cheese

Cook the dumplings in:
>   Tomato juice

QUICK CHEESE
DUMPLINGS

[Ten 2-Inch Dumplings]
Have ready:
>   ⅔ cup grated cheese

Add 2 tablespoons of this
cheese to:
>   2 cups commercial biscuit
>   mix

and prepare the recipe on the
label. Pat out the dough to a ⅛
inch thickness and cut into 3
inch rounds. Place in the center of each round a tablespoon
of the cheese. Wet the edges of
the rounds with cold water.
Gather them up to form a ball.
Pinch them well. Have ready in
a lidded pot:
>   6 to 8 cups boiling water

Drop the dumplings in, cover
at once and ◆ reduce heat. ◆
Simmer covered about 15 minutes. Meanwhile heat:
>   Quick Tomato Sauce,
>   page 376

Drain the dumplings and serve
at once on hot plates covered
with the sauce and:
>   Finely chopped parsley

CORN MEAL DUMPLINGS

Cooking in the United States is
on the up and coming side but
it seemed to us that a peak was

reached in a small Kentucky town where we were served chicken with dumplings. The latter were like thistledown. "Oh yes!" said the hotel proprietress wearily when we exclaimed over them. "They are always like that when our cook is drunk."

Far be it from us to limit your sources of inspiration, but we are convinced that the following recipe will give you superlative dumplings without dissipation. Have simmering:

> 5 or 6 cups corned beef stock, consommé or any clear soup or stock

Sift:

> 1 cup corn meal
> ¼ cup all-purpose flour
> 1 teaspoon any baking powder
> ½ teaspoon salt

Beat:

> 2 eggs
> ½ cup milk

Combine the egg mixture and the dry ingredients. Stir in:

> 1 tablespoon melted butter

Drop the batter from a spoon into the hot stock. Cover the pan closely. Simmer the dumplings for about 15 minutes. Remove them at once from the liquor.

FARINA DUMPLINGS COCKAIGNE [6]

Please read About Dumplings, page 146. Prepare:

> Farina Balls Cockaigne, page 147

These remain after many tests the queen of dumplings. Though usually served in soup they may be simmered in stock or boiling water, then served with meat gravy. They may be drained, placed in a greased baking dish and covered with a cup of cream sauce, to which you may add onion juice and parsley, or chopped chives. Sprinkle the top with ¼ cup grated Parmesan cheese, dot it with butter and bake the dish in an oven for about 15 minutes.

SPATZEN, SPAETZLE OR GERMAN EGG DUMPLINGS [4]

Spatzen are good at any time but they are particularly good served with roast veal. Beat:

> 2 eggs

Combine them with:

> 1½ cups flour
> ½ cup water
> ½ teaspoon salt
> ¼ teaspoon any baking powder
> (A small grating of nutmeg)

Beat these ingredients well. Drop small bits of the batter from a spoon into simmering salted water or stock, or put the batter through a colander, or a sliding cutter as shown below or use a pastry bag as shown on page 157. Spatzen should be very light and delicate. Try out a sample and if it is too heavy, add water to the batter. Simmer them until they are done. Drain them, place them in a dish and cover them with:

> Croutons, or ¼ cup bread crumbs sautéed in ½ cup butter

Spatzen may be cooked and served in soup. Pie Dough (II, 293), cut into strips or shapes, simmered in stock, is frequently substituted for a dumpling mixture. Remember the good Vegetable Noodles on page 149.

POTATO DUMPLINGS OR KARTOFFELKLOESSE

These are light and tender, especially good with beef à la mode or other roast gravy. It is traditional to serve them with Sauerbraten.
Boil uncovered in their jackets until tender:

6 medium-sized mature baking potatoes

Peel and coarsely grate or rice them. Add:

2 eggs
1½ teaspoons salt
½ cup flour

Beat the batter with a fork until it is fluffy. Roll it lightly into balls 1 inch in diameter. Many cooks prefer to put croutons in the balls. Put 1 crouton into the center of each 1 inch ball. If you wish to make large balls, roll several croutons into each ball. Drop them into gently boiling salted water for about 10 minutes. Drain them well. Melt:

½ cup butter or drippings

Stir in:

¼ cup dry bread crumbs

Or prepare:

½ cup Croutons, page 390

Pour them over the dumplings.

KARTOFFEL-   [6 to 8] KLOESSE WITH RAW POTATOES

This recipe, contributed by Claire Gregory, is a favorite of her far West German village. Coarsely grate into a bowl of cold water:

5 lbs. peeled mature baking potatoes

Reserve the small ends and pieces that cannot be grated and put them in a small pan covered with water. Squeeze the grated potatoes in a muslin towel until dry and in a firm ball, saving the pressed-out water in a bowl and letting it stand to settle the potato starch.

In the meantime, cook the small pieces of potato in a small amount of water until tender. Drain, mash and add:

3 cups boiling milk

to make a smooth paste.
Correct the seasoning then add the grated raw potato. Drain off the water from the settled potato starch and add the starch to the potato and paste mixture. Mix together by hand and form patties 3 inches in diameter and about ¼ inch thick. Place in the center of each patty:

Small diced buttered croutons, diced liverwurst or sausage

Then press the potato patty around this to enclose it in the center of the ball. Drop these balls into a large pot of:

Boiling salted water

When the pot begins to boil again ▶ reduce the heat and simmer for 25 to 30 minutes. Serve with:

Fat meats
Game
Cabbage with hot melted butter

ABOUT QUENELLES

Once eaten, never forgotten is the texture of a well-made quenelle. Success lies not only in the mixing but in the very shaping. The ground mixture, which may be fish, chicken, veal or game, is placed in a large bowl ▶ set in a bowl of ice, see below.

It is then worked into a smooth paste with a wooden spoon.

♦ To shape, you may roll quenelles in flour but this is not the method for best results. We suggest the following classic spoon molding—letting the size of the spoon determine the size of the quenelle. They will expand to about double their original size. Have ready a well-buttered cooking pan and 2 spoons of equal size. Put one spoon in a bowl of hot water. With the other spoon, lightly scoop out enough of the quenelle mixture to just fill it. Invert the other hot, moist spoon over the filled spoon, shaping as shown. ♦ Do not press hard —only smooth the surface. After shaping the point, invert the little egg shapes into the buttered pan. Continue to shape and place the quenelles in neat rows, allowing for expansion space. ♦ To poach the quenelles, pour almost boiling salted water or stock very gently into the pan from the sides so as not to dislodge them. The stock should come half-way up the quenelles. ♦ Simmer gently for 8 to 10 minutes. The water should be barely quivering. As quenelles cook on the bottom, they become light and rise and turn over, but the weight of the uncooked portion will keep them submerged until they are thoroughly done and float.

Although they are not quite as delicate as when served at once, you may hold the quenelles for several hours if you poach them as described above. Place them gently in a bowl of cold water to cool, then drain off onto a cloth and place on a plate. ♦ Butter the surfaces to keep from crusting.

If you want quenelles very small, as a garnish, cut a parchment paper the size of the pan in which you plan to poach them. Use a decorating bag with a small round tip, fill with the quenelle mixture and force out small units on the parchment paper in uniformly spaced rows. Lift the whole paper into the pan and as with larger quenelles, pour the water gently from the side of the pan until the quenelles are only half-covered. As they simmer for 5 to 8 minutes, they will float free and roll over. When floating, skim off and place in a bowl of warm, mildly salted water until ready to use.

If fancy shapes are desired, pack the quenelle mixture into buttered decorative individual molds. To poach, place the molds into a pan of hot water so that they are completely covered. When the quenelle mixture is cooked, it will release itself, rise to the surface and can be removed for serving.

Reheat quenelles by simmering them in the sauce or soup in which they are to be served. Or place the quenelles in a buttered mold in a pan of hot water. Cover with a buttered poaching paper, page 84, and bake for 50 to 60 minutes at 350° until firm.

POACHED OR BAKED QUENELLES   [6]

♦ Please read About Quenelles, above.

Run through the finest blade of a food chopper 3 times:

    1½ lbs. fresh pike, sole,

shrimp or lobster

Place the ground mixture in a large bowl ◗ set in a bowl of ice. With a wooden spoon, work it to a smooth paste. Gradually ◗ by small additions work in:

2 egg whites

Season with:

Grated fresh nutmeg
Salt
White pepper
Dash of cognac
Dash of cayenne or hot
pepper sauce

Mix well. At this point the quenelle mixture should be very firm. Still over ice, add ◗ very, very gradually and mix well with a wooden spoon:

3 cups well-chilled
whipping cream

The consistency now should be like a firm whipped cream. To form and poach or bake, follow above directions. Serve with:

Newburg Sauce,
page 361
Poulette Sauce, page 362

FISH QUENELLE IN [6]
LOBSTER SAUCE

Preheat oven to 350°.
This is a deluxe fish course for a special dinner party.
Prepare the mixture for:

Quenelles, page 180

using:

Dover sole

Put the quenelle mixture into a buttered mold. Place the mold in a pan of hot water. Cover with a buttered poaching paper and bake 50 to 60 minutes until firm. ◗ Test for doneness as for cake (II, 336). Remove the hot mold from the oven, allowing it to rest 5 minutes before unmolding. Then drain off the accumulated liquid and unmold onto a hot deep serving tray and cover with:

Newburg Sauce,
page 361

Garnish with:

Parsley

and serve immediately.

YORKSHIRE PUDDING [6]

Preheat oven to 400°.

It was customary to cook this old and delicious dish in the pan with the roast or under the roast, letting the drippings fall upon it. As many of us now cook roast beef in a slow oven and no longer have extravagant drippings, we must revise the preparation of Yorkshire pudding. It is best to cook it separately in the hot oven required to puff it up and brown it quickly. Serve it from the dish in which it was cooked, cut into squares. In Yorkshire it is served before the meat course as a hefty pudding. We always substitute the pudding for the usual starch served with a main course.

◗ The ingredients must be at room temperature when mixed or they will not puff. Sift into a bowl:

⅞ cup flour
½ teaspoon salt

Make a well in the center, into which pour:

½ cup milk

Stir in the milk. Beat until fluffy:

2 eggs

Beat them into the batter. Add:

½ cup water

Beat the batter well until large bubbles rise to the surface. You may permit this to stand covered and refrigerated for 1 hour and then beat it again. Have ready a hot ovenproof dish about 9 x 12, or hot muffin tins containing about ¼ inch hot beef drippings or melted butter. Pour in the batter. It should be about ⅝ inch high. Bake the pudding for about 20 minutes. ◗ Reduce the heat to 350° and bake it 10 to 15 minutes longer. Some cooks recommend a 350° oven for ½ hour or longer. Serve it at once.

EGGS, SOUFFLÉS AND TIMBALES

ABOUT EGG DISHES

Egg dishes are maids of all work in most households. They are nutritious, economical, usually quickly assembled and can be served in any number of appealing combinations—pleasing to the eye and to the palate. Every country in the world seems to have its own special knack of cooking eggs or combining them with something which brings up their flavor. The light, fluffy, golden omelet was born in France. East Indians like their eggs curried. And the Chinese, while partial to Eggs Foo Yoong, are reputed to be connoisseurs of vintage eggs.

To us, no egg dish can be good unless the eggs are "strictly fresh" and cooked with due regard for their delicacy and great sensitivity to heat. Let us not say of an egg, like the curate breakfasting with the bishop, "Oh, no, my Lord, parts of it are excellent!" For more details ♦ please read About Eggs (II, 179). Eggs and egg dishes can be served at any meal in the day: fried, scrambled, boiled, poached, baked or cooked in omelets or soufflés. And almost unlimited variations of meat, vegetables or fish may accompany or be folded into them. They are an excellent means of adding extra protein to a light meal, whether it be hot or cold.

♦ Always keep in mind that eggs must cook on very gentle heat. In combining eggs with soufflés and sauces let them partially cook on the stored heat in the pan. Do not put them back on direct heat—because they never will have as good a texture in sauces and will not function properly in soufflés.

SOFT, HARD-COOKED AND CODDLED EGGS

The difference in soft-cooked, hard-cooked and coddled eggs is more a matter of timing than method.

Place in a sauce pan, preferably glass or enamel:

    Unshelled eggs

Cover them with:

    Cold water

Put the pan over medium heat and bring the water to boiling point. ♦ Reduce the heat to below boiling point and let the water ♦ simmer. Now watch your time, which will depend on how large and how cold your eggs are. Allow the following times for 70° eggs. If they come right out of the refrigerator, you will have to add at least 2 minutes to the timing given below:

I. Soft-Cooked Eggs
Remove them from the water 2 to 3 minutes after you reduce the heat.

II. Medium-Soft-Cooked Eggs
Allow about 4 minutes after you reduce the heat.

III. Hard-Cooked Eggs
Allow about 15 minutes after you reduce the heat. Plunge the

finished hard-cooked eggs in cold water at once to arrest further cooking and to prevent the yolks from discoloring.

IV. Coddled Eggs

Place the eggs in boiling water by lowering them in gently with a tablespoon. Turn off the heat and cover the pan. Allow 6 minutes for delicately coddled eggs; 8 minutes for firmly coddled eggs; and 30 to 35 minutes for hard-cooked eggs. We repeat, plunge hard-cooked eggs, when done, into cold water. If you want the eggs to remain shapely, turn them several times within the first few minutes of coddling so that the white of the egg solidifies evenly in the air space and the yolk is centered.

♦ To shell hard-cooked eggs, crack the shell and roll the egg between the palms of the hands to free the thin tough skin from the egg and make shelling easier. If eggs are very fresh, they are more difficult to shell. If you want to slice the eggs smoothly, dip a knife in water before using.

Soft-cooked eggs may be served shelled, in the various ways suggested for Poached Eggs, opposite.

Recipes and suggestions for serving hard-cooked eggs follow. Others will be found in Hors d'Oeuvre and Salads.

SAUTÉED OR FRIED EGGS [4]

Melt in a skillet over low heat:
  1 or 2 tablespoons butter
Break into a saucer one at a time and slip from the saucer into the skillet:
  4 eggs
Baste the eggs with the hot butter. Cook them over a very low heat until they are done. To get a firm white ♦ cover the pan

with a lid at once. If you like a softer white, you may at once pour over the eggs:
  1 tablespoon boiling water
then cover the skillet and cook for about 1 minute. When the eggs are firm, serve them seasoned with:
  Salt and pepper

ADDITIONS TO SAUTÉED EGGS

It is the extras that often give punch to eggs, especially in brunch and luncheon dishes. Try eggs on a small mound of:
  Boiled rice, noodles, potatoes or rounds of toast
Pour over them:
  Well-seasoned leftover gravy
  Mushroom, tomato or onion sauce
  Canned Soup Sauce, page 375
  Cream sauce seasoned with mustard or curry powder, herbs, onion, celery, green peppers, capers, anchovies or cheese, Black Butter, page 383, with a few capers, or Brown Butter, page 383

POACHED EGGS

[Individual Serving]
I. Poached eggs, unless made in individual molds, are apt to produce "streamers" that you may trim off with scissors before serving.

Grease the bottom of a 6 to 8-inch pot. Put in enough slightly salted boiling water to fill to twice the depth of an egg. While the water comes to a boil, put in a small bowl:
  1 egg
Swirl the water into a mad vortex with a wooden spoon. Drop the egg into the well formed in the center of the pot. ♦ The

swirling water should round the egg. ◗ Reduce the heat. ◗ Simmer 4 to 5 minutes or let stand off the heat for 8 minutes. The white should be firm and the yolk soft by this time. Remove with a skimmer and drain well. If not using the egg immediately, plunge at once into cold water to stop the cooking. Repeat the process for each egg. To reheat the eggs, use hot—not boiling—water.

II. This method will produce a flattened poached egg rather than the rounded "egg-shaped" one described previously.
Put enough water to cover the eggs in a shallow skillet. Add:
        ½ teaspoon salt
        1 teaspoon vinegar
Bring to a boil. Break into a saucer:
        1 egg
Take the skillet from the heat and slip the egg into the hot water. Repeat the process for as many eggs as you require. Let the eggs stand in hot water for about 3 to 5 minutes, or until the white is firm. Remove with a skimmer and drain well. Eggs may be poached in a small amount of milk, cream or stock. If these liquids are used, omit the vinegar. For other additions, see below. To store for later use—but not later than 24 hours after the original cooking—put the poached eggs in a bowl of ice-cold water in the refrigerator. This is a good way to prepare eggs in advance for use the following day in Eggs Benedict, page 186, or any other recipe calling for poached eggs. The heat from platter, toast and sauce warms up the egg.

ADDITIONS TO POACHED EGGS

I. Arrange them in a shallow buttered baking dish.   •

Cover with:
        Sauce Mornay, page 361
Sprinkle with:
        Grated cheese
        Bread crumbs
and brown quickly under a hot broiler.

II. Cover the bottom of a shallow buttered baking dish with:
        Creamed Spinach,
        page 326
Arrange the poached eggs on the spinach and proceed as for Poached Eggs Mornay, above, to produce Eggs Florentine.

III. Hollow out a hard roll, insert egg, cover with Seafood Spaghetti Sauce, page 379, and garnish with cooked shrimp, mussels and oysters.

IV. Serve on toast, covered with Hunter's Sauce or Aurore Sauce, pages 366, 362.

V. Poach eggs in:
        Creole Sauce, page 380

EGGS POACHED IN   [4]
SOUP

The following recipe makes a good, attractive, light meal—prepared in a few minutes. Combine in an 8-inch skillet and heat to the boiling point over low heat:
        1 can tomato soup:
        10½ oz.
diluted with:
        ½ cup water
Add:
        (½ teaspoon dried basil)
        (¼ teaspoon sugar)
◗ Reduce the heat and keep the liquid below the boiling point. Add to the soup:
        4 eggs
◗ Simmer 4 to 5 minutes or until the eggs firm up. Serve the eggs on:
        Rounds of toast
covered with the soup. Sprinkle them with:
        Chopped parsley

EGGS POACHED IN [6] WINE

Combine in a skillet:
>1 cup dry red wine
>1 crushed clove garlic
>2 tablespoons minced onion
>   or shallot
>¼ teaspoon salt
>⅛ teaspoon pepper
>A Bouquet Garni
>   (II, 220)

Heat to boiling point ▶ reduce heat and simmer for about 3 minutes, then remove the bouquet garni. Slide into the wine from a saucer, one at a time:
>6 eggs

Poach them until the whites are firm. Remove and put them on:
>Slices of fried bread
>   (rubbed with garlic)

Strain the wine, put it back into the skillet and thicken with:
>Kneaded Butter,
>   page 357

Pour the sauce over the eggs.

EGGS BENEDICT [6]

Toast:
>6 rounds of bread or halves
>   of English muffins

Cover each with:
>A thin slice of cold or
>   hot ham, minced cooked
>   bacon or deviled ham

Top with:
>A Poached Egg, page 184

Serve them hot, covered with:
>Hollandaise Sauce,
>   page 369

POACHED EGGS [6] BLACKSTONE

Sauté, then mince:
>3 slices bacon

Reserve the drippings. Cut:
>6 slices tomato, ½ inch
>   thick

Season them with:
>Salt and white pepper

Dip the slices in flour. Sauté them in the bacon fat. Sprinkle them with the minced bacon. Cover each slice with:
>A Poached Egg, page 184

Pour over the eggs:
>Hollandaise Sauce,
>   page 369

SMOKED SALMON WITH EGGS

A good winter breakfast or luncheon dish. Perpare:
>Buttered toast or a slice
>   of pumpernickel bread

Dip into boiling water:
>Very thin slices smoked
>   salmon

Dry them. Place them on the toast. Cover them with:
>Poached or sautéed eggs

Sprinkle with:
>(Dill seed)

HUEVOS RANCHEROS [4] OR COWBOY EGGS

A traditional Spanish and Latin American dish. These eggs can be baked in the following sauce or poached or sautéed with the sauce poured over afterward. Heat in a skillet:
>¼ cup olive oil

and sauté in it for 5 minutes:
>1 crushed clove garlic

Remove the garlic and add, sautéing until soft:
>2 medium-sized finely
>   chopped onions
>1 large finely chopped
>   green pepper

Add:
>1 cup peeled, seeded and
>   chopped fresh tomatoes
>½ teaspoon salt
>¼ teaspoon freshly ground
>   black pepper
>2 teaspoons chili powder
>¼ teaspoon oregano
>⅛ teaspoon powdered
>   cumin

Simmer covered until thick and well blended.
>Correct the seasoning

The sauce should be very hot and well flavored. At this point, pour it over:

8 poached or sautéed eggs

allowing 2 eggs per serving.
Or, to bake, preheat oven to 450°.
Pour the sauce into a heatproof shallow dish or 4 individual casseroles and nest the uncooked eggs in the same. Garnish with:

Strips of red pimiento

Sprinkle with:

A little grated cheese

Bake until eggs are set. Serve with:

Hot Pepper Sauce, or
Mexican Sauce, page 378

ABOUT OMELETS

The name "omelet" is loosely applied to many kinds of egg dishes. In America, you often get a great puffy, soufflélike, rather dry dish in which the egg whites have been beaten separately and folded into the yolks. In France an entire mystique surrounds a simple process in which the egg is combined as unobtrusively as possible to avoid incorporating air and this marbleized mixture is quickly turned into a three-fold delicacy, filled or unfilled. In an Italian frittata, the food is often mixed at once with the stirred egg and this thin pancakelike mixture is cooked in a little oil, first on one side and then on the other, with a result not unlike a large edition of Eggs Foo Yoong, page 190.

Since omelet making is so rapid, see that you have ready everything you are going to serve the omelet with or on and be sure you have your diners captive. For more details about equipment, see French Omelet, following.

The quality that all of these so-called omelets have in common is that ♦ the pan and the fat in which they are cooked must be hot enough to form an envelope almost at once to hold together the softer egg layers above it, but not too hot to let it toughen before the rest of the egg cooks.

♦ Eggs, therefore, and any food incorporated with them, must be at least 70° before being put in the pan. More omelet failures are due to eggs used direct from the refrigerator than to any other cause. There is always, too, discussion about salting. As salt tends to toughen the egg structure, this flavoring can be allowed to come in the delicate tidbits added to the omelet.

Glazing omelets makes them look prettier but also tends to toughen them. ♦ To glaze an omelet, brush it with butter. Or, if it is a sweet omelet, sprinkle it with sugar and run it under the broiler briefly or use a hot salamander or brander. If you want a real finished job, put the omelet on an ovenproof server. Coat it lightly with a thin Mornay Sauce, page 361, and run it under a broiler for 2 minutes.

♦ To fill and garnish an omelet with mushrooms, seafood, ham, truffles or tongue, put them into the hot butter before the eggs are added. Creamed food, cheese, herbs, garlic or any foods demanding low heat go on top of the eggs the minute the eggs are added to the pan and before stirring begins. Have ready about ½ to ¾ of a cup of the mixture. Place ¼ cup on the upper half of the omelet. Reserve the remaining mixture for the final garnish on top. Or, a simple method is to fold the omelet as sketched on page 188, then cut an incision along the top and insert the hot food. For other fillings, see Additions for Scrambled Eggs, page 191.

ABOUT OMELET PANS

Much fuss is always made about an omelet pan. It is said that it should be kept for that purpose and that alone and should never be washed but simply rubbed with a handful of salt and soft toweling. The argument for a separate pan goes further. For not only should this surface smoothness be maintained, but any pan used for braising is apt to have developed hot spots. But those of us who resent giving kitchen space to a pan for one use only find an all-purpose skillet—cleaned with modern detergents—usable ▶ provided the pan surface is smooth so the eggs can slide freely over it. The pan should be heavy enough to be slowly but thoroughly heated. Otherwise the egg cannot stand what one French authority calls the too great brutality of the quick heat. The next thing to consider is the omelet in relation to the pan size. Since French omelets are made so quickly, we never try more than 2 to 3 eggs at a time—cooked in 1 tablespoon of sweet butter. If more than one omelet is needed, have some extra butter already melted to save preparation time. We use a skillet with a long handle and a 5-inch base flaring gently to a 7-inch top, as shown in the sketches. For larger omelets—and they can be made successfully with up to 8 to 10 eggs—see that the similarly-shaped pan is big enough to keep the egg no deeper than ¼ inch, and add a proportionate amount of butter.

FRENCH OMELET

▶ Please read About Omelets, page 187. Remember that an omelet of this type takes only 30 to 50 seconds to make, depending on your preference for soft or firm results. Mix briefly in a bowl with a dinner fork:

3 eggs

Put in a 7-inch omelet pan:

1 tablespoon clarified
sweet butter

To avoid sticking, clarified butter is best. Roll it over the bottom and sides of the pan. When it is hot and ▶ has reached the point of fragrance, but is not brown, pour in the eggs. Meanwhile, agitate the pan forward and backward with the left hand. Keep the egg mass sliding as a whole over the pan bottom. Quickly pick up a dinner fork and swirl the eggs with a circular motion, as shown on the left below. Hold the fork so the tines are parallel to, but not scraping, the base of the pan. At this point, the heat in the pan may be sufficient to cook the eggs and you may want to lift the pan from the heat as you gently swirl the eggs, as illustrated, in circular scrolls from the edges to the center. Pay no attention to the ridges formed by the fork. The rhythm of the pan and the stirring is like a child's trick of patting the head while rubbing the stomach. ♦ Have ready a hot serving plate —a heat-resistant one if you plan to glaze the omelet. A heated plate helps to inflate the omelet. To fold it—whether you fill, see page 188, or serve a plain omelet—grasp the handle of the pan so the right palm is up, as shown. Tip the pan down away from the handle and, with the fork, flip about one third of the omelet over, away from the handle, as shown in the center. If the omelet shows any tendency to stick, discard the fork and, by giving the pan handle a sharp rap or two with the fist, as sketched, the omelet will even flip over without the use of a fork and will start to slide. Quickly pick up the hot plate with the left hand. Slant the pan to 90° or more until the omelet makes a second fold in sliding out of the pan and lies with its ends folded under on the plate —ready to serve. Glaze and garnish if you wish and serve at once. For fillings, see About Omelets.

FLUFFY OR SOUFFLÉED OMELET [4]

If you have 1 or 2 extra egg whites, add these and omit the baking powder. You may add some grated Parmesan cheese or chopped parsley, chives and chervil to the egg mixture before cooking it, or sprinkle these on top before putting the omelet in the oven.

Combine and beat with a fork:

¼ cup milk
4 egg yolks
1 teaspoon any baking powder

Beat until stiff, but not dry:

4 egg whites

Melt in a heavy skillet over slow heat:

1 tablespoon butter

Fold the yolk mixture lightly into the egg whites. Pour the batter into the skillet. Cover the skillet with a lid. As the omelet cooks, slash through it several times with a knife to permit the heat to penetrate the lower crust. When the omelet is half done— after about 5 minutes—it may be placed uncovered on the center rack of a 350° oven until the top is set. Jet-propel this to the table as it comes out of the oven, as it will collapse quite quickly. Do not try to fold it as it will crack and become flat and tough. It may be garnished with any of the fillings or sauces suggested for a French omelet, or use poached, drained, chopped oysters. Serve it cut in pie-shaped wedges.

BAKED OMELET [4]

Preheat oven to 325°.
Beat until very light:

4 egg yolks
¼ cup sugar

Add:

½ teaspoon vanilla

Whip until stiff:

4 egg whites

Fold them lightly into the yolk mixture. Place these ingredients in a flat, 8-inch, round baking dish. Slash the top lightly. The soufflé should be about 1-inch high. Bake it until firm, about 25 minutes. Dust it with:

Powdered sugar

Warm and pour over it:

¼ cup rum, Cointreau or kirsch

Ignite the rum at table and let

it burn down. This may be
served with:

>Crushed sweetened
>berries

FIRM OMELET [4]

For the beginner, the texture of
this omelet is a little more man-
ageable.

Beat with a fork until blended:

>4 eggs

Beat in:

>¼ cup milk or cream
>½ teaspoon salt
>⅛ teaspoon paprika

Melt in a skillet:

>1½ tablespoons butter

When this is fairly hot, add the
egg mixture. Cook it over low
heat. Lift the edges with a pancake turner and tilt the skillet
to permit the uncooked custard
to run to the bottom or stick it
with a fork in the soft spots to
permit the heat to penetrate the
bottom crust. When it is all an
even consistency, fold the omelet over and serve it. The Japanese make a good omelet by
this rule, substituting stock for
milk or cream.

SWEET OMELET

See (II, 448) for other sweet
omelets.

I. Follow the preceding recipe
for:

>Fluffy Omelet

Add to the yolk mixture:

>1 tablespoon sugar

Just before serving spread the
omelet with:

>Jam or jelly

Sprinkle the top with:

>Confectioners' sugar

Fruit juice may be substituted
for the milk and the omelet may
be spread with cooked or raw
sweetened fruit instead of jelly.

II. Prepare:

>Fluffy Omelet, above

Add to the egg yolks:

>1 tablespoon brandy

>1 tablespoon curaçao

When finished, sprinkle with:

>Castor sugar

and Flambé, page 80.

SHRIMP EGGS FOO YOONG

Foo Yoong is really a rich omelet made with additions of
cooked vegetables, fish and
meat.

Clean or drain:

>2 cups bean sprouts

Heat:

>A little cooking oil

in a skillet and stir-fry, page
253, until translucent and crisp:

>1 slice minced gingerroot
>6 chopped green onions
>1 stalk thinly sliced celery
>1 cup shredded cooked
>fish or finely diced
>cooked meat

Have ready and combine with
the above ingredients:

>6 well-beaten eggs
>1 teaspoon salt
>½ teaspoon pepper

Heat an additional:

>1 tablespoon cooking oil

in another small skillet. Drop the
above mixture into it to form
small omelets, golden brown on
both sides. Serve with:

>Soy sauce

FRITTATA [3]

This Italian omelet usually has
the filling mixed into the eggs
before they are cooked. You
may use any of the suggested
fillings for the basic French
omelet, except the creamed or
sauced ones, allowing about 1
cup of filling to 3 eggs. The
frittata is usually turned when
the bottom has set firm.

Prepare and keep warm:

>2 cups diced cooked
>vegetables, chicken,
>seafood, ham, etc., in
>any combination

Beat with a fork until blended:

>6 eggs

Stir in the filling and

Correct the seasoning

How much salt and pepper you add will depend on how highly seasoned your filling is. Have ready a 10-inch greased omelet pan. Into another 10-inch pan which has been heated, put:

1½ tablespoons olive oil

Pour in the egg mixture and proceed as in the basic French Omelet, above, until the bottom of the frittata is set and the top is still like creamy scrambled eggs. Place the greased skillet with the greased side over the frittata like a lid. Reverse the position of the skillets so the ungreased side of the frittata falls into the lid, and this lid then becomes the skillet which is heated to complete the cooking of the dish, a matter of 1 to 2 minutes more. Serve at once on a hot platter.

SCRAMBLED EGGS [2]

Beaten egg whites may be added to whole eggs in the proportion of one additional white to 3 whole eggs.

Melt in a skillet over slow heat or in a well-greased double boiler ▶ over—not in—hot water:

1 tablespoon butter

Beat and pour in:

3 eggs
⅛ teaspoon salt
⅛ teaspoon paprika
(3 tablespoons cream)

When the eggs begin to thicken, break them into shreds with a fork or stir with a wooden spoon. When they have thickened, serve them on:

Hot toast lightly buttered or spread with fish paste, deviled ham or liver sausage; or in a hollowed-out hard roll

An attractive way to serve scrambled eggs is to put them in individual well-buttered ring molds while the eggs are still rather creamy in consistency. Let them finish cooking in their own heat, which will set them. Turn out and fill the center with any of the additions listed below.

ADDITIONS TO SCRAMBLED EGGS

Small amounts of the following may be stirred into the egg mixture before scrambling. They should be at least 70°.

Grated or crumbled cheese
Chopped, peeled, seeded, sautéed tomatoes flavored with basil
Cultured sour cream and chives
Canned chopped sardines
Crab meat, seasoned with curry powder
Capers
Chopped canned anchovies
Chopped sautéed onions
Crisp bacon bits
Small pieces of broiled sausage
Sautéed mushrooms
Poached calf brains

EGGS SCRAMBLED [4] WITH CREAM CHEESE

Melt in a double boiler over simmering water:

1 package cream cheese: 3 oz.
1 tablespoon butter

Scald and stir in:

1 cup cream

Add:

½ teaspoon salt
¼ teaspoon paprika

Break into the sauce:

6 eggs

Before the egg whites are firm, stir the eggs gently with a fork until thick. Add:

1½ tablespoons sherry

SCOTCH WOODCOCK [2]

Toast:

2 slices bread

Cut it into fingers. Butter well and spread with a thin layer of:

Anchovy paste

Beat together:

3 or 4 egg yolks

½ cup cream

⅛ teaspoon pepper

⅛ teaspoon salt

Melt in a double boiler:

2 tablespoons butter

Add the egg mixture and scramble until creamy. Arrange the anchovy toast on a hot dish and cover with the egg mixture. Garnish with:

Chopped parsley

SHIRRED OR BAKED EGGS OR EGGS EN COCOTTE

[Individual Serving]

Baked eggs always have great "eye appeal" served in little ramekins, casseroles or cocotte dishes. Care must be taken that they are not overcooked, as the white can become quite hard and rubbery and the ramekin will retain the heat and continue to cook the egg after it is removed from the oven. If you put a poaching paper, page 83, over the ramekin, this will return enough heat to the topside of the egg to set it. The centers should be soft, the whites just set. Don't try to hurry baked eggs; they must be cooked in gentle oven heat.

Preheat oven to 350°.

Grease small bakers or ramekins. Break carefully into each one:

1 egg

Add lightly:

Salt

Sprinkle over the top:

1 teaspoon cream or melted butter

Bake for about 8 to 10 minutes. You may garnish with:

Chopped or sliced truffles

Sautéed pieces of chicken liver

BAKED EGGS ON TOAST

[Individual Serving]

Carefully prepared, this makes a delicious dish.

Preheat oven to 325°.

Grease warmed individual molds with:

Butter

Place in each one:

1 teaspoon chopped celery, chives or parsley

Break into each one:

1 or 2 eggs

Season them with:

Salt and paprika

Cover each mold with a small poaching paper. Place the molds in a pan of hot water, deep enough to reach to within ½ inch of the top of the mold. Bake until the eggs are firm. Turn them out on:

Rounds of hot buttered toast

Serve them with well-seasoned:

Cream Sauce I, page 359, or Tomato Sauce, page 376

Or serve with one of the Additions to Baked Eggs, listed below.

ADDITIONS TO BAKED EGGS

For interesting variations to baked eggs try adding: cooked mushrooms, asparagus tips, tomatoes or other vegetables, such as creamed spinach. Or add chicken hash, small bits of bacon, sausage or anchovy. Or place a round of toast covered with Gruyère cheese in the bottom of the baker before the eggs are added. Instead of butter, you may also cover the eggs with a cheese or tomato sauce before baking. Other tasteful sauce additions are: one cup cream sauce flavored with 1 teaspoon prepared mustard; creamed mushrooms or canned soup—celery, mushroom, asparagus, etc. Dilute the latter with milk or water to the consistency of cream sauce. Eggs are also good baked in 1 cup or more of Creamed Onions, page 301.

EGGS IN A NEST [1 to 2]

A gala-looking dish:
Preheat oven to 350°.
Beat until very stiff.

> 2 egg whites

Heap them in a greased ovenproof dish. Make 2 cavities an equal distance apart, not too near the edge. Slip into them:

> 2 unbroken egg yolks

Bake for 10 minutes or until the eggs are set. Season with:

> Salt and white pepper

Sprinkle with:

> (Chopped chives)

EGGS BAKED IN BACON RINGS

[Individual Servings]
Preheat oven to 325°.
Sauté or broil lightly:

> Strips of bacon

Grease the bottom of muffin pans. Line the sides with the bacon. Place in each pan:

> (1 tablespoon chili sauce)

Drop into it:

> 1 egg

Pour over the egg:

> 1 teaspoon melted butter

Sprinkle with:

> Salt and paprika

Bake for about 10 minutes or until the eggs are set. Turn them out onto:

> Rounds of toast or slices of drained pineapple

Garnish with:

> Parsley

HAM CAKES AND EGGS [4]

Preheat oven to 325°.
Combine:

> 1 cup cooked ground ham

> 1 egg
> 1 tablespoon water
> ⅛ teaspoon paprika or pepper

Press these ingredients into 4 greased muffin tins. Leave a large hollow in each one. Drop into the hollows:

> 4 eggs

Bake the cakes until the eggs are firm. Turn out the cakes on:

> Rounds of toast

Garnish them with:

> Parsley or chopped chervil

HARD-COOKED EGG [5] AND VEGETABLE CASSEROLE

Preheat oven to 350°.
Combine:

> 1 cup cooked vegetables
> 1 cup Cream Sauce I, page 359
> 1 cup Creole Sauce, page 380

You may add:

> 2 teaspoons chopped fresh parsley, thyme, basil, etc.

Dill or celery seeds are wonderful. Prepare:

> 5 Hard-Cooked Eggs, page 183

Slice them. Grease a baking dish. Place alternate layers of eggs, etc., and sauce in the dish. Top with:

> Au Gratin III, page 389

Bake for about 15 minutes.

CURRIED EGGS [4]

An occasional curry dish is a treat.
Cook:

> 6 Hard-Cooked Eggs, page 183

Shell and slice them or cut them in half, lengthwise. Prepare:

> 2 cups Curry Sauce I or II, page 363

You may pound and add:

> (¼ cup blanched almonds)

Add the eggs. Heat them well. Serve on:

                    Hot buttered toast
garnished with:
            Parsley

CREAMED EGGS AND   [6]
ASPARAGUS COCKAIGNE

We use both versions of this, depending on the time at hand.
The texture is lovely if the asparagus is well drained and the
sauce is not overheated.
I. Drain well and cut in 1-inch
pieces:
            2 cups cooked or canned
              asparagus tips
Reserve the liquid. Have ready:
            6 hard-cooked, shelled,
              sliced eggs
Prepare:
            2 cups Quick White Sauce,
              page 360
using milk and the reserved asparagus liquor. When the sauce
is hot, gently fold in the asparagus and sliced eggs. Either heat
this further in the top of a
double boiler ◗ over—not in—
hot water or preheat oven to
350° and place in a baker. Cover
with:
            Au Gratin I, page 389
and bake until the eggs and
asparagus are heated through.
Serve with:
            Slices of ham
            Hot French Bread
            (II, 245)

II.   [4]
Preheat oven to 350°.
Have ready:
            4 to 6 sliced hard-cooked
              eggs
        1½ cups well-drained canned
              asparagus, cut in 1-inch
              lengths
            1 can cream of chicken
              soup
diluted with:
            ¼ cup asparagus liquor
Place in 4 individual baking
dishes. Alternate layers of eggs
and asparagus. Cover each dish
equally with soup mixture. Cover

and bake about 15 minutes or
until thoroughly heated.

CREAMED EGGS   [4]
AU GRATIN

Preheat broiler.
Slice into a baking dish:
            4 hard-cooked eggs
Combine:
        1½ cups Cream Sauce II,
              page 359
            ¼ cup chili sauce
Pour this mixture over the eggs.
Top with:
            Au Gratin II, page 389
Place the dish under the broiler
until the crumbs are golden.

SCOTCH EGGS

[Individual Servings]
Preheat deep fryer to 375°.
◗ Please read About Deep-Fat
Frying, pages 75–79.
Some people use pork sausage
meat, bound with egg and bread
crumbs for the coating. Make a
forcemeat with:
            Finely chopped or
              minced cooked ham
        2 or 3 mashed anchovies
              in oil
            Fresh bread crumbs
            Salt
            Pepper
Coat thickly with the forcemeat:
            Hard-cooked eggs
Bind with:
            Raw egg
Dip in:
            Egg and bread crumbs
Deep fry until the coating is
brown. Slice in half and serve
on:
            Croutons

MASKED EGGS

[Allow 1 Egg to a Person]
Chill and shell:
            Hard-Cooked Eggs,
              page 183
Cut them into halves, lengthwise. Place them cut side down
on:

Water cress or shredded
lettuce
Pour over them:
Mayonnaise thinned with
a little lemon juice or
cream, Mayonnaise
Collé, page 387, or
Chaud-Froid Sauce,
page 388
Sprinkle them with:
Capers, chopped
anchovies, bits of ham
or cooked bacon

STUFFED EGGS ON ROSETTES WITH SAVORY SAUCE [8]

This dish is elaborate, but capable of prefabrication. The rosettes, the sauce and eggs may be made the day before they are served.
Prepare:
8 hard-cooked eggs
Cut them crosswise into halves.
Remove the yolks. Combine them with an equal part of:
Cooked, finely chopped
seasoned spinach or
Creamed Spinach,
page 326
Fill the egg whites with the mixture. Prepare:
2 cups Cream Sauce I,
page 359
Season it with:
2 tablespoons
Worcestershire sauce
2 tablespoons dry sherry
¾ cup chili sauce
Salt and pepper
When the sauce is smooth and hot, add:
2 cups cooked or canned
shrimp or diced cooked
sweetbreads
Prepare:
16 Rosettes, page 209
Place a stuffed egg half on each rosette and cover with sauce. Serve them at once or, if you have made the sauce and the rosettes ahead of time, reheat the sauce in a double boiler.

Reheat the rosettes in a 400° oven.

PICKLED EGGS

Prepare:
6 hard-cooked eggs
Shell and stick into each egg:
4 cloves—24 in all
Boil:
2 cups vinegar
Make a smooth paste of:
½ teaspoon ground mustard
½ teaspoon salt
½ teaspoon pepper
with a little cold vinegar and add to the boiling vinegar. Stir for about 1 minute. Put the eggs in a glass fruit jar and pour the boiling vinegar over them. Cover and refrigerate for about 2 weeks. Use with cold cuts and in salads.

DEVILED OR STUFFED EGGS

The blandness of hard-cooked eggs is a challenge to adventurous cooks and a few suggestions to vary this basic ingredient with supplies from your pantry shelves follow:
Prepare:
Hard-Cooked Eggs,
page 183
Shell the eggs. Cut them in half lengthwise or slice off both ends, which leaves a barrel-shaped container. Remove yolks carefully so as not to damage the whites. Crush the yolks without packing them and moisten them pleasantly with:
French dressing or
mayonnaise, sweet or
cultured sour cream,
soft butter with vinegar
and sugar, lemon juice
or sweet pickle juice
Season to taste with:
Salt and paprika
Or one or more of the following:
A little dry mustard
Catsup
A dash of cayenne, curry,

or hot pepper sauce
Worcestershire sauce
Exotic additions to the yolks are:
Anchovy or sardine paste
Liver sausage paste or
foie gras
Chopped sautéed chicken
livers
Chopped ginger and
cream cheese
Chutney
Caviar
Smoked salmon
Deviled ham or tongue
Grated Roquefort
Chopped chives,
tarragon, chervil, parsley,
burnet or basil
Garnish with:
Olives, capers or truffles
Put the filling back in the whites.
You may use a pastry tube for
elaborate effects. Remove from
the refrigerator ½ hour before
serving for improved flavor and
texture.

DEVILED EGGS [4]
IN SAUCE

Preheat oven to 425°.
Prepare:
4 Deviled Eggs, page 195
Place the halves in a greased
dish. Pour over them:
1 cup Tomato Sauce, page
376, Mornay Sauce, page
361, Béchamel Sauce,
page 360, or Mushroom
Sauce, page 367, or a
Shrimp Sauce for Fish,
page 377
Coat the sauce with:
Au Gratin II or III,
page 389
Bake the dish until the top is
brown.

ABOUT SOUFFLÉS AND
TIMBALES

The soufflé is considered the
prima donna of the culinary
world. The timbale is her more
even-tempered relative. On
closer acquaintance, both become quite tractable and are
great glamorizers for leftover
foods. ♦ Cooked foods are best
to use, as they release less moisture into the mixture than do
raw ones.

The soufflé is usually based
on a Béchamel or cream sauce,
the timbale often on cream and
eggs only. The timbale may
seem the more fragile of the
two, but ♦ steaming—the distinctive process in the timbale—
gives this custardlike dish much
more stamina. The soufflé, which
is baked ♦ must always be kept
away from drafts and be served
at once in the ovenproof straight-
sided dish in which it is cooked.

A timbale is made in a mold
and can be reversed onto a
hot dish or into a pastry shell
that was previously baked and
cooled. It looks particularly attractive in a ring mold. It is
often coated or served with a
sauce. If a delay is even a possibility, turn your ingredients
into a timbale, which will even
submit to the indignity of reheating.

If your guests are assembled,
prepare a soufflé. If not it may
be like the beauty Horace Wal-
pole commented on: "She is
pretty with the bloom of youth
but has no features and her
beauty cannot last."

ABOUT SOUFFLÉS

Soufflés have the same kind of
life as the "breath" for which
they are named, some slightly
longer than others, but with a
predictable endurance for puffi-
ness. If well made, you can
count on about 10 short minutes
in a holding oven ♦ but beware
of drafts. Since they ♦ depend
on egg white and steam for their
ascent ♦ no second should be
wasted from the beating of the
whites until the soufflé is popped
quickly into the ♦ preheated

oven. With very few exceptions, every action, including ▶ immediate serving after baking, should contribute to hold their "breath" as long as possible. These tours de force, based on cream sauce with egg yolks and whipped whites, are easy to make if the pointers are carefully heeded. The cream sauce should be a rather firm one ▶ heated just to a boil. Remove it from the heat for ½ minute before the 70° eggs and any other ingredients —also at 70°—are added. The egg whites should be ▶ stiff, but not dry (II, 180). ▶ Soufflés can always be made lighter if an extra egg white is added for every 2 whole eggs.

▶ To prepare soufflé dishes for baking, use a straight-sided ovenproof baker. Grease the bottom and sides well with butter and then coat the buttered surfaces with a thorough dusting of flour, sugar or dry grated cheese—depending on the flavor of your soufflé. It will also climb up the sides of an ungreased baker, but it will not rise as high and the lovely brown crust will stick and have to be scraped off the sides rather than form a glossy coating which adds so much to the look of the individual serving.

Next, be sure the oven is heated to the indicated temperature. ▶ A soufflé needs quick bottom heat. ▶ If your electric oven has a top element, be sure to remove it, as the heat in it is often enough to stiffen the top surface of the soufflé too quickly and not allow for its fullest expansion during the baking period. ▶ For oven placement of soufflé bakers, see sketch, page 100. Some recipes suggest making soufflés in the top of a double boiler ▶ over—not in—hot water. This is advisable only if an oven is not available, as the resulting texture is closer to

a timbale than a soufflé. ▶ To make a soufflé with a crown— a "high-hat soufflé"—just before putting the soufflé into the oven take a large spoon or a rubber scraper and run a groove about 1½ inches deep all around the top, about 1¼ inches from the edge of the dish. A crown may also be made by extending the height of the baker with a piece of parchment paper tied firmly around the dish. We find this satisfactory only with so-called cold soufflés based on cream gelatins (II, 449).

MADE-IN-ADVANCE CHEESE SOUFFLÉ [6]

Preheat oven to 475°.
You can mix this soufflé as much as 3 hours before baking time, if you like, and set in the refrigerator. Remove it about 20 minutes before putting it in the preheated oven.
Prepare a 10-inch soufflé baker, opposite.
Melt:
　½ cup butter
in a double boiler ▶ over—not in—boiling water. Add:
　½ cup sifted flour
　1½ teaspoons salt
　½ teaspoon paprika
　　Dash cayenne or hot
　　pepper sauce
Mix well. Gradually stir in:
　2 cups milk
Cook ▶ stirring constantly until sauce is thick. Dice:
　½ lb. sharp cheddar cheese
Stir in cream sauce until cheese melts. Remove from heat. Beat until light:
　8 egg yolks
▶ Gradually pour yolks into cheese sauce, stirring constantly. Wash beater. Beat ▶ until stiff, but not dry:
　8 egg whites
Fold cheese sauce into egg whites. Pour mixture into baker and refrigerate if you wish. Bake

10 minutes. ◗ Reduce heat to
400° and bake 25 minutes longer.
Serve with:

> Tossed Green Salad,
> page 33, or Grapefruit
> and Orange Salad, page
> 55

⅄ BLENDER   [4 to 5]
CHEESE SOUFFLÉ

A somewhat firm but acceptable
soufflé. ◗ To prepare baker,
please read About Soufflés,
page 196.
Preheat oven to 325°.
Dice into cubes:

> 6 oz. sharp cheddar cheese

Heat to just below boiling:

> 1½ cups milk

Pour the milk into blender container and quickly add:

> 2 teaspoons butter
> 6 to 8 pieces crustless
> bread, torn into large
> pieces
> ½ teaspoon salt
> ⅓ teaspoon pepper or a
> few grains of cayenne
> (⅛ teaspoon mustard)

Blend until thickened. Add the
cubed cheese. Beat in a large
bowl until lemon colored:

> 4 egg yolks

Add the blended cheese mixture
◗ very slowly, beating constantly. Beat until stiff, but not
dry and fold in gently:

> 4 egg whites

Place the mixture in a prepared
8-inch soufflé baker and bake
about 50 minutes or until set.

ADDITIONS TO CHEESE
SOUFFLÉS

For a more complete dish, consider adding one of the following to cheese soufflé:

> ½ cup ground or finely
> chopped ham
> ½ to 1 cup cooked,
> well-drained and
> chopped or ground
> vegetables, such as
> celery or carrots

> 3 tablespoons Italian
> tomato paste

CHEESE SOUFFLÉ   [4]
COCKAIGNE

Preheat oven to 350°.
◗ Please read About Soufflés,
page 196.
Prepare:

> 1 cup Cream Sauce II,
> page 359

Bring to a boil. Remove from
heat ½ minute. Add, stirring
well:

> 5 tablespoons grated
> Parmesan cheese
> 2 tablespoons grated
> Gruyère cheese
> 3 beaten egg yolks

Fold into the cheese mixture.
Pour into one 7-inch or 4 individual ◗ prepared soufflé bakers.
You may decorate the soufflés
before baking with:

> Paper thin slices of Swiss
> cheese cut into fancy
> shapes

Bake for about 25 to 30 minutes
or until set.

VEGETABLE SOUFFLÉ   [4]

Preheat oven to 350°.
Cooked oyster plant, eggplant,
cauliflower, peas, onions, carrots,
celery, canned or fresh asparagus, etc., may be used alone or
in any good combination. Small
quantities of leftover vegetables
may be combined with minced
raw carrots, celery and onions.
Prepare:

> 1 cup Cream Sauce II,
> page 359: ⅓ cup cream
> and ⅔ cup vegetable
> stock

When the sauce is boiling, stir
in:

> 1 cup minced drained
> vegetables

When the vegetables are hot,
reduce the heat and add:

> 3 beaten egg yolks

Cook and stir for 1 minute
longer to permit the yolks to

thicken. Season as required with:

> Salt and pepper
> (Nutmeg)

Cool this mixture slightly. Whip until stiff, but not dry:

> 3 egg whites

Fold them lightly into the vegetable mixture. Bake the soufflé in a greased 7-inch baking dish for about 40 minutes or until firm. If you wish a dish that is a course in itself, serve the soufflé with:

> Mushroom Sauce, page 367

CORN SOUFFLÉ

Follow the preceding recipe. Use in place of the minced vegetables:

> ¾ cup well-drained corn, canned or cooked, cut from the cob

Add:

> (1 chopped pimiento)
> (1 chopped green pepper)

ONION SOUFFLÉ [4]

One of our pet accompaniments to an otherwise slim meal.
Preheat oven to 325°.
Prepare:

> 1 cup Steamed Onions, page 301

Drain and mince them. Melt:

> 2 tablespoons butter

Stir in until blended:

> 2 tablespoons flour

Combine and stir in slowly:

> ½ cup milk
> ½ cup evaporated milk or cream

When the sauce is smooth and hot, stir in the minced onion. When the onions are hot ♦ remove from the heat and stir in:

> 3 beaten egg yolks

Cook ♦ but do not boil, and stir for about 1 minute longer to permit the yolks to thicken. Season with:

> Salt, paprika and nutmeg
> 2 tablespoons chopped

parsley or ½ teaspoon dried basil

Cook these ingredients slightly. Whip until stiff, but not dry:

> 3 egg whites

Fold them lightly into the onion mixture. Bake the soufflé in a greased or prepared 7-inch baker until it is firm, about 40 minutes.

SWEET POTATO AND [6] PINEAPPLE OR APPLESAUCE SOUFFLÉ

This is fine with cold or hot ham.
Preheat oven to 350°.
Prepare:

> 3 cups Boiled Sweet Potatoes, page 322

Add and beat with a fork until the potatoes are fluffy:

> 3 tablespoons butter
> ½ teaspoon salt
> ½ teaspoon grated lemon rind
> 2 beaten egg yolks

Drain well and fold in:

> ½ to ¾ cup drained crushed pineapple or tart applesauce

Cool these ingredients slightly. Whip until stiff and fold in:

> 2 egg whites

Bake the soufflé in a greased 7-inch baker for about 40 minutes.

EGGPLANT SOUFFLÉ

Preheat oven to 325°.
Prepare:

> A Stuffed Eggplant, page 292

Combine the cooked mashed pulp with:

> ¾ cup soft bread crumbs
> 2 beaten egg yolks
> 1 tablespoon melted butter
> ½ cup chopped nut meats or grated cheese
> Salt and pepper
> Grated nutmeg

If the filling seems stiff, add:

> 1 tablespoon or more milk

Beat until stiff but not dry:
  2 egg whites
Fold them lightly into the other
ingredients. Fill the shells. Cover
the tops with:
  Buttered crumbs or
    cornflakes
Place them in a pan with a little
water and bake for about 30
minutes.

CHICKEN SOUFFLÉ

[16 Individual Soufflés]
This soufflé makes a good luncheon dish, as it has more "body"
than most of the other soufflé
recipes. Serve in individual
bakers.
▶ Please read About Soufflés,
page 196.
Preheat oven to 325°.
Mince:
  2¼ cups cooked chicken
Prepare:
  3 cups Cream Sauce II,
    page 359
using chicken fat to replace the
butter and stock or cream as the
liquid. When the sauce is hot,
stir in the minced chicken and:
  1 cup chopped nut meats
  1 cup chopped cooked
    vegetables or raw celery,
    carrots and onions
When these ingredients are hot,
remove from the heat and add:
  9 beaten egg yolks
Season with:
  Salt and pepper
  Nutmeg
Let cool slightly. Whip ▶ until
stiff, but not dry:
  9 egg whites
Fold them lightly into the
chicken mixture. Pour until ⅔
full into prepared soufflé bakers,
page 196. Bake until firm, about
20 to 25 minutes. Serve the
soufflé with:
  Mushroom Sauce, page
    367, or
  Poulette Sauce, page
    362, etc.

LEFTOVER CHICKEN   [5]
SOUFFLÉ

A glamorous way to use chicken
leftovers.
Preheat oven to 325°.
Prepare:
  1 cup Cream Sauce II,
    page 359
using Chicken Stock and cream
for the liquid. When the sauce
is hot, add:
  1 cup solids: minced
    chicken, nut meats,
    minced and drained
    cooked vegetables
Remove from the heat and add:
  3 beaten egg yolks
Season with:
  Salt and pepper
  Freshly grated nutmeg
Let cook slightly. Whip ▶ until
stiff, but not dry:
  3 or 4 egg whites
Fold them lightly into the
chicken mixture. Bake the soufflé
in a prepared 8-inch baker until
firm, about 40 minutes.

COOKED FISH OR   [4]
MEAT SOUFFLÉ

▶ Please read About Soufflés,
page 196.
Preheat oven to 325°.
Prepare:
  1 cup Cream Sauce II,
    page 359
When it is smooth and hot, stir
in:
  ¾ to 1 cup flaked cooked
    fish: tuna, crab, clams,
    lobster, shrimp, etc., or
    finely chopped, cooked
    meat
  ¼ cup finely chopped raw
    carrots, celery and
    parsley
When these ingredients are hot,
remove from the heat and stir
in:
  3 beaten egg yolks
Season with:
  Salt and paprika
  Nutmeg
  Lemon juice, Worcester-

shire sauce or tomato
catsup
(⅓ cup sliced olives)
Let cool slightly. Whip ♦ until
stiff, but not dry:
  3 to 4 egg whites
Fold them lightly into the mixture. Bake in a greased 7-inch
soufflé baker until firm, about 40
minutes. Serve the soufflé with:
  (Tomato Sauce, page
  376)

OYSTER SOUFFLÉ   [4]

This soufflé is very delicate.
Preheat oven to 325°.
Drain, but save the liquor from:
  ½ to 1 pint oysters
Dry on a towel. Prepare:
  1 cup Cream Sauce II,
  page 359, using part
  cream and part oyster
  liquor
When it is hot, remove from
heat and add the oysters. Add:
  3 beaten egg yolks
Season with:
  Salt and pepper
  Nutmeg
  (Lemon juice)
Let cool slightly. Whip ♦ until
stiff, but not dry:
  3 to 4 egg whites
Fold them lightly into the oyster
mixture. Bake in a ♦ prepared
7-inch soufflé baker until firm,
about 40 minutes.

SHAD ROE SOUFFLÉ   [4]

♦ Please read About Soufflés
and Timbales, page 196.
Preheat oven to 375°.
Poach for 3 to 5 minutes:
  1 fresh shad roe
Remove outer integument and
veins. Crumble the roe and combine it with:
  2 beaten eggs
  1 cup whipped cream
  A grating of nutmeg
  Correct the seasoning
Fill individual molds ¾ full of
this mixture. Set molds in a pan

of hot water. Bake about 25
minutes. Serve with:
  Allemande Sauce, page
  362, or
  Béarnaise Sauce,
  page 370

ABOUT TIMBALES

♦ Please read About Soufflés
and Timbales, page 196.
  Butter individual or larger
molds lightly. Fill them about
two-thirds full with the timbale
mixture. ♦ Place them on a rack
in a pan of hot, but not boiling,
water. The water should be as
high as the filling in the molds.
If a rack is not available, fold
several thicknesses of paper and
place the molds on it. ♦ Check
the heat occasionally to make
sure that the water around the
mold never boils—just simmers.
  It is wise to protect the top of
the timbale with a poaching
paper, page 83.
  Bake the timbales in a ♦ moderate oven, about 325°, for
about 20 to 50 minutes, depending on the size of the mold.
The timbales are done when a
knife blade inserted in the center of the mold comes out un-
coated.

CUSTARD FOR   [4]
VEGETABLE TIMBALES

In France the salad is served
with the meat course and the
vegetable is served in solitary
state. It is usually worthy of this
exalted position. Sometimes it is
accompanied by a mound or
ring of delicious custard.
Preheat oven to 325°.
Combine and beat with a wire
whisk:
  1½ cups warm cream or ½
  cup cream and 1 cup
  chicken stock
  4 eggs
  ¾ teaspoon salt
  ½ teaspoon paprika

(⅛ teaspoon grated nutmeg
 or celery salt)
(1 tablespoon chopped
 parsley)
(A few drops onion or
 lemon juice)

To bake, unmold and serve, see
About Soufflés and Timbales,
page 196. Serve the timbales
with:

Creamed vegetables or
Mushroom Sauce,
page 367

For a brunch, garnish with:
Crisp bacon
Parsley

LEFTOVER   [5 to 6]
TIMBALES

Use any good combination of
cooked vegetables and meat.
Preheat oven to 325°.
Follow the rule for:

Custard for Vegetable
Timbales, above

using milk instead of cream.
Omit the seasoning. Cut into
small pieces and add:

1 to 1½ cups leftover food
(Chopped parsley)
(Grated onion)

After the food has been added
to the timbale mixture, season
it to taste. If the food is dry, no
additional thickening is needed.
If it is slightly moist, add to the
leftovers, before combining them
with the custard, until they
form a moderately thick paste:

Cracker crumbs or bread
crumbs

To bake, unmold and serve, see
About Soufflés and Timbales,
page 196. Serve with:

Tomato Sauce, page 379

BROCCOLI OR   [5 to 6]
CAULIFLOWER TIMBALES

Preheat oven to 325°.
Prepare:

Custard for Vegetable
Timbales, page 201

Add to the custard:
1 to 1½ cups cooked well-
drained broccoli or
cauliflower, chopped or
put through a food mill

Add seasoning if required. To
bake, unmold and serve, see
About Soufflés and Timbales,
page 196. Garnish with:

Hollandaise Sauce,
page 369

MUSHROOM   [5 to 6]
TIMBALES

Preheat oven to 325°.
Prepare:

Custard for Vegetable
Timbales, page 201

Add:
2 cups drained, chopped,
sautéed mushrooms

To bake, unmold and serve, see
About Soufflés and Timbales,
page 196.

SPINACH   [5 to 6]
TIMBALES

Preheat oven to 325°.
Prepare:

Cream Sauce I, page 359

Add to it:
2 cups cooked, drained,
finely chopped spinach
3 beaten eggs
½ cup grated cheese
¼ cup Veal Stock or other
stock (II, 142)
Salt and pepper
A few grains cayenne

To bake, unmold and serve, see
About Soufflés and Timbales,
page 196.

CORN, EGG AND   [4]
CHEESE TIMBALES

Preheat oven to 325°.
Combine:

1⅓ cups canned cream style
corn
½ cup grated Swiss cheese
2 to 3 beaten eggs
¼ teaspoon salt
⅛ teaspoon paprika
¼ teaspoon mustard
A few grains cayenne

To bake, unmold and serve, see About Soufflés and Timbales, page 196.

ASPARAGUS TIMBALES [4]

Wonderful balanced by a fruit or vegetable salad.
Preheat oven to 325°.
Grease 4 deep custard cups or a 7-inch ring mold. Place around the sides of each container:
>3 to 5 well-drained canned or cooked asparagus tips, heads down

Fill the cups with:
>Custard for Vegetable Timbales, page 201

To bake, unmold and serve see About Soufflés and Timbales, page 196. Place between the inverted timbales:
>Hollandaise Sauce, page 369

Garnish them with:
>Parsley

and surround them with:
>Broiled or boiled link sausages

CHEESE TIMBALES OR CRUSTLESS QUICHE

Preheat oven to 325°.
Prepare the filling for:
>Cheese Custard Pie, page 214

To bake, unmold and serve, see About Soufflés and Timbales, page 196. Good served with:
>Green peas, spinach or broccoli

RICE TIMBALES

A good garnish for a fish platter.
Preheat oven to 350°.
Pack greased molds with leftover:
>Vegetable Rice, page 164
>Pilaf, page 166
>Curried Rice, page 159, or
>Spanish Rice, page 160

Bake them in a pan of hot water

for 10 minutes. Invert them and garnish with:
>Parsley

Serve with:
>Onion Sauce, page 363

CHICKEN OR HAM TIMBALES [6]

Preheat oven to 325°.
Grind twice or blend:
>2 cups cooked white chicken meat or 1 cup each chicken and cooked ham

Stir into it very slowly to form a paste:
>¾ cup cold thick cream
>¼ teaspoon salt
>⅛ teaspoon paprika

Whip until stiff:
>4 egg whites

Fold them lightly into the chicken mixture. Line greased timbale molds with:
>(Pieces of truffles, ripe olives or pimiento)

To bake, unmold and serve, see About Soufflés and Timbales, page 196. Serve them with:
>Mushroom Sauce, or chicken gravy with chopped parsley

CHICKEN LIVER TIMBALES [4]

Very light and delicate.
Preheat oven to 325°.
Put through a ricer, grinder or blender:
>¾ cup cooked chicken livers
>½ cup Boiled Rice, page 158

Add:
>A scant ¼ teaspoon salt
>A few grains cayenne and nutmeg
>½ teaspoon prepared mustard

Whip until stiff:
>2 egg whites

In a separate bowl, whip until stiff:
>¼ cup whipping cream

Fold these ingredients lightly

into the chicken-liver mixture. To bake, unmold and serve, see About Soufflés and Timbales, page 196. Serve with:

Mushroom Sauce, page 367, or
Poulette Sauce, page 362

VEAL TIMBALES [4]

Preheat oven to 325°.
Grind twice or blend:

1¼ cups cold cooked veal

Beat slightly and add:

3 egg yolks

Stir the ingredients well. Our French recipe says pound them in a mortar. Continue to stir while adding:

⅓ cup whipping cream
¼ cup dry white wine or
2 tablespoons lemon juice
⅛ teaspoon paprika
Salt, as needed

Beat until stiff:

3 egg whites
(¼ teaspoon mace)

Fold these into the other ingredients. To bake, unmold and serve, see About Soufflés and Timbales, page 196. Serve with:

Mushroom Sauce, page 367, or
Tomato Sauce, page 376

FISH TIMBALES [5 to 6]

Preheat oven to 325°.
Flake and chop until very fine:

2 cups cooked fish

Season it with:

¼ teaspoon salt
⅛ teaspoon paprika
½ teaspoon grated lemon rind
1½ teaspoons lemon juice

Whip until stiff:

½ cup whipping cream

In a separate bowl, whip until stiff:

3 egg whites

Fold the cream into the fish mixture, then fold in the egg whites. To bake, unmold and serve, see About Soufflés and

Timbales, page 196. Serve them with:

Shrimp Sauce, page 377,
Béchamel Sauce, page 359, or Tartare Sauce, page 349

FISH TIMBALES OR [6] MOUSSE

Cooked fish may be substituted, but uncooked fish gives a better result.
♦ Please read About Soufflé and Timbales, page 196.
Preheat oven to 350°.
Grind, put through a ricer or ⅄ blend:

1 lb. uncooked fish: 2 cups

Heat over a low burner:

1½ tablespoons butter

Stir in, until blended:

1 tablespoon flour

Stir in:

¼ cup milk

♦ Remove from heat. Beat and stir in:

2 egg yolks

Season these ingredients with:

½ teaspoon salt
⅛ teaspoon paprika

Stir the yolk mixture for 1 to 2 minutes. Permit it to thicken slightly. Add the ground fish. Cool the mixture. Whip ♦ until stiff, but not dry:

2 egg whites

Whip until stiff:

1 cup whipping cream

Fold these ingredients lightly into the fish mixture. Garnish a greased 9-inch ring mold with:

Strips of pimiento
(Strips of green pepper)

Pour the fish mixture into the mold. Set the mold in a pan of hot water. Bake it for about ½ hour. Serve it with:

Hollandaise Sauce, page 369
Hot Shrimp Sauce, page 377
Horseradish Sauce, page 362
Oyster Sauce, page 361

SPINACH OR BROCCOLI [4] RING MOLD

♦ Please read About Soufflés and Timbales, page 196.
Preheat oven to 325°.
Have ready:

    1 cup cooked spinach or broccoli

Drain, chop until fine, put through a purée strainer or ✕ blend. Melt in a skillet:

    3 tablespoons butter

Add and sauté for about 1 minute:

    1 tablespoon chopped onion

Stir in until blended:

    3 tablespoons flour

Combine and stir in slowly:

    ½ cup milk or Stock (II, 141)
    ½ cup cream or evaporated milk

When the sauce is boiling, stir in the spinach. Remove from heat and stir in:

    3 beaten egg yolks

Cook and stir for about 1 minute longer to permit the yolks to thicken. Season with:

    Salt and pepper
    Nutmeg
    (½ cup grated cheese)

Cool slightly. You may add just for looks:

    A few drops green coloring

Whip until ♦ stiff, but not dry:

    3 egg whites

Fold them lightly into the spinach mixture. Place these ingredients in a greased 7-inch ring mold set in a pan of hot water. Bake the mixture until it is firm, about 30 minutes. Invert it on a platter and serve it filled with:

    Creamed Mushrooms, page 296
    Some other creamed dish

CELERY ROOT RING [6] MOLD

♦ Please read About Soufflés and Timbales, page 196.
Preheat oven to 325°.
Cook, page 283:

    4 medium-sized celery roots

Drain them well. Put them through a grinder, using a coarse knife, or through a ricer. Soak:

    2 slices white bread

in:

    3 tablespoons milk

Stir this into the celery and add:

    2 tablespoons melted butter
    1 teaspoon grated onion
    2 tablespoons cream
    4 beaten egg yolks
    ¾ teaspoon salt
    ½ teaspoon paprika
    A fresh grating nutmeg

Whip until ♦ stiff, but not dry:

    4 egg whites

Fold them into the celery mixture. Bake the mixture in a greased ring mold set in a pan of hot water for about 45 minutes. Invert it onto a hot plate. Fill the center with:

    Buttered peas, sautéed mushrooms, etc.

CHESTNUT RING [4] MOLD

A delightful way to use chestnuts—the egg white lightens the consistency of the mixture.
♦ Please read About Soufflés and Timbales, page 196.
Preheat oven to 325°.
Combine:

    2 tablespoons flour
    1 teaspoon salt
    ¼ teaspoon paprika
    1 cup riced Boiled Chestnuts, page 283
    ½ teaspoon grated onion

Add gradually:

    ½ cup milk

Stir and cook these ingredients over low heat for about 5 minutes. Cool slightly. Whip until ♦ stiff, but not dry, then fold in:

    3 egg whites

Bake the mixture in a 7-inch ring mold set in a pan of hot water for about ½ hour. Invert

it onto a hot plate. Fill it with:
>   Buttered green peas
>   Chopped parsley

It may be served with:
>   Mushroom Sauce, page
>   367

to which add:
>   2 tablespoons dry sherry

MUSHROOM RING [8] MOLD WITH SWEET-BREADS OR CHICKEN

♦ Please read About Soufflés and Timbales, page 196.
Preheat oven to 325°.
Parboil, page 537:
>   1 pair sweetbreads or use
>   1 cup cooked minced
>   chicken

Remove the skin and membrane and mince the sweetbreads. Prepare:
>   1 cup Cream Sauce II,
>   page 359

Melt in a pan:
>   2 tablespoons butter

Add and sauté for about 3 minutes:
>   2 slices onion

Remove the onion. Add to the pan:
>   1½ cups finely minced
>   mushrooms

and the sweetbreads or chicken. Heat the cream sauce to the boiling point and combine it with the mushroom mixture. Remove from heat and stir in:
>   ¼ cup dry bread crumbs
>   1 chopped pimiento
>   ¼ teaspoon salt
>   2 beaten egg yolks

Cook and stir about 1 minute longer to permit the yolks to thicken. Cool these ingredients slightly. Whip until ♦ stiff, but not dry:
>   2 egg whites

Fold them lightly into the mushroom mixture. Place the mixture in a greased ring mold set in a pan of hot water and bake covered with a piece of buttered paper for 35 minutes or until

firm. Invert the mold onto a platter and serve filled with:
>   Asparagus spears
>   Peas, etc.

and pass with:
>   Suprème Sauce, page 363

STEAMED VEAL MOLD [8]

The following is an excellent pudding.
Combine:
>   1½ lbs. ground veal
>   ½ lb. ground pork
>   1½ cups finely rolled cracker
>   crumbs
>   3 egg yolks
>   ¾ cup milk
>   ¼ teaspoon nutmeg
>   1 tablespoon melted butter
>   1 tablespoon onion juice
>   1¼ teaspoons salt
>   ¼ teaspoon pepper
>   ¼ cup chopped celery
>   ⅛ cup chopped parsley

Beat until ♦ stiff, but not dry:
>   3 egg whites

Fold them into the other ingredients. Grease a pudding mold, fill it with the mixture, close it tightly and steam for 2½ hours. ♦ Please read about Steamed Puddings (II, 463). Serve with:
>   Mushroom Sauce, page
>   367, or
>   Poulette Sauce, page 362

or with the always admirable:
>   Quick Tomato Sauce,
>   page 376

HALIBUT RING MOLD [4]

♦Please read About Soufflés and Timbales, page 196.
Preheat oven to 350°.
Combine and cook to a paste:
>   1 cup bread crumbs
>   ½ cup cream

When it is hot, add:
>   ½ lb. finely chopped raw
>   halibut

Season with:
>   teaspoon salt

⅛ teaspoon paprika

Cool these ingredients slightly. Whip until ▶ stiff, but not dry:

2 egg whites

Fold them lightly into the fish mixture. Place the mixture in a 7-inch buttered baking dish; set it in a pan of hot water. Bake it for about 40 minutes. Serve with:

Oyster Sauce, page 361, or

Poulette Sauce, page 362

Garnish with:

Tomatoes

Water cress

BRUNCH, LUNCH AND SUPPER DISHES

This is a chapter, we admit, for which we have a special fondness. In it, we call attention to the many delicious ways you can combine those foods you have already cooked, as well as the staples in your larder—whether they are dried, preserved, canned or frozen. Do not neglect other combinations in the egg, pasta and cereal chapters. From many of these recipes attractive meals may be prepared in less than half an hour's time.

Care in cooking, distinction in seasoning and presentation, can make even a tin of tuna memorable. The large gratinéed casserole, the individual lidded baking dish or one of the following cases for food—as well as garnishes made from simple materials—all lend distinction in making a quick dish a gracious one.

Keep in mind that many fresh fish and shellfish recipes are almost as rapidly cooked as those involving a preprocessed food. For other quick dishes, refer also to the section on Ground Meats, page 514, Variety Meats, page 534, and Vegetables, page 249. For the quickest of sauces, see Soup-Based Sauces, page 375.

ABOUT CASES FOR FOOD

We have left behind the era of trenchers—those coarse loaves that served as dishes and were eaten when empty by trenchermen. But none of us has lost a taste for the sauce-flavored pastry, pancake, tortilla or toast. All manner of creamed foods—meat, vegetable or fish mixtures, cheese concoctions, as well as farces and stews can be placed in one of the following cases and then served with a sauce.

Patty Shells (II, 304)
Popovers (II, 283)
Brioches (II, 258)
Rounds of buttered and toasted bread or French Toast (II, 290)
Rusks lightly buttered and heated
A loaf of bread that has been hollowed, buttered lightly and toasted in a 300° oven
A Rice Loaf, page 161
Pies or Tart Shells (II, 292)
Large or individual Noodle Rings, page 173
Large or individual Rice Rings, page 162
A Pastry Roll, page 311
Biscuits or Shortcakes (II, 283)
A Mashed Potato Ring, page 311
A Bread Dressing Ring, page 225
Stuffed Pancakes (II, 113)
Waffles (II, 118)
Noodle Baskets or Potato Baskets, page 319
Stuffed vegetables
Sandwich Loaf (II, 52)
Barquettes (II, 54)
Turnovers (II, 54)
Leaf Wrappings, page 85

Coconut shells
Sea shells
And the 9 recipes that follow.

ROLL CASES

Preheat oven to 300°.
Hollow out:
Small rolls
Spread the hollows with:
Melted butter
Toast in the oven until crisp.

BREAD CASES

Preheat oven to 300°.
With a biscuit cutter make
rounds from:
1¼-inch-thick slices of bread
With a smaller cutter, press out
an inner round, but do not let
the cutter go beyond 1 inch
deep. Hollow out these smaller
rounds and brush the hollows
with:
Melted butter
Toast in the oven until crisp and
golden.

MELBA TOAST BASKETS

Preheat oven to 275°.
Lightly butter on both sides:
Thin crustless bread slices
Press them into muffin tins, letting the corners of the bread
protrude slightly. Toast in the
oven until crisp and golden.

ROSETTES

[About Thirty-Six 2½-inch
Rosettes]
Rosettes are shaped with a small
iron made for the purpose. They
are very good served as a base
for creamed chicken or sweetbreads. For dessert, serve with
sweet sauce, stewed fruit or
alone with coffee.
▶ This batter makes a thinner,
crisper confection if it is allowed
to rest refrigerated for 2 hours
or more.
Beat until blended:
2 eggs
Add and beat:

¼ teaspoon salt
1 tablespoon sugar
If the rosettes are to be used as
patties, omit the sugar. Sift before measuring:
1 cup all-purpose flour
Stir it into the egg mixture, alternately with:
1 cup milk
2 tablespoons melted butter
To deep fry rosettes, prepare the
iron by immersing the head of
it in deep fat. You can use a
rather small deep pan, slightly
larger than the head of the iron,
with about 2½ inches of fat in
it. Heat the fat to 375°. Dip the
hot iron in the batter, but do
not let it run over the top of the
iron, for then it is difficult to
get the rosette off when cooked.
Return the batter-coated iron to
the fat, immersing it completely

from 20 to 35 seconds. Remove
the rosette with a fork. Reheat
the iron in the deep fat and
repeat the process. Drain the
rosettes on absorbent paper and,
if served as a dessert, dust with:
Confectioners' sugar

TIMBALE CASES
FOR FOOD

Select a timbale iron that is
fluted, see above. It is easier to
handle than a plain one.
Sift:
¾ cup all-purpose flour
½ teaspoon salt
Combine and beat:
1 egg
½ cup milk
Combine the liquid and the

sifted ingredients with a few swift strokes. Add:

1 teaspoon olive oil or melted butter

Let the batter stand for 1 hour to avoid bubbles which disfigure the timbales. For a crisper, thinner case, rest the batter 2 hours or longer covered and refrigerated. To fry timbale cases, prepare the iron by immersing its head in deep fat. Heat the fat to 370°—hot enough to brown a cube of bread in 1 minute. Wipe the iron with a cloth wrapped around a fork. Plunge the iron into the batter, within ¾ inch of the top. Remove it. Allow the batter to dry slightly on the iron. Fry the timbale in the hot fat until it is golden brown, about 1 to 1½ minutes. Remove it from the iron and drain it on a paper towel. Repeat the process.

ABOUT MEAT PASTRIES

How we'd love to judge a competition of housewives, each turning out her native meat pastry! The doughs would range from the resilient to the flaky, with fillings running a full gamut of flavor. They would include: Won Ton, Ravioli, Kreplach, Piroshki, Rissoles, Enchiladas, Pot Pies. It is in such homely functional dishes, varied according to the season and by the individual cook, that the true cuisine of a country dwells. Many of these specialties call for precooked fillings which, already encased, need only a brief cooking of the dough and reheating of the filler, either by simmering in a broth, deep-fat frying, sautéing or baking.

Take your pick of the recipes following and those in hors d'oeuvre and soup garnishes. Size often dictates their placement in the menu.

◗ Cooking method will deter-

mine whether or not to vent the pastry. A baked meat pie will need a vent. Some cooks leave a hole in the center by which to add more gravy, if necessary. Others just prick the surface to allow the steam to escape and to prevent a soggy crust. If simmered like Won Ton, page 112, or fried like Rissoles (II, 54) do not vent. If covering a stew with biscuits, allow steam to escape by leaving spaces between the biscuits. This wide spacing also applies to dumpling toppings.

TURNOVERS, PIROSHKI [6] OR ROLLS FILLED WITH MEAT, ETC.

Preheat oven to 450°.

This recipe and the following one make excellent hot canapés. For canapés cut the dough into small, attractive shapes. For hot luncheon sandwiches, make them a more generous size. If prepared in advance, keep them chilled until ready to bake.

Prepare, using about 2 cups of flour:

Biscuit or Pie Dough (II, 283, 292)

Pat or roll it until thin. This is a matter of taste—about ¼ inch for biscuit dough, ⅛ inch for pie dough. Cut it into 3 x 3-inch squares or rounds. Place a filling on each piece of dough—as much as they will hold properly. Moisten the edges, fold over and pinch down with a fork. Place the triangles or crescents in a pan. Brush them lightly with:

(Soft butter)

Bake them until the dough is done, about 20 minutes. This may be served with:

Brown Sauce, page 365

Fillings
I. Lightly moisten:
Ground or minced cooked meat

with:

> Gravy or cream, Brown
> Sauce, page 365, or
> canned Soup Sauce,
> page 376

Season it well with:

> Salt and pepper
> Worcestershire sauce
> or chili sauce

II. Moisten braunschweiger sausage with chili sauce or tomato soup.

III. Use:

> 1½ cups cooked ground ham
> ½ cup Cream Sauce II,
> page 359
> thick cream or
> evaporated milk
> 2 tablespoons chopped
> pickles
> 1 tablespoon chopped onion
> 1½ tablespoons catsup
> Salt and pepper, if needed

IV. Sauté gently until yellow:

> 2 cups chopped onions

in:

> 2 tablespoons olive or
> anchovy oil

Add:

> ¼ cup or more chopped
> ripe olives
> 6 or 8 chopped anchovies

V. Use any good cooked seafood filling and taste before seasoning.

MEAT PIE ROLL OR PIN WHEELS   [4]

Preheat oven to 450°.
This is a palatable, quickly made, everyday dish—an attractive way to serve a small quantity of leftover meat.
Use one of the fillings given in the previous recipe.
Use the recipes on (II, 283, 293), or a biscuit mix to make:

> Biscuit Dough or Pie
> Dough: use 2 cups of
> flour

If you use biscuit dough, make it a little drier than for ordinary biscuits, otherwise it will be difficult to handle. Roll it until very thin. Cut it into an oblong. Use a pastry brush and brush it lightly with:

> 1 egg white or soft butter

This will keep the crust from being soggy. Spread the dough with the meat filling, being careful to leave about 1 inch at the sides uncovered. Begin to roll it loosely. Moisten the end with water and plaster it down. Moisten the sides and pinch them together. Bake the roll until it is done, about 20 minutes. Or cut the roll into ¾-inch slices. Place the slices in a lightly greased pan. Dot the tops with:

> Butter

This roll may be prepared in advance and placed in the refrigerator until ready for use. Bake the slices until the dough is done. Serve them very hot with:

> Brown Sauce, page 365,
> or Tomato Sauce, page
> 376

MEAT SHORTCAKES

[10 Cakes]
Preheat oven to 350°.
Prepare, omitting the sugar:

> Fluffy Biscuit Dough
> (II, 286)

If a richer dough is desired, use an additional tablespoon of butter. Combine:

> ¼ cup cream
> ¾ cup deviled ham

Ground cooked ham or other meat may be substituted. In that case ¼ teaspoon prepared mustard, 2 teaspoons minced onion or other seasoning may be added. Roll out the dough on a lightly floured board to the thickness of ¼ to ⅓ inch. Spread ½ of it with the ham mixture. Fold over the other ½, so that the ham is between the layers

of dough. Cut the dough with
a biscuit cutter. Bake the cakes
for about 15 minutes until done.

QUICK CHICKEN OR
BEEF POT PIE

Preheat oven to 400°.
An easy dish if you have precooked chicken or beef and precooked pie crust shells. We find
the precooked shell more convenient and tastier than the
crust which has to be exposed
to long, slow cooking.
Have ready:
> A baked Pie Shell
> (II, 296)
formed to fit your casserole or
individual bakers. Heat:
> Creamed chicken,
> Chicken or Turkey
> Hash, page 226, or
> Beef Hash, page 223
Fill the shell with the meat
filling and top with:
> A prebaked pie topping,
> Biscuit Dough (II, 284),
> or slices of bread
> buttered on both sides
Bake until thoroughly heated
and the top is light brown.

CORN BREAD   [6]
TAMALE PIE

Preheat oven to 425°.
This can be prepared up to the
point of adding the corn bread
topping; then cooled and refrigerated until 45 minutes before
serving time. Place the casserole
in the oven and let it warm
while you are mixing the corn
bread topping.
Sauté in a lightly greased skillet:
> 1 pound ground beef
> 1 chopped onion
When the meat is lightly
browned and the onion translucent, add:
> 1 can tomato soup
> 1 cup water or stock
> ¼ teaspoon pepper
> 1 teaspoon salt
> 1 tablespoon chili powder

> 1 cup drained whole kernel
> corn
> ½ cup chopped green
> pepper, seeds and fiber
> removed
Simmer for 15 minutes. Meanwhile, sift and mix together:
> ¾ cup corn meal
> 1 tablespoon flour
> 1 tablespoon sugar
> ½ teaspoon salt
> 1½ teaspoons baking powder
Moisten with:
> 1 beaten egg
> ⅓ cup milk
Mix lightly and fold in:
> 1 tablespoon cooking oil
Place meat mixture in a greased
2-quart casserole and cover with
the corn bread topping. The
topping will disappear into the
meat mixture, but will rise during baking and form a good
layer of corn bread. Place in
oven and bake for about 20 to
25 minutes or until corn bread
is brown.

CHINESE EGG ROLLS

[6 Servings or 12 Egg Rolls]
Egg rolls are frequently used for
hors d'oeuvre or you may serve
them as the main dish at luncheon. The pancake-like skins are
available at Chinese grocery
stores, although in an emergency
you may make a thin Won Ton
dough, page 112, or use the
follʌwing:
Sift into a bowl:
> 1 cup flour
Beat in:
> 2 eggs
> ½ teaspoon salt
Add gradually to make a thin,
smooth batter:
> 2 cups water
Grease a 6-inch-diameter skillet
and put over ♦ low heat. Beat
the batter again and pour 1
tablespoon into the pan. Let it
spread over the surface of the
pan to form a very thin, flexible
pancake. When it shrinks away

from the sides, turn it and let it set on the other side. Do not let it become brown or crisp. Remove each pancake to a dish when done and cover all with a damp cloth until ready to use. You may prepare the filling the day before, as it should be chilled before being enclosed in the pancake envelope. Bring to a boil in ½ cup water, then drain:

>   ½ cup finely chopped celery
>   ¾ cup shredded cabbage

Heat in a skillet:

>   3 tablespoons salad oil

Stir-fry, see page 253, for 3 minutes:

>   ½ cup diced cooked shrimp
>   ½ cup diced cooked pork

Add and stir-fry for 5 more minutes:

>   4 finely chopped scallions
>   ½ cup drained and finely
>   chopped water chestnuts
>   1 minced clove garlic
>   ¼ cup soy sauce

Place 4 tablespoons of filling in rectangular shape on the center of each pancake and fold up envelope-style, sealing the last flap with a paste made of:

>   1 tablespoon flour
>   2 tablespoons cold water

Preheat deep fryer to 375°. Fry rolls until golden brown. Or fill a deep skillet with oil about 1 inch deep up the sides and fry the egg rolls until golden brown. Serve with:

>   Chinese Mustard
>   Soy sauce
>   Chinese Sweet-Sour
>   Sauce I, page 371

PIZZAS

These Italian pies—pizza is the Italian word for pie—have become very popular luncheon and supper dishes. The pizza began as a use for leftover bread dough. The Italians sometimes use pastry as the base and, in an emergency, we have successfully used sliced English muffins. A slice of cheese over the whole first—before the sauce—keeps it from getting soggy. To make pizza dough, mix as for Bread (II, 243), using the following ingredients, but do not let it rise a second time:

>   4 cups sifted flour
>   1 cake yeast in 1⅓ cups
>   85° water
>   2 tablespoons salad or
>   olive oil
>   1 teaspoon salt

Knead for 10 minutes. Cover with damp cloth and let rise about 2 hours. Have ready two oiled 12-inch pizza pans. Pat and stretch the dough in the pans, pinching up a collar around the edge to hold the filling. Prick dough in about 6 places.

Preheat oven to 400°.

Spread each pizza with your preferred filling and rest it for about 10 minutes. (At this stage the pizzas may be frozen for at least a week before baking.) Bake for about 25 minutes until light brown and serve at once very hot.

I. Spread the pizza with:

>   (A thin slice of cheese)
>   Thickened Tomato
>   Sauce, page 376, or
>   Italian Tomato Paste,
>   page 377

Arrange on top:

>   12 to 14 anchovies or sliced
>   Italian sausage,
>   pepperoni, Prosciutto
>   ham or Salami

Sprinkle with:

>   Orégano
>   Olive oil
>   Chopped parsley
>   (Parmesan or Romano
>   cheese)

II. Use a highly seasoned:

>   Meat Sauce for Spaghetti,
>   page 378, or other meat
>   pasta sauce

Cover with a layer of:
> Fontina or Mozzarella
> cheese

III. Use as a base:
> Thickened Tomato
> Sauce, page 376

Add:
> 1 cup chopped or sliced
> mushrooms

IV. Cover the base with:
> Lightly sautéed onions
> Black olives
> Anchovies

Brush with:
> Olive oil

ENCHILADAS

[About 2 Dozen]
Preheat oven to 350°.
Have ready:
> Baked tortillas

In a heavy saucepan, heat:
> 2 tablespoons olive oil

Sauté until golden:
> ½ cup chopped onion
> 1 minced clove garlic

Add:
> 2 teaspoons to 1 tablespoon
> chili powder
> 1 cup tomato purée
> ½ cup chicken or beef stock

Season with:
> Salt and pepper
> 1 teaspoon cumin

Spread some sauce over the tortillas and fill the centers with equal quantities of:
> Chopped raw onion
> Chopped Mozzarella
> cheese

Roll the tortillas and place in an ovenproof dish. Pour more sauce over the tops and sprinkle with:
> Chopped Mozzarella
> cheese

Heat thoroughly about 15 minutes in the oven.

ABOUT QUICHES

Early recipes for Quiche called for bacon and cream, but gradually cheese was added. When

sautéed onions were included, the dish was called Alsacienne. Cool the onions before adding them.

Quiche makes a hefty brunch or an hors d'oeuvre baked in tiny tarts no larger than the lining of muffin tins. As it is always served lukewarm, time it accordingly. Following are several variations on a Quiche theme.

QUICHE LORRAINE　　[6]

Preheat oven to 375°.
Prepare a 9-inch pie shell of:
> A Pie Crust (II, 293)

Brush it with:
> The white of an egg

and prick it well. Slice in 1-inch lengths:
> ¼ lb. sliced bacon

Cook the bacon in a heavy skillet, stirring constantly, until the fat is almost rendered out but the bacon is not yet crisp. Drain on absorbent toweling. Scald to hasten the cooking time:
> 2 cups milk or cream

Cool slightly, then beat together with:
> 3 whole eggs
> ¼ teaspoon salt
> ⅛ teaspoon white pepper
> A fresh grating of nutmeg
> 1 teaspoon chopped chives

Sprinkle in the bottom of the pie shell the bacon and:
> ½ cup diced Swiss cheese

Pour the custard mixture over it. Bake 35 to 40 minutes or until the top is a golden brown. For safety, you may test as for Custard (II, 436).

CHEESE CUSTARD PIE　　[4]

Preheat oven to 325°.
In Switzerland we had a vile-tempered cook named Marguerite. Her one idea, after being generally disagreeable, was to earn enough to own a small chalet on some high peak where she could cater to moun-

tain climbers. While she was certainly not born with a silver spoon in her mouth—although it was large enough to accommodate several—she did arrive with a cooking spoon in her hand. If she has attained her ideal, many a climber will feel it worth while to scale a perilous peak to reach her kitchen. The following Cheese Custard Pie was always served in solitary state. Its flavor varied with Marguerite's moods and her supply of cheese. It was never twice the same, as she had no written recipe, but we have endeavored to make one like hers, for it would be a pity to relegate so good a dish to inaccessible roosts.

Prepare and bake:

> An 8-inch baked Pie
> Crust (II, 293)

It should be at least 2 inches deep. When cool, brush with:

> Egg white

Scald:

> 1¾ cups milk or cream

Reduce the heat and add:

> 1 cup grated cheese

Stir until the cheese is melted. Add:

> ½ teaspoon salt
> ¼ teaspoon paprika
> ½ teaspoon grated onion
> A few grains cayenne

Remove the mixture from the heat and beat in, one at a time:

> 3 eggs

Fill the pie crust and bake it until the custard is firm, about 45 minutes.

ONION SHORTCAKE [6]

Preheat oven to 425°.
Peel and slice:

> 10 medium-sized white
> onions

Sprinkle them with:

> ½ teaspoon salt

Melt in a saucepan:

> 3 tablespoons butter

Add the onions. Cover and sim-

mer until they are tender. Cool them. Prepare ½ the amount on (II, 286):

> **Fluffy Biscuit Dough**

omitting the sugar.
Spread the dough in a deep greased ovenproof dish. Cover it with the cooked onions. Add:

> ¼ teaspoon paprika
> 2 teaspoons chopped
> parsley
> (¼ cup diced cooked ham)
> A grating nutmeg or
> white pepper

Prepare:

> 1 cup Cream Sauce I,
> page 359

Beat into the sauce:

> 1 egg

Pour the sauce over the onions. The top may be sprinkled with:

> ¼ cup grated cheese

Bake the cake for about 20 minutes or until the dough is done.

ONION OR LEEK PIE

Preheat oven to 450°.
Richer and more sophisticated than the preceding Onion Shortcake. Serve Onion Shortcake with a meat course. Have Onion Pie as a main dish with a green salad.
Line a 9-inch pie pan with:

> Pie Dough (II, 293)

Prick and chill it. Skin and slice thinly:

> 2½ lbs. Bermuda onions or
> leeks

Melt in a heavy saucepan:

> 3 tablespoons butter

Add the onions. Stir and cook them over low heat until they are clear. Cool them well. Combine and heat slowly until blended:

> 3 eggs
> 1 cup cultured sour cream
> ¼ cup dry sherry
> 1 teaspoon salt
> ¼ teaspoon freshly ground
> pepper
> (1 tablespoon minced fresh

herb or 1 teaspoon dill
or celery seed)
Stir this mixture into the onions.
Brush the bottom of the cooled
pie shell with:

1 slightly beaten egg white
Fill it with the slightly cooled
onion mixture. Place over the
top:

(4 strips bacon cut into
squares)
(Small cooked link
sausages)

Bake the pie in a 450° oven for
10 minutes. ♦ Reduce the heat
to 300° and bake the pie until
the crust is light brown, about
½ hour. Serve it piping hot.

QUICK TOMATO TART [6]

Preheat oven to 350°.
Have ready:

6 baked, unsweetened,
2½-inch tart shells
(II, 296)

Slice ½ inch thick:

3 peeled seeded fresh
tomatoes

Mix and heat well:

¼ cup sautéed sliced
mushrooms
¼ cup canned cream of
chicken soup
¼ cup Italian tomato purée
¼ teaspoon sugar
¼ cup softened liver sausage
4 large chopped stuffed
olives
2 teaspoons fresh chopped
basil
¼ teaspoon salt

First place a layer of this hot
sauce in each tart shell, then a
tomato slice. Cover with the remaining hot mixture. Dust each
tart with:

Grated Parmesan cheese
Heat the filled tarts on a baking
sheet in the oven for about 15
minutes or until well heated.

MIXED VEGETABLE GRILL

A good Lenten dish if you omit
the bacon and sausages.

Preheat broiler.
Cut into slices:

Tomatoes
Brush them with:

Melted butter
Season them with:

Salt and pepper
Brown sugar
Prepare for cooking:

Mushrooms
Brush them with:

Melted butter or heavy
cream
Season them lightly with:

Salt
(Lemon juice)
Grease the broiler. Place on it
the tomato slices, mushrooms
and:

(Sliced bacon)
(Sausages)
Broil these ingredients until they
are done. Meanwhile sauté or
poach:

Eggs
Serve the eggs on a hot platter,
surrounded by the grilled food.
Garnish the platter with:

Parsley, olives, radishes,
etc.

ROAST BEEF IN SAUCE [4]

I.
Cut into ½-inch cubes:

2 cups cooked roast beef
Prepare:

Hot Cumberland Sauce,
page 372
Add the beef and heat the sauce,
but do not boil. Serve at once
on:

Hot toast

II. Prepare:

Creole Sauce, page 380,
or Curry Sauce II, page
363
Arrange very thin slices of:

Cooked roast beef
on a hot platter. Pour the hot
sauce over them. Sprinkle the
top with:

Chopped parsley or
chopped chives

BOEUF MIROTON

Make a sauce by melting:

2 tablespoons butter

Sauté in it until golden:

1 coarsely sliced onion

Sprinkle over all and mix rapidly with a wooden spoon:

1 tablespoon flour

Add and stir until boiling:

1 cup bouillon
Salt and pepper

Reduce the heat and add:

1 to 2 teaspoons vinegar

Simmer about 15 minutes. Arrange on a heatproof platter:

Thin slices of boiled or roasted beef

Cover the slices with the above hot sauce. Keep on low heat for about 20 minutes and serve.

DEVILED LEFTOVER MEAT

Preheat broiler.

Spread:

Cooked sliced meat

with:

Prepared mustard or catsup

Roll the slices in:

Buttered bread crumbs

Broil them until browned. Serve the meat with:

Leftover gravy, Piquant Sauce, page 367, or Brown Onion Sauce, page 366

CREAMED LEFTOVER [6] VEAL

Melt in a chafing dish or electric skillet:

¼ cup butter

Add and sauté for about 5 minutes:

½ lb. sliced mushrooms
¼ cup diced green pepper, seeds and membranes removed

Add and stir well:

¼ cup flour

Pour over the mixture and stir until thickened:

½ cup cream
1 cup veal or chicken stock

Correct the seasoning and add:

2 cups diced cooked veal
2 tablespoons minced pimiento
¼ teaspoon marjoram
½ cup dry white wine

Simmer about 5 minutes longer and serve over:

Rice, noodles or macaroni

Garnish with:

Chopped parsley

VEAL AND SPINACH DISH

Preheat oven to 425°.

Place in a casserole a 1-inch layer or more of:

Creamed spinach

which has been delicately flavored with a little:

Grated onion

Place over it:

Slices of roast veal or lamb, etc.

If you have gravy, pour a little of it over the meat or use a little thick cream. Cover the top with:

Au Gratin III, page 389

Bake the dish until the top is brown. Garnish it with:

Parsley

COOKED CURRIED [4] VEAL OR LAMB AND RICE

This combination of meat, apple and curry is luscious. Peel and slice:

1 cup onions
(½ cup celery)

Core, peel and slice:

2 medium-sized apples

Melt in a saucepan:

3 tablespoons butter

Add:

½ to 1 teaspoon curry powder

Caution: use only ½ teaspoon curry to begin with if you are unfamiliar with it. Add the onions and apples and sauté until the onions are tender. Re-

move them from the pan. Brown
lightly in the pan about:
  2 cups sliced or diced
    cooked veal or lamb
Remove it from the pan. Stir
into the pan juices:
  2 teaspoons flour
Stir in slowly:
  1 cup Stock (II, 141)
When the sauce is smooth and
boiling, add the onions, apples
and meat. Stir in:
  1 tablespoon lemon juice
    Correct the seasoning
and serve the meat with:
    Steamed or boiled rice

LAMB TERRAPIN   [4]

Cut into dice:
  2 cups cold cooked lamb
Chop or rice:
  2 hard-cooked eggs
Combine the lamb, the eggs and:
  2 tablespoons olive oil
  1 tablespoon lemon juice
Melt:
  2 tablespoons butter
Stir in until blended:
  3 tablespoons flour
  1 teaspoon dry mustard
Stir in slowly:
  2 cups lamb stock or milk
Add:
  1 teaspoon Worcestershire
    sauce
    Salt, as needed
Cook and stir the sauce until it
is boiling. Add the lamb and
egg mixture. Heat the terrapin
thoroughly. Serve it on:
    Hot toast

CHOP SUEY OR   [4]
CHOW MEIN

These vaguely Chinese dishes
which can be made with cooked
pork, chicken or seafood, differ
in that Chop Suey is served over
steamed rice, and Chow Mein
over fried noodles. They resemble some Chinese porcelain patterns originally made strictly for
export. To get the feeling of
true Chinese food, read Mrs.

Buwei Yang Chao's delightful
"How to Cook and Eat in Chinese."
Cut into 2-inch julienne strips
about ¼ inch in section:
  2 cups cooked pork roast
Slice diagonally, see page 484:
  ½ cup celery with tender
    leaves
  ½ cup green onions
  1 cup mushrooms
Chop coarsely:
  1 green pepper, seeds and
    membrane removed
Drain:
  1 cup bean sprouts
Heat well in a deep heavy skillet:
  2 tablespoons cooking oil
Stir-fry, page 253, the onion and
celery for about 3 minutes. Then
add the mushrooms, pork, peppers and the bean sprouts. Continue to stir-fry for 2 to 3
minutes longer. Then add:
  (½ cup fresh, peeled, seeded,
    and slivered tomatoes)
    Jellied juices from the
    roast or a bit of Meat
    Glaze (II, 145)
  1 cup strong consommé
Season with:
    Salt and pepper
  1 tablespoon soy sauce
  3 tablespoons dry sherry
You may thicken the juices with:
    Cornstarch
Serve at once.

LEFTOVERS IN BACON

Preheat oven to 450°.
Measure:
    Cooked ground meat,
    meat loaf, etc.
Add ⅓ this measure of:
    Boiled Rice
Moisten it lightly with:
    Gravy or cream
Season it well with:
    Salt and pepper
    Minced onion or onion
    juice
Roll the mixture into small balls,

flatten them slightly and wrap around them:

Slices of bacon

Secure the bacon with toothpicks. Place the patties in a greased pan or dish and bake them until the bacon is crisp, about 15 minutes. Serve them with:

Tomato Sauce, page 376

HAM LOAF WITH COOKED HAM [6]

Preheat oven to 350°.
Combine:

2 cups cooked ground ham
1 cup bread or cracker crumbs or crushed cornflakes
2 eggs
2 tablespoons grated onion
⅛ teaspoon pepper
1 cup milk
2 tablespoons chili sauce
2 to 4 tablespoons chopped parsley or celery

Bake these ingredients in a greased loaf pan for about 45 minutes. Serve the loaf with:

Tomato, Horseradish, Mustard, Mushroom or some other sauce, page 367

STUFFED HAM ROLLS [4]

I.

Make these when you have leftover rice. Preheat oven to 400°.
Trim:

8 thin slices baked or boiled ham

Spread them lightly with:
Mustard

Place on each slice part of the following filling. Combine:

1½ cups cooked rice
⅓ cup chopped raisins
1 beaten egg
¼ teaspoon paprika
½ teaspoon Worcestershire sauce
(¼ cup chopped celery)
(½ teaspoon basil)

Roll the slices and secure them with toothpicks. Brush them with:

Milk

Bake the rolls until they are thoroughly heated. Serve them with:

Hot Cumberland Sauce, page 372

II. Prepare, as for above:
Slices of ham

Place on each side:
4 asparagus tips

Roll, brush and heat the ham, as directed. Serve the rolls with:

1½ cups Cheese Sauce, page 364

III. [4]

Preheat oven to 350°.
Prepare, as for above:
8 large slices ham

Combine and mix well:
¾ cup cultured sour cream
1 cup sieved creamy cottage cheese
1 slightly beaten egg
¼ cup minced onions
½ cup drained chopped cooked spinach
½ teaspoon dry mustard
¼ teaspoon salt

Place about 2 tablespoons filling on each slice of ham. Roll and tuck in the edges. Put in a shallow baking dish and cover with the following mixture:

1 can cream of mushroom soup: 10½ oz.
¼ cup cultured sour cream

Bake for 20 to 25 minutes.

GROUND HAM ON PINEAPPLE SLICES [4]

Preheat oven to 400°.
Combine:

1 cup cooked ground ham
1 teaspoon prepared mustard
2 tablespoons mayonnaise

Spread this mixture on:
4 slices drained pineapple

Bake the slices in a greased pan for about 10 minutes.

HAM AND POTATO CAKES [4]

Combine:
  1 cup mashed potatoes
  1 cup ground cooked ham
  1 tablespoon chopped parsley
  ½ teaspoon grated onion
  ⅛ teaspoon pepper
  Salt, if needed
Shape this mixture into flat cakes. Dip them lightly in:
  Flour
Sauté them in:
  Bacon drippings or other fat

HAM CAKES WITH PINEAPPLE AND SWEET POTATOES [6]

Boil by the recipe on page 322:
  3 large sweet potatoes
Preheat oven to 375°.
Combine:
  2 cups cooked chopped or ground ham
  ½ cup dry bread crumbs
  2 eggs
  ⅛ teaspoon salt
  1 teaspoon prepared mustard
Shape these ingredients into 6 flat cakes. Melt in a skillet:
  5 tablespoons bacon drippings
Brown lightly in the skillet:
  6 slices drained pineapple
Remove them and brown the ham cakes in the skillet. Place the pineapple slices in a baking dish and cover each slice with a ham cake. Peel the sweet potatoes. Cut them lengthwise into halves. Combine and sprinkle over them:
  ¼ teaspoon cloves
  ¼ cup brown sugar
Cook them slowly in the skillet until they are well caramelized. Place them in the baking dish. Baste them with:
  Pineapple juice
Bake the dish for about 10 minutes.

HAM À LA KING [6]

Prepare:
  2 cups Cream Sauce I, page 359
When the sauce is boiling, add:
  2 cups cooked diced ham
  2 diced hard-cooked eggs
  1 cup Sautéed Mushrooms, page 296 or canned mushrooms with sliced stuffed olives
  1 tablespoon chopped green pepper
  1 tablespoon chopped pimiento
Serve the ham very hot on:
  Rounds of toast, on rusks, in bread cases or on corn bread squares
Garnish with:
  Chopped parsley

▤ BARBECUED FRANKFURTERS, WIENERS OR HOT DOGS

Preheat broiler or grill.
Grill or put:
  Frankfurters, wieners or hot dogs
on a rack in a roasting pan. During the cooking baste them
▶ constantly with:
  Barbecue Sauce, page 374

▤ FRANKFURTER KEBABS [8]

Preheat grill or broiler.
Cut into about 4 pieces each:
  8 frankfurters
Marinate about 30 minutes in:
  French Dressing, page 341
Skewer the pieces alternately with bits of:
  Bacon
  Small canned pickled onions
  Green pepper
Grill or broil, turning often.

FRANKFURTERS OR SAUSAGE IN SAUCES

I. [3]

Preheat oven to 400°.
Place in a shallow pan:

6 frankfurter sausages

Prepare:

1 cup Tomato Sauce, page 376, or Barbecue Sauce, page 374

Add:

(Chopped green peppers, seeded and veined)
(Grated onions or chives)

Pour these ingredients over the sausages. Bake them until they swell and the sauce thickens.

II. Prepare, using no salt:

Creole Sauce, page 380, or Quick Tomato Sauce, page 376

Season it well with:

Paprika

Cook:

Vienna Sausages, page 531

Drain them. Heat them in the sauce. Serve with:

Boiled Rice, Noodles, page 192, or Mashed Potatoes, page 311

SAUSAGE BAKED WITH APPLES [4]

Preheat oven to 400°.
Arrange in a baking dish:

8 partially cooked pork sausages

Core:

6 tart apples

Cut them into ¼-inch slices and place them around the sausages. Sprinkle them with:

¾ cup brown sugar

Bake the dish in a hot oven 400° for 10 minutes. ◗ Reduce the heat to 350° and continue baking for about 15 minutes longer. Baste with the drippings.

SAUSAGES AND MUSHROOMS

Fine for brunch.
Prepare:

Mashed Potatoes, page 311, or Boiled Mashed Chestnuts, page 283

Heap them in a mound on a hot platter. Keep them hot. Cook:

Sausages, page 531

Place them around the potatoes. Sauté in the drippings:

Mushrooms, page 296

Garnish the platter with them and:

Sprigs of parsley

Pour the drippings over the potatoes.

SAUSAGE AND ONIONS [4]

Heat in a skillet:

2 tablespoons oil or fat

Add:

1½ cups slivered onions

Cook and stir these over low heat for about 15 minutes until light brown. Cut a lengthwise slit in:

8 wiener sausages or frankfurters

Fill them with the onions. Fasten them with toothpicks. Broil them slowly on both sides. You may place them in:

Lightly toasted buns

LENTIL AND SAUSAGE CASSEROLE [4]

Preheat oven to 400°.
Place in a greased ovenproof dish:

1 cup cooked lentils

Place in boiling water and simmer for 10 minutes:

1 lb. small link or other sausages

Drain them. Place them on top of the lentils. Bake the dish uncovered until the sausages are brown.

PIGS IN POTATOES [3]

Preheat deep-fat fryer to 375°.
Combine and beat well:

1 teaspoon minced onion
1 teaspoon minced parsley

2 cups Mashed Potatoes,
　　page 311
1 egg yolk
Cook:
6 small Vienna sausages
or use:
Precooked pork sausages
Coat them with the potato mixture. Roll in:
Finely crushed bread
　　crumbs
then in:
1 egg diluted with 1
　　tablespoon water or milk
then again in the crumbs. Fry
the piggies until they are a
golden brown.

BAKED CORN BEEF

Preheat oven to 350°.
Remove whole from the can:
Corned beef
Stud it with:
Whole cloves
Make a paste by stirring a little
water into:
¼ cup brown sugar
1 teaspoon chili powder
Add to it:
2 tablespoons chopped
　　pickles
Spread the beef with the paste.
Bake it for about 10 minutes.

CREAMED CHIPPED BEEF

[4 Large Servings]
◗ Do not oversalt.
Pull apart:
8 oz. chipped beef
Melt:
3 tablespoons butter
Sauté in it until light brown:
3 tablespoons minced onion
3 tablespoons minced
　　green pepper
Sprinkle these with:
3 tablespoons flour
Add slowly, stirring constantly:
2 cups milk
Add the beef. Simmer these ingredients until they thicken. Remove from the heat and season
with:

1 tablespoon chopped
　　parsley or chives
¼ teaspoon paprika
2 tablespoons dry sherry
(2 tablespoons capers or
　　chopped pickles)
Serve the beef on:
Hot buttered toast

CHIPPED BEEF IN　　　[3]
CREOLE SAUCE

◗ Do not oversalt.
Prepare:
Quick Creole Sauce,
　　page 376
Melt:
1 tablespoon butter
Sauté in it for 1 minute:
4 oz. shredded chipped
　　beef
Add the sauce. Heat the dish.
Serve it on:
Buttered toast

CHIPPED BEEF IN　　　[2]
CHEESE SAUCE

◗ Do not oversalt.
Prepare:
1 cup Cheese Sauce,
　　page 364
Add to it:
4 oz. or more shredded
　　chipped beef
Heat it. Serve it over:
Hot corn bread squares
This may be served in pancakes.

CHIPPED BEEF AND　　[5]
SWEET POTATO
CASSEROLE

Preheat oven to 375°.
◗ Do not oversalt.
Cut into cubes:
5 cooked or canned sweet
　　potatoes
Shred:
¼ lb. dried beef
Prepare:
¼ cup grated onion
1½ cups Cream Sauce I,
　　page 359, or canned
　　cream soup
Place these ingredients in layers

in a greased casserole. Cover the top with:

Crushed cornflakes

Dot it with:

Butter or cheese

Bake for ½ hour.

CHIPPED BEEF OR CORNED BEEF IN CANNED SOUP [4 to 5]

◗ Do not oversalt.

Combine and heat:

1 can cream soup—
  mushroom, celery,
  asparagus, etc.: 10½ oz.

6 tablespoons milk or Stock
  (II, 141)

⅛ teaspoon freshly ground
  nutmeg

A grating of black
  pepper

Add:

8 oz. shredded chipped
  beef or 1 cup canned
  diced corned beef

1 cup leftover vegetables

Heat these ingredients. Serve them on:

Toast or hot biscuits

sprinkled with:

Chopped parsley, chives
  or grated cheese

Or you may boil until nearly tender:

10 small onions

Drain them and place them in a baking dish, pour the soup and beef mixture over them. Cover the top with:

Crushed potato chips

Bake the dish in a 400° oven for about 15 minutes.

ABOUT HASH

Hash has its ups and downs.

The Irish cook was praised for her hash and she said: "Beef ain't nothing. Onions ain't nothing. Seasoning's nothing. But when I throw myself into my hash, that's hash!" The usual way to make hash is to cut the meat from a chicken or turkey carcass or from a roast beef, combine it with leftover gravy, reheat it briefly and season it acceptably. Never overcook it. There should be about ½ as much gravy as other ingredients. Have sauce or gravy boiling vigorously. Put in the solids ◗ reduce the heat at once and let them warm through thoroughly. If heating hash in the oven, be sure to use a lid or a topping, see Gratins, page 389.

You may add, in addition to the meat, cooked mushrooms, celery or potatoes, chopped olives, green peppers, parsley or some other herb or anything else that seems suitable. The proportions may be varied. This is a matter of taste and expediency. In the absence of gravy, sweet or sour cream or a sauce—cream, tomato, creole, etc.—may be substituted. Or you may add a sauce or cream to the gravy to obtain the desired amount. When using cream, reheat the hash in a double boiler as boiling thins it. Sherry, Madeira or dry wine may be added. Hash may be served in a pastry shell, in a rice or noodle ring, etc.

BEEF AND HAM HASH WITH POTATOES AND MUSHROOMS

Cut into cubes equal parts of:

Cooked roast beef and
cooked or smoked ham
Raw pared potatoes

Reserve the beef. Place in a saucepan the ham and potatoes. Cover them with:

Brown Sauce, page 365

Cover these ingredients and simmer for 15 minutes. Add:

½ lb. or more sliced
  mushrooms

Simmer them covered for 15 minutes longer. Add the beef. Reheat the hash, but do not permit it to boil. Season it with:

Garlic salt

A pinch basil, thyme or
savory
Dry sherry
Salt, if needed
Serve it on:
Hot toast
garnished with:
Chopped parsley
This dish may be made without
the ham.

SAUTÉED OR [4]
BROWNED HASH

Combine and grind:
1½ cups cooked meat
½ cup raw cubed potatoes
with or without skins
1 medium-sized onion
Season with:
Salt, pepper, celery seed
Turn these ingredients into a
hot well-greased skillet. Cook
the hash over medium heat until
a crust forms on the bottom,
turn it and brown the other
side. Stir it from time to time to
let the hash brown throughout.
Shortly before it is done, pat it
down firmly to form an unbroken cake. This requires about
½ hour cooking in all. Serve
the hash with:
Catsup or Tomato Sauce,
page 376

QUICK HASH [4]

Heat over very low heat:
1 can cream of mushroom
soup: 10½ oz.
Stir in gradually:
¼ cup milk
Add:
1 cup cubed cooked ham
or meat: frankfurters,
hamburgers, etc.
2 sliced hard-cooked eggs
Season the hash with:
A pinch dried basil or
thyme
Salt and pepper
(Chopped parsley)
Serve it over:
Hot corn bread or toast

HASH WITH [6]
VEGETABLES

This is an excellent combination. If it is not feasible to use
all the ingredients given, it will
still be good.
Preheat oven to 350°.
Prepare:
½ cup cooked diced
potatoes
⅓ cup cooked diced onions
⅓ cup seeded sliced green
peppers
⅓ cup cooked chopped
celery
3 tablespoons diced
pimientos
2 cups cold cooked meat,
cut into ⅓-inch cubes
Combine and heat to boiling:
1 cup leftover gravy
⅓ cup tomato purée
1 tablespoon butter
Salt and pepper, as
required
1 teaspoon Worcestershire
sauce
Add the meat and vegetables.
If there is no available gravy,
make it with 2 tablespoons butter, 2 tablespoons flour and 1
cup of vegetable stock or water
in which 1 beef cube has been
dissolved. Pour the hash into 1
large baking dish or into 6 individual baking dishes. Sprinkle
the top with:
Au Gratin III, page 389
Or cover it with green pepper
rings and seasoned slices of tomatoes dotted with butter.
Brown the dish in the oven.

HASH IN CREAMED
CABBAGE

Preheat oven to 400°.
Prepare:
Creamed Cabbage III,
page 275
Place ½ the cabbage in a
greased ovenproof dish. Place on
top of it a layer of:
Hash moistened lightly
with gravy or cream

Cover it with the remaining cabbage. Sprinkle the top with:

Au Gratin II or III,
page 389

Bake the cabbage until the top is light brown.

SHEPHERD'S PIE

I. Preheat oven to 400°.
Prepare:

Hash

Spread it in a baking dish.
Cover it with fresh hot:

Mashed Potatoes,
page 311

Spread the top with:

Melted butter

Bake the dish until the potatoes are brown.

II. Preheat oven to 400°.
A very good way of using a small quantity of cold mashed potatoes and bits of meat or vegetable scraps.
Line individual molds with a wall ¼ inch thick of:

Leftover mashed
potatoes

If the potatoes are very hard, soften them with:

1 or 2 tablespoons hot milk

Brush the inner walls with:

1 egg white

Moisten:

Chopped cooked meat
and vegetables

with a small amount of:

Gravy, Tomato Sauce,
page 376, Cream Sauce,
page 359, or cream

Fill the molds and cover them with a layer of mashed potatoes.
Brush the tops with:

Soft butter

Place the molds in a pan of hot water in the oven for 15 minutes or until the potatoes are brown.

BREAD DRESSING IN A RING FILLED WITH HASH, ETC.

Preheat oven to 400°.
Grease a ring mold. Fill it with:

Bread Dressing, page
560, Apple and Onion
Dressing, page 563, etc.

Bake it until it is brown. Invert it onto a hot plate. Fill the center with:

Hash, or stewed creamed
fresh or leftover
vegetables

Good served with:

Leftover gravy or other
sauce

CORNED BEEF HASH [6] AND POTATOES

Grind, using coarse blade, or dice:

1½ lbs. cooked or canned
corned beef: about 3
cups

Dice:

2 cups boiled potatoes

Melt in a large saucepan:

2 tablespoons butter

Stir in and simmer until tender:

½ cup chopped onion
1 diced green pepper, seeds
and fibers removed
2 ribs chopped celery
(1 clove garlic)
(1 cup mushrooms)

Remove the garlic. Add the beef and potatoes and:

1 tablespoon
Worcestershire sauce
2 tablespoons minced
parsley or chives
Salt and pepper, as
needed

Cook and stir lightly over medium heat while adding gradually:

⅓ to ⅔ cup Stock (II, 141),
or Cream Sauce III,
page 359

Stir and cook till well blended and thoroughly heated. Place on a hot platter and serve topped with:

6 Poached Eggs, page 184

Or sauté the hash in a greased skillet until well browned on the bottom. Remove carefully, folding like an omelet, to serve.

CANNED CORNED [4]
BEEF HASH PATTIES

Sauté:
> 3 tablespoons chopped
> onion

in:
> 2 tablespoons butter

Add:
> 2 tablespoons horseradish
> ½ teaspoon thyme
> 2 cups canned corned beef
> hash

Form patties of this mixture.
Sauté them on both sides in:
> Hot butter or drippings

Sauté in the same pan:
> Slices firm tomato

Season them with:
> Brown sugar
> Salt and pepper

Arrange the tomatoes and patties on a platter, garnished with:
> Parsley

Or serve the patties with:
> 1½ cups Cream Sauce I,
> page 359

to which you may add:
> 2 chopped hard-cooked
> eggs
> 2 tablespoons chopped
> pickles

CHICKEN OR [4]
TURKEY HASH

◗ Please read About Hash, page 223.

Combine and heat:
> 1½ cups diced cooked
> chicken or turkey
> ½ cup cooked drained
> celery or boiled potato
> cubes
> 1 cup leftover chicken or
> turkey gravy or sauce
> 1 tablespoon chopped
> parsley or chives
> Seasoning, as required

Serve the hash as suggested in About Hash, page 223.

CREAMED CHICKEN [4]
OR VEAL

There is no reason why this dish should not be delicious, whether it is made in a luxurious way or with leftover food. Proportions, seasonings, etc., are unimportant, provided that good combinations are chosen.

Prepare:
> 1 cup Cream Sauce I,
> page 359

Use cream and chicken stock or vegetable water, with part gravy and part milk, etc. Add:
> 2 tablespoons chopped
> parsley
> 2 cups minced cooked
> chicken or veal
> (½ cup Sautéed Mushrooms,
> page 296)

Part of this may be cooked or canned vegetables. Season these ingredients with:
> 1 teaspoon lemon juice
> or ½ teaspoon
> Worcestershire sauce or
> 2 teaspoons dry sherry
> (3 tablespoons chopped
> pickles or olives)

Add:
> Salt and pepper
> (Celery salt)

Grease a baking dish and put the creamed mixture in it. Sprinkle the top with:
> Au Gratin II or III,
> page 389
> (½ cup blanched shredded
> almonds)

Place the dish under the broiler until the crumbs are brown. The creamed ingredients may be served unbreaded on:
> Hot Waffles or in a
> Noodle or Rice Ring,
> pages 173, 162

CHICKEN À LA KING [4]

Cut into dice:
> 1 cup cooked chicken
> ½ cup Sautéed Mushrooms,
> page 296
> ¼ cup canned pimiento

Melt:
> 3 tablespoons chicken fat
> or butter

Stir in and blend:

3 tablespoons flour
Add slowly:
1½ cups Chicken Stock (II, 142), or cream
When the sauce is smooth and boiling, add the chicken, mushrooms and pimiento. Reduce the heat. Pour some sauce over:
1 egg yolk
Return mixture to pan. Stir and permit it to thicken slightly. Add:
Seasoning, if required
(¼ cup blanched slivered almonds)
(1 tablespoon dry sherry)
Serve the chicken at once. To reheat, place in a saucepan over boiling water.

TURKEY OR CHICKEN CASSEROLE WITH VEGETABLES [4]

Prepare by cutting into cubes:
2 cups cooked turkey or chicken
Melt:
3 tablespoons butter
Stir in and sauté gently until lightly browned:
½ cup diced celery
⅓ cup thinly sliced onions
⅓ cup thinly sliced green pepper, seeds and fibrous portions removed
Sprinkle over the top, stir in and cook slowly for 5 minutes:
3 tablespoons flour
Stir in gradually:
1½ cups turkey or chicken stock
Remove the pot from the heat. Stir in:
2 lightly beaten egg yolks
Seasoning, as required
and the turkey meat. Stir over low heat just long enough to let the sauce thicken slightly. You may add:
3 tablespoons dry white wine
Correct the seasoning
Place the mixture in one large

or in individual casseroles.
Sprinkle the top with:
Minced chives or parsley, nut meats or grated cheese
Serve at once. Good with rice or spoon bread or on toast.

QUICK CHICKEN CREOLE [8]

Melt:
3 tablespoons chicken fat
Sauté in it:
2 tablespoons chopped onion
2 tablespoons chopped green pepper
(1 minced clove garlic)
Stir in:
3 tablespoons flour
¼ teaspoon salt
¼ teaspoon paprika
Add:
½ cup tomato purée or strained tomatoes
1 cup chicken broth
Stir and cook these ingredients until they boil. Add:
1 teaspoon lemon juice
½ teaspoon horseradish
2 cups cooked diced chicken meat
½ cup sliced Sautéed Mushrooms, page 296
½ cup chopped pimiento
Salt, as needed
Serve the chicken in a:
Rice Ring, page 162, or Noodle Ring, page 173
Just before serving, top with:
(1 cup cultured sour cream)

COOKED TURKEY, CHICKEN OR VEAL LOAF [4 to 6]

Preheat oven to 350°.
Cook and stir for 1 minute:
1½ tablespoons grated onion in:
1 tablespoon butter
Add it to:
2 cups diced cooked turkey, chicken or veal
¾ teaspoon salt
1 cup cracker crumbs

¾ cup gravy or thickened
   Chicken Stock (II, 142)
¾ cup milk
2 beaten eggs
(½ cup finely chopped
   celery)
(¾ teaspoon chili powder)

Place these ingredients in a well-greased loaf pan set in a pan of hot water. Bake the loaf for about 50 minutes. Serve it with:

Leftover gravy with
   chopped olives
Mushroom Sauce, page
   367, or cream sauce with
   lots of chopped parsley
   or chives

QUANTITY   [16 to 24]
CHICKEN LOAF

This is a wonderfully stretchable recipe to serve at group meetings. It is rather firm and serves well sliced, covered with a sauce. Preheat oven to 350°. Remove meat carefully from:

A 4 to 5 lb. stewed
   chicken

Shred it. Combine lightly with a fork:

2 to 4 cups dry bread
   crumbs
1 to 3 cups cooked rice
1½ to 2 cups chicken broth,
   depending on how much
   rice and crumbs are
   added
3 to 4 lightly beaten eggs
Correct the seasoning
(½ cup chopped ripe olives)
(½ cup slivered pistachio
   nuts)

Bake ♦ uncovered for about 25 to 30 minutes. Serve with:

Chicken pan gravy, page
   359, seasoned with a
   little lemon rind, parsley
   and ⅟₁₆ teaspoon saffron

or with:

Quick à la King Sauce,
   page 375, or Mushroom
   Sauce, page 367, or
   Poulette Sauce, page 362

SWEETBREAD AND   [4]
CHICKEN IN PATTY
SHELLS OR BOUCHÉES À
LA REINE

A good party dish.
Prepare and keep warm:

Timbale Cases, Bread
   Cases, page 209, or Patty
   Shells, page 596

Prepare:

1 cup Cream Sauce I,
   page 359

seasoned with a small amount of:

Chablis or dry sherry

Add:

½ cup blanched button
   mushroom caps
¾ cup coarsely chopped
   cooked white chicken
   meat
1 pair coarsely diced
   cooked sweetbreads

Heat thoroughly, but do not boil and, just before serving, fill the above cases to overflowing with the creamed mixture. Garnish with:

Chopped parsley

CHICKEN OR TURKEY   [4]
DIVAN

Preheat oven to 400°.
Butter a 12 x 9-inch shallow heatproof dish or use individual oval steak platters. Place on the dish:

(4 slices hot buttered toast
   or make a layer of
   buttered crackers)

Next place a layer of:

Slices of cooked chicken
   or turkey

The white meat is best. Allow 2 or 3 slices per serving. Partially cook and lay on top of the meat:

1 package frozen broccoli
   or asparagus spears,
   cooked and well drained

Or use leftover cooked broccoli or asparagus. Cover the whole with:

2 cups Mornay Sauce,
          page 361
Sprinkle with:
          Grated Parmesan cheese
and heat in the oven until the
sauce is browned and bubbling.
Serve at once.

DUCK PILAF   [4]

A leftover duck and rice dish.
Remove the meat from:
          Roast duck
There should be about 2 cups.
Break the carcasses apart. Add
to them:
          4 cups water
          1 chopped onion
          Some celery leaves
Simmer this stock covered for 1
hour. Strain. Bring to boiling
point. Stir in slowly, not disturbing the boiling:
          ⅔ cup rice
Cook the rice until it is tender,
for about ½ hour. Strain it. Reserve the liquor. Melt:
          2 tablespoons butter
Add and sauté covered for 5
minutes:
          ¾ cup finely chopped
              celery
          1 teaspoon grated onion
Add the duck scraps, the rice
and:
          1 cup leftover gravy, duck
              liquor or cream
              combined
Mix these ingredients well with
a fork. Season them, if needed,
with:
          Salt and paprika
Serve the pilaf hot with:
          Stewed plums or apricots

SEAFOOD À LA KING   [4]

Combine:
          1 cup canned lobster, crab
              meat, etc.
          3 peeled, diced, hard-
              cooked eggs
          1 chopped pimiento
Sauté, page 296, and add:
          ½ cup chopped mushrooms

Cook until tender in boiling
water, drain and add:
          ¼ cup chopped sweet red
              peppers
Prepare:
          Cream Sauce I, page 359
When the sauce is smooth and
boiling, add the other ingredients.
          Correct the seasoning
and add:
          1 teaspoon Worcestershire
              sauce, 1 tablespoon
              lemon juice or 2 table-
              spoons dry white wine
Serve the seafood over:
          French Toast (II, 290)
          rusks, or in a patty shell
          or au gratin in ramekins
Or toast bread triangles and
spread with:
          Mashed avocado and
              lemon juice

CREAMED SEAFOOD   [6]
AU GRATIN

Preheat oven to 350°.
Combine 3 or 4 kinds of raw
fish or shellfish.
For example:
          ½ lb. chopped lobster meat
          1 cup drained oysters
          1 cup minced fillet of
              haddock
Prepare:
          1½ cups Sautéed
              Mushrooms, page 296
          4 cups Cream Sauce I,
              page 359
using cream as the liquid. When
the sauce is smooth and hot,
fold in the fish. Add the mushrooms.
          Correct the seasoning
Fill ramekins or shells with the
mixture. Cover the tops with:
          Au Gratin II, page 389
Bake the fish for about 25 minutes.

QUICK TUNA OR   [4]
SEAFOOD CASSEROLE

Prepare:
          1½ cups Cream Sauce I,

page 359, or Poulette
Sauce, page 362

Add:
  1 cup canned tuna, shrimp,
    clams, etc.
Just before serving, heat through
and add:
  ½ to 1 cup coarsely
    chopped watercress
  1 diced avocado
Serve over:
  Toast or rusks

CREAMED SEAFOOD [4]
AND VEGETABLES

Preheat broiler.
Cook:
  1 cup chopped celery,
    eggplant or cucumber
Drain it well. Prepare:
  ¾ cup Cream Sauce I,
    page 359
When the sauce is boiling, add
the celery and:
  ¾ lb. cooked shrimp, crab
    meat, etc.
Season with:
  Salt, if needed
  ⅛ teaspoon paprika
  (½ teaspoon Worcestershire
    sauce)
Place these ingredients in
greased ramekins. Cover with:
  Au Gratin I, page 389
Brown them under the broiler.

SHRIMP WITH CHEESE [4]
AND ONION SAUCE

Preheat broiler.
Shell and clean:
  1 lb. poached Shrimp,
    page 442
Melt:
  ¼ cup butter
Add:
  ½ cup minced onion
Sauté the onion for about 3 minutes. Stir in:
  ½ cup grated cheese
  ½ teaspoon dry mustard
  ½ teaspoon salt
  (½ minced clove garlic)
Cook and stir these ingredients
over very low heat until the

cheese has melted. Add the
shrimp and:
  6 tablespoons dry sherry
Butter individual baking dishes.
Place the shrimp in them.
Brown lightly under a broiler.
Shortly before they are done
sprinkle the tops with:
  Grated coconut
Serve very hot when the coco-
nut is light brown.

KEDGEREE OF [6]
LOBSTER OR OTHER FISH

Combine:
  2 cups cooked rice
  1 lb. cooked flaked lobster
    or cod fillets
  4 minced hard-cooked eggs
  ¼ cup butter
  ¼ cup cream
  2 tablespoons minced
    parsley
  Salt and cayenne
Heat these ingredients in a
double boiler.

SEAFOOD CASSEROLE [4]
IN CREOLE SAUCE

Prepare:
  ¾ lb. cooked shrimp or
    other seafood
Melt in a skillet:
  2 tablespoons butter
Add the shrimp. Stir and cook
over high heat for about 2 minutes. Add:
  2 cups Creole Sauce,
    page 380
  ¼ cup dry white wine
Simmer the shrimp covered for
about 5 minutes. You may add:
  (Salt and pepper)
  (A few grains cayenne)
  (3 diced hard-cooked eggs)
Serve the shrimp with:
  Boiled Rice

LOBSTER OR SEAFOOD [4]
CURRY

Heat in a double boiler:
  2 cups Curry Sauce I,
    page 363

Add, stir and cook for about 3 minutes:

> 2 cups boiled diced lobster meat or 2 cups cooked seafood

You may add:

> (3 chopped sautéed ribs celery)
>
> (½ chopped sautéed green pepper, seeds and fibrous portions removed)
>
> (1 teaspoon grated sautéed onion)
>
> Correct the seasoning

▶ Simmer until well heated. May be served at once with:

> Boiled Rice, Chutney (II, 592), or slivered almonds

Or place in individual baking dishes or a casserole and cover with:

> Au Gratin II, page 389

Heat in a 425° oven until the crumbs are lightly browned.

LOBSTER OR SEAFOOD [4] NEWBURG

I.

Melt in a double boiler:

> 4 tablespoons butter

Add, stir and cook for 3 minutes:

> 2 cups boiled diced lobster meat

Add:

> ¼ cup dry sherry or Madeira

Cook gently about 2 minutes more. Add:

> ½ teaspoon paprika
>
> (⅓ teaspoon nutmeg)

Beat and add:

> 3 egg yolks
>
> 1 cup cream

Cook and stir these ingredients until they thicken. Do not permit them to boil.

> Correct the seasoning

Serve the lobster at once on:

> Hot buttered toast

II. Heat in a double boiler:

> 2 cups Newburg Sauce, page 361

Add, stir and cook for about 3 minutes:

> 2 cups boiled diced lobster meat or 2 cups cooked seafood

You may add:

> (1 lb. sliced sautéed mushrooms)
>
> Correct the seasoning

Serve at once on:

> Hot buttered toast or Boiled Rice

QUICK SEAFOOD [4] DIVAN

Preheat oven to 325°.
Prepare and heat:

> 1½ cups Cream Sauce I, page 359, condensed cream of celery or mushroom soup sauce, or Quick Creole Sauce, page 380

Have ready:

> 1 cup cooked shrimp, crab meat, etc.
>
> Correct the seasoning

Put in a hot baking dish:

> 2 cups cooked asparagus, broccoli, cauliflower, etc.
>
> ½ cup Sautéed Mushrooms
>
> 2 teaspoons diced pimientos

Cover the vegetables with a close layer of the seafood. Pour the hot sauce over the seafood. Sprinkle lightly all over:

> Grated cheese

Bake for about 25 minutes.

QUICK CRAB MEAT OR [4] LOBSTER MONGOLE

For a perfect luncheon or supper, serve with rice and a salad. Combine and heat in a double boiler:

> ¾ cup canned tomato soup
>
> ¾ cup canned pea soup
>
> ¾ cup cream

Heat in a double boiler:

> 1 cup canned crab or lobster meat

Pour a little of the sauce over

it. Serve it garnished with:
    Parsley
    Boiled Rice, page 158
and the remaining sauce. All the
sauce may be added to the crab.
In that case, the dish becomes
a thick soup.

CRAB MEAT CUSTARD [8]

Preheat oven to 325°.
In the bottom of a large but-
tered casserole place:
    4 slices crustless bread
Place on top of the bread:
    1 large can flaked crab
        meat: 2 cups
    ½ cup grated American
        cheese
    Salt and pepper
Beat together:
    4 eggs
    3 cups milk
    ½ teaspoon salt
    Dash of cayenne
Pour this mixture over the fish
and top with:
    ½ cup grated American
        cheese
Bake as for a Custard (II, 437),
until done. Serve with:
    A mixed green salad

DEVILED CRAB [4]

Flake and pick over:
    1½ cups canned or cooked
        crab meat
Melt in a saucepan:
    1 tablespoon butter
Add:
    1½ tablespoons cracker
        crumbs
    ¾ cup milk or cream
Cook these ingredients until
they are thick. Remove from the
heat. Beat and add:
    2 small eggs
    ¼ teaspoon salt
    1½ teaspoons prepared
        mustard
    A few grains cayenne
Add the crab meat. Pack these
ingredients into crab shells or
ramekins. Brush the tops with:
    Melted butter

Brown them in a 400° oven or
under a broiler.

INDIVIDUAL TUNA [6] FISH PIES

Any other fish or seafood may
be substituted. Bake 6 individual Pie Shells (II, 296).
Combine:
    1 cup flaked tuna fish
    1 or 1½ cups thick Cream
        Sauce II, page 359, or
        condensed cream soup
        slightly diluted with
        milk
Heat this mixture. Season it with
a choice of:
    2 tablespoons fresh
        chopped parsley or
        chervil
    ¼ teaspoon curry powder
    ½ teaspoon Worcestershire
        sauce
Place the hot tuna mixture in the
hot pie shells. Serve them garnished with:
    Parsley sprigs
sprinkle with:
    Parmesan cheese or
        chives

TUNA AND POTATO [4] CHIP LOAF

Preheat oven to 350°.
Pat lightly until broken:
    3 oz. potato chips
Flake and add:
    1 cup canned tuna fish
Combine these ingredients
lightly with:
    1 can mushroom soup:
        10½ oz.
Add, if desired:
    Chopped pimiento,
        stuffed olives or
        chopped parsley
Bake the loaf in a greased pan
for about ½ hour.

⋏ LOBSTER PARFAIT [6]

This is an exceedingly elegant
way of serving cold lobster—fit

for a pavilion! Serve with iced champagne.

Purée in the ⅄ blender:

    The meat of 1 freshly killed and cooked 2½ lb. lobster or 2 cups cooked meat from frozen lobster tails

with:

    3 tablespoons tomato purée
    2 tablespoons lemon juice
    1 tablespoon dry sherry
    2 teaspoons cognac
    ½ cup water

Mix in:

    1 minced clove garlic
    1 finely chopped shallot

Cook the mixture over a low heat until reduced by ⅓. Cool, then add:

    2 cups mayonnaise
    1½ tablespoons heavy cream
    ½ teaspoon paprika
    1 teaspoon salt
    ½ teaspoon monosodium glutamate

Chill for 1½ hours. Arrange additional:

    4 oz. lobster meat per serving

in 6 parfait glasses. Cover the meat with the above sauce, letting it trickle down in parfait style. Garnish with:

    Chilled whipped cream
    Water cress

Serve at once.

HOT LOBSTER RING   [5]

Preheat oven to 325°.

Melt:

    2 tablespoons butter

Stir in, until blended:

    3 tablespoons flour

Stir in gradually:

    2 cups chicken bouillon or 1 cup bouillon and 1 cup cream

Add:

    1 tablespoon minced parsley
    ½ cup grated bread crumbs —not toasted

    4 beaten egg yolks
    2 cups boiled diced lobster meat
    Salt and white pepper

Whip until stiff, but not dry:

    4 egg whites

Fold lightly into the other ingredients. Bake the lobster mixture in a well-oiled 9-inch ring mold until firm, about 20 minutes. Unmold and serve with:

    Mushroom Sauce, page 367

QUICK FISH LOAF   [4]

Preheat oven to 400°.

Drain, then flake:

    1 lb. cooked or canned fish: 2 cups

Combine and beat:

    1 egg
    ¼ cup undiluted evaporated milk or rich cream
    ¾ cup soft bread crumbs
    ½ teaspoon salt
    ¼ teaspoon paprika
    2 teaspoons lemon juice or 1 teaspoon Worcestershire sauce
    1 tablespoon melted butter
    3 tablespoons minced parsley
    2 tablespoons chopped celery, onion, green pepper or olives

Add the fish. Place these ingredients in a greased baking dish. Bake them for about 30 minutes. This loaf may be served hot with:

    Cream, Tomato or Cheese Sauce, or Caper Sauce

or cold with:

    Mayonnaise

TUNA FISH BALLS

[About 4 Servings]

Also use as a hot hors d'oeuvre.

Combine and mix well:

    1 cup grated or flaked tuna fish
    1 cup mashed potatoes
    4 or 6 chopped olives

6 or 8 capers
½ minced clove garlic or 1
teaspoon grated onion
1 tablespoon minced
parsley
Salt and paprika
1 teaspoon brandy or dry
sherry
(1 teaspoon dried basil)

Shape the mixture into 1-inch balls. Sauté them for 2 or 3 minutes in:

½ cup hot olive oil or butter

Drain the balls, roll them in:

¾ cup ground nut meats

EMERGENCY FISH CAKES

Excellent cakes may be made quickly by combining cooked seafood with condensed cream soup. Keep your mixture rather stiff. Treat it as you would any other fish ball or cake.

CRAB, CLAM OR OYSTER CAKES

[Six 3-Inch Cakes]

You may combine the fish or use them separately.

Melt:

2 tablespoons butter

Add, stir and simmer for 3 minutes:

2 tablespoons minced
onion
½ cup soft bread crumbs

Combine and add:

2 beaten eggs
½ cup cream
2 cups minced oysters,
canned clams or flaked
crab meat
½ cup minced celery
½ teaspoon dry mustard or
1 tablespoon lemon juice
2 tablespoons chopped
parsley
½ teaspoon salt
½ teaspoon paprika

Chill this mixture for 2 hours. Shape into cakes. Dust them lightly with:

Flour or bread crumbs

Melt in a skillet:

1 tablespoon butter

Quickly brown the cakes on both sides. ▶ Lower the heat and cook the cakes slowly for about 6 minutes longer. You may dip the cakes in crumbs, then in 1 egg diluted with 1 tablespoon water and again in crumbs. If you do, permit them to dry for 15 minutes, then fry until golden in deep fat heated to 375°.

SALMON CAKES   [6]

Flake the contents of:

2 cups canned salmon

Stir in:

½ cup cracker crumbs
2 beaten eggs
½ teaspoon salt
⅛ teaspoon paprika

Form these ingredients into cakes. Sauté them until brown in:

Butter

Serve the cakes with:

Mushroom Sauce,
page 367
Celery Soup Sauce III,
page 375, etc.

SALMON POTATO   [6]
CAKES

Prepare:

Leftover Potato Cakes,
page 320

Use the egg and 2 cups mashed potatoes. Add in small flakes:

1 cup or more cooked
salmon

Season with:

Chopped parsley, onion
juice or celery seed

Shape the mixture into cakes. Dip them in:

Crushed cornflakes or
bread crumbs

Sauté them slowly in:

Butter, oil or drippings

SALMON PUFFS   [6]

Preheat oven to 350°.
Remove skin and bones, drain, then flake:

2 cups canned salmon

Add and stir lightly to blend:

½ cup fresh bread crumbs
2 tablespoons grated onion
1 tablespoon lemon juice
1 tablespoon melted butter
¼ teaspoon salt
¼ teaspoon pepper

Beat:

1 egg

Add and beat in:

½ cup milk

Combine with the salmon mixture. Place in 6 well-greased baking cups set in hot water. Bake for about 45 minutes. Unmold onto a hot platter. Serve with:

Velouté Sauce, page 362

SALMON CASSEROLE [4]

Preheat oven to 425°.
Skin, bone and flake:

2 cups cooked or canned salmon or other fish

Add:

Salt—lightly
Freshly ground pepper
Freshly ground nutmeg

Place the fish in a greased baking dish. Pour over it:

Béchamel Sauce, page 359, Cream Sauce, page 359, or Canned Soup Sauce, page 375, etc.

Cover the top with:

Au Gratin II, page 389

You may add a border of:

Mashed potatoes

Bake the dish until the top is lightly browned.

SALMON LOAF WITH CHEESE SAUCE [6]

Preheat oven to 350°.
Prepare:

1 cup Cream Sauce I, page 359

Stir in over low heat until melted:

¼ lb. grated cheese

Season the sauce with:

¼ teaspoon salt
⅛ teaspoon paprika

A few grains cayenne

Prepare:

1½ cups Mashed Potatoes, page 311

Grease a baking dish and spread the mashed potatoes in it. Cover them with ½ the sauce. Drain, skin, then flake the contents of:

2 cups canned salmon

Place it over the sauce. Cover it with the remaining sauce. Bake the dish for about 30 minutes. Serve it with:

Tomato Sauce, page 376

The cheese may be omitted in the cream sauce and a well-seasoned Cream Sauce I, page 359, may be used. Add herbs.

SALMON POT PIE [8]

Preheat oven to 425°.
A meal in one dish. The salmon mixture may be prepared in advance, so may the dough, and combined shortly before baking. A fine thing for the hurry-up housekeeper. Canned vegetables —peas, asparagus, etc.—and, of course, other fish—crab, shrimp, tuna, etc.—may be substituted.

Drain, reserving the oil:

2 cups canned salmon

Prepare:

Biscuit Dough (II, 284)

Prepare:

1 cup cooked celery
1 cup cooked peas

Drain the vegetables, reserving the liquid. Melt:

¼ cup butter

Sauté in it for about 2 minutes:

1½ tablespoons minced onion

Stir in until smooth:

6 tablespoons flour

Stir in until boiling:

¾ cup vegetable water
1½ cups milk

Add:

1 teaspoon salt
⅛ teaspoon paprika
1 tablespoon lemon juice or 1 teaspoon Worcestershire sauce

1 teaspoon or more
    chopped parsley or chives

Break the salmon into large pieces. Fold the vegetables and the salmon into the cream sauce. Add, if needed, more salt and flavoring. Place the mixture in a large casserole. Roll the biscuit dough to the thickness of about ¼ inch. Cut it into rounds. Top the salmon mixture with biscuits. Bake until it is done, for about 12 minutes.

SALMON AND TOMATO SCALLOP

[4 Large Servings]
Preheat oven to 375°.
Drain:
    2 cups canned salmon
Combine them with:
    3 cups soft bread crumbs
    2 tablespoons butter
    ¼ cup chopped onion
    ½ teaspoon salt
    1 teaspoon sugar
    ¼ teaspoon paprika or
        pepper
    2½ cups tomatoes
    (1 chopped seeded green
        pepper)
    (1 beaten egg)
    (1 teaspoon Worcestershire
        sauce or lemon juice)
    (¼ cup white wine)
Place these ingredients in a greased baking dish. The top may be sprinkled with:
    Grated cheese
Bake the dish until the top is brown and the interior heated.

SALMON IN PARSLEY   [6]
SAUCE WITH RICE OR
NOODLE RING

Drain:
    2 cups canned salmon
Remove skin and bones. Break the fish into large flakes. Combine:
    1½ teaspoons dry mustard
    1½ teaspoons salt
    ⅛ teaspoon pepper
    ½ teaspoon paprika

    3 tablespoons flour
Combine and beat into the dry ingredients:
    1 cup milk
    ¾ cup salmon liquid and
        water
Place in double boiler ◗ over— not in—boiling water and beat with a wire whisk:
    1 egg
    2 tablespoons lemon juice
Add the milk mixture and stir and cook until the sauce has thickened. Add the salmon and:
    2 tablespoons butter
    ½ cup finely minced parsley
    1 teaspoon Worcestershire
        sauce
Heat well and serve in:
    Rice Ring, page 162, or
    Noodle Ring, page 173

CREAMED CANNED   [2]
SHAD ROE

Sauté:
    1 cup canned shad roe
in:
    Butter
with:
    ½ teaspoon curry powder
Add:
    Salt and paprika
    ¾ cup cream
Reheat but do not boil the roe. Serve it on:
    Toast
See other roe recipes on page 416.

BROILED CANNED   [2]
SHAD ROE

Preheat broiler.
Separate into pieces:
    1 cup canned shad roe or
        other canned fish roe
Dry them with a paper towel. Brush them with:
    Melted butter
Sprinkle them with:
    Lemon juice
    Paprika
Place them in a shallow greased pan or on a greased broiler. Broil the roe gently for about

10 minutes. Turn it once. Baste it frequently with:

Melted butter

Serve it on toast, garnished with:

Slices of lemon
Chopped parsley

CANNED FISH ROE [3]
IN RAMEKINS

Preheat oven to 325°.
Combine:

1 cup drained canned fish roe
1½ teaspoons bread crumbs
1½ teaspoons butter
1 beaten egg
Salt, if needed
¼ teaspoon paprika
2 teaspoons chopped parsley
½ cup milk

Fill four greased ramekins. Bake them in a pan of hot water until firm—about 20 minutes. Serve the roe with:

Slices of lemon

ABOUT CHEESE DISHES

If you want to know the secrets of cheese cookery, please read About Cheese (II, 175).

WELSH RAREBITS

Our correspondence is closed on the subject of rarebit vs. rabbit. We stick to rarebit because rabbit already means something else. But we can only answer the controversy with a story. A stranger mollifying a small crying boy: "I wouldn't cry like that if I were you!" Small boy, "You cry your way and I'll cry mine." Good Welsh rarebit can now be bought canned, ready to be heated and served.

I. With Beer [6 to 8]

Grate or grind:

1 lb. aged yellow cheese

Melt in a double boiler:

1 tablespoon butter

Stir in:

1 cup beer

When the beer is warm, stir in the cheese. Stir constantly with a fork until the cheese is melted. Beat slightly and add:

1 whole egg

Season the rarebit with:

1 teaspoon Worcestershire sauce
1 teaspoon salt
(½ teaspoon paprika)
A few grains red pepper
(¼ teaspoon curry powder)
¼ teaspoon mustard

Serve the rarebit at once on:

Crackers, hot toast or Grilled Tomatoes

II. With Milk [4]

Melt in a pan over hot water:

1 tablespoon butter

Stir in and melt:

1½ cups diced aged cheese

Add:

⅓ teaspoon salt
¼ teaspoon dry mustard
A few grains cayenne
1 teaspoon Worcestershire sauce

Stir in slowly:

½ to ¾ cup cream or top milk

When the mixture is hot, remove the pan from the heat. Beat in:

1 egg yolk

Serve the rarebit at once over:

Hot toasted crackers or bread

TOMATO RAREBIT OR [4]
WOODCHUCK

I.

Combine and bring to the boiling point:

1 can tomato soup:
10½ oz.
½ cup water

Add and cook slowly until tender:

(¾ cup thinly sliced onions)

Add and stir until melted:

¾ lb. or more thinly sliced aged cheese

Remove the pan from the heat.
Combine, beat and add:
>   2 egg yolks
>   1 teaspoon Worcestershire
>   sauce
>   1 teaspoon dry mustard
>   1 teaspoon salt
>   ¼ teaspoon paprika
>   ⅛ teaspoon white pepper

Stir these ingredients over low
heat for 1 or 2 minutes to permit
the yolks to thicken slightly.
Whip until ▶ stiff, but not dry:
>   2 egg whites

Fold them into the hot cheese
mixture. Serve the rarebit on:
>   Hot toast or crackers

II.   [4]

Stir and melt over low heat:
>   ½ lb. grated aged cheese:
>   2 cups

Add, stir and heat:
>   1 can condensed tomato
>   soup: 10½ oz.
>   3 tablespoons water
>   ½ teaspoon salt
>   A few grains cayenne

Serve the rarebit on:
>   Toast or toasted crackers

CHEESE CASSEROLE

This inexpensive luncheon or
supper dish is good balanced by
a green vegetable, a salad or
orange and grapefruit cups. A
fine addition to this dish is ½
pound cooked or canned shrimp.

I.   [4]

Preheat oven to 350°.
Cut ½ inch thick:
>   7 slices bread

Spread the slices lightly with:
>   Butter

Cut 2 of the slices twice across
on the bias, making 8 triangular
pieces. Cut the remaining bread
into cubes. There should be
about 4 cups of diced buttered
bread. Place layers of diced
bread in a buttered baking dish.
Sprinkle the layers with:
>   1 cup grated cheese

Combine and beat:
>   2 eggs
>   1 cup milk
>   1 teaspoon salt
>   ¼ teaspoon paprika
>   A few grains cayenne
>   ½ teaspoon dry mustard

Pour these ingredients over the
cheese. Place the triangle of
bread upright around the edge
to form a crown. Bake the dish
for about 25 minutes. Serve at
once.

II.   [4]

Preheat oven to 350°.
Trim the crust from:
>   8 slices bread

Cut them in half on the bias.
Place ½ of them in the bottom
of a greased 8-inch ovenproof
dish, spiral fashion, not letting
them overlap. They should resemble a pinwheel. Cut into
slices ¼-inch thick:
>   6 oz. cheese: cheddar,
>   American, Swiss, etc.

Cover the bread layer with the
cheese slices, not letting them
overlap. Cover the cheese with
the rest of the bread, again in
spiral fashion. Beat lightly:
>   3 eggs

Add and beat well:
>   ¼ teaspoon salt
>   ⅛ teaspoon paprika
>   A few grains cayenne
>   2 cups rich milk
>   (1 teaspoon grated onion,
>   1 tablespoon parsley or
>   chives or ¼ teaspoon
>   mustard)

Pour this mixture over the
bread. Permit the dish to stand
for 1 hour. Bake it for about 1
hour or until well browned.
Serve it hot.

CHEESE NUT AND   [6]
BREAD LOAF

Preheat oven to 350°.
Combine well:
>   2 cups fresh bread crumbs

1 cup minced walnut or
   pecan meats
1 cup grated American
   cheese
1 cup milk
¾ teaspoon salt
½ teaspoon paprika
1 tablespoon finely
   chopped onion
1 tablespoon minced
   parsley
1 beaten egg

Shape these ingredients in a
loaf by placing them in a bread
pan. Bake the loaf for about 25
minutes. Serve it with:

Quick Tomato Sauce,
   page 376,
Mushroom Sauce, page
   367, or
Onion Sauce, page 363

ABOUT FONDUE

For so simple an affair, the controversy involved in the making
of this dish is vast indeed. Its
confecting is a ritual that varies
with each Swiss household. Experiment has led to the following conclusions, no matter how
simple or how complex a version
you choose to make. The cheese
or combination of cheeses used
must be ◗ a natural cheese, not
pasteurized types. Whatever
kind of wine, it must be ◗ a dry
white wine. Although kirsch is
de rigueur, you may substitute a

nonsweet liqueur like slivovitz,
a cognac or an applejack. ◗
Measure all ingredients and have
them ready to add with one
hand. For your other hand will
be busy stirring the mixture
with a wooden spoon—from the
time the wine is hot enough for
the cheese until the fondue is
ready to be eaten. Altogether,
this is a matter of about 10 minutes of cooking.

Have ready a bread basket or
bowl filled with crusty French or
Italian bread cut into 1 x 1 x ¾-
inch pieces, making sure that
each piece has one side of crust.
At this point the guests, each
equipped with a heatproof-
handled fork—preferably two or
three-tined—spear the bread
from the soft side and dip the
impaled bit into the well-
warmed cheese. The fondue will
at first be on the thin side, but
will thicken as the process progresses. There is seldom much
left by the time another 10 minutes has elapsed. Serve with
fresh fruit and tea.

FONDUE   [4]

Grate:
   1 lb. Emmenthaler or ½ lb.
      Emmenthaler and ½ lb.
      Gruyère cheese
Rub a heavy saucepan with:
   A clove of garlic
Put into the pan:
   2 cups dry white wine
While this is heating ◗ uncovered, over moderately high heat,
pour into a cup:
   3 tablespoons kirsch
This is the classic flavoring, although one of the other dry
liqueurs mentioned above may
be used. Stir into the kirsch until
well dissolved:
   1 teaspoon cornstarch
By this time the wine will begin
to show small foamy bubbles
over its surface. When it is almost covered with this fine foam

◗ but is not yet boiling, add the coarsely shredded cheese gradually ◗ stirring constantly. Keep the heat high, but do not let the fondue boil. Continue to add the cheese until you can feel a very slight resistance to the spoon as you stir. Then, still stirring vigorously, add the kirsch and cornstarch mixture. Continue to cook until the fondue begins to thicken. Add to taste:

> Nutmeg, white pepper or paprika

Quickly transfer it to a heatproof heavy pan which can be placed over an alcohol lamp or chafing dish or transfer it to an electric skillet adjusted to ◗ low heat. After this transferral the cooking continues on low heat and the guests take over as described previously.

ABOUT SANDWICHES

Innumerable hostesses—not to mention quick-lunch stands— keep green the memory of Lord Sandwich, whose mania for gambling gave the world the well-known concoction that bears his name.

Sandwiches range in size and complexity until they rival a Dagwood. But don't neglect the Canapé chapter, where many delectable smaller versions are found. To keep sandwiches fresh, wrap in wax paper, foil or a dampened cloth.

TOASTED SANDWICHES

These are offered as luncheon suggestions. Many of the sandwich fillings given in the chapter on Canapés (II, 59), may be spread between slices of toast. The sandwiches may be served with a hot sauce or a cold dressing.

Put between:

> 2 slices toast

any of the following combinations:

Sliced chicken
2 strips sautéed bacon
Grated cheese
Mushroom Sauce, page 367

Creamed chicken
Parmesan cheese
Grilled tomatoes and bacon

Baked ham
Creamed chicken and mushrooms

Ham, chicken and lettuce, with mayonnaise

Braunschweiger
Sliced tomatoes
Lettuce
Tart mayonnaise

Sliced tongue
Sliced tomatoes
Mayonnaise
Sautéed bacon

Creamed mushrooms
Sliced tomatoes
Grated cheese on top, broiled until it is melted

Sliced ham
Creamed mushrooms

Lettuce, French dressing
Sliced tomato and avocado
2 slices crisp sautéed bacon

Asparagus tips
2 slices crisp bacon
Welsh Rarebit, page 237

Lettuce, sliced tomato
Sliced chicken
Crumbled Roquefort cheese
2 slices crisp bacon

SAUTÉED OR GRILLED SANDWICHES

Melt in a small skillet large

enough to accommodate one sandwich:

    1½ teaspoons butter

Sauté a sandwich slowly on one side until browned. Add to the skillet:

    1½ teaspoons butter

Brown the second side. Especially good with a thin slice of cheese, mustard, salt and paprika between the bread slices or with deviled ham, meat mixtures, jam or jelly.

WAFFLE OR TOASTED SANDWICHES

Cut into thin slices:

    White or dark bread

Spread it lightly with:

    Soft butter

Cut off the crusts and spread between the slices:

    Cheese Spread or other
    sandwich fillings, pages
    (II, 59) and 240

Cut the sandwiches to fit the sections of a waffle iron. Wrap them in a moist cloth until ready to toast. Heat a waffle iron, arrange the sandwiches upon the iron, lower the top and toast them until they are crisp.

FINGER ROLL FILLINGS

Very good picnic sandwiches. Cut into lengthwise halves:

    Soft finger rolls

Hollow them slightly. Fill the hollows with any palatable sandwich spread. These are easy to handle. They are delicious filled with:

    Chicken Salad, page 51
    Tuna Fish Salad, page 51
    Braunschweiger sausage
    Canapé Filling (II, 63)
    Chopped celery and
    mayonnaise
    Chopped olives and
    cream cheese, etc.

Also see the many spreads in Canapés (II, 59 to 62).

HOT BISCUITS BAKED WITH FILLINGS

[About Eighteen 2½-Inch Biscuits]
Combine:

    1 cup cooked, shredded
    meat: chicken, fish, ham,
    veal, roast, etc.
    ½ cup thick gravy, cream
    sauce or condensed soup
    1 tablespoon grated onion
    1 chopped hard-cooked egg
    2 tablespoons chopped
    pickles or olives
    Seasoning

Prepare:

    Baking Powder Biscuit
    Dough (II, 284)

Roll it to the thickness of ¼ inch. Cut it into rounds. Place on one round 1 tablespoon of the above meat mixture.
Moisten the edges and cover it with another round. Seal the edges with a fork. Prick the tops. Place the biscuits on a baking sheet and bake them until brown in a very hot oven —450°. You may serve these with:

    Mushroom Sauce,
    page 367

MEAL-IN-ONE SANDWICH

[4 Servings—But
Better Call It 2]
On your toes when you make this. It's easy if you have all your ingredients ready before you poach the eggs.
Prepare:

    4 large slices of toast
    8 sautéed bacon slices
    4 skinned and sliced large
    tomatoes
    ½ cup French dressing
    1 cup Cream Sauce I,
    page 359
    1 cup grated cheese

Place the toast on a baking sheet, cover it with the bacon, tomatoes and dressing.
Poach:

    4 eggs

Place an egg on each piece of garnished toast, cover it with ¼ of the cream sauce and ¼ of the grated cheese. Place the toast under the broiler until the cheese melts. Serve the sandwiches piping hot.

HOT ROAST BEEF [4] SANDWICH

Slice:
    Cold roast beef
Prepare:
    1 cup Brown Sauce, page 365
Add to it:
    1 tablespoon finely minced sour pickle or ½ cup chopped olives
Cut:
    6 thin slices of light or dark bread
Beat until soft:
    2 tablespoons butter
    ¼ teaspoon prepared mustard or 1 teaspoon horseradish
Spread the bread with this mixture. Dip the beef slices in the hot sauce. Place them between the slices of bread. Serve the sandwiches on a hot platter, covered with remaining sauce.

CORNED BEEF OR [6] DRIED BEEF AND CHEESE SANDWICHES

Cut into tiny slivers:
    ¼ cup sharp American cheese
Cream the cheese well with:
    2 tablespoons mayonnaise
Shred finely and add:
    4 oz. canned corned beef or dried beef
Chop until fine and add:
    ¼ cup sweet-sour pickles
    1 tablespoon grated onion
    (2 tablespoons minced celery or parsley)
Season the spread, as needed, with:
    Salt and pepper

Curry powder, mustard or Worcestershire sauce
Spread it between:
    Slices of bread
The sandwiches may be toasted or served with sliced tomatoes and lettuce between the layers.

CORNED BEEF AND TOMATO SANDWICHES

Preheat broiler.
Prepare:
    Slices of buttered toast
Cover them with:
    Sliced corned beef
seasoned with:
    Mustard or horseradish
    Tomatoes seasoned with French dressing
Sprinkle the tops with:
    Grated cheese
Broil the sandwiches until the cheese is melted.

SANDWICH [1] SAVOYARDE

Preheat broiler.
Place on a shallow baker:
    ½ English muffin
Then add:
    A large thin slice of ham
Make a:
    2 egg French Omelet, page 188
large enough to cover the ham. Do not fold the omelet, but slip it flat onto the above. Sprinkle with:
    Grated Swiss cheese
Run under broiler until cheese melts. Serve at once.

HAM OR TONGUE SALAD SANDWICHES

I. Combine:
    Ground cooked ham or tongue
    Chopped onion or chives
    Chopped celery
Moisten them with:
    Cream or salad dressing
If cream is used, season with:

Paprika and salt, if
needed
Spread the filling between:
Thin slices of bread

II. Combine and mix:
2 tablespoons chopped
onion
2 tablespoons catsup
2 tablespoons chopped
green pepper
2 tablespoons chopped
pickles
½ lb. chopped sharp cheese
3 oz. deviled ham or ½ cup
finely cut cooked ham
¼ cup cream, melted butter
or oil
Serve in hollowed hard rolls.

HAWAIIAN TOAST   [4]
WITH BACON SANDWICH

Cut:
4 to 6 slices stale bread,
½ inch thick
Beat until light:
2 eggs
Beat in:
1 cup pineapple juice
½ teaspoon salt
Dip the bread in the egg mixture. Soak it well. Sauté in a
skillet:
8 slices bacon
Remove them to a hot platter.
Keep them hot. Fry the bread
in the bacon drippings, brown
one side and then the other. Remove the bread to the hot platter. Sauté in the bacon drippings:
4 slices drained pineapple,
cut into halves
Garnish the platter with the
bacon and the pineapple. Serve
the toast at once.

HAM, TOMATO AND EGG
SANDWICH

Slice and butter:
Rye bread
Place on it:
Slices boiled ham

Lettuce leaves
Sliced tomatoes
Garnish the sandwiches with:
Slices hard-cooked egg
Sprigs parsley
Serve them with:
Horseradish Dressing,
page 343, or Russian
Dressing, page 349

TOAST ROLLS WITH   [4]
HAM AND ASPARAGUS

A fine luncheon or supper dish
with a molded grapefruit salad
and coffee.
Preheat oven to 400°.
Drain:
2 cups asparagus tips
Remove the crusts from:
8 thin slices bread
Brush them lightly on both sides
with:
Melted butter
Place on each slice:
A slice boiled ham
Several asparagus tips
Roll the bread around the tips
or bring 2 corners together.
Fasten the bread with tooth-
picks. Bake these rolls on a
baking sheet until they are
lightly browned. Use the aspara-
gus water and cream to make:
Cream Sauce, page 359
Serve the rolls piping hot with
the sauce.

HAM AND PINEAPPLE
FRENCH TOAST
SANDWICH

Combine equal parts:
Ground ham
Crushed pineapple
Season these ingredients with:
French mustard
Spread this filling between slices
of:
Buttered bread
See French Toast (II, 290).
Spread the outside of the sand-
wiches with the egg mixture and
sauté them as directed.

TOASTED DEVILED HAM AND CHEESE SANDWICHES

Cover:
> Thin slices of toast

with a paste made of:
> Deviled ham, French
> mustard or horseradish

Or use:
> (Thin slices boiled ham)

Cover the ham with thin slices of:
> American cheese

Dot with:
> Capers

Press the sandwiches and refrigerate 6 hours. Then sauté until toasted in:
> Butter

Serve hot.

POOR BOY, SUBMARINE [4] OR HERO SANDWICH

Cut in half lengthwise a long loaf of:
> French Bread (II, 245)

Spread both cuts with:
> Butter

On the bottom half, arrange layers of:
> Sliced salami sausage
> Sliced sharp cheese
> Thinly sliced boiled ham
> (Thin slices tomato)

Put the top half of bread on to make a sandwich and cut into 4 pieces. Mix together:
> ¼ cup dry mustard
> 1 tablespoon dry white
> wine

Serve this with the sandwich.

TOASTED BRAUNSCHWEIGER SANDWICH

Braunschweiger is a refined version of the rather heavy smoked liver sausage.
Combine and stir to a smooth paste:
> Braunschweiger sausage
> Canned tomato soup or
> tomato paste
> (A few drops of cream or
> Worcestershire sauce)

Cut the crusts from:
> Thin slices of bread

Spread them with the sausage mixture. Roll the bread or make double-deck sandwiches. Toast and serve them very hot.

BACON AND CHEESE [4] SANDWICH

Preheat broiler.
Toast on either one or both sides, or use untoasted:
> 4 slices bread

Place on each slice:
> (A thick slice tomato)
> (Chopped onion and
> green peppers)
> (Sliced olives or pickles)
> A slice of American
> cheese

Spread the cheese with:
> Mustard or chili sauce

Cover each sandwich with:
> 2 slices bacon

Crisp the slices of bacon under the broiler and serve immediately. Also good with:
> (Hot Cheese Sauce)

EGG AND CHEESE [4] SANDWICH WITH TOMATO SAUCE

Rub:
> 4 slices French bread

with:
> (Garlic)

Dip them quickly in:
> Milk seasoned with a
> pinch of salt

Brown them in:
> Olive oil

Place them on a hot ovenproof plate. Cover them with:
> 4 chopped hard-cooked
> eggs
> 1 cup or more grated
> cheese
> 6 or more chopped olives
> Dots of butter

Place the slices under a broiler until the cheese is melted. Serve them with:
> Tomato Sauce, page 376

FRENCH TOAST [4] AND CHEESE

Preheat oven to 350°.
Prepare, omitting the sugar:
  French Toast (II, 290)
Toast the bread in the oven on
a buttered ovenproof plate for
about 5 minutes. Stir over very
low heat until smooth:
  ½ lb. grated or minced
    cheese
  ½ teaspoon salt
  A few grains cayenne
  ¼ cup milk
  3 tablespoons butter
Spread the toast with the cheese
mixture. Return it to the oven
to brown lightly.

FRENCH TOMATO TOAST

Beat until light:
  2 eggs
  ½ teaspoon salt
  ¼ teaspoon paprika
  ½ cup condensed tomato
    soup
Dip in this:
  6 slices of bread
Sauté the slices in hot:
  Butter or drippings
When a good brown, serve them
with:
  Cheese Sauce, page 364
  Minced parsley or chives

CHEESE SANDWICH WITH MUSHROOM SAUCE

Trim the crusts from:
  Slices light or dark bread
Spread them with:
  Butter
Place on each piece:
  Slices of cheese
  Lettuce leaves
  Slices tomato or
    cucumber
  Slices hard-cooked egg
  Sliced olives or pickles
Serve the sandwiches with:
  Mushroom Sauce,
    page 367

PUFFED CHEESE WITH [4] MUSHROOMS ON TOAST

Preheat oven to 375°.
Melt in a saucepan:
  1 tablespoon butter
Add and sauté until tender:
  ½ cup finely sliced
    mushrooms
  1 teaspoon grated onion
Combine:
  2 unbeaten egg yolks
  ½ lb. grated Swiss cheese:
    2 cups
  ¾ teaspoon salt
  ¼ teaspoon pepper
  A few grains cayenne
Stir in the mushroom and onion
mixture. Beat until stiff, but not
dry:
  2 egg whites
Fold them into the mixture.
Toast on one side:
  6 slices bread
Place them toasted side down on
a cookie sheet. Spread the untoasted sides lightly with:
  Butter
Heap the cheese mixture on the
bread. Bake the slices until they
are firm to the touch and well
puffed.

PEANUT BUTTER AND TOMATO SANDWICH

Preheat broiler.
Toast on one side:
  A slice of bread
Spread the untoasted side with:
  Peanut butter
mixed with:
  Chopped cooked bacon
  Bacon drippings
You may top this with:
  A thick slice of tomato
Season the tomato with:
  ¼ teaspoon brown sugar
  Salt and paprika
Put the sandwich under a broiler
for a minute or two.

PEANUT BUTTER AND [4] BACON SANDWICH

Preheat broiler.
Virtue, however admirable, is

frequently dull. Peanut butter needs enlivening. Try this mixture on the unconverted.
Combine:

> ¾ cup peanut butter
> ¼ cup mayonnaise
> ¼ teaspoon salt
> 2 tablespoons pickle relish or chili sauce
> ¼ cup cooked minced bacon

Toast on one side:

> 4 slices bread

Spread the untoasted side with the mixture. Broil the sandwiches until the tops are brown. Slice them diagonally.

CLUB SANDWICH

[Individual Serving]
Prepare:

> 3 large square slices of toast

Cover slice 1 with:

> A lettuce leaf
> 3 crisp slices hot bacon
> Slices of tomato
> 1 tablespoon mayonnaise (Drained slices pineapple)

Place slice 2 over slice 1 mixture and cover it with:

> Slices of cold cooked chicken
> 1 tablespoon mayonnaise

Place slice 3 over slice 2 mixture and cut the sandwich on the bias.

FRUIT STICKS

I. Cut into strips 3 by 1½ inches wide and ½ inch thick:

> White bread

Toast them on 3 sides. Place them on a baking sheet with the untoasted side up. Drain:

> Pineapple or apricot slices

Place them on the untoasted sides. Sprinkle them well with a mixture of:

> Brown sugar and cinnamon

Dot them with:

> Butter

Brown them under a broiler.

II. Preheat oven to 450°.
Prepare:

> Pie Dough (II, 293)

Roll it until very thin. Cut it into oblongs. Sprinkle:

> Pineapple or apricot slices

with:

> Cinnamon and brown sugar

Wrap the slices in the oblongs. Moisten the edges with water. Bake the slices for about 20 minutes.

LAMB OR CHICKEN SANDWICH

Trim the crusts from:

> Large slices rye bread

Spread them with:

> Butter

Place on each piece:

> Slices cold lamb or chicken
> Lettuce leaves
> Slices tomato
> Slices hard-cooked egg

Serve the sandwich with:

> Russian Dressing, page 349

CHICKEN AND CREAM CHEESE SANDWICHES

Spread:

> Slices of whole-wheat bread

with:

> Cream cheese softened with cream

Add:

> Slices of cooked chicken
> Chopped green olives
> Salt

HOT CHICKEN SANDWICHES

I. Cut into slices:

> Cold cooked chicken

Dip the slices in:

> Mayonnaise

Prepare:

> Biscuits (II, 284)

While hot, open and spread them with:

Butter

Place the chicken slices in the biscuits. Serve them hot with:

Chicken gravy, Cheese Sauce, page 364, or Mushroom Sauce, page 367

II. Using biscuits, as in the previous recipe, fill with:

Chicken Salad, page 51

or combine:

½ cup cooked minced chicken
1 chopped hard-cooked egg
6 chopped stuffed olives
¼ cup mayonnaise
(2 tablespoons chopped parsley)

Serve hot with one of the sauces mentioned previously.

III.

Preheat oven to 375°.

Prepare:

Buttered toast

Cover the toast with:

Sliced chicken

Sprinkle it with:

Crumbled Roquefort cheese

Cover it with:

Strips of notched bacon

Bake for about 10 minutes, until the bacon is crisp. Sliced tomatoes may be placed on the toast.

OPEN-FACED SEAFOOD SALAD AND TOMATO SANDWICHES

I. Prepare:

Slices of buttered bread

Cover them with:

Slices of tomato

Top the tomatoes with mounds of:

Tuna Salad, page 51, or other seafood

Garnish with:

Chopped parsley, olives or chives
Chopped sautéed bacon

II. Cut crosswise into 2 sections:

A large round loaf of bread

Spread cut sides with:

Butter

Place around the outer edges of each piece:

Thinly sliced tomatoes

Sprinkle with:

Salt and pepper
Chopped fresh basil or chives

Arrange like spokes of a wagon wheel, in the center of each piece:

Canned sardines

Decorate with:

Sliced black olives

Sprinkle some of the sardine oil over all, cut the pieces into 6 wedges each and serve.

TOASTED ROLLS WITH [4] CRAB MEAT AND CHEESE

Fine with beer or cider.

Preheat broiler.

Cut into halves:

4 rolls

Cover the 4 lower halves with:

Lettuce leaves

Combine:

¾ cup canned crab meat
¼ cup mayonnaise

Spread this on the lettuce. Spread the remaining halves with:

Butter
Slices of cheese
(Mustard)

Toast the cheese under a broiler until it is soft. Combine the halves.

LOBSTER SANDWICHES

Flake:

6 oz. canned lobster or other seafood

Sprinkle over it:

1 teaspoon lemon juice

Add:

½ cup minced celery

1 tablespoon minced onion
    or chives
½ cup mayonnaise

Mayonnaise, if too thick, is fine
thinned with sour cream. Season
with:
    (Worcestershire sauce,
    curry powder or freshly
    grated nutmeg)
Add:
    (Capers, chopped olives,
    pickles or parsley, etc.)
Spread these ingredients on:
    Buttered rye bread
You may add:
    Crisp lettuce leaves

SHRIMP SANDWICHES [3] WITH CHEESE SAUCE

Clean:
    1½ cups cooked shrimp
Melt:
    2 tablespoons butter
Add:
    1 tablespoon grated onion
    (1 sliced pimiento)
and the shrimp. Stir over low
heat for 1 minute. Prepare:
    6 slices toast
Heap the shrimp on the toast.
Serve with:
    Cheese Sauce, pag. 364

VEGETABLES

It is probably true that more outrages are perpetrated against vegetables than against any other basic foods. These outrages often begin when the seeds are sown —in impoverished ground; they may continue during the plant's development, because of inadequate moisture; and then reach some sort of climax in the almost uniformly careless handling that produce is subjected to on its way to the point of sale.

To preserve their true, delicate flavor, as well as their natural sugars and nutrients and enjoy green vegetables at their wholesome best, they should be ▶ washed just before cooking ▶ cooked just after picking ▶ just to the point of doneness, not a moment more, and ▶ eaten just off the heat.

▶ The longer vegetables take to reach maturity, the coarser their cellulose. The greater the period between picking and cooking, the longer the time needed to make them palatable. Naturally, longer cooking periods impair nutritive values, color and especially flavor—that quality a family considers first.

Here are ways to get the best out of the less than perfect vegetables we are often forced to buy. Market on days when supplies reach your store— buying so that you hold them the least possible time before use. ▶ Apply to each kind of vegetable the tests for ripeness we describe later.

If stocks are limited, always prefer a fresh, fluffy, country or garden lettuce over a bruised Bibb and a crisp bunch of carrots over darkened, leathery artichokes. Care in cooking, piquancy of seasoning and ingenuity in combining familiar varieties can compensate for the more commonplace choice.

If the vegetable is old, dress it up with seasoned butters, herbs, spices and sauces. If young, drain it, toss it in butter, allowing 1 tablespoon to every cup of vegetable and season it very lightly, so that its own tender flavor prevails. You will find that young vegetables have an abundance of natural sugars but that ▶ older ones often profit by an added pinch of sugar in cooking. You will notice varied seasonings suggested in our individual recipes. Add them with a light hand; the exception being dried legumes and canned vegetables, which are greatly improved by a bold and imaginative approach. ▶ Salting just after the onset of cooking will slightly firm vegetable structure and help retain color and flavor. ▶ Allow about ¼ teaspoon of salt to each cup of water. But see the steaming method we prefer, page 252.

ABOUT STORING VEGETABLES

Certain vegetables and fruits should not be stored together. Apples give off an ethylene gas that makes carrots bitter, for example, and onions hasten the spoilage of potatoes. Watch for other such relationships. Do not wash vegetables until you are ready to use them and then do not soak them, except as indicated, because moisture tends to leach away the water-soluble vitamins.

A good general rule ♦ for leaf vegetables, peas and green beans is to store them unwashed at about 45° in plastic bags. There is enough moisture within the vegetables to keep them fresh this way. The exception is water cress, page 31. Cut the leaves from root vegetables before storing, for the flow of sap continues to the leaf at the expense of the root. Store thick-skinned vegetables like potatoes, rutabagas and turnips unwashed in a dry, dark, cool place. The ideal temperature is 55° to 65°.

ABOUT PREPARING VEGETABLES FOR COOKING

Some vegetables may simply be scrubbed and steamed or baked unpeeled. These methods keep vitamin losses to a minimum, provided cooking is not overly prolonged. Sometimes vegetables are scrubbed, scraped or thinly pared before cooking. Remember that most of the vitamins lie near the skin and that deep paring will mean losing them. Prepare peeled vegetables and cook them immediately to minimize their exposure to air. ♦ Never soak after slicing, if the greatest amount of nutrient values is to be retained. Whether you cook vegetables whole or sliced ♦ see that pieces are uniform in size, so they will all be done and tender simultaneously.

Many chopping and slicing devices are advertised, but nothing can replace a skilled relaxed wrist and a sharp French knife. Acquire this indispensable trick and you will be forever grateful. Practice with a mushroom, which is yielding and not slip-

pery when placed cap down, and work up to an onion, which is resistant and evasive. In either case ♦ to slice, first cut the onion or apple or whatever you are slicing, so that it rests on a flat, not a rolling base, then hold this object as shown in the sketch below. For a good view, showing how the knife handle is held relaxed between the thumb and forefinger, see Soufflé Potatoes, page 317. ♦ The point of the knife is never lifted from the cutting board but forms a pivot. The cutting edge is never lifted above the first joint of the left forefinger.

The handle end of the knife is raised high enough to be eased gently up and down, its wide blade guided by the perpendicular left forefinger and midfinger. As the slicing progresses, inch a slow retreat with the left hand without releasing a firm grasp on the object.

If celery or Chinese cabbage, for instance, are to be sliced on the diagonal, the two guide fingers are set at an angle, as shown next. But the knife in the right hand continues its relaxed accurate slicing, while the left makes way without losing control of the stalks. To peel very hard, round vegetables, see a trick sketched on page 338.

If you are really determined to lure your family into eating vegetables, you will find they will respond more readily if the vegetables are attractive in shape and perhaps rather sparse in number. Think of the irresistible charm of vegetables floating like flowers in a Japanese lacquered bowl. The French are also very adept at presentation, if more lavish, and they disguise the same old carrots, beans and potatoes under a mass of impressive aliases. As printanière, they are spring-grown, young, tender and thinly sliced. As brunoise, salpicon, mirepoix and macédoine, they are ageless, and sliced respectively from ⅛ to ¼ to ⅜ inch, which latter size we call just plain "diced." As jardinière, julienne or allumette, they are taller and thinner, about 2 to 3 inches long and ⅛ inch through. When they are round in shape and small, you may call them pearls; if they are elliptical, call them olivette at ⅜ inch, noisette at ½ inch and Parisienne, if about 1 inch at their narrowest diameter. Utilize whatever scraps are left over in ⅃ blender soups or, unless they are starchy ones, in the stockpot.

ABOUT MAINTAINING FLAVOR AND COLOR DURING VEGETABLE COOKING

There are bound to be some nutritional losses, especially of vitamin C, in any cooking process. It does not follow that eating vegetables raw is the whole answer. Cooked carrots and spinach, in spite of losses during cooking, will have more nutrients available for absorption by the body than raw. ◗ The greatest losses probably come in mashing and puréeing. If done when the vegetables are hot, exposure to air during these processes will involve losses of ¼ to ½ of the vitamin C content. If you prepare mashed or puréed vegetables, compensate by serving a salad or citrus fruit at the same meal. All in all, you will do best nutritionally with fresh vegetables; next, with frozen ones that have been held below 0° for less than 2 months; last, with canned vegetables, provided the liquid in the can is utilized. Dehydrated vegetables, frozen and nonfrozen, suffer great loss of nutrients, the latter, especially, if improperly packaged. For cooking frozen vegetables, see page 254.

No one method of vegetable cooking can claim superiority over all other methods, but ◗ those processes which retain the best color and flavor are most apt to retain the most nutrients. ◗ Color should never be maintained by the addition of baking soda, for this method not only destroys nutrient values but makes the vegetable mushy in texture. Color may, however, be lost without accompanying nutrient loss if you cook in hard water, see (II, 147). ◗ The addition of vinegar or lemon juice to the cooking water will stabilize color. Greens, cauliflower, cabbage, onions, turnips and beets will need about 1 teaspoon for each 2 cups of water. Another method of preserving color without losing nutrients is to cook vegetables in milk. This tenderizes them more rapidly too, although sometimes, due to acid in the vegetable, the milk may curdle harmlessly.

It is advisable to cook most vegetables ‣ covered and with a small amount of water. ‣ Exceptions are the cabbage and onion tribes, turnips, parsnips, beets and wild greens which, when boiled, require water to cover. All are cooked uncovered. They react adversely under too great heat and too long a period of cooking. The greens become slimy and the strong, volatile oils of all these vegetables give off unpleasant odors—and they discolor. It is often wise to parblanch, page 88, this whole group of vegetables, briefly. ‣ Both when putting them into hot water which has reached a rolling boil for the blanching and again for the cooking, add them gradually so as not to disturb the boiling. These vegetables also tend to discolor badly, especially if covered. Blanching, page 88, helps to retain their color, as does cooking Cauliflower à blanc (II, 147). Do not cover any vegetable completely after the cooking is over, but allow the steam to escape and the dish will have much better color.

No matter which method of cooking you use, be sure ‣ to keep the vegetable waters unless they taste too strong. Use them for their invaluable nutritional qualities and flavoring powers (II, 138).

ABOUT STEAMING VEGETABLES

Steaming vegetables, we find, gives the most consistently good results. See the sketches of steamers on page 253. Our favorite method ‣ when time is short, is a French steamer used with a pressure cooker. If you ✪ pressure-steam, add a minute or

two to the time we indicate for pressure cooked vegetables. Expel all air from the pan before cl..ing the vent, Time carefully, for vegetables may be quickly overcooked by this method. Or use regular heat under a double boiler with a specially built steamer inset—sketched on page 253. Steaming is such a superior method, we feel, that, if you have no adequate equipment, it is worthwhile to improvise a steamer by placing a colander in any pot with a tight-fitting lid.

In any steaming, not matter what accessory you use, be sure that ‣ the water is boiling before you set the perforated container over it. ‣ Cover at once and cook 3 to 5 minutes longer than when vegetables are processed in boiling water.

ABOUT PANNING VEGETABLES

Panning, also known as braising or covered-skillet cooking, as well as stir-frying—discussed later—are very good and quick methods for tender vegetables and those very finely and evenly sliced. ‣ They are prepared the same way for both methods: sliced fine and usually cut on the diagonal for any that tend to be stringy. If leaves are coarse, remove mid-ribs and stem ends. For 4 servings, allow about 1 lb. kale, cabbage, okra, celery or celery cabbage, about 1½ lbs. of spinach or chard, ¾ lb. beans.

Skillet and panning cookery requires about 1 tablespoon of oil or butter per pound of vegetables. If the vegetables are dry, sprinkle them lightly with water before adding them to the hot fat. To pan, braise or skillet-cook any tender vegetable, have ready a pan with a tight-fitting lid. Heat the pan, put in the fat and heat to the point of fragrance. Quickly add the ▶ uniformly sliced vegetables and clap the lid on at once to retain as much steam as possible. When the steam comes up vigorously ▶ reduce the heat at once and cook over low heat until the vegetable is just tender. Shake the pan repeatedly to be sure the contents do not stick.

The braising or panning method is also an effective, if somewhat slower, way to do small quantities of podded vegetables. Let them remain in the pod and shell them just before serving. Allow about 1½ to 2 lbs. of these vegetables—depending on how full the pods are—for 4 servings. Depending also on the thickness of the pod, add from ⅓ to ¾ cup boiling water for each pound of vegetables and cook 15 to 20 minutes or until tender. No fat is necessary if the vegetables are podded. Butter them after shelling.

ABOUT STIR-FRYING

This is the method so typical of Chinese cooking, which allows the vegetables to remain tender, crisp and of very good color. They are traditionally stirred in a big open conical pan held erect by a ring stand ▶ over really fierce heat. Stir-frying is an ideal way to cook mixed tender vegetables quickly—the whole process lasting only 3 or 4 minutes. Preparation is the slow part, as the vegetables

must all be cut uniformly as for panning, page 252. Those which need longer cooking are put in first and the tenderer ones later, so they are all done at the same time.

Use any cooking oil, other than olive. Allow 2 teaspoons of oil to 1 pound of vegetables. ▶ Have the pan very hot and heat the oil to the point of fragrance. A slice or two of fresh ginger root or garlic may be put in at this time and discarded before the vegetables are added. Stir the vegetables rapidly to make sure they are well coated with the oil. Continue to cook ▶ uncovered, over high heat, stirring constantly until the vegetables are just tender.

Watery vegetables like cucumber, tomato and zucchini, and thin-leafed types like spinach, Chinese cabbage, bean sprouts and salad greens may need no water. Beans and root vegetables will require about ¾ cup of stock or water for each pound. Cook these a little longer —about 5 to 8 minutes in all.

When the vegetables are just tender, you may add Chinese Sauce for Vegetables, page 372. Stir it into the vegetables—and cooked meat, if you are using any. ▶ Cover the pan briefly until the sauce reaches the boiling point and serve at once.

▶ To ensure crispness, bring your guests to the table the moment you have finished cooking. Be sure also ▶ to preheat lidded dishes from which to serve the food.

The preceding description applies primarily to meat-and-vegetable dishes, but it may be ♦ adapted to meat combinations, too—although ♦ we do not recommend it for raw pork. First, cook thin slices or slivers of lean meat briefly in the pan. Remove the meat and set it aside —keeping it warm. Cook the vegetables in the same fat with the meat juices. When they are ready, add the meat to them just before serving. It is advisable to cook no more than one pound of meat at a time by this method.

❂ ABOUT PRESSURE COOKED VEGETABLES

Please see About Pressure Cooking, page 81. Rather than cook directly in a small amount of water, we prefer to pressure steam, as described previously in About Steamed Vegetables. For pressure timing, see individual recipes. Be sure to save the cooking juices for the stock pot.

⅄ ABOUT BLENDED PURÉED VEGETABLES

The blender is a real find for mothers of young children who want to cook fresh vegetables all at once for the whole family and then purée the very young children's portion. As an alternative, well-washed and scrubbed, tender, raw vegetables may be blended and then cooked to the boiling point. Tough ones should be briefly parboiled, cooled and then blended. You may reheat briefly in butter or cream before serving.

▤ ABOUT CAMPFIRE VEGETABLES

Here are 2 simple, potless ways to cook vegetables for an outdoor barbecue. For the first, use frozen or sliced and washed vegetables. Place them on heavy-weight aluminum foil and season them. Use the drugstore wrap (II, 550). Place the foil-wrapped vegetables on a grill or under or on hot coals for 10 to 15 minutes.

For the second method, place —directly on a greased grill above the coals—thick slices of tomato, mushroom, pepper, parboiled onion. Cover with an inverted colander. Cook until tender.

✳ ABOUT COOKING FROZEN VEGETABLES

♦ Please read about Thawing and Cooking of Frozen Foods (II, 552). To cook these convenience foods so they are all heated through at the same time, use a frozen-food steamer.

❂ To pressure cook frozen foods, allow about ½ as long as for the regular pressure cooking times given in individual recipes, but use the same amounts of water.

If using an electric skillet, place the hard-frozen vegetables, except for spinach and corn on the cob, which must be partially thawed, in the skillet and cover. Set at 350° until steam escapes. Then turn to 300° until the vegetable is tender.

▲ ABOUT COOKING VEGETABLES AT HIGH ALTITUDES

In baking vegetables at high altitudes, use approximately the same temperatures and timing given for sea-level cooking. In cooking vegetables at high altitude by any process involving moisture, both more liquid and a longer cooking time are needed, as the vegetables boil at lower temperatures. Frequently, the longer time can be reduced if the vegetables are thinly sliced or cut into small units. To avoid tough stems and overcooked leaves on leafy vegetables, remove the mid rib and use it in the stock pot.

Make these adjustments as an approximate time guide: for each 1000 feet of elevation, add to the cooking time given in the recipes about 10% for whole beets, carrots and onions, and about 7% for green beans, squash, green cabbage, turnips and parsnips. ▲ ✳ In cooking frozen vegetables at high altitudes, whole carrots and beans may require as much as 5 to 12 minutes of additional cooking, while other frozen vegetables may need only 1 to 2 more minutes.

The extension division of most land grant colleges will test the gauge of your pressure cooker and probably provide a pressure chart for your area free of charge.

In pressuring vegetables at high altitude, you will have to increase the liquid in your cooker ¼ to ½ cup for every 2 cups of vegetables, depending on their respective length of cooking time. As with other vegetable-cooking at high altitudes, sliced or shredded vegetables, as well as peas, corn and spinach may cook almost as rapidly as at sea level, at 15 lbs. pressure. But you may find that, with some of the leafy greens, 10 lbs. of pressure and a slightly longer cooking period gives a better result. This has been found true for asparagus, celery, turnips and cauliflower. Don't be surprised if whole potatoes, beets, yams and beans need considerably more time than at sea level.

ABOUT REHEATED VEGETABLES

Reheating vegetables is frowned on—both from a culinary and health standpoint. If you do reheat them, put them with a few teaspoons of water or stock in the top of a covered double boiler or reheat or bake them in a hot sauce. Allow about ¼ to ½ as much sauce as vegetables. Reheating in a sauce is one of the best ways to serve vegetables which must be held. The sautéing and browning of cooked vegetables diminish vitamins. Try serving leftover vegetables vinaigretted in a salad, remembering—contrary to at least one precept we learned at mother's knee—that cold food is as nutritious as hot.

Canned or frozen vegetables have, of course, already suffered some loss of flavor and vitamins. Reheating before serving increases this loss. ◗ Be sure to retain the canning or cooking water for use in soup or sauce or as the medium in which to reheat.

◗ Always clean off tops before opening cans, as they may be dusty or have been sprayed with poisonous insecticides while in the store. Also ◗ avoid metal slivers in opening a can, by starting to open it beyond the side seam and stopping before you cut through it. Food may be stored safely in opened cans, covered and refrigerated, but a metallic taste results, especially if the food is acid.

ABOUT CREAMED, BUTTERED AND SAUCED VEGETABLES

Practically any vegetables may be served in or with a sauce. They may be steamed or even deep fried before saucing. ◗ Drain them well before combining with sauces or butter.

The amount to allow for garnishing will depend so largely on the richness of the sauce, from ½ to 1 tablespoon of butter per cup of cooked vegetables —on up to 4 tablespoons of a cream sauce garnish. If the vegetable is heated in the sauce, allow about 2 to 3 tablespoons for each cup of vegetables, using less if it is a rich sour cream dressing—more, perhaps, if based on cream soup. Consider, too, if the vegetable is to be presented in individual deep dishes or from a big serving bowl onto a flat plate.

If you are casseroling the vegetable in a sauce, allow enough sauce to just cover the vegetables. Such casseroles are often finished off Au Gratin, page 389.

Add to vegetable butters and sauces, if not already indicated in the recipe, citrus juices and pinches of zests (II, 219), fresh or dried herbs, curry powder, mustard, chili powder, horseradish or grated cheese; and don't forget the onion (II, 209).

ABOUT VEGETABLES FONDUES

Although the term fondue is usually associated with cheese, page 239, or Boeuf Fondu Bourguignonne, page 475, it applies also to vegetables reduced to a pulp by very, very slow cooking in butter, as for Tomato Pudding II. Some other vegetables that lend themselves well to such dishes are carrots, celery, eggplant, sweet pepper, onion, leek and lettuce.

To prepare them for this method of cooking, first rid them of excess moisture in one of the following ways. Except for tomatoes, they may be parblanched, page 88, from 3 to 5 minutes. Eggplant and cucumber may be sliced, salted generously and allowed to drain on a rack. Salting clears them of a rather unpleasant astringent quality they sometimes acquire. They may also be thinly sliced, salted, placed in a bowl and weighted to force out excess moisture.

Mushrooms and green onions may be wrapped in a dish towel and wrung out. If you are strong enough, you may be able to extract enough juices for the stock pot.

Tomatoes for fondues may be cut at the stem end and squeezed toward the cut end to get rid of both moisture and seeds.

Cook fondue vegetables covered, until they reach a naturally puréed state.

ABOUT STUFFED VEGETABLES

Tomatoes, peppers, squashes, cucumbers, onions, mushrooms, all make decorative and delicious vegetable cases. For a "new dimension," fill them with other vegetables, contrasting in color or flavor; or point up the bland ones with a farce of cooked food, with buttered, crumbed, cooked vegetables or with creamed mixtures. Raw foods needing long cooking should not be used in vegetable stuffings.

As vegetable cases need different timing for blanching, see recipes under individual vegetables for this information. Other factors remain the same. After draining, place the filled cases on a rack, in a pan containing about ¼ inch of water.

Heat the cases through in a 400° oven, unless otherwise indicated, before serving. Or, if you want to serve them Au Gratin I or II, page 389, you may find they have better color if you run them first under a broiler and then bake as above to heat them. With Au Gratin III, the cheese will probably brown the tops sufficiently in the baking alone without using a broiler at all.

ABOUT VEGETABLES À LA GRECQUE

These mixed vegetables, left whole if small or cut into attractive shapes, see page 250, become aromatic as the result of being boiled in a court bouillon of highly seasoned oil and water. They are served at between 70° and 90° or, at most, slightly chilled, so that the oil will not be evident. They make convenient hors d'oeuvre, meat tray or salad garnishes, as they keep well if covered and refrigerated. They are excellent for an antipasto tray. Prepare one of the following court bouillons in which to cook:

1 lb. mixed vegetables

Suitable vegetables include artichoke hearts, julienned carrots, cauliflower florets, celery, fennel, green beans, leeks, mushrooms, pearl onions, peppers and pickled whole olives. Cucumber and eggplant slices or strips are delicious but these should have excess moisture removed, see page 288.

Squeeze over the cut vegetables, to keep them white:

Juice of 2 lemons

I. Place in a 3-quart stainless or enamel pan:

4 cups water
⅓ to ½ cup olive oil
1 teaspoon salt
2 peeled cloves garlic
(3 peeled shallots)

and the following herbs and spices, tied in a cheesecloth bag:

6 sprigs parsley
2 teaspoons fresh thyme
12 peppercorns
(3 coriander seeds or ¼
    teaspoon orégano)
(⅛ teaspoon fennel or celery
    seeds)

Add for flavor 2 of the squeezed lemon halves. Bring the mixture to a boil, then remove from the heat to season for about 15 minutes. Remove the spice bag and garlic. Bring the court bouillon again slowly to a ◗ simmer. Add in turn the most delicately flavored of the prepared vegetables. Once more bring the oil just to a boil, reduce the heat and let the vegetables heat through and then cool in the marinade. Drain them and place them in a jar, using a slotted wooden spoon. Now, use the marinade to cook the next most delicately flavored vegetable. Continue till each one has been cooked and cooled in the marinade. When they are all in the jar, mixed or separate, cover them with the marinade to store. After the vegetables have been eaten, use the marinade for sauces.

II. Combine in a stainless or enamel pan:

1 cup wine
2 cups olive oil
½ cup vinegar
½ to ¾ cup water
2 cloves garlic
3 sprigs parsley
6 peppercorns
2 sliced lemons
¼ teaspoon salt

Cook the vegetables in the heated mixture, as in I.

III. This rather off-beat version is a pleasant change.

Combine in a stainless or enamel pan:

¾ cup olive oil
½ cup wine vinegar
¾ cup catsup
½ cup chili sauce
1 clove garlic
1 teaspoon Worcestershire
    sauce

Cook the vegetables in the heated mixture, as in I.

ABOUT VEGETABLES BAKED UNPEELED

We have always liked the snug phrase "baked in their jackets" to describe this process. But we are told that at least one young cook, after encountering it, called a home economist of the local utility company and complained that her grocer was unable to supply her with potato-jackets!

Only to a degree true is the concept that unpeeled baking is the very best way of cooking to preserve vitamins in vegetables. Since most vitamins lie just under the skin ▶ those most sensitive to heat will be destroyed if baking is too protracted and the skin becomes too crusty. Proper baking, however, destroys few and we can cheerfully put up with the loss in gaining the distinctive baked flavor.

ABOUT VEGETABLES FOR A ROAST

To cook vegetables for a roast, it is better on several scores to process them separately. For one thing, if they are placed in the roasting pan, the steam they exude tends to give a moister oven heat than is desirable for meat roasting. For another, typical root vegtables such as potatoes, carrots, onions and turnips themselves profit by separate cooking. Steam them, page 252, first, then drain and dry. Cook them in butter in a ▶ heavy, covered pan until almost tender and finish browning them uncovered.

GLAZED ROOT VEGETABLES

Choose:
  2 cups young vegetables—

onions, carrots, turnips or potatoes
Simmer, covered, in a very heavy pan with:
  1 cup veal or chicken stock
  ½ teaspoon salt
  2 teaspoons sugar
  2 tablespoons butter
When the vegetables are tender and the liquid has been almost absorbed ▶ uncover and continue to cook, shaking the pan constantly over brisk heat until they are coated with a golden glaze.

ABOUT DEEP FAT FRIED VEGETABLES

The French have made the fried potato famous in floured strips, page 318, the English in chips, page 401. The Italians, by using either a beaten egg coating or a batter, produce their famous vegetable and other mixtures as fritto misto—and the Japanese, who learned this trick from Portuguese sailors way back in the 16th century, prepare them today under the term tempura.

Since success depends so largely on the ▶ quality of the fat and avoiding its excess absorption, please read About Deep Fat Frying, page 75. ▶ Be sure to have the vegetables dry before applying the coating. It is also best to let the coating dry for about 10 minutes before immersing the food in fat brought to between 350° and 375°. Cook until the vegetables are golden.

Vegetables suitable for this type of cooking are long green beans; ⅓ inch thick eggplant slices—barely nicked with tiny knife marks at ½ inch intervals, all around the bands of skin; mushrooms and tiny green peppers—whole or cut in half vertically; cucumber, squash, zucchini or sweet potato rounds, cut lotus roots or bamboo shoots, small bundles of julienned onions, asparagus tips, finely shredded cabbage, cauliflower or broccoli florets, artichoke hearts or stems.

After preparing the vegetables, be sure to sprinkle any which may discolor with lemon juice.

ARTICHOKES

Artichokes of the globe type, sketched, differ in shape, taste and method of cooking from Jerusalem artichokes, page 260. If the leaves are spreading or discolored, the artichokes are not tender. They are served whole or cored and eaten with the fingers after cooking. Serve one to each diner. The leaves are dipped, one at a time, in a sauce and the lower end is simply pulled through the teeth to extract the tender edible portion. The leaf is then discarded. Continue to eat them until a light-colored cone of young leaves appears. Pull this up with one movement. Then lift the fuzzy center out and discard it. Eat the remaining heart with a fork, dipping each piece in sauce first.

To prepare, hold by the stem end and dash up and down, quickly, in a deep bowl of water:

    Artichokes

Cut off the stems. Pull off the tough bottom row of leaves and cut off ¼ of the tops. For this, you may use scissors. To avoid discoloration, dip the cut parts in:

    Lemon juice

◆ Steam, page 252, or place the artichokes upright on a trivet, with 1 to 2 inches of boiling water beneath. Add:

    1 sliced onion or 1 mashed
      clove garlic
    2 celery ribs with leaves

    1½ tablespoons lemon juice,
      wine or vinegar
    (2 tablespoons salad oil)
    (A bay leaf)

Cook them covered for 45 minutes or until tender. Drain and serve them hot with:

    Melted butter,
    Mayonnaise, page 345,
    Hollandaise Sauce, page
      368, Béchamel Sauce,
      page 359, or Vinaigrette
      Sauce, page 341

Cooked artichokes may be served chilled. ⊘ Pressure cook large artichokes at 15 lbs. about 15 minutes, small ones 8 minutes at 15 lbs.

CORED ARTICHOKES

Clean and trim, as described previously

    Artichokes

Turn them upside down. Press hard to force the leaves apart. Reverse and insert a grapefruit corer. Press the handles down to cut out the choke. Remove it. Tie artichokes into shape with string. ◆ Steam them, page 252, or cook as in previous recipe. Drain them well, untie and serve either warm or cold, the centers filled with:

    Hollandaise Sauce,
      page 368

If they are too hot when filled, the Hollandaise may separate. Or serve cold with:

    Marinated shrimp and
      mayonnaise

ARTICHOKE HEARTS

Remove all leaves and chokes from:

Artichokes

Steam them, page 252, or drop the hearts into 1 inch of:

Boiling water

to which you may add:

Lemon juice

Simmer them, covered, for 20 minutes or until tender. Serve them with:

Brown Butter, page 383, or Hollandaise Sauce, page 368

Cooked or canned artichoke hearts, well drained, may be sautéed until hot in:

Butter or drippings

to which you may add:

Garlic, shallots or onions

Season them with:

Salt and paprika
Lemon juice

Serve hot or cold. For a good way to stuff cold artichoke hearts, see Salads, pages 40–41.

STUFFED BAKED ARTICHOKES

Preheat oven to 350°.
I. Roman Style
Clean, trim and blanch, page 88:

Artichokes

Drain them well. Make a dressing of:

Bread crumbs
Minced garlic or onion
Chopped celery
Chopped anchovies or anchovy paste
Grated Parmesan cheese
Chopped parsley
Salt and paprika

Push the dressing down between the leaves. The choke may be removed, as described previously, if desired, and the center filled with the dressing. Pour over the artichokes a little:

Olive oil

Place them in a baking dish and cover the bottom of the dish with ½ inch of:

Boiling water or stock

Bake them, covered, until they are done, about 1 hour.

II. Or fill the artichokes with either:

Ham or sausage stuffing, or Stuffed Mushrooms, page 297, or Creamed Spinach, page 326, and grated cheese

JERUSALEM ARTICHOKES

This tall, yellow blooming composite of our roadsides has been miraculously hybridized and should be better known. Its nubbly roots proliferate to furnish us that extra vegetable we always wish we could find. They do need watching while being cooked.

Wash:

1½ lbs. Jerusalem artichokes

◗ Steam them, page 252, or drop them into:

Boiling water

To prevent discoloration, add:

1 teaspoon mild vinegar or white wine

Cook them ◗ covered, until they are tender only. If permitted to cook beyond this point, they will again become tough. Test them with a toothpick after 15 minutes. Drain them. Remove the peel. Melt:

2 to 3 tablespoons butter

Add:

2 drops hot pepper sauce
2 tablespoons chopped parsley

Pour these ingredients over the artichokes or cream them, page 255. Or, cut into halves and ⊘ pressure cook at 15 lbs. for 10 minutes.

ASPARAGUS

The Romans used to say if they wanted to do something in a

hurry, "Do it in less time than it takes to cook asparagus."

I.   **4 to 6 Servings**

Wash:

     2 lbs. asparagus

Cut off or snap off the lower part of the stalks. Keep the trimmings for soup. It is seldom necessary to skin green asparagus. If it is white, skin from below the head, increasing the depth of cut into the stalk as you approach the base to remove any bitter flavor in the skin. Tie the asparagus in serving bunches with white string. Place them upright in a deep stewpan or in the bottom part of a double boiler, the lower ends in:

     ½ cup boiling water

Cook the asparagus ▶ closely covered 12 minutes or until ten-

der. An inverted double boiler top may be used. The steam will cook the tips. Drain the asparagus well. Reserve the liquor. Add:

     ½ teaspoon salt

Melt:

     ⅓ cup butter

Sauté in it, for 1 minute:

     1 cup bread crumbs

Pour this mixture over the tips of the asparagus or serve them with:

     1 cup Cream Sauce I, page 359, made with half cream and half asparagus liquor, Egg Sauce, page 360, or Hollandaise Sauce, page 368

II. Sometimes, if asparagus must be held, both the color and texture are improved if this recipe is used—although we do not guarantee nutritive value.

Arrange in a flat pan:

     2 lbs. cleaned asparagus

Place them not more than 3 or 4 deep. Add:

     ½ teaspoon salt

Cover with cold water. Prepare and cover with a poaching paper, page 83. Bring them to a boil, reduce the heat at once and ▶ simmer about 15 minutes. Keep lukewarm until ready to serve.

Drain when ready to serve.

BAMBOO SHOOTS

These slightly acid shoots, which complement mushrooms and meat, must be young and tender and from an edible bamboo plant.

If fresh, boil:

     Bamboo shoots

in:

     Water

about 10 to 15 minutes. Discard the water and then the shoots are ready to use. If using canned shoots, scrape off the calcium deposits. If you want to use only part of a can, store the remainder by first draining. Re-cover with cold water and refrigerate ▶ covered, for about 1 week.

ABOUT FRESH BEANS

Green or snap beans, formerly called string because their strings had to be removed, have in many instances been hybridized so that now they snap clean and need only have the ends snipped off. Kentucky wonders and wax beans, however, still need both snipping and stringing. To prepare broad beans, see Lima Beans, page 268. To prepare immature fava beans or marrow-fat beans, see Podded Peas, page 307. For ma-

ture green favas, see Lima
Beans. For dried favas, see
Dried Legumes, page 264. Haricots verts, with their okra-like
flavored overtones, are otherwise much like green beans.
◗ To avoid toughening any
beans, salt when cooking is half
finished.

GREEN OR SNAP [4]
BEANS

This vegetable is available fresh
the year around and lends itself
to endless variations.
Wash:
    1 lb. green beans
Snip off the ends. You may then
sliver them, French them on the
diagonal or leave them whole. If
the latter, tie them in individual
bunches before cooking. When
cooked and drained, arrange
them on a platter and cover
with one of the garnishes or
sauces suggested below. To cook
green beans ◗ steam, page 252,
or drop them into:
    Boiling water or part
    water and part stock
Reduce the heat at once. Place
on top of the beans:
    (1 whole peeled onion)
Cook partially covered, page
251, if you wish to preserve the
color; or covered, if you wish to
preserve more nutrients. Simmer until barely tender, no
longer—about 20 minutes. Before draining, you may remove
the onion.
    Correct the seasoning
Cover with:
    1 tablespoon melted butter

ADDITIONS TO GREEN
BEANS

To further flavor beans during
the cooking, add:
    (1 small cut-up onion)
    (1- to 2-inch cube of salt
    pork)
To garnish or sauce, use for 1
lb. of beans:

    1 tablespoon butter or
    browned butter, or ¼
    cup buttered crumbs, or
    2 tablespoons brown
    onion butter, or 2
    tablespoons crumbled
    bacon and drippings
Add to the above fats:
    (1 teaspoon celery or dill
    seed) or (1 teaspoon fresh
    summer savory or basil)
Or garnish with:
    Anchovy Butter or Oil,
    page 384, or Almond
    Garnish, page 390
Or add:
    ½ cup sautéed mushrooms
    ⅓ to ½ cup cultured sour
    cream
    2 tablespoons chopped
    parsley
Or add:
    2 tablespoons wine vinegar
    ¼ teaspoon mustard
    1 tablespoon
    Worcestershire sauce
    A drop of hot pepper
    sauce
Or add:
    2 tablespoons butter
    ¼ cup toasted slivered
    almonds
    ¼ cup sliced water
    chestnuts
    ¼ cup sliced cooked
    mushrooms
If the beans are left long, cover
with:
    A Cream Sauce
    Variation, page 359, or
    1 can Cream of Chicken
    or Mushroom Soup and
    herbs, or Quick
    Tomato Sauce, page 376
    or Egg Sauce I, page 360

CASSEROLE GREEN [6]
BEANS

I.
Preheat oven to 350°.
What becomes of the onions
and peppers? They frequently
disappear, leaving marvelously
seasoned beans. An easy dish for

the hostess who cooks her own dinner.
Trim:

>1 lb. green beans

Skin and chop:

>4 medium-size white onions

Remove the seeds and membrane from:

>2 medium-size green
>peppers

Chop the peppers. Butter a baking dish. Place in it alternate layers of the vegetables, beginning and ending with a layer of beans. Sprinkle each layer with:

>Salt and paprika

Dot each layer with:

>Butter

Bake the vegetables ▶ covered, for about 1¼ hours or until the beans are tender. Before serving, garnish with:

>Au Gratin II, page 389

II. Preheat oven to 350°.
Prepare for cooking:

>1 lb. green beans

Place them in a greased casserole. Cover with:

>1 can cream of tomato soup
>3 tablespoons prepared
>horseradish
>2 teaspoons Worcestershire
>sauce
>¼ teaspoon salt
>¼ teaspoon paprika

Bake ▶ covered, for about 1 hour or until tender. Remove the lid and garnish with:

>Au Gratin III, page 389

Serve when the cheese is melted.

GREEN BEANS, [4]
POTATOES AND SMOKED MEAT

Cook until nearly tender in water to cover:

>A piece of smoked meat:
>ham, picnic, Canadian
>bacon, etc.

If using already cooked or leftover ham or bone, just bring to a boil before adding:

>1 lb. green beans

>4 halved, pared, medium
>potatoes
>(1 onion)

Simmer, covered, about 20 to 25 minutes.

>Correct the seasoning.

Serve from a large platter, garnished with:

>Lemon wedges

SWEET-SOUR BEANS [4]

Trim and shred lengthwise:

>1 lb. green beans

▶Steam them, page 252, or drop them into:

>Boiling water

to barely cover. Cook them, covered, about 20 minutes. Now, render the fat slowly from:

>3 pieces lean bacon

Cook with it:

>2 tablespoons chopped
>onions

When the bacon is crisp, remove it and swirl in the pan:

>1 tablespoon white wine
>vinegar
>1 tablespoon sugar
>½ teaspoon salt

Drain the liquid from the beans and add it to the skillet mixture. Then combine with the beans and cut-up bacon and serve. A good variation to this dish is the addition of:

>Bean sprouts

PURÉED GREEN BEANS, PEAS OR LIMAS

In winter, these are a fresh note if used as a base for soup, as a lining in serving sautéed mushrooms or as a puréed vegetable, garnished with parsley.
Purée:

>2 cups cooked beans or
>peas

Use a ⅄ blender or a food mill.
Add:

>2 tablespoons butter
>Correct the seasoning

and serve as soon as possible after puréeing. If the purée must be held over, cover it while hot

with whipping cream and, in reheating in a double boiler ♦ over
hot water, beat in the cream
before serving.

COOKED BEAN   [4]
SPROUTS

As with other vegetables, cooked
sprouted beans have less vitamin
C than if eaten raw just after
sprouting.
Bring to a boil:
    ¾ cup water
Add:
    4 cups sprouted beans,
        Mung or edible soybeans
        or lentils
♦ Simmer, covered, until almost
soft, just long enough to remove
the raw bean flavor. Season
with:
    Salt
    (Soy sauce)

ABOUT DRIED LEGUMES

Dried peas and beans, being
rather on the dull side, much
like dull people respond readily
to the right contacts. Do not
scorn them, for they have valuable, if incomplete, proteins, see
page 2. Combine them with tomatoes, onions, chili and cheese.
They are also much more tem-
peramental than one would
think. Their cooking time depends on the locality in which
they were grown and on their
age—usually two unknowns for
the cook; plus the type of water
used in cooking them, see About
Water (II, 147). Wash, unless
the package states otherwise.
Do not use soda, see About
Soda (II, 164). Soak in 3 to 4
times as much water as beans.
Remove any beans that float. If
the beans are not preprocessed,
usually they are soaked overnight. Bring the beans to a slow
boil in the water in which they
were soaked, unless it is bitter,
as happens sometimes with soy-

beans. Reduce the heat and ♦
simmer them. All beans should
be cooked until tender. One test,
provided you discard the beans
you have tested, is to blow on a
few of them in a spoon. If the
skins burst, they are sufficiently
cooked.

If you have forgotten to soak,
a quick method to tenderize
them for cooking is to cover
with cold water. Bring up to a
boil and simmer for 2 minutes.
Remove from heat and let stand,
tightly covered, for 1 hour. Or,
blanching the beans for 2 minutes is almost equivalent to 8
hours of soaking.

You may use pre-processed
beans which require no soaking.
But remember that some nutrients have been lost in the
preparation. Lentils and split
peas are better for soaking, but
do not require it.

Remember that 1 cup of
beans, peas or lentils will expand to 2 to 2½ cups after
cooking.

There are over 25 types of
beans and peas available in our
stores. They include red, kidney,
black-eyed peas or beans, edible
soys, pinto, strawberry, cow peas
or Mexican frijoles, chick peas
or Garbanzos or flageolets—
which is the French haricot,
dried and shelled.

White beans, which the white
man learned of from the Indians
and then took sailing, became
our navy beans. They are usually the toughest beans and take
up to 3 hours simmering. Dried
Limas, after soaking for 8 hours,
may cook almost as rapidly as
the fresh ones—in about ½
hour. Lentils take about 1½
hours to cook.

Other people know a trick or
two with navy beans. In Europe,
where chestnuts are highly
prized, bean purée often replaces
chestnut purée in strongly seasoned chestnut dishes. ⊙ Dried

legumes can be pressure cooked, but can be dangerous, see page 81; therefore, long, slow cooking is preferable. Never fill the pressure cooker more than ¾ full of liquid. Pressure cook at 15 lbs.: black-eyed peas for 10 minutes; Great Northern beans for 20 minutes; kidney beans for 30 minutes; lentils for 20 minutes; Lima beans, small, for 25 minutes—large for 30 minutes; navy beans for 30 minutes; pea beans for 20 minutes and soy beans for 35 minutes. Cool pan normally for all dried vegetables for about 5 minutes, then place under cold water faucet.

PURÉE OF DRIED LEGUMES

Cook until tender:
> Dried Lentils, Beans or Peas, page 264

You may add:
> A clove of garlic

After draining the lentils, put them through a fine sieve, a purée strainer or ⅄ blender. Allow to every cup of purée:
> 1 tablespoon butter
> A scant ½ teaspoon salt
> ¼ teaspoon pepper or paprika or a dash of clove

You may brown in the butter:
> 1 tablespoon flour

Whip the purée over a high heat. Serve in a mound, garnished with:
> Sautéed onions
> Chopped parsley

✪ For pressure cooking time, see About Dried Legumes, above.

DRIED BEAN PATTIES [4]

Grind and mash:
> 2 cups cooked dried beans: soy, Lima, navy

Add to them:
> 1 chopped onion
> ¼ cup chopped parsley

Beat and add:

> 2 egg yolks
> 2 tablespoons cream or evaporated milk
> ¼ teaspoon pepper
> 1 teaspoon salt

Shape these ingredients into balls. Flatten them. Dip them in:
> Flour

Chill the patties for 1 hour or more. Sauté them slowly, until brown, in:
> Butter, drippings or other fat

Serve them with any:
> Barbecue Sauce, page 374

GREEN SOY BEANS

Use the young vegetable type, not field varieties of beans. The fuzzy pods should still be green. Immerse them in boiling water. ▶ Cover the pot. After 5 minutes, drain and cool them. Squeeze the pods to press out the beans. Cook the beans in boiling water until tender, approximately 10 to 15 minutes. Use them as directed in About Lima Beans, etc., page 268.

The cooked beans may also be spread in a greased pan, dotted with butter and roasted in a 350° oven until brown or they may be browned in deep fat, pages 75-76.

Soy milk, see page 487, and cheese can also be made from them.

BEAN DINNER IN   [4]
ONE DISH

Preheat oven to 350°.
Combine:
> 1 cup cooked corn
> 1 cup cooked navy beans
> 1 cup lightly drained canned tomatoes
> ¾ teaspoon salt
> ¼ teaspoon paprika
> ½ teaspoon brown sugar
> 1 teaspoon grated onion

Place in a greased baking dish.
Sprinkle the top with:

> Browned bread crumbs
> or grated peanuts

Bake ◗ covered, for about 45
minutes.

BAKED BEANS   [4]

Did you know that baked beans
are as traditional in Sweden as
they are in Boston?
◗ Please read About Dried Legumes, pages 264–265.
If quick-cooking or precooked
beans are used, follow the directions on the package. Otherwise, soak:

> 1½ cups dried beans

Cover them with water. Bring
them to a boil, then simmer
them slowly for ½ hour or more,
until tender.
Preheat oven to 250°.
Drain the beans, reserving the
cooking water and add:

> ¼ cup chopped onion
> 2 tablespoons or more dark
>   molasses
> 2 or 3 tablespoons catsup
> 1 tablespoon dry mustard
> 1 teaspoon salt
> ½ cup boiling bean water
>   or beer
> (½ teaspoon vinegar)
> (1 teaspoon curry powder)
> (1 tablespoon Worcester-
>   shire sauce)

Place them in a greased baker,
decorate them with:

> ¼ lb. sliced salt pork

and bake them, covered, for 6 to
9 hours. If they become dry,
add a little:

> Well-seasoned stock or
>   reserved bean water

Uncover the beans for the last
hour of cooking.

CANNED BAKED   [6]
BEANS WITH FRUIT

This is a good brunch dish.
Preheat oven to 250°.
Arrange:

> 2 cans beans without sauce

in layers in a casserole with:

> 2 sliced apples
> 2 sliced oranges or 4
>   canned apricot halves or
>   pineapple slices
> (2 large onions, sliced)

Top with:

> ½ lb. salt pork

Cover with:

> 1 cup molasses

Bake about 1 to 3 hours.

BOILED BEANS   [5]

Soak, page 264, then drain:

> 1 lb. dried beans: kidney,
>   navy, marrow-fat or
>   Limas

Place them in a heavy saucepan.
Cover them with water. Add:

> 6 tablespoons butter
> ⅓ cup chopped onion
> 3 whole cloves
> 2 teaspoons salt
> ¼ teaspoon freshly ground
>   pepper
> ¼ teaspoon dried thyme

Simmer the beans, covered, from
1 to 1½ hours. Stir them from
time to time. Add and cook for
about 20 minutes longer:

> 1 cup dry red wine or stock

When the beans are tender,
serve them hot, garnished with:

> Chopped chives or
>   parsley

✪ We do not recommend the
pressure cooking of dried beans,
because of the danger of froth-
ing.

▤ CAMPFIRE BEANS

Have ready at least 2 to 3 quarts
of hot coals. Dig a hole deep
enough and wide enough to
hold a covered iron kettle, allowing about 4 extra inches to
the depth of the hole. Get ready
for cooking:

> Baked Beans

Put half the coals in the bottom
of the hole. Sink the covered
kettle. Cover the lid with a large
piece of foil to keep out dirt. Put
the rest of the coals on the ket-

tle lid. Now, fill in the rest of the hole with dirt and put at least 3 inches of dirt on top of the kettle. Don't dig in to peek for at least 4 hours.

CANNED BAKED BEANS AND BACON OR FRANKFURTERS [6]

Preheat oven to 350°.
To jazz up pepless canned beans, add to:

2½ cups canned beans

approximately:

¼ cup catsup
2 tablespoons molasses
2 tablespoons brown sugar
2 tablespoons bacon
    drippings
Minced onion, celery and
    green pepper
Salt if needed
(3 drops hot pepper sauce,
    a few grains of red
    pepper or 1 tablespoon
    mustard)

to make them moist and palatable. Place the beans in a greased, shallow, ovenproof dish. Cover the top with:

Bacon, very thin strips of
    salt pork or skinned
    sliced frankfurters

Bake beans ▶ covered, about 30 minutes. ▶ Uncover. Bake 30 minutes more.

CANNED KIDNEY BEANS AND TOMATOES

[4 Large Servings]
Preheat oven to 350°.
Grease a baking dish. Have ready:

2½ cups canned red kidney
    beans
1 cup canned tomatoes or
    diluted tomato soup
¼ cup chopped onion
¼ lb. chopped bacon

Cover the bottom of the dish with a layer of beans. Sprinkle it with some of the bacon and onions. Repeat the process. Pour the tomatoes over the whole. Cover the top with:

Bread crumbs or
    cornflakes

Dot it with:

Butter

or sprinkle it with:

Grated cheese

Bake the dish until the top is browned, for about 30 minutes.

PINTO BEANS AND RICE [4]

A combination often found in South American countries.
Soak:

½ cup pinto beans

in:

3 cups ham broth

Gently boil the beans in the broth until they are almost done.
Add:

½ cup chopped cooked ham
½ cup rice

Cover and cook for about 20 to 30 minutes, until the rice is tender.

LENTILS [6]

▶ Please read About Dried Legumes, page 264.

I. Add to:

2 cups lentils
3 sprigs parsley or a celery
    rib with leaves
¼ cup sliced onions
½ bay leaf
    (A piece of fat corned
    beef, ham skin or bacon
    rind, tried-out pork fat or
    smoked sausage)
(2 cloves without heads)
    (A slice of garlic)

Cover with:

4 cups water

Cook, covered, about 1½ hours. Add boiling water, if necessary, during the cooking. Drain the lentils and serve with:

Tomato Sauce, page 376

Or serve as a Purée, page 254. If you omit the bacon or pork flavorings above, serve the lentils with:

> Roast Pork, page 485

II. Wash but do not soak:

> 1 cup lentils

Sauté, until golden brown:

> 1 minced onion

in:

> ¼ cup olive oil

Add the lentils and let them absorb the oil. Pour over them:

> 3½ cups boiling water

Cover the pan and simmer about 1½ hours.

> Correct the seasoning

and serve hot or cold. If used for a salad, serve with French dressing and hard-cooked egg slices.

LENTILS AND PRUNES   [4]

Please read About Dried Legumes, pages 264–265. Wash and cook:

> 1 cup lentils

Cook:

> 1 cup Stewed Dried Prunes (II, 108)

Pit the prunes and mash them. Add them to the lentils with:

> ¼ cup dry sherry
> 1 teaspoon salt
> (Lemon juice and spices)

Cook over low heat until thoroughly heated.

ABOUT LIMA, BUTTER OR BROAD BEANS

The following cooked beans, whether canned, frozen, fresh or dry, may be substituted for one another in most recipes: Fordhooks or baby Limas, Sieva types or fava beans and the European broad beans—which really taste more like peas.

If you are hulling fresh Limas, cut a thin strip along inner edge of the pod to which the beans are attached. The beans will pop out easily. One pound in the pods will yield 2 servings.

For that famous combination called Succotash, see page 286.

LIMA BEANS   [6]

▶ Steam, page 252, or cover:

> 1 quart fresh shelled Lima beans

with:

> 1 inch boiling water

Add:

> 1 tablespoon butter

Simmer the beans for 15 minutes. Add:

> 1 teaspoon salt

Simmer the beans, covered, until tender, for about 20 minutes more. Add:

> 1 tablespoon butter or olive oil
> 1½ tablespoons lemon juice
> 1 tablespoon chopped parsley, chives or dill

Or dress them with:

> Warm cultured sour cream and freshly ground white pepper

Or serve them with:

> Sautéed onions, creamed mushrooms or a sprinkling of crisp bacon

✪ Pressure cook Lima beans at 15 lbs. for about 2 minutes.

LIMA BEANS WITH   [4]
PIQUANT SAUCE

In order to provide a canned Lima bean with glamor, you must do a fan dance with it! Drain:

> 1½ cups canned or cooked Lima beans

Reserve the liquor. If necessary,

add to it, to make 1½ cups of liquid:

    Cream

Melt:

    3 tablespoons butter or drippings

Sauté in it until golden brown:

    ¼ cup chopped onion
    (¼ cup chopped celery)

Stir in, until it bubbles:

    2½ tablespoons flour

Stir in the liquid slowly. Reduce the heat and stir in until melted:

    ¼ cup or more minced cheese

Season the sauce with:

    ½ teaspoon salt
    ⅛ teaspoon paprika
    A few grains red pepper
    ¼ teaspoon mustard
    2 teaspoons Worcestershire sauce
    A pinch of 3 herbs— marjoram, thyme, savory, etc.

Add the beans and heat them. Serve them garnished with:

    Chopped parsley

FRENCH LIMA BEANS [4]

Place in a heavy saucepan:

    1 quart fresh Lima beans
    1 small clove garlic
    2 tablespoons peeled, seeded, finely diced tomatoes

Barely cover with:

    1 inch water or half water and half olive oil

Cover and simmer about 15 minutes. Remove garlic. Add:

    2 tablespoons butter
    ¼ teaspoon salt
    1 tablespoon chopped parsley

Continue cooking, covered, until beans are tender.

LIMA BEAN CASSEROLE [4]

This is a fine main dish.
Preheat oven to 375°.
To:

    1 cup cooked or canned Lima beans

add:

    6 sliced frankfurters or sausages
    1 chopped and seeded green pepper
    2 chopped tomatoes

You may wish to purée the beans, page 254. Place these ingredients in a baking dish and cover the top with:

    Au Gratin II, page 389

Bake the beans for about 15 minutes. This dish, puréed, makes a fine stuffing for peppers or onions.

LIMA BEANS WITH CHEESE [4]

Preheat oven to 350°.
Prepare:

    2½ cups cooked Lima beans

Stir into them:

    ½ cup chicken stock

Or melt:

    2 tablespoons butter

Add and sauté for 3 minutes:

    ¼ cup minced onion

Stir into the stock or butter, over low heat, until melted:

    ½ lb. grated cheese

Add the beans and:

    ½ teaspoon salt
    ¼ teaspoon pepper
    1 teaspoon dried basil or thyme
    A few grains cayenne
    (1 cup chopped nut meats)

Bake the beans for about ½ hour. Serve them with:

    Tomato Sauce, page 376

CHILI LIMA BEANS [6]

Preheat oven to 350°.
Drain:

    2 cups cooked Lima beans

Add:

    ¼ lb. salt pork, cut in strips
    1 large minced onion
    1 tablespoon molasses
    2 cups cooked tomatoes
    1 tablespoon brown sugar

¼ teaspoon chili powder or
    pepper
1 teaspoon salt
Bake these ingredients in a
greased casserole for about 1
hour.

LIMA BEANS AND [6]
MUSHROOMS

Serve this with crisp bacon and
grapefruit salad.
Have ready:
    2 cups fresh, cooked or
      canned Lima beans
Drain them. Sauté:
    ½ lb. mushrooms
Drain them, saving the liquor if
there is any. Add to the liquor
and melt:
    1 tablespoon butter
Stir in:
    2 tablespoons flour
Cook and stir these ingredients
until they are well blended. Stir
in slowly:
    ½ cup Chicken Stock (II,
      142), or stock and bean
      liquor
    ½ cup top milk
    Correct the seasoning.
Add the beans and mushrooms.
Heat them. Add before serving:
    (1 tablespoon sherry)
The dish may be served with:
    Au Gratin II, page 389
Place it under a broiler until the
crumbs are brown.

BEETS [8]

Cut the tops from:
    2 lbs. beets
leaving 1 inch of stem. Wash the
beeets. ▶ Steam them, page 252,
or half cover them with:
    Boiling water
Cover pot and cook until tender.
Allow ½ to 1 hour for young
beets, 1 to 2 hours for old beets.
Add boiling water as needed.
When the beets are done, cool
them slightly and slip off the
skins. Cut them into quarters,
chop or put them through a
ricer.

    Correct the seasoning
Then either pour over them:
    Melted butter
    Chopped parsley
or serve the beets in:
    Cream Sauce II,
    page 359
seasoned with:
    Mustard, curry powder,
      horseradish or ¼ cup
      sautéed onions
or prepare:
    Cream Sauce II,
    page 359
using in place of the milk, half
orange juice and half water.
Add:
    3 tablespoons brown sugar
    2 teaspoons grated orange
      rind
✿ Pressure cook small beets 12
minutes, large beets 18 minutes
at 15 lbs.

CASSEROLED BEETS [8]

Preheat oven to 400°.
Pare, then slice or chop fine:
    16 medium-sized beets
Grease a 7-inch baking dish.
Place the beets in it in layers.
Season them with:
    ¼ cup sugar
    ¾ teaspoon salt
    ¼ teaspoon paprika
Dot them with:
    3 tablespoons butter
Add:
    1 tablespoon lemon juice or
      a sliver of fresh ginger
    ⅓ cup water
    (Grated or sliced onions)
Cover the dish closely and bake
the beets for 30 minutes or until
they are tender. Stir them twice.

SWEET-SOUR OR [6]
HARVARD BEETS

For a cold version of sweet-sour,
see Pickled Beet Salad, page 42.
Slice or dice:
    3 cups freshly cooked or
      canned beets
Stir in a double boiler until
smooth:

½ cup sugar
1 tablespoon cornstarch
½ teaspoon salt
2 whole cloves
½ cup mild cider vinegar
or dry white wine

Cook and stir these ingredients until they are clear. Add the beets and place them over hot water for about 30 minutes. Just before serving, heat, but do not boil, the beets and add:

2 tablespoons butter
(1 tablespoon orange
marmalade)

BOILED BEETS IN [4]
SOUR CREAM

Combine in a double boiler:

3 cups cooked or canned
sliced beets
½ cup cultured sour cream
1 tablespoon prepared
horseradish
1 tablespoon chopped
chives
Salt, as needed
(1 teaspoon grated onion)

Heat these ingredients ▶ over hot water.

SWEET-SOUR APPLE [4]
BEETS

Preheat oven to 325°.
Grease a casserole. Mix together and put into it:

2 cups chopped cooked
beets
2 cups chopped tart apples
¼ to ½ cup thinly sliced
onions
1½ teaspoons salt
A generous grating of
nutmeg

If the apples are very tart, add:

(1 tablespoon sugar)

If they are bland:

(2 tablespoons lemon juice)

Dot with:

2 to 3 tablespoons butter

Cover and bake for about 1 hour.

BAKED BEETS

I. Beets may be baked like potatoes—in their jackets.
Preheat oven to 325°.
Wash:

Beets

Trim the tops, leaving 1 inch of stem. Place them on a pan and bake them until they are tender. Allow at least ½ hour for young beets and 1 hour for old beets. Pull off the skins. Season the beets with:

Salt and paprika

Serve them with:

Melted butter

II. Have ready a preheated 325° oven or ☰ hot coals in the grill. Pare and slice:

Beets
Correct the seasoning

and add:

Butter

to each serving, before wrapping in aluminum foil. Bake until tender.

YOUNG BEETS AND [4]
LEAVES

Scrub well and dice, unpared, into ¼-inch cubes:

6 or 8 beet roots

Drop them into:

¾ cup hot milk

Stir until you are sure that all surfaces have been coated with the milk. Cook, covered, over slow heat, 8 to 12 minutes, depending on age of beets. Cut into ½-inch shreds:

Beet leaves

Add them to the diced beets. Re-cover the pan and continue to simmer 6 to 8 minutes longer. Season with:

Salt and paprika
Freshly ground nutmeg
or cloves

BEET GREENS [4]

Beet greens may be prepared like Spinach, page 325. Put the

beets in a ring, serve the greens in the center, dressed with melted butter, and garnish with horseradish sauce. Or, heat in a frying pan:

    2 tablespoons butter or
      cooking oil

Add and simmer:

    2 cups cooked, chopped
      beet greens
    1 teaspoon grated onion
    ¼ teaspoon salt
    ½ tablespoon prepared
      mustard
    1 tablespoon horseradish

Remove from the heat and add:

    ½ cup cultured sour cream

✪ Pressure cook at 15 lbs. for about 3 minutes.

BREADFRUIT

If ever your fate is that of Robinson Crusoe, remember that you can eat raw any breadfruit that has seeds. The seeds are treated like Chestnuts, page 283. All seedless varieties must be cooked.

The breadfruit is one of the most beautiful of tropical trees, with a highly romantic history. The fruit is 6 to 8 inches in diameter and greenish brown or yellow when ripe. The slightly fibrous meat is light yellow and sweet. You may remove the center core with its seed, if it has one, before or after cooking. Season and serve it as you would sweet potato.

I. To boil, choose mature, firm fruit, with rind still green in color. Core and dice:

    4 cups peeled breadfruit

Drop into:

    3 cups boiling water

and simmer, covered, about 1 hour, until tender. Drain, season and serve.

II. Preheat oven to 375°.
To bake, place in a baking pan:

    1 unpeeled breadfruit

Have enough water in the pan to keep it from burning. Bake until tender, about 1 hour, then the stem and core will pull out easily. Cut in half. Season with:

    Salt and pepper or sugar
      and butter

III. To steam, remove skin, stem and core:

    1 breadfruit

Cut into halves or quarters and place the pieces in a pan to steam, covered, page 252, for 2 hours. Season with:

    Butter
    Salt and pepper

You may steam ¾-inch-thick breadfruit slices, roll in flour and fry in deep fat until a golden brown color.

BREADFRUIT SEEDS

These are so close to chestnuts in flavor and texture that they may be substituted in any chestnut recipe.
Wash well:

    1 lb. breadfruit seeds

Drop them into:

    1 quart boiling water
    3 tablespoons salt

Cook covered for about 45 minutes. Drain and serve hot.

BROCCOLI   [4]

Choose heads that are all green. If yellow appears, the bloom is coming up and the broccoli is apt to be tough. Soak for 10 minutes in cold water:

    2 lbs. broccoli

Drain it well. Remove the large leaves and the tough part of the stalks. Cut deep gashes in the bottom of the stalks. If the broccoli is mature, cook it like cabbage, page 274. If it is young ▸ steam it, page 252, or place it upright so only the stems are in water and the heads steam, see Asparagus, page 260. Or, to retain excellent color, use a poaching paper, page 83. Add:

1 inch boiling water
Cook it ♦ closely covered, until
it is barely tender, 10 to 12 minutes. Drain and sprinkle with:
    ½ teaspoon salt
Serve it with:
        Buttered crumbs, melted
        butter or lemon juice
to which add:
    (¼ cup chopped salted
        almonds)
or try serving it:
        Au Gratin II, page 389
or with one of the following
sauces:
        Hot Vinaigrette Sauce,
        page 341
        Hollandaise Sauce,
        page 368
        Cheese Sauce, page 364
        Onion Sauce, page 363
        Sour Cream Dressing,
        page 351
        Allemande Sauce,
        page 362
❂ Pressure cook broccoli at 15
lbs. for about 2 minutes.

QUICK CREAMED BROCCOLI   [4]

Preheat broiler to 550°.
Prepare:
    2 cups hot, cooked broccoli
Drain. Either cover it with:
        Hot canned cream soup
        sauce
or dice the broccoli and fold it
gently into the sauce. Place it
in a buttered casserole and sprinkle with:
        Crushed cornflakes
        (Grated Romano cheese)
Run it under the broiler until
golden.

DEEP FRIED BROCCOLI

Preheat deep fryer to 375°.
Prepare:
        Cooked broccoli
Drain it before it is tender. Cut
it into quarters. Dip in:
        Batter for Vegetables,
        page 221

Fry the broccoli in deep fat,
page 75, until golden brown.

BRAISED BROCCOLI   [6]

Preheat oven to 350°.
Cut off the tough stems and
slice:
    2 lbs. broccoli
Wash and drain it. Prepare and
place in a baking dish:
    ¼ cup chopped celery or
        carrots
    ¼ cup chopped onions
Add the broccoli, cover it with:
        Well-seasoned Chicken
        Stock (II, 142)
Bake the vegetables, covered,
until they are tender—about 1
hour. Serve:
        Au Gratin I or III,
        page 389
❂ Pressure cook broccoli at 15
lbs. for about 2 minutes.

BRUSSELS SPROUTS   [6]

If wilted, pull the outer leaves
from:
    1 lb. Brussels sprouts
Cut off the stems. Soak the
sprouts for 10 minutes in cold
water to which a little salt has
been added. Drain them. Cut
crosswise gashes into the stem
ends. ♦ Steam, page 252, or drop
them into a quantity of rapidly
boiling:
        Water
♦ Reduce heat and simmer, uncovered, until they are barely
tender, about 10 minutes. Do
not overcook. Drain and serve
with:
        1 tablespoon melted butter
        (Grated Parmesan cheese
        and chopped parsley or
        1 tablespoon lemon juice
        or a grating of nutmeg)
or sauté in the butter:
        1 tablespoon grated onion,
        or 2 tablespoons bread
        crumbs and ¼ teaspoon
        mustard
or serve with:
        Canned Cream Soup

Sauce, page 375
into which you may put at the
last moment:
(½ cup finely chopped fresh
celery)
or, best of all, with lots of:
Hollandaise Sauce,
page 369
○ Pressure cook Brussels
sprouts at 15 lbs. for about 3
minutes.

BAKED BRUSSELS [6]
SPROUTS AND CHESTNUTS

Preheat oven to 350°.
Have ready:
2 cups cooked Brussels
sprouts
½ lb. cooked chestnuts
Butter a baking dish. Fill it with
alternate layers of sprouts and
chestnuts. Dot the layers with:
Butter
Correct the seasoning
Moisten them lightly with:
Stock
Cover with:
Au Gratin II, page 389
Bake them, uncovered, for about
20 to 30 minutes.

ABOUT CABBAGE

Cabbage types are as different
as the uses of the word. In
France, "mon petit chou" is a
term of endearment—but call
anyone a cabbage in English
and see what happens!
Savoys, which are a loose-
leaved cabbage, endear themselves to us for their elegance of
texture. They are usually available only in the fall. As a rule,
whether cabbage is green or red,
choose a head that is firm. Cabbage lends itself to stuffing as do
the leaves, see Dolmas, page
522.
All cabbage types, if fresh,
are a high and inexpensive
source for vitamin C. To preserve the vitamins, keep cabbage
wrapped before cooking. And

use the cooked cabbage water
in sauces and soups. The old
way of cooking cabbage is to
cut it in sections and boil it for
hours. The new way is to shred
it finely or quarter it and barely
cook it—allowing only 7 minutes if shredded, 15 if quartered.
♦ To shred cabbage, cut the
head in half and place flat side
down on a board. Hold the cabbage with the left hand and
slice into long shreds with a
sharp knife. The longer growing periods required for winter
and Savoy cabbages demand in
turn more time to break down
their coarser cellulose. Use a
longer cooking period, about 20
minutes. ○ Pressure cook 2- to
3-inch wedges of cabbage at 15
lbs. pressure for 3 to 5 minutes.

I. Remove the outer leaves
from:
½ head cabbage
Drop it into a quantity of rapidly boiling:
Water
♦ Reduce the heat to a simmer.
Cook it ♦ uncovered, until it is
tender but still crisp. Drain it.
Add:
½ teaspoon salt
Place it in a serving dish and
pour over it:
Melted butter—1
tablespoon to 1 cup
cabbage
Add to the butter:
(Bread crumbs or
caraway, chilis, or poppy
seeds or a few drops
lemon juice and a
tablespoon chopped
parsley)
or place the cooked cabbage in
a baking dish and cover with:
A Creole Sauce, page
380, or Au Gratin III,
page 389
Heat through in a 350° oven.

II. All rules have exceptions, so
try out this cabbage dish which

calls for little water. Cut into wedges:

A head of cabbage

Trim off part of the core. Drop the wedges into:

½ inch boiling water

Cover and cook the cabbage for about 10 minutes. Drain it well. Dress it with:

1 cup Cream Sauce I,
page 359

to which has been added:

½ teaspoon freshly grated
nutmeg or 2 teaspoons
prepared mustard or ½
cup grated cheese

or use:

1 cup Horseradish Cream
Sauce, page 362, or 1
cup creamed canned
condensed soup, or
Allemande Sauce,
page 362

No matter which sauce you use, combine it with the cabbage and serve at once.

III.   **[6]**

This method makes young cabbage very delicate and is a great help in disguising the age of a mature cabbage, but you may be losing some nutrients. Cut into very fine shreds:

3 cups cabbage

Drop it gradually into:

¾ cup boiling milk

Boil it for 2 minutes. Drain and discard the milk. Drop the cabbage into hot:

Cream Sauce I, page 359

Simmer for 3 minutes longer and serve at once with:

Broiled sausages

**CABBAGE, POTATOES   [4]
AND HAM**

Cook until nearly tender, in water to cover:

A piece of smoked ham:
Cali, picnic, butt, shank
or cottage ham or roll

If using already cooked or left-over ham or bone, just bring to a boil before adding:

1 large quartered cabbage
4 halved and pared
medium size potatoes

Simmer, covered, about 20 to 25 minutes.

Correct the seasoning

Serve from a large platter, garnished with:

Lemon wedges

BAKED CABBAGE   **[4]**

Preheat oven to 325°.

Put in a buttered baking dish:

3 cups shredded cabbage

Pour over it a mixture of:

¾ cup cream
1 tablespoon sugar
½ teaspoon salt
½ teaspoon paprika
(½ cup chopped nuts)

Sprinkle the top with:

½ cup bread crumbs

Bake for about 45 minutes. Just before serving, sprinkle the top with:

⅓ cup grated cheese

and run under the broiler until melted.

SAUTÉED CABBAGE   **[4]**

Preheat oven to 375°.

Shred:

A small head cabbage

Sauté it lightly in:

Butter or bacon drippings

Add to the hot fat:

½ teaspoon salt
¼ teaspoon paprika
Minced garlic or onion

Place the cabbage in a greased baking dish. Pour over it:

1 cup cultured sour or
sweet cream

Bake it for about 20 minutes.

FRENCH FRIED CABBAGE

Preheat deep fryer to 375°.

Crisp in cold water:

Finely shredded cabbage

Drain and dry it. Dip it in:

Milk

then in:

Flour

Fry a small amount at a time in deep fat, see page 258. Drain it on absorbent paper.

Correct the seasoning

CABBAGE OR LETTUCE AND RICE DISH [6]

This is a good dish to make in the trail of a salad luncheon. You may use the outer leaves of lettuce. Melt:

2 tablespoons bacon drippings
2 tablespoons butter or 3 tablespoons other fat

Stir in, cover and cook gently for about 10 minutes:

3 cups finely shredded cabbage or lettuce
½ cup finely chopped onion
1 seeded, chopped green pepper

Stir these ingredients frequently. Stir in and cook until well heated:

1 cup cooked rice
2 cups tomato pulp or thick stewed tomatoes
Salt and pepper

This is good served with:
Crisp bacon or cold ham

CABBAGE OR SAVORY STRUDEL [12 to 14]

Prepare:
Strudel Dough (II, 307)

Steam blanch, page 89, for 5 minutes:
4 lbs. shredded cabbage

Press out any excess moisture and place on the dough with:

1½ cups heavy cultured sour cream
(teaspoon caraway seed)
(4 chopped hard-cooked eggs)

To roll and bake the strudel, see (II, 307).

SCALLOPED CABBAGE [8]

Rather luxurious treatment for this good bourgeois vegetable. Preheat oven to 375°.
Chop, then cook:

1 medium-sized head cabbage

Drain it well. Prepare:
1½ cups Cream Sauce I (II, 359)

Prepare:
2 tablespoons chopped seeded green peppers
2 tablespoons chopped pimientos

Sauté and mince:
(6 slices bacon)

Melt:
2 tablespoons bacon fat or butter

Toss lightly in this:
½ cup bread crumbs

Place layers of drained cabbage in a greased baking dish. Sprinkle them with the minced bacon and peppers and:

1 cup or less grated cheese

Cover them with the cream sauce. Top the dish with the sautéed bread crumbs. Bake the cabbage for about 10 minutes.

CABBAGE WITH TOMATO SAUCE [6]

A practical, all-purpose vegetable dish. Good made with Brussels sprouts as well. Prepare by any recipe for Cooked Cabbage, page 274:

A small, firm head cabbage

While the cabbage boils, prepare this sauce. Dice and sauté until crisp:

4 slices bacon

Remove and reserve the bacon. Sauté in the bacon fat, until tender:

1 small minced onion

Add:
1 cup tomato purée
Salt and pepper
(2 teaspoons brown sugar)

When the sauce is boiling, add the well-drained cabbage and the bits of bacon. Serve very hot, garnished with:

2 tablespoons minced parsley

CABBAGE, TOMATO [6]
AND CHEESE DISH

Preheat oven to 325°.
Cook for 5 minutes, page 274:
    3 cups finely shredded
        cabbage
Drain it well. Cook:
    1½ cups Stewed Tomatoes,
        page 332
    ¾ teaspoon salt
    ¼ teaspoon paprika
    (2 teaspoons brown sugar)
Butter a baking dish. Place in it
alternate layers of tomatoes and
cabbage, beginning with tomatoes. Sprinkle the layers with:
    Au Gratin III, page 389
Bake the dish for about ½ hour
or until the crumbs are brown.

CABBAGE ROLLS [6]
STUFFED WITH RICE
AND CHEESE

To prepare, see:
    Dolmas, page 522
Omit the vegetables if desired.
Substitute for the meat:
    ¾ cup grated American
        cheese
Season well with:
    Cayenne, paprika and
        salt

CABBAGE STUFFED [4]
WITH CORNED BEEF
HASH

Trim the outer leaves and the
stem from:
    A medium-sized head of
        cabbage
Cook it, uncovered, until it is
barely tender in:
    2 quarts boiling water
Do not overcook cabbage. It is
best when still slightly crisp.
Drain it well. Scoop out the inside, leaving a 1½-inch shell.
Place the shell in a greased
ovenproof dish. Keep it hot.
Chop the removed part. Add it
to the contents of:
    1 can minced corned beef
        hash: 16 oz.

    ¼ cup or more sautéed
        onions
    A pinch of thyme
Moisten it with:
    (Cream, evaporated milk
        or bacon drippings)
Heat these ingredients. Fill the
shell. Cover the top with:
    Buttered cornflakes
The cabbage may be heated in
a 425° oven for about 10 minutes. It may be served with:
    Dried Onion Soup Sauce,
        page 375

CABBAGE STUFFED [6]
WITH HAM AND CHEESE

Trim the loose outer leaves
from:
    A firm head cabbage
Cut out enough from the stem
end to make a deep well. Prepare a filling by combining:
    2 cups cooked ground or
        chopped ham
    1 cup bread crumbs
    ¾ cup grated American
        cheese
    ½ teaspoon dry mustard
    Salt
    ½ teaspoon paprika
    A few grains cayenne
Fill the center of the cabbage
with this filling. Steam in an im-
provised steamer made of a colander or frying basket, if necessary, until it is tender—from 1
to 2 hours. Place it over boiling
water. Cover it with a bowl or
lid or wrap the cabbage in heavy
foil and bake it from 1 to 2
hours. Serve it with:
    Cheese Sauce, page 364,
    or Tomato Cheese Sauce,
        page 376

RED CABBAGE

An old favorite to serve with
game—cooked either for a long
time as in this recipe or for a
shorter time as in the next. Pull
the outer leaves from:
    A head of red cabbage:
        about 2 lbs.

Cut it into sections. Remove the hard core, shred the cabbage and soak in cold water. Cook over low heat until some fat is rendered out:

     4 slices chopped bacon or
          use 3 tablespoons melted
          butter

Sauté with the bacon or butter, until golden:

     3 or 4 tablespoons finely
          chopped onions

Lift the cabbage from the water with the hands, leaving it moist. Place it in a heatproof glass or enameled iron casserole, cover it and let it simmer for 10 minutes. Core and cut into very thin slices:

     2 apples
     (⅛ teaspoon caraway seeds)

Add them to the cabbage with:

     ¼ teaspoon salt, if bacon is
          used, or 1 teaspoon salt,
          if unsalted butter is used
     ¼ cup vinegar or ½ cup
          red wine or a mixture of
     2 tablespoons honey and
     2 tablespoons vinegar

Add the sautéed onion and stir these ingredients. Cover the pan and simmer the cabbage very slowly for 1 hour and 20 minutes. Add boiling water during cooking, if necessary. If the water has not been absorbed when the cabbage is done, uncover the pot and cook it gently until it is absorbed.

RED CABBAGE AND   [6]
CHESTNUTS

In "The House of Exile," the Chinese serve red cabbage in green peppers, see Stuffed Peppers, page 307. This dish is attractive. Have ready:

     1 cup blanched chopped
          chestnuts

Shred until very fine:

     1 small head red cabbage

Place it in a bowl. Cover it with:

     Boiling water

Add:

     ¼ cup dry white wine or
          vinegar

Permit it to soak for 15 minutes. Drain it well. Heat in a saucepan:

     2½ tablespoons bacon
          drippings or butter

Add the cabbage. Sprinkle it lightly with:

     Salt and pepper

Sauté the cabbage until it is limp. Cover and simmer for ten minutes. Sprinkle over the cabbage:

     1 tablespoon flour

Meanwhile, in a separate saucepan, combine the chestnuts with:

     1 cup water
     1½ tablespoons sugar
     ¼ cup dry white wine or
          vinegar
     ⅓ cup seedless raisins
     1 peeled, thinly sliced
          apple

Simmer these ingredients, covered, until the chestnuts are tender. Add to the cabbage mixture. Cook these ingredients until they are well blended.

     Correct the seasoning

and serve them hot.

SAUERKRAUT   [6]

The healthful quality of sauerkraut was recognized in 200 B.C. when, history records, it was served to the laborers working on the Great Wall of China. To retain its full flavor, serve it raw or barely heated through. Cooking makes kraut milder.

Melt in a skillet:

     2 tablespoons butter or
          bacon drippings

Add and sauté until clear:

     ½ cup sliced onion or
          shallots

Add and sauté for about 5 minutes:

     1 quart fresh or canned
          sauerkraut

Peel, grate and add:

1 medium-sized potato or
tart apple
Cover the kraut with:
Boiling Stock (II, 141),
or water
(¼ cup dry wine)
Cook the kraut, uncovered, for
30 minutes, cover it and cook or
bake it in a 325° oven for about
30 minutes longer. It may be
seasoned with:
1 or 2 tablespoons brown
sugar
1 teaspoon caraway or
celery seed
Serve with:
Frankfurters, roast pork
or spareribs

SAUERKRAUT AND [8]
TOMATO CASSEROLE

Lovers of sauerkraut will welcome this old friend in a new
guise.
Preheat oven to 350°.
Drain well:
4 cups canned sauerkraut
Put through a strainer:
3½ cups canned tomatoes
Melt:
2 tablespoons bacon or
other fat
Add, cook and stir about until
golden:
1 small chopped onion
Add the strained tomatoes and:
¼ cup brown sugar
Freshly ground pepper
Add the drained sauerkraut.
Place the mixture in a covered
casserole and bake for about 1
hour. ◗ Uncover the last 20
minutes of cooking. Garnish the
top with:
Crumbled crisp bacon

CARDOONS

A vegetable of the thistle family,
like artichoke—but the tender
stalks and root are eaten, rather
than the flower. Generally used
for soups. Wash well. Discard
outside stalks, trim the strings
as for celery. Leave the heart

whole. Cut into 3-inch pieces:
Tender stalks of cardoon
Parblanch, page 88, in:
Court Bouillon Blanc
(II, 146)
for 5 to 7 minutes, to keep it
from discoloring. Drain and
rinse at once in cold water to
remove bitterness. Simmer, cov-
ered, for about 1½ to 2 hours or
until tender in:
Boiling Acidulated
Water (II, 148) to cover
Correct the seasoning
and serve with:
Cream, butter or Cream
Sauce I, page 359
Slice the heart and arrange it as
a garnish.

CARROTS

Carrots are frequently boring—
but that may be the cook's fault.
For good results, combine them
with onions, celery, green peppers, olives, mushrooms, etc.
Peel or scrape them; or use unpeeled, cut into slices, or diced.
If small, they may be served
whole. If large, they may be
more attractive if cut Parisienne, page 250. Wash and
scrape:
Carrots
◗ Steam, page 252, or place
them in a small quantity of:
Boiling water or stock
Cook them, covered, until they
are tender, from 20 to 30 minutes. Allow a shorter cooking
period for cut-up carrots. Permit
them to absorb the water in
which they are cooked. If necessary, add a small quantity of
boiling water. Celery, onions,
etc., may be cooked with peeled
carrots or they may be cooked
separately and added later.
Serve the carrots with:
(Seasoned chopped
parsley)
Bercy Butter, page 384,
or
Cream Sauce, page 359

or add to 2 cups cooked carrots:
    1 or 2 tablespoons butter
    1 or 2 tablespoons sugar,
      honey or orange
      marmalade
    (½ teaspoon ginger, ginger
      root or cinnamon)
Simmer the carrots in this mixture until well glazed. Or try the glaze in:
    Candied Sweet Potatoes,
    page 323
❂ Pressure cook carrots whole for 4 minutes—sliced, 2 minutes—at 15 lbs.

CARROTS IN BUNCHES

Steam or cook as in preceding recipe:
    Small, shapely carrots in
    their jackets
Cool them. Skin them. Reheat them by placing them over steam or by sautéing them for about 12 minutes in a little butter. Serve them in 2 bunches—one at each end of a meat platter. Place at the blunt ends, to represent carrot greens:
    Sprigs of parsley
Pour over them:
    Melted seasoned butter
Season with:
    A dash of cloves

MASHED CARROTS OR   [4]
CARROT RING

Cook as above:
    2 bunches young carrots in
    their jackets
Skin the carrots and use a ⅄ blender or put them through a ricer or mash them with a potato masher. Beat in:
    1 tablespoon butter
    Salt and pepper
    1 tablespoon chopped
      parsley or chives
    (A dash of cloves)
Heap the carrots in a mound or in individual mounds. Garnish them with:
    Sprigs of parsley
To make a ring, beat in:

    1 to 2 egg yolks
Place in a greased mold and heat over hot water in a 350° oven until set, for about 20 to 30 minutes. Invert the mold. Fill the center of the ring with:
    Green Peas, page 305

CARROTS VICHY   [4]

Place in a saucepan:
    2 cups scraped, sliced
      carrots
    ½ cup boiling water
    2 tablespoons butter
    1 tablespoon sugar
    ¼ teaspoon salt
    (1 teaspoon lemon juice)
Cover the pan closely. Cook the carrots over quick heat until the water evaporates. Permit them to brown in the butter. Serve them sprinkled with:
    Chopped chives or
    parsley

BAKED CARROTS   [4]

Preheat oven to 350°.
Melt:
    3 tablespoons butter
Sauté in it for about 3 minutes:
    ¼ cup chopped onion
Add:
    2 cups peeled, shredded
      carrots
Place these ingredients in a baking dish. Sprinkle them with:
    ¾ teaspoon salt
    1 teaspoon sugar
Pour over them:
    ½ cup water or stock
Cover the dish. Bake the carrots until they are tender.

WATERLESS CARROTS   [5]

Peel or scrape:
    2 bunches carrots
Slice them in long, thin strips. Place them in a heavy saucepan with:
    2 tablespoons butter
    ½ teaspoon sugar
    ½ teaspoon salt

1 tablespoon chopped
parsley
You may sauté in the butter:
3 tablespoons chopped
onion
Cover the pan closely. Simmer
the carrots on top of the stove
for about 20 minutes or place
them in a 350° oven until they
are done. Add:
1 tablespoon cream
Cook them about 2 minutes
longer.

CARAMELIZED CARROTS

A good way to treat mature car-
rots.
Steam in their jackets, page 252:
Carrots
Skin them. Cut them into halves
or quarters. Dip them in:
Melted butter
Sprinkle them with:
Salt, paprika and brown
sugar
Place them in a heavy skillet
over low heat until they are well
glazed. Baste them from time to
time with a little melted butter.

CAULIFLOWER [4]

Cut off the tough end of the
stem, remove the leaves and soak
in cold salted water, head down
for 10 minutes:
1 medium-sized head
cauliflower
Drain it. You may break it into
florets. Cut deep gashes into the
stalks. ◗ Steam, page 252, or
place it uncovered, head up, in
about 1 inch of:
Boiling water or milk
The milk will help keep it white,
as will:
(Juice of ½ lemon)
Reduce the heat to a simmer
and cook ◗ partially covered,
until the stalk is barely tender.
Test for tenderness after 12 minutes. Drain the cauliflower well
and place it in a serving dish.
Serve it with:

Brown Buttered Bread
Crumbs (II, 159)
and you have prepared Cauli-
flower Polonaise.
Or cream it, page 255. Or use:
Hollandaise Sauce,
page 368
Egg Sauce I, page 360
(with crumbled bacon)
Creole Sauce, page 380
Lemon Butter, page 384
✪ Pressure cook whole cauli-
flower at 15 lbs. for about 7
minutes.

SAUTÉED [5]
CAULIFLOWER

Cook as above:
Boiled or steamed
cauliflower
Break it into florets. Heat:
2 tablespoons butter
2 tablespoons salad oil
Add and cook for 2 minutes:
½ clove garlic or
2 teaspoons grated onion
Remove the garlic. Sauté the
florets in the fat until they are
well coated. Cover and cook for
several minutes. Season with:
Salt and paprika
A fresh grating of nutmeg
or serve the cauliflower with:
Chopped parsley or
chives

DEEP FRIED
CAULIFLOWER

Drain:
Cooked cauliflower
Separate the florets.
Preheat deep fryer to 380°.
Dip each section of cauliflower
in:
Fritter Batter for
Vegetables (II, 125)
Drain, and deep fry, page 75,
until golden. Serve with:
Hollandaise Sauce, page
368, or Sour Cream
Dressing, page 351
or cream them, page 255

CAULIFLOWER AND [6]
MUSHROOMS IN
CHEESE SAUCE

Cook:
>   1 large cauliflower

Drain it well and put it in a greased baking dish. Place it where it will keep hot. Melt in a skillet:

>   2 tablespoons butter

Sauté in it for 2 minutes:

>   ½ lb. mushrooms

Cook:

>   1½ cups Cream Sauce I,
>   page 359

Stir into the hot sauce ▶ off the heat:

>   ¾ cup grated cheese

When the cheese is melted, add the sautéed sauce and pour the sauce over the cauliflower. Serve it at once.

CELERY [4]

Wash:

>   2 cups chopped celery

▶ Steam, page 252, or drop it gradually into:

>   ½ inch boiling water

Cook it, covered, until it is tender, for about 8 minutes, allowing it to absorb the water. Should there be any liquid, drain the celery and reserve the liquid for the sauce. Brown the celery in:

>   Seasoned butter

Or, drop the celery into:

>   1 cup Cream Sauce I, page
>   359, made with cream
>   and celery liquor

Season the sauce with:

>   Curry powder
>   Celery, dill or sunflower
>   seeds
>   Freshly grated nutmeg
>   Herbs (II, 200)

Serve:

>   Au Gratin III, page 389

✪ Pressure cook celery at 15 lbs. pressure for 1½ minutes.

BRAISED OR [4]
GLAZED CELERY

Not only celery, but Belgian endive and Boston lettuce are choice prepared in this way. Do blanch the endive and lettuce briefly first.
Wash and trim:

>   1½ lbs. celery

Cut into 3- to 4-inch lengths. Arrange them attractively in the bottom of a buttered heatproof ▶ glass, enamel or stainless steel casserole. Squeeze over them:

>   3 tablespoons lemon juice

Add:

>   ½ cup chicken or veal stock
>   ½ teaspoon salt
>   1 tablespoon sugar
>   2 tablespoons butter

Bring the liquid to a boil, then cover with a poaching paper, page 83. Now, cover the casserole with a lid and simmer for about 25 minutes or until tender. Place the celery on a heated serving dish and keep warm. Reduce the pan liquid to about ½ a cup. Add:

>   1 tablespoon butter or
>   Beurre Manié, page 357

Pour this glaze over the celery.

CELERY CABBAGE OR
CHINESE CABBAGE

Use raw as a salad or prepare this vegetable by any of the recipes for cabbage; or stir-fry it as the Chinese do, page 372. If young, it may require only a few minutes' cooking.
▶ Steam, page 252, or place a stalk of:

>   Whole or shredded celery
>   cabbage

in:

>   ½ cup boiling water

Cook until it is barely tender. Drain thoroughly. Add:

>   ½ teaspoon salt

Serve it with:

>   Melted butter or Mock
>   Hollandaise Sauce, page
>   370

or season with:

    ½ teaspoon **turmeric**

and garnish with:

    ¼ cup freshly grated
      coconut

CELERY ROOT [4]
OR CELERIAC

This knobby tough **root**, also
called **celerirave**, is often woody
if too old, but can be one of the
most subtly flavored vegetables.
It is difficult to peel, so cut into
slices first. See page 338. To
make the flavor more delicate
for use in salads and hors
d'oeuvre, blanch 1 to 2 minutes
after peeling to keep it white—
by using lemon juice or ascorbic
acid in the water. Scrub well:

    1½ lbs. celery root

◗ Steam, page 252, or cover it
with:

    Boiling water

Cook uncovered, until it is tender—about 25 minutes. Drain
the celery root. Cover with:

    1½ cups Cream Sauce II,
      page 359

or serve with:

    Au Gratin III, page 389

✪ Pressure cook at 15 lbs. about
5 minutes.

SWISS CHARD

Prepare:

    Chard leaves

as you would spinach, but remove the coarse middle rib before cooking. If cooking the ribs,
cook as for asparagus.

CHAYOTES [4]

This pear-shaped vegetable belongs to the gourd family and is
also called **Christophenes**. Treat
it much as you would zucchini
or other squash. It may be served
chilled with mayonnaise, combines well with meats, seafoods
and is even good in some desserts.

Pare and cut crosswise in ¾-
inch slices:

    1 lb. chayotes

Drop into:

    Boiling water to cover

Reduce the heat at once and ◗
simmer 45 minutes, if young, or
as long as 1 hour, if mature—
or until tender. Drain it. You
mya also ✪ pressure cook whole
chayotes at 15 lbs. for 6 to 8
minutes and, if diced, for 2 minutes. Dress with:

    Salt
    Butter
    Black Butter, page 383,
      etc., or cream sauce and
      grated cheese

They are delicious if steamed
whole and stuffed with:

    Mushrooms and cheese

BOILED CHESTNUTS [4]

I. To use as a vegetable, shell
and skin (II, 188):

    1 lb. chestnuts

or use ½ lb. dried chestnuts that
have been soaked overnight. Use
this water. Drop the chestnuts
into:

    Boiling water or milk

To which add:

    3 chopped ribs celery
    1 small, peeled, chopped
      onion
    (1 tablespoon vinegar)
    (⅛ teaspoon anise)

Cook them until they are tender.
Drain them well. Mash them
with:

    1 tablespoon butter
    Correct the seasoning

Add:

    2 or more tablespoons
      warm cream

Beat the chestnuts until they are
fluffy. Keep them hot over hot
water. Immediately before serving them, stir in:

    (1 cup or more finely diced
      raw celery)

II. To use as a compote, shell,
skin, boil, as above:

    1 lb. chestnuts

in:

> **Boiling water or milk**

Drain. Save the liquid and add sufficient to make about 2 cups. Make a sirup by adding:

> 2 cups sugar
> Juice and grated rind of 2 lemons
> Juice and grated rind of 1 orange
> 4 whole cloves
> 1 stick cinnamon
> ¼ teaspoon ground ginger
> (½ cup raisins)
> (½ cup chopped nuts)

Simmer the sirup gently until slightly reduced, then fold into the mashed chestnuts and serve.

BAKED CHESTNUTS   [4]

Preheat oven to 325°.
Prepare and cook:

> 3 cups chestnuts, above

Season them with:

> (2 tablespoons or more brown sugar)

Grease a baking dish. Place the chestnuts in it. Pour over them:

> 1¾ cups chicken stock

Cover them and bake for about 3 hours. Pour off the stock and reserve. Melt:

> 2 tablespoons butter

Stir in until blended:

> 1 tablespoon flour

Stir the stock in slowly. When the sauce is smooth and boiling, pour it over the chestnuts and serve them.

CHICORY

Witloof chicory and French or Belgian endive may be treated just as for any recipe calling for cooked lettuce or celery. Differentiate the above from the sunburst-centered, highly ruffled or frisée endive, common in our store and usually used raw only.

ABOUT CORN

Some years ago a Frenchman wrote to the Paris Herald to ask: "Why do Americans put their elbows on the table?" The answer, published the following day, was conclusive: "It comes from eating green corn."

When cooked corn is called for in the following recipes, it can be canned, fresh cooked or frozen cooked. Cooked just after picking, young corn is naturally sweet. A few hours off the stalk brings about changes which lessen this flavor. Try cutting fresh corn for puddings and fritters by scraping with either of the tools sketched here—and notice the superior results this

preparation gives. If you must use a knife to cut off the kernels, do not cut deeply. Then press along the rows with the dull side of a knife to retrieve the richly flavored juice and heart of the kernel. ♦ To avoid toughness in cooking corn, add salt when the cooking period is half over.

If ✪ pressure cooking ✻ frozen corn on the cob ♦ be sure to thaw partially before cooking at 15 lbs. for about 4 minutes.

CORN ON THE COB

I. Remove the husks and silk from:

> **Ears of fresh corn**

♦ Steam, page 252, or drop them, ear by ear, so as not to disturb the boiling, into:

> 1 inch boiling water or half milk and half water

Add:

> (1 tablespoon or more sugar)

Cover the kettle and boil the corn rapidly until it is tender, from 4 to 10 minutes, depending on maturity. Drain and serve it with:

> Butter
> Salt
> Freshly ground pepper

II. Remove the husks and silk from:

> Very young, freshly
> picked corn

In a large kettle which you can cover tightly, bring to a rolling boil:

> Enough water to cover
> corn generously

Slip the ears into the water one by one. Cover the kettle and remove it from the heat at once. Allow the corn to remain in the hot water for about 5 minutes or until tender. Drain and serve at once.

FRESH CORN CUT FROM THE COB

Cut or grate from the cob:

> Fresh corn

Simmer it, covered, for several minutes, until it is tender, in its own juice and a little:

> Butter

Season it with:

> Salt and white pepper

Moisten it with:

> Milk or cream

You may devil it by adding:

> 1 tablespoon
> Worcestershire sauce
> Minced garlic

▤ GRILLED OR ROASTED CORN

Preheat oven to 400° or have ready a good bed of coals.
I. Pull down husk to remove silk and any damaged portions of the ear on:

> Young roasting corn

Replace the husk. Run into the husk as much:

> Water

as it will hold. Drain and close the husk by twisting it. Put the ears on a rack over the hot coals or in the preheated oven and bake 20 to 25 minutes. Husk before serving.

II. Strip the husk and silk from:

> Roasting ears

Remove any damaged portions. Rub with:

> Butter
> Salt and pepper

Wrap in foil and roast 20 to 30 minutes, depending on the size of the ears.

FRESH CORN   [8]
PUDDING COCKAIGNE

This is a luscious dish, but it is a little difficult to give an exact recipe for it because the corn differs with the season. If the corn is watery when scraped, it is sometimes necessary to add a tablespoon of flour. This is apt to be the case early in the season. Later on, it may be necessary to use more cream—up to 1 cup. When the corn mixture is right, it looks like thick, curdled cream when scraped.
Preheat oven to 325°.
Scrape, but ▶ do not cut:

> 2 cups fresh corn

Add:

> 1 teaspoon sugar
> ½ to ¾ cup cream
> Salt and white pepper

Place these ingredients in a generously buttered flat baking dish. Dot the top with:

> Butter

Bake the pudding for about 1 hour. ✳ This dish may be frozen.

CORN PUDDING   [5]

A good hefty corn dish.
Preheat oven to 350°.
Drain:

> 1 No. 2 can kernel corn:
> 2½ cups

Reserve the liquid. Melt:

2 tablespoons butter
Stir in until blended:
    2 tablespoons flour
Combine and stir in slowly:
    **The corn liquid and
    enough cream to make
    1 cup**
When the sauce is smooth and
hot, stir in the drained corn and:
    ¼ cup chopped seeded
        green pepper
    1 chopped pimiento
When this mixture reaches a
boil ▶ reduce heat. Beat well:
    2 egg yolks
Pour part of the corn mixture
over them off the heat. Beat it
and return to corn mixture. Stir
and cook for several minutes to
permit the yolks to thicken
slightly.
Add:
    ¾ teaspoon salt
    ¼ teaspoon paprika
    (¼ cup crisply cooked,
        crumbled bacon)
or you may cover the bottom of
the dish with:
    (Minced ham)
Place on a platter and whip ▶
until stiff, but not dry:
    2 egg whites
Fold them lightly into the corn
mixture. Bake the pudding in a
baking dish ▶ prepared as for a
soufflé baker, page 196, for about
30 minutes.

SCALLOPED CORN   [4]

Preheat oven to 325°.
Combine:
    2 cups uncooked corn,
        scraped or cut from
        the ear
    2 beaten eggs
    ½ teaspoon salt
    (¼ cup minced seeded
        green peppers with
        membrane removed, or
        chopped olives)
    ¾ cup cream
Place in a baking dish, prepared
as for a soufflé baker, page 196.
Sprinkle with:

Au Gratin II, page 389
Bake the corn for about ½ hour.

CORN SUCCOTASH   [4]

This is also good made with
canned or frozen vegetables.
Combine, then heat in a double
boiler ▶ over—not in—hot
water.
    1 cup cooked fresh corn
    1 cup cooked fresh Lima
        or finely shredded green
        beans
    2 tablespoons butter
    ½ teaspoon salt
    ⅛ teaspoon paprika
    Chopped parsley

CORN CREOLE   [6]

Seed, remove membranes and
chop:
    ¼ cup green pepper
Skin and chop:
    1 small onion
Melt:
    2 tablespoons butter
Sauté the vegetables in the but-
ter until they are translucent.
Heat in the top of a double
boiler:
    1 cup drained canned or
        fresh cooked tomatoes
Add the sautéed vegetables and:
    ½ teaspoon salt
    ⅛ teaspoon pepper
    A few grains cayenne
Cook and stir these ingredients
▶ over—not in—boiling water
about 5 minutes. Add:
    ⅔ cup cooked corn
Heat 2 minutes longer. Stir in,
until melted:
    1⅓ cups grated cheese

CORN FRITTERS WITH
FRESH CORN

For a short period one of our
local newspapers devoted a column to masculine taste in culinary matters. The author of the
following graciously permitted
us to use it when we told him
how much it pleased us.

"When I was a child, one of eight, my father frequently promised us a marvelous treat. He, being an amateur horticulturist and arboriculturist, would tell us of a fritter tree he was going to plant on the banks of a small lake filled with molasses, maple sirup or honey, to be located in our back yard. When one of us children felt the urge for the most delectable repast, all we had to do was to shake the tree, the fritters would drop into the lake and we could fish them out and eat fritters to our hearts' content.

"Mother was a good cook and a good helpmate, so she developed the fritter that was to grow on and fall from the tree into the lake of molasses or maple sirup or honey, as the case might be. Her recipe, as preserved in our family, is:

"Grate 12 ears of corn, preferably sugar corn, then beat the yolks of 3 eggs with a very small amount of flour—about a teaspoonful—and a scant teaspoon of salt; beat the whites thoroughly. Mix the grated corn and yolks, then fold in the beaten whites.

"Fry in butter like pancakes and serve hot. You will want more; so will your guests."

Who could resist the delightful idea of a fritter tree in full fruit?

For 4 Servings
Grate:
    2½ cups fresh corn
Add:
    1 well-beaten egg yolk
    (2 teaspoons flour)
    ¼ teaspoon salt
Whip until ▶ stiff, but not dry:
    1 egg white
Fold the egg white into the corn mixture. Into a hot buttered skillet, drop the mixture as for pancakes and sauté until light brown and fluffy. Do not overcook.

CORN FRITTERS OR CORN OYSTERS WITH FRESH OR CANNED CORN

[About 16 Fritters]
For best results, make the batter immediately before using it. Drain, then mash with a potato masher:
    1 cup freshly scraped corn or canned, cream-style corn
Beat until light and add:
    2 eggs
Add:
    6 tablespoons flour
    ½ teaspoon double-acting baking powder
    ¼ teaspoon salt
    ⅛ teaspoon nutmeg
Melt in a small skillet:
    3 tablespoons butter
When it has reached the point of fragrance, add the batter with a tablespoon. Permit the bottom of the cakes to brown, reverse them and brown the other side. Serve at once with:
    Mushroom Sauce, page 367, or maple sirup

TAMALES

[20 Tamales]
A curious call used to rend the air on hot summer nights, one that brought a sense of adventure to our limited childhood world. It was the Mexican tamale man, whose forbidden, hence desirable, wares long remained a mystery. These varied, leaf-wrapped confections, like individual puddings, may be spicy as mole, filled with cheese and peppers, or sweet with almond, citron and coconut.

Tamales steam slowly to allow the wrapping, either corn husks or banana leaves, to both protect and flavor the contents. Soften the leaves by soaking for 5 minutes in hot water and then draining before using. Most tamales have two ingredients not easily available. First a pastate or tortilla base—that moistened mixture of unslaked lime and dried corn which is ground into flour in a matate; and second, a combination of tequesquite and transparent green tomato parings which make the puddings puff up. The following tamale filling, for which we can get authentic ingredients, is made from fresh corn.

Remove the husks from 20 ears of:

Tender corn

and reserve the largest leaves. Soak for 5 minutes in hot water and drain. You will need 3 to 4 large leaves for each tamale. Scrape the kernels from the cobs, using the scraper illustrated on page 284. Mix these tender bits with:

¾ cup cultured sour cream
1 to 1¼ cups milk

Use the larger quantity if the corn is absolutely not fresh picked. Add:

¼ cup sugar
½ teaspoon salt
½ cup raisins

Overlap 3 or 4 leaves, see page 86. Place about 3 tablespoons of the corn mixture lengthwise down the center of the overlapped leaves. Roll the filling so the husks completely encase it, tucking up the short ends and tying with a white string. Put several layers of the remaining husks in the bottom element of the steamer and cover with about 1 to 1½ inches of boiling water. Place the carefully wrapped rolls ▶ upright in some form of vegetable steamer, see types illustrated on page 252. Close the steamer tightly and steam the tamales over low heat for about 1 hour. Remove the strings, allow the puddings to cool slightly and serve still wrapped in the inedible husks. The fillings should be firm enough to leave the husks easily. You may pass as a garnish:

Cultured sour cream
Cinnamon

ABOUT CUCUMBERS

How often the Japanese draw these decorative plants! That their formal values were missed when the cold weather came was poignantly noted by Isaiah when he said, "as desolate as a cottage in a cucumber garden abandoned in winter."

A cucumber ready to use is rigid and all green. It should have a lustrous skin—but do not be misled by the heavy, waxy, man-applied finish on some of those now in the markets. Never use a skin so waxed. If not waxed, it is perfectly edible. Some people who are allergic to this delicious vegetable find they can enjoy it if it is cooked. ▶ Use any recipe for summer squash or one of the following:

MULLED CUCUMBERS

I.   [4]

Pare, seed and cut into strips:

2 cups cucumbers

Drop them into:

1½ cups boiling water

▶ Simmer them until they are nearly tender—but no longer, as they will not retain their color. Drain them well. Place in a double boiler:

¾ cup Cream Sauce I, page 359

Season the sauce with:

Salt and white pepper
Freshly grated nutmeg or
1 teaspoon chopped fresh herbs or dill or celery seeds
1 teaspoon or more lemon juice

When the sauce reaches a boil, add the drained cucumbers. Place the pan over hot water and steam them, uncovered, for a few minutes before serving.

II. Prepare:
>   Mulled Cucumbers I,
>   above

substituting for the Cream Sauce:
>   Lemon Butter, page 384,
>   with capers or Tomato
>   Sauce, page 376, with
>   basil or Soubise or Onion
>   Sauce, page 363

CUCUMBER OR [4]
MOCK-OYSTER CASSEROLE

Preheat oven to 400°.
Prepare:
>   2 cups Mulled Cucumbers,
>   as above

Drain the vegetable well. Prepare:
>   1 cup Cream Sauce,
>   page 359

seasoned with:
>   1 tablespoon anchovy paste

Place the vegetable in a baking dish. Pour the hot sauce over it. Cover the top with:
>   Au Gratin III, page 389

Bake the dish until the top is brown.

CUCUMBER CREOLE [4]
CASSEROLE

Preheat oven to 375°.
Pare and seed:
>   3 large cucumbers

Cut them into ¼-inch slices. Combine with half the recipe for:
>   Creole Sauce, page 380

Place in the bottom of a greased ovenproof dish:
>   ½ cup dry bread crumbs

Add the cucumbers. Pour the sauce over them. Cover it with:
>   Au Gratin I, page 389

Bake the dish for about 35 minutes.

ABOUT DASHEEN OR TARO

This versatile vegetable, a form of the elephant ears we all know as a decorative plant, has a potato-like root that becomes grayish or violet when cooked. It is used as a vegetable or as a base for puddings and confections. Fermented, it is the famous poi of tropical countries, see following recipe. The spinach-flavored leaves are boiled as for greens but must be cooked from 45 minutes to 1 hour.

To bake, parboil the unpared root for 15 minutes and then time as for potato baking, but make certain the oven is not over 375°.

POI

[About 5 Cups]
Poi may be held at room temperature if unmixed with water. If refrigerated, mix with water. Dice into 1-inch cubes:
>   2½ lbs. cooked taro roots,
>   above

Mash in a wooden bowl with a wooden potato masher until starchy paste forms. Work in gradually with the hands:
>   2½ cups water

To remove lumps and fiber, force through several thicknesses of cheesecloth. Store in a cool place and serve at once or let it stand 2 to 3 days until it ferments and has a sour taste.

ABOUT EGGPLANT
OR AUBERGINE

These vegetables, lovely when stuffed, also make beautiful individual servings with their green caps against the polished purple of the cases. We have tried alternating them with green and red stuffed peppers for an effective buffet platter.

There are several important things to keep in mind in cooking eggplant. ◗ It may become very watery. Get rid of excess moisture by salting and draining on a rack before using in unthickened recipes; or stack the slices, cover with a plate, place a heavy weight on top and let stand until moisture is squeezed out. ◗ Eggplant discolors quickly when cut and should be sprinkled or rubbed with lemon juice. Also, because of discoloration ◗ cook in pottery, enamel, glass or stainless steel. One lb. of eggplant equals 3 cups diced.

Eggplant has a blotter-like capacity for oil or butter, well pointed up by this Near East tale. The imam or priest was so fetched by the eggplant dish his fiancée prepared that he asked that her dowry be the oil in which to cook it. Great Ali Baba jars of oil were stored in their new home. The first night the eggplant was delicious, also the second; but on the third night, his favorite dish was not waiting for him. "Alas," said the wife, "the first two nights have exhausted the supply of oil." And then the priest fainted! Imam Baaldi, the current and classic dish which carries the priest's name, calls for halved egg-plant, stuffed and completely covered in oil and casseroled covered, page 84, for 1½ hours.

EGGPLANT SLICES

These slices, after frying, sautéeing or broiling, are used in many ways.

I. Top with:
    Creamed Spinach,
        page 326
Sprinkle with:
    Gruyère cheese
and run under broiler.

II. Put in a casserole and cover with:
    Creole Sauce, page 380
Sprinkle with:
    Au Gratin I, page 389
Run under a broiler.

III. Place on each slice:
    A slice of Tomato
    Provençale, page 333

IV. Place on eggplant slice:
    A grilled tomato slice
Cover with:
    A poached egg
Serve with:
    Cheese Sauce, page 364

V. Place on an eggplant slice:
    Creamed ham or hash

BAKED EGGPLANT   [4]
SLICES

Preheat oven to 400°.
Pare:
    An eggplant
Cut it crosswise into slices ½ inch thick. Spread the slices on both sides with a mixture of:
    Soft butter or salad oil
Seasoned with:
    Salt and pepper
    Grated onion, lemon
    juice or basil
Place them on a baking sheet and bake until tender, about 12 minutes, turning them once. Garnish with:
    Chopped parsley or
    chervil

BAKED EGGPLANT   [4]
HALVES

Preheat oven to 400°.
Wash, dry, then cut into halves lengthwise:
    An eggplant
Crisscross the top with gashes about 1 inch deep. Sauté the halves cut side down for about 10 minutes in:
    3 tablespoons hot olive oil
Set them upright in a shallow ovenproof dish. Make a paste by mashing together until well blended:
    8 flat, minced anchovy
    fillets
    2 skinned, chopped cloves
    garlic
    ¼ cup bread crumbs
    2 tablespoons strong beef
    stock
    ⅛ teaspoon freshly ground
    pepper

Spread this over the tops of the eggplant. Sprinkle them with:

> Dry bread crumbs
> Finely minced parsley
> A little oil or dabs of
> butter

Bake the dish for about ½ hour.

SCALLOPED [4]
EGGPLANT

Preheat oven to 375°.
Pare and cut into dice:

> A medium-sized eggplant

Simmer it until tender in:

> ½ cup boiling water

Drain it well. Sprinkle it with:

> (2 tablespoons chopped
> parsley)

Chop until very fine:

> 1 small onion

Melt:

> 1 tablespoon butter

Sauté the onion in this until it is golden. Add it to the eggplant with:

> ½ cup milk
> (2 well-beaten eggs)

Melt:

> 3 tablespoons butter

Stir into it, until the butter is absorbed:

> ¾ cup cracker crumbs or
> ½ cup bread crumbs

Place layers of eggplant and layers of crumbs in a baking dish. Season them, if the crackers are unsalted, with:

> ¼ teaspoon salt
> ⅛ teaspoon paprika

Halve the top layer of crumbs. Place on the top:

> (Thin slices of cheese or
> grated cheese)

Bake the eggplant for about ½ hour. Garnish it with:

> Crisp crumbled bacon,
> page 491, or thin strips
> of pepperoni

DEEP FRIED [4]
EGGPLANT SLICES

The classic method is to dip eggplant in batter and fry it in deep fat.

◗ Please read About Deep Fat Fried Vegetables, page 258.
Preheat deep fryer to 370°.
Pare, cut into ½-inch slices or sticks:

> An eggplant

Dip it in:

> Fritter Batter for
> Vegetables (II, 125)

Fry it in deep fat until golden. Drain on absorbent paper and serve after adding:

> Salt

SAUTÉED EGGPLANT [4]
SLICES

Peel and cut into ½-inch slices, cubes or sticks:

> An eggplant

Dip the pieces in:

> Milk

Dredge them in:

> Seasoned flour, crumbs
> or cornmeal

For easier handling, place slices on a rack to dry for 15 minutes before cooking: Melt in a skillet:

> Butter or oil

Sauté the pieces until tender. Serve while very hot with:

> Chopped parsley or
> tarragon
> A sliced lemon or Tomato
> Sauce, page 376

EGGPLANT CASSEROLE [8]
OR RATATOUILLE
PROVENÇALE

This ends up looking in color like a Braque still life.
Put in a deep skillet or heavy casserole:

> ⅓ cup olive oil

Sauté until golden:

> ¾ cup thinly sliced onions
> 2 cloves garlic

Remove the onions and garlic from the casserole and combine in layers with:

> 4 julienned green peppers
> 2½ cups peeled, diced
> eggplant
> 3 cups zucchini in ½-inch
> slices

2 cups peeled, seeded,
    quartered tomatoes
Add to each layer:
    Salt and pepper
Sprinkle the top with:
    Olive oil
Simmer, covered, over very low
heat 35 to 45 minutes. ▸ Uncover and continue to heat 10
minutes longer to reduce the
amount of liquid. Serve hot or
cold.

STUFFED EGGPLANT   [4]
OR EGGPLANT FARCIE

Eggplant makes a wonderful
"background" food, due to its
color and shape. Cut eggplant,
just under and following the
lines of the leafy green cap. This
then forms an attractive lid. Or
slice it into two oval halves. The
cases may be filled with any desired combination of food, to
which the cooked eggplant pulp
is added.
Preheat oven to 400°.
Cut as described:
    A medium-sized eggplant
Scoop out the pulp, leaving a
thick shell. Then, drop the pulp
into a small quantity of boiling
water or stock and cook it until
it is tender. Drain it well and
mash it. Combine with:
    Farce, page 564, or
    chopped or ground
    cooked meat: lamb or
    ham or rice and shrimp

Fill the shell. Cover the top with
the cap or
    Au Gratin II or III,
    page 389

Bake the eggplant until filling is
heated.

STUFFED EGGPLANT   [4]
CREOLE

Cut into halves:
    A small eggplant
Scoop out the pulp and chop it.
Leave a shell ¼ inch thick.
Mince and heat in a skillet:
    2 strips bacon
Add to it and sauté until the
bacon is cooked:
    ¼ cup minced onion
    ¼ cup minced seeded green
    pepper with membrane
    removed
Add the eggplant pulp and:
    2 cups drained canned
    tomatoes
    ¼ cup diced celery
Simmer these ingredients until
the eggplant is tender. Beat
them with a fork until they are
well blended. Thicken them
with:
    ⅓ cup bread crumbs
Season them with:
    Salt and freshly ground
    pepper
Add to them:
    ½ cup Sautéed Mush-
    rooms, page 296
Preheat oven to 350°.
Fill the eggplant shells with the
mixture. Cover the tops with:
    Au Gratin III, page 389
Place the eggplant in a pan with
a very little water and bake until
it is thoroughly heated, about
15 minutes.

BRAISED OR GLAZED
ENDIVE

Prepare as for:
    Braised Celery, page 282

ABOUT FENNEL OR
ANISE

Florence fennel, which is found
in season at Italian markets, can
be eaten raw and is a choice
hors d'oeuvre or a substitute for

celery with rice in stuffings. If you enjoy the anise flavor, use the bulbous root and stalk as for celery and try seasoning with olive oil. The leaves can also be used discreetly for seasoning, but the usual plant for this purpose is Foeniculium vulgare (II, 206).

ABOUT FERN SHOOTS OR FRESH BRACKEN

In the Spring, cut ferns while the shoots are still curled in crosiers. Wash and tie in bundles of 6 to 8 fronds. Stand upright and steam about 20 minutes or until just tender.
Serve with:
> Hollandaise Sauce, page 368

ABOUT GREENS

Greens, such as turnips, mustard, kale, collards, corn salad, comfrey, borage, etc.—are seldom creamed. However, there is no reason why they should not be. The old-fashioned custom is to cook them to death, for an hour or more, with bacon, salt pork or ham hocks and to serve them with vinegar. To retain color and nutrients, try cooking by the following methods.

I. Prepare greens by washing carefully to remove grit and cut out any blemished areas or tough stems. Simmer for 2 hours in water to cover:
> A 2 lb. piece side meat:
> bacon or cottage ham
Add:
> 2 to 3 lbs. greens
And simmer about 35 to 40 minutes, until just tender.

II. If the greens are very young, cook them as for:
> Panned Spinach, page 326
allowing about 15 minutes cooking time.

ABOUT WILD GREENS

If you are in earnest about pursuing the hobby of greens collecting, try to consult a local enthusiast. If he is not available, make a slow approach, trying the greens you are absolutely sure of, like dandelion. Then experiment with poke, dock, lambs quarters, marsh marigold leaves, emerging ferns, yellow rocket cress, young milkweed shoots, pigweed, mustard, purslane.

Many plants are poisonous in part or in whole and most wild greens are bitter unless blanched, page 88, sometimes more than once before cooking. Young milkweeds, marsh marigold, plantains, purslane and nettles are relatively mild, while dock and dandelion, even when young, are better blanched.

Poke, for instance, has a poisonous root and leaf, although the shoot is both edible and delicious. In any case, use these wild greens in small quantities until you know your own reaction to them.

KOHLRABI [4]

Wash:
> 8 large kohlrabi
Cut off the tops and pare the roots. Slice the roots and drop them into a quantity of rapidly:
> Boiling water
Cook them, uncovered, until they are barely tender. Drain them well. Boil the tops separately in the same manner. Drain them well, chop them until they are very fine or purée them and combine them with the roots. Prepare:
> Cream Sauce I, page 359
Add:
> (A grating of nutmeg)
When the sauce is smooth and hot, add the kohlrabi.

ABOUT LEEKS OR POIREAUX

How we wish that leeks were as common here as in France, where they are known as the "asparagus of the poor." Leeks, like other onion types (II, 209), make a wonderful seasoning. When cooked as a vegetable, they must be carefully washed to free the interlacing leaves from grit; and only the white portion is used. Cook as for Asparagus, page 260, or braise as for Celery, page 282.

PURÉE OF LEEKS

Good as a meat garnish or stuffing in tomatoes.
Prepare and cook:
Leeks, as above
Drain them well. Chop them coarsely. For each cup add:
2 tablespoons butter
½ cup fresh bread crumbs
Salt and pepper
Stir and simmer them gently until blended. If they become too thick, add:
A little cream
Serve the purée very hot with:
Finely chopped parsley

COOKED LETTUCE

Home gardeners in their enthusiasm find themselves with sudden surpluses of lettuce and wish they had rabbits instead of children—failing to realize that nibbling is not the only approach to this vegetable. Try these delectable alternatives: cook lettuce as a Cream Soup, page 131; cream it like Spinach,

page 326; cook with peas; stuff it like Cabbage, page 277; cook and smother it with stewed tomatoes or braise as for Celery, page 282, allowing the lettuce to simmer only a few minutes before reducing the sauce.

ABOUT MUSHROOMS

Who would expect a lot of sunshine vitamin D in plants that flourish in cellars and caves? Yet this is only one of the many valuable nutrients in mushrooms. They delight us too with their almost total lack of calories and then promptly fool us by a blotter-like capacity for butter, oil and cream.

They can fool the experts in other ways. Some of the poisonous types resemble edible forms during various stages of development. ◗ There is no simple way to identify mushrooms and other edible fungi. Experts prefer to have about 10 specimens for identification before committing themselves.

The amanitas, for instance, include types so deadly they may well have been the rumored secret poison of the Borgias. These rather common growths are white gilled and they have a ruptured basal cup and a torn veil or ring left by that veil on the stem. So, collectors should stick to a safer family, like the puffballs, which have neither stems nor gills. They are edible if they grow above ground and the flesh inside is white. Lycoperdon giganteum, shown first on the left, varies from marble to canteloupe size and Lycoperdon craniforme resembles a skull slightly shrivelled, even when in prime eating condition.

Rural families return, season after season, to the same mushroom clumps and fairy rings which appear like magic when moisture conditions are just right. The hidden roots of mushrooms are often as stable as an oak. To preserve these seasonal mushrooms, see (II, 221).

♦ Never use any mushroom that shows signs of decay. It harbors ptomaines and toxins just like any other decaying vegetation. ♦ Never cook light-colored mushrooms in aluminum as it darkens them. And don't worry about mushrooms packaged by reputable firms. These firms guard their beds intensively against harmful invading spores. Don't bother to buy spawn blocks to grow your own mushrooms if your cellar is warmer than about 55°.

Agaricus campestris, shown in the center, is the type most often found fresh at the market. The young, pale buttons are succulent, the older, drier ones are best for sauces, as the flavor lies in the dark gills. The completely dried **Gyromitra esculenta** usually imported from Europe is also very strong in flavor when reconstituted, see below. Strangely enough, it can never be eaten raw as it has a poisonous alkaloid which, with this mushroom, disappears entirely in drying or parboiling. But cooking will not destroy the poison ♦ with the most poisonous types.

Shown second from the left, page 294 are a **morel,** a spring growth, and second from the right, **chanterelle,** a summer one. On the far right is **Boletus edulis,** a great European favorite known to gourmets as cêpe or Steinpilz. For truffles, those diamonds of the kitchen, see page 299.

♦ To prepare fresh mushrooms, brush or wipe with a cloth. If they must be washed, dry thoroughly. As the most intense flavor lies in the skin, do not remove it. Some people use only the caps, as the stems tend to be tougher. Should you be so extravagant, turn the mushroom on its side and cut the stem so enough is left within the cap to prevent subsequent shrinkage at the center during the cooking. Be sure to use the stems in Stock Making (II, 139) in Farces, page 564, or in Duxelles, page 540. Another way to keep the mushroom plump and to use most of the stem is to turn it, as sketched, and slice lengthwise.

One of the choicest garnishes for looks is the channelled mushroom. To channel these curving lines on the rather firm but spongy textured mushroom evenly with a sharp knife requires considerable skill, but we find the point of a curved grapefruit knife is quick and easy for the amateur. We have even been tempted to use a V-shaped linoleum carving tool.

♦ To keep mushrooms light in color, sprinkle with lemon juice or white wine or cook À Blanc (II, 146). ♦ To reconstitute dried mushrooms, soak from ½ to 4 hours in tepid water to cover. Drain and use as for fresh mushrooms. Use the water

for sauces or soups. Store dried mushrooms, uncovered, in a glass container in a light place.
♦ 3 oz. dried mushrooms reconstituted equal 1 lb.

To keep mushrooms or truffles impaled on food as a garnish, use tiny lemon thyme branches as picks.

STEAMED MUSHROOMS

This is a fine way to prepare very large mushrooms for stuffing.
♦ Please read About Mushrooms, page 294.
Prepare:

    1 lb. mushrooms

Place them in the top of a double boiler ♦ over—not in—hot water. Dot them with:

    2 tablespoons butter

Add:

    ¼ teaspoon salt
    ⅛ teaspoon paprika
    (½ cup milk)

Cover closely. Steam for about 20 minutes or until tender. The broth that results is superlative. Serve with salt or use this broth in sauces.

SAUTÉED   [4]
MUSHROOMS

Prepare for cooking, using caps or pieces sliced to uniform thickness:

    1 lb. mushrooms

Melt in a skillet over moderately high heat until they reach the point of fragrance:

    2 tablespoons butter
    1 tablespoon cooking oil

or use:

    (3 tablespoons clarified
    butter)

Add the mushrooms and ♦ shake the pan, so the mushrooms are coated without scorching. Drop in:

    (1 clove garlic)

Continue to cook over moderately high heat ♦ uncovered, shaking the pan frequently. At first the mushrooms will seem dry and will almost invisibly absorb the fat. Continue to shake the pan for 3 to 5 minutes, depending on the size of the pieces. Remove the garlic. If you are holding the mushrooms to add to other food, do not cover, as this will draw out their juices. If using as a garnish or vegetable, serve at once on:

    Toast rounds
    Grilled tomatoes or
    eggplant

or on a bed of:

    Puréed Peas, page 306

CREAMED   [4]
MUSHROOMS

Sauté, as for Sautéed Mushrooms, above:

    1 lb. sliced mushrooms
    1 tablespoon finely
    chopped onion

Combine the above with:

    1 cup hot Cream Sauce II,
    page 359, or Velouté
    Sauce, page 362

Season with:

    Salt and paprika
    2 tablespoons dry white
    wine
    A pinch of herbs

Marjoram is the traditional touch. Chives and parsley are recommended too. Serve over a baked potato or serve in a casserole, covered with:

    Au Gratin II, page 389

MUSHROOMS À LA   [4]
SCHOENER

A Viennese specialty.
Wipe off with a clean cloth:

    1 lb. button mushrooms

Choose mushrooms with about a 1- to 1½-inch cap and cut off the stems ¼ to ½ inch below the caps. Sprinkle with:

    Lemon juice
    Salt

Dip them in:
> Fritter Batter with Beer
> (II, 126)

and deep-fat fry them at 375°, until a golden brown. You may hold them for a very short time in a 200° oven, covered with a paper towel. Just before serving, dust them with:
> Chopped parsley or chervil

Serve with:
> Cold Tartare Sauce, page 349

BROILED MUSHROOMS

Preheat broiler.
Wipe with a dry cloth and remove the stems from:
> Mushrooms

Brush them lightly with:
> Butter or oil

Place them cap side down on a hot greased broiler and broil them for about 2½ minutes to a side, turning them once. Put in each cap a small lump of:
> Butter or a square of bacon

Season the mushrooms with:
> Salt, as needed and paprika
> Chopped parsley and lemon juice

They are usually done when the butter has been absorbed. Serve them at once on:
> Hot toast

After adding the butter, keep the cap side up to preserve the juices.

BROILED STUFFED MUSHROOMS COCKAIGNE

[4 Small Servings]
Preheat broiler.
There are wonderful farces of sweetbreads, sausages or just seasoned puréed peas with a sprig of lemon thyme. The mushroom stems may be incorporated with them to form the stuffings. Our particular favorite is given below.

Remove stems. Wipe with a damp cloth:
> 12 large mushroom caps

Chop the stems. Simmer them for 2 minutes in:
> 1 tablespoon butter

or, if the stems are very large, cook them, first in the top of a double boiler in:
> Milk

Add:
> 1½ cups dry bread crumbs
> ¼ cup chopped blanched almonds, pecans or other nut meats
> (1 pressed clove garlic)
> 1½ tablespoons chopped chives, basil or tarragon

Bind these ingredients with:
> 2 tablespoons cream, stock or part stock and part sherry

Season with:
> Salt and paprika

Brush the caps with:
> Butter or olive oil

Fill them with the above dressing and sprinkle with:
> Grated Parmesan cheese

Place them cap side up on a well-greased pan. Broil for about 5 minutes and serve them sizzling hot on:
> Toast

MUSHROOMS STUFFED WITH CLAMS OR OYSTERS

Preheat broiler.
Remove the stems and wipe with a dry cloth:
> Large mushrooms

Dip the caps in:
> Melted butter

Place on each one:
> A clam or oyster

Cover each clam with:
> 1 teaspoon horseradish
> 1 teaspoon or more mayonnaise
> A drop or 2 hot pepper sauce or Worcestershire sauce

Place the mushrooms in a pan.

Broil them about 6 inches from
the source of heat, until the tops
begin to color. Serve them hot.

MUSHROOMS   [4]
FLORENTINE

Preheat broiler.
Prepare as for Broiled Stuffed
Mushrooms Cockaigne, page
297:

> 12 large mushrooms

Add to the stems and the juice
in the pan:

> 2 teaspoons grated onion
> 2 tablespoons chopped
>   parsley
> (1 teaspoon anchovy paste)

Cook these ingredients gently
for about 3 minutes. Add:

> 1/3 cup or more creamed
>   spinach

Brush the caps with:

> Butter or olive oil

Fill them with the above mixture and broil them cap side up
on a greased pan for about 5
minutes. Serve as a garnish for
individual steaks or scrambled
eggs.

MUSHROOMS STUFFED   [4]
WITH SEAFOOD OR
SNAILS

Preheat broiler.
Remove the stems from:

> 8 large mushrooms

Wipe caps and stems with a dry
cloth. Chop the stems. Shell,
then chop:

> 1/2 lb. cooked shrimp, snails
>   or crab meat

Prepare the sauce. Melt:

> 3 tablespoons olive oil or
>   butter

Stir in:

> 1/4 cup flour

Add:

> 2 cups shrimp, chicken or
>   clam stock

Add the mushroom stems. ♦
Lower the heat. Stir and simmer
the sauce for 2 minutes. Add the
seafood and:

> 2 teaspoons chopped
>   chives, parsley or
>   other herb

Stir gently until well blended.
Correct the seasoning
and add:

> 1/8 teaspoon curry powder
>   or 1 tablespoon sherry

Brush the caps with:

> Butter or olive oil

Fill them with the above dressing, place cap side up on a well-
greased pan and broil for about
5 minutes. While the caps are
cooking, prepare:

> 8 rounds of buttered toast,
>   about same size as
>   mushrooms

Place the cooked caps on the
toast. Put the remaining filling
in the center of a platter and
surround it with the caps on
toast. Garnish with:

> Parsley

If you want to make this a main
dish, add curls of:

> Broiled bacon

MUSHROOMS AND   [4]
ONIONS IN WINE

Fine for a chafing dish.
Prepare for cooking:

> 1 lb. mushrooms

Melt:

> 1/2 cup butter

Skin, add, stir and sauté for 5
minutes:

> 16 tiny white onions

Add the mushrooms. When they
are coated with butter add:

> 2 tablespoons flour
> 1/4 cup chopped parsley
> 1/2 bay leaf
> 1/4 teaspoon freshly grated
>   nutmeg
> 1/2 cup bouillon or stock

Cook and stir these ingredients
until the onions are tender. Add:

> 1/4 cup Madeira or dry
>   sherry

Serve garnished with:

> Croutons, page 390
> Sprigs of parsley

MUSHROOM RING [6] OR MOUSSE

Preheat oven to 325°.
Put through a food chopper:

> 1 lb. mushrooms

Melt:

> 2 tablespoons butter

Stir in:

> 2 tablespoons flour

Brown the flour slightly. Sauté
the mushrooms in this mixture
for 2 minutes. Cool them. Beat
in:

> 4 beaten egg yolks
> ½ teaspoon salt
> ¼ teaspoon paprika

Whip until stiff:

> 1 cup heavy cream

In another bowl ▶ whip until
stiff, but not dry:

> 2 egg whites

Fold the cream lightly into the
mushroom mixture. Fold in the
egg whites. Butter a 9-inch ring
mold. Pour in the mousse. Cover
it with a piece of buttered paper.
Place the ring mold in a pan of
hot water. Bake it for about 1
hour. Invert the mousse onto a
platter. Fill center with:

> Buttered peas and parsley

MUSHROOMS UNDER [4] GLASS

In former years the following
dish was always a mark of ex-
treme luxury. Today it is within
the reach of anyone with an
ovenproof glass bowl that fits
closely over a baking dish.
Preheat oven to 375°.
Trim the stems from and channel, page 295:

> 1 lb. mushrooms

Beat until creamy:

> ¼ cup butter

Stir in very slowly:

> 2 teaspoons lemon juice

Add:

> 1 tablespoon chopped
>   celery
> ⅓ teaspoon salt
> ¼ teaspoon paprika

Cut with a biscuit cutter and
toast:

> 4 rounds bread, ½ inch
>   thick

When cold, spread them on both
sides with ½ the butter mixture. Spread the rest on the tops
of the mushroom caps. Place the
toast in the bottom of a small
baking dish and heap the mushrooms upon them. Pour over
them:

> ½ cup cream

Cover them closely with a glass
bowl. Bake them for about 25
minutes. Add more cream if they
become dry. Just before serving,
add:

> 2 tablespoons dry sherry

Serve the mushrooms garnished
with:

> **Parsley**

ABOUT TRUFFLES

When we found them at a gas
stop in the Indiana hills one
winter day, in their imported
cans, both as rubbings and
whole, we knew they had become common currency. So common that when a friend asked
the proprietor of a small fruit
market if he had any truffles,
he, being a little hard of hear-
ing, shrugged his shoulders elo-
quently and replied, "And who
hasn't?"

Like other "storied" foods,
truffles are best appreciated
where they are grown: in Péri-
gord, they lock them up in hotel
safes. For even where they are
most plentiful they are expensive and treasured, as they defy
cultivation. French are the black
truffles, rooted from their under-
ground depths by trick pigs.
Dogs are used in Italy for digging the whites. They are called
white only in contrast to the best
French ones, for they are really
pale brown and beige and are
in season from October to
March.

Too bad there isn't a truffle Geiger counter, but since these fungi have a symbiotic relationship to oak trees, that's the place to start digging.

The terms **Périgordine, Piémontaise** or **Lucullus** are often applied to truffled dishes. Famous dishes seasoned with truffles are:

Pâté de foie in pastry
Scrambled eggs
Garnishes for hors d'oeuvres
Farce for artichokes

♦ To prepare truffles, wash fresh ones in several waters. As the skin is rough, scrub them. They should be sliced very thin, for their aroma is overpowering. To take advantage of it, place thin slices on food and store overnight in a closed container in the refrigerator. Save all parings and mince finely for sauce or soup. Add truffles to dishes at the end of the cooking period, as they should be cooked with the food to flavor it—but not overcooked. If using canned truffles, merely heat with the food or use as a garnish. If you open a can and use only a portion, cover the remainder with oil or sherry. It will keep refrigerated a month.

✻ Truffles may be frozen in their own juice; or add some Madeira wine if juice is lacking.

⅄ TRUFFLE GARNISHES

I. To get truffles in economical quantity for decorating, put in a blender:

7 tablespoons truffle bits, peelings and juice
1 tablespoon gelatin

Dissolved in:

¾ cup water

If this blended mixture is not dark enough to suit you, heat it over hot water until it colors to your satisfaction. Spread the mixture thin on a cookie tin and cool it in the refrigerator. Cut into any desired form and use on cold food, see Chaud-froid, page 388. This same process may be used for pimientos.

II. White truffles can be used raw over risotto or fondue, puréed for canapés, processed in foie gras or cooked 2 to 3 minutes in butter with Parmesan cheese.

ABOUT OKRA

This vegetable is often combined in stews, where its gluey sap helps thicken the sauce and gives to such dishes the name of **Gumbo.** See also page 118.

STEWED OKRA   [3]

Wash:

2 cups young okra

If the pods are small, leave them whole, in which case less sap is released. If they are large, cut off the stems and slice into 1-inch pieces. Drop the okra into a small amount of:

Boiling water

enough to cover the bottom of the pan by ⅛ inch. Simmer it, covered, until tender. If whole, it will take about 8 minutes—if cut, about 5. Or the okra may be cooked until half tender, drained and then cooked, covered, in the butter over low heat until it is tender. Drain it.

Correct the seasoning

Serve it hot with:

Melted butter—1 tablespoon to 1 cup okra

or serve with:

Hollandaise Sauce, page 368

or serve it:

Vinaigrette, page 341

❂ Pressure cook okra cut into 1-inch slices at 15 lbs. for 4 minutes.

SAUTÉED OKRA [6]

Wash:

    1 quart okra: 1 lb.

Dry it well, cut off the stem ends and slice the okra crosswise in thin slices. Melt:

    2 tablespoons butter

Add the okra, cover it and simmer gently for about 10 minutes. Stir it frequently. Remove the cover and continue cooking the okra until it is tender and a golden brown.

ABOUT ONIONS

Onions are supposed to be the secret of health. But how can they keep that secret? For vari-

ous suggestions to disguise their lesser virtues and exploit their potential ♦ please read About Onions as Seasoning (II, 209), where you will also find a full discussion of this marvelous family with the qualities each member contributes.

A pleasant way to skin onions is to drop them into rapidly boiling water and leave for about 8 seconds. Drain, chill; and the skin should slip off.

To avoid weeping, you may also pare them under running water, as sketched. Onions all rebel under high heat or too long a cooking period by both discoloring and releasing an unpleasant clinging odor from their sulphur

compounds. In sautéing them, be sure they are evenly sliced so they all cook golden at the same time and none remains raw and unpleasant in taste. Give them care in cooking and you will be amply rewarded by the flavor that results.

STEAMED ONIONS [4]

This method is recommended in place of stewing because onion, like cabbage, releases sulphur compounds under too great heat, causing odors and discoloration. Place on a rack ♦ over—not in —hot water:

    10 medium, dry, unpeeled onions

Cover the pan and cook them until tender, for 30 minutes or more. Peel and serve with:

    (1 cup browned buttered bread crumbs (II, 159)

or dress them with:

    ¼ cup melted butter
    ½ teaspoon salt
    ½ teaspoon cinnamon or cloves
    (1 teaspoon sugar)

CREAMED ONIONS [4]

Prepare:

    Steamed Onions, above

Cover with:

    1 cup Cream Sauce I, page 359, and Au Gratin III, page 389, 1 cup Allemande Sauce, page 362, or 1 cup Tomato Sauce, page 376

You may use ¼ onion water and ¾ cream. Cook the onions and the sauce together for 1 minute. Add:

    ¼ cup chopped parsley
    A dash of cloves
    ¼ teaspoon paprika
    (2 tablespoons sherry)

A wonderful addition is:

    (½ cup Sautéed Mushrooms, page 296)

or:

(Minced celery, cooked
or raw)
If using one of the above sauces,
you may serve the onions on:
(Toast)

YOUNG GREEN ONIONS OR SCALLIONS

Place:
Young green onions
in a very small quantity of:
Boiling water
Cook them, uncovered, until
they are nearly tender, about
25 minutes. Drain them well.
Place them in rows, on very
thin:
Slices of toast
Season them with:
Salt and freshly grated
white pepper or nutmeg
Pour over them:
Melted butter or
Hollandaise Sauce,
page 369
Or cut the onions into small
pieces, cook them and combine
them with other cooked vege-
tables—peas, beans, or new po-
tatoes.

WHOLE BAKED ONIONS

I. Preheat oven to 375°.
Wash:
Medium-sized onions
Bake them in a buttered baking
dish until they are tender, for
about 1½ hours. Cut a slice
from the root end. Squeeze the
onions to force out the centers.
Discard the outer shells. Pour
over the onions:
Melted butter
Season them with:
Salt and paprika
Cover them with:
(Grated cheese or
chopped parsley)

II. ▤ Cook, as you would potatoes, in a bed of coals for about
45 minutes:
Whole onions
The outer skin forms a protection. When they are tender,
puncture the skin to let the
steam escape. Scoop out the centers and serve with:
Salt and pepper

SAUTÉED ONIONS   [2]

These can be useful also as a
garnish for a greater number
than two.
Skin:
4 medium-sized onions
Cut them into very thin slices
or chop them. Melt in a skillet:
2 tablespoons butter or
bacon drippings
Add the onions and sauté them
until they are golden brown. Stir
them frequently to keep them
from burning. Before serving,
season with:
Salt
(Worcestershire sauce)

SMALL BRAISED ONIONS

Skin:
Small onions
Pour over them, to the depth of
½ inch:
Boiling Stock (II, 141)
Simmer them, covered, over slow
heat. Let them absorb the liquid
until they are tender, about 35
minutes. Add additional stock,
if necessary. When they are
tender
Correct the seasoning
and add:
(Seeded raisins)

GLAZED ONIONS   [4]

These onions are good with pork
roast.
Skin:
12 small onions
Prick them through the center
and place them on a rack above:
1 inch boiling water
Cook them, covered, until they
are nearly tender, for about 25
minutes. Dry them on a cloth.
Melt:
¼ cup butter
Add:

½ teaspoon salt
2 tablespoons brown sugar

Cook this sirup for 1 minute. Add the onions and move them about until they are well coated. Cook them over low heat for about 15 minutes, using an asbestos mat under the pot, if needed, toward the end.

SCALLOPED ONIONS [4]
WITH CHEESE

Preheat oven to 350°.
I. Peel, slice crosswise and poach in:

Milk

until tender:

6 large white onions

Drain them well. Place in a buttered baking dish:

4 slices buttered toast

Arrange the onions on the toast. Sprinkle them with:

½ cup grated American
cheese

Beat well:

1 egg
1 cup milk
½ teaspoon salt
⅛ teaspoon paprika

Pour this mixture over the onions. Dot the top with:

1 tablespoon butter

Bake the dish for 40 minutes. Serve with:

Crisp bacon
Parsley

II. Or, as a substitute for scalloping which gives much the same result, cook the onions, as described above, until tender. Then make a generous spread of grated cheese, Worcestershire sauce and seasonings. Place the parboiled onions on the toast, spread them with the paste, broil them until the cheese is melted.

FRENCH FRIED ONION [4]
RINGS OR SHOESTRING
ONIONS

▶ Please read About Deep-Fat Frying, pages 75–79.

Skin and cut crosswise into ¼-inch slices or shred paper-thin.

2 large onions

Combine:

1 cup milk
1 cup water

Soak the onions in this for ½ hour. Drain them, spread them on absorbent paper and dredge them with:

Fritter Batter for
Vegetables (II, 125)

Fry in a deep fryer, preheated to 350°–370°, until light brown. Drain on absorbent paper.

STUFFED ONIONS

Onions make attractive garnishes or individual servings when filled.
▶ Please read About Stuffed Vegetables, page 256.
Skin and parboil, page 88, for about 10 minutes:

Medium-sized onions

Drain well. Cut a slice from the top and remove all but ¾ inch of shell. Chop the removed pulp with:

Bread crumbs or cooked
rice, chopped cooked fish,
meat or sausage, baked
beans, mushrooms and
bacon, deviled ham or
nutmeats

Moisten these ingredients with:

Cream Sauce I, page 359,
melted butter, stock,
cream or gravy
Correct the seasoning

and add:

Chopped fresh herbs

Fill the onion cases. Cover the tops with:

Au Gratin III, page 389

Place the filled onions in a pan with enough water to keep them from scorching and bake them in a preheated 375° oven until they are tender, about 30 to 40 minutes, depending on size and type. If they are too soft to hold their shape well, bake them in well-greased muffin tins.

ONIONS STUFFED [4]
WITH SAUERKRAUT

Preheat oven to 400°.
Prepare:
6 onion cases, above
Combine the chopped pulp and:
1 cup drained sauerkraut
½ cup soft bread crumbs
¼ teaspoon salt
(¼ teaspoon caraway or
celery seed)
Heap the mixture into the onion
cases. Sprinkle the tops generously with:
Buttered crumbs
Bake the onions in a pan with
a very little water until they are
well heated and tender, about
35 minutes.

ONION AND APPLE [4]
CASSEROLE

This is a complete meal served
with green salad, a beverage and
bread.
Preheat oven to 375°.
Peel and cut crosswise into ⅛-
inch slices:
6 medium-sized onions
Peel, core and cut in the same
way.
4 medium-sized apples
Sauté, remove from the pan and
mince:
8 slices bacon
Take out 2 tablespoons of the
bacon fat. In the remainder,
toss:
½ cup soft bread crumbs
Grease a baking dish. Arrange
the onions, apples and bacon in
alternate layers. Combine and
pour over them:
¾ cup hot Stock (II, 141),
or water
½ teaspoon salt
Cover the top with the bread
crumbs. Cover the dish and bake
it for 30 minutes. Uncover and
cook it about 15 minutes longer.

ABOUT OYSTER PLANT
OR SALSIFY

Salsify, as usually found in the
market, is white-skinned. If you
plan growing a salsify, pick
scorzonera—the black-skinned
type which is better flavored.
The best flavor results if the
vegetable is stored for several
weeks at temperatures just above
32°.
This root discolors on exposure to air. To avoid this, cook
it unpeeled or, if peeled, cook
it à blanc, as below.

OYSTER PLANT À BLANC

Have ready:
3 cups boiling water
in which you have dissolved:
1 tablespoon flour
2 teaspoons lemon juice
½ teaspoon salt
Drop in:
2 cups peeled oyster plant
and cook for 7 to 10 minutes.
Serve in:
Cream Sauce I, page 359
or with:
2 tablespoons melted butter
(Chopped chives or
parsley)
or season it with:
1 tablespoon brown sugar
A grating of nutmeg
½ cup whipping cream

SAUTÉED OYSTER PLANT

Wash and peel:
Oyster plant
Dip at once in:
Milk
Drain and season it with:
Salt and pepper
Roll it in:
Flour, bread crumbs or
crushed cornflakes
Sauté it slowly until golden in:
Butter

ABOUT HEARTS OF PALM

This ivory-layered vegetable,
also known as swamp cabbage,
usually weighs between 2 to 3
lbs. when trimmed. Unless available where grown, it is found

canned—for it loses flavor and
discolors quickly after removal
from its sheath.

♦ To boil, remove the outer
covering of the heart, leaving a
cylindrical portion, the base of
which should be tested for bitterness. Remove fibrous upper
portion. Slice thin and soak for
1 hour. Use the same water to
blanch à blanc (II, 146), the
palm for 5 minutes—if there is
any trace of bitterness. Now
drain and plunge into boiling
water again. Cook, covered,
about 45 minutes. Drain and
serve with:

> Hollandaise Sauce,
> page 368

or in:

> Cream Sauce I,
> page 359

♦ To roast, leave the heart in its
sheath. Roast in a 400° oven
until tender. Lay back the
sheath. Slice the heart crosswise
and serve with:

> Lemon juice and salt

DEEP FRIED PARSLEY

♦ Please read About Deep-Fat
Frying, pages 75–79.
Fried parsley was used merely
as a decoration by Ranhofer, the
great chef at Delmonicos, who
wrote "The Epicurean." Today,
try to keep guests from eating it!
This is so delicious if properly
fried, but becomes limp if the
fat is not hot enough and olive
green if the fat is too hot. It
should be both crisp and a
bright dark green. To obtain
this crispness and color have at
least 2 to 3 inches of fat per
cup of parsley and bring the fat
you are using just to the smoking point. The parsley must be
carefully stemmed, washed and
placed between towels until absolutely dry. Put in a frying
basket:

> 1 cup clean, fresh,

> well-dried, stemmed
> parsley

Immerse the basket in:

> Hot cooking oil

which has just reached the smoking point and leave it 1 to 2
minutes or until no hissing noise
is heard. Remove and drain on
paper. Serve immediately!

PARSNIPS   [4]

To bring out the best flavor of
this vegetable, store for several
weeks at temperatures just above
32°. Parsnips discolor easily. To
avoid this see Oyster Plant, page
304.

Preheat oven to 375°.
Pare, then cut into halves:

> 4 medium-sized parsnips:
> 1 lb.

Place them in a buttered ovenproof dish. Brush them with:

> 2½ tablespoons butter

Sprinkle them with:

> ½ teaspoon salt

Add to the dish:

> ¾ cup stock or water

Cover the dish and bake until
the parsnips are tender, for
about 45 minutes. Serve with:

> Parsley butter

✪ Pressure cook parsnips at 15
lbs. for 7 minutes.

FRENCH PARSNIPS

Prepare as for:

> Carrots Vichy, page 280

GREEN PEAS   [2 to 3]

Young peas have always elicited
paeans of praise, but what to
do with old ones? The skins
toughen easily. Try salting when
cooking is about half over or try
Puréed Peas I, below. ♦ One
pound of fairly well-filled pods
will yield about 1 cup hulled
peas. Wash, then hull:

> 1 lb. green peas

Steam them, page 252, or cook
them, covered, in:

⅛ inch boiling water or
light stock
to keep them from scorching.
Add:

½ teaspoon lemon juice
to help preserve color. There is
a tradition that one must add to
peas:

(A pinch of sugar)
Two or three pea pods may be
cooked with the peas for flavor.
Simmer 10 to 15 minutes. When
the peas are tender, drain them
if there is any water left. Season
them with:

Melted butter or hot
cream
to which you may add:

Chopped parsley or mint
✪ Pressure cook peas at 15 lbs.
for 2 minutes.

GREEN PEAS AND LETTUCE

I. [2 to 3]
Wash, and remove the heart
from:

A head of lettuce
Wash, then hull:

1 cup green peas
Season them with:

Salt and pepper
Pinch of sugar
Fill the head of lettuce with the
peas, tie up the leaves and place
the head in a small quantity of:

Boiling water
Steam the peas, covered, until
tender, about 30 minutes. Serve
them with:

Melted butter or cream
The lettuce leaves may be
chopped and served with the
peas.

II. [2 to 3]
Wash, then hull:

1 cup green peas
Place them in the top of a double boiler. Cover them with large
moist:

Lettuce leaves or
purslane
Cook them, covered, until ten-

der, over boiling water. This is
sometimes a slow process, dependent upon the size of the
peas, about ¾ of an hour. Remove the lettuce or purslane.

Correct the seasoning
and add:

Butter or cream
Serve the peas sprinkled with:

Chopped parsley

PURÉE OF PEAS

These make a lovely base on
which to place stuffed mushrooms.

I. Prepare:

2 cups cooked frozen peas
⅄ Blend them, when tender,
with:

3 tablespoons cream
Correct the seasoning
and serve at once.

II. Prepare:

¼ cup minced onions,
scallions or chives
Sauté them until tender in:

3 tablespoons butter
Heat in a double boiler the contents of:

2 cans condensed cream of
pea soup: 21 oz.
Stir in the onions. Serve:

Au Gratin, page 389

PEAS AND CARROTS

Prepare:

Hot, drained Carrots,
page 279
Combine them in any proportion
with:

Hot canned or cooked
green peas
Drain the vegetables well.

Correct the seasoning
Pour over them:

Melted butter:
1 tablespoon to 1 cup
vegetables
Chopped parsley
Serve at once.

PEAS AND MUSHROOMS

Prepare as for:

Peas and Carrots, above

substituting for the carrots:

Sautéed Mushrooms,
page 279

PODDED PEAS

These sought-after varieties,
known also as sugar peas, snow
peas and mange-tout, are often
available in Chinese shops. If
they are not young, slice them
diagonally, page 250.
Wash, cut off the ends, string
and cook as for:

Green or Snap Beans,
page 262

or you may stir-fry, page 253,
about 5 minutes. Serve while
still crisp.

ABOUT SWEET PEPPERS OR PIMIENTOS

Many people in the Midwest
call sweet bell peppers man-
goes. Do not confuse them with
the tropical fruit of the same
name (II, 103). Peppers and
their hot cousins (II, 213) are
chock-full of vitamin C and are
also reported as having antibac-
terial values as well. The seeds
cause excruciating pain when in
contact with eyes or lips, so
♦ always remove, before use, the
stem and fibrous portions that
hold the seeds. ♦ To peel peppers, put under the broiler and
turn often until they blister.

These are one of the few vegetables that can be ✻ frozen
without blanching. So buy when
they are plentiful. Peppers are
delicious stuffed, but ♦ never
overcook them as they become
bitter.

GREEN PEPPERS IN SAUCE

Stewed green peppers combine
well with other vegetables—for
example, green peppers with
celery or onions. Remove stem,
seeds and fibrous portions from:

Green peppers

Cut the peppers into oblongs or
strips. Drop them into:

½ inch boiling water

Boil them until they are tender,
for about 10 minutes. Drain
them well. Serve them in:

Cheese sauce or a canned
soup sauce

Season either one with:

Salt
Worcestershire sauce

Allow about ½ as much sauce
as peppers.

ONIONS AND   [4]
GREEN PEPPERS

This is a good accompaniment
to cold meat.
Skin, then cut into thin slices:

6 medium-sized onions

Cut coarsely, after removing
seeds and membranes:

3 green peppers

Melt in a large skillet:

3 tablespoon butter, ham
fat or olive oil

Sauté the onions and peppers in
this for about 10 minutes. Add:

2 tablespoons stock or
water

Correct the seasoning

Cover the skillet. Simmer the
vegetables until the onions are
tender, for about 10 minutes.
Serve with:

Tomato Sauce, page 376

STUFFED PEPPERS

Should you want to fill peppers
with heated, precooked food,
blanch them, page 88, for about
5 minutes. Fill and serve. Or,
cover the filling with Au Gratin
I, II, or III, page 389, and run
briefly under broiler until the
crumbs are golden. You may fill
pepper cases with any of the
fillings suggested for Stuffed
Tomato, page 336, or one of the
following: parslied, buttered
Lima beans; creamed spinach,

peas or celery; creamed asparagus with shredded almonds;
Stuffings of precooked food;
Macaroni and Cheese au Gratin,
page 170, or Corn Creole, page
286.

PEPPERS STUFFED   [4]
WITH ANCHOVY
DRESSING

▶ Please read About Stuffed
Vegetables, page 256.
Preheat oven to 350°.
Prepare:
    4 pepper cases
Fill the pepper cases with a
mixture of:
    1⅔ cups dried bread crumbs
      2 tablespoons melted butter
      6 crushed anchovy fillets
      2 tablespoons capers
      ½ cup sliced green olives
      ½ teaspoon salt
     1¼ cups undrained canned
        tomatoes
Bake, as directed, about 10 to
15 minutes.

PEPPERS STUFFED   [4]
WITH RICE

▶ Please read About Stuffed
Vegetables, page 256.
Preheat broiler.
Prepare:
    4 pepper cases
Have ready:
    1 cup hot cooked rice
Add:
    ½ cup stock, cream or
      tomato pulp
      Salt and pepper
      A few grains cayenne
    ½ teaspoon curry powder
      or a bare pinch of
      oregano
    ½ cup or more grated
      cheese
Fill the pepper cases. Cover tops
with:
    Au Gratin I or II,
      page 389
Brown briefly under a broiler.

PEPPERS STUFFED WITH
FISH OR MEAT

Fine for creamed turkey or
shrimp.
▶ Please read About Stuffed
Vegetables, page 256.
Line individual molds with:
    Pimientos, whole or in
      strips
Prepare in Cream Sauce II, page
359.
    Chopped cooked fish or
      meat
Use ½ as much cream sauce as
fish or meat. Season these ingredients with:
    Worcestershire sauce,
      lemon juice or sherry
Fill the molds and place them
in a pan of hot water on top of
the stove. Steam them gently
until they are well heated, about
10 minutes. Serve them hot with:
    Thickened Tomato
      Sauce, page 376
to which add:
    2 tablespoons chopped
      parsley
Or chill them, unmold and serve
cold with:
    Mayonnaise

PEPPERS STUFFED   [4]
WITH MEAT AND RICE

▶ Please read About Stuffed
Vegetables, page 256.
Preheat oven to 350°.
Cook until nearly tender:
    4 pepper cases
Melt:
    2 tablespoons drippings or
      butter
Add, stir and sauté until light
colored:
    ½ lb. ground beef
      3 tablespoons minced
        onions
Add:
    1 cup hot cooked rice
    2 well-beaten eggs
    ½ teaspoon salt
    ⅛ teaspoon paprika
    ¼ teaspoon celery seed,
      curry powder, dried

herb or Worcestershire
sauce

Fill the pepper cases. Bake, as
directed, about 10 or 15 minutes.

PEPPERS STUFFED [6]
WITH CORN À LA KING

◗ Please read About Stuffed
Vegetables, page 256.

Prepare:

   6 pepper cases

Place in a double boiler and
cook for 20 minutes:

   2½ cups corn niblets: 1 No.
      2 can
   1 shredded green pepper
   1 chopped pimiento

You may add:

   (4 slices sautéed minced
      bacon)
   2 tablespoons minced onion
      that has been sautéed
      in the bacon fat and
      drained

Combine and beat:

   1 egg
   ½ cup milk
   1 tablespoon soft butter
   ¾ teaspoon salt
   ⅛ teaspoon paprika

Add these ingredients to the
vegetables. Cook and stir over
low heat until they are slightly
thickened. Fill the peppers with
this hot mixture and serve.

PEPPERS STUFFED [4]
WITH CREAMED OYSTERS

◗ Please read About Stuffed
Vegetables, page 256.

Preheat broiler.

Prepare:

   4 pepper cases
   ½ pint Creamed Oysters,
      page 424, using ½ the
      amount

Add:

   2 tablespoons chopped
      parsley

Fill the pepper cases with the
hot oysters. Cover the tops with:

   Au Gratin II or III,
      page 389

Brown the tops briefly under a
broiler.

ABOUT PLANTAIN

These 9- to 12-inch bananas
must be cooked to avoid a
starchy, raw flavor. They are not
sweet, even when ripe. They get
bitter when overcooked, due to
a tannin component, but can be
put into omelets, soups or stews
if finely diced and added the
last minutes before serving.

Remove the fibrous strings
before cooking, as they darken.
Peel green plantains under running water to keep from staining
the hands. ◗ Simmer 30 minutes
in rapidly boiling water. Season
and serve with butter. If plantains are ripe, slice fine and
deep-fat fry as for Potato Chips,
page 319, or cook as for Candied
Sweet Potatoes, page 323. The
purple bud end of the banana
can be roasted in its husk. Only
the heart is eaten. Serve with
crumbled bacon or cracklings.

ABOUT POTATOES

Anyone who has visited Hirsch-
horn, in the sweetly romantic
Neckar Valley, and who has
climbed the hill to the partly
ruined castle that dominates the
little village, will remember
being confronted by a "Potato
Monument" dedicated piously
"To God and Francis Drake,
who brought to Europe for the
everlasting benefit of the poor—
the Potato."

But, in recent years, potatoes
have been maligned as too caloric—although they are only
equal to the same-sized apple or
a baking powder biscuit. They
are full of B, C, and G vitamins,
plus many minerals and even
some high-class protein. Do include them regularly in the diet,
but don't use potatoes whose
skins are greenish, as they are
apt to be bitter, or sprouted

potatoes or frost-bitten ones, which are watery and have a black ring under the skin when cut in cross sections.

If you wonder why there are no recommendations for ✳ freezing potatoes in this chapter, let us say that this operation is not possible with success in home freezers. Potatoes purchased frozen have all been treated to a quick-vacuum partial dehydration and instant freezing, to which home freezing equipment does not lend itself.

In the following recipes we have tried to give these delicious vegetables a renewed status. ◗ Be sure, if a potato type is specified, to use that type only—and remember that ◗ once a potato is cold, mealiness can never be returned to it.

Potatoes are often combined and mashed with other cooked vegetables, as: ⅔ celeriac, ⅓ potato, or in equal parts with turnips or ¼ fresh avocado, ¾ potato.

BOILED MATURE POTATOES   [4]

Wash well, remove sprouts and blemishes, then pare:

      6 medium-sized potatoes

When in haste, cut them into quarters. Cook them, covered, from 20 to 40 minutes in:

      4 cups boiling water
      ½ teaspoon salt

When they are tender, drain them well. Reserve the stock for a thick soup base.

To make the potatoes mealy, place a folded towel over the pot for 5 minutes. Shake the pot well. Remove the towel, which will have absorbed excess steam. Roll the potatoes in:

      2 to 3 tablespoons melted butter
      3 to 4 tablespoons chopped parsley or chives

⊗ Pressure cook large potatoes at 15 lbs. for about 15 minutes.

BOILED NEW POTATOES   [4]

There are many lovely things to do with small new potatoes, one of which is serving them in their skins, so all of their delicate goodness is held until the very moment they are eaten. Wash well:

      12 new potatoes

Drop them in:

      Boiling water to cover

Cook them, covered, until they are tender, from 20 to 30 minutes. Remove the skins and serve the potatoes with:

      Chopped parsley, mint or chives

Or melt in a skillet:

      3 to 6 tablespoons butter

Add the potatoes and shake them gently over low heat until they are well coated. Serve them sprinkled with:

      Salt
      Chopped parsley or chopped fresh dill or fennel

Or add to the butter in the pan:

      3 to 4 tablespoons freshly grated horseradish

and shake the potatoes until coated. This last is particularly good with cold cuts.

⊗ Pressure cook small new potatoes at 15 lbs. for about 2½ minutes.

RICED POTATOES   [6]

A fine foil for meat with a rich gravy.
Prepare:

      Boiled Mature Potatoes, this page

When the potatoes are tender and dried, put them through a food mill, ricer or strainer. Heap them on a dish and pour over them:

      (2 tablespoons melted butter)

MASHED POTATOES [6]

Mashed potatoes should be served at once but, in a pinch, can be kept warm by placing the pan in a larger pan of hot water. Or put them in a greased casserole, run a slight film of cream over the top and keep in a warm oven. The cream should brown to an attractive color.
Prepare:

> Boiled Mature Potatoes, page 310

You may add to the water a small onion or a cut clove of garlic, a piece of bay leaf and a rib of celery with leaves. Remove these extraneous ingredients. Mash the potatoes with a fork or a potato masher or put them through a food mill, ⅄ blender or electric mixer. Add to them:

> 3 tablespoons butter
> 1 teaspoon salt
> ⅓ cup hot milk or cream

Beat them with a fork or heavy whisk until they are creamy. Grated or sautéed onions with the drippings, minced crisp bacon, chopped parsley, chives or water cress are good additions to mashed potatoes. To help fluff the potatoes, cover the pan after they are mashed and place over very slow heat for about 5 minutes.

MASHED POTATO CHEESE PUFFS

[6 Puffs]
This is a tempting potato dish and a good-looking one.
Preheat oven to 350°.
Beat:

> 2 egg yolks

Add and beat until fluffy:

> 1⅓ cups hot or cold Mashed Potatoes, above
> 3 tablespoons hot milk
> ⅓ cup grated cheese

Season these ingredients with:

> ¼ teaspoon salt
> ¼ teaspoon paprika
> ¼ teaspoon celery salt
> ½ teaspoon finely grated onion
> 1 teaspoon chopped green pepper or parsley

Beat until stiff, then fold in:

> 2 egg whites

Place the batter in mounds in a greased pan. Brush the tops with:

> 1½ tablespoons soft butter

Bake the potatoes for about 20 minutes.

CHANTILLY POTATOES [6]

The use of whipping cream is what makes a dish Chantilly.
Preheat oven to 375°.
Prepare:

> 3 cups Mashed Potatoes, this page

Whip until stiff:

> ½ cup whipping cream

Season it with:

> Salt and white pepper
> A few grains cayenne

Combine it with:

> ½ cup grated cheese

Shape the potatoes into a mound on an ovenproof plate. Cover the mound with the whipped cream mixture. Bake the plate until the cheese is melted and the potatoes are lightly browned.

BAKED MASHED POTATO BALLS [4]

Preheat oven to 350°.
Have ready:

> 2 cups well-seasoned, hot Mashed Potatoes, this page: 4 medium-sized potatoes

Beat in:

> 2 egg yolks
> 1 tablespoon chopped parsley

Cool these ingredients slightly.
Beat until stiff:

> 2 egg whites

Fold them lightly into the potato mixture. Shape the mixture into balls. Bake the potatoes in lightly greased muffin tins or drop them on a greased sheet. Bake them until crisp. Turn them to brown evenly.

CREAMED POTATOES

Prepare:
    Boiled New Potatoes,
    page 310
Drain and dry off potatoes over very low heat. Peel and cut into ½-inch dice. Serve at once in:
    Cream Sauce II,
    page 359
flavored with:
    Dill seed

CREAMED POTATO CASSEROLE

Prepare as for:
    Boiled New Potatoes,
    page 310
using mature baking potatoes. When nearly done, in about 35 to 40 minutes, drain and dry off the potatoes by shaking the pan over low heat. Peel and cut into ½-inch dice.
Preheat oven to 400°.
Prepare, for every 2 cups diced potatoes:
    1 cup Cream Sauce II,
    page 359
Line a buttered casserole with the potatoes. Add the cream sauce and sprinkle the top with:
    Au Gratin III, page 389
Bake the potatoes for 20 minutes, longer if the casserole has been refrigerated.

SCALLOPED   [4]
POTATOES

Preheat oven to 350°.
I. Grease a 10-inch baking dish. Place in it, in 3 layers:
    3 cups pared, very thinly
    sliced potatoes
Dredge the layers with flour and dot them with butter. Use in all:
    2 tablespoons flour
    3 to 6 tablespoons butter

There are many tidbits you can put between the layers. Try:
    (¼ cup finely chopped chives
    or onions)
    (12 anchovies or 3 slices
    minced crisp bacon—but
    then reduce the salt in
    the recipe)
    (¼ cup finely sliced sweet
    peppers)
Heat:
    1¼ cups milk or cream
Season with:
    1¼ teaspoons salt
    ¼ teaspoon paprika
    (¼ teaspoon mustard)
Pour the milk over the potatoes. Bake them for about 1½ hours. They may be covered for the first ½ hour.

II. Prepare:
    Scalloped Potatoes I,
    above
Omit the flour, using, instead of the hot milk mixture:
    1¼ cups hot condensed
    mushroom or celery
    soup or hot Cheese
    Sauce, page 364
Bake, as directed above.

POTATOES   [6]
SCALLOPED IN BUTTER

Preheat oven to 425°.
Wash and pare:
    4 cups mature baking
    potatoes
Cut them in slices ⅛ inch thick. Place them in cold water to cover for 15 minutes. Drain them. Dry them between towels. Butter a shallow 9-inch baking dish generously. Sprinkle it with:
    Fine dry bread crumbs
Cover the bottom carefully with the potato slices. Dot them generously with:
    Butter
Use in all about ⅛ cup. Sprinkle them lightly with:
    Salt and white pepper
    (Grated Swiss cheese)

Repeat this process until the
dish is filled. Cover the dish.
Bake the potatoes for about ¾
hour or until tender. Turn them
out onto a platter. Garnish them
with:

> Parsley

BAKED POTATOES

The best baked potatoes are
flaky when served—so start with
mature baking types like Idahos.
Although new potatoes can be
used, they will never have the
desired quality and will need
only half as much baking time.
The present rage for wrapping
potatoes in foil will not allow
them to become flaky as too
much moisture is retained. In
fact, to draw moisture out of
bakers, they are often placed on
a bed of rock salt. One of the
treats of baked potatoes is eating the skin, under which the
greatest proportion of its minerals, vitamins and protein lie.
Preheat oven to 425°.
Wash and scrub even-sized,
shapely:

> Baking potatoes

Dry them and grease them
lightly with:

> Butter

Bake the potatoes for 40 minutes
to 1 hour, depending on their
size. When potatoes are ½
done, pull out rack, quickly
puncture skin once with fork,
permitting steam to escape. Return to oven and finish baking.
When done, serve them at once
with:

> Butter or thick sweet or
> cultured sour cream
> Chopped chives or
> parsley

1 tablespoon deviled ham
or serve with:

> Cheese Sauce, page 364

STUFFED POTATOES   [6]

Prepare:

> 6 Baked Potatoes, above

Cut them in halves crosswise,
lengthwise like boats, or leave
them whole, cutting a small
ellipse on the flat top. Scoop out
the pulp. Add to the pulp:

> 3 to 4 tablespoons butter
> 3 tablespoons hot milk or
> cream
> 1 teaspoon salt

Sauté:

> (2 tablespoons grated onion)

in the butter or, if you plan to
serve these with fish, add, for
piquancy:

> (1 tablespoon horseradish)

along with the butter and
cream. Beat these ingredients
until they are smooth. Whip
until stiff:

> (2 egg whites)

Fold them into the potato mixture. Fill the potato shells.
Sprinkle the exposed potato
with:

> ½ cup grated cheese
> Paprika

Broil them under low heat until
the cheese is melted.

BAKED POTATOES   [8]
STUFFED WITH
VEGETABLES

Preheat oven to 400°.
Prepare:

> 4 Baked Potatoes, this
> page

Have ready:

> 1 cup Cream Sauce I,
> page 359

Mix into the sauce:

> ¼ teaspoon salt
> ½ cup grated cheese
> ½ cup cooked peas
> ½ cup cooked chopped
> carrots
> ¼ cup diced green peppers
> 2 tablespoons diced
> pimientos

Cut the potatoes lengthwise into
halves. Remove the pulp without breaking the skin. Mash the
pulp and fold in the sauce and
vegetables. Fill the potato shells

with the mixture. Cover them
with:

>Au Gratin II, page 389

Place the potato shells in the
oven until the tops are brown.
Serve with:

>Hot or cold meat

BAKED POTATOES [6]
STUFFED WITH HASH

Creamed leftover vegetables
and/or meat or fish may be substituted.
Preheat oven to 400°.
Bake:

>6 medium-sized baking
>potatoes

Cut a thin slice off the flat side.
With a spoon, remove as much
as you can of the potato without
breaking the skin. Do not mash
the potato. Add to it and work
lightly with a fork until blended:

>1 tablespoon butter
>1 tablespoon cream
>½ teaspoon salt
>¼ teaspoon paprika
>1 teaspoon onion juice
>1 tablespoon minced
>parsley
>1 cup chopped cooked
>meat
>(¼ minced celery)

Moisten these ingredients with:

>Gravy or stock

Season them with:

>2 teaspoons Worcestershire
>sauce

Combine them with the potato
mixture. Fill the skins, heap the
tops. Place on each potato:

>½ teaspoon butter

or sprinkle it with:

>Grated cheese

Brown the potatoes in the oven.

STUFFED POTATO CUPS

▶ Please read About Deep-Fat
Frying, pages 75–79.
Preheat deep fryer to 385°.
Pare oval:

>Potatoes

Hollow out the centers to make

cups or boat shapes. Parboil for
10 minutes in:

>Boiling water

Drain and dry them. Fry the
potato cups in the hot deep fat
until they are well browned.
Drain well and sprinkle them
with:

>Salt

Fill them with hot:

>Creamed meat, fish or
>vegetables

TINY NEW POTATOES, [4]
SAUTÉED

Scrub and scrape well:

>24 very small whole new
>potatoes

Heat in a heavy saucepan:

>2 to 3 tablespoons olive oil
>or clarified butter

Turn the potatoes in the oil,
cover them closely and cook
them slowly until tender. Shake
the pan from time to time.
Sprinkle the potatoes with:

>Salt and paprika
>(Chopped chives or
>parsley)

LYONNAISE POTATOES

Prepare:

>6 medium, waxy, Boiled
>New Potatoes, page 310

While hot, peel and slice thinly.
Sauté them to an even brown in
a heavy skillet in:

>2 tablespoons butter
>2 tablespoons cooking oil

While they are cooking, sauté
until golden in another pan:

>½ cup finely sliced onions

in:

>2 tablespoons butter

Mix onions and potatoes together gently.

>Correct the seasoning

Sprinkle with:

>Parsley

and serve at once.

FRANCONIA OR BROWNED
POTATOES

We love browned potatoes, but

have an aversion to the hard-crusted, grease-soaked variety so often served. To insure a tender crust, we suggest preparing:

> 6 boiled mature potatoes, about 2-inch diameter

Cook them until they are ◆ not quite done, so that there is still resistance to the testing fork. Preheat oven to 350°.
Melt in a small, heavy iron skillet or casserole a mixture of:

> Butter and cooking oil

to the depth of about ¼ inch. When the fat is hot, but not quite to the point of fragrance, put in the potatoes. Let them cook ◆ covered, in the oven for about 20 minutes, turning them for even coloring. On the last turn, put in:

> 2 tablespoons finely chopped parsley

Bake them ◆ uncovered, about 10 minutes longer.

POTATOES ANNA   [6]

One of the most beautiful of all culinary wares is the lidded copper Potatoes Anna dish, about 8 inches in diameter and 3½ inches high. The lid, which has side handles, fits down over it to a 1½ inch depth during the oven period, but is reversed to hold the potatoes for serving. You may substitute a heavy skillet.
To get even rounds, cut cylinders from big potatoes with a corer the size of a small biscuit cutter. Cut the cylinders into ³⁄₁₆-inch even slices to make:

> 4 cups potatoes

Soak them in ice water for 10 minutes. Drain. Dry carefully in a towel. Heat in an 8-inch skillet with sloping sides:

> 2 to 3 tablespoons butter
> 2 tablespoons cooking oil

Do not brown the fats, but let them just reach the point of fragrance. Put the potatoes in the butter in slightly overlapping

spirals until the base of the pan is filled. Shake vigorously while filling, so the potatoes will not stick. Add a sprinkling of:

> Salt
> Grated onion
> Parmesan cheese

The butter will bubble up. But make sure, before adding another layer of slightly overlapping potato slices, that the first layer is coated with additional:

> Butter

Continue this process for the first 2 layers, letting the potatoes color slightly. Be sure the layers are welded together. Add a sprinkling of salt, onion and butter each time. It is not necessary to continue adding butter if you have used about ½ cup. The moisture from the cooking potatoes will make it bubble up. In building the next layer or two, omit the butter. Shake the pan constantly to make sure the contents are not sticking. Cover the pan and bake in a 375° oven for 45 minutes to 1 hour. Just before the potatoes are done, turn the entire mass over—to brown the upper side.

HASHED BROWN   [4]
POTATOES

Combine with a fork:

> 3 cups finely diced raw potatoes
> 1 teaspoon grated onion
> 1 tablespoon chopped parsley
> ½ teaspoon salt
> ¼ teaspoon black pepper
> (1 teaspoon lemon juice)

Heat in a 9-inch skillet:

> 3 tablespoons bacon drippings, oil or other fat

Spread the potato mixture over this. Press it with a broad knife into a cake. Sauté the potatoes slowly, shaking them from time to time to keep them from sticking. When the bottom is brown, cut the potato layer in half and turn each half with 2 spatulas. Pour over them slowly:

    ¼ cup cream

Brown the second side and serve the potatoes piping hot.

POTATO PANCAKES

[About Twelve 3-Inch Cakes]
▶ This recipe demands mature potatoes.
Pare and grate coarsely until you have:

    2 cups grated mature
        potatoes

Place the gratings on a muslin towel and wring the towel to extract as much moisture from the potatoes as possible. Place them in a bowl. Beat well, then stir in:

    3 eggs

Combine and sift:

    1½ tablespoons all-purpose
        flour
    1¼ teaspoons salt

Add the flour to the potato mixture with:

    (1 to 3 teaspoons grated
        onion)

Shape it into ¼-inch thick 3-inch diameter patties. Sauté in ¼ inch or more hot fat. Turn and brown the second side until crisp. These are usually served hot with:

    Applesauce (II, 95)

They are best, like all pancakes, served hot out of the pan. If you must hold them until all the batter is cooked, place them on a rack above a baking sheet in a 200° oven. Then serve all of them at once after draining on absorbent paper to remove any excess grease.

GRATED POTATOES,   [4]
PAN-BROILED

Very good, quick—something like a potato pancake. Wash, grate on a medium grater, skin and all:

    3 medium-sized mature
        baking potatoes

    (2 tablespoons grated onion)

Melt in a skillet to the point of fragrance:

    2 tablespoons butter
    2 tablespoons cooking oil

Spread the potatoes in the skillet to a depth of about ¼ inch. Cook, covered, over medium slow heat until the bottom is brown. Reverse and brown the other side. Season with:

    Salt

Serve piping hot.

SOUFFLÉ OR PUFFED   [6]
POTATOES

▶ Please read About Deep-Fat Frying, pages 75–79.
Legendary or not, we like this version of the origin of these delicacies. Louis XIV, diverted for the moment by his favorite pastime of fighting the Dutch, was inspecting his army at the front. He was to dine at a given point, at a given time, and a fitting repast had been prepared for him.

His sumptuous traveling coach, that little palace on wheels which was the scene of so many intrigues—or so many tender affairs—was swinging along on its great springs when it was delayed by torrential rains that made the rough roads almost impassable.

Whenever the King made his entrance he would undoubtedly demand food at once to appease his phenomenal appetite. The cook was frantic. His delicious dinner was kept hot over steam, but the potatoes, unfortunately fried ones, appeared limp and cold. A tremendous bustle heralded the arrival of the King and, in despair, the unfortunate cook immersed the potatoes in the hot fat for the second time, agitated them madly, and, behold—the dish that was to make him rich and famous!

There were several more coincidences that the cook may not have been aware of. His potatoes must have been old, so that the starch content was just right to make them puff. He must have had a very systematic apprentice who cut the potatoes all with the grain and to a very uniform thickness, as sketched. In his relief at having something to serve, he evidently didn't mind a 10% failure, for even experts who make these daily count on that great a percentage of duds. All this is just to encourage you if, like us, you expect a 100% return on your efforts. The duds, by the way, are edible as good French fries, if not as glamorous as the puffs. Choose:

8 large mature potatoes

Restaurants famous for this dish age their own to the point where you can no longer pierce or scrape the skin off with your fingernail, but must use a knife to pierce it. There should be about 80% starch in the potato. Idahos and Burbanks are especially recommended, although Pierre Adrian, who is very expert at this, says there is nothing like a Holland potato, grown on Spanish soil. Cut from the unpared potato the largest possible

oblong ◗ with the grain—that is, the long way, as sketched—into ◗ ⅛-inch slices that are of uniform thickness from one end to the other. In restaurants, this accuracy is produced by a slicing machine. Once you have these long, even slices, you can cut them into the classic shape with polygonal ends, as sketched, or into triangles, circles or fancy ovals with crimped edges. ◗ But whatever the final shape, always start with the long piece—cut with the grain—and have it ⅛ inch thick for its entire length. Soak the slices for at least 25 minutes in:

Ice water

Dry them thoroughly. Have ready a deep-fat frying kettle ⅓ filled with:

Rendered kidney suet or cooking oil

heated to 250°. Drop the slices in separately. ◗ Do not crowd the pan. The slices will sink. This next admonition is not without danger for the unskilled. ◗ When, after a few seconds, they rise, use a continuous shaking motion with the pan, which will set up a wave-like action to keep the floating strips bathed in the fat. Continue to cook them at 250° until they begin to clarify toward the centers and show a marked difference in texture at the cut edges, to a depth of about 1/16 of an inch. Drain them on absorbent paper. If you do not want to use them at once, they may be refrigerated before the second cooking, but ◗ bring them to room temperature before immersing in the hot fat the second time. If you want to proceed at once, let them cool off and drain for about 5 minutes before the second cooking.

Just before you are ready to serve them, drop them again one by one into a kettle filled ⅓ full with frying oil which has reached 375°. Again agitate the pan, as described. The once-fried slices should puff at once, although they always retain a seam wherever you have made an original perimeter cut. Cook to a golden brown. Drain. Dry them on absorbent paper. Salt and serve the puffed ones at once. If they are not crisp enough, return them to the fat for a few seconds. Drain again. Sometimes it is worth trying the duds once more, after they have cooled.

NEVER-FAIL FRENCH FRIES

The following recipe, like Soufflé Potatoes, calls for a two-stage frying operation. After the first stage, you may drain and cool the potatoes on absorbent paper. Cook the second stage just before serving.
♦ Please read About Deep-Fat Frying, pages 75–79.
Preheat deep fryer to 300° to 330°.
As with all successful potato frying, much depends on the maturity of the potato, so choose:
    Mature baking potatoes
Pare and slice them into strips about 2¼ inches long and about ⅜ inches through. If you are using cold storage potatoes and want a good, light-colored result, soak the potatoes for 15 minutes in 90° water. Wipe well with a towel to remove surface moisture and excess starch. Slowly heat to 300° to 330°:
    Cooking oil or rendered beef kidney fat
When the fat is ready, drop in the potatoes—about 1 cup at a time—and cook about 2 minutes, until all sputtering ceases. Skim out the rather limp potatoes, drain on absorbent paper and cool at least 5 minutes before starting the second stage.
♦ Heat the oil to 375°. Place the potatoes in a frying basket. This will assure quick and easy removal for them, in just the right condition. Finish frying them for about 3 minutes. They should be golden brown and will be crisp when drained on absorbent paper. ♦ Never cover them, as they will get flabby. Serve at once, in a napkin-lined basket.

SHOESTRING POTATOES

Cut into very thin strips, not more than 3/16 inch thick:
    Mature baking potatoes
Cook as for:
    Never-Fail French Fries, above

BAKED "FRENCH [4] FRIED" POTATOES

Preheat oven to 450°.
Pare:
    4 medium-sized potatoes:
    2 cups
Cut them lengthwise into strips about ½ inch thick. You may soak them in cold water for 10 minutes. Dry them well between towels. Spread them in a single layer in a flat ovenproof dish. Pour over them:
    ¼ cup melted butter, bacon drippings or cooking oil
Stir them about until coated. Bake them for about 30 to 40 minutes. Turn them several times during this period. Drain them on absorbent paper. Sprinkle them with:
    ½ teaspoon salt
    ¼ teaspoon paprika

POTATO PUFFS [4]

Preheat deep fryer to 385°.
Combine:
    ½ cup sifted flour
    1 teaspoon double-acting baking powder
    ¼ teaspoon salt
Add and mix:
    1 cup mashed potatoes
The potatoes should be soft at room temperature. If they are

not, add a little hot milk or water and beat. Add:

1 slightly beaten egg
1 teaspoon minced parsley

Drop by spoonfuls into hot fat. Fry to a golden brown. Drain on absorbent paper.

BAKED POTATO WAFERS

Potatoes prepared in this way have a distinctive flavor.
Preheat oven to 375°.
Select large, well-shaped:

Potatoes

Scrub them well. Rub them with:

Butter

Cut them, without peeling, in rounds ¼ inch thick. Place them in a generously buttered skillet or baking pan, flat side down. Sprinkle them with:

Salt and white pepper

Cover and bake for 20 minutes or until they are tender. Turn the slices as they brown. Serve them, garnished with:

Minced parsley

POTATO OR SARATOGA CHIPS

▶ Please read About Deep-Fat Frying, pages 75–79.
As with Soufflé Potatoes, page 316, and French Fries, page 318, it is very important to have properly aged potatoes. Or try unpeeled sweet potatoes. Use either of these chips as a vegetable, a garnish or a cocktail snack.
Using a vegetable slicer, slice as thin as possible:

Peeled Idaho potatoes

Soak the slices for 2 hours in cold water, changing the water twice. Drain and dry well. ▶ Very slowly, heat to 380°:

Peanut or corn oil

If you want a good luster on your cooled chips, bring the cooking oil to 75° before heating it. Drop the separated slices into the hot fat in a frying bas-

ket. Shake the basket or stir the potatoes several times to prevent the chips from sticking together. Cook until they are golden. Drain and place on absorbent paper to get rid of excess fat.

POTATO BASKETS

▶ Please read About Noodle Baskets, page 173.
Preheat deep fryer to 390°.
Use a shredder to cut into long ¼-inch strips:

Peeled potatoes

Soak them for 30 minutes in ice water. Drain them well and dry them between towels. Line the larger strainer, as directed for noodle baskets. Fit the smaller strainer over it. Fry the potato basket 3 to 4 minutes. Remove from the fat and drain. Bring the fryer up to 390° again and immerse basket for 1 minute more. Drain on absorbent paper and serve at once.

DUCHESS POTATOES [4]

I. Prepare:

Riced Potatoes, page 310

Add:

¼ cup butter
2 beaten egg yolks
(A dash of mustard)
Correct the seasoning

and allow this mixture to cool briefly.
Preheat oven to 400°.
Now shape the potato mixture into flat cakes on a floured board. Place the cakes on a buttered baking sheet. Brush with:

A slightly beaten egg

Bake until golden and serve at once.

II. This version is for decorating the edges of planks or baking dishes.
Prepare:

Duchess Potatoes I,
above

using:

1 egg yolk
3 to 4 tablespoons milk

Be sure there are no lumps to block the nozzle of the pastry tube or to destroy the smooth surface. Use a fluted tube to shape ruffles or wavy scallops. Brown in oven.

DAUPHINE POTATOES

If you add about 2 tablespoons of grated Gruyère cheese to each cup of potatoes called for in this recipe, you will have Potatoes Lorette.
♦ Please read About Deep-Fat Frying, pages 75–79.
For every cup:

> Freshly Mashed Potatoes, page 311

add:

> ⅓ to ½ cup Pâte à Choux (II, 305)

made without sugar and seasoned with:

> A grating of nutmeg

Shape the potato mixture into 1 to 1½ inch balls or fill into a pastry bag with a large plain tube. If you use the tube, shape as for Spaetzle, page 179. Roll in:

> (White dry bread crumbs)

Deep-fat fry for 3 or 4 minutes and allow the heat of the fat to increase to 370° until the potato balls are golden. Drain on absorbent paper. Add:

> Salt

and serve at once.

FRIED POTATO BALLS   [6]

A simpler version, not unlike Dauphine Potatoes.
♦ Please read About Deep-Fat Frying, pages 75–79.
Preheat deep fryer to 385°.
Prepare:

> 2 cups hot Riced Potatoes, page 310: 4 medium-sized potatoes

Add to them:

> 2 tablespoons butter

½ cup grated cheese
½ teaspoon salt
  A few grains cayenne
2 tablespoons cream
2 beaten egg yolks
½ teaspoon any baking powder

Whip these ingredients until they are light. Shape them into balls. Roll the balls in:

> Flour

then in:

> 1 egg, diluted and beaten with 2 tablespoons water

and in:

> Sifted bread crumbs

Fry the balls in deep fat. Drain them on absorbent paper. Serve at once.

ABOUT LEFTOVER POTATOES

Not for nothing do we use the phrase "cold potato" as a disagreeable appellation. Once cold after cooking, potatoes lose their mealiness and the good, earthy flavor of a freshly cooked potato is forever gone. They are probably most frugally used ⅄ blended into or used with a soup base. If you do use them, see that the base liquid is hot before combining with the cold potato. We give the following recipes as rather sorry bargains.

LEFTOVER MASHED POTATOES

To reheat, try placing in the top of a double boiler:

> Leftover mashed potatoes

Add, if necessary:

> A little hot milk

Beat the mixture well with a fork. Cover and cook ♦ over—not in—hot water until thoroughly heated.

LEFTOVER BAKED POTATOES

Have ready:

> 2 baked potatoes, 24 hours old

Grate them on the coarsest side of a hand grater. Melt in a 10-inch skillet:

> 2 tablespoons cooking oil

When the oil is hot, sprinkle the potato evenly and thinly over the bottom of the pan. Cook until the entire mass can be turned as one. Before turning, dribble over the uncooked surface of the potatoes:

> 2 tablespoons melted butter

Now cook the second side until glazed and brown. Serve at once, garnished with:

> 2 tablespoons yogurt and chives

LEFTOVER GERMAN [4] FRIED POTATOES

Melt in a skillet:

> 2 or more tablespoons fat

Add:

> 2 cups cold, sliced, boiled potatoes
> Salt and paprika
> (1 or more teaspoons minced onion)

Sauté the potatoes slowly until they are light brown. Turn them frequently.

LEFTOVER POTATOES [6] O'BRIEN

Preheat oven to 350°.
Dice:

> 6 medium-sized leftover boiled potatoes

Add:

> 1 chopped seeded green pepper
> 1 chopped onion
> 1 tablespoon flour
> Salt and pepper
> A few grains cayenne
> (¾ cup grated cheese)

Place these ingredients in a greased baking dish. Pour over them:

> 1 cup hot milk

Cover them with:

> Au Gratin II, page 389

Bake them for about 30 minutes.

LEFTOVER POTATO CAKES

I. Shape into little cakes:

> Leftover mashed potatoes

Add:

> (A beaten egg)
> (Chopped parsley)
> (Chopped celery)
> (Celery seed)
> (Grated onion or ¼ cup chopped sautéed onions)
> (A grating of nutmeg)

Dip the cakes in:

> Flour, bread crumbs or crushed cornflakes

Melt in a skillet:

> Butter or other fat

Brown the cakes in this on one side, reverse them and brown the other side.

II. Preheat oven to 375°.
Have ready:

> 2 cups leftover mashed potatoes

Roll the potatoes into balls and flatten them. Dip in:

> Melted butter

Roll in:

> Crushed cornflakes

Place them in a greased pan. Bake the balls until they are well heated.

LEFTOVER AU GRATIN POTATOES

Cut into dice:

> Leftover boiled potatoes

Prepare:

> Cream Sauce—½ as much sauce as there are potatoes, page 359

Combine the potatoes and the sauce. Add:

> (Chopped parsley, minced onion or chives)

Heat these ingredients in a double boiler for 30 minutes or put them in a greased baking dish. Cover them with:

> Au Gratin II, page 389

Bake them in a 400° oven until the crumbs are brown. To prepare the potatoes with cheese, omit the parsley, etc., and substitute grated cheese or place alternate layers of potatoes and cream sauce in a baking dish and sprinkle the layers with:

>Grated cheese

Season with:

>Paprika or a dash of cayenne

Cover top with:

>Au Gratin III, page 389

Bake the potatoes, as directed.

ABOUT SWEET POTATOES OR YAMS

It was George Washington Carver who really brought attention to the many ways in which this highly nutritious tuber could increase the health of our South. Sweet potatoes, whether the light yellow, dryish Jersey types or the orangey, moist varieties affectionately called yams, are both extremely high in vitamin A. Buy only enough for immediate use as they spoil rather easily.

They lend themselves to most of the cooking methods used for potatoes, and are especially good when combined with fruits and fruit flavoring.

Six medium-sized sweet potatoes will yield about 2 cups of riced sweet potatoes. Cooked sweet potatoes lend themselves to reheating better than leftover "Irish" potatoes, page 255.

BOILED SWEET POTATOES

To cook sweet potatoes in their jackets, drop them into boiling water to cover and cook ▶ covered, until tender, about 25 minutes. They may also be pared, dropped in ¼ cup boiling water and cook ▶ uncovered, until tender, about 15 minutes. Salt before serving.

MASHED SWEET [4] POTATOES

Prepare:

>6 Boiled Sweet Potatoes, above

Put them through a ricer or mash them with a potato masher. Add:

>2 tablespoons butter
>½ teaspoon salt
>A little hot milk, cream, lemon juice or dry sherry
>(2 teaspoons brown sugar)

Beat them with a fork or whisk until they are very light. Sprinkle them with:

>Grated orange or lemon rind, cloves or cinnamon

Chopped dates and nut meats may be added. Good served with ham.

BAKED SWEET POTATOES

Follow the recipe for:

>Baked Potatoes, page 313
>▶ Be sure to cut a small slice off one end or to puncture a sweet potato when half cooked, as a safety valve to prevent its bursting.

STUFFED SWEET [4 to 6] POTATOES

Preheat oven to 375°.
I. Prepare and bake as for Baked Potatoes, page 313:

>6 shapely sweet potatoes

Cut them lengthwise into halves and scrape out the pulp. Add:

>2 tablespoons butter
>¼ cup hot cream or ¾ cup crushed pineapple
>½ teaspoon salt
>(1 tablespoon dry sherry)

Southern people say "use lots of butter, some brown sugar, nutmeg and black walnut meats; and replace the sherry with 2 tablespoons bourbon whisky." Beat these ingredients with a fork until they are fluffy. Fill the shells and cover the tops with:

>Au Gratin III, page 389

Marshmallows may be substituted for the bread crumbs and butter. These are a matter of taste, or lack of taste. Bake the potatoes until they are brown.

II. These make a good cold weather lunch. Bake:

Sweet potatoes

Just before serving, insert in each potato:

1 tablespoon deviled ham

CANDIED SWEET POTATOES [4]

Cook, covered, in boiling water to cover until nearly tender:

6 sweet potatoes

Preheat oven to 375°.
Pare and cut them lengthwise in ½-inch slices. Place them in a shallow greased baking dish. Season with:

Salt and paprika

Sprinkle with:

¾ cup brown sugar or ⅓ cup maple sirup

½ teaspoon grated lemon rind

1½ tablespoons lemon juice or ⅛ teaspoon ginger

Dot them with:

2 tablespoons butter

Bake them, uncovered, for about 20 minutes.

CARAMELIZED SWEET POTATOES

Slice:

4 medium-sized boiled sweet potatoes

Melt:

3 tablespoons orange marmalade or Sauce Cockaigne (II, 474)

Cook the sweet potatoes gently in the sauce until they are glazed and brown.

SAUTÉED SWEET POTATOES

Dice into a skillet:

4 medium-sized boiled or

baked hot sweet potatoes

Add to them:

3 tablespoons melted butter
Grated rind and juice of 1 small orange

½ cup brown sugar

2 tablespoons chopped parsley or chives

Shake the sweet potatoes over quick heat until they are hot.

DEEP-FRIED SWEET POTATOES

▶ Please read About Deep-Fat Frying, pages 75–79.
Preheat deep fryer to 380°.
I. Wash, then parboil for 10 minutes:

Large sweet potatoes

Pare and cut them into strips. Fry the sweet potato strips in the deep fat until they are a golden brown. Drain them on absorbent paper. Sprinkle with:

Salt

▶ To flambé, just before serving, put the drained potatoes in a pan. Sprinkle over them:

2 tablespoons warm brandy, applejack or rum

Light and tilt the pan back and forth until the flame burns low.

II. Pare, then cut into ¼-inch slices:

Sweet potatoes

Deep fry them in hot fat until done. Drain them on absorbent paper. Sprinkle with:

Brown sugar
Salt
Freshly grated nutmeg

SWEET POTATO PUFFS

Preheat oven to 500°.
Have ready:

2 cups riced, cooked sweet potatoes

Peel, mash and add:

1 large ripe banana

Combine these ingredients and beat them into:

1½ tablespoons melted butter

1 egg yolk
1½ teaspoons salt
⅓ to ¼ cup hot milk or
cream
(⅛ teaspoon nutmeg or
ginger)
Beat until stiff:
1 egg white
Fold it lightly into the potato
mixture. Drop the batter with
a tablespoon in mounds—well
apart—on a greased tin, or place
the mixture in buttered ramekins. Bake the puffs for about
12 minutes.

SWEET POTATOES   [4]
AND APPLES

This tart dish is exceptionally
good with roast pork, baked
ham or game. Cook, covered,
until nearly done in boiling
water to cover:
6 medium-sized
sweet potatoes
Peel and cut them into ½-
inch slices. Cook, covered, until
nearly done in a very little
boiling water:
1½ to 2 cups thinly sliced
apples
If the apples are not tart, sprinkle them with:
Lemon juice
Preheat oven to 350°.
Grease a baking dish and place
in it alternate layers of sweet
potatoes and apples. Sprinkle
the layers with:
½ cup or more brown sugar
A dash cinnamon or
grated lemon rind
Dot them with:
¼ cup butter
Pour over them:
½ cup apple water or water
Bake them for about 1 hour.

SWEET POTATOES WITH
OTHER FRUITS

Follow the recipe for:
Sweet Potatoes and
Apples, above
Omit the sugar and substitute

for the apples:
½ cup puréed, sweetened,
dried apricots (II, 96),
½ cup Sauce Cockaigne
(II, 474), or ½ cup
crushed pineapple

SWEET POTATOES AND
ORANGE JUICE

Preheat oven to 375°.
Cook and mash:
Sweet potatoes
Allow to every cup of potatoes:
1¼ tablespoons butter
1 tablespoon brown sugar
½ teaspoon grated orange
or lemon rind
3 tablespoons orange juice
½ teaspoon salt
Combine these ingredients and
place them in a baking dish or
in hollow orange rinds made
into cups, placed in a baking
pan. Sprinkle the top with:
Brown sugar
Paprika
Cover the dish or the cups
closely. Bake the potatoes for 30
minutes in the dish, 15 minutes
in the cups. Remove the cover
and bake them until they are
brown.

PURSLANE   [3]

Wash well:
2 lbs. purslane
Use only the tender tips and
leaves. Blanch, page 88, briefly
in
Salted boiling water
Drain well. Reheat in:
2 tablespoons butter
Correct the seasoning
and serve at once.

ABOUT RADISHES

We all enjoy red and white radish garnishes and, if we've read
Pepys, we know he ate them
buttered at William Penn's—
worth trying, too, especially
with black radishes. Radishes
are also good prepared as for

Celeriac Remoulade, page 43. The large Japanese radish, Daikon, and the red and white ones, if you have a plethora in your garden, are good cooked by any recipe for Turnips, pages 338–339.

To store radishes before using, cut off the leaves.

COOKED RADISHES

Peel and slice:
>Radishes
Drop them into:
>Boiling salted water
>to cover
Simmer, uncovered, about 6 to 8 minutes or until tender. Drain.
>Correct the seasoning
Serve in:
>Cream or Cream Sauce I,
>page 359

RUTABAGAS [4]
OR SWEDES

These may be French fried as for Shoestring Potatoes, page 318, or baked like Potatoes, page 313.
To boil, pare and dice:
>4 medium rutabagas
♦ Do not use the leaves. Drop the pieces into:
>Boiling water
Cook them, uncovered, until tender, about ½ hour. Drain them well. Add:
>½ teaspoon salt
Serve them with:
>Melted butter
to which you have added generously:
>Lemon juice
>Chopped parsley
or mash the turnips and add them in any proportion to mashed potatoes with lots of:
>Chopped parsley or
>cultured sour cream
>and nutmeg

ABOUT SKIRRET

Cook as for any recipe using carrots, but never peel before boiling as the flavor is lost. Be sure to remove the inner hard core before serving.

ABOUT SORREL

Rather heavy in oxalic acid, this vegetable is seldom served by itself, but is combined with spinach, chard or other greens. It lends itself to flavoring with meat glaze, eggs and cream.

Prepare as for Panned Spinach, page 326, and season with butter; or purée it and season with mustard and tarragon as a bed for fish.

ABOUT SPINACH

Forced down the throats of a generation as a source of iron, spinach is today in bad repute for its calcium-robbing activity. Perhaps we had better forget both these factors and just eat it in moderation for its true goodness. It is a special treat as a garnish with other foods, where its presence is usually heralded by the title **Florentine**.

We suggest 3 servings to the pound as the cooked amount is so variable—depending on age.

Spinach requires little salt. Its astringent taste comes from alum and iron. Never serve it in silver.

✻ If using frozen spinach, thaw partially before cooking.

✪ Pressure cook spinach at 15 lbs. for 1 minute.

BOILED SPINACH [3 to 4]

Pick over and cut the roots and tough stems from:
>¼ peck spinach: 1 lb.
Wash it quickly in several waters until it is free from sand and soil. If it is young and tender, cook it as for Panned Spinach, page 326. If old, place the spinach in:
>2 cups rapidly boiling water
♦ Reduce heat and simmer, cov-

ered, until tender, for about 20 minutes. Discard the water if it is strong in flavor. If not, keep it for use in soups and sauces. Drain the spinach well. ↧ Blend briefly or cut up the spinach with 2 sharp knives or a triple chopper until it is as fine as you like it. Sauté:

2 tablespoons diced sweet red pepper, 2 tablespoons minced onion or a clove of garlic

in:

Butter or drippings

Add:

Lemon juice
Correct the seasoning

▶ being careful not to over salt. Serve the seasonings over the spinach. Other garnishes for spinach include:

Hard-boiled egg
Crumbled bacon
Fine buttered croutons
Hollandaise Sauce, page 369
Au Gratin III, page 349

CREAMED SPINACH   [3]

Prepare:

2 cups Boiled Spinach, above

↧ Blend, rice or chop it until it is a fine purée. Melt in a skillet which may be rubbed lightly with a clove of garlic:

1½ to 2 tablespoons butter

Add and cook for 1 minute or, if preferred, until golden:

(1 tablespoon or more very finely chopped onion)

Stir in, until blended:

1 tablespoon flour or 2 tablespoons browned flour

Stir in slowly:

½ cup hot cream, top milk or stock
1 teaspoon sugar

When the sauce is smooth and hot, add the spinach. Stir and cook it for 3 minutes. Season it well with:

Salt and pepper
(Freshly grated nutmeg or grated rind of ½ lemon)

Serve it garnished with slices of:

1 hard-cooked egg

PANNED OR SICILIAN   [3]
SPINACH

The seasonings in this dish are also good used with canned spinach.

Wash well and remove the coarse stems from:

1 lb. spinach

Shake off as much water as possible. Heat in a large, heavy skillet:

1 tablespoon butter
2 tablespoons olive oil

Add:

(1 clove minced garlic)

Add the spinach. Cover at once and cook over high heat until steam appears. ▶ Reduce the heat and simmer until tender, 5 to 6 minutes in all.

Correct the seasoning

To turn this into Sicilian Spinach, add:

(2 or more chopped anchovies)

SPINACH WITH   [4]
TOMATOES

Cook:

1 lb. spinach

Drain and ↧ blend or chop fine.

Add:

6 or 8 oz. Italian tomato paste or tomato purée

Sauté:

1 pressed clove garlic or 3 tablespoons minced onion

in:

3 or 4 tablespoons olive oil

Add the spinach mixture and
Correct the seasoning

SPINACH, TOMATO   [8]
AND CHEESE LOAF

Preheat oven to 350°.
Place in a bowl:

2 cups cooked, drained
   spinach
2¼ cups canned tomatoes
¼ cup chili sauce
½ lb. grated cheese
1 cup cracker crumbs
   Juice of ½ onion
¼ teaspoon salt
¼ teaspoon freshly ground
   pepper

Toss these ingredients until they
are blended. Place them in a
greased loaf pan. Bake the dish
for about 1 hour. Serve it garnished with:

   Crisp Bacon, page 491

SPINACH IN PANCAKES

Prepare:
   Creamed Spinach, page
   326
Prepare:
   French Pancakes (II,
   113)
   Chopped Sautéed
   Mushrooms, page 296

Place the spinach and mushrooms on the pancakes. Roll
them like a jelly roll. The tops
may be sprinkled with:
   Grated cheese
Place the rolls under a broiler
until the cheese is melted. Serve
at once.

⅄ BLENDER SPINACH [3]

Cook and drain:
   Boiled Spinach, page 325
Put it very briefly through a
blender. Stir into it:
   ¼ cup cultured sour cream
   or condensed cream of
   chicken soup
   A grinding of nutmeg or
   ⅛ teaspoon prepared
   mustard
   (1 teaspoon horseradish)
   Correct the seasoning
Heat briefly and serve.

GROUND SPINACH [3]

Cooked in this way, spinach
seems to retain all its flavor.

Wash:
   1 lb. spinach
Drain it well. Shortly before you
are ready to serve the spinach,
run it through a food chopper
with:
   1 small onion
Reserve the juices. Place it in a
saucepan with the juices and:
   ½ teaspoon sugar
Cover and cook it slowly for 3
minutes. Add before serving:
   1½ to 2 tablespoons butter
   (2 teaspoons lemon juice)
   Correct the seasoning

ABOUT SQUASHES

Perhaps no other vegetable has
so wide a tolerance of growing
conditions. You will quickly
know after cooking if the variety you have is cultivated, for
the wild ones are very bitter.
Cross-pollination from wild species grown in subtropical climates may explain the occasional bitterness you find in
squash from the market.

These plants divide into summer and winter types. We often
call for special varieties of each
type in the recipes which follow; but others may be substituted, as long as they belong to
the respective type.

SUMMER SQUASHES OR CYMLINGS

Whether green, yellow, white,
long, round or scalloped, these
are all thin-skinned and easily
punctured with a fingernail—
the classic marketer's gesture
and the grocer's despair. They
should be firm and heavy. Avoid
them if the rind is tough or the
stem dry or black. If they are
young, there is no need to pare
nor to discard the seeds. If only
hard-rinded ones are available,
do both. Summer squash do not
store well.

You may have your favorites.
Ours are undoubtedly zucchini
or the closely related cocozelle.

Remember these squash may also be prepared by recipes for cucumber and eggplant. As shown above, from left to right, they are **straight neck, crooked neck, cymling, cocozelle** and **zucchini.**

WINTER SQUASHES

These are of many colors and shapes and remain on the market from fall to early spring. Except for butternut, they have hard-shelled skins. Choose the others for their hard rinds. Avoid winter squash with watery spots which indicate decay. The winter types sketched from left to right below, are **Golden Delicious, acorn, buttercup** or **turban, butternut** and **Hubbard.** For ways to cook pumpkin, the most famous winter squash, see (II, 319). Unless you bake them whole, remove the seeds and stringy portions. Peel and cut into small pieces. They need from 10 to 45 minutes of cooking.

Because squash is so bland in flavor, it can stand a good deal of "doctoring" and is ideal for stuffing. Cut small squash into boats and fill. ♦ To stuff a whole

squash cut off the ends, core the center and, after stuffing, secure the ends with toothpick closures. For fillings, see Farces, page 564.

If it is a tender summer type, you may combine the removed portion with the farce, which may include vegetables, bread crumbs, nuts, mushrooms or cooked meat.

STEAMED SUMMER   [4]
SQUASH

♦ Please read About Squashes, page 327.
I. Wash and cut into small pieces:

    2 cups any summer squash:
    zucchini, yellow crooked
    neck, etc.

If very tender, the squash may even be left whole. Steam it, covered, in a strainer over boiling water until it is tender. Drain it very well. Sprinkle it generously with:

    Grated Parmesan cheese
    and melted butter

II. Prepare the squash as above, then mash it with a fork. Beat it until it is fluffy. Beat in:

    1 tablespoon cream

1 tablespoon butter or
olive oil

⅛ teaspoon pepper

(1 teaspoon grated onion or
chopped fresh herb or a
touch of saffron)

Reheat the squash briefly and
serve.

STUFFED SQUASH
BLOSSOMS

Do you wonder why so many of
your squash blossoms fall off
without maturing? These are
male blooms and after they close
and drop make decorative, as
well as edible, cases for Forcemeat, see page 564. Open each
flower and put in only enough
of the forcemeat to allow the
petals to close again. Place
stuffed blossoms side by side
in a greased baking dish, in a
moderate oven, until thoroughly
heated. Serve them alone or as
a platter garnish.

BAKED SUMMER [4]
SQUASH

◆ Please read About Squashes,
page 327.
Preheat oven to 350°.
If summer squash is young, it
need not be pared. Cut into
strips:

3 cups any summer squash

Place in a greased baking dish.
Dot with:

2 tablespoons butter

Sprinkle with:

1 teaspoon salt

¼ teaspoon paprika

(A grating of nutmeg or
1 teaspoon fresh lemon
thyme)

Pour over it:

¼ cup milk

(1 teaspoon grated onion)

Cover the dish. Bake the squash
for about ½ hour or until it is
tender. Garnish with:

Crisp crumbled bacon

SAUTÉED SUMMER [4]
SQUASH

◆ Please read About Squashes,
page 327.
Wash and cut into dice:

2 cups any summer squash

Melt in a saucepan:

3 tablespoons butter or
olive oil

Add and sauté until golden:

1 cup minced onion

Add the squash and:

½ teaspoon salt

¼ teaspoon freshly ground
white pepper

Cover the pan and cook the
squash until tender, for about 10
minutes, shaking the pan occasionally to keep from sticking.
Serve it sprinkled with:

Chopped parsley or basil
Grated Parmesan cheese
or Tomato Sauce, page
376

STUFFED COOKED
SUMMER SQUASH

I. [4]

◆ Please read About Squashes,
page 327.
Wash thoroughly, then cut the
stem ends from:

4 small summer squashes

Steam them as for Steamed Summer Squash, but leave them
whole. When almost tender,
drain the squashes, cool them.
Scoop out the centers, leaving
a shell about ½ inch thick.
Chop the removed pulp. Add
to it:

¼ teaspoon paprika

½ teaspoon Worcestershire
sauce

Minced garlic or onion

¼ teaspoon salt

1 tablespoon butter

3 tablespoons dry bread
crumbs

¼ cup grated cheese

A few grains cayenne

⅛ teaspoon curry powder or
dry mustard

Preheat oven to 400°.

Refill the shells. Place them in a pan, in a very little water or on a rack above the water. Bake until hot, about 10 minutes.

II. Or fill these cooked squash cases while hot with:

> Heated creamed chicken, ham, fish or spinach

Garnish with:

> Parsley or tiny sprigs of lemon thyme

STUFFED RAW SUMMER SQUASH [4]

◗ Please read About Squashes, page 327.
Preheat oven to 350°.
Wash:

> 4 small squashes

Cut them down the middle, either crosswise or horizontally. Scoop out the pulp, leaving a ½-inch shell. Combine the squash pulp and:

> 2 tablespoons chopped sautéed onions
> ½ cup grated cheese
> ½ teaspoon salt
> ¼ teaspoon paprika
> A dash of nutmeg or cloves

Stir and cook these ingredients until hot. Remove from the heat. Add:

> 1 beaten egg
> ½ cup dry bread crumbs

You may rub the squash shells with:

> Butter or drippings

Fill them with the stuffing. Place them in an ovenproof dish. Cover the bottom with ⅛ inch water or stock. Sprinkle the tops with:

> Au Gratin II, page 389

Bake the squashes until tender, about 20 to 25 minutes, depending on their size.

SUMMER SQUASH CREOLE

◗ Please read About Squashes, page 327.
Have ready:

> 2½ cups well-drained, cooked zucchini, yellow crooked neck, etc. summer squash

Place it in a greased baking dish and proceed as for:

> Stuffed Eggplant Creole, page 292

substituting the squash for the eggplant.

DEEP FRIED ZUCCHINI

◗ Please read About Deep-Fat Frying, pages 75–79, and About Squashes, page 327.
Preheat deep fryer to 365°.
Wash, dry and slice into ¼- to ½-inch slices:

> Zucchini

Dry it well. Dip it in:

> Fritter Batter for Vegetables (II, 125)

Fry it in deep fat until golden. Serve at once.

SUMMER SQUASH [4] CASSEROLE COCKAIGNE

We are particularly fond of zucchini in this dish.
◗ Please read About Squashes, page 327.
Cut into small pieces:

> 3 cups summer squash

Simmer the squash, covered, until tender, for about 6 to 8 minutes, in a small amount of boiling water. Shake the pan to keep from sticking. Drain well. Combine:

> ¼ cup cultured sour cream
> 1 tablespoon butter
> 1 tablespoon grated cheese
> ½ teaspoon salt
> ⅛ teaspoon paprika

Stir this mixture over low heat until the cheese is melted. Remove it from the heat. Stir in:

> 1 beaten egg yolk
> 1 tablespoon chopped chives

Add the squash. Place the mixture in a baking dish. Cover the top with:

> Au Gratin III, page 389

Brown it in a heated 375° oven.

BAKED WINTER SQUASH

▶ Please read About Squashes, page 327.

Preheat oven to 375°.
If the squash is small, like:

> Acorn or butternut
> squash

it may be washed, dried, greased and treated just like Baked Potatoes, page 313. Bake at least 1 to 1½ hours. The smaller baked winter squashes make attractive cases for:

> Creamed spinach, ham,
> etc., or buttered
> vegetables

Serve garnished with:

> (Pimiento strips or Au
> Gratin, page 389)

MASHED WINTER SQUASH

▶ Please read About Squashes, page 327.

I.

Preheat oven to 375°.
Scrub:

> A 3 to 4 lb. Hubbard or
> other winter squash

Place it on a rack and bake it until it can be pierced easily with a toothpick. Cut it in halves, remove the seeds. Peel the squash and mash the pulp. To:

> 1 cup squash

add:

> 1 tablespoon butter
> 1 teaspoon brown sugar
> ¼ teaspoon salt
> ⅛ teaspoon ginger

Beat this well, with enough:

> Warm cream or orange
> juice

to make it a good consistency. Place it in a serving dish. Sprinkle it with:

> Raisins or nut meats
> ¼ cup crushed pineapple

II. ✳ If using frozen or canned squash, season with:

> Sautéed onions
> Cultured sour cream

> A pinch allspice
> Chopped parsley

Heat it in a double boiler.

STUFFED WINTER SQUASH

Small acorn or butternut squash are ideal for individual service. You may fill the raw shell as in I or make it first, as in Baked Winter Squash, and then fill it with the hot, creamed foods suggested below.

▶ Please read About Stuffed Vegetables, page 256, and About Squashes, page 327.

I. Preheat oven to 375°.

Prepare uncooked:

> Acorn squash cases

by washing, cutting the squash in half lengthwise and scooping out the seeds. Fill them with:

> Sausage meat or Ham à
> la King, page 220

Bake them for about 1 hour.

II. Prepare cooked:

> Acorn squash cases, see
> above

Fill them with:

> Creamed oysters,
> chicken, chipped beef,
> crab, fish, mushrooms,
> hash, hash and vege-
> tables, hot applesauce
> or crushed pineapple

Garnish the tops with:

> Parsley

Reheat for 10 to 15 minutes in a 350° oven.

ABOUT PUMPKIN

We think of this squash first as pie (II, 319), and next as soup, but it is also good as a vegetable. Cook by any recipe calling for a winter squash. About ½ lb. will serve 1 person.

ABOUT TOMATOES

Really a fruit, beautifully colored and unsurpassed for flavoring, tomatoes, like lemons, are one of the most satisfactory things to have on hand fresh or canned—also in the form of juice, purée, paste, catsup or chili sauce. Since they are an acid fruit and often home grown, they can be easily home processed (II, 537). Try growing the more meaty pear-shaped Italian varieties, which are both sweeter and sharper than American types.

To use fresh tomatoes in cooking where their juiciness is sometimes not an asset, slit the stem end and remove it. Holding your hand palm down above a bowl, press the tomato tightly in the palm to eject excess juice and seeds. To skin tomatoes, see pages 48 and (II, 537).

When the recipes call for strained, canned tomatoes, watch for 2 things: Be sure to force the pulp through the sieve well, so you make the most of its thickening and seasoning powers; also watch your brands: the cheaper ones are often watery.

We cannot leave this eulogy without comment on the high vitamin C and A values of tomatoes. To retain them and the best color ♦ store in good light, not sunlight, unwrapped, between 65° and 75°. If you have any choice in the matter, do not pick until they have reached their full size. Ripened 5 to 6 days off the vine, unless over-ripe, they retain good vitamin values. Once ripe, store refrigerated. ♦ Immature green tomatoes will not ripen off the vine, so use at once for pickles. To retain food value, prepare tomatoes just before using.

Prepare them stuffed, not only for Salads, page 48, but as cases for other Vegetables, page 256.

STEWED TOMATOES   [4]

Wash and skin (II, 537):
    6 large quartered tomatoes

or 2½ cups canned
    tomatoes
Place them in a heavy pan over slow heat, about 20 minutes for the fresh tomatoes—10 for the canned. You may add:
    (1 teaspoon minced onion)
    (½ cup chopped celery)
    (2 or 3 cloves)
Stir them occasionally to keep them from scorching. Season them with:
    ¾ teaspoon salt
    ¼ teaspoon paprika
    2 teaspoons white or brown sugar
    ⅛ teaspoon curry powder or 1 teaspoon chopped parsley or basil
    1 tablespoon butter
Tomatoes may be thickened with:
    (½ cup bread crumbs)

STEWED GREEN   [4]
TOMATOES

Sauté until light brown:
    2 tablespoons minced onion
in:
    2 tablespoons butter
Add:
    2 cups sliced green tomatoes
Stir and cook the tomatoes slowly until they are tender. Season with:
    ¾ teaspoon salt
    ¼ teaspoon paprika
    ½ teaspoon curry powder
Garnish the tomatoes with:
    1 tablespoon chopped parsley

SEASONED SAUTÉED   [4]
TOMATOES

This recipe is much like the preceding one, but it may be useful when broiling or baking is out of the question. Wash:
    6 firm, medium-sized, red or green tomatoes
Slice them in ¼-inch slices. Bread them with:

Seasoned Flour (II, 160)

Rub a skillet with garlic. Melt in it:

3 tablespoons butter or bacon drippings

Add the tomato slices. Sauté them gently on both sides. Place the tomatoes on:

Rounds of toast or squares of corn bread

Blend the butter and crumbs left in the skillet with:

¾ cup cream
1 teaspoon chopped fresh basil or chopped parsley

When the sauce is smooth and hot ▶ but not boiling, pour it over the tomatoes.

CREAMED CANNED TOMATOES [4]

Simmer gently for about 10 minutes:

2 cups canned tomatoes
2 tablespoons minced onion
¾ teaspoon salt
¼ teaspoon paprika
2 teaspoons brown sugar
(½ cup chopped celery)

Combine until smooth and bring just to a boil:

1 tablespoon flour
½ cup cream or milk

If you use the milk, add 2 tablespoons of butter to the tomato mixture. Add the tomato mixture slowly to the cream or milk. ▶ To avoid curdling, be careful not to reverse the process, and stir constantly over very low heat until the raw-flour taste is gone, about 3 to 5 minutes.

BAKED TOMATOES [4]

Preheat oven to 400°.
Cut deep, narrow holes in:

6 firm tomatoes

Season them—pushing the seasoning into the hollows—with:

3 tablespoons brown sugar
1½ teaspoons salt
2 tablespoons butter

Fill the remaining space with:

(¼ cup Au Gratin II, page 389)

Place the tomatoes in a well-buttered shallow baking dish on a rack or in greased muffin tins. Bake them for about 15 minutes. You may top each tomato with:

Crisp crumbled bacon

TOMATO PROVENCALE

This garnish looks very professional if you have a broiler and an oven you can use in quick succession. Choose:

Firm ripe tomatoes

Slice off a deep enough section horizontally on the stem end to get an even surface. Do the same on the base. Divide the remaining tomato horizontally. Place these thick slices on a rack to drain. Sprinkle on top of each:

Salt and black pepper
Sweet basil
A slight pinch of orégano

Melt enough:

Butter

to coat the tomato slices. Place in the butter:

A split clove of garlic

Or, as an alternative to the butter, squeeze a little garlic on a thin square of:

(Parmesan cheese)

that will almost cover the tomato slice. Allow the seasoned tomatoes to remain at 70° for 1 hour.

Preheat broiler and preheat oven to 350°

Put the slices on a greased baking sheet. Run them under a broiler first to brown slightly and then bake them for 15 minutes. Serve at once.

GRILLED TOMATOES [4]

Preheat broiler.
Wash:

4 large, firm tomatoes

Cut them crosswise into even ½-inch slices. Season them well with:

1 teaspoon salt
¼ teaspoon pepper
White or brown sugar
(Celery salt)

Place in a greased pan and cover
them closely with:

About 1 cup Au Gratin
III, page 389
(2 tablespoons or more
grated onion)

Broil them for about 10 minutes
♦ about 5 inches from the heat
source.

BROILED BREADED
TOMATOES

Preheat oven to 375°.
Wash and cut a piece off the
stem end horizontally, so the
surface is even, and cut another
off the base of:

Tomatoes

Cut them in half, crosswise and
sprinkle the halves with:

Salt and pepper
(Brown sugar)

Dip them in:

Bound Breading III
(II, 160)

Bake them on a greased sheet
until they are nearly soft, then
broil them under moderate heat,
turning them once, until they
are brown.

CANDIED TOMATOES   [4]

Melt:

2 tablespoons butter

Sauté in the butter until brown:

¼ cup chopped onion

Add:

1 quart canned tomatoes
6 tablespoons brown sugar

Cook these ingredients very
slowly, using an asbestos mat,
until the juice has been absorbed. Place the tomatoes in a
baking dish. Sprinkle them with:

¾ teaspoon salt
2 tablespoons brown sugar
1½ cups buttered bread
crumbs

Bake them in a 375° oven until
the crumbs are brown.

TOMATOES CREOLE   [4]

In contrast to the above, a very
good quickie!
Melt in a saucepan:

2 tablespoons butter

Add:

4 large, skinned, sliced,
tomatoes or 1½ cups
canned tomatoes
1 large minced onion
2 tablespoons minced
celery
(1 shredded green pepper)

Cook the vegetables until they
are tender, about 12 minutes.
Add:

¾ teaspoon salt
¼ teaspoon paprika
2½ teaspoons brown sugar
(¾ teaspoon curry powder)

Strain the juice from the vegetables and add to it enough:

Cream

to make 1½ cups of liquid. Stir
in:

1½ teaspoons flour

Simmer and stir the sauce until
it is thick and smooth. Combine
it with the vegetables and serve
them hot on:

Toast

with:

Sautéed bacon

Or use to fill pepper or squash
cases.

TOMATO OLIVE   [3]
CASSEROLE

If you have any prejudice
against tapioca, please dismiss it
long enough to try out this fine
dish. Serve it with ham, scrambled eggs, omelet, etc.
Preheat oven to 350°.
Heat and ♦ strain well, discard-
ing the seeds:

1½ cups canned tomatoes

Melt in the top of a double
boiler:

1 tablespoon butter

Add and sauté until golden:

¼ cup minced onion or 1
pressed clove garlic

Add the strained tomato and:

3 tablespoons
quick-cooking tapioca
½ teaspoon salt
½ teaspoon sugar
⅛ teaspoon paprika

Cook and stir these ingredients in a double boiler ♦ over—not in—hot water for about 7 minutes. Chop coarsely:

18 stuffed or ripe olives

Grease a baking dish. Fill it with alternate layers of tomato mixture and olives. Sprinkle the layers with:

(½ cup grated cheese)

Cover the top with:

Au Gratin I, page 389

Bake the dish for about 30 minutes.

TOMATO CUSTARD   [6]

Preheat oven to 325°.
Skin and squeeze well, page 331, to rid them of excess liquid and seeds and put through a coarse sieve:

Enough tomatoes to
make 2 cups

Beat together with:

3 eggs
1 cup milk
¼ to ½ cup sugar
½ teaspoon salt
⅛ teaspoon nutmeg

Bake in custard cups for about 30 minutes or until set. Serve hot or cold.

TOMATO PUDDING COCKAIGNE

Either of these recipes should serve 6, but we find the demand for this favorite makes 4 servings a safer count.

I. Preheat oven to 375°.
In winter, place in a saucepan:

1¼ cups tomato purée
¼ cup boiling water

Heat to the boiling point and add:

¼ teaspoon salt
6 tablespoons brown sugar
½ teaspoon dried basil

Place in a 9-inch baking dish:

1 cup fresh white bread
crumbs (II, 159)

Pour over them:

¼ cup melted butter

Add the tomato mixture and:

(2 tablespoons chopped
stuffed olives)

♦ Cover the dish closely. Bake the pudding about 30 minutes. Do not lift the lid until ready to serve.

II. Preheat oven to 325°.
In summer, substitute for the dried basil:

1½ to 2 teaspoons fresh
chopped basil
1 teaspoon chopped chives
1 teaspoon chopped parsley

and for the tomato purée and water, substitute:

14 skinned, seeded, sliced
tomatoes

Bake the dish for 2½ to 3 hours until it has cooked down to a pastelike consistency.

TOMATO TART   [6]

Have ready:

6 baked 2-inch Tart Shells
(II, 296)

Prepare a filling of:

¾ cup tomato purée
¾ cup Cream Sauce III,
page 359
3 tablespoons sautéed
chopped onions
½ cup sautéed chopped
chicken livers
2 tablespoons chopped
stuffed olives

Just before serving, preheat the oven to 400°. Fill the tarts and bake until thoroughly heated. Serve at once.

ABOUT HOT STUFFED TOMATOES

♦ Please read About Stuffed Vegetables, page 256.
To prepare cases for hot food, cut large hollows in very firm unpeeled tomatoes. Salt them

and invert them on a rack to
drain for about 15 minutes. Fill
the tomato cases with any of
the following cooked foods and
cover the tops with:

> Au Gratin I, II, or III,
> page 389

Place the tomato cases in a pan
with enough water to keep them
from scorching and bake them
in a preheated 350° oven for
10 or 15 minutes. If they are
too soft to hold their shape, bake
them in well-greased muffin tins.
For fillings, try:

> Creamed ham or sausage
> and mushrooms
> Bread crumbs and deviled
> ham
> Chestnuts and rice or
> wild rice, seasoned with
> salt and brown sugar
> Creamed green peas,
> parsley or mushrooms
> Mashed potatoes and nuts
> Creamed Spinach, or
> Florentine

Or see Farces, page 564, Fillings
for Vegetable Cases, page 48; or
use one of the following recipes.

TOMATOES STUFFED [4]
WITH PINEAPPLE

◗ Please read About Stuffed To-
matoes, above.
Preheat oven to 350°.
Prepare:

> 4 medium-sized tomato
> cases

Sprinkle each hollow with:

> 1 teaspoon brown sugar

Place in each hollow some of the
following mixture:

> 1 tablespoon chili sauce
> 1 cup drained crushed
> pineapple
> 2 tablespoons dry bread
> crumbs

Sprinkle the tops with:

> Au Gratin II, page 389

Bake, as directed above and
serve on:

> Toast rounds

TOMATOES STUFFED [4]
WITH CORN

◗ Please read About Stuffed To-
matoes, page 335.
Preheat oven to 350°.
Prepare:

> 4 tomato cases

Sauté, then mince:

> 4 slices bacon

Combine:

> 1 cup cooked, drained
> corn
> 1 chopped pimiento
> ½ chopped green pepper
> 2 tablespoons chopped
> celery
> ½ cup bread crumbs
> 2 tablespoons corn liquor
> or cream
> ½ teaspoon salt
> ¼ teaspoon paprika
> ½ teaspoon sugar, if the
> corn is green

Add the minced bacon. Fill the
tomato cases. Sprinkle the tops
with:

> Au Gratin I or III,
> page 389

Bake as directed above.

TOMATOES FILLED [6]
WITH ONIONS

◗ Please read About Stuffed To-
matoes, page 335.
Preheat oven to 350°.
Prepare:

> 6 tomato cases

Melt:

> 2 tablespoons bacon
> drippings or butter

Add and sauté until golden:

> ½ cup finely chopped onion

Chop the pulp taken from the
tomatoes and combine it with
the onions. Add:

> 1½ teaspoons brown sugar
> ½ teaspoon salt
> 1 tablespoon celery seed

Simmer these ingredients for
about 10 minutes. If the filling
is too moist, it may be thickened
with:

> (Bread crumbs)

If it is too dry, it may be moistened with:

 Cream or milk

Fill the tomato cases. Cover the tops with:

 Au Gratin II or III,
 page 389

Bake them, as directed above.

TOMATOES STUFFED [6] WITH BREAD CRUMBS AND ANCHOVIES

▶ Please read About Stuffed Tomatoes, page 335.

Preheat oven to 350°.

Prepare:

 6 medium-sized tomato
  cases

Season the cases with:

 3 tablespoons brown sugar

Chop the pulp taken from the tomatoes. Combine it with an equal amount of:

 Soft bread crumbs

add:

 2 tablespoons sautéed
  chopped onion
 2 tablespoons sautéed
  chopped pepper
 4 chopped anchovies

Taste before

 Correcting the seasoning

as anchovies are salty. Fill the tomato cases. Bake, as directed above.

TOMATOES STUFFED [6] WITH CREAMED SWEETBREADS

▶ Please read About Stuffed Tomatoes, page 335.

Prepare:

 6 tomato cases

Sauté:

 ¼ lb. Mushrooms, page 296

Cook:

 ¼ lb. Sweetbreads, page 537

The mushrooms and sweetbread proportions may be varied. Cook by the recipe on page 389:

 Cream Sauce I—as much
  as there are mushrooms
  and sweetbreads
  combined

Add the other ingredients to the boiling cream sauce. Thicken them with:

 (¼ cup bread crumbs)

Preheat oven to 350°.

Fill the tomato cases. Cover the tops with:

 Au Gratin II or III,
 page 389

Bake them, as directed above.

TOMATOES STUFFED [6] WITH CRAB MEAT

▶ Please read About Stuffed Tomatoes, page 335.

Preheat oven to 350°.

Prepare:

 6 tomato cases

Melt over low heat:

 1½ tablespoons butter

Add and cook for 3 minutes:

 3 tablespoons minced green
  pepper
 3 tablespoons minced onion

Stir in, until blended:

 1½ tablespoons flour

Stir in slowly:

 1½ cups milk

When sauce is thick and hot, add:

 1½ cups crab meat
 ⅓ teaspoon salt
 A few grains red pepper
 2 teaspoons Worcestershire
  sauce
 1 cup grated American
  cheese

Simmer and stir these ingredients until the cheese is melted. Fill the tomato cases with this mixture. Bake, as directed above.

TOMATOES STUFFED [6] WITH SHRIMP

▶ Please read About Stuffed Tomatoes, page 335.

Preheat oven to 350°.

Prepare:

 6 tomato cases

Chop the tomato pulp removed from the centers. Melt:

 1 tablespoon butter

Sauté in it for 2 minutes:

2 tablespoons finely
chopped onion
Add the tomato pulp and:
1 cup chopped, cooked or
canned shrimp
Stir in:
1 tablespoon chopped
parsley
3 tablespoons crushed
cracker crumbs
Paprika and salt, if
needed
Fill the tomatoes with this mixture. Dust the tops with:
Au Gratin I or II,
page 389
Bake them, as directed in the 2
previous recipes.

ABOUT TURNIPS

A turnip is not necessarily a de-
pressant, as so many people seem
to feel. Children often enjoy
them well-washed and raw, like
apples; and the knowing choose
them as an accompaniment to
game. They make a good change,
if browned, to serve instead of
potatoes around a roast, page
258. A favorite peasanty dish,
Himmel und Erde, is made of
mashed turnips, potatoes and
seasoned apples, combined in
any proportion.
Discard woody turnips and
parblanch old ones for 3 to 5
minutes before cooking. ◗ One
pound turnips will yield about
3½ cups sliced and 2½ cups
cooked.
Cut off the tops at once and
store in a dark cool place. The
tops, if tender, may be used as
greens, page 293.
◗ Pressure cook turnips at 15
lbs. for 5 minutes.

COOKED TURNIPS   [4]

I. If young, wash, pare and place
in a steamer:
1 lb. sliced young turnips
Steam, page 252, for 20 to 30
minutes. Drain.
Correct the seasoning

and dress with:
Butter
Lemon juice and vinegar
or mash or cream as for Potatoes,
page 311.

II. If old, you may parblanch,
page 88, 3 to 5 minutes:
Sliced or whole turnips
Drop them into rapidly boiling
water to cover. Add:
½ teaspoon salt
½ teaspoon sugar
Cook, uncovered, 15 to 20 minutes if sliced, 20 to 25 minutes
if whole or until tender. Proceed
as for I.

SCALLOPED TURNIPS

Prepare:
Scalloped Potatoes,
page 312
substituting just turnips or turnips and sliced onions for the
potatoes.

GLAZED TURNIPS

Cook as directed previously:
Young turnips
Drain and dry them well. Brown
them in:
Hot melted butter
Season them with:
Paprika and sugar
The sugar helps with the brown-
ing. Use Meat Glaze (II, 145),
or dissolve in a little boiling
water:
A beef cube
Pour it over the turnips.
Correct the seasoning
Serve them at once, rolled in:
Chopped parsley

STUFFED TURNIP CUPS   [8]

◗ Please read About Stuffed Vegetables, page 256.
Preheat oven to 350°.
I. Pare, then blanch, page 88, for 3 to 5 minutes:

8 medium-sized turnips

Hollow into cups, reserving and chopping the pulp. Melt:

1 tablespoon butter

Sauté in it for about 3 minutes:

1 tablespoon grated onion
2 tablespoons cooked, seasoned peas

You may use the peas alone, omitting the onion. Combine the pulp with the onion and peas. Season with:

Salt and pepper

Thicken it slightly with:

Cracker crumbs or bread crumbs

Fill the turnip cups with this mixture. Place them in a greased baking dish. Combine and pour around them:

½ cup milk
⅛ teaspoon salt

Bake until tender, about 15 minutes.

II. Proceed as above, using a filling of leftover sauced foods, a cooked Farce, page 564, or creamed peas.

ABOUT WATER CRESS

Usually thought of only as salad and sandwich material, water cress not only adds greatly in flavoring soups and vegetables but is good cooked with other greens or by itself. Prepare as for Creamed Spinach, page 326. Serve with grills or chops.

WATER CHESTNUTS

Please read About Water Chestnuts (II, 188).
These crisp vegetables are added usually as a garnish to other vegetables.
◗ Add for the last 2 or 3 minutes of cooking only.

SALAD DRESSINGS, SAUCES, GRAVIES, MARINADES, GLAZES AND SEASONED BUTTERS

ABOUT COLD SAUCES AND DRESSINGS

Some dressings seem designed to turn a salad into a costume piece. To demonstrate how welcome a switch to simplicity can be—after more elaborate recipes —follow our instructions for Tossed Salad, page 33. This dressing consists of nothing whatever but oil and vinegar, both of first quality, plus a sprinkling of salt. Good salad dressings should complement— never repeat—the salad ingredients they grace.

A word to dieters: while a salad is an unimpeachable slenderizer, a salad dressing most definitely is not. The fat content in commercial French dressings may be 35% and generally goes up to 40%; commercial mayonnaise must, by law, consist of 65% fat; and these amounts are almost always exceeded in their homemade counterparts. If you diet, then, be a spendthrift with the greenstuff, a miser with dressing. To help along, we have included in this section some low calorie formulas. The recipes given later may inspire you to make spiced or herb vinegars in quantity; also to add to individual bottles of salad dressing that certain something which gives them a personalized appeal. ♦ Store refrigerated, in closed containers, all egg-based dressings like mayonnaise. Please read About Salads, page 30, About Oil (II, 173) and Vinegar (II, 150). For heavier dressings, see Dips (II, 83).

ABOUT SAUCE TOOLS

Handy-size simple tools hanging above the cooking area encourage the addition of interesting ingredients to sauces. ♦ The 3 hand-beaters, sketched on the left, make lumps vanish. The third from the left is particularly useful for beating an egg in a cup. For that little grating of cheese, onion or bread crumbs, try the rotary grater shown next. Kitchen shears with a self-releasing hinge are easy to keep clean and unrusted. Use them to snip herbs quickly, right into the sauce.

A garlic press, center, will squeeze enough juice to give an ineffable flavor to your sauces, and the hand grater is good for a shaving of lemon rind or nutmeg. Also have ready a bar-type strainer for the quick clearing of very small quantities of sauce. For larger ones, use a Chinese hat or conical strainer, shown on page 145, and for very careful straining, line this with muslin.

By all means have some very hard wooden spoons for delicate sauces which may be broken down by the more vigorous metal tools. A sauce spoon with one pointed end will scrape the pan edges clean easily and help avoid lumping. If you should use a metal spoon, make sure it is stainless steel, so as not to discolor a delicate sauce.

♦ If the recipe calls for beating over ice, please see illustration, page 180.

Electric beaters and ⅃ blenders are great labor-savers in the kitchen and will beat out lumps very quickly. They do, however, change the texture and flavor of the sauce as they whip in a great deal of air and will make a thickened sauce foamy and less tasty and a brown sauce much lighter in color.

OIL DRESSING

Pour the following over salad greens:
    ½ cup olive oil
    1 clove garlic
    ½ teaspoon salt
Before serving, grate over greens:
    Fresh lemon peel

FRENCH DRESSING OR SAUCE VINAIGRETTE

[About ½ Cup]
The dressing is best made just before use and can become part of the salad-making if you like. See Tossed Salad, page 33. The classic proportions are 3 to 4 parts of oil to one part lemon juice, lime juice or vinegar, and salt and pepper to taste. Many other condiments may be added,

including Worcestershire sauce, chili sauce, chutney, Roquefort cheese, spices, sweet and sour cream and, of course, herbs and garlic. The garlic clove should be removed after 24 hours if the dressing is to be stored refrigerated. ♦ Fresh herbs should be added only when the sauce is to be used at once, because they become strong and unpleasant if left in the oil for any length of time.

Combine in a small bowl:
    ¼ teaspoon salt
    ¼ teaspoon pepper
    1 tablespoon olive oil
    1 tablespoon vinegar or lemon juice
    (¼ teaspoon dry mustard)
Beat these ingredients well with a wire whisk or a fork until they are smooth. Add:
    2 tablespoons olive oil
Beat well again. Add:
    1 tablespoon vinegar or lemon juice
    3 tablespoons olive oil
Peel and add:
    (1 clove garlic)
Place the dressing in a jar, cover it well. Put it in a cold place ready for use. Shake well before using.

FRENCH FRUIT-SALAD DRESSING

[About ⅔ Cup]
Prepare:
    ½ cup French dressing
Substitute for the vinegar:
    3 tablespoons grapefruit or lemon juice

FRENCH DRESSING WITH CREAM CHEESE

[About ⅞ Cup]

Serve this dressing over a green salad or a vegetable salad.
Mash with a fork and beat until smooth:

 1 package cream cheese:
   3 oz.

Beat in:

 1 teaspoon finely minced
   onion
 ½ teaspoon dry mustard
 1 teaspoon salt
   Freshly ground black
   pepper
 2 tablespoons chopped
   parsley

Beat in gradually:

 ¼ cup salad oil
 1½ tablespoons vinegar

AVOCADO DRESSING

I. [About ¾ Cup]

Good on sliced tomatoes.
Peel and mash:

 ½ avocado

Add gradually:

 ½ cup French dressing

and beat until smooth. Use immediately.

II. Use this as a heavy dressing or as a filling for tomatoes, cucumbers, celery or endive. See Salads, page 33, and Hors d'Oeuvre (II, 66).
Mash:

   A ripe avocado

with:

   Lemon juice or vinegar
   to taste

and

   Correct the seasoning.

RAVIGOTE SAUCE

[About 1⅓ Cups]

Good with cold meat or fish.
Prepare:

 1 cup French dressing

Add:

 ½ cup finely chopped onion

 1 tablespoon finely chopped
   capers
 1 teaspoon chopped parsley
 ½ teaspoon chopped fresh
   tarragon
 ½ teaspoon chopped fresh
   chervil

LORENZO DRESSING

[About ½ Cup]

Combine:

 ½ cup French dressing
 2 tablespoons chili sauce
 2 tablespoons chopped
   water cress

ANCHOVY DRESSING

[About ½ Cup]

Prepare:

 ½ cup French dressing

Beat into it:

 1 tablespoon or more
   anchovy or other
   fish paste

ANCHOVY AND BEET DRESSING

[About 1 Cup]

Place in a jar with a screw top:

 ½ cup French dressing
 3 or 4 chopped anchovies
 2 small chopped cooked
   beets
 1 chopped hard-cooked egg

Season the dressing highly.
Shake the jar well. Pour the dressing over a large bowlful of:

   Endive or lettuce

SALSA VERDE

[About ¾ Cup]

To be used with salads and fish.
Combine:

 ½ cup chopped parsley
 1½ tablespoons capers
 2 garlic cloves
 3 anchovy fillets or
   ½ teaspoon anchovy
   paste

Add:

 1 crustless slice white bread

soaked in:

 ¼ cup vinegar
 3 tablespoons olive oil

2 tablespoons sugar
Correct the seasoning
Any of the following may be
added:
(Horseradish, pickles,
green olives, green
peppers)

ROQUEFORT OR BLEU CHEESE FRENCH DRESSING

[About ⅔ Cup]
Prepare:
½ cup French dressing
Beat into it:
2 tablespoons or more
crumbled Roquefort or
bleu cheese

⅄ BLENDER ANCHOVY AND ROQUEFORT DRESSING

[About 1½ Cups]
Place in container of electric
blender and blend until smooth:
⅔ cup olive oil
1 can anchovies with oil
3 tablespoons vinegar
3 tablespoons lemon juice
¼ teaspoon paprika
(1 clove garlic)
½ teaspoon mustard
½ teaspoon sugar
½ teaspoon celery salt
A dash of Worcestershire
sauce and hot pepper
sauce
A 3-inch wedge Roquefort
cheese

HORSERADISH DRESSING

[About ½ Cup]
Prepare:
½ cup French dressing
Beat into it:
1 tablespoon or more fresh
or prepared horseradish

FROZEN HORSERADISH SAUCE

[About 1½ Cups]
This comes out rather like a
sherbet and is delicious with
boiled beef.
Combine:
¼ cup grated horseradish
¼ cup fresh orange juice
1 teaspoon sugar
and fold into:
1 cup stiffly whipped cream
Freeze about 3 to 4 hours in a
tray and spoon out into a bowl
to serve. Do not hold frozen for
long periods.

CUMBERLAND SAUCE

[About ¾ Cup]
Good with cold ham and game.
Combine and blend well:
Grated rind of 1 lemon
Juice of 1 lemon
Grated rind of 1 orange
1 tablespoon confectioners'
sugar
1 teaspoon prepared
mustard
½ cup melted red currant
jelly
1 tablespoon port wine
If the jelly is very stiff, it may
have to be diluted over heat
with:
(1 or 2 tablespoons hot
water)

WATER CRESS DRESSING

[About 2 Cups]
Excellent over salad greens or
Cucumber Gelatin Salad, page
64, and Shrimp, page 441.
Combine:
2 tablespoons lemon juice
1 tablespoon tarragon
vinegar
½ cup olive oil
1 teaspoon salt
⅛ teaspoon pepper
Stir in:
2 finely chopped bunches
water cress

⅄ BLENDER CRESS DRESSING

Blend to a paste in an electric
blender:

2 hard-cooked eggs
2 tablespoons olive oil
¾ cup cut water cress,
    packed lightly
Dilute this paste with:
    French dressing
to the consistency you like.

⅄ BLENDER VEGETABLE SAUCE

[About 1 Cup]
Serve this sauce over bland foods, sweetbreads, cold veal, hot or cold fish.
Combine:
ん¾ cup tomato purée or
    2 large, raw, skinned
    tomatoes—the juice
    pressed from them
1 medium-sized onion
1 green pepper, seeds and
    membrane removed
¼ cup celery or 1 teaspoon
    celery and/or dill seeds
2 tablespoons parsley or
    chives
½ teaspoon salt
¼ teaspoon freshly ground
    pepper
(2 tablespoons French
    dressing)
Chill the sauce for about ½ hour.

CHIFFONADE DRESSING

[About 1½ Cups]
Prepare:
    ½ cup French dressing
Add to it:
2 chopped hard-cooked
    eggs
2 tablespoons julienned
    cooked beet root
2 tablespoons chopped
    parsley
2 teaspoons chopped chives
1 teaspoon chopped onion

COCKTAIL SAUCE

[About 1 Cup]
Good for dunking or garnishing shellfish, small sausages or other hors d'oeuvre.

Combine:
¾ cup catsup
⅛ to ¼ cup prepared
    horseradish
    Juice of 1 lemon
1 dash hot pepper sauce

CHUTNEY DRESSING

[About 1 Cup]
Combine in a bottle and chill:
1 tablespoon chopped
    hard-cooked egg
1 tablespoon chopped
    chutney
¼ teaspoon curry powder
1 tablespoon lemon juice
½ cup olive oil
3 tablespoons vinegar
¼ teaspoon salt
1 teaspoon sugar
    A few grains black pepper
Shortly before serving the dressing, beat it well with a fork.

COLD MUSTARD SAUCE

I.
For boiled or cold meats or fish. This is in the nature of a relish.
Combine:
2 teaspoons grated onion
1 tablespoon prepared
    mustard
1½ teaspoons sugar
1 to 2 tablespoons oil
2 tablespoons vinegar
(2 hard-cooked egg yolks)
(1 tablespoon cream)

II. [About 1 Cup]
Try this over raw or cooked vegetables or seafood.
Combine:
¾ cup Italian tomato paste
1 teaspoon dry mustard
1 tablespoon sugar
½ teaspoon salt
1 tablespoon vinegar
1 tablespoon drained
    horseradish
(1 tablespoon chopped
    onion, chives or fresh
    herbs)

III.

A highly seasoned sauce for cold meats or broiled sausages. Blend gradually:

>2 tablespoons or more dry mustard

with a little:

>Water

until it is the consistency of thick cream. Fold this paste into:

>½ cup heavy cream or evaporated milk, whipped (II, 133)

Season the sauce, if desired, with:

>Salt and paprika

DRESSING WITHOUT OIL

[About ¾ Cup]

No, it isn't particularly good, but it may be eaten by the bulging with a clear conscience.
Soak:

>1 teaspoon gelatin

in:

>1 tablespoon cold water

Dissolve it in:

>¼ cup boiling water

Add:

>1 tablespoon sugar
>½ teaspoon salt

Cool this mixture. Add:

>1 teaspoon grated lemon rind
>½ cup lemon juice
>⅛ teaspoon dry mustard
>¼ teaspoon paprika
>A few grains cayenne
>⅛ teaspoon pepper
>¼ teaspoon onion juice
>(⅛ teaspoon curry powder)

Shake the dressing. Chill it. Before serving it, beat it well with a wire beater. Add, if you wish:

>2 tablespoons minced parsley
>1 tablespoon minced chives

SWEET-SOUR LOW CALORIE DRESSING

[1 Cup]

Serve on a green salad.
Combine:

>⅓ cup lemon juice
>⅔ cup water
>1 teaspoon sugar
>¼ teaspoon salt

CHINESE LOW CALORIE DRESSING

[About ½ Cup]

Good on sliced cucumber and tomato.
Combine:

>3 tablespoons lemon juice
>3 tablespoons soy sauce
>1 tablespoon sugar
>(1 teaspoon finely chopped candied ginger)

LOW CALORIE THOUSAND ISLAND DRESSING

[About 2 Cups]

Combine in a large screw-top jar:

>¾ cup tarragon vinegar
>1 can condensed tomato soup: 10½ oz.
>1 minced garlic clove
>A few grains cayenne
>2 tablespoons chopped dill pickle
>2 tablespoons finely chopped celery
>2 tablespoons finely chopped parsley
>1 tablespoon Worcestershire sauce
>1 teaspoon paprika
>1 teaspoon prepared mustard

MAYONNAISE

The making of a perfect mayonnaise is the Sunday job for Papa in France and rivalry for quality between households is intense. Mayonnaise or Mahonnaise—as it was first called, after a French victory over the British at Port Mahon on the Island of Minorca —is a great favorite, not only as a dressing, but for combining with other foods. It has been made by hand for some 300 years. But, with care, we can now make it with an electric mixer or in the ⅄ blender. Blender mayonnaise is made more quickly, has greater volume and fluffier texture, but cannot duplicate the smooth, rich-looking glisten of hand-beaten mayonnaise. We believe it is slightly less adaptable to some mayonnaise variations, such as mayonnaise collée. Care must be used in ◗ storing all mayonnaise combinations under refrigeration, as they are subject to bacterial activity which may be very toxic without showing any evidence of spoilage. Cooked foods to be mixed with mayonnaise keep much better and help deter bacteria if they have been marinated in vinegar or lemon juice or are mixed with pickle. But, even if they have this added acid content, they must be kept thoroughly refrigerated. Freezing mayonnaise combinations is also chancy, as the spoilage is only arrested and not destroyed and then accelerates when the food is defrosted. ◗ Don't try to make mayonnaise if a thunderstorm threatens or is in progress, as it simply will not bind.

If you have to resort to bottled mayonnaise, beating in 1 to 2 tablespoons good olive oil until all trace of it has disappeared will give it a good flavor and make it stiffer and heavier. Sour cream, according to taste, can also do wonders for commercial mayonnaise—if well beaten in. Please note that commercial "Salad Dressing" is not mayonnaise and the above suggestions will not work if it is used.

◗ Eggs, oil, bowl and mixer must all be at room temperature, 70°. Warm the oil slightly if it has been refrigerated, rinse your bowl in hot water and dry it.

I. [About 1¼ Cups]

Place in a medium-sized bowl and beat with a wire whisk or wooden spoon until lemon color:

2 egg yolks

Beat in:
   ¼ to ½ teaspoon dry
      mustard
   ½ teaspoon salt
      A few grains cayenne
   ½ teaspoon vinegar or
      lemon juice
   ½ teaspoon confectioners'
      sugar

Beat in, very slowly, ½ teaspoon at a time:
   ½ cup olive oil

The mixture will begin to thicken and emulsify. Now you can relax! Combine in a cup or small pitcher:
   1½ tablespoons vinegar
   2 tablespoons lemon juice

Have ready:
   ½ cup olive oil

Alternate the oil ◗ drop by drop, with a few drops of the lemon and vinegar mixture. If the oil is added slowly during constant beating, this will make a good thick sauce. Sometimes the sauce will break, because you have either added your oil too fast toward the end or added too much of it—figure no more than ½ to ¾ cup oil to each large yolk. It may also break if your oil has been cold and your egg yolks warm. Do not despair: a curdled mayonnaise can be reconstituted by placing 1 egg yolk in a bowl. Stir it constantly and add the curdled dressing to it very, very slowly at first and continue slowly as the mixture thickens. If the dressing is too heavy, thin it with cream.

II. ⅄ [About 1¾ Cups]

You may make the above recipe following exactly the same procedure, in the same order, using an electric mixer on medium speed or the speed indicated for whipping cream.

III. ⅄ [About 1¾ Cups]

Blender mayonnaise differs from the first recipe in that it uses a whole egg. If your beating arm is rather weak, we suggest you try this method as the emulsifying is taken care of by the action of the blender.

Put in blender container:

    1 egg
    1 teaspoon ground mustard
    1 teaspoon salt
    A dash of cayenne
    1 teaspoon sugar
    ¼ cup salad oil

Cover and blend until thoroughly combined. With blender still running, take off the cover and slowly add:

    ½ cup salad oil

and then:

    3 tablespoons lemon juice

until thoroughly blended. Then add slowly:

    ½ cup salad oil

and blend until thick. You may have to stop and start the blender to stir down the mayonnaise.

AIOLI OR GARLIC SAUCE

[1 Cup]

This is a garlic sauce very popular in France where it is sometimes known as "Beurre de Provence." Some recipes omit the eggs. Serve over fish, cold boiled potatoes, beet rounds and boiled beef.

Skin, then chop very finely the:

    4 garlic clove sections

that give the sauce its name. Beat in:

    2 egg yolks
    ⅛ teaspoon salt
    (1 slice dry French bread
        without crust, soaked in
        milk and wrung out)

Add, as for mayonnaise, very slowly and beating constantly:

    1 cup olive oil

As the sauce thickens, beat in:

    ½ teaspoon cold water
    1 teaspoon lemon juice

In the case the sauce fails to thicken, treat as a defeated Mayonnaise, above.

SKORDALIA

[1 Cup]

Prepare:

    Aioli Sauce, as above

adding, after the sauce has thickened:

    ¼ cup ground almonds
    ¼ cup fresh bread crumbs
    3 teaspoons lemon juice
    2 tablespoons chopped
        parsley

ROUILLE SAUCE

A strongly flavored sauce, served with Mediterranean fish soups or bouillabaisse. Pound together in a bowl or mortar to make a smooth paste:

    1 blanched, seeded, skinned
        red pimiento or 1 canned
        pimiento
    1 small red chili, boiled
        until tender or a dash of
        hot pepper sauce
    ¼ cup white bread crumbs
        soaked in water and
        squeezed dry
    2 mashed cloves garlic

Beat in, very slowly, as in Mayonnaise:

    ¼ cup olive oil

Thin the sauce just before serving with:

    2 to 3 tablespoons of the
        soup you are serving

Pass with the soup.

SAUCE FOR SMOKED FOOD

Combine:

    2 tablespoons mayonnaise
    1 teaspoon horseradish
    1 tablespoon cultured sour
        cream

ANDALOUSE SAUCE

[2 Cups]

For vegetable salads, cold fish or egg dishes.

Combine:

    2 cups mayonnaise
    1 chopped tomato, with

seeds and juice removed
or ½ cup tomato purée
¼ julienned red pimiento

FRUIT-SALAD MAYONNAISE

[1½ Cups]
Combine:
1 cup mayonnaise
½ cup pineapple juice
1 teaspoon grated orange rind
1 tablespoon orange curaçao

CREAM OR CHANTILLY MAYONNAISE

[2 Cups]
Serve with fruit salad.
Prepare:
1 cup mayonnaise
Add to it, shortly before serving:
1 cup whipped cream

CURRY MAYONNAISE

[About 1 Cup]
For fruit or fish.
Combine:
1 cup mayonnaise
¼ teaspoon ginger
½ to 1 teaspoon curry powder
1 mashed clove garlic
1 teaspoon honey
1 tablespoon lime juice
It is very good for molded chicken salad or shrimp with these additions:
(1 tablespoon chopped chutney)
(1 tablespoon chopped kumquats)
(1 tablespoon blanched slivered almonds)

MAYONNAISE GRENACHE

[About 2½ Cups]
Serve with smoked turkey or smoked tongue.
Combine:
1 cup mayonnaise
½ cup red currant jelly

3 tablespoons grated horseradish
¼ teaspoon salt
⅛ teaspoon freshly ground pepper
2 tablespoons dessert sherry or Madeira
Fold in:
½ cup whipped cream

GREEN GODDESS DRESSING

[About 2 Cups]
Use on fish or shellfish.
Combine:
1 cup mayonnaise
1 minced clove garlic
3 minced anchovy fillets
¼ cup finely minced chives or green onions
¼ cup minced parsley
1 tablespoon lemon juice
1 tablespoon tarragon vinegar
½ teaspoon salt
Ground black pepper
½ cup cultured sour cream

GREEN MAYONNAISE OR SAUCE VERTE

[1 Cup]
For cold shellfish or vegetables.
Chop, blanch, page 88, for 2 minutes and drain:
2 tablespoons parsley
2 tablespoons tarragon, fennel or dill
2 tablespoons chives
2 tablespoons spinach or finely chopped cucumber
2 tablespoons water cress
Rub through a sieve and combine to make a paste with:
2 hard-cooked egg yolks
Add to:
1 cup stiff mayonnaise

HARD-COOKED EGG MAYONNAISE OR SAUCE GRIBICHE

[About 3 Cups]
For fish and cold meat.

Mash in a bowl until smooth:
    3 hard-cooked egg yolks
Add:
    ½ teaspoon salt
    A dash of pepper
    1 teaspoon prepared
      Dijon-type mustard
Add very gradually and beat
constantly:
    1½ cups olive oil
    ½ cup vinegar
The mixture will thicken. Then
stir in:
    3 finely julienned egg
      whites
    ½ cup mixed, finely
      chopped sour pickles and
      capers, with the moisture
      squeezed out
    2 tablespoons finely
      chopped mixed parsley,
      chervil, tarragon and
      chives

REMOULADE SAUCE

[About 1⅓ Cups]
For cold meat and poultry—also
shellfish, with which it is especially good.
Combine:
    1 cup mayonnaise
    1 tablespoon drained, finely
      chopped cucumber pickle
    1 tablespoon drained,
      chopped capers
    2 teaspoons French
      mustard
    1 teaspoon finely chopped
      parsley
    ½ teaspoon chopped fresh
      tarragon
    ½ teaspoon chervil
    (½ teaspoon anchovy paste)

RUSSIAN DRESSING

[About 1¾ Cups]
Use on arranged salads, eggs,
shellfish or in chicken sandwiches, instead of butter or
mayonnaise.
Combine:
    1 cup mayonnaise
    1 tablespoon grated
      horseradish

    (3 tablespoons imported
      caviar)
    (1 teaspoon Worcestershire
      sauce)
    ¼ cup chili sauce or catsup
    1 teaspoon grated onion

TARTARE SAUCE

[About 1⅓ Cups]
A good old stand-by for fried
fish.
Combine:
    1 cup firm mayonnaise
    1 teaspoon French
      mustard
    1 tablespoon finely chopped
      parsley
    1 teaspoon minced shallots
    1 tablespoon chopped,
      drained sweet pickle
    (1 tablespoon chopped,
      drained green olives)
    1 finely chopped hard-
      boiled egg
    1 tablespoon chopped,
      drained capers
    Correct the seasoning
You may thin the sauce with:
    A little wine vinegar or
      lemon juice

THOUSAND ISLAND DRESSING

[About 1½ Cups]
Serve over iceberg lettuce
wedges, eggs, etc.
Combine:
    1 cup mayonnaise
    ¼ cup chili sauce or catsup
    2 tablespoons minced
      stuffed olives
    1 tablespoon chopped
      green pepper
    1 tablespoon minced onion
      or chives
    1 chopped hard-cooked egg
    2 teaspoons chopped
      parsley

WATER CRESS SAUCE OR SAUCE AU CRESSON

[About 1 Cup]
This is excellent with cold fish
dishes.

Combine:

    ¼ cup finely chopped water
    cress
    ¾ cup mayonnaise
    1 tablespoon lemon juice
    Correct the seasoning

SAUCE LOUIS

[About 2 Cups]

This is good with stuffed artichokes, shrimp or crab. It is the sauce used for Crab Louis, page 50.

Combine:

    1 cup mayonnaise
    ¼ cup heavy cream
    ¼ cup chili sauce
    1 teaspoon Worcestershire
    sauce
    ¼ cup chopped green
    pepper
    ¼ cup chopped green onion
    2 tablespoons lemon juice
    Correct the seasoning

HALF AND HALF DRESSING

[About 2½ Cups]

Serve on tossed salad, combination salads or hearts of lettuce.

Combine:

    1 cup mayonnaise
    1 cup French dressing
    1 minced garlic clove
    1 teaspoon mashed
    anchovies
    ½ cup Parmesan cheese

BOILED SALAD DRESSINGS

Three recipes for boiled salad dressings are given. No. I, made with 1 egg or 2 yolks, is a very economical, acceptable boiled dressing. It may be thinned with cream, but is good as it is over vegetable and potato salad. No. II is made with milk and whole eggs. Use this dressing over slaw, tomatoes, aspics, etc. No. III is a fruit salad dressing. Keep these dressings well refrigerated.

I. [About 1¼ Cups]

Dissolve:

    ½ to 1 teaspoon dry
    mustard
    1 to 2 tablespoons sugar
    ½ teaspoon salt
    2 tablespoons flour
    ¼ teaspoon paprika

in:

    ½ cup cold water

Beat in the top of double boiler:

    1 whole egg or 2 yolks
    ¼ cup vinegar

Add the dissolved ingredients. Cook and stir the dressing ♦ over —not in—boiling water, until it is thick and smooth. Add:

    2 tablespoons butter

Chill the dressing. It may be thinned with:

    Sweet or cultured sour
    cream

II. [About 1½ Cups]

Beat in the top of a double boiler:

    2 egg yolks
    2 teaspoons sugar
    1 tablespoon melted butter
    ⅔ cup milk
    ¼ cup vinegar
    2 teaspoons salt
    A few grains cayenne
    1 teaspoon dry mustard

Dissolve:

    2 teaspoons cornstarch

in:

    ⅓ cup milk

Add it to the ingredients in the double boiler. Cook and stir the dressing ♦ over—not in—boiling water, until it is thick. Cool it. You may add chopped parsley, chives or other herbs, celery or dill seeds, etc. Fold it into:

    2 stiffly beaten egg whites

III. [About 1¼ Cups]

Beat in the top of a double boiler:

    1 teaspoon salt
    ⅓ teaspoon paprika
    ¼ to ½ cup sugar
    2 tablespoons melted butter

6 tablespoons cream
3 eggs
(½ teaspoon mustard)

Stir and cook the dressing ▶ over—not in—boiling water, until it is thick. Add slowly:

6 tablespoons lemon juice

The dressing may be thinned with:

Fruit juice or cream

SOUR CREAM HORSERADISH DRESSING OR DRESDEN SAUCE

[1 Cup]

A fine change from the well-liked but often monotonous butter or cream sauce. Usually served with smoked or boiled fish. Combine and stir:

1 cup cultured sour cream
½ teaspoon prepared mustard
½ teaspoon horseradish
¼ teaspoon salt

CREAM HORSERADISH DRESSING

[About 1¼ Cups]

This dressing is good with cold meat.

Beat until stiff:

½ cup heavy cream

Add slowly, beating constantly:

3 tablespoons lemon juice or vinegar
¼ teaspoon salt
⅛ teaspoon paprika
A few grains cayenne
2 tablespoons grated horseradish
(3 tablespoons mayonnaise)

SOUR CREAM DRESSING FOR VEGETABLE SALAD

[About 1 Cup]

Beat until smooth:

1 cup thick cultured sour cream

Add to it:

1 teaspoon grated onion or fresh onion juice

1 teaspoon celery or dill seed
½ teaspoon salt
A fresh grating of white pepper
(2 tablespoons chopped green or sweet red pepper)

CUCUMBER SAUCE

[About 1½ Cups]

For fish or meat, preferably cold food, such as salmon.

Beat until stiff:

¾ cup heavy sweet or cultured sour cream

If the cream is sweet, add slowly:

2 tablespoons vinegar or lemon juice

Season the sauce with:

¼ teaspoon salt
⅛ teaspoon paprika

Pare, seed, cut finely and drain well:

1 large cucumber

Add it to the sauce with:

(2 teaspoons finely chopped chives or dill)

YOGURT DRESSING

Yogurt (II, 135), simple and unadorned, is excellent on honeydew and cantaloupe melon balls in a lettuce cup. Try it on other fresh fruits or on crisp salad greens on hot summer days. Good for dieters, too.

SOUR CREAM SAUCE FOR BAKED POTATOES

[1 Cup]

Combine:

1 cup cultured sour cream
1 teaspoon Worcestershire sauce
A dash of hot pepper sauce
½ teaspoon monosodium glutamate
½ teaspoon salt
Freshly ground black pepper

Garnish with:

Chopped chives

CAVIAR SAUCE

[About 1⅓ Cups]

Try on baked potatoes or as a dip for cold vegetables in hors d'oeuvre or salad.

Combine:

1 cup cultured sour cream
1 teaspoon onion or shallot juice
2 teaspoons capers
¼ cup red caviar

HONEY DRESSING

[1 Cup]

For fruit salads:

Combine:

½ cup honey
½ cup lime juice
(A pinch of ground ginger)

CELERY SEED DRESSING

[About 2 Cups]

Add to fruit salad just before serving. This may be made with an electric ⅄ blender or mixer. Constant beating to blend the ingredients is the secret of success here.

Combine:

½ cup sugar
1 teaspoon dry mustard
1 teaspoon salt
1 to 2 teaspoons celery seed

Add:

3 tablespoons grated onion

Gradually add, beating constantly:

1 cup salad oil
⅓ cup vinegar

Garnish with:

(A few finely cut sprigs lemon thyme)

CREAM CHEESE DRESSING FOR FRUIT SALAD

[About 1¼ Cups]

Mash with a fork and beat until smooth:

1 package cream cheese:
3 oz.

Beat in slowly:

1 tablespoon lemon juice
2 tablespoons currant jelly
½ cup cream

Chill the dressing for 1 hour or more before serving it.

LEMON AND SHERRY DRESSING FOR FRUIT SALAD

[About ½ Cup]

Delightful over tart fruit, apples, grapefruit, etc.

Combine:

¼ cup lemon juice
⅛ teaspoon salt

Stir in slowly:

¼ cup sugar

Add:

2 tablespoons dry sherry

CURRY DRESSING FOR FRUIT SALAD

[About 1 Cup]

Combine:

2 tablespoons mild vinegar
1 tablespoon lemon juice
¼ to ½ teaspoon curry
1 teaspoon sugar

Stir in:

1 cup cultured sour cream

See also Curry Mayonnaise, page 348.

ABOUT HOT SAUCE TYPES

There are certain old dowagers who try to dominate "sauciety." Call them the mother sauces, as the French do, if you like. Each has her strong peculiarities of individual makeup; each traditionally queens it over a whole coterie of dishes. The ubiquitous member of the clan—the one who is always close by—is pan gravy: she knows what's cooking, because she carries its essence.

Her roux-based cousins have more solid and dependable backgrounds and take more abuse in heating, reheating and storing—for their flour and butter base combines into as stable an ingredient as any in the kitchen. There are the delicate pale members of the roux family, descended from Béchamel, who accept the company of eggs, cream and even shallots. There are the robust characters originating in browned flours, who have picked up acquaintanceships with strange foreign spices, who love tomatoes and who, on occasion, set their caps for garlic. Both rely for authenticity on two principles. Their roux base must be cooked to rid it and them of any trace of plebeian floury origin and must always be hot when added to cold liquids or cold when added to hot.

There are the plush sauce aristocracy who scorn flour altogether and derive their stamina from eggs. Like a lot of other sauces for cold food, the mayonnaise branch performs this elegant trick without requiring heat. While its cousins, the Hollandaise-Béarnaise group, must have heat, they need it only in small doses and for short periods.

Most showy and demonstrative of all are the wine sauces, the vinaigrettes, the playful tenderizing sweet-sours or agrodulces, the marinades, the barbecues and, of course, the truly sweet dessert sauces (II, 473), which are the simpering sentimentalists of the whole colony.

Although these rather simple divisions mark the major sauce families, don't feel overconfident about your acquaintanceship until you can spot a rare nonidentical twin—with arrowroot as thickener—or an occasional reveler in fancy dress, tricked out with beurre manié or butter swirls. These wayward collaterals are among the most treasured, if fleeting, personalities of all.

When you once feel at home in sauce circles, you will learn rapidly how to make them welcome members of your culinary life. You will learn how to skillfully blend the hot ingredients, so that they may receive food without thinning. You will discover that adding the wine before—not after—the eggs and cream will avoid curdling and that a mixture can be stabilized with that extra bit of cream when separation threatens.

Of course, there is always the ⋏ blender to fall back on in a crisis of this kind, but the texture of the sauce can never be as smooth or thick as if it had been properly made in the first place. In sauces based on cornstarch, overbeating itself can disturb consistency—and this factor alone may cause thinning. The use of a light whisk or a wooden spoon is a help in avoiding this condition. Another reason for thinning in sauces may be the addition of acid in the form of fruit juice or wine. Sauces will also lose body if covered and held heated, for the excess steam created thins them and tends to cause separation. ◗ To lessen separation in frozen sauces, see Waxy Rice Flour (II, 157).

ABOUT COLOR IN SAUCES

A well-prepared sauce really has its color built in and should need no artificial coloring. ◗ To maintain and develop color for sauces, see page 353.

Rich beef stock combined with some tomato, browned meat—in the case of a stew—browned onions and carrots and a brown roux will result in a rich brown sauce needing no addition of caramel to bring up the color. If you feel obliged to add caramel to gravies, add it sparingly. Some cooks use yellow coloring for chicken gravies and sauces to try to hide the omission of chicken fat and egg yolks. Should you use saffron, do beware of its overpowering flavor. A tomato sauce will keep a good color if you do not cook it too quickly or too long.

ABOUT SAUCES IN QUANTITY

◗ If you are making gravies or sauces in quantity, it will take considerably longer to get rid of the raw flour taste after the liquid has been added to the roux than when you are making only 1 or 2 cups for immediate family use. We advise heating these larger amounts ◗ uncovered, in a slow oven for ½ to ¾ of an hour and straining the sauce before serving, to remove any crusting or lumps. But if you stir the sauce from time to time, it may not be necessary to strain it.

When doubling the ingredients in sauce recipes, taste before adding the full amount of seasoning. It is easy to overdo it.

ABOUT KEEPING SAUCES

You may keep Velouté, Tomato and Brown Sauces in the refrigerator for at least a week. To store, strain the sauce, pour it into a container and cover with a thin layer of fat or sherry. If you have not used all the sauce at the end of a week, you may reheat it, put it in a clean jar, cover again with a little melted fat and return it to the refrigerator, where it will keep at least another week.

You can also ✳ freeze the sauces mentioned above, as well as Béchamel, in ice-cube trays and keep the cubes in your freezer in a plastic bag, taking out as many as you need for immediate use. They may be melted in a double boiler—4 large cubes melt down to about ½ cup of sauce. You may also freeze Hollandaise Sauce, page 369, but be very careful when reheating. Do not try to freeze mayonnaise; it will break. And, in general, do not try to keep sauces made with eggs, cream or milk for more than 2 or 3 days in the refrigerator.

ABOUT SAUCE INGREDIENTS

Sauces in general are spoken of as savory or sweet. Many of those in the first category are made with some sort of pan gravy. Pan residues, unless from fish or from strong variety meats, like kidneys, are a most desirable flavoring ingredient. ◗ To make pan gravies, see page 358.

Pan residues for sauces also include those which are left over from browning and sautéing meats. Browning lends attractive color and the addition of some rendered fat serves to intensify the characteristic meat flavor. It is always best, if you sauté with butter—and the butter should be sweet, not salted —to clarify it, page 383, or to combine it with a little cooking oil to raise its smoking point, so as to prevent scorching and bitter overtones. If economy is a factor and margarine has been substituted for butter, you may wish to improve the flavor of the final product by finishing the sauce off with a Butter Swirl, page 357.

Good strong, fat-free Stocks (II, 138) are invaluable sauce ingredients, too, especially when reduced to a Glaze (II, 145). Where possible, the stock should reflect the food it is to flavor: chicken stock for chicken, lamb stock for lamb, etc. Although meat stocks, including those of poultry and game, are often combined in sauce-making—favorites being those of chicken—and veal—fish and shellfish Fumets (II, 143) should be reserved only for fish and shellfish dishes.

Such broths always make better sauce ingredients if left to stand refrigerated for 24 hours and then de-fatted.

When pan residues or stocks are scanty, turn to wine. ♦ Please read About Cooking With Wine (II, 149). Use, as a rule of thumb, dry white wines in sauces for fish or white meats; dry red wines for red meats. Strong game sauces sometimes support stronger liquors like rum, brandy or Madeira, but whisky is never added to them.

♦ In any wine sauce, add egg, milk, cream or butter swirls after the wine has been incorporated.

ABOUT THICKENERS FOR SAUCES

Sauces not made by deglazing with liquids, as described above, are generally ♦ thickened just enough to coat food lightly and yet not run off.

ROUX

The most common thickeners for savory sauces are the ♦ roux —white, blonde or brown. All of these are made of the same ingredients to begin with, but change in character as heat is applied. These mixtures of flour and fats are blended gently ♦ over very low heat from 5 minutes to a much longer period, depending on your available time and your patience. White roux should not color; blonde, barely; and brown should reach the color of hazelnut and smell deliciously baked.

♦ Unless a roux is cooked long enough to dispel the raw taste of flour, this unpleasant flavor will dominate the strongest stocks and seasonings. And unless the flour and butter are stirred to distribute the heat and to allow the starch granules to swell evenly, they will later fail to absorb the liquid. Therefore the sauce will be thin. ♦ This heated blending period is important. Using too high heat to try hurrying it will burn the flour, giving it a bitter taste and it will shrink the starch, making it incapable of continuing to swell.

For white roux-based sauces, see Béchamel, page 359; for blonde, see Blanquette de Veau, page 504; for brown, see Sauce Espagnole, page 365. Since most cooks use some form of roux every day, you may find it a time-saver to make one in advance and store it in tablespoon-sized units under refrigeration. It will keep in the ✳ freezer, too, for several months if you do the following: when the roux has been cooked to the desired color and is still soft, measure it by tablespoons on a baking sheet and freeze. Transfer the frozen wafers to a plastic bag or wide-topped container and store in the freezer. To thicken sauce, drop several wafers of the original roux in the sauce to reach the thickness desired. Or you may soften the wafers in a double boiler over hot water and proceed as usual with the making of the sauce.

BROWNED FLOUR

This variant is used in gravies to enhance color and flavor. The slow but inexpensive procedure by which it is made is worth trying. Place:

1 cup all-purpose flour
in a heavy dry skillet. ♦ Stir constantly over very low direct

heat until golden brown; or place the skillet in a 350° oven until the flour is golden brown, about 30 minutes. Stir frequently, scraping the flour from the sides and bottom of the pan. In a very slow oven, the flour, when ready, should smell nutty and baked. Do not let it get too dark or, as with brown roux, it will become bitter and lose its thickening power altogether. ♦ Even properly browned flour has only about ½ the thickening power of all-purpose flour. It may be stored in a tightly covered jar in a cool place.

FLOUR PASTE

This is sometimes pressed into service to thicken emergency gravies and sauces, but the results are never as palatable as when even a quick roux is used. Make a paste of flour and cold water or stock. Use about 2 parts water and one part flour. Stir as much of the paste as needed into the boiling stock or drippings. Permit the sauce to heat until it thickens and ♦ simmer for at least 3 minutes more to reduce the raw taste of the flour. Stir frequently with a wire whisk.

CORNSTARCH

Cornstarch is often used where translucency is desirable, as in some Chinese or dessert sauces. It should be mixed with a little cold water before being added to the hot liquid. One tablespoon cornstarch will thicken 1½ to 2 cups of liquid. Most Chinese sauces are finished over direct heat. But dessert sauces are better cooked in the top of a double boiler ♦ over—not in —hot water until the raw taste of the cornstarch disappears. ♦ Do not overbeat cornstarch-based sauces for this thins them.

ARROWROOT

Of all the thickeners, this makes the most delicately textured sauces. ♦ But use it only when the sauce is to be served within 10 minutes of thickening. It will not hold, nor will it reheat. Since the flavor of arrowroot is neutral and it does not have to be cooked to remove rawness, as do flour and cornstarch, and since it thickens at a lower temperature than either of them, it is ideal for use in egg and other sauces which should not boil. Allow 2½ teaspoons to 1 cup liquid. See also (II, 158).

POTATO STARCH OR FECULA

This is preferred by some cooks, rather than flour, as a thickener in certain delicate sauces. When it is used, less simmering is required and the sauce gains some transparency. ♦ Heated beyond 176° the sauce will thin out. Serve soon after it has thickened, as it has no holding power. One tablespoon of potato starch will moderately thicken 1 cup of liquid.

EGG YOLKS

Egg yolks not only thicken but also enrich a sauce. ♦ Never add egg yolks directly to hot liquid. Stir them into a little cream, then incorporate with them some of the hot sauce you want to thicken. Stir this mixture into the remainder of the hot liquid and continue to stir over low heat until the sauce thickens. ♦ Do not allow the sauce to boil, or it will curdle. If this happens, plunge pot into cold water and stir; or beat in a small amount of chilled cream. It is generally safer to add egg yolks to a mixture in a double boiler ♦ over— not in—hot water, unless you can control the heat source very exactly. Two or three egg yolks with a little cream will thicken 1 cup of liquid. Egg yolks added very slowly to melted butter or oil with constant stirring will produce an emulsion which is quite thick. Suitably seasoned, this becomes the base for Hollandaise or mayonnaise. Hard-cooked egg yolks and oil will also emulsify, see Sauce Gribiche, page 349.

BLOOD

Blood from the animal or bird the sauce is to accompany is a desirable thickener. To save the blood from a freshly killed hare, rabbit or chicken, see (II, 540). You may store it refrigerated for a day or two, mixed with 1 or 2 tablespoons vinegar to prevent clotting. Strain it and add it to the sauce at the last minute just before serving, swirling it in as you would butter, below. Simmer gently, but ◗ never allow the sauce to boil after the blood is added. For other thickening suggestions, see Thickeners for Soups, page 108, and Ingredients.

REDUCTION

This is another classic way to thicken sauces. Béchamel and Espagnole may be thickened during very slow simmering by the evaporation of liquid to achieve a more perfect consistency. If you intend to thicken a sauce by reducing it, season ◗ after you have brought it down to the right viscosity, otherwise you may find it highly overseasoned or unpleasantly salty. There are a good many recipes for tomato sauces which demand long cooking and reducing. Unless you can keep these sauces—or, in fact, any thickened sauces—on very low heat, they will cook too fast and flavor will be impaired. In the case of roux-thickened sauces

which call for reducing, do use an oven. It is a great labor-saver and the heat can be controlled much more exactly. ◗ Almost all reduced sauces, to be perfect in texture, should be strained before serving.

BUTTER SWIRLS

These finish off many fine, rich sauces, both white and brown, after straining and final heating. This can only be done if the sauce is to be served at once. ◗ It must not be reheated after the butter has been added. In addition to improving the flavor, the butter swirl also, very slightly, thickens the sauce. To make a sauce "finie au beurre" after straining and heating, add ◗ unsalted, unmelted butter bit by bit to the sauce, moving the pan in a circular motion, so that the butter makes an actual swirl in the hot sauce as it melts. Remove the pan from the heat before the butter is fully melted and continue to swirl. ◗ Do not use a spoon to stir it and do not try to reheat it. About 1 tablespoon butter is generally used to "finish" 1 cup of sauce.

KNEADED BUTTER OR BEURRE MANIÉ

This a magic panacea for rectifying sauces or thickening thin ones at the end of the cooking process. Do not use it for those which require long simmering. After adding kneaded butter ◗ do not boil the sauce. Simmer only long enough to dispel the floury taste. Manipulate with your fingers, as though you were rubbing for fine pastry, 2 tablespoons butter and 2 tablespoons flour. Form into small balls and drop into the hot liquid, stirring constantly until the ingredients are well blended and the sauce thickens. This amount will be sufficient for 1 cup of thin liquid.

ABOUT ATTRACTIVE WAYS TO SERVE SAUCES

Apart from the usual gravy boat or deep bowl and ladle, there are a number of attractive ways to serve sauces. Cold sauces and dips with a mayonnaise or sour cream base may be served in a crisp hollowed-out cabbage (II, 67), or individually in tomato or pepper cases, page 39. Suggest the marine flavor of cold shrimp or poached salmon with a delicate pink mayonnaise or Remoulade Sauce in a large sea shell.

Hot sauces can be served in ramekins, tin-lined copper pans or other small heatproof containers. The doll house instinct rises in all of us at the sight of these miniature individual pitchers and pots that are so appropriate when serving hot lobster, artichokes or asparagus. Sauces on the buffet table may be kept hot in small French three-legged saucepans, placed over a candle or—in the case of egg-based sauces—in wide-mouthed vacuum bottles or in chafing dishes. Like the food it accompanies, sauce, if it is meant to be hot, must be kept hot. However, ▶ any sauce that is worth its salt won't keep indefinitely on a steam table or in a casserole. There is a point of maximum goodness at which it should be served.

Cold sauces and seasoned butters can be kept chilled on a mound of crushed ice. Molds and pats of seasoned butter may be placed directly on the ice. Don't use ice cubes—the butter slips down between them.

ABOUT SAUCES MADE BY DEGLAZING

These are such a welcome change after the monotonous flour-thickened type. Pan juices and scrapings are precious and are frequently used as the base for many delicious sauces accompanying sautéed as well as roasted fowl and meat dishes. In initially roasting meat, be sure to grease the pans lightly to keep from burning any juices which may drip, before the fats from the meat have covered the bottom of the roasting pan. The addition of a cup of Mirepoix (II, 221) to the pan after the browning period will make both roast and pan gravy more flavorful. When the meat is done, remove it from the pan and pour off the fat. Add ¼ cup or more hot water or stock to the pan and cook on top of the stove—stirring and scraping the solidified juices from the bottom and sides. The addition of wine or dry sherry will hasten the deglazing process and heighten the flavorful aroma. Use the stock appropriate to your meat or fowl and the kind of wine you would normally drink with it. This, with a Butter Swirl, page 357, or Beurre Manié, page 357, or a little cream or more wine, can make the finest of all sauces.

ABOUT PAN GRAVY

If you use drippings for sauces, you may want to strain them first and remove excess fat. Reheat some of the fat because it will absorb the flour better. Add flour until it has the consistency of heavy cream.

PAN GRAVY

[1 Cup]
Remove the meat from the pan. Place it where it will remain hot. Pour off all but:

2 tablespoons drippings

Blend into them:

1 or 2 tablespoons flour

Stir with a wire whisk until the

flour has thickened and until well combined and smooth. Continue to cook slowly and stir constantly, while adding:

> The degreased pan juices and enough milk, water, stock, cream or beer to make 1 cup

The beer may be "still." Season the gravy with:

> Salt
> Pepper
> Fresh or dried minced herbs
> Grated lemon rind, etc.

Color, if necessary, with:

> A few drops Caramel
> (II, 169)

You may strain the gravy, reheat and serve it. If you are using a thickener other than flour, please read About Thickeners, page 355, for the correct amount of cornstarch or arrowroot to be added for the above amount of liquid.

CHICKEN PAN GRAVY

[About 2 Cups]
Strain the juices from the roast chicken. Pour off the fat. Heat:

> ¼ cup fat

Add and stir until blended:

> ¼ cup flour

Stir in slowly:

> 2 cups pan juices and Chicken Stock (II, 142)

Cook and stir the gravy until smooth and ◗ simmer for 5 minutes. Add:

> The cooked chopped chicken giblets
> (¼ cup or more cream)

◗ If the gravy is very rich, it may separate. Add the cream slowly. Stir it constantly. This will usually forestall any difficulty.

> Correct the seasoning

and serve.

CREAM SAUCE I OR BÉCHAMEL

[1 Cup]

This sauce, actually made with milk, is used for creaming foods like vegetables and fish and as a base for other sauces. Melt over low heat:

> 2 tablespoons butter

For a delicate flavor, even commercial establishments have found no substitute for butter. Add and blend over low heat for 3 to 5 minutes:

> 1½ to 2 tablespoons flour

Stir in slowly:

> 1 cup milk

For better consistency, you may scald the milk beforehand; but be sure—to avoid lumping—that the roux is cool when you add it. Add:

> 1 small onion studded with 2 or 3 whole cloves
> ½ small bay leaf

Cook and stir the sauce with a wire whisk or wooden spoon until thickened and smooth. Place in a 350° oven for 20 minutes to cook slowly. The oven interval also saves your time and hands for other kitchen jobs. Strain the sauce,

> Correct the seasoning

and serve. For creamed dishes, use about ½ as much sauce as solids.

CREAM SAUCE II OR HEAVY BÉCHAMEL

[1 Cup]
This sauce is used in soufflés.
Prepare:

> Cream Sauce I

Use in all:

> 3 tablespoons butter
> 3 tablespoons flour
> 1 cup liquid

CREAM SAUCE III OR BINDING BÉCHAMEL

[1 Cup]
This sauce is used in croquettes.
Prepare:

> Cream Sauce I, above

Use in all:

> 3 tablespoons butter

⅓ cup flour
1 cup liquid

CREAM SAUCE IV OR ENRICHED BÉCHAMEL

Reduce:
    1 cup Cream Sauce I
to ¾ of its volume. Stir in:
    ¼ cup heavy cream
and bring to boiling point. If
the sauce is for fish, add:
    (½ to 1 teaspoon lemon
    juice)

QUICK WHITE SAUCE

If you are in a hurry, this base
can be flavored and modified in
many ways. Melt over low heat:
    2 tablespoons butter
Add ◆ still over low heat and
stirring about 3 to 4 minutes or
until well blended and the taste
of raw flour has vanished:
    1½ to 2 tablespoons flour
Stir in slowly:
    1 cup milk, milk and light
    stock, light stock or light
    stock and cream
    Correct the seasoning
and vary the flavor with one or
more of the following:
    Celery salt
    A grating of nutmeg
    1 teaspoon lemon juice
    ½ teaspoon Worcestershire
    sauce
    1 teaspoon sherry
    1 teaspoon onion juice
    2 tablespoons chopped
    parsley
    2 tablespoons chopped
    chives
◆ Simmer and stir the sauce
with a wire whisk until it has
thickened and is smooth and
hot. Combine it with other ingredients just as it boils, so that
it will not become watery. For
creamed dishes, use about ½ as
much sauce as there are solids.

CREAM SAUCE MIX

[4 Cups Dry Mix]

This can be stored in a covered
container, refrigerated several
months. It will thicken, in all,
about 2½ to 3 quarts of sauce.
Rub:
    1 cup butter
into:
    1 cup flour
Stir in and blend thoroughly:
    2 cups nonfat milk solids
To make sauce, stir to a paste
in a saucepan ⅓ cup of the
above mixture with:
    ⅓ cup water or stock
then add:
    ⅔ cup water or stock
gradually over low heat and stir
constantly until the sauce thickens.
    Correct the seasoning

EGG CREAM SAUCE

[1¼ Cups]
This is good made with chicken
stock and cream.
Prepare:
    Cream Sauce I, page 359
Add to it:
    2 chopped hard-cooked
    eggs
    1 tablespoon capers or
    chopped pickles

FLORENTINE SAUCE

[About 2 Cups]
Combine:
    1 cup Cream Sauce I,
    page 359
    A dash of hot pepper
    sauce
    2 drops Worcestershire
    sauce
    (A dash of monosodium
    glutamate)
    1 cup finely chopped
    spinach
    A fresh grating of nutmeg
    1 tablespoon finely
    chopped parsley
If using cold for fish, do not
thin. If you use it hot, you may
thin it with:
    Cream or dry white wine

MORNAY SAUCE

[About 1¼ Cups]

Excellent for masking fish, egg and vegetable dishes. If you are using it in a dish to be browned in the oven or under the broiler, sprinkle a little grated cheese over the top first. Prepare:

>1 cup Cream Sauce I,
>   flavored with onion or
>   shallot, page 359

Beat together until blended:

>1 egg yolk
>2 tablespoons cream

▶ Add a little of the sauce to the egg yolk and cream, stirring constantly, then return the mixture to the rest of the sauce and cook until well heated. Then add:

>2 tablespoons grated
>   Parmesan cheese
>2 tablespoons grated
>   Gruyère cheese

Keep stirring with a small whisk to help melt the cheese and keep the sauce smooth while it thickens.

>Correct the seasoning

with:

>Salt and a few grains of
>   cayenne

NANTUA SAUCE

[About 1½ Cups]

For fish.

Prepare:

>1 cup Cream Sauce I,
>   page 359

Add:

>½ cup whipping cream

Rub through a fine sieve:

>2 tablespoons Shrimp
>   Buttter, page 385

Instead of the shrimp butter, you may add 1 tablespoon finely ground shrimp made into a smooth paste with 1 tablespoon butter. Heat to boiling point.

>Correct the seasoning

Garnish with:

>Finely chopped shrimp

NEWBURG SAUCE

I. [About 1 Cup]

Melt in a double boiler:

>½ cup Lobster Butter,
>   page 385

Add and cook gently until translucent:

>1 teaspoon finely chopped
>   shallots

Add and continue to cook about 3 minutes:

>¼ cup sherry or Madeira

Into:

>1 cup cream

beat:

>3 egg yolks

Add the two mixtures, stirring constantly until the sauce thickens. Use at once.

II. If you want a pink sauce for shrimp or lobster, add to the above:

>1 tablespoon tomato paste
>(1 tablespoon cognac or
>   brandy)

OYSTER SAUCE FOR FISH

[About 2 Cups]

Prepare:

>1 cup Cream Sauce II,
>   page 359

Season it well with:

>Salt
>(1 teaspoon Worcestershire
>   sauce)

Shortly before serving, bring the sauce to the boiling point and add:

>3 tablespoons chopped
>   parsley
>1 cup finely chopped
>   poached oysters and
>   juice

ANCHOVY SAUCE FOR FISH

[1 Cup]

Prepare:

>Cream Sauce I, page 359

Add to it:

>3 fillets of anchovy,
>   washed and pounded to
>   a paste

Blend it well with the sauce.

HORSERADISH SAUCE OR SAUCE ALBERT

[1 Cup]
Usually used with boiled beef or corned beef.
Prepare:
    Cream Sauce I, page 359
Remove it from the heat. Add:
    3 tablespoons prepared horseradish
    2 tablespoons whipping cream
    1 teaspoon sugar
    1 teaspoon dry mustard
    1 tablespoon vinegar
Reheat but do not boil. Serve immediately.

VELOUTÉ SAUCE OR SAUCE BLANCHE

[1½ Cups]
This is a white cream sauce made from a roux and stock base. The stock may be chicken, veal or fish, depending on the dish the sauce is to accompany. A quick Velouté may be made like Cream Sauce I, using stock in place of milk, but for a classic sauce of fine texture, proceed as directed below. ♦ The sauce should never be cooked in aluminum pans because they discolor it badly. Melt in the top of a double boiler:
    2 tablespoons butter
Stir in:
    2 tablespoons flour
When blended, add gradually:
    2 cups chicken, veal or fish stock
and stir over low heat until well combined and thickened. Add:
    ¼ cup mushroom peelings
Place in the double boiler and simmer ♦ over—not in—hot water for about 1 hour, stirring occasionally. Strain through a fine sieve, then add:
    A pinch of nutmeg
    Correct the seasoning
and stir occasionally during the cooling process to prevent a crust from forming.

AURORE SAUCE

[About 2 Cups]
Fine with fish.
Prepare:
    Velouté Sauce
Add:
    2 tablespoons tomato purée
to the sauce and mix. Let boil a little before pouring through a sieve and adding:
    A Butter Swirl

ALLEMANDE SAUCE OR THICKENED VELOUTÉ

[1½ Cups]
This is an enriched Velouté Sauce, to be used with poached chicken or vegetables. ♦ Do not let this sauce boil or it will curdle.
Prepare:
    1½ cups Velouté Sauce, above
Stir in:
    ¾ cup strong chicken stock
Blend well and reduce on medium heat to ⅔ of its original volume. Remove from the heat and add:
    1 egg yolk mixed with 2 tablespoons cream
Stir the sauce until it is slightly thickened. Just before serving, stir in:
    1 tablespoon lemon juice
    1 tablespoon butter

POULETTE SAUCE

[1½ Cups]
Prepare:
    1½ cups Allemande Sauce, above
Just before serving, add:
    1 tablespoon finely chopped parsley

PAPRIKA OR HUNGARIAN SAUCE

[About 1½ Cups]
Use for fish, poultry or veal.
Sauté until golden:
    1 finely chopped onion
in:

1 tablespoon butter

Add:

2 tablespoons mild
Hungarian paprika

and stir for 1 minute. Add gradually, stirring constantly:

1 cup cream
⅓ cup Velouté Sauce, above
Correct the seasoning

CAPER SAUCE

[1½ Cups]
For poached or broiled fish, or
mutton.
Prepare:

1½ cups Velouté or
Allemande Sauce, above

Just before serving, add:

2 tablespoons drained
chopped capers

CURRY SAUCE

I. [1½ Cups]
Pour over whole poached fish or
fish fillets.
Prepare:

1½ cups Allemande Sauce,
page 362

A few minutes before serving,
stir in:

1 teaspoon good curry
powder

II. [About 2 Cups]
Sauté slowly until tender:

¼ cup chopped onion
¼ cup chopped tart apple

in:

¼ cup butter

Stir in and cook, without browning, for 4 or 5 minutes:

2½ tablespoons flour
½ to 2 teaspoons curry
powder

Add slowly, stirring constantly
and simmer until well blended:

1 cup chicken broth
1 cup cream
½ teaspoon grated lemon
peel

If you wish to have a perfectly
smooth sauce, add the chicken
broth and grated lemon peel
only, cook for 10 minutes, strain

through a sieve, add the cream
and bring back to a boil. You
may liven up this sauce, if you
like a hot curry, with dashes of:

Hot pepper sauce
Cayenne
Ginger
Chopped chutney
Dry sherry

MUSTARD SAUCE

[1½ Cups]
Serve with poached or broiled
fish.
Prepare:

1½ cups Allemande Sauce,
page 362

Add, just before serving:

½ teaspoon dry mustard or
1 teaspoon prepared
mustard
¼ teaspoon salt
½ teaspoon freshly ground
black pepper

SOUBISE OR WHITE
ONION SAUCE

[About 1½ Cups]
This is a delicate onion-flavored
sauce for fish, poultry or vegetables.
Prepare:

1½ cups Velouté Sauce,
page 362

Sauté until transparent:

2 medium chopped onions

in:

2 tablespoons butter

Add the onions to the Velouté
Sauce and simmer over low heat
for 30 minutes, stirring occasionally. Rub the whole sauce
through a fine sieve. Finish off
the sauce with:

2 tablespoons whipping
cream
Correct the seasoning

SUPREME SAUCE

[About 2 Cups]
For fish, poultry and eggs. The
special characteristics of Supreme Sauce are its perfect

whiteness and delicacy.
Prepare:

> 1½ cups Velouté Sauce, page
> 362, made with chicken
> stock

Add:

> 1 cup strong white chicken
> stock
> ¼ cup mushroom peelings

Bring to a boil, reduce the heat
and simmer, stirring occasionally, until the sauce is reduced
to 1½ cups. Strain through a
fine sieve and add, stirring constantly:

> ½ cup whipping cream

Stir in:

> 1 tablespoon butter
> Correct the seasoning

HOT RAVIGOTE SAUCE

This sauce is served lukewarm
over variety meats, boiled fish,
light meats and poultry. Chop
until very fine:

> 2 shallots

Add:

> 1 tablespoon wine vinegar

Cook these ingredients rapidly,
stirring constantly for about 3
minutes. Add:

> 1 cup Velouté Sauce,
> page 362

to the shallots and simmer the
sauce for about 10 minutes. Stir
it from time to time. Add:

> Salt and freshly ground
> pepper

Cool the sauce to lukewarm.
Add:

> 1 tablespoon chopped
> parsley
> (1 teaspoon prepared
> mustard)
> 1 tablespoon chopped
> chervil
> 1 tablespoon chopped
> capers
> ½ teaspoon chopped chives
> ½ teaspoon chopped
> tarragon
> (A grating of fresh
> nutmeg)

SMITANE SAUCE

[About 2 Cups]
Use for roast poultry or game—
especially pheasant.
Melt in a saucepan:

> 1 tablespoon butter

Add:

> ¼ cup finely chopped
> onions

and cook until transparent, then
add:

> ½ cup dry white wine

and cook until the mixture is reduced to ½. Add:

> 1 cup Velouté, page 362
> or Brown Sauce,
> page 365

Blend and simmer 5 minutes
then add:

> 1 cup cultured sour cream
> Correct the seasoning

If a sourer effect is wanted, add:

> (A little lemon juice)

Do not allow the sauce to boil
after adding the sour cream or
it will curdle.

BREAD SAUCE

[About 3 Cups]
Usually served with small
roasted wild birds or roast meat.
Skin:

> A small onion

Stud it with:

> 3 whole cloves

Place the onion in a saucepan
with:

> 2 cups milk
> 2 tablespoons butter

Bring the milk to a boil. Add:

> 1 cup fresh white bread
> crumbs

Simmer for 15 minutes. Remove
the onion. Beat the sauce smooth
and stir in, until blended:

> 3 tablespoons cream

CHEESE SAUCE

[About 2 Cups]
Melt in a saucepan:

> 3 tablespoons butter

Stir in, until blended:

> 3 tablespoons flour

Stir in slowly:

1½ cups milk

When the sauce is smooth and hot, reduce the heat and stir in:

1 cup or less mild grated cheese or diced processed cheese

Season the sauce with:

½ teaspoon salt

⅛ teaspoon paprika

A few grains cayenne

(½ teaspoon dry mustard)

Stir the sauce until the cheese is melted.

BROWN SAUCE OR SAUCE ESPAGNOLE

[About 6 Cups]

This is one of the "sauces mères" of the French cuisine, the basis for many other sauces and dishes. Diat has said that the making of a good Espagnole is the mark of an accomplished saucier.

▶ Always stir, never whip, a Brown Sauce and use good, strong, clear beef stock. The flavor comes from the gradual "reduction" of the sauce by very slow simmering, which, if you are a perfectionist, can be 8 to 12 hours. Here is a rather more time-saving method.

Melt in a heavy saucepan:

½ cup beef or veal drippings

Add:

1 cup Mirepoix (II, 221)

When this begins to brown, add:

½ cup flour

and stir until the flour is a good brown. Then add:

10 black peppercorns

2 cups drained, peeled tomatoes or 2 cups tomato purée

½ cup coarsely chopped parsley

Stir and mix well, then add:

8 cups good beef stock

Simmer on the stove for about 2 to 2½ hours or until reduced by

½. Stir occasionally and skim off the fat as it rises to the top. Strain the sauce and stir occasionally as it cools to prevent a skin forming. The sauce should be the consistency of whipping cream, no thicker. If you are using this sauce "as is,"

Correct the seasoning

DEMI-GLAZE SAUCE

[About 4½ Cups]

This is the Espagnole, above, reduced to the nth degree. Serve with filet mignon or any meat with which Madeira Sauce is generally used.

Combine in a heavy saucepan:

4 cups Brown Sauce, above

4 cups good beef stock, flavored with mushroom trimmings

Simmer slowly, until reduced by half. Strain into a double boiler and keep warm, over hot water, while adding:

½ cup dry sherry

ORANGE SAUCE FOR DUCK OR GOOSE

[About 2 Cups]

For a true Bigarade, see page 588.

Pour off the fat from the pan in which you have roasted the bird. Deglaze the pan with:

1 cup Game Stock (II, 143)

Thicken with:

1 teaspoon arrowroot or cornstarch

mixed first with a little of the stock. In another pan, cook together until light brown:

2 tablespoons vinegar

2 tablespoons sugar

Add the sauce from the roasting pan and cook 4 or 5 minutes, then add:

1 tablespoon julienned and blanched orange rind

½ cup hot orange juice

1 teaspoon lemon juice

2 tablespoons curaçao
Correct the seasoning

Serve immediately over goose or wild or domestic duck and garnish with:

Orange sections

BORDELAISE SAUCE

For sweetbreads, chops, steaks, grilled meats.

Cook together in a saucepan:

½ cup dry red wine
4 or 5 crushed black peppercorns

until reduced to ¾, then add:

1 cup Brown Sauce, above

Simmer for 15 minutes. Add, just before serving:

¼ cup diced beef marrow, poached for a few minutes and drained
(½ teaspoon lemon juice)
½ teaspoon chopped parsley

QUICK BROWN SAUCE OR GRAVY

[About 1 Cup]

You may rub your pan with:

½ clove garlic

Melt:

2 tablespoons butter

Stir in, until blended:

2 tablespoons flour

Stir in:

1 cup canned bouillon or 1 or 2 bouillon cubes dissolved in 1 cup boiling water

Permit the gravy to reach the boiling point. Stir it constantly. Season it as required with:

Salt and pepper or paprika
Dry sherry or Worcestershire sauce
Lemon juice, catsup or chili sauce
Dried herbs

HUNTER'S SAUCE OR SAUCE CHASSEUR

[About 2 Cups]

Sauté gently until very tender:

2 tablespoons minced onion or shallots

in:

2 tablespoons butter

Stir in and sauté gently for about 2 minutes:

1 cup sliced mushrooms

Add:

½ cup dry white wine
(2 tablespoons brandy)

Simmer until reduced by ½. Add:

½ cup tomato sauce or purée
1 cup Brown Sauce, page 365

Cook for 5 minutes, then:

Correct the seasoning

and add:

1 teaspoon chopped parsley

MADEIRA SAUCE

[About 1 Cup]

This sauce may also be made with dry sherry. It is good with game or fillet of beef.

Reduce:

1 cup Brown Sauce, page 365

to ¾ its volume, then add:

¼ cup Madeira
(1 teaspoon Meat Glaze (II, 145))

Finish with a:

Butter Swirl, page 357

and another:

2 tablespoons Madeira

Keep hot, but do not allow to boil after adding the butter. You may also make this in the pan in which you have sautéed the meat. Remove the meat and pour off the fat. Deglaze the pan with the above quantity of Madeira until the wine is reduced by half, then add the Brown Sauce and cook for 10 minutes before finishing, as described above.

LYONNAISE SAUCE OR BROWN ONION SAUCE

[1¼ Cups]

A good sauce to use for leftover meat.

Melt in a saucepan:

2 tablespoons butter

Add:

2 finely chopped onions

and cook until golden brown. Add:

⅓ cup dry white wine or 2 tablespoons vinegar

If you use the wine, simmer until reduced by ½. Then add:

1 cup Brown Sauce, page 365

and simmer for 15 minutes. Just before serving, add:

1 tablespoon finely chopped parsley

MARCHAND DE VIN SAUCE

[About 2 Cups]

Serve with broiled steak.

Sauté:

1 cup finely sliced mushrooms

in:

2 tablespoons butter

Add:

½ cup hot beef stock

▶ Simmer for 10 minutes. Add:

1 cup Brown Sauce, page 365

½ cup dry red wine

▶ Simmer for 20 minutes, then:

Correct the seasoning

You may add:

(Juice of ½ lemon)

MUSHROOM SAUCE

[About 2 Cups]

For roast meat, chicken and casseroles.

Sauté:

¼ lb. sliced mushrooms

in:

2 tablespoons butter

Remove the mushrooms from the skillet. Add to the drippings:

1 cup Brown Sauce, page 365, or Quick Brown Sauce, page 366

When the sauce is heated, add the sautéed mushrooms.

SAUCE PÉRIGUEUX

[1 Cup]

Use for croquettes, shirred eggs and chicken.

Prepare:

Madeira Sauce, page 366

Just before adding the butter swirl, stir in:

1 tablespoon chopped truffles

Very similar is Sauce Périgourdine, but the truffles are finely diced instead of chopped and a dice of foie gras is added.

PIQUANT SAUCE

[About 1¼ Cups]

This sauce is excellent for giving extra zip to bland meats and for reheating leftover meat. A good sauce for pork and pigs' feet.

Lightly brown:

2 tablespoons minced onion

in:

1 tablespoon butter

Add:

2 tablespoons dry white wine or 2 tablespoons vinegar or lemon juice

and cook until the liquid is almost evaporated. Add:

1 cup Brown Sauce, page 365

and simmer for 10 minutes. Just before serving, add:

1 tablespoon chopped parsley or chopped mixed parsley, tarragon and chervil

1 tablespoon chopped sour pickles

1 tablespoon chopped capers

Correct the seasoning

SAUCE ROBERT

[1¼ Cups]

Prepare:

Piquant Sauce, above

doubling the amount of onion and omitting the parsley, chervil and tarragon. Just before serving, stir in:

1 teaspoon prepared Dijon-
type mustard
A pinch of powdered
sugar

POIVRADE OR PEPPER SAUCE

[3 Cups]

This is the traditional sauce to
serve with venison and consti-
tutes the basis of several other
game sauces. As the name suggests, it is quite peppery.
Heat:

¼ cup cooking oil

Sauté in it, until brown:

1 chopped carrot
1 chopped onion
(Game bones, trimmings
and giblets, if available)

Add:

3 sprigs parsley
1 bay leaf
A pinch of thyme
¼ cup vinegar or ¼ cup
marinade liquid, if the
game has been marinated
before cooking

Simmer until reduced to ⅓ original quantity. Add:

3 cups Brown Sauce, page
365

Bring to a boil ◗ reduce heat
and simmer for 1 hour. Add:

10 peppercorns

and simmer 5 more minutes.
Strain the sauce into another
saucepan and add again:

¼ cup marinade liquid

Cook slowly for 30 minutes
more, then add:

½ cup dry red wine
Correct the seasoning

Add enough:

Freshly ground black
pepper

to make a hot sauce.

ROSEMARY WINE SAUCE

[1 Cup]

Serve with Calf's Head, or turtle
meat.
Heat to boiling point:

½ cup good Madeira or dry
sherry

Add:

1 teaspoon mixed dried
marjoram, rosemary,
sage, bay leaf, thyme
and basil

This strongly flavored combination of herbs is known as herbs
"à tortue" in France. Remove
from heat and let stand 5 to 10
minutes. Strain off the herb-
flavored wine and add it to:

1 cup hot Brown Sauce,
page 365

ABOUT HOLLANDAISE AND OTHER EGG-THICKENED SAUCES

These delicious sauces, loaded
with calories, make a superb
dish out of the plainest and
simplest cooked vegetables or
broiled or roasted meat. But
nothing can make a cook more
frenzied than a Hollandaise
which suddenly breaks or fails
to thicken just as dinner is to
be served. To avoid such dis-
asters, here are a few tricks.
Don't try to make Hollandaise
or Béarnaise, on a very humid
day, unless you use Clarified
Butter, page 383. You will remove the cords from the egg
yolks as they make the sauce
lumpy. Cook these sauces ◗ over
—not in—hot, but not boiling,
water. If you use a heatproof
glass double boiler you can see
when the water begins to boil
and add 1 or 2 tablespoons of
cold water. ◗ Keep stirring the
sauce all the time and ◗ add the
melted butter very, very slowly
at first. Scrape the mixture away
from the sides and bottom of
the pan as you stir, to keep the
sauce smooth. As with Mayonnaise, page 345, a wooden spoon
or a whisk is the best tool for
making Hollandaise. A professional chef will make Hollandaise over low direct heat, but

don't try this unless you have a drummer's quick wrist—as it needs both fast and practiced stirring. ♦ To hold egg sauces for several hours, prepare and stir in wide-mouthed vacuum bottles, as sketched. Some of our friends freeze Hollandaise just as one can roux-based sauces.

Reheat it in a double boiler ♦ over—not in—hot water, stirring constantly so that it does not break. Should any of these egg sauces break, beat into them at once 1 to 2 tablespoons cream. Or a slightly curdled sauce can be rescued in a blender, although the texture will not be as good as an originally well-made sauce. Or it can be reconstituted, using a fresh egg yolk as for Mayonnaise, page 345.

NEVER-FAIL HOLLANDAISE SAUCE

♦ Please read About Hollandaise Sauce, page 369
[1 Cup]
Our cook calls this "holiday sauce"—isn't that a grand name for it?
Melt slowly and keep warm:
    ½ cup butter
Barely heat:
    1½ tablespoons lemon juice, dry sherry or tarragon vinegar

Have ready a small saucepan of boiling water and a tablespoon with which to measure it when ready. Place in the top of a double boiler ♦ over—not in—hot water:
    3 egg yolks
Beat the yolks with a wire whisk until they begin to thicken. Add:
    1 tablespoon boiling water
Beat again until the eggs begin to thicken. Repeat this process until you have added:
    3 more tablespoons water
Then beat in the warm lemon juice. Remove the double boiler from the heat. Beat the sauce well with a wire whisk. Beat constantly while adding the melted butter slowly and:
    ¼ teaspoon salt
    A few grains cayenne
Beat until the sauce is thick. Serve at once.

⅄ BLENDER HOLLANDAISE

[About 1 Cup]
This is easy, but not as flavorful as handmade Hollandaise. It is also paler in color. ♦ Do not make in a smaller quantity than given here, as there is, then, not enough heat to cook the eggs properly.
Have ready in your blender:
    3 egg yolks
    2 tablespoons lemon juice
    A pinch of cayenne
    ¼ teaspoon salt
Heat to bubbling stage, but do not brown:
    ½ cup butter
Cover container and turn motor on "High." After 3 seconds, remove the lid and pour the butter over the eggs in a steady stream. By the time the butter is poured in—about 30 seconds—the sauce should be finished. If not, blend on "High" about 5 seconds longer. Serve at once or keep warm by immersing blender container in warm water. This

sauce may be frozen and reconstituted over hot water.

MOCK HOLLANDAISE

For less rich versions, try one of the following or if you are in a hurry, prepare Hot Mayonnaise.

I. [About 1¼ Cups]
Mix in the top of a double boiler:

> 1 cup cultured sour cream
> Juice of 1 lemon
> 2 egg yolks
> ½ teaspoon salt
> ¼ teaspoon paprika

Stir ◗ over—not in—hot water until thick.

II. [4]
Good over vegetables such as Cauliflower, see page 281.
Place in a double boiler ◗ over —not in—boiling water:

> 2 beaten eggs
> ¼ cup cream
> ⅛ teaspoon salt
> ⅛ teaspoon freshly ground nutmeg
> 1 tablespoon lemon juice

Cook and stir these ingredients until they are thick, then add a little at a time:

> 2 tablespoons butter

Serve at once.

HOT MAYONNAISE SAUCE

[About 1 Cup]
Good over steak and fish.
Heat in a double boiler and stir:

> 1 cup mayonnaise

Add:

> Lemon juice and capers

MOUSSELINE SAUCE

[1¼ Cups]
Use for any vegetable or fish on which Hollandaise is served.
Just before serving, add:

> ½ cup whipped cream

to:

> 1 cup Hollandaise Sauce, above

Serve hot or cold.

FIGARO SAUCE

Prepare:

> 1 cup Hollandaise Sauce, above

Beat in very slowly:

> ¼ cup warm tomato purée

Add:

> 1 to 2 tablespoons chopped parsley
> Correct the seasoning

and serve.

MALTAISE SAUCE

[About 1 Cup]
Interesting on asparagus.
Add:

> 2 to 3 tablespoons orange juice
> 1 teaspoon grated orange rind

to:

> 1 cup Hollandaise Sauce, above

SAUCE BÉARNAISE

[About 1½ Cups]
Heavenly on most broiled red meat, especially beef tenderloin. It is also quite at home on fish and eggs.
Combine in the top of a double boiler:

> ½ cup white wine or red wine
> 2 tablespoons tarragon vinegar
> 1 tablespoon finely chopped shallots or onion
> 2 crushed peppercorns
> 2 sprigs chopped tarragon
> 1 sprig finely chopped chervil
> (1 sprig parsley)

Cook over direct heat until reduced by half. ◗ If you have used dried tarragon or coarsely chopped onion, now strain the mixture. Allow it to cool. Then, beating briskly ◗ over—not in— hot water, add alternately a little at a time and beat steadily

so that they are well combined
before you add in all:

    3 egg yolks
    ¾ cup melted butter
    Correct the seasoning

When you have added all the
butter, the sauce should have
the consistency of Hollandaise.

SOUFFLÉD [6]
MAYONNAISE SAUCE
FOR FISH

This is also good as a masking
for broiled tomatoes.
Broil until nearly done, see page
399:

    3 lbs. fish

Transfer them to a hot ovenproof dish. Combine and beat
well:

    ½ cup mayonnaise
    ¼ cup pickle relish
    2 tablespoons chopped
        parsley
    1 tablespoon lemon juice
    ¼ teaspoon salt
    A few grains cayenne

Beat until stiff, but not dry:

    2 egg whites

Fold them into the mayonnaise
mixture. Spread the sauce evenly
on the fish. Broil it until the
sauce is puffed and golden.

MINT SAUCE

[About 1 Cup]
The usual accompaniment to
roast lamb.
Heat:

    3 tablespoons water

Dissolve in it:

    1½ tablespoons
        confectioners' sugar

Cool the sirup and add:

    ⅓ cup finely chopped mint
        leaves
    ½ cup strong vinegar

This is best made ½ hour before serving.

SWEET-SOUR MUSTARD
SAUCE

[About 2½ Cups]
Use for ham or tongue.

Combine in a double boiler ▶
over—not in—hot water:

    ½ cup sugar
    1 tablespoon flour
    4 teaspoons dry mustard

Add gradually:

    2 cups cream

mixed with:

    2 egg yolks

Cook until thick. Stir in, gradually:

    ½ cup vinegar

SWEET-SOUR CREAM
DRESSING

[About 1 Cup]
For snap beans, cabbage, etc.
Combine and stir over very low
heat until the sauce thickens
slightly:

    1 beaten egg
    ½ cup cultured sour cream
    2 tablespoons sugar
    ¼ cup vinegar
    ½ teaspoon salt
    ¼ teaspoon paprika

Serve it hot over hot vegetables
or cold over chilled vegetables.

SWEET-SOUR BACON
SAUCE

[About 1 Cup]
Fine for green beans.
Slowly render, until crisp:

    4 thin slices of cut-up
        bacon

At the same time, you may cook
until transparent:

    (1 teaspoon minced onion)

Remove the bacon and onion
and pour off all but:

    2 tablespoons bacon grease

Add to the grease:

    ¾ cup of the bean or
        vegetable stock
    2 tablespoons vinegar
    1 to 2 tablespoons sugar

CHINESE SWEET-SOUR
SAUCE

I. [1 Cup]
Heat:

    ½ cup pineapple juice

3 tablespoons oil
2 tablespoons brown sugar
1 teaspoon soy sauce or
salt
½ teaspoon pepper
¼ cup mild vinegar

II. [2½ to 3 Cups]
Serve with Chinese Meat Balls,
page 519, or Sweet-Sour Pork,
page 488.
Have ready a paste of:

2 tablespoons cornstarch
½ cup chicken broth
2 tablespoons soy sauce

Melt in a heavy pan:

2 tablespoons butter

Add:

1 cup chicken broth
¾ to 1 cup diced green
peppers
6 slices diced canned
pineapple

Cover and simmer for 5 minutes. Add the cornstarch paste
and the following ingredients to
the peppers and pineapple:

½ cup vinegar
¾ cup pineapple juice
½ cup sugar
½ teaspoon salt
¼ teaspoon ginger

Simmer, stirring constantly, until
the mixture thickens.

CHINESE SAUCE FOR VEGETABLES

[For About 1 lb. Vegetables]
Blend until smooth:

1 tablespoon cornstarch
3 tablespoons cold water

Add:

½ teaspoon salt
1 tablespoon soy sauce
½ teaspoon finely grated
gingerroot

Pour over vegetables that are
cooking. Stir well until the
whole mixture comes to a boil.

CURRANT JELLY SAUCES

I. [About 1¼ Cups]
For game or cold meat.

Heat in a double boiler just before serving:

¾ cup currant jelly

Stir in:

½ cup Indian chutney
1 teaspoon lemon juice
1 tablespoon brandy
Salt

II. [About ½ Cup]
Make a simplified version by
mixing:

½ cup jelly
2 tablespoons horseradish
½ teaspoon dry mustard

HOT CUMBERLAND SAUCE

[About 2 Cups]
This calls for many ingredients,
but you may omit some or substitute others.
Combine:

1 teaspoon dry mustard
1 tablespoon brown sugar
¼ teaspoon powdered
ginger
A few grains cayenne
¼ teaspoon salt
¼ teaspoon ground cloves
1½ cups red wine, preferably
port
(½ cup seedless raisins)
(½ cup blanched slivered
almonds)

Simmer the sauce, covered, for
8 minutes.
Dissolve:

2 tablespoons cornstarch

in:

2 tablespoons cold water

Stir this into the sauce. Let it
simmer for about 2 minutes.
Stir in:

¼ cup red currant jelly
1 tablespoon grated orange
and lemon rind
¼ cup orange juice
2 tablespoons lemon juice

BURGUNDY SAUCE OR SAUCE BOURGUIGNONNE

[1 Cup]
For snails and egg dishes.
Reduce by ½ a mixture of:

2 cups dry red wine,
preferably red Burgundy
2 minced shallots
A few sprigs parsley
A pinch of thyme
¼ bay leaf
(Mushroom peelings)

Strain the mixture. When ready to serve, heat and add:

1 to 1½ tablespoons
Kneaded Butter, page
357
(A dash of cayenne)

RAISIN CIDER OR BEER SAUCE

[About 1½ Cups]
Good with hot or cold ham or smoked tongue.
Combine in a saucepan:

¼ cup firmly packed brown
sugar
1½ tablespoons cornstarch
⅛ teaspoon salt

Stir in:

1 cup fresh cider or beer
¼ cup raisins, cut in halves

Put in a cheese cloth bag and hang it in the cooking sauce from the edge of the pan:

8 whole cloves
1 two-inch stick cinnamon

Cook and stir for about 10 minutes. Add:

1 tablespoon butter

Remove the spices. Serve the sauce very hot.

SAUCE FOR LIGHT MEAT GAME

After roasting the game bird, which is barded with salt pork or bacon and basted with equal quantities of butter and white wine, flame it in:

⅛ cup cognac: 1 oz.

Remove the game and keep warm. Degrease the pan juices and reduce them over low heat for 1 minute. Then add, for each small bird:

1 egg yolk

Beat in:

½ cup whipping cream

Stir until thickened ◗ but do not allow the sauce to boil. Season well.

BERCY SAUCE

[¼ Cup]
White wine is best for this sauce, which is served on fish.
Cook until transparent:

1 teaspoon finely chopped
shallots

in:

1 tablespoon butter

Add:

¼ cup dry white or red
wine
¼ cup Fish Fumet (II,
143)

and simmer until reduced by ½. Thicken the mixture with:

Kneaded butter, made by
creaming together 1
teaspoon flour and
2 tablespoons butter

stirring it in briskly until well blended.
Add:

1 teaspoon chopped parsley
Correct the seasoning

WHITE WINE SAUCE FOR FISH

[About 1¼ Cups]
Reduce by ½ over medium heat a mixture of:

¼ cup white wine
1 bay leaf
2 cloves
2 black peppercorns
(1½-inch piece gingerroot)
¼ cup fish stock
1 teaspoon chopped shallot

Strain and add to:

1 cup strained Cream
Sauce I, page 359

To make a sauce that coats well and browns beautifully, add:

2 tablespoons whipped
cream

WHITE WINE SAUCE FOR LIGHT MEATS

[About 1 Cup]
Serve over Sautéed Brains, page

540, or other light meats.
Add to the pan drippings and
sauté until light yellow:

>1 tablespoon chopped
>onion

Stir in until smooth:

>1½ tablespoons flour

Stir in gradually, until the sauce
is smooth and very hot:

>½ cup chicken or veal
>stock
>½ cup dry white wine

Add:

>1 tablespoon chopped
>parsley or chives
>Salt, as needed

SOYER'S UNIVERSAL DEVIL SAUCE

We have chosen this sauce from
Alexis Soyer's "Culinary Cam-
paign," a fabulous account of the
Crimean War, through which he
cooked his way with abandon.
No one brought more conviction
to his work, whether changing
the diet of the British armed
forces, cooking at the Reform
Club or remolding the cooking
habits of the English lower
classes—which he attempted
through his Shilling Cook Book.
The original recipe called for a
tablespoon of cayenne pepper.
We have changed it to a small
pinch, for in Soyer's day cayenne
was baked into a sort of bread
and then ground, making it
about the same strength as a
mild paprika.
Rub any deviled food with the
following mixture:

>1 good tablespoon Durham
>mustard
>¼ cup chili vinegar
>1 tablespoon grated
>horseradish
>2 bruised shallots
>1 teaspoon salt
>A few grains cayenne
>½ teaspoon black pepper
>1 teaspoon sugar
>(2 teaspoons chopped
>chilies)

>(2 raw egg yolks)

Soyer's instructions are to "broil
slowly at first and end as near as
possible the Pandemonium Fire."

BARBECUE SAUCES

Please read About Skewer Cooking, page 174. It is important to
baste with barbecue sauces
only during the last 15 minutes
of cooking. Too long cooking of
the sauce will make the spices
bitter.

I. [About 2 Cups]
Sauté until brown:

>¼ cup chopped onions

in:

>1 tablespoon drippings or
>other fat

Add and simmer for 20 minutes:

>½ cup water
>2 tablespoons vinegar
>1 tablespoon
>Worcestershire sauce
>¼ cup lemon juice
>2 tablespoons brown sugar
>1 cup chili sauce
>½ teaspoon salt
>¼ teaspoon paprika
>1 teaspoon pepper
>1 teaspoon mustard

II. [About 1½ Cups]
Simmer for 15 minutes, stirring
frequently:

>12 to 14 oz. tomato catsup
>½ cup white distilled
>vinegar
>1 teaspoon sugar
>A liberal seasoning of red
>and black pepper
>⅛ teaspoon salt

FEROCIOUS BARBECUE SAUCE

Combine and heat:

>1½ cups Barbecue Sauce II,
>above
>¼ of a seeded lemon, diced
>fine
>½ teaspoon ground cumin
>1 teaspoon ground
>coriander
>⅛ teaspoon Spanish paprika

⅛ teaspoon saffron
¼ teaspoon ground ginger

BARBECUE SAUCE
FOR FOWL

[For 1 Fowl]
I. Combine and heat:
    4 teaspoons lemon juice
    1 teaspoon Worcestershire
        sauce
    1 teaspoon tomato catsup
    1 tablespoon butter

II. Cook slowly until golden:
    1 medium chopped onion
    1 minced clove garlic
in:
    3 tablespoons fat
Add and simmer for 30 minutes:
    3 tablespoons soy or
        Worcestershire sauce
    1 cup water
    1 red pepper
    2 tablespoons vinegar
    2 to 4 tablespoons brown
        sugar
    1 cup catsup
    1 teaspoon prepared
        mustard
    ½ cup celery
    ½ teaspoon salt
Then add:
    ¼ cup lemon juice

QUICK CANNED SOUP
SAUCES

Not only can the thin canned
consommés and broths be used
for flavoring sauces, but some
of the condensed cream soups
can be quickly made into acceptable sauces. ◗ Taste before
salting them.
I. [1¼ Cups]
For chicken, veal and fish.
Heat:
    1 cup condensed cream of
        chicken soup
    2 tablespoons butter
    2 to 4 tablespoons rich
        chicken or vegetable
        stock
    A grating of lemon rind

II. [1¼ Cups]
For beef hash.
Heat:
    1 cup cream of mushroom
        soup
    2 to 4 tablespoons strong
        beef stock
    ½ teaspoon meat glaze
        Few drops garlic juice
    1 tablespoon butter

III. [1¼ Cups]
For creaming vegetables.
Heat:
    1 cup cream of celery soup
    2 tablespoons butter
    2 to 4 tablespoons chicken
        stock
    1 tablespoon chopped
        chives

DRIED SOUP SAUCES   [4]

These are not as quick as the
canned ones but can provide a
well-flavored base when reconstituted with half the amount of
liquid called for normally. Use
in making sauces for casseroles.
The dried vegetables swell as
the casserole cooks.
Try heating:
    1 package dried cream of
        leek, cream of mushroom
        or smoky pea soup
    1½ cups light cream or top
        milk
Use with leftover chicken or
veal, with rice or noodles in a
casserole. Or combine and heat:
    1 package dried onion soup
    1½ to 2 cups water
and add to meat and vege-
tables in a casserole. Again, do
not salt—and go easy on other
seasonings in these sauces—until
they have cooked for about 20
minutes and you have tasted
them.

QUICK À LA KING SAUCE

[About 1½ Cups]
To the rescue, whenever this
type of sauce is required.
Sauté until tender:

1 minced green pepper in:

1 tablespoon butter

Add the contents of:

1 can condensed mushroom
soup: 10½ oz.
¼ cup milk

Heat the sauce and add:

1 pimiento, cut into strips
(2 tablespoons dry sherry)

QUICK CREOLE SAUCE

[2½ Cups]
To:

2 cups Quick Tomato
Sauce, page 377

Add:

½ cup finely chopped green
peppers, onion, celery,
olives and pimiento

QUICK TOMATO CHEESE SAUCE

[About 1½ Cups]
Good over eggs.
Heat in a double boiler:

1 can condensed tomato
soup: 10½ oz.

Add:

¼ teaspoon salt
¼ teaspoon pepper or
paprika

Stir and cook these ingredients
until they are hot. Beat in:

1 cup or more grated
cheese

Use a wire whisk. Beat the sauce
until the cheese is melted.

UNTHICKENED TOMATO SAUCE

[About 4 Cups]
Place over low heat:

3 tablespoons olive oil

Add and stir for about 3 minutes:

1 large chopped Bermuda
onion
2 chopped celery ribs with
leaves
1 carrot, cut in small pieces
(½ chopped green pepper,
seeds and fibrous portions
removed)

(1 chopped clove garlic)

Add:

4 cups canned tomatoes or
6 large fresh tomatoes

If these are very juicy, peel and
squeeze slightly to get rid of
excess liquid and seeds. Add:

1 sprig thyme, basil or
tarragon
1 teaspoon salt
⅛ teaspoon pepper
1 teaspoon sugar

Cook the sauce gently, uncovered, until thick, for about 45
minutes. ◗ Watch it, so that it
does not burn. Put it through a
fine strainer. Add seasoning, if
needed. This sauce will keep for
several days.

THICKENED TOMATO SAUCE

[About 1½ Cups]
Bring to a boil and then ◗ simmer for 30 minutes before sieving:

2 cups canned tomatoes
1 onion, stuck with 3 cloves
2 chopped celery ribs with
leaves
1 diced carrot
1 Bouquet Garni (II, 220)
1 bay leaf
(½ chopped green pepper)

◗ Be sure to get all the pulpy
residue when sieving, so that
only cloves, leaves and seeds remain in the sieve. This well-flavored pulp helps thicken the
sauce. Melt in a saucepan:

3 tablespoons butter

Stir in, until blended:

2 tablespoons flour

Add the strained thickish stock
slowly with:

¼ teaspoon sugar

◗ Simmer and stir the stock for
about 5 to 10 minutes.

Correct the seasoning

Flavor with:

(1 tablespoon fresh basil)

QUICK TOMATO SAUCE

[About 3 Cups]

Strain:

    1 large can Italian
        tomatoes

Add:

    ½ can tomato paste: 6 oz.
    ½ teaspoon salt
    1 tablespoon onion juice
        or 2 tablespoons finely
        grated onion
    ½ teaspoon sugar

Bring to a boil and simmer
gently for 15 to 20 minutes.

SHRIMP SAUCE FOR FISH

[3½ Cups]

This is an elaborate sauce. Do
not hesitate to deduct from, add
to or alter it.
Prepare:

    2 cups Thickened Tomato
        Sauce, page 376, or 2
        cups Cream Sauce I,
        page 359

Season the sauce well. Add and
heat to the boiling point:

    1 teaspoon Worcestershire
        or 2 teaspoons chili sauce
    2 tablespoons chopped
        parsley
    ¼ cup chopped olives
    ½ cup boiled or canned
        shrimp
    ½ cup sautéed or canned
        mushrooms
    ¼ cup finely chopped celery

Serve the sauce with baked or
boiled fish or place the fish on a
platter and pour the sauce over
it. Heat it under a broiler.

ITALIAN TOMATO PASTE

This flavorful paste is diluted in
a little boiling water or stock
and added to sauces and soups.
Fine in spaghetti and noodle
dishes and as a dressing for
cooked vegetables or salads.
Wash and cut into slices:

    1½ pecks ripe Italian
        tomatoes: 6 quarts

Add:

    3 teaspoons salt

You may add:

    1 large celery stalk, cut up
        with some leaves
    ¾ cup chopped onion
    3 tablespoons fresh herbs
        or 1 tablespoon dried
        herbs
    ¾ teaspoon peppercorns
    12 cloves
    1 two-inch stick cinnamon
    (1 minced clove garlic)

Simmer these ingredients until
the tomatoes are soft. Stir frequently. Put the vegetables
through a fine sieve. Simmer the
pulp over hot water or simmer
it over direct heat with some
means of protecting it from the
bottom by using an asbestos
pad. Stir it frequently, as it
burns easily. After several hours,
when the pulp is thick and reduced by about ½, spread the
paste to the depth of ½ inch
on moist plates. Cut into the
paste to permit the air to penetrate. Place the paste in the sun
to dry or dry it in a 250° oven.
When the paste is dry enough,
roll it into balls. They may be
dipped in salad oil. Store them
in airtight jars or store the paste
in a tin box with waxed paper
between the layers.

TOMATO PASTE
OR VELVET

[About ¾ Cup]

Wash, then mash:

    6 large ripe tomatoes

Melt:

    2 tablespoons butter

Add the tomatoes and:

    1 teaspoon brown sugar
    ¼ teaspoon paprika
    ¾ teaspoon salt

Cook the tomatoes over low
heat, stirring constantly or in a
double boiler, until they are the
consistency of thick paste. Put
the paste through a strainer.
This makes a relish or fine addition to sauces.

MEXICAN SAUCE

[About 1 Cup]
Just what you might expect.
You will feel hot inside, down
to your toes. Use with Cowboy
Eggs, page 186.
Place in a small saucepan and
simmer until fairly thick:

¾ cup canned tomatoes or
   about 3 large, skinned
   and quartered, peeled
   and seeded fresh
   tomatoes
6 tablespoons chili sauce
2 teaspoons dry mustard
3 tablespoons grated or
   prepared horseradish
½ teaspoon sugar
¾ teaspoon salt
¼ teaspoon pepper
   A few grains cayenne
¾ teaspoon curry powder
6 tablespoons vinegar
1 teaspoon onion juice
1 sliced clove garlic
Strain the sauce. Add:
1 teaspoon dried or
   1 tablespoon fresh herbs
This may be served—in discreet
quantities—by itself but it combines excellently with hot cream
sauce or hot or cold mayonnaise.
Use as much of the Mexican
sauce as you find palatable.

SPAGHETTI MEAT SAUCE

[About 2½ Quarts]
Mince and cook over very slow
heat:
3 slices bacon
Stir in and sauté:
¼ cup chopped onion
½ lb. ground round steak
When the meat is nearly done,
add:
2½ cups pressed drained
   tomatoes
½ cup chopped green
   peppers
1 cup chopped mushrooms
   or ½ lb. to 1 lb. fresh
   sliced Sautéed
   Mushrooms, page 296
   Salt, cayenne or paprika

½ lb. grated cheese: 2 cups
Simmer ♦ uncovered 20 or 30
minutes. If more liquid is needed
after adding the spaghetti, add:
½ cup hot stock or canned
   bouillon

ITALIAN MEAT SAUCE
FOR SPAGHETTI

[About 1 Quart]
Heat:
½ cup olive oil
Add:
1 pressed clove garlic
1 lb. ground round steak
¼ lb. ground lean pork
2 cups Italian tomatoes
½ cup Italian tomato paste
½ cup beef or veal stock
1½ teaspoons salt
¼ teaspoon pepper
1 bay leaf
Simmer the sauce uncovered for
about 1 hour. Add the last 15
minutes:
(½ cup sliced mushrooms)
Season it with:
1 to 2 tablespoons fresh
   basil
Serve over:
Cooked spaghetti or
   noodles
with:
Grated Parmesan cheese

SPAGHETTI SAUCE   [4]
WITH LIVER

Melt:
2 tablespoons butter or
   drippings
Sauté in it until light brown:
½ cup chopped onions
Add and sauté very lightly:
1 cup cubed liver or
   chicken livers
Add and simmer for about 15
minutes:
½ cup tomato sauce
Season with:
1 teaspoon salt
⅛ teaspoon pepper
(¼ teaspoon basil)
Serve the sauce over noodles,

spaghetti, etc., garnished with:
Parsley

BOLOGNESE SAUCE

[About 2 Cups]
This is an interesting variation
on the usual meat sauce for
pasta.
Melt in a large saucepan:
⅓ cup butter
Add:
¼ cup minced lean ham or
Canadian bacon
¼ cup finely chopped carrot
¼ cup finely chopped onion
Stir and cook for 1 or 2 minutes. Add:
1 cup chopped lean beef
and brown it over medium heat,
stirring occasionally, then add:
2 tablespoons tomato paste
1 strip lemon peel
A pinch of nutmeg
1 cup beef stock
(½ cup dry white wine)
Partially cover and simmer
slowly for 1 hour. Remove from
heat, take out the lemon peel
and stir in:
¼ cup whipping cream
just before serving with:
Green Noodles, page 149,
or Lasagne, page 176

MARINARA SAUCE

[About 1½ Cups]
Keep this sauce on hand. Use a
little on green beans or serve
over meatless spaghetti.
Sauté lightly:
1 minced clove garlic
in:
2 tablespoons olive oil and
the oil from the anchovies
Add slowly:
2½ cups canned pressed and
drained whole or Italian
tomatoes
then stir in:
6 finely chopped anchovies
½ teaspoon orégano
1 tablespoon chopped
parsley
Bring to a boil then ▶ reduce

heat and simmer uncovered 15
to 20 minutes, stirring occasionally. If served with spaghetti,
pass with:
Grated Parmesan cheese
Try omitting the orégano and
adding:
(5 chopped canned
artichoke hearts)
Simmer 3 or 4 minutes more.

SEA FOOD SPAGHETTI SAUCE

[About 1 Quart]
Heat:
1½ cups condensed tomato
soup
Melt in a saucepan over slow
heat:
¼ cup olive oil or butter
Stir in and cook until transparent:
¼ cup or more chopped
onion
¾ cup chopped green
pepper
Stir in slowly:
½ cup Stock (II, 141)
When the sauce is hot, add very
slowly, stirring constantly:
½ lb. cooked or canned
diced lobster, crab,
shrimp or tuna
Remove from heat and add:
½ lb. diced cheese:
Mozzarella or Scamorza
Correct the seasoning
and stir in cheese until melted.
Pour over cooked spaghetti.

QUICK SHRIMP AND CLAM SAUCE FOR PASTA

[Enough for 1 lb. Pasta]
Heat in a skillet:
6 tablespoons olive oil
Add:
3 minced cloves garlic
and cook gently for 5 minutes.
Add:
¾ cup finely chopped
parsley
1 cup minced clams or
mussels with liquid

½ lb. shelled raw shrimp,
cut in bite size pieces
(⅛ teaspoon orégano)

Heat until bubbling and the shrimp is pink. Serve at once over hot cooked sea shell pasta —conchiglie—to complete the marine flavor. This goes down well with seafood addicts who don't care for the usual tomato sauces. Pass with:

Grated Parmesan or
Romano cheese

OCTOPUS PASTA SAUCE

[For 1 lb. Linguini Pasta]

Heat in a large saucepan:

1 to 1¼ cups olive oil

Add:

1¼ cups seeded, peeled fresh
tomatoes
⅔ to 1 cup finely chopped
parsley
1 teaspoon salt
2 cloves garlic

To remove the garlic before serving, see (II, 210). Simmer the mixture for 15 to 20 minutes. Add:

1½ cups cooked octopus, cut
into bite size pieces

Simmer for another 15 to 20 minutes. Toss with the cooked, drained pasta and serve at once.

CREOLE SAUCE

[About 2 Cups]

Melt over low heat:

2 tablespoons butter

Add and cook, covered, for about 2 minutes:

¼ cup chopped onion
1 minced clove garlic
6 shredded green olives

Add and cook until the sauce is thick, about 50 minutes:

1½ cups canned tomatoes or
½ cup tomatoes and
1 cup Brown Sauce,
page 365
½ chopped green pepper,
with seeds and
membranes removed
½ bay leaf

A pinch of thyme
1 teaspoon chopped
parsley
1 teaspoon white or brown
sugar
⅓ teaspoon salt
A few grains cayenne
(1 tablespoon dry sherry)
(¼ cup chili sauce)
(2 tablespoons diced ham)
(½ cup sliced mushrooms)

ABOUT MARINADES

Never underestimate the power of a marinade. ▶ Choose your type carefully if an originally delicate food flavor is to be preserved. These aromatic tenderizing liquids are easily abused. There is usually an acid in their make-up, so any dish in which they are soaked should be glass, glazed or impervious metal—like stainless steel or stainless enamel. Use wooden spoons in stirring or turning.

The simplest marinades are, first, a means of spreading flavor or preserving a better color; and immersion may last only a few minutes. Spicier, stronger marinades may be devised to make bland food more interesting or to mask off-flavor. But perhaps the most important function of a marinade is to tenderize tougher foods. Sometimes these replace and sometimes are combined with papaya extract, which tenderizes.

Marinades may be either raw or cooked. ▶ The cooked ones make their flavor more available to the food and should be prepared in advance and ▶ thoroughly chilled before use. They are best to use if the marinade exceeds 12 hours. Marinating is hastened by higher temperatures, but so is the danger of bacterial activity.

▶ Refrigerate any foods in their marinade if the marination period indicated is 1 hour or more or if the weather is hot or stormy.

A marinade is also used in finishing a sauce. So do not discard it before deciding whether you need it for your meat when it has been cooked. Sauce Poivrade for venison is an example. And some dishes, such as Hasenpfeffer and Sauerbraten, are cooked in the marinade, which is then converted into a sauce proper—just before serving.

When using the same marinade for cubed meat or one whole piece, soak the cubes for only 2 to 3 hours and the whole 4- or 5-lb. piece overnight. Longer marination may be too pungent and kill the flavor of the meat. In an emergency, try mixing oil and vinegar with packaged dried salad seasonings for a quickly prepared marinade.

MARINADES FOR VEGETABLES

Marinated vegetables are usually served cold as hors d'oeuvre or salads. French dressing seasoned with herbs, Vinaigrette and Ravigote Sauces are all suitable for the short-term marinating of vegetables. See also Vegetables à la Grecque, page 257.

FISH OR LAMB MARINADE

[Enough for 1 lb. Lamb Kebabs]
I. Combine:

    2 tablespoons lemon juice
    ¼ cup olive oil
    1 teaspoon salt
    ⅛ teaspoon pepper

Marinate refrigerated and covered for at least 3 hours. Turn frequently.

II. Combine:

    ½ teaspoon turmeric
    ½ teaspoon powdered ginger
    1 small pressed clove garlic
    1 tablespoon lemon juice
    ½ teaspoon grated lemon rind

Toss the meat in this mixture and leave to marinate covered and refrigerated for 24 hours.

II. Combine:

    ¼ cup pineapple juice
    2 teaspoons soy sauce
    2 teaspoons lemon juice
    1 minced clove garlic

Marinate covered and refrigerated for 2 hours, turning the meat frequently.

LAMB OR GAME MARINADE

[About 1 Cup]
For marinated leg of lamb.
Combine:

    ½ cup dry red wine
    ¼ cup vinegar
    ¼ cup olive oil
    3 to 4 juniper berries
    A sprig of parsley
    A sprig of thyme
    2 bay leaves
    1 crushed clove garlic
    2 slices onion
    A pinch of nutmeg
    1 tablespoon sugar
    1 teaspoon salt
    A dash of hot pepper sauce

Marinate the meat, covered and refrigerated, for 24 hours.

MARINADE FOR VENISON

[For 5 lbs. Meat]
Cover venison with:

    1 cup each of water and dry red wine

Add:

    6 or 8 black peppercorns
    1 bay leaf
    8 to 10 whole cloves
    1 sliced onion
    (1 small sprig rosemary)

Permit the meat to remain in the marinade, covered and refrigerated, from 1 to 3 days. Turn it from time to time.

SASSATIES SAUCE
OR MARINADE

[For a 3-lb. Lamb]
Soak overnight:
>½ cup dried apricots

Cook them until soft and press through a sieve or purée in the ⅄ blender. Sauté until golden:
>3 large sliced onions
>1 minced clove garlic

in:
>2 tablespoons butter

Add and cook for a minute longer:
>1 tablespoon curry powder

Then add the apricot purée with:
>1 tablespoon sugar
>½ teaspoon salt
>3 tablespoons vinegar
>A few grains cayenne
>6 lemon or orange leaves

Bring to a boil, then remove from heat, cool and pour over raw meat, which marinates overnight in the sauce. Fry or grill the meat, which should be cut into small, thin, round pieces. Heat the sauce to boiling and pour over the grilled pieces of meat. Serve with rice.

COOKED MARINADE
FOR GAME

[About 8 Cups]
This is a cooked marinade, which can be stored in the refrigerator and used as needed for venison, mutton or hare.
Sauté a combination of:
>1 cup chopped celery
>1 cup chopped carrot
>1 cup chopped onion

in:
>¼ cup cooking oil

until they begin to color. Then add:
>8 cups vinegar
>4 cups water
>½ cup coarsely chopped parsley
>3 bay leaves
>1 tablespoon thyme
>1 tablespoon basil
>1 tablespoon cloves

>1 tablespoon allspice berries
>A pinch of mace
>1 tablespoon crushed peppercorns
>6 crushed cloves garlic

Simmer for 1 hour. Strain and cool.

BEER MARINADE

I. [2 Cups]
Use for beef.
Combine:
>1½ cups beer
>½ cup salad oil

stirring the oil in slowly. Then add:
>1 clove garlic
>2 tablespoons lemon juice
>1 tablespoon sugar
>1 teaspoon salt
>3 cloves

II. [2 Cups]
A more pungent mix for beef or pork.
Combine:
>1½ cups beer
>½ teaspoon salt
>1 tablespoon dry mustard
>1 teaspoon ground ginger
>3 tablespoons soy sauce
>⅛ teaspoon hot pepper sauce
>2 tablespoons sugar
>4 tablespoons marmalade
>2 cloves minced garlic

PORK MARINADE

[Enough for 1 lb. of
Pork Chops]
Combine:
>3 tablespoons chili sauce
>1½ tablespoons lemon juice
>1 tablespoon grated onion
>¼ teaspoon dry mustard
>2 teaspoons Worcestershire sauce
>½ teaspoon salt
>¼ teaspoon paprika

MARINADE FOR CHICKEN

[¾ Cup]

Use for chicken to be broiled or grilled.

Combine:

> ¼ cup cooking oil
> ½ cup dry white wine
> 1 minced clove garlic
> 1 finely chopped medium-sized onion
> ½ teaspoon celery salt
> ½ teaspoon salt
> ½ teaspoon coarsely ground black pepper
> ¼ teaspoon dried thyme, tarragon or rosemary

Mix well. Chill several hours in covered jar or dish. Shake well, then pour over chicken pieces. Chill about 3 hours, turning pieces at least once.

ABOUT SEASONED BUTTERS AND BUTTER SAUCES

Butter sauces are quick, tasty and simple. The main thing is to use fresh, good butter, preferably unsalted. For other seasoned butters used as Spreads, see (II, 56). For Snail Butters, see page 384.

Allow about 1 tablespoon butter per serving for butter sauces. A few butter sauces are melted, but most seasoned butters are creamed and served in solid form, being allowed to melt on the hot fish, meat or vegetables. You may form the butter into fancy shapes and molds, see page 56. Most of the solid seasoned butters may be prepared more quickly and taste almost as good, when made, as melted butter sauces. But if you use melted butter, dress the food in the kitchen. Make sure you spoon out the seasonings with the butter. They will sink to the bottom if you serve the melted butter at table in a sauce boat. There are some butters, such as shrimp and lobster, which are used to flavor and finish sauces,

but rarely are served by themselves as sauces.

Seasoned butters may be ❄ frozen for several weeks. But they ▶ should not be refrigerated longer than 24 hours, as the herbs deteriorate quickly.

DRAWN OR CLARIFIED BUTTER

There is no mystery about drawn or clarified butter. It is merely melted butter with the sediment removed. But, as it is used in so many different ways—as a sauce for cooked lobster, to make brown and black butter and as a baking ingredient— here is the recipe.

Melt over low heat:

> Butter

When completely melted, remove from heat, let stand for a few minutes, allowing the milk solids to settle to the bottom. Skim the butter fat from the top and place in a container. This is the clarified drawn butter ready for use.

BROWN BUTTER OR [4] BEURRE NOISETTE

Brown and black butters can only be made successfully with clarified butter. The sediment in unclarified butter will tend to brown and make sauce speckled and bitter. Use for asparagus, broccoli and brains.

Melt in a saucepan and cook slowly until light brown:

> ¼ cup clarified butter

BLACK BUTTER OR [4] BEURRE NOIR

Use for fish, eggs, vegetables and brains. Melt very slowly, until very dark brown:

> ¼ cup clarified butter

Stir in at once:

> 1 teaspoon vinegar or lemon juice

If served with brains or fish, you may add:

1 tablespoon chopped
capers

Serve immediately.

MEUNIÈRE OR LEMON [4] BUTTER

Prepare:

Brown Butter, page 383

Add:

1 tablespoon chopped
parsley
1 teaspoon lemon juice
Correct the seasoning

ALMOND BUTTER

[⅓ Cup]

This is often used in cream sauces, for sautéed chicken and other "amandine" dishes. Another version for such dishes is Amandine Garnish, page 390.

Cream:

¼ cup butter

Blanch:

¼ cup Almonds (II, 189)

Remove the skins and pound the almonds to a paste with:

1 teaspoon water

Add gradually to the butter, blending well. Rub through a fine sieve.

ANCHOVY BUTTER [4]

Fine spread on hot broiled fish, steak or canapés.

Cream until soft:

¼ cup butter

Beat in:

1 teaspoon anchovy paste
⅛ teaspoon onion juice
¼ teaspoon lemon juice
A few grains cayenne

BERCY BUTTER [4]

Simmer in a saucepan:

2 teaspoons finely chopped
shallots
¾ cup dry white wine

until reduced to ¼ original quantity. Cool. Cream together

and blend into the wine and shallot mixture:

¼ cup butter
2 teaspoons finely chopped
parsley
Correct the seasoning

and serve on broiled meats.

CAVIAR BUTTER [6 to 8]

A lovely fish garnish.

Cream:

½ cup butter

Add:

1 tablespoon lemon juice
¼ cup black caviar
Salt, if necessary

Chill slightly, mold or cut into shapes and serve.

MAÎTRE D'HÔTEL [4] BUTTER

Good over broiled steak.

Cream until it is soft:

¼ cup butter

Add:

½ teaspoon salt
⅛ teaspoon white pepper
1 teaspoon chopped parsley

Add very slowly, stirring the sauce constantly:

¾ to 1½ tablespoons lemon
juice

COLBERT BUTTER [4]

Use on fish and roasted meats.

Cream together:

¼ cup Maître d'Hôtel
Butter, above
½ teaspoon melted beef
extract or meat glaze
¼ teaspoon finely chopped
fresh tarragon

SNAIL BUTTER

[About 1 Cup]

Should any of this be left from stuffing the snails ✻ freeze for a short period for use on steaks, fish or vegetables.

Cream until soft:

¾ cup butter

Work into it:

1 to 2 tablespoons minced
shallots
1 to 2 well-crushed cloves
garlic
(1 tablespoon minced
celery)
1 tablespoon minced
parsley
½ teaspoon salt
Freshly ground pepper

DEVILED BUTTER [4]
FOR SEAFOOD

Work until soft:
¼ cup butter
Combine it with:
½ teaspoon dry mustard
2 teaspoons wine vinegar
2 teaspoons Worcestershire
sauce
¼ teaspoon salt
1/16 teaspoon cayenne
2 egg yolks
Beat well.

GARLIC BUTTER [4]

This is good on steak, if you are
a garlic fancier, or it can be
used for garlic bread. Boil in a
little water for 5 or 6 minutes:
1 to 3 cloves garlic
Drain, crush and pound well in
a mortar with:
¼ cup butter

GREEN OR RAVIGOTE
BUTTER

Use for broiled fish, to give
sauces a green color or in the
making of Ravigote Sauce, page
364.
Chop until fine:
2 shallots
1 teaspoon fresh tarragon
1 teaspoon fresh chervil
1 teaspoon fresh parsley
6 to 8 spinach leaves
Blanch these ingredients for 5
minutes, then plunge in cold
water, drain and dry in a towel.
Pound them in a mortar or bowl.
Work in gradually:
¼ cup butter
Salt, if needed

SHRIMP OR LOBSTER
BUTTER

[½ Cup]
This should appeal to frugal
cooks. It uses every last bit of
your shellfish, and a deliciously
flavored pinkish butter is the
result. Use for finishing cream
sauces served with fish or with
the shellfish you have used for
the butter.
Dry the shells from:
1 lb. shrimp or 1 large
lobster
in a low oven for a short time.
Pound them in a mortar or put
them through the food grinder,
so that they are broken up as
finely as possible. Melt:
½ cup butter
in a double boiler ▶ over—not
in—hot water. Add the shells
and:
2 tablespoons water
Simmer for 10 minutes. ▶ Do
not let the butter boil. Line a
sieve with cheesecloth or fine
muslin and strain the hot butter
into a bowl of ice water. Refrigerate and skim off the butter
when it hardens.

WHITE BUTTER [4]

Use for poached fish, making the
fumet required from the same
type of fish. Simmer together,
until reduced to ¼ original volume:
1 teaspoon finely chopped
shallots
¼ cup wine vinegar
¼ cup Fish Fumet
(II, 143)
Cool and add, a little at a time:
¼ cup softened butter
beating constantly with a sauce
whisk until the sauce is creamy
and whitened, rather like
whipped cream.
Correct the seasoning
Add:
(1 teaspoon chopped
parsley)
2 tablespoons mixture of

chopped fresh fennel,
parsley, chives, basil,
chervil or tarragon or
1 tablespoon of the
dried herbs

POLONAISE OR [4]
BROWNED CRUMB SAUCE

A garnish for vegetables.
Brown:
    1/3 cup fine dry bread crumbs
in:
    Meunière Butter,
    page 384
Garnish the vegetable with:
    Hard-cooked, finely
    chopped egg
and pour the sauce over it. If
you wish, you may sauté:
    (1 tablespoon minced
    onion)
in the butter, until transparent,
before adding the bread crumbs.

BUTTER SAUCE FOR
CANNED OR BOILED
VEGETABLES

Drain the vegetables. Permit the
stock or juice to boil until it is
reduced by 1/2. Add to it:
    Melted butter
    Seasonings

ABOUT GLAZES
AND GLAÇAGE

These terms are among the very
trickiest in the cooking vocabulary and we might try to
straighten them out right here.
They apply to both glazes for
candies, nuts and desserts and
to the desserts themselves. They
also apply to a number of important processes and coatings
for savory items.

Let's get rid of the sweet ones
first, by referring to the following: Glacé or Ice (II, 493);
Crème Glacé or Ice Cream (II,
483); Glacé, as in Meringue
(II, 522); Fruit Glaze for Tarts
(II, 434); and Caramel Glaze
as in Crème Brulée (II, 438);

transparent glaze as in Nuts
Glacé (II, 515) and Fruits
Glacé (II, 523).

And then turn to the non-
sweet processes and coatings,
which do so much to add color
and flavor to food. ♦ To glaze
meats is an expression that can
be interpreted in a number of
ways. If food has been Braised,
page 538, or prepared à l'étouffée, page 85, it acquires, in
the cooking, reduced juices
which may be further reduced.
Place it ♦ uncovered in an oven
if the food was braised. Or hold
it ♦ covered in the skillet or
poêle if the food is covered with
a poaching paper, before lidding. Meats may also be glazed
by the use of Glacé de Viande,
or Meat Glaze (II, 145)—a
specially prepared, potent and
wonderful substance to use with
discretion.

♦ To glaze a sauce can mean
to run it under a hot broiler until
it becomes golden brown.

♦ To glaze an hors d'oeuvre
or sandwich may mean to apply
to it an aspic coating.

♦ You can, in cooking vegetables, let the butter in which
they are cooked combine with
their reduced juices to form a
glaze. This is usually done over
carefully controlled heat. Often
a little sugar or honey is added,
see page 387.

♦ You can coat eggs or fish
with a rich white sauce—which
process can be referred to as
glazing them.

And last but not least, let's
read about ♦ deglazing, a most
vital process—usually neglected
—but one that can mean so
much, see page 358.

TO GLAZE A SAUCE ON A
CASSEROLE

Preheat broiler.
Try this only if you have preheated your broiler well. Then

run your dish quickly under the heat, until it browns delicately. Should the broiler not be hot enough and your sauce boil before it colors, it will separate into an oily, watery mass. ◗ Be sure the sauce does not touch the edge of the pot. Allow an empty area all around for expansion. It is also a wise precaution to protect the casserole by putting it in a pan of hot water. Do not leave it longer than 3 minutes. A perfect all-over brown glaze on the sauce coating fish dishes or Chicken Divan can be achieved by the following method: Reserve some of the Béchamel or Mornay Sauce and fold in whipped cream, at least 4 tablespoons to 1 cup of sauce. The more whipped cream, the smoother the browning. Put under the hot broiler and watch closely.

SPIRIT GLAZE FOR HAM

Combine:
    ½ to 1 cup dry red wine
    ½ to 1 cup bourbon whisky
    1 cup brown sugar
    6 cloves
    2 tablespoons grated
        orange peel
Spread on the ham after it is skinned and continue to baste during the last ½ hour of cooking.

CRANBERRY GLAZE FOR FOWL

Combine:
    1 cup canned cranberries
    ½ cup brown sugar
    2 tablespoons lemon juice

HONEY GLAZE FOR MEAT OR ONIONS

Combine:
    ¼ cup honey
    ¼ cup soy sauce
    1 teaspoon mustard

ASPIC GLAZE

Use this for cold meats, fish, salads and canapés.
Soak:
    1 tablespoon gelatin
in:
    ½ cup meat or vegetable
        stock
Dissolve it over hot water. Add it to:
    1½ cups clarified stock
Season it mildly. Chill it until it thickens somewhat. Spoon it over cold roast, cold fish, canapés, etc.

MAYONNAISE COLLÉE OR GELATIN MAYONNAISE

This coating, also known as Mayonnaise Chaud-Froid, is ordinarily used to coat or mask aspics, cold fish, meat or fowl dishes. But if you make it fairly stiff, it can be piped through a pastry tube and you can achieve the same rococo flights of fancy as when icing a wedding cake. You may also use delicately tinted mayonnaise collée, made from Green Mayonnaise, see page 348, but please avoid highly colored mayonnaise which looks unappetizingly artificial. Note that this stiffened mayonnaise serves much the same purpose as the Béchamel-based Chaud-Froid Sauce on page 388, but it does not hold as well or as long for the heavy oil content may cause oozing. ◗ Have the dish you wish to coat well chilled and dry.
I. Soak:
    1½ to 2 teaspoons gelatin
in:
    1½ to tablespoons water
Beat into:
    1 cup heavy mayonnaise

II. Or beat:
    1 cup mayonnaise
into:
    ¼ cup Aspic Glaze, above
    The Aspic Glaze should be at

about 70°—tepid and still liquid. Once it has begun to jell, it will not beat into the mayonnaise properly. Spread it as you would frosting, with firm strokes of a spatula. Work quickly, for this mayonnaise will set at room temperature. Chill the dish until the mayonnaise is set, then decorate as described later. After the decorations have set, place the whole dish on a rack with a platter under it and glaze it with aspic glaze, which should be about the consistency of thick sirup. Your food should be very cold, so that the aspic almost sets at the moment of contact. Use a ladle which holds about 1 cup glaze and pour it on with the motion illustrated for Petits Fours (II, 360). You should give the whole dish two or three coats, which should be perfectly smooth. There should be no streaks or lumps if you have used aspic of the consistency described. You may re-use the aspic which has fallen through the rack onto the platter, after straining, for the second and third coats.

SAUCE CHAUD-FROID

Chaud-Froid is so-called because it begins as a heated sauce and is served as a cold one. It has an advantage over Mayonnaise Collée, because it emphasizes the flavor of the dish it coats—for you make the sauce with the stock resulting from the dish itself. It is often used to coat whole cooked chickens, ham or veal roasts, fish or other cold buffet items.
Prepare:
2 cups Béchamel Sauce, page 359, slightly overseasoned
using chicken or veal stock or Fish Fumet (II, 143)—according to the dish you intend to mask. Chaud-Froid may also be made with a Brown Sauce for meats or chicken. The brown color is more appetizing to many people. Add:
2 tablespoons gelatin
softened in:
3 or 4 tablespoons stock
again using the appropriate flavor for the dish. Stir constantly over medium heat until thoroughly combined. Remove from heat and cool, stirring from time to time to prevent a skin forming. ◗ When cool enough to coat a spoon, but not set, ladle it over the cold chicken or fish in the way described above. Chill to set. The dish may need more than one coat of the sauce. Decorate and glaze.

ABOUT DECORATIONS FOR CHAUD-FROID

Decorations on dishes masked with Sauce Chaud-Froid or Mayonnaise Collée, can be as fanciful as you wish. And professional chefs achieve masterful effects. With a little practice, you can produce the same elegantly curving sprays of flowers, leaves and stems from leeks, chives, eggplant skin or green peppers. To make them pliable, they must be blanched for about 3 minutes in salted water, then cooled immediately on crushed ice to retain their color. Chives form the stems, and leeks, etc. can be cut into leaf shapes—free-hand or with fancy cutters sketched in the illustration on page 39.
Lemon rind, carrot and red pepper, blanched as above, can be used for flower petals. Or use paper-thin slices of ham. Other materials suitable for decoration are: truffles; black olives —you can use the skins of ripe olives as a truffle substitute; pickles, hard-cooked eggs and grapes; parsley and other herbs

—blanched for 1 minute; peas, capers and wilted cucumber slices.

The decorations are first dipped in clear Aspic Glaze, page 387, then applied to the dish to be ornamented, as described on page 387. If they slip after the first application of clear glaze, replace carefully with tweezers. If the decorating proves slow, be sure to chill periodically so that the chaud-froid does not darken.

Chaud-froids are often garnished with aspic jelly, chopped or cut in fancy shapes; and you may use on a suitable meat dish, foie gras balls rolled in chopped Truffles, see page 299. Lemon wedges, sprinkled with finely chopped parsley and other fancy lemon shapes are shown (II, 101). To garnish with hard-cooked eggs, see (II, 74).

ABOUT AU GRATIN

"Au gratin" is a term that, in America, is usually associated with cheese. But the term may merely refer to a light but thorough coating of fine fresh or dry bread crumbs or even crushed corn flakes, cracker crumbs or finely ground nuts placed on top of scalloped or sauced dishes. These are then browned in the oven or under the broiler to form a crisp golden crust. Such dishes are usually combinations of cooked shellfish, fish, meats, vegetables or eggs, bound by a white or brown sauce and served in the dish in which they are cooked. If the sauce is heavy in fat, it is wise to place the scalloped dish in a pan of hot water before running it under a broiler. Or you may set the casserole or baking dish on a piece of foil, with the shiny side down to deflect the heat. Or just put the casserole in a baking tin.

Raw food may also be covered with one of the above toppings before cooking. See Scalloped Potatoes, page 312. ◗ To make au gratin mixtures quickly, put them in a blender ⅄ in the proportion and amount you need.

AU GRATIN

I. Place:

> Dry bread crumbs

in a thorough, but light, covering over the sauced food. Bake in a 350° to 375° oven— or run it under a preheated broiler, 3 inches below the source of heat until a golden brown crisp crust forms.

II. Place:

> Dry bread crumbs and
> dots of butter

to make a thorough but light covering over the food, before baking it in a 350° oven—or running it under a preheated broiler, 5 inches from the source of heat, to produce a crisp golden crust.

III. Completely cover the food to be au gratined with:

> Dry bread crumbs, dots
> of butter and grated
> cheese

Run it under a preheated broiler, 5 inches below the source of heat, to form a glazed golden crust. The finished result should be neither powdery nor rubbery but "fondant." It will be more "fondant" if you use natural-aged American or cheddar cheese, and dried if you use Parmesan or Romano.

BUTTERED CRUMBS

Sauté

> 1 cup bread crumbs

in:

> ⅓ cup hot butter or bacon
> drippings

You may add a choice of:

>   Chopped minced bacon
>   Minced onions
>   Chopped parsley
>   Chopped nut meats
>   Curry powder
>   Paprika
>   Grated cheese

CROUTONS

These dry or fried seasoned fresh breads come in all sizes. As coarse crumbs, they are an attractive garnish for noodles, dumplings or Spaetzle. In small dice, they add glamour to pea and other soups. Use in tiny dice and mound them around game, or, as larger toasts, under game or a chop. They can be spread with a pâté or be used as a spongy surface for the natural juices. In large size, they can also be placed under a dripping rack during the roasting of meats to catch and hold the juices.

I. Dice bread, fresh or dry, and sauté it in butter until it is an even brown. Or butter slices of bread, cut them into dice and brown them in a 375° oven.

II. When croutons have been sautéed or browned in the oven, drop them while still hot into a bag containing:

>   1 teaspoon salt
>   1 teaspoon paprika
>   Ground Parmesan cheese
>   or very finely minced
>   fresh herbs

Close the bag. Shake it until the croutons are evenly coated. Add them to hot soup.

III. Use for soup, noodles or Caesar Salad. Cut into ½-inch cubes:

>   Bread

Sauté the cubes in:

>   Hot butter or olive oil

You may rub the skillet with garlic or add grated onion to the butter. Stir them gently or shake the skillet until they are coated. Sprinkle with:

>   Grated cheese or herbs

ELABORATE TOPPING OR GRATIN

[About 1½ Cups]
Combine:

>   ¼ cup melted butter
>   2 tablespoons crumbled
>   potato chips
>   ½ cup cracker or bread
>   crumbs
>   ½ teaspoon paprika
>   2 tablespoons grated
>   Parmesan
>   ½ cup dry sherry

ALMOND OR AMANDINE GARNISH

[A Scant ½ Cup]
This garnish is a classic. It glorifies the most commonplace dish.
Melt:

>   ¼ cup butter

Stir and sauté in it over low heat, to avoid scorching, until lightly browned:

>   ¼ cup blanched shredded
>   almonds
>   Salt, as needed

As a variation on almonds as a vegetable garnish, try:

>   (Roasted pumpkin,
>   squash or sesame seeds)

EGG AND CHEESE GRATIN

[About 1 Cup]
This is a good topping for spaghetti or noodle casserole dishes which have to wait for tardy guests, as it prevents the spaghetti from drying out.
Beat until light yellow and foamy:

>   3 eggs

Stir in, to form a thick paste:

>   ⅔ cup grated Parmesan
>   cheese

Spread over the top of the dish and bake in a 400° oven until the eggs and cheese are set and browned.

CHICKEN LIVER TOPPING FOR PASTA DISHES

Sauté until just done:

1 cup chicken livers

in:

¼ cup cooking or olive oil

Remove the livers from the pan and cut up coarsely. In the same pan, sauté for 5 minutes:

1 cup sliced mushrooms

then add:

½ cup halved, ripe, pitted olives

and the chicken liver pieces. Stir and deglaze the pan with:

½ cup dry sherry

Spread the topping over the spaghetti in an even layer and sprinkle as evenly as possible with:

½ cup chopped hard New York cheese

Run under the broiler until the cheese is toasted, about 2 minutes.

FISH

ABOUT FISH

As demographers concern themselves about our exploding population they begin more and more to consider—as a source of abundant high-grade protein—the creatures of the lakes, the rivers, and the seven seas. There are schemes for reaping the fantastically numerous, infinitely tiny plankton. There are projects for fertilizing the spawning ground of the world's more conventionally edible water-life and so harvesting familiar species more intensively than ever before.

The amateur angler, too, has been doing his bit. With America gone fishing-crazy, no housewife knows when she will answer a knock at the kitchen door and be suddenly faced with a neighbor's surplus catch in all its chill, scaly impersonality. This need not be a moment of consternation. If it happens to you, judge the gift—after, of course, enthusiastically thanking the donor—as critically as you would judge a fish offered at market. To test its freshness ♦ make sure that its eyes are bulging and its gills are reddish, that the scales are adhering firmly to the skin, and that the flesh, when you press it, is firm to the touch. The scales should have a high sheen. Also be certain that the fish has no offensive odor—especially around the gills or the belly. If it is very fresh, and you cannot use it at once ♦ see directions for freezing fish and

for cooking frozen fish, page 397, and (II, 562). Should you be buying fish, remember that in some stores ♦ thawed frozen fish is sold with no sign or comment to indicate the important fact that it should be used at once and never refrozen. If you are in doubt about the freshness of a fish, place it in cold water. A fresh fish will float.

♦ To choose a method of cooking appropriate to a particular type of fish and to the kind of meat at hand—whether whole, filleted or cut for steaks —see the generalized recipes which come first in this chapter.

Many fish are seasonal delicacies. Available all year round are rock bass, carp, cod, eel, flounder, grouper, haddock, hake, halibut, herring, mullet, red snapper, sole and tuna.

If you are adventuring with eel, herring, some types of sole —or an officious stranger like octopus—consult the Index to see if we have some extra special suggestions for preparing, cooking or seasoning them.

SEAFISH

These include: bass, bluefish, butterfish, cod, croaker, cusk, flounder, grouper, haddock, hake, halibut, Atlantic herring, Pacific herring, lingcod, mackerel, mullet, pilchard, pollock, pompano, porgy, red snapper, rosefish, sea bass, sea trout, shad, the soles, swordfish, tuna, turbot and whiting.

These include: buffalo fish, carp, catfish, crappie, lake herring, mullet, muskellunge, yellow perch, yellow pike, pickerel, sheepshead, sucker, sunfish, brook trout, lake trout, and whitefish.

Either sea or fresh fish—depending on age and season—are eel, elver and salmon.

For those of you concerned with lean and fat fish, the following are considered in the fattest category: bloaters, bluefish, herring, kipper, pilchard, salmon, sardine, shad, smelt, and sprat, beginning at 15% fat and achieving about 30% with eel.

Now, a few more general comments. Many fish respond to Deep Fat Frying, pages 75-79, Sautéing, page 79, Pan-Frying, page 80, Broiling, page 399 and Baking, page 402. And there are fish that steam or poach well. In the latter category—a more descriptive term with which we like to replace the word "boiled"—are: cod, buffalo fish, hake, haddock, sheepshead, red snapper, grouper, pollock, halibut and salmon. Some very oily fish respond to smoking (II, 545). Some others are available fresh or salted, page 407. Some fish, strong in flavor or dry in texture, respond to Marinating, pages 409, 411.

Whatever kind of fish you choose ♦ don't overcook it.

ABOUT CLEANING AND PREPARING FISH

♦ To prepare a fish for baking and stuffing, begin by spreading on a firm work surface several layers of newsprint covered with 3 thicknesses of brown paper. If the fish needs scaling, cut off the fins with scissors so they will not nick you while you are working. Wash the fish briefly

in cold water—scales are more easily removed from a wet fish. Grasp the fish firmly near the base of the tail. If it is very slippery you may want to hold it in a cloth. Begin at the tail, pressing a rigid knife blade at a slight angle from the vertical position to raise the scales as you strip them off. Work against the "nap"—up toward the head. A serrated scaler or a grater will be of great help in scaling. Be sure to remove the scales around the base of the head and the fins. After scaling, discard the first layer of brown paper with the scales on it. Next draw the fish. Cut the entire length of the belly from the vent to the head and remove the entrails. As they are all contained in a pouch-like integument which is easily freed from the flesh, evisceration need not be a messy job. Now, cut around the pelvic and ventral fins on the lower side and remove them. If you are removing the head, cut above the collarbone and break

the backbone by snapping it off on the edge of the work surface as shown above. The head and pectoral fins, if they were not previously cut off, should come with it. Then remove the tail by slicing right through the body just above it. Wrap and discard the entrails, keeping the choicer trimmings for making Fumet (II, 143).

If the fish does not need scaling and you are preparing it for stuffing, you can remove the dorsal fin in such a way as to release unwanted bones. Cut first down to either side of it for its full length. Then give a quick pull forward toward the head end to release it, and with it the bones that are attached to it, as sketched below.

Wash the fish in cold running water, removing any blood, bits of viscera or membrane. ▶ Be sure the blood line under the backbone has been removed. Dry the fish well. It is then ready to use steamed, baked, stuffed or unstuffed, or as steaks.

▶ To cut a fish into steaks or darnes, begin at the head end and cut evenly, as shown, into cross sections of desired thickness.
▶ To clean small fish like smelts, spread open the outer gills, take hold of the inner gills with the forefinger and pull gently. The parts unfit for food are all attached to these inner gills and come out together,

leaving the fish ready to cook after rinsing.

If you cannot use a fish at once, store it at 39° temperature, preferably lidded, so that its penetrating odor does not permeate other foods in the refrigerator. Fish may be kept directly on ice if drainage is provided to prevent it from soaking up water. Length of fish storage depends largely on the condition in which it reaches you. The sooner it can be used the better, for its fragile gelatinous substances break down and dry out quickly as the fish ages, destroying flavor as they dry.

ABOUT FILLETING FISH

To prepare skinned fillets, you need not scale the fish, remove its fins, or draw it.

▶ To fillet—place on the work surface several thicknesses of newsprint covered by brown paper. Cut the fish, as shown, along the back ridge from the tail to a point just behind the head. Then slice down at a slight angle behind the collar bone beyond the gill—until you feel the backbone against the knife. Turn the knife flat with the cutting edge toward the tail and the point toward the cut edge of the backbone. Keep the blade flat and in the same plane with the backbone. Now, cut with a sliding motion along the backbone until you have freed the fillet all the way to the tail, see below. It should come off in one piece.

▶ To skin, place the fillet skin side down. Hold the tail firmly with your free hand as shown. Cut through the flesh of the fillet about ½ inch above the tail. Flatten the knife against the skin with the blade pointing toward the top of the fillet. Work the knife forward, keeping in the same plane and close against the skin while your left hand continues to hold the skin taut.

An exception to the above procedure must be made with a certain group of very flat fish, some of which, rather disconcertingly, have both eyes on their upper surface. All of them are skinned and filleted in a special way; and they may all be cooked by recipes for sole or flounder, including turbot, which is less flat than most.

The true English or Dover sole, whose eyes are normally

situated, has the most delicate flavor and texture of them all. But fillets of flounder, plaice, dab, lemon or gray sole are often palmed off on the unsuspecting purchaser as the genuine article.

▶ To fillet these flat varieties, first skin the fish by cutting a gash through the skin above the tail. Peel back the skin for about ¾ of an inch. Grasp the released skin firmly in the right hand as shown. Hold the tail flat in the left hand while pulling steadily toward the head with the right. When skinned, flat fish reveal an indentation down the center which separates a double set of fillets—2 on the dark side and 2 on the light side. Cut through the flesh on either side of the spine. Slip the knife under the fillet—close to the bone—and cut the fillet loose from the backbone toward the outside edge of the fish. Having freed the fillets, refrigerate them, and wrap for discard in the papers on which you were working all the unusable entrails. You may keep the bone structure, skin, heads and tails for Fumet (II, 143), unless the fish is a strong-flavored or oily one.

ABOUT COOKING FISH

▶ While in cooking and timing, the size and shape of the fish, and whether it is whole or divided, must be taken into consideration, the methods themselves are much the same. A good cook knows through experience how long to cook her fish, but even she will watch the proceedings with a vigilant eye to guard against overdoneness. For details of each method of cooking see the following pages. ◗ Cooking times in individual recipes apply to fish which has been removed from the refrigerator long enough to reach 70°; but no warmer.

You will sometimes see ◗ suggestions for gashing fish before cooking. This procedure is adopted chiefly for firm-fleshed fish when cooked unskinned, to prevent them from curling. Slashes may be made, too, before baking, if the fish is a very tough-skinned one, to allow the heat to penetrate, or when the area of skin is large, as in turbot, to keep the skin from bursting.

◗ To test a fish for doneness you may insert a thermometer at an angle in the thickest portion of the flesh behind the gills. Fish is edible when the internal heat reaches 140°. At 150° its tissues begin to break down, allowing both juices and flavor to escape. Remove the fish from the heat, surely by 145°. Remember that because fish needs so little heat to cook, it will continue to do so on a hot platter.

If you have no thermometer, stick a toothpick into the thickest part of the fish near the backbone and separate the meat from the bone. The fish is done when the flesh is no longer translucent and flakes readily. One of the best ways ◗ to test a soft-fleshed fish is to touch it as you would a cake to see if the flesh responds by returning to its original shape after imprinting a finger.

Many fish are bland in flavor and profit by a sauce. If, on the contrary, the fish is strong in flavor, many expert cooks ◗ discard the butter or cooking oil in which it has been cooked. Otherwise, deglaze the pan, page 358.

◗ Most of our fish recipes call for cooking in ovenproof dishes. Service is simplified if such dishes are attractive enough to appear at table. This way, fish —being fragile—undergoes less handling, and you have fewer "fishy" dishes to clean up later. Single-dish service also, of course, keeps the fish warmer; but do watch for overcooking from the added heat of the dish.

◗ To keep a whole fish warm, put it on a heated serving platter in a very low oven. Leave the door ajar. For fillets, treat as above, but cover them with a damp warm paper towel or cloth. ◗ Be sure that any sauce served on the fish is very hot.

◗ To keep a sauced fish warm, use a double boiler ◗ uncovered, or place the baker in which you plan to serve the fish in a pan of boiling water and hold ◗ uncovered.

◗ If cooked fish is to be served cold keep refrigerated until the very last minute. If served buffet, place it over cracked ice.

◗ Allow per serving 1 lb. whole small fish, ¾ lb. if entrails, head, tail and fins are removed; ½ lb. fish steaks; or ⅓ lb. fish fillets.

◗ To minimize fish tastes and odors, use lemon, wine, vinegar, ginger, spring onions, or garlic in the marinating or cooking.

To remove the odor of fish from utensils and dishcloths use a solution of 1 teaspoon baking soda to 1 quart water. Pans may be washed in hot suds, rinsed and dried, and then scalded with a little vinegar. To remove the odor of fish from the hands, rub them with lemon juice, vinegar or salt before washing them.

Frozen fish should preferably be thawed before cooking but may be cooked while still frozen.

Use thawed fish immediately, and do not re-freeze. You may also thaw at room temperature if you are in a hurry, and speed up the process even more by covering the fish and placing it in front of an electric fan, see (II, 562). ◗ Frozen fish, when thawed, may be cooked in the same way as its fresh counterpart. ◗ If cooked frozen, it is best baked, broiled, or cooked "en papillote" or in aluminum foil. Double the cooking time given for fresh fish, and in foil cooking add another 15 minutes to allow the heat to penetrate the foil. Freezing processes for fish have improved greatly in the last few years, and have brought us varieties hitherto not available, such as rainbow trout. But we still think that frozen fish cannot compare with fresh fish for flavor and texture. It is apt to be dry, as the gelatins lose their delicate quality, and thus needs a well-flavored sauce or a good deal of moisture or fat in the cooking process. ◗ If you are buying frozen fish from frozen food cabinets, buy only solidly frozen packages. They should not be torn or misshapen or show evidence of refreezing. ◗ Skin frozen fish before cooking it.

CURED FISH

Smoked, dried, salted or pickled —some of these cured fish can be eaten as they come, others must be cooked first. Haddock and several kinds of herring are usually ◗ Cold-Smoked (II, 545). They have been salted and smoked over a smoldering fire to the dry stage, but have not been cooked. Whitefish, chub and salmon are usually ◗ Hot-Smoked (II, 545), so that they cook in the heat of the smoking fire, and so can be used without further cooking. Haddock, when smoked, becomes finnan haddie. A smoked herring is known as a kipper—actually, the general term for any smoked fish. An unsalted, smoked herring is known as a bloater. It will not keep as long as a kipper. ◗ Store all smoked fish refrigerated in airtight containers to lengthen their keeping period.

Cod, mackerel and herring are often ◗ salted and air-dried, and before cooking should be soaked in water for several hours—skin side down. If soaking in fresh running water is not practical, change the water frequently during the soaking period. For ways to cook, see Salt Cod, page 408. Fish was often ◗ pickled in the days before refrigeration, and in eighteenth century English and American cookbooks you will find recipes for "caveaching" fish in spices, oil and vinegar. We imagine there is a close relationship between the French "Escabèche," and its Spanish variant, page 406, in both word derivation and method. Nowadays, herring and mackerel are usually reserved for pickling, although Escabèche can be used for small fish, like fresh anchovies, sardines, young mullet and whiting.

◗ To prepare fish dishes based on cooked fish and shellfish, see Luncheon Dishes, pages 229–237, and Hors d'Oeuvre (II, 79) and Canapés (II, 63). ◗ To prepare Fish Stews and Soups, see pages 132–138.

There are any number of attractive ways to serve and garnish fish. Handsome bases for cold dishes are salmon, lake trout, chicken halibut, turbot, filleted Dover sole, wall-eyed pike and carp. For directions for Cold Salmon, see page 415.

A gala way to serve a hot fish in summer is to place it on a grill above a bed of dry fennel stalks and flame it for several seconds before serving. This may also be done directly on a heatproof platter. Another decorative and delicious addition to fish is Fried Parsley, page 305.

ABOUT STEAMING, POACHING OR BRAISING FISH

Steaming is one of the better ways to treat a delicate lean fish as far as retaining flavor is concerned; although—unlike meat —fish will lose more weight processed in this way than in poaching. Poaching—sometimes also called braising in fish cookery—runs steaming a close second.

A steamer has a perforated tray support designed to hold the fish above the water level. In a poacher, which is otherwise very similar, the tray is not elevated and allows the fish to be immersed in the liquid. ♦ A poaching tray is always greased before the fish is placed on it. Fish may be poached in Fumets (II, 143), Court Bouillons (II, 146), in Light Stocks (II, 142), or à Blanc (II, 146)—depending on the flavor you wish to impart or the degree of whiteness you desire. If you are chiefly concerned with preserving the true flavor of the fish, salted water may be all you care to use. Allow 1 tablespoon of salt for every quart of water. For details, see individual recipes.

♦ If fumet or light stock is used for the steaming or poaching liquid, you may want to use some of it either as it is, or re-duced, in the fish sauce. ♦ Court bouillons are not used in this way, nor are à blanc liquids, because they are both apt to contain too much vinegar and salt.

♦ Please read the general principles of Poaching, page 83, which apply here. Small fish or cut pieces are started in a boiling liquid which is at once reduced to a simmer. ♦ Large pieces are started in cold liquid. This is especially important because immersing a fish of any considerable size in boiling water causes the skin to shrink and burst. Fragile fillets profit by the use of a poaching paper. Large fish will tolerate more liquid. In either case, allow about 5 to 8 minutes to the pound, depending on the size of the fish, from the moment the cooking liquid reaches the boiling point, and then ♦ reduce to a simmer for the remainder of the cooking period. If you do not have a poacher there is the problem, with large fish, of keeping them constantly bathed in liquid; and after cooking, of lifting them out of the pan without breaking them. Both can be solved either by cooking them tied in a muslin cloth or by using a cloth as described below.

A roasting or baking pan is

best. If a large pan is not available, cut the fish in two and place it in a smaller pan with the halves dovetailed. The fish can be reassembled on a platter later. If served hot or cold, it can be masked with a sauce without anyone being the wiser for your subterfuge. Put in the pan with the fish several onion and lemon slices, a chopped carrot and a few celery stalks. Fill the pan with Court Bouillon (II, 146) to within an inch of the top. Cover the fish completely with a piece of turkish toweling or a heavy muslin which is large enough to hang down into the liquid. Baste the cloth with the court bouillon in which the fish is cooking as it ▶ simmers on the stove or in the oven. ▶ See that the cloth is always completely soaked. The top of the fish will then cook as quickly as the bottom. If you have already wrapped the fish in muslin as described previously, it will serve exactly the same purpose as a piece of cloth over the top; so will a close-fitting domed lid or a poaching paper if the pot is sufficiently deep.

After the cooking period the fish is sometimes allowed to cool in the water. We do not recommend this practice, as it leads to overcooking and waterlogging. ▶ If the fish is to be served cold it is easier to remove the skin and trim the fish while it is still warm.

ABOUT COOKING FISH "AU BLEU"

It is the skin of the fish only, of course, which turns blue during this cooking process. The important point about cooking "au bleu" is to have available a very fresh fish—alive, if possible. The fish should not be washed or scaled, and should be handled as little as possible, merely being eviscerated. Small fish are sometimes cleaned through the gills, see page 393. Larger ones, such as carp and pike, are slit along the belly to clean them. And, if this involves less handling, slit the small fish, too. Both may then be poached in a vinegar Court Bouillon (II, 146). The natural slime of the fish, coupled if you wish with a preliminary sprinkling of boiling hot vinegar all over, "blues" the skin. See Blue Trout, page 419. They may be served hot or cold.

ABOUT BROILING FISH

"Ruling a large kingdom," observed Lao-Tzu, "is like cooking a small fish." What he meant was that both should be gently handled, and the treatment never overdone. We have usually respected the old philosopher's advice. But in broiling fish we have discovered that they taste even better when they can be subjected to quite high and intense, rather than gentle, heat. The following cooking procedure, for instance, is most effective.

For a 2½-lb. fish, unskinned, broil in the bottom of a preheated broiler at 400° for 5 minutes, then move to a top broiler for 5 minutes more at a preheated 800°. The 800° is not a misprint. But it requires coil or burner capacity that most household ranges are simply not equipped to supply, see page 74. The closest practical home approach is to use a vertical pair of charcoal grills—set as sketched—which produce what is known in France as a "roti" rather than a grill. But most of us must be content with our range broilers preheated to 550°. ◗ It helps to warm up the broiling rack in advance—thus transferring some heat at once to the fish; but be sure to ◗ grease the rack after heating so the fish will not stick. If the fish is to be turned, the hinged rack which fits into the vertical grill, as sketched, may also be conveniently used in the oven broiler pan. Grease it with cooking oil, and the fish with clarified butter. A lean fish may be floured before dotting with butter.

Fillets, flat and split fish are usually placed about two inches from the source of heat. If unskinned, place them skin side down. It is not necessary to turn them, but advisable to baste several times during the cooking period.

If thick fish steaks or large fish are being broiled, place the rack about 6 inches from the source of heat. They may take as long to cook as 5 or 6 minutes to a side.

Types of fish good for broiling include: halibut or salmon steaks, sole and its cousins, split herring, mackerel and sea trout. For swordfish steaks, be sure to baste with plenty of butter, as they tend to become dry. Melted butter, lemon wedges and parsley adequately garnish broiled fish. If the fish is fat, try a spicy sauce, like Tomato, page 376, Mustard, page 363, Tartare, page 349, or Devil Sauce, page 374; if lean, Hollandaise, page 368, Béarnaise, page 370, or one of the seasoned butters.

▤ FISH KEBABS

[Serves 6]
Prepare:

    2 lbs. firm-fleshed fish:
      swordfish, halibut, cod
      or haddock

Cut into 1-inch cubes. Place in a glass, enameled or stainless steel pan and marinate for 30 minutes in:

    ¾ cup cooking oil
    ½ cup lemon juice
    ¼ teaspoon powdered bay
      leaf
    4 drops soy sauce

Stir once or twice to thoroughly coat fish. Preheat broiler.
Thread on skewers alternating with thick slices of:

    2 cucumbers, and
    Stuffed olives

Broil or grill for 10 minutes, turning frequently and basting with the marinade.

FRIED FISH

Scale, if necessary, and clean, page 393:

    A large fish or several
      small pan fish: crappie,
      brook trout, sun fish, or
      perch

Cut the large fish into Steaks or Darnes, page 394, before rolling them in:

    Seasoned flour or corn
      meal or Bound Breading
      (II, 160)

Melt in a skillet to the depth of ⅛ inch:

    Clarified butter and
      cooking oil

◗ It is inadvisable to use butter, when sautéing large fish, without the addition of cooking oil, as it burns more readily than other shortening or drippings. When the fat is hot place the fish in it. To keep the fat from spattering your hands you may cover the pan with an inverted colander. Reduce the heat slightly and cook the fish until done, from 3 to 5 minutes. Our former cook, Virginia Turner, taught us to complete cooking one side of the fish entirely before turning and cooking the other side until done. Larger fish may be sautéed on both sides until seared, then placed in a 375° oven about 10 minutes.

DEEP FAT FRIED FISH

[Allow About ⅓ Pound
Per Serving]
Preheat deep fryer to 370°
◗ Please read About Deep Fat Frying, pages 75–79. Have fish at 70°. Clean and prepare for cooking:

    Small fish or pieces of fish
      not thicker than 1 inch
Dip them in:
    Fritter Batter for Fish
      (II, 125), or Bound
      Breading (II, 160)
Fry in deep fat for 5 to 8 minutes, or until a golden brown. The fish will rise to the surface when done. Drain on absorbent paper. Serve very hot with:
    Lemon wedges or
    Tartare Sauce, page 349

MARINATED DEEP FAT [3]
FRIED FISH

Preheat deep fryer to 370°.
◗ Please read About Deep Fat Frying, pages 75–79. Skin and cut into pieces:
    1½ lbs. fish steaks
Marinate for 30 minutes in:
    6 tablespoons dry white
      wine or
    2 tablespoons lemon juice
Drain dry and dip each piece separately in:
    6 tablespoons cream
then in:
    Flour
Fry the fish in deep fat for about 7 minutes. Serve with:
    Tartare Sauce, page 349

FISH AND CHIPS [4]

Preheat deep fryer to 375°.
◗ Please read About Deep Fat Frying, pages 75–79.
Cut into uniform serving pieces:
    1½ lbs. fillet of flounder
Coat with:
    Fritter Batter for Fish
      (II, 125)
Cut into thick uniform strips, slightly larger than for French fries:
    1½ lbs. mature baking
      potatoes
Soak in cold water for ½ hour. Drain and dry thoroughly. Fry in the hot fat until golden brown. Remove, drain and keep warm. Deep fry the breaded fish until golden brown. Arrange the potatoes and fish on a platter and serve as a dip:
    Hot cider vinegar

OVEN-FRIED SMALL FISH
FILLETS OR STICKS

[Allow About ⅓ Pound
Per Serving]
Preheat for cooking:
    Small fish, pieces of fish
      or fish fillets
Dip the fish in:
    ¼ cup rich milk or cream
then in:
    Seasoned bread crumbs
      or crushed cornflakes
Let the fish dry on a rack for ½ hour. Preheat oven to 350°. Bake in an ovenproof dish until firm and golden. Baste twice during the cooking period with:
    Melted butter

FILLETS OF FISH
SAUTÉED AMANDINE

[Allow ⅓ Pound Per Serving]
Dip:
    Fillets of Sole
in:
    Milk
Dust with:
    Flour

Melt in a skillet enough to cover the bottom well:

    Butter

Sauté the fillets in the pan. Turn once. Place on a hot platter. Melt additional:

    Butter

Brown in it lightly:

    Blanched shredded almonds

Pour them over the fillets. Garnish the dish with:

    Lemon and parsley

FRESH FILLETS   [2]
SAUTÉED PALM BEACH

Bread if you like:

    2 small skinned fish fillets

Sauté until golden brown in:

    2 tablespoons clarified butter

Serve with 3 or 4 alternate sections of:

    Grapefruit and orange

on each fillet. Pour the pan gravy over the garnished fillets and serve at once.

BAKED UNSTUFFED FISH

[Allow ½ Pound Per Person]
Preheat oven to 325°.
Scale, remove the entrails and clean:

    A 3-lb. fish

A larger fish may be used, but will require longer, but not proportionately longer, baking, see page 395. If the fish has a tough skin slash it in several places. Place it on a well-greased ovenproof platter. Rub generously with:

    Clarified Butter, page 383

If the fish is ▶ lean, you may bard it, page 453. If it is not barded, baste it frequently with:

    Clarified Butter

Bake about 30 minutes or until done. Serve on a hot platter garnished with:

    Slices of lemon
    Sprigs of parsley

    Stuffed Tomatoes, page 335

Suitable sauces are:

    Almond Sauce, page 390,
    Shrimp Sauce, page 377,
    or Mustard Sauce, page 363

▶ To carve an unstuffed fish, remove the skin and cut a line down the middle of the exposed side from head to tail. To either side of this line, cut pieces 2½ to 3 inches wide. Lift off above the bone structure and serve. Pry up the backbone, beginning at the tail. Slide it up and out the dorsal ridge. Break the spine at the neck. Lift it out and lay it aside. The exposed lower fillet will then be ready to carve just as the upper one was.

POACHED FISH   [3]
STEAKS

Cut into pieces suitable for individual servings:

    1½ lbs. halibut or other fish steak

Place it in a skillet. Cover with:

    Boiling water

Season with:

    4 whole peppercorns
    ½ bay leaf
    2 teaspoons lemon juice

Simmer about 10 minutes, or until tender. Remove to a hot platter. Strain the stock and use it to make the sauce. Try:

    Curry Sauce I, page 363,
    or Poulette Sauce, page 362, or Mustard Sauce, page 363, or Anchovy Sauce for Fish, page 361

FISH FILLETS À LA   [4]
BONNE FEMME

Cut, wipe with a damp cloth and dry:

    4 Flatfish Fillets, page 395

Place in a buttered shallow casserole. Cover with:

    ¾ cup finely sliced mushrooms
    1 minced shallot

1 teaspoon chopped
parsley
Pour gently into the dish:
⅔ cup dry white wine
Cover with a Poaching Paper,
page 86, and ▶ simmer 10 to 15
minutes. Remove the fish onto a
hot shallow ovenproof serving
dish. Reduce the wine by half.
Stir into it gradually until well
blended:
⅔ cup Velouté Sauce,
page 362
using fish stock. You may swirl
in:
2 tablespoons butter
Pour the sauce over the fillets
and run them under a broiler
until the sauce is lightly
browned. Serve with:
Boiled New Potatoes,
page 310

FISH STEAKS OR [6] FILLETS MARGUÉRY BAKED IN SEA FOOD SAUCE

Preheat oven to 350°.
Place in boiling water or milk
and simmer until nearly tender:
6 fillets or 3 steaks
This will be a quick process if
the fillets are thin. Drain the
fillets. Place in a greased baking
dish or platter. Keep them
where they will remain hot.
Melt:
¼ cup butter
Stir and sauté in it until done:
½ lb. mushrooms
Stir in:
¼ cup flour
Stir in gradually:
1¾ cups milk
Simmer in their liquor until
plump:
½ pint oysters: 1 cup
Strain and reserve the liquor.
Dry in a towel and add the
oysters to the hot cream sauce.
Stir in:
¼ lb. cooked shelled
shrimp, split lengthwise
Remove the sauce from the heat.

Add the oyster liquor and:
½ cup dry white wine
Correct the seasoning
Pour the sauce over the fillets.
Bake about 10 minutes or until
firm when pressed.

FILLETS OF FISH ON [3] SPINACH WITH SHRIMP AND MUSHROOMS

Cook, page 359, drain and chop:
1 lb. spinach or broccoli
Poach, page 398:
1 lb. fish fillets
Cook, then shell, page 441:
½ lb. shrimp cut lengthwise
Sauté:
½ lb. mushrooms
Prepare:
1 cup Cream Sauce,
page 359
using part of the stock in which
the fish was poached, and part
cream. Combine:
1 egg yolk
¼ cup dry white wine
Add these ingredients to the
cream sauce. Thicken the sauce
by stirring over low heat, but
do not let it boil. Place the spinach on a buttered ovenproof
dish, place the fillets on it. Pour
the sauce over them. Surround
them with the mushrooms and
shrimp. Place the dish in a preheated 400° oven until well
heated.

QUICK BAKED [3] FILLETS OF FISH

Preheat oven to 350°.
Place in an ovenproof dish:
1 lb. small skinned fish
fillets
Stir and heat until smooth:
⅔ cup condensed soup:
tomato, celery, mushroom
or asparagus
2 tablespoons milk, stock,
or dry white wine
Add:
A few grains cayenne
Pour the sauce over the fish.

Bake ♦ uncovered 10 minutes.
Serve with:
    Steamed Rice

BAKED STUFFED FISH   [6]

♦ If you bone a fish before stuffing be sure to leave the skin intact. Stuffed fish, like stuffed meats, need a longer baking period to the pound. See About Cooking Fish, page 395.

Dressing for fish should not be so bold in seasoning as to destroy the naturally delicate fish flavor. Scandinavians would object to this counsel, and make lavish use of fennel in preparing many of their traditional seafood dishes.
Scale, eviscerate and clean:
    A 3-lb. fish
Preheat oven to 325°.
Stuff fish with:
    1½ cups Oyster Bread
        Dressing, page 561, or
        Bread Dressing for Fish,
        page 561, or Green
        Dressing, page 562
or with a combination of:
    Pressed cucumbers,
        bread crumbs and
        almonds
Bake about 40 minutes or until done.
Serve with a sauce of equal parts of:
    Butter and sauterne
and:
    Lime wedges

BAKED FILLETS OF   [4]
FISH IN WINE

Preheat oven to 350°.
Place in a greased ovenproof dish:
    1½ lbs. fillets of sole or
        other fish
If the fillets are large they may be cut in half. Pour over them:
    1 cup dry white wine
    (2 tablespoons dry sherry)
Bake until just done, see page 396. Serve covered with the liquid from the dish, which you

may reduce slightly. Garnish with:
    Lemon wedges
    Sautéed mushroom caps

BAKED FISH WITH   [8]
SOUR CREAM

Preheat oven to 350°.
Split and remove the bones from:
    A 4-lb. whitefish
Flatten it out. Rub inside and out with:
    Paprika and butter
Place on an ovenproof dish.
Cover with:
    2 cups cultured sour cream
Lid the dish. Bake the fish for about ¾ hour, or until done, see page 396. Before serving sprinkle with:
    Chopped parsley

FISH BAKED IN A   [4]
COVERED DISH

Preheat oven to 350°.
This is a simple way to bring out the flavor of a delicate fish.
Combine:
    2 tablespoons Clarified
        Butter, page 383
    ¼ teaspoon pepper or
        paprika
    A fresh grating of
        nutmeg
Rub well over:
    2 lbs. fish, preferably in 1
        chunky piece
Place the fish in an ovenproof dish. Cover with a closely fitting lid. Bake 20 to 25 minutes, or until done. The time depends largely on the shape of the fish.
Add while cooking:
    (2 tablespoons dry white
        wine)
Place the fish on a hot platter.
Melt:
    3 tablespoons butter
Add:
    2 tablespoons capers
    1 teaspoon chopped
        parsley
    1 teaspoon chopped chives

2 teaspoons lemon juice
    Correct the seasoning
Pour this or some other suitable
sauce over the fish.

▤ FISH BAKED IN FOIL

[Individual Serving]
Preheat oven to 350°.
Clean a small fish. Rub with:
    Seasoned Butter,
    page 383
Place on a piece of buttered
aluminum foil large enough to
make a generous fold at the
edges. Do not include more than
1 lb. in each packet. Bake 35
to 40 minutes to the pound.

MOLDED FILLED   [4]
FILLETS OF FISH OR
PAUPIETTES

Preheat oven to 375°.
Have ready:
    8 fillets of Dover sole or
    blue fish, or any other
    very thin fillet
Butter 4 individual molds. Line
each mold by placing 2 fillets
crisscrossed at right angles, filling the center with the farce
below, or with a Fish Quenelle
Mixture, page 180, and overlapping the ends of the fillets to
make a casing. Combine and stir
with a fork a farce made of:
    ¼ cup melted butter
    1½ cups soft bread crumbs
    ¼ cup chopped celery
    1 teaspoon grated onion
    1 tablespoon chopped
    parsley
    (⅛ teaspoon dried burnet or
    basil)
    ¼ teaspoon salt
Fill the molds with this filling.
Place the molds in a pan of hot
water. Bake for about ½ hour.
Unmold on a hot platter. Garnish with:
    Lemon wedges
    Parsley or watercress
Serve with:
    Lemon Butter, page 384,
    or a seafood sauce, page

377, or Oyster Sauce for
    Fish, page 361

PLANKED FISH   [6]

▶ Please read About Planking,
page 80.
Preheat oven to 350°.
Scale, clean, wash in running
water and dry:
    A 3 to 4 lb. fish
Brush with:
    Clarified butter or
    cooking oil
Place the fish on a well-greased
ovenproof or metal platter,
about 18 x 13 inches. A Seasoned Plank, page 80, may be
used ▶ but if used, should in
the future be reserved solely for
fish. Bake the fish 40 to 60 minutes; ▶ if stuffed, about 10 minutes longer.
Preheat broiler.
Garnish the platter with a decorative edging of:
    Duchess Potatoes,
    page 319
Broil 6 to 8 minutes, 8 inches
from the source of heat or until
the potato garnish is delicately
browned. Further garnish the
plank with:
    A stuffed vegetable
    Parsley, fennel or
    watercress
and serve.

FISH IN ASPIC   [5]
COCKAIGNE

Prepare for cooking, page 393,
then cut into 4 or 5 pieces:
    A fish weighing about
    2½ lbs.
Bring to the boiling point:
    5 cups water
    3 or 4 ribs celery with
    leaves
    1 small sliced onion
    4 or 5 sprigs parsley
    3 tablespoons lemon juice
    1 inch lemon rind
    3 peppercorns
    ½ teaspoon dried herbs:
    tarragon, basil, etc.

½ teaspoon paprika
1 teaspoon salt

Drop the fish into the boiling stock. ♦ Simmer until tender. Do not let it boil at any time. This is a quick process, requiring only 12 to 15 minutes or so. To test for doneness, see page 396. Remove it at once from the stock. Strain the stock. There should be about 3½ cups. If there is not, add water or chicken stock to make up the difference. Soak:

2 tablespoons gelatin

in:

¼ cup cold fish stock

Dissolve it in the hot stock. Add:

2 tablespoons or more
   capers
2 to 3 tablespoons lemon
   juice or dry white wine
Correct the seasoning

Chill until it begins to thicken. Remove the skin and bone from the fish. Leave it in large flakes or pieces. Place a layer of aspic in a wet mold, cover it with flaked fish and repeat this process, winding up with aspic on top. Chill. Serve the aspic very cold with:

Mayonnaise, page 345,
   or cultured sour cream

to either of which you may add:

1 to 2 tablespoons chopped
   herbs: chives, tarragon,
   parsley, etc.
Diced cucumbers

Decorate the platter with watercress or shredded lettuce, and surround it with deviled eggs, radishes and olives. Serve with:

Brioche Loaf Cockaigne
   (II, 245), or Garlic
   Bread (II, 289)

PICKLED FISH OR ESCABÈCHE

[Allow ½ Pound Per Serving]
Preheat deep fryer to 375°.
♦ Please read About Deep Fat Frying, pages 75–79.

Use smelts, fresh anchovies, sardines, whitings or mullets not over ½ inch thick. For an alternate method, see (II, 79).
Clean, wash, dry and flour:

1 lb. small whole fish

Plunge them into:

Hot cooking oil

for 5 to 10 seconds, according to size. Remove them, drain, and arrange in a shallow ovenproof glass or earthenware dish. Using 3 tablespoons of the oil, sauté until the onion is translucent:

2 tablespoons finely minced
   carrot
1 small finely minced
   onion
4 whole cloves garlic

Add:

⅔ cup wine vinegar
¼ cup water
A small bay leaf
A sprig of thyme
Salt
2 small red hot peppers

Simmer for 10 minutes, then pour sauce over the fish. When cooled, refrigerate for 24 hours. Serve the fish in the same dish in which it was marinated.

GEFÜLLTE FISH OR POACHED FISH BALLS

[Allow ½ Pound Per Person]
Using two varieties of fish, lean and fat, remove the skin and bone from:

3 lbs. of fish: jack salmon
   and white

Put the fish through a fine food chopper with:

3 large onions

Place this ground mixture in a large bowl. Slowly add, mixing well until fluffy:

1 well-beaten egg
¾ cup cold water
1 teaspoon salt
¼ cup soft white bread
   crumbs or matzo meal
½ teaspoon pepper

Place heads, skins and bones of fish in a large pan and add:

Water to cover
1 large sliced onion
2 thinly sliced carrots
Salt and pepper

Bring to a boil. Wet hands to facilitate handling. Form the ground fish mixture into small balls. Drop the balls into the boiling stock. Reduce the heat, cover the kettle and ◖ simmer for 2 hours. Remove the fish balls. The fish liquid may be strained and thickened with egg yolks, page 356, to make the sauce.

SOUTHERN FRIED CATFISH

Preheat deep fryer to 370°.
Clean and skin:
A catfish
Dredge with:
Seasoned white corn meal
Fry in hot fat until golden brown. Serve with:
Hush Puppies (II, 279)
Sliced Tomatoes, page 47

ABOUT CARP

These great, languid, soft-finned fish, whose portraits we admire on Chinese scrolls, can be admirable eating too. But be sure to hold them alive for several days in clear, running water—to rid them of the muddiness they acquire in their native haunts. To enjoy carp at their best, they should be killed just before cooking. If you cannot appoint a Lord High Executioner and must perform the act yourself, we recommend a preliminary perusal of the chapter called "Murder in the Kitchen," in Alice B. Toklas' weird and wonderful "Cookbook."

Carp lend themselves to cooking Au Bleu, page 399; are delicious baked, stuffed or braised; in red wine (II, 149); and eaten hot or cold. Serve with new potatoes and Celeriac, page 283.

ABOUT COD

Through the ages cod has been one of the mainstays of the Lenten diet. It has endless variations. Salt cod, often very tough, is pounded before desalting. To freshen salt cod, leave it under running water for 6 hours; or soak it up to 48 hours in several changes of water in a glass, enamel or stainless steel pan.

Salt cod is most often used flaked. To prepare for flaking, put the desalted fish in cold unsalted Court Bouillon (II, 146) to cover, then bring it to a boil and ◖ simmer for 20 to 30 minutes. Skin, bone and flake it. One lb. dried salt cod will yield about 2 cups cooked flaked fish.

SCALLOPED COD [4]

Preheat oven to 375°.
◖ Please read About Cod, above.
Cook and flake:
1 lb. dried salt cod
Combine:
1 tablespoon flour
2 cups milk
1 well-beaten egg
Cook and stir these ingredients until they are thick in the top of a double boiler ◖ over, not in, hot water.
Correct the seasoning
Prepare:
1½ cups bread crumbs
1½ cups finely chopped celery
Grease a baking dish. Place in it ½ the fish and a layer of ⅓ the crumbs and celery. Cover with ½ the sauce and repeat the process. Sprinkle the remaining crumbs on the top. Dot with:
Butter or grated cheese
Bake for about 20 minutes, or until the crumbs are golden brown.

CODFISH BALLS OR [4]
CAKES

♦ Please read About Cod, page 407.

Soak in water for 12 hours, drain, place in boiling water, and simmer for 15 minutes:

    1 cup salt cod

Drain and flake it. Rice or mash:

    6 medium-sized boiled
      potatoes

Combine the fish and potatoes. Beat in one at a time:

    2 eggs

Beat in until fluffy:

    2 tablespoons cream
    (1 teaspoon grated onion)
      Correct the seasoning

Shape the mixture into balls or patties, and use one of the following cooking methods.

I. Form the mixture into 2-inch cakes, dip in flour and sauté in butter until brown. Serve at once.

II. Preheat deep fryer to 375°. Form into 1-inch balls, dip in milk, roll in flour. Fry until golden brown.

III. Preheat oven to 375°. Form into patties and bake in a greased pan about ½ hour. Dot with butter and serve.

FRESH COD À LA [4]
PORTUGAISE

Season:

    4 thick cod fillets

with:

    Pepper

Place the fish in a heavy saucepan. Add:

    1 finely chopped onion
    1 crushed clove garlic
    ¼ cup coarsely chopped
      parsley
    A sprig of thyme
    3 peeled, seeded and
      coarsely chopped
      tomatoes
    ½ cup dry white wine

Bring to boiling point, ♦ reduce the heat and simmer gently ♦ covered for about 10 minutes. Remove the fish carefully. Arrange it on a hot serving dish and keep warm. Reduce the cooking liquid by ⅓.

Correct the seasoning and finish with a Butter Swirl, page 357. Pour the sauce over the fish and serve at once.

SALT COD OR MORUE [4]
À LA PROVENÇALE

♦ Please read About Cod, page 407.

Cook, drain, cut into 2-inch cubes and reserve:

    1 lb. salt cod

In a large saucepan fry gently until golden:

    3 tablespoons olive oil
    1 minced clove garlic
    3 large chopped onions
    1 large sliced leek, white
      part only

Add and simmer gently for about 15 minutes:

    1 quart hot water
    ¼ cup tomato paste
    ¼ teaspoon each dried sage,
      thyme, and rosemary
    1 bay leaf
    1 small hot Spanish pepper
    1 chopped green pepper,
      seeds and membrane
      removed

Add to the sauce and simmer until tender:

    2 cups peeled potatoes cut
      Parisienne, page 250

Add the cod to the hot sauce and set the pan over very low heat until the cod is heated through. Garnish with:

    Triangles of fried French
      bread
    Chopped parsley

COD SOUNDS AND
TONGUES

[Allow About ¼ Pound
Per Serving]
Sounds—or cheeks—and tongues

may come fresh or salted. If salted, they must be soaked overnight, drained, simmered for 5 minutes in water started cold, then drained again. To poach, cover with boiling water, ▶ reduce the heat and simmer about 5 minutes. Drain. Serve this way with Mornay Sauce, page 361, or Poulette Sauce, page 362. Or you may sauté them until golden brown. Serve with Maître d'Hôtel Butter, page 384.

FRESH COD [4]
BOULANGÈRE

Preheat oven to 350°.
Parboil in separate pans:
   16 small peeled potatoes
   12 small white onions
Place in a shallow buttered heat-proof dish:
   A center cut of cod or a
      whole small cleaned cod
Arrange the onions and potatoes around it and sprinkle with:
   A pinch of thyme
   Correct the seasoning
Brush with:
   Melted butter
Baste frequently with melted butter during the baking process. Bake about ½ hour. Serve in the same dish garnished with:
   Chopped parsley
   Slices of lemon

BROILED FRESH SCROD

[Allow ½ Pound Per Serving]
Split, then remove the bones from:
   A young codfish: scrod
Leave it whole, flatten it out, or cut it in pieces. Broil as described on page 399.

ABOUT EEL

The eel is a fish which believes in long journeys. It is spawned in the Sargasso Sea in the western Atlantic, and from there will travel back to its fresh water haunts in this country or in Europe to feed and grow up in the rivers and streams frequented by its parents. The young eel or elver is still only 2 or 3 inches longer after its immense journey, and is transparent and yellowish. Little eels can be cooked and larger ones smoked or pickled to make a delicious addition to Hors d'Oeuvre or Antipasto (II, 69). As with cats, there is more than one way to skin a fresh eel. We prefer the following. Slip a noose around the eel's head and hang the other end of the cord on a hook, high on the wall. Cut the eel skin about 3 inches below the head all around, so as not to penetrate the gall bladder which lies close to the head. Peel the skin back, pulling down hard—if necessary with a pair of pliers—until the whole skin comes off like a glove. Clean the fish by slitting the white belly and removing the gut which lies close to the thin belly skin.
Eel may be sautéed as for:
   Trout à la Meunière,
      page 419
poached for 9 to 10 minutes and then served with a:
   Velouté Sauce, page 362
or one of its variations, made from the eel stock. Skinned, cleaned, boned and cut into 3-inch pieces and dried, eel may be dipped in:
   Batter (II, 125)
   Bound Breading (II,
      160)
and deep fried until golden brown. Serve this way with:
   Fried Parsley, page 305
      and lemon wedges,
   Tartare Sauce or Tomato
      Sauce, page 376
Eel may also be broiled as for any fat fish, page 399.

MARINATED [6]
FLOUNDER FILLETS

Marinate for 10 minutes:

2 lbs. flounder fillets
in:
  1 cup tarragon vinegar
Drain, and coat with a mixture
of:
  ½ cup yellow corn meal
  ½ cup flour
  ¼ teaspoon salt
  ⅛ teaspoon freshly ground
    pepper
Sauté the fillets in:
  ¼ cup butter
until golden brown, about 4
minutes on each side. Serve
with:
  Hot Ravigote Sauce,
    page 364, or Cucumber
    Sauce, page 251

ABOUT HADDOCK

Fresh haddock may be prepared
as in any recipe for cod, flounder or other lean white fish. It
may be baked plain or stuffed,
its fillets fried, sautéed, or
poached. Smoked haddock—or
finnan haddie—may be broiled,
well basted in butter, or baked,
as in the following recipe.

CREAMED FINNAN
HADDIE

Barely cover:
  Finnan haddie: smoked
haddock
with:
  Milk
Soak for 1 hour. Bring slowly
to the boiling point. Simmer for
20 minutes. Drain. Flake and
remove the skin and bones.
Place the fish in very hot:
  Cream Sauce I, page 359
Use about ⅔ as much sauce as
you have fish. Add for each cup
of flaked fish:
  1 chopped hard-cooked egg
  1 teaspoon chopped green
    pepper, seeds and
    membrane removed
  1 teaspoon chopped
    pimiento
Serve fish on:
  Rounds of toast

sprinkled with:
  Lemon juice
  Chopped chives or
    parsley

BAKED STUFFED   [6]
FRESH HADDOCK

Preheat oven to 375°.
Sauté in a large saucepan for
about 5 minutes:
  ½ cup chopped onion
  ¼ cup chopped celery
  ½ cup chopped fresh
    mushrooms
in:
  3 tablespoons butter
Stir into the sautéed vegetables:
  2 cups soft bread crumbs
  1 teaspoon salt
  ⅛ teaspoon pepper
    A pinch of dried tarragon
    (A pinch of dried
    rosemary)
Arrange in a layer on a greased
large shallow baking dish:
  2 lbs. haddock fillets
Sprinkle the fish with:
  Lemon juice
and spread the stuffing over it.
Cover with:
  3 or 4 peeled sliced
    tomatoes
Bake uncovered for 35 to 40
minutes.
Serve with:
  Boiled Potatoes, page
    310

BAKED FINNAN   [6]
HADDIE

Preheat oven to 350°.
Prepare for cooking:
  2 lbs. finnan haddie:
    smoked haddock
Soak it in warm water for ½
hour, skin side down. Pour off
the water. Put the fish on a
greased ovenproof pan and
cover it with:
  1 cup cream
Dot generously with:
  Butter
Sprinkle with:

¼ cup chopped onions
   Paprika

Bake for about 40 minutes. If cream evaporates, use additional cream. The dish may be served with:

   Cream Sauce I, page 359

BAKED FRESH   [4]
FILLETS OF HADDOCK
IN CREAM SAUCE

Preheat oven to 350°

Place on an ovenproof dish:
   4 haddock or other lean
     fish fillets

Prepare:
   2 cups Cream Sauce I,
     page 359, or
     Cheese Sauce, page 364

Season the sauce well, adding:
   1 teaspoon Worcestershire
     sauce or ½ teaspoon dry
     mustard or 1 teaspoon
     fennel, dill or celery seed
     (2 tablespoons dry sherry)

Pour it over the fillets. Bake the fish until done, see page 396. You may sprinkle over it:
   1 cup or more freshly
     cooked or canned shrimp
     or crab meat

Place the dish under a broiler until the top is heated. Sprinkle with:

   Chopped parsley

ABOUT HERRING

Herring is one of the cheapest, most nutritious and plentiful fish one can buy. It is very fat, with a calcium content twice that of milk. Split, salted and smoked, it is known as a **kipper**; smoke-cured without salt, as a **bloater**. Bloaters are very perishable and should be eaten right after curing. Perhaps the reason herring is not more popular is because it has innumerable tiny, fine bones. If you split a herring down the center of the back with a sharp knife, lever up the backbone and carefully pull it out, most of these small bones will come with it. After cleaning, page 393, you may then cook the herring in one piece or split it in two.

Marinated herring comes in various disguises. Rollmops are fresh herring fillets seasoned and rolled—like Paupiettes, page 405—around a pickle or cucumber. **Bismarck herring** is the flat fillet in a sour marinade; **matjes** or virgin herring can be sour or salted. Herring also comes with the roe or milt sieved and thinned with sour cream as a dressing over the fish, pages 351 and 416.

BAKED HERRING AND   [4]
POTATOES

Preheat oven to 375°.

I. To prepare salt herring, soak overnight in water or milk to cover:
   2 large salt herring

Drain and split them. Remove and discard skin and bones. They can now be used as a garnish for hors d'oeuvre, on lasagne; or as follows. Cut fillets into 1-inch-wide pieces. Pare and slice very thinly:
   6 raw potatoes
   2 medium-sized onions

Butter a baking dish. Place in it alternate layers of potatoes, onions and herring, beginning and ending with potatoes. Cover the top with:

   Au Gratin II, page 389

Bake for 45 minutes or more.

II. A Yorkshire version substitutes:

   Sour apples

for the onions, and uses:

   Fresh herring

In this case, prepare as above, but season with:

   Salt and pepper

after each layer of herring.

MARINATED HERRING [12]

Soak for 3 hours in water to cover:

24 milter herring
Change the water twice. Cut off
the heads and tails. Split the
herring. Remove the milt, page
416. Reserve it. Remove the
bones as described, page 411.
Discard them. Cut the fillets into
pieces about 3 inches long. Place
in a crock in alternate layers
with the herring:
    ½ the milt
    2 very thinly sliced lemons
    2 skinned and thinly sliced
        onions
    ⅓ cup mixed pickle spices
    1 tablespoon sugar
Cover these ingredients with:
    Malt vinegar or other
        vinegar
Crush with a fork and add:
    The remaining milt
Dilute the vinegar with a little
water if it is very strong. ▸
Cover the crock and put it in a
cool place. The herring will be
ready to serve after 2 weeks.

MARINATED HERRING
WITH SOUR CREAM

Prepare, as above:
    6 milter herring
using only 1 lemon, 1 onion,
2½ tablespoons mixed spices
and ¼ cup vinegar.
Add:
    1 cup cultured sour cream
Keep in a cool place. Serve after
48 hours.

SCOTCH FRIED HERRING

[Allow 1 Herring Per Serving]
This must be made with:
    Fresh caught herring
You may fry them whole but
they are better split down the
backbone and boned, as described, page 411. Cut off head,
tail and fins. Roll in:
    Medium-ground seasoned
        Scotch oatmeal
pressing a little to make it stick.
Fry the herring on both sides in:
    Bacon fat or olive oil
Serve with:

    Lemon wedges
    A pat of butter
or with:
    Mustard Sauce, page 363
Garnish with:
    Parsley

GRILLED OR BAKED
KIPPERS OR BLOATERS

[Allow ½ Pound Per Serving]
Preheat broiler.
An excellent breakfast dish with
scrambled eggs. Do not try to
grill canned kippers; they are
too wet. Place:
    Kippers or bloaters
skin side down on a hot oiled
grill. Dot with:
    Butter
Grill 5 to 7 minutes. Serve very
hot. You may also bake them in
a 350° oven for 10 minutes, or
En Papillote, page 87, for 15
minutes at the same temperature. Season with:
    A little lemon juice
    Pepper

ABOUT OCTOPUS AND
SQUID

These fish are similar in shape,
treatment and taste. They both
have long edible arms, a body
that can be formed into a natural sack for stuffing if desired,
and an ink-expelling mechanism. The transparent cartilage
must be removed from squid
and octopus before they are
ready for the kitchen; and some
of it, after heating and drying,
becomes the cuttlebone one sees
in birdcages.

Of much greater importance
to us is the ink. Not only does
it furnish the pigment known as
sepia, but it may be used in
recipes just as blood is used,
page 357, to color, flavor and
give body to a sauce. When the
ink is not available, it is sometimes "faked" by the use of
chocolate, as in Mole Sauce,
page 586.

To prepare octopus and squid, remove the beaklike mouth, anal portion and the eyes—being careful not to pierce the ink sack which lies close by. If inkfish are small, this may be done with scissors; if large and tough, you will need a knife to penetrate far enough to slip them inside out and remove and discard the yellowish pouch and the attached membranes. On octopus the very ends of the tentacles are also discarded. Wash well in running water to remove gelatinous portions. Octopus, which has 8 arms, comes in enormous sizes, but is apt to be very tough if over 2 to 2½ lbs. in weight. Both these and the 8 to 12 inch squid, which have 6 arms and 2 tentacles, need tenderizing. This can be done in 2 ways: by merciless beating—native fishermen pound them on the rocks— or by adding tenderizer to a marinade.

The arms and tentacles are cut crosswise in 1 to 1¼ inch rounds and the white portions of the body meat are often cut in diamond shapes of about the same size to equalize the cooking time. ‣ To skin these sections, Parblanch, page 88, briefly 1 to 2 minutes, and arrest further cooking by plunging them into cold water. If you do not deep fat fry as for other fish, page 401—a matter of 3 to 4 minutes at 375°—long slow cooking is necessary. Even after marinating, the simmering time may run close to 3 hours, unless the specimens are very young and well pounded, when 45 minutes should suffice.

Squid is available ready to use in cans and is sometimes found frozen or dried. ‣ To use dried squid, marinate in a combination of water, gin and ginger for 45 minutes and then use in recipes as for the fresh meat. ‣ Allow about ½ lb. of fresh squid or octopus per serving.

CASSEROLED OCTOPUS

[Allow ½ lb. Per Person]
Clean, pound, and cut up as described previously and place in a casserole:

> 6 small octopus
> ½ cup olive oil
> ⅓ cup vinegar or ½ cup dry wine
> 2 cups julienned mushrooms
> 1 cup chopped onions
> 1 pressed clove garlic
> 1 tablespoon each fresh chopped parsley, chervil and basil
> ⅓ bay leaf

Cover and bring just to a boil. ‣ Reduce the heat at once and ‣ simmer, very tightly covered, 2½ to 3 hours. You may add the ink to the pan drippings just before serving. ‣ Do not boil. Serve with:

> Creamed Spinach, page 326

BOILED SALT MACKEREL

[Allow ⅓ to ½ Pound Per Serving]
Soak overnight, skin side up, well covered with cold water:

> Salt mackerel

Drain, place in a shallow pan, cover with water and simmer until tender, for about 12 minutes. Drain well. Place on a hot platter. Pour over the fish:

> Melted butter

to which add:

> Chopped chives or parsley, lemon juice or Worcestershire sauce

BROILED FRESH MACKEREL

Preheat broiler.
Split and bone:

> A Mackerel, page 392

Place it skin down in a greased
pan. Sprinkle with:

Paprika

Brush with:

Melted butter or olive oil

Broil slowly on one side only
until firm, about 20 minutes.
Baste with the drippings while
cooking. Remove to a hot platter. Spread with:

**Anchovy Butter, page
384**

Garnish with:

Parsley and lemon slices

BROILED SALT MACKEREL

[Allow ⅓ to ½ Pound Per
Serving]

Soak by the preceding recipe:

Salt mackerel

Drain, then wipe dry.
Preheat broiler.
Brush with:

Melted butter

Broil, skin side down. Baste
twice with melted butter while
cooking. Remove to a hot
platter. Pour over the fish:

**½ cup Cream Sauce I,
page 359**

Garnish with:

Chopped parsley

ABOUT PIKE, PICKEREL AND MUSKELLUNGE

These fish, which are naturally
dry, may be marinated or not,
as desired, before cooking. Many
cooks prefer to bake or braise
them, page 398.

POMPANO EN PAPILLOTE

[Individual Serving]

Preheat oven to 450°.
Place on heart-shaped parchment paper, page 86.

**2 medium-sized skinned
pompano fillets**

Cover with:

**2 tablespoons Velouté
Sauce, page 362**

2 chopped cooked shrimp

**2 tablespoons chopped
cooked crab meat**

Close the parchment paper, fold
the edge and bake for about 15
minutes until the paper is
browned and puffed. Serve immediately. For a party, make individual packets ahead of time,
allow them to reach about 60°.
Preheat oven and bake as above.

ABOUT SALMON

Atlantic salmon, pink and prized,
comes to our markets mainly in
fresh form. Pacific salmon
reaches us in many forms. These
include the choice King or
Chinook from Alaska and the
Columbia River areas. They may
be pink or white-fleshed, and
are about 17% fat. Included also
are the red-fleshed sockeye, the
pinkish silver Coho and the
yellowish-fleshed, almost fat-
free, dog salmon. ◊ All smoked
salmon is highly perishable and
should be kept refrigerated even
when canned. Regular canned
salmon, if in tall cans, is tail
meat; if in squat cans it comes
from the center cuts.

BROILED SALMON STEAKS OR DARNES

[Allow ½ Pound Per Serving]

Preheat broiler.
To cut steaks or darnes, see
page 394.
Brush preheated broiler rack
and:

¾-inch-thick salmon steaks

well with:

Clarified Butter, page 383

Place rack 6 inches from the
source of heat. Broil 5 minutes.
Baste, turn, baste again and continue to broil 5 to 8 minutes. To
test for doneness, see if you can
lift out the central bone without bringing any of the flesh
with it. Serve with:

**Freshly grated horse-
radish**

The steak shape lends itself to
attractive service as the hollow
may be filled with:

A stuffed tomato, or
A mound of vegetables, or
Potatoes garnished with parsley

COLD GLAZED SALMON

[Allow ½ Pound Per Serving]
This method of preparation applies to any fish you wish to glaze and serve cold.
Poach, page 398, leaving head and tail on:

1 large cleaned salmon

Remove from the poaching water as soon as it is done. Leaving the head and tail as it is, and working with the grain, skin and trim the rest of the fish, removing the fins and the gray, fatty portions until just the pink flesh is left. Place on a large serving platter and refrigerate. If you have an emergency, the fish may be eaten just this way with mayonnaise. But to glaze—read on. ◗ Work quickly to prevent the glaze from darkening, and keep chilling between processes. Coat the visible pink portion of the fish evenly and smoothly with:

Mayonnaise Collée, page 387, or
Sauce Chaud-Froid, page 388

Rechill until this sauce has set. Decorate as described in the Sauce Chaud-Froid recipe. Chill again. Coat the whole surface, head and tail too, with:

Aspic Glaze, page 387

Chill and continue coating and chilling until you have built up an even clear ¼ inch of aspic. Clean the platter by removing aspic dribbles. Save any leftover aspic and chill it in sheet form. Chop it fine and surround the fish with an edging of little sparkling tidbits. Serve the fish with:

Cold Mousseline Sauce, page 370, or

Green Mayonnaise, page 348

The classic garnish is:
Tiny tomatoes stuffed with Russian Salad, page 40

We suggest also:
Cold Leeks Vinaigrette

ABOUT SARDINES

Sardines were to us something that came out of a can on laundry day until one summer we had a Breton guest. Her family had for centuries lived an amicably divided life in seaside castles on opposite sides of a river inlet. Her uncle's fleets dredged seaweed from which chemicals were produced. Her father's fleet sailed from Maine to Spain—following those Atlantic sardines which were fit even for the Czar of Russia, himself, to whom they were purveyed. But fish, like people, may change habits suddenly. For three years the fleet failed to find the sardine runs. Sonar might have changed Odette's fate, but Brittany's loss was our vivacious and warmhearted gain.
Pacific sardines are almost twice as large as the Atlantic kind, and both are bigger than the type of pilchards originally caught off Sardinia. Anchovies are even smaller sardines. When smoked, sardines are referred to as sprats. Treat fresh sardines as for Smelts, page 417.

If you want to present canned sardines in an interesting way, skin and bone:

12 canned sardines

Mash 6 of them with:
1 teaspoon minced onion
2 teaspoons butter
½ teaspoon prepared mustard
1 teaspoon lemon juice

Spread:
6 narrow toasts

with this mixture. Place a whole sardine on each toast and run under the broiler. Before serving garnish with:

> Finely chopped fennel
> A grating of black pepper

ABOUT SEA SQUAB OR BLOWFISH

These puffers are related to the sought after Japanese fugu. As the ovaries and liver are very poisonous be sure to discard all but the back flesh before cooking. Prepare as for any delicate fish.

ABOUT ROE AND MILT

The eggs of the female fish are known as roe or hard roe; the male fish's sperm is known as milt or soft roe, as its texture is creamy rather than grainy. Both types are used in cooking and the roe of certain fish is more valued than the fish itself, see Caviar (II, 79).

Shad roe is considered choice. You may serve the roe or milt of other fish such as herring, mackerel, flounder, salmon, or cod as in the following recipes for shad roe. The milt of salmon must have the vein removed.

Hard roe, to be cooked and served alone, should be pricked with a needle to prevent the membrane from bursting and splattering the little eggs. Cook roe gently with very slow heat. Overcooked, it is hard, dry, and tasteless. It may be served as a luncheon dish; as a savory; as stuffing or garnish for the fish from which it comes. Or it may be used raw, as in Marinated Herring, page 411, or as an hors d'oeuvre. Also see Canned Roe Dishes, page 236.
♦ Allow 6 oz. Per Serving.

PARBOILED SHAD ROE

♦ Please read About Roe, above. Prick with a needle in several places and cover with boiling water:

> Shad roe

Add to it:

> 2 tablespoons lemon juice
> or 3 tablespoons dry
> white wine

Simmer from 3 to 12 minutes, according to size. Drain and cool. Remove the membrane. Add salt if needed. The roe is now ready to be sautéed, sauced, or used in a garnish or hors d'oeuvre.

BAKED SHAD ROE

Preheat oven to 375°.
Parboil:

> Shad roe

Place in a buttered pan. Cover with:

> Creole Sauce, page
> 376, or
> Mushroom Sauce, page
> 367

Bake for 15 or 20 minutes, basting every 5 minutes.

SAUTÉED SHAD ROE

Heat until light brown:

> 2 tablespoons Clarified
> Butter, page 383

Sauté in this until delicately browned on both sides:

> Parboiled Shad Roe, see
> above

Correct the seasoning
Remove to a hot platter. Add to the drippings and heat:

> 2 teaspoons lemon juice
> ½ teaspoon chopped chives
> ½ teaspoon chopped
> parsley
> 1 minced shallot
> ½ teaspoon dried tarragon,
> chervil or basil

Pour the sauce over the roe. Sautéed roe is frequently served with Tartare Sauce, page 349. Or sprinkle with:

> Chopped parsley, lemon
> juice and Brown Butter,
> page 383

Surround with:
        Orange sections

BROILED SHAD ROE

Preheat broiler.
Parboil, page 88, wipe dry and place on a greased rack:
        Shad roe
Sprinkle with:
        Lemon juice
Bard with:
        Bacon
Broil from 5 to 7 minutes. If the roe is large, you may have to turn it, baste with drippings and cook until firm. Serve on toast garnished with:
        Maître d'Hôtel Butter, page 384
        Parsley

BAKED SHAD WITH [6 to 8] CREAMED ROE

Preheat oven to 350°.
Parboil, page 88:
        Shad roe
▶ Simmer for 15 minutes. Drain. Remove the outside membrane. Mash the roe. Melt in a saucepan:
        2 tablespoons butter
You may add and sauté for about 3 minutes:
        1 tablespoon grated onion
Add the roe and stir in:
        2 tablespoons flour
        ½ cup cream
When these ingredients begin to boil, remove from heat. Stir in:
        2 egg yolks
Season the roe mixture well with:
        Dry white wine or lemon juice
Keep hot. Bone, page 395:
        A 3 or 4 lb. shad
Place it skin side down on a well-greased broiler rack or a flat pan. Brush it with:
        Melted butter
Bake, allowing about 8 minutes per pound. Remove from the oven and spread the thin part of the fish with the creamed roe.

Cover the fish with:
        Au Gratin Sauce II, page 389
Return to the broiler and brown evenly. Serve at once garnished with:
        Lemon slices
        Parsley or water cress
        Pickled beets or cucumbers

ABOUT CARVING SHAD

Carving shad is a very direct process. Before cooking, every effort must be made to remove as many bones as possible. Even tweezers may be resorted to. When carving time comes, the fish is sliced completely through its entire thickness in about 4-inch parallel widths. Any exposed bones may again be removed with tweezers before the cut pieces are put on the individual plates.

ABOUT SHARK

If you care to adventure, you will find that shark meat—close to and along the backbone—responds to recipes for Fish Fillets, pages 401–405, or to Poaching, page 490. The belly sections need long simmering.

SMELTS   [2]

Clean, see page 393, rinse thoroughly and wipe dry:
        12 smelts
Leave whole. Season with:
        Lemon juice
Let them stand covered for 15 minutes. Roll the smelts in:
        Cream
Dip in:
        Flour or corn meal
I. Melt:
        ¼ cup butter
Sauté the smelts gently until they are done.

II. Bake smelts in a buttered pan in a 450° oven for about 5 minutes. Place them on a hot

platter. Add to the butter in the
pan:

Juice of 1 lemon
2 tablespoons chopped
parsley or chives

Pour the sauce over the smelts.

III. ◆ Please read About Deep
Fat Frying, pages 75–79.
Smelts may be dipped in crumbs
or egg and crumbs and fried in
deep fat at 370° about 3 minutes. Serve with:

Tartare Sauce, page 349

BAKED RED   [4 to 6]
SNAPPER WITH SAVORY
TOMATO SAUCE

Preheat oven to 350°.
Prepare for cooking:

A 3-lb. red snapper or
other large fish

Dredge it inside and out with:
Seasoned flour

Place in a baking pan. Melt:
6 tablespoons butter

Add and simmer for 15 minutes:
½ cup chopped onion
2 cups chopped celery
¼ cup chopped green
pepper, seeds and
membrane removed

Add and simmer until the celery
is tender:

3 cups canned tomatoes
1 tablespoon Worcester-
shire sauce
1 tablespoon catsup
1 teaspoon chili powder
½ finely sliced lemon
2 bay leaves
1 minced clove garlic
1 teaspoon salt
A few grains red pepper

Press these ingredients through
a potato ricer or food mill. Pour
the sauce around the fish. Bake
the fish for about ¾ hour, basting frequently with the sauce.

SOLE AMBASSADOR

[Allow ½ lb. Per Person]
Prepare for poaching:
10 fillets of sole, lemon or

English, trout or halibut
Place them in a buttered heatproof dish or skillet and sprinkle
with:

1 tablespoon finely
chopped shallot or onion
Salt and pepper

Add:
½ cup dry white wine
Juice of 1 lemon

Cover with a buttered poaching
paper, page 84, and simmer
until the fillets are done, see
page 395. While they are cooking, melt in a heavy casserole:

1 tablespoon butter
Sauté:

1 cup finely chopped
mushrooms
Juice of ½ lemon
Salt and pepper

Cook over high heat for about
3 minutes, until the juices disappear. Reduce heat.
Add:

½ cup whipping cream
◆ Simmer until reduced by ⅓.
Remove from the heat and beat
in:

1 egg yolk
Drain and save the stock from
the fish. On a heatproof serving
platter, spread the mushroom
mixture, and arrange the fillets
over it. Heat the fish stock and
add:

Kneaded Butter, page
357

Beat in well until thickened.
Add:

½ cup whipping cream
Heat to the boiling point. ◆ Remove from the heat and add:

3 egg yolks
Strain the sauce and pour it
over the fish fillets. Glaze under
the broiler until brown. Serve at
once.

FILLET OF SOLE   [6]
FLORENTINE

Poach, page 398:
6 fillets of sole or other
fish

In the bottom of an ovenproof platter, put a layer of:

1½ cups Creamed Spinach, page 398

Arrange the poached, drained fillets on top. Cover with:

1 cup seasoned Cream Sauce II, page 359

Sprinkle over it:

Au Gratin III, page 389

Run under the broiler to heat through until the sauce is glazed.

SWORDFISH STEAKS

Prepare as for:

Salmon Steaks, page 414

As this fish dries out even when in prime condition, be sure to use plenty of butter in the cooking.

BROOK TROUT MEUNIÈRE [4]

Clean and wash:

4 brook trout: 8 inches each

Cut off the fins. Leave the head and tail on. Dip in:

Seasoned flour

Melt:

¼ cup Clarified Butter, page 383

Sauté the trout until they are firm and nicely browned. Remove to a hot platter. Add to the drippings in the pan:

3 tablespoons clarified butter

Let it brown. Cover the fish with:

Chopped parsley

Pour the browned butter over the fish. Garnish with:

Lemon wedges

BROILED LAKE TROUT OR WHITEFISH

[Allow About ½ Pound Per Serving]
Preheat broiler.
Bone, page 393:

A large fish, lake trout, whitefish, etc.

Flatten it out or cut it into pieces. Rub a saucer with

Garlic

Place in it and mix:

1 or 2 tablespoons olive oil
¼ teaspoon white pepper

Rub the fish on both sides with these ingredients. Place it in a greased shallow pan. Broil until brown, turning it once. Spread with:

Maître d'Hôtel Butter, page 384, or Lemon Butter, page 384

Garnish with:

Parsley
Cucumbers in Sour Cream, page 44

BLUE TROUT OR TRUITE AU BLEU

[Allow One 4 to 6½ Ounce Trout Per Person]
Please read About Cooking Fish "Au Bleu," page 399. The amazingly brilliant blue color of this dish can be achieved only if your fish is alive when ready for the pot. We ate these first in the Black Forest at an inn bordering a stream, but we think of them always in connection with Joseph Wechsberg's zestful book, "Blue Trout and Black Truffles."

Have ready and boiling:

Seasoned Acidulated Water with lemon juice or vinegar (II, 148)

allowing 2 tablespoons acid per fish. Kill the fish with one sharp blow on the head. Split and clean it with one stroke if possible. Be careful not to disturb the slime on the body of the fish. Plunge it at once into the boiling water. Let this come to a boil again, then remove the pan from the heat and cover it. Let stand for about 5 minutes. Slightly larger fish may need another 2 or 3 minutes. The white eyeballs pop out when the fish is done. Remove the fish and drain well. The classic service is on a napkin on your best silver salver, accompanied by a garnish of:

Parsley

with:

Boiled or steamed
potatoes and
sweet butter balls, or
melted butter

You may also serve other fancy butters or:

Hollandaise Sauce, page
368

But why add earrings to an elephant? If you serve the fish cold, pass:

Gribiche Sauce, page
348 or
Ravigote Sauce, page
342

FRESH TUNA OR BONITO

[Allow ½ Pound Per Serving]
Clean:

A fresh tuna or bonito

Braise or roast as for veal, or brush the delicate stomach sections with:

Cooking oil

and broil. For recipes for canned tuna, see Index.

POACHED TURBOT

[Allow ½ Pound Per Serving]
This firm-fleshed, very white flat fish may be skinned and filleted, page 395, and poached in Court Bouillon (II, 146), part wine or part milk to reinforce its whiteness, and cooked as for any

recipe for Sole, page 418. As both the skin and the gelatinous areas near the fins are considered delicacies, turbot is often prepared and served unskinned. To keep it from curling or bursting cut a long gash down the center of the under or brown side before poaching.
To cook in the skin, place the fish in a greased pan; float it in a cool:

Court Bouillon

Cover with a poaching paper, page 84. Bring the liquid to a boil. ♦ Reduce the heat at once. Barely simmer for about 30 minutes, basting several times during the cooking. Be sure to replace the paper after each basting.

WHALE

[Allow ½ Pound Per Serving]
Last—but vast.
If whale meat is frozen, thaw before cooking. Whether fresh or frozen, soak for 1 hour in a solution of:

1 tablespoon baking soda to
1 quart water

Rinse well and marinate 1 to 2 hours ♦ covered with a liquid made up of:

3 cups water
1 cup vinegar

Cut across the grain into thin steaks not over ½-inch thick. Sprinkle with:

Lemon juice

and pound, page 452, to tenderize further. Stew, braise or sauté as for beef, which it resembles more than it does fish.

SHELLFISH

ABOUT MOLLUSKS AND CRUSTACEANS

Connoisseurs dispute as to which stretches of the world's seacoast provide the best breeding grounds for shellfish and are ready to do battle over the relative merits of oysters and mussels versus lobsters and crabs. We hope to sidestep most of these controversies in the pages which follow. We hope also to clarify the distinction, along the way, between lobster, page 436, langouste, page 436, and langoustine, page 441, and between crevettes, scampi, page 437, and écrevisses, page 444; sneaking in a few succulent freshwater anomalies like crawfish and frogs, as well as the land-based snail. And we will put our chief emphasis on how to cook so as to retain a just-caught flavor. Details for handling and keeping are given in each shellfish category.

In cooking, we beg you to ◗ use low heat, unless otherwise indicated, to ◗ use the shortest possible cooking period and to serve at once. If these delicacies are eaten raw, be sure they are served properly chilled. Shrimps, prawns, lobsters and crabs are regarded as rather indigestible. Consider an accompanying citrus or vinegar sauce, which will both stimulate the gastric juices and help break down food fibers. Keep in mind that ◗ commercial shellfish collection is permitted only in areas where the waters are unpolluted and that if you collect on your own, be sure the water in the area is safe. ◗ Recipes for mussels, oysters and clams are fairly interchangeable; and some exciting dishes may be created by combining mollusks and crustaceans.

Seafood is often seasoned with wines. For every 6 servings, allow 2 tablespoons dry sherry, 4 tablespoons white wine or 1 tablespoon cognac.

SHELLFISH COCKTAILS

Serve these well chilled, preferably in glasses imbedded in ice. If serving individually, allow about ⅓ cup of seafood per person with about ¼ cup sauce. You may pour the sauce over the seafood, serve it separately for dipping or toss the seafood in the sauce and serve it on lettuce, endive or cress. For appropriate sauces, see:

> Russian, page 349, or
> Seafood Dips and Sauces,
> pages (II, 84) and 343

Serve with these cocktails:
> Oyster crackers
> Cheese crackers
> Pretzel sticks
> Potato chips
> Olives

ADDED COLOR AND FLAVOR IN SEAFOOD DISHES

To 3 well crushed lobster shells and 2 lbs. shrimp shells, add ½ bottle of white wine. Reduce to ½ to ⅓. A bright red sauce results which, when tepid, can be added with puréed shrimp or lobster to Hollandaise Sauce. Purée of pimiento can also be used.

ABOUT OYSTERS

These shellfish, edible at any time, are best in flavor when they are not spawning. As Southern oysters spawn all during the year, they do not have the fine flavor of Northern types and are, therefore, often served highly condimented. These bivalves have one shallow and one deep shell and it is in the deeper shell that they are served raw or baked. Some canny diners have been known to ask for them in restaurants on the shallow shell, in the hope of getting them absolutely freshly opened. Oysters in the shell should be alive. If they gape and do not close quickly in handling, discard them. Also discard any with broken shells.

♦ To open oyster shells, provide yourself first with a strainer and a bowl in which to catch the juices. Hold a well-scrubbed oyster, deep shell down, in a folded napkin in the palm of one hand—work over the strainer and bowl. Insert the edge of an oyster knife into the hinge of the shell. Turn the knife to pry and lift the upper shell enough to insert the knife to cut the hinge muscle. Then run the knife along between the shells to open. The oysters are then ready to be served on the half shell. This procedure is not easy until you have the knack. Should you grow desperate in this shucking process, you may be willing to sacrifice some flavor for convenience. If so, place the oysters in a 400° oven from 5 to 7 minutes, depending on size, drop them briefly into ice water and drain. They should open easily. ♦ To shuck, no matter how you open them, release the oysters from the shell with a knife. Examine each oyster with your fingers to be sure no bit of shell is adhering to it. Drop the oyster into a strainer. If the oysters are sandy, you may rinse them in a separate bowl, allowing ½ cup cold water to each quart of shucked oysters. Pour it over the oysters and reserve the water. In using the oyster liquor and the water mixture, be sure to strain it through a fine muslin to free it from grit. ♦ Before using oysters in any fried or creamed dish, dry them carefully in an absorbent towel.

If oysters have been bought already opened, in bulk, be sure to free them of bits of shell. They should be plump and creamy in color. The liquor should be clear, not cloudy, and should have no sour or unpleasant odor. If plump oysters burst during the cooking, they have been previously soaked in fresh water to plump them and their flavor as well as their texture has been ruined. Oystermen claim they can easily tell the sex of oysters and insist that females should be fried and males should be stewed. ♦ Allow 1 quart undrained, shucked oysters for 6 servings. It is hard to estimate amounts for oysters on the shell, as they vary in size—6 moderate-sized Eastern oysters would equal about 20 Olympia West Coast oysters.

♦ To store oysters in the shell, refrigerate at 39°, not directly on ice. Keep dry. Store shucked oysters at the same temperature, covered by their liquor, in a closed container. The container may be put in crushed ice, up to about ¾ its height. If you received them fresh, oysters may be stored in this way up to 5 days.

For other oyster suggestions, see Hors d'Oeuvre and Canapés (II, 64, 81 and 82). For cooked oyster suggestions and oyster cakes, see Luncheon Dishes, page 229. Champagne is a fine accompaniment.

OYSTERS ON THE HALF SHELL

[Allow 5 to 6 Oysters per Serving]
♦ Please read About Oysters, page 422.
Scrub well and ♦ open just before serving:
Oysters
Chill them well. Arrange them in cracked ice on the serving plates. You may place, in the center, a small glass of:
Cocktail Sauce, page 344, or Lorenzo Dressing, page 342
or you may serve them with:
Lemon wedges and horseradish sauce

BROILED OYSTERS

[Allow 6 Oysters per Serving]
♦ Please read About Oysters, page 422.
Preheat broiler.
Shuck, drain and dry in a towel:
Oysters
Place them on a well-buttered baking sheet. Broil them for about 3 minutes, turning once during this time. They should be lightly browned. Serve them with:
Lemon wedges, Parsley or Lemon Butter

▤ GRILLED OYSTERS

[Allow 6 Oysters per Serving]
You may grill Western oysters—except Olympias—right on the coals without toughening them, but if you have Eastern oysters put them on a piece of foil in which you have punched holes, before placing them on your grill over a bed of coals.
I. Put on the foil:
Scrubbed, unopened oysters in their shells
Grill until the shells pop. Season and serve with:
Lemon wedges
Melted butter

II. Open:
Scrubbed oysters
Sprinkle them with a:
Gremolata (II, 222)
Heat for a few minutes on the grill over moderate coals.

DEEP-FAT FRIED OYSTERS [2]

♦ Please read About Deep-Fat Frying, pages 75–79.
Preheat deep fryer to 375°.
Drain:
12 large shucked oysters
Dry them well between towels.
Beat together:
1 egg
2 tablespoons water
Inserting a fork in the tough muscle of the oysters, dip them in the egg, then in:
Seasoned bread crumbs
in the egg again and again in the crumbs. Permit the oysters to dry on a rack for ½ hour. Fry them in deep fat for about 4 minutes.

SAUTÉED OYSTERS [2]

Bread, as above, for Deep-Fat Fried Oysters:

12 large shucked oysters

When they are dry, sauté them until they are golden in a combination of:

3 tablespoons cooking oil
2 tablespoons butter

Serve at once.

BAKED OYSTERS

[6 Oysters per Serving]

Preheat oven to 475°.

Have ready:

Oysters on the half shell

Cover them with:

1 tablespoon Creamed Seafood, page 425

Sprinkle them with:

Bread crumbs

Bake for about 10 minutes or until golden.

CREAMED OYSTERS   [4]

▶ Please read About Oysters, page 422.

Drain and dry:

1 pint oysters

Reserve the liquor. Melt in a saucepan:

2 tablespoons butter

Add and stir until blended:

2 tablespoons flour

Stir in slowly:

1 cup oyster liquor or oyster liquor and cream, milk or chicken stock

Add:

½ teaspoon salt
⅛ teaspoon paprika or cayenne
(½ to 1 teaspoon curry powder)

When the sauce is smooth and hot, add the drained oysters. Heat them to the boiling point, but do not allow the sauce to boil. When the oysters are thoroughly heated, season them with:

1 teaspoon lemon juice,
½ teaspoon Worcestershire sauce or
2 tablespoons dry sherry

Serve them at once in:

Bread Cases, page 209,

patty shells or on hot buttered toast:

Sprinkle them generously with:

Chopped parsley

SCALLOPED OYSTERS   [6]

Preheat oven to 350°.

Have ready:

1 quart shucked oysters in their liquor

and a deep buttered casserole.

Place in the bottom a:

½-inch layer of coarsely crushed soda crackers

Put in a layer of the oysters.

Season with:

Salt and pepper
Bits of butter
2 cups cream

Sprinkle with another layer of:

Crushed crackers

Bake 45 to 50 minutes.

OYSTERS SCALLOPED   [6]
IN CANNED SOUP

▶ Please read About Oysters, page 422.

Preheat broiler.

Drain and dry, reserving the liquor:

1 pint small oysters: 2 cups

Combine:

1 cup dry bread or cracker crumbs
3 tablespoons melted butter
¼ teaspoon salt
1 teaspoon minced parsley

Heat to the boiling point:

1 can cream of celery, mushroom or chicken soup: 10½ oz.
The oyster liquor or
4 tablespoons water

or replace 1 tablespoon of the liquor with:

(Catsup)

Add the oysters. Cook them until the edges begin to curl. Place ½ the buttered crumbs in a hot casserole, add the oysters and soup. Top with the remaining crumbs. Place the dish under a broiler until the top is brown.

OYSTER CELERY   [4]

Preheat oven to 350°.
Prepare:

Creamed Oysters, page
424

Before adding the oysters
thicken with:

2 egg yolks

Season with:

Dry sherry

Place in a baking dish:

¾ cup white, peeled, diced
celery

Cover with the creamed oysters
and dust with:

Parmesan cheese

Bake until golden, about 15
minutes.

BAKED CREAMED   [6]
OYSTERS AND SEAFOOD

Do not take this dish too literally. Change the proportions and
substitute crab, tuna, etc., to
suit yourself. It's a grand basic
dish with which to work.
Preheat oven to 375°.
Prepare:

Creamed Oysters, page
424

Add:

1 cup cooked chopped
shrimp, lobster, crab
meat, tuna, scallops or
leftover cooked fish

Cover with:

Au Gratin II or III,
page 389

Bake about 10 minutes.

OYSTERS IN   [4]
MUSHROOMS AU GRATIN

Preheat oven to 375°.
Sauté, page 296:

20 large mushroom caps

in:

3 tablespoons butter

Place the mushrooms, cavity side
up, in a greased baking dish.
Fill them with:

20 large drained oysters

and cover them with:

1 cup hot Cream Sauce I,
page 359

seasoned with:

Dry sherry

Sprinkle the top with:

Grated Parmesan cheese

Place the dish in the oven until
the top is brown or omit the
cream sauce and dot each oyster
with:

¼ teaspoon butter
A few drops lemon juice

Bake about 10 minutes, until the
oysters are plump. Serve on:

Creamed Spinach,
page 326

OYSTER RAREBIT   [4]

Cook in their liquor until plump:

2 cups oysters: 1 pint

Drain. Keep them hot and reserve the liquor. Cook in a
double boiler and stir until
smooth:

2 tablespoons butter
¼ lb. diced Swiss or
Gruyère cheese
½ teaspoon salt
A few grains cayenne

Add and stir until thick:

The oyster liquor

If there is not enough oyster
liquor to make a good sauce,
add rich milk until it is the right
consistency. Add:

2 beaten eggs

Add the oysters and:

Salt
1 teaspoon Worcestershire
sauce or 2 tablespoons
dry sherry

Serve it on:

Toast or rusks

Garnish it with a sprinkling of:

Paprika

OYSTERS ROCKEFELLER

[Allow 6 Oysters per Serving]
Preheat oven to 475°.
I. This dish is best with oysters
in the shell but, if they are not
available, this recipe is a good
way to dress up bulk oysters in
separately bought shells.
Season and cover the oysters in
turn with:

Butter, creamed with
onion juice and chopped
parsley—reserve some
of this
Salt
A few grains cayenne
Cooked, minced bacon
Puréed spinach
Bread crumbs and some
of the remaining butter
A dash of Spice
Parisienne

It is a New Orleans idea to
sprinkle the oysters with ab-
sinthe. The shells are then imbedded in pans of rock salt.
Bake for about 10 minutes or
until plump. Run them under a
broiler to brown and serve at
once.

II. A simpler version.
Half fill a shell with:
Creamed Spinach,
page 326
Place on spinach:
1 large oyster
Cover with:
1 teaspoon chopped parsley
A few drops lemon juice
and Worcestershire sauce
A square inch of bacon
Cook as in I.

III. Fill half the shell, as above,
with:
Creamed Spinach,
page 326
Place the oyster on the spinach
and cover with:
1 teaspoon well-seasoned
Cream Sauce I, page 359
1 teaspoon grated
Parmesan Cheese
Bake as above.

OYSTERS CASINO   [4]

▶ Please read About Oysters,
page 422.
Preheat oven to 450°.
Prepare:
24 oysters on the half shell
Imbed them in pans of rock salt.
Cream together:

½ cup sweet butter
⅓ cup finely chopped
shallots
¼ cup finely chopped
parsley
¼ cup finely chopped
green pepper
¼ cup finely chopped white
celery
Juice of 1 lemon
Put a piece of the butter mixture
on each oyster, plus:
½ teaspoon of chopped
pimiento
Small square of partially
cooked bacon
Bake until the bacon is browned,
from 5 to 8 minutes.

ABOUT MUSSELS

Mussels are sometimes called
"the oysters of the poor," which
only goes to show that there are
various definitions of poverty.
These delicious mollusks do,
however, deteriorate rapidly and,
if uncooked, may be the cause
of infections.

▶ To test mussels for freshness, try to slide the two halves
of the shell across each other.
If they budge, the shell is probably filled with mud, not mussel.
Mussels are distinguished by a
beard. They may be served
either with or without it.

Wash mussels in a colander
in running water. Keep agitating
the colander, so as to keep them
from opening their shells and
dying. Scrub them with a stiff
brush. You may clip the beards
with scissors. Mussels may be
steamed, removed from the shell,
bearded and served much like
oysters or clams or served with
a sauce, shell and all. It is per-
missible—probably because it is
necessary—to use the hands in
separating the shells. Gourmets
suggest that a half shell be used
to spoon up the liquor to the
last drop. ▶ For 4 servings allow
about 1 quart undrained shucked

or 3 quarts unshucked mussels. Cockles may also be cooked as for mussels.

STEAMED [3 to 4] MUSSELS OR MOULES MARINIÈRE

▶ Please read About Mussels, page 426.
In:

    ¼ cup butter
sauté until golden:

    6 chopped shallots
    1 clove garlic
Cook in a deep, heavy skillet for about 2 minutes:

    ¼ cup dry white wine
    ⅓ bay leaf
Add the sautéed shallots and:

    3 quarts scrubbed, bearded mussels
Cook ▶ closely covered, over lively heat about 6 to 8 minutes. Agitate the pan sufficiently during this time to cook the mussels evenly but ▶ remove from heat the moment the shells are open. Pour the mussels, shells and all, and the sauce into heated bowls and serve garnished with:

    ¼ cup chopped parsley
If you prefer, you may drain the sauce off and quickly thicken it with:

    2 tablespoons fresh bread crumbs
before pouring it over the mussels.

BAKED BUTTERED MUSSELS

Preheat oven to 450°.
Place well-cleaned mussels in a large pan, in:

    2 tablespoons olive oil
in the oven until the shells open. Do not overcook them. Remove the upper shell and beard or fringe. Reserve the liquor. If any has escaped io the pan, strain and add it to the reserved liquor from the shell. Serve the mussels on the lower shell with:

    Melted butter or melted garlic butter
and the liquor in small cups or glasses. See Steamed Clams, page 430.

ABOUT CLAMS

All clams are sandy, especially surf clams. Unshucked, they should be scrubbed and washed in several waters, then soaked in a cold brine of ⅓ cup salt to 1 gallon of water; and it may even be necessary later to put the cooked clams under cold running water to rid them completely of sand. Clams are sold in the shell or shucked. If in the shell ▶ test to see that the clams are tightly closed or, if slightly open, that they close tightly at once upon being touched. ▶ Discard any that float, or have broken shells.

▶ Eight quarts of clams in the shell will yield about 1 quart of clams shucked. ▶ Allow about 1 quart of unshucked clams per person for steamed clams, 6 to 8 clams if served in some other way.

SOFT OR LONGNECK CLAMS

Found mostly north of Cape Cod, these are the preferred East Coast type for eating raw or steamed whole. They are easily opened by running a sharp knife along the edge of the top shell. Work over a bowl, so as to trap the juices. Cut the meat from the bottom shell. Slit the skin of the neck or siphon, as sketched, and pull off the neck skin.

This skin is too tough to eat as it is, but may be chopped or ground and used in chowders or creamed dishes with other clam meat.

HARD-SHELL CLAMS

These include **butter clams** and **quahogs** which in turn are called **cherrystones** in junior sizes; in medium sizes, they are called **littlenecks.** The large, strongly flavored hard-shells are preferred for chowders. The smaller sizes are suitable for eating on the half shell. If in the shell, you may wash them in several waters. Then cover them with a cold brine of ⅓ cup salt for each gallon of water and sprinkle on the top ¼ cup corn meal to every quart of clams. Leave them in this bath 3 to, preferably, 12 hours. This whitens them, rids them of sand and causes them to eject the black material in their stomachs. After soaking, wash them again in clear water.

Quahogs are difficult to open but, if covered for 5 minutes with water and then gently picked up, you may be able to insert a knife quickly in the opening. Or, if you are using them in a cooked dish and do

not mind a small loss in flavor, you may place them in a pan in a moderate oven until they open. After opening, cut through the muscle holding the shells together. If they have not had a

corn meal bath, open the stomachs with sharp shears and scrape out and discard the contents. Large hard-shelled clams have a tough portion, which may be separated from the tender portion, chopped or ground and used in various dishes, creamed, scalloped, in fritters, chowders, etc., using any of the recipes for oysters, or any of the following clam recipes.

RAZOR CLAMS

Especially the Pacific Coast variety, these are unsurpassed for flavor.

SURF CLAMS

These may be used in chowders, broth or cocktails, but their sweetness should be counteracted with salt. They are the sandiest of all clams.

▶ For other recipes, see Soups and Chowders, page 135, or Luncheon Dishes, page 229.

ABOUT CLAMBAKES

Whatever the size of your bake, dig your clams the day before. Scrub them well to remove sand. Put them in a bucket, well covered with sea water. Add corn meal, allowing ½ cup to 2 quarts water. The cereal helps rid the clams of sand and internal waste. Leave the clams in a ▶ cool place. Rinse and drain them just before using. A big bake is described in I; a smaller one, often more practical, in II, with amounts proportionately cut.

▤ CLAMBAKE

I.   **[20]**
Allow:
    200 soft-shell clams
    (50 hard-shell clams)
Start preparations at least 4 hours before you plan to serve. Dig a sand pit about 1 foot deep and 3½ feet across. Line it with

smooth round rocks. ◗ Be sure
the rocks have not been baked
before. Have a wet tarpaulin—
generous enough to overlap the
pit area by 1 foot all around—
and a few rocks handy to weight
the edges. Build a fire over the
rock surface, using hardwood,
and keep feeding it for the next
2½ to 3 hours while the rocks
are heating. Gather and wash
about 4 bushels of wet rock seaweed. In fact, it is wise to soak
the seaweed for at least 45 minutes before use. Have a pail of
sea water at hand. Partially husk
about:

4 dozen ears of corn

Do not pull them quite clean
but leave on the last layer or
two. Rip these back far enough
to remove the silk. Then replace
them, so the kernels are fully
protected. Reserve the pulled
husks. Quarter:

5 broiling chickens

Have ready:

10 sweet potatoes
(20 frankfurters)

You may wrap the chicken
pieces in cheesecloth or divide
the food into 20 individual
cheesecloth-wrapped servings, so
that each person's food can later
be removed as one unit. Scrub:

20 1½-lb. lobsters or 5 pecks
soft-shell crabs

Now you are ready to arrange
for the "bake." Rake the embers
free of the hot stones, remove
them from the pit and line it
with the wet seaweed covering
the stones. The lining should be
about six inches deep. Put over
it, if you wish, a piece of chicken
wire. If you haven't wrapped the
individual servings in cheesecloth, now pack the pit in layers.
For added flavor, put down first
a layer of hard-shell clams, then
the frankfurters if you use them,
then the lobsters or crabs, the
chicken, the corn and the soft-
shell clams. You may also put
seaweed between the layers.

Cover the layered food with the
reserved corn husks and sprinkle
the whole with the bucket of
sea water. Quickly cover with
the wet tarp. ◗ Weight the tarp
down well with rocks. The whole
should steam ◗ covered, about
1 hour. During the steaming, it
will puff up, which is a sign of
a satisfactory "bake." To test,
lift the tarp carefully at one corner ◗ so as not to get sand into
the pit and see if the clams have
opened. If so, the whole feast
should be cooked just to the
right point. Have handy plenty
of towels and:

Melted butter

Serve with the "bake":

Beer

and afterwards:

Watermelon
Coffee

II. [8]

A well-timed bake in a wash
boiler on a stove or outdoor grill.
Soak for 45 minutes and remove
sand from seaweed in several
rinsings. Line the bottom of the
boiler with a 4-inch layer of it.
Add about:

1 quart water

When water boils, add:

8 foil-wrapped potatoes

◗ Cover boiler and cook gently
15 minutes. Wrap in cheesecloth:

2 cut-up broiler chickens

and place on top of the potatoes.
Cook 15 minutes more, before
adding:

8 well-scrubbed 1½ lb.
lobsters

Cover and cook 8 minutes more,
then place on top of the lobsters:

8 shucked foil-wrapped
ears of corn

Cook 10 minutes, still covered
and add:

48 well-scrubbed soft-shell
clams

Cover and steam until the clams
open, from 5 to 10 minutes
longer. In serving, use:

Melted butter

The drained kettle liquid is to be drunk, but it is wise to drain this through a cloth-lined sieve before serving.

III.   [4]

For amounts, cut those in II in half. Use a clean 8-inch stove pipe, about 20 inches deep. Dig and line a circular 18-inch-diameter pit with stones, as described in I—about 12 inches deep—and build the same type fire. When ready to cook, center the stove pipe over the embers. Put in an 8-inch layer of well-soaked seaweed, followed by 4 units of food wrapped in cheese-cloth, as described in I, placing seaweed between them. Top with 8 inches of seaweed and heap sand against the stove pipe in volcano shape. Put a wet tarp over the top and weight with rocks. Cook about 1 hour.

STEAMED SOFT-SHELL CLAMS WITH BROTH

[Allow 2 Dozen Unshucked Clams per Serving]

Scrub thoroughly with a brush and wash in several waters:

Soft-shell clams

Place them close together in the top of a steamer, as sketched on the right, page 398, or on a rack in a stock pot with a spigot, as shown on (II, 139). Place in the bottom of the steamer or stock pot:

½ inch water

Cover the kettle closely. Steam the clams over moderate heat until they open, but no longer—from 5 to 10 minutes. Overcooking makes clams tough. Lift them out. Place in individual soup bowls. Serve with individual dishes of:

Melted butter
Lemon wedges

The broth is served in cups along with the clams or it is used for

clam juice cocktail later. ◆ To eat clams, pick them up from the shell by the neck with the fingers, dip in broth to remove any possible sand, then in butter. All of the clam is edible, except the neck sheath. The broth is delicious to drink, but don't entirely drain the cup, so as to avoid the sand at the bottom.

BAKED SOFT-SHELL   [4]
CLAMS

Preheat oven to 425°.

Scrub with a brush and wash in several waters:

36 soft-shell clams

Place them flat in a pan in depressions in crumpled foil or rock salt to keep shells steady. Bake them about 15 minutes until the shells open. Remove the top shell carefully to avoid spilling the juices. Serve the clams in individual plates with:

Butter and celery salt
Pepper and lemon
wedges

CLAMS BROILED ON THE HALF SHELL

[Allow 6 to 8 Clams per Person]

Preheat broiler.

Place on an ovenproof dish, in which foil has been crumpled to keep shells steady:

Cherrystone clams on
the half shell

Cover each clam with:

A dash of Worcestershire
sauce
A square of bacon

Broil the clams until the bacon is done.

FRIED CLAMS

[Allow 6 to 8 Clams per Person]

◆ Please read About Clams, page 427.

Shuck, wash well in a colander under running water:

Soft-shell clams

Dry them between towels. Cut

away the black skin of the neck or siphon. Prepare as for Fried Oysters, page 423. Serve with

> **Tartare Sauce, page 349, or catsup**

CLAM BROTH FROM STEAMED HARD-SHELL CLAMS

The meat of these clams is used for chowder, fritters or sauced dishes, the broth for soup or as sauce stock. Prepare as for:

> **Steamed Soft-Shell Clams, opposite**

Strain the broth through 2 thicknesses of cheesecloth. You will have about 1 quart of strong broth. It may be diluted with scalded cream or milk but do not boil it after these additions. Or it may be combined with:

> **Water, chicken broth, consommé or tomato juice**

Each cup of broth may be topped with a spoonful of:

> **(Unsweetened whipped cream)**

Sprinkled with:

> **(Chopped chives)**

To prepare the clam meat for use ◗ please read About Hard-Shell Clams, page 428, and add to broth, if desired.

ABOUT SCALLOPS

These beautiful mollusks known on menus as Coquilles St. Jacques are emblematic of the pilgrims who visited the shrine of St. James of Compostella. They ate the mollusks as penance—surely not a rigorous one —and afterwards fastened the cockle shells to their hats. Scallops are also responsible for the cooking term "scalloped," which originally meant seafood creamed, heated and served in a shell. If you get scallops in the shell, wash and scrub them thoroughly. Place in a 300° oven, deep shell down, until they open. Remove the hinge muscle. In Europe, the handsome beanlike coral and beard are both used. The former is treated as for any roe and the latter cut up, sautéed briefly and then simmered ◗ covered, in white wine for ½ hour. When you buy scallops, try for the small, tender, creamy pink or tan bay scallops rather than the large, firmer, whiter sea scallops. Both types are illustrated on (II, 80). If only the large ones are available, slice them—after cooking—in 3 parts, against the grain, for use in salads and creamed dishes or sauces.

◗ To test scallops for freshness, see that they have a sweetish odor. If in bulk, they should be free of liquid. Allow about ⅓ lb. of sea scallops or ¼ lb. of bay scallops per serving for sautéing or broiling. Cooked scallops may be used in any recipe for fish salads or creamed fish or may be skewered and grilled, see below. See the seafood suggestions in Luncheon Dishes, page 229.

SCALLOPS MEUNIÈRE [4]

In:

> **A Bound Breading (II, 160)**

dip:

> **1 lb. bay or sea scallops**

You may let them dry on a rack about 15 minutes. Heat in a heavy skillet large enough so the scallops will be only 1 layer deep:

> **2 tablespoons butter**
> **2 tablespoons cooking oil**

Sauté ◗ agitating frequently, about 5 minutes for bay scallops, 8 minutes for sea scallops. Just before the cooking time is over, sprinkle with:

> **Lemon juice**
> **Finely chopped parsley**

Serve with:

> **Tomatoes Florentine, page 336**

BAY SCALLOPS FONDU [4] BOURGUIGNONNE

◗ Please read about Boeuf Fondu Bourguignonne, page 473, using instead of beef:
    1 lb. bay scallops
Serve as sauces:
        Seasoned Butters for Fish, page 383, or Hollandaise Sauce, page 368

☰ SCALLOP KEBABS

[Allow ¼ lb. Bay or ⅓ lb. Sea Scallops per Person]
Preheat broiler or grill.
If scallops are large or old, drop into boiling water and allow them to stay immersed, but removed from heat, for 1 minute. Drain and dry. If tender, simply brush:
        Scallops
with:
        Cooking oil
Dip in:
        Fine bread crumbs
Skewer alternately with:
    1-inch squares of bacon
Grill over moderate heat for 10 minutes or until golden brown or broil 4 inches from the source of heat, turning several times during the cooking period. Serve with:
        Lemon wedges
        Fried Parsley, page 305

DEEP-FAT FRIED [6 to 8] SCALLOPS

Preheat deep fryer to 385°.
Wash and pick over:
    1 quart scallops: about 2 lbs.
Drain. Dry between towels. Season with:
        White pepper
        Celery salt
Dip them in a:
        Bound Breading (II, 160)
Fry for 2 minutes in deep fat. Drain on absorbent paper. Serve with:

        Tartare Sauce, page 349, Béarnaise Sauce, page 370, or Tomato Sauce, page 376

SCALLOPS IN [6 to 8] WINE

Wash well:
    2 lbs. scallops
◗ Simmer in:
    2 cups dry white wine
Drain and reserve the liquid.
Melt:
    ¼ cup butter
Sauté:
    4 finely chopped shallots
    24 finely sliced mushroom caps
    2 tablespoons minced parsley
Stir in, until blended:
    2 tablespoons flour
Add the reserved liquid and:
    2 to 4 tablespoons whipping cream
Add the scallops to the hot sauce. Place in a shallow casserole. Cover with:
        Au Gratin II, page 389
and run under a broiler until golden brown.

CREAMED SCALLOPS [4] OR OYSTERS AND MUSHROOMS

Simmer until tender, for about 5 minutes:
    2 cups scallops
in:
        Water or light stock to cover
Drain well. Sauté for 5 minutes:
    ½ lb. mushrooms
in:
    2 tablespoons butter
Prepare:
    1 cup Cream Sauce I, page 359
using half cream and half chicken broth or milk. When the sauce is smooth and hot, stir in the scallops and the mushrooms. Simmer gently for about

3 minutes if bay scallops, 5 minutes if sea scallops.

Correct the seasoning
An unusual variation is to add:

2 cups of minced cooked ham

to the above mixture. When oysters are substituted, cook them in their own juice until the edges begin to curl. Drain. Substitute the juice for part of the milk.

SCALLOPED SCALLOPS [6] OR SCALLOPS MORNAY

Preheat broiler.
Poach:

3 cups scallops

in:

1½ cups dry white wine and Light Stock (II, 142), or Fumet (II, 143)

Drain and slice the scallops. Coat each of the deep halves of 12 scallop shells with:

1 tablespoon hot Mornay Sauce, page 361

You may edge the shell, using a forcing bag, with a decorative rim of:

(Duchess Potato, page 319)

Almost fill the shell with the sliced scallops. Coat each shell, staying within the rim of the potatoes, with:

Hot Mornay Sauce, page 361

Dust the sauce coating with:

Grated Parmesan or Gruyère cheese

Run under a broiler until the sauce is lightly browned. Serve at once.

ABOUT ABALONE

The foot of this delicious shellfish—contraband if shipped from California—comes to our markets canned or frozen from Mexico and Japan, shelled, pounded and ready to cook. If you get it in the shell, remove the edible portion by running a knife between the shell and the meat. Trim off the dark portion. Abalone, like inkfish, needs prodigious pounding to tenderize it, if it has died in a state of tension. Leave it whole or cut it in ¼-inch strips for pounding with an even, not too hard, motion. The meat is ready to cook when it looks like Dali's limp watches. ◗ For steaks, slice against the grain. Bread it if you like and sauté or boil as for any fish, page 399. Beat and chop it for Chowder, or for Fritters (II, 125). ◗Allow 1 lb. for 2 to 3 servings.

SAUTÉED [2 to 3] ABALONE

Cut into ⅜-inch-thick steaks across the grain and pound:

1 lb. abalone

Dip in a:

Bound Breading (II, 160)

Melt in a heavy skillet:

2 tablespoons cooking oil or clarified butter

When the fat reaches the point of fragrance, sauté the abalone steaks, allowing 1½ to 2 minutes to each side.

ABOUT CRABS

Recipes for cooking crab meat apply to almost all species of edible crab, but both the type of crab and the part of the crab from which the meat is taken may make a difference in color, taste and texture.

BLUE CRABS

These comprise three-fourths of the fresh crabs in the market. Lump or back-fin meat, taken from the body, is choice for looks and white in color. Flake meat, while less shapely, is also white. Claw meat is brownish, but very choice as to taste.

DUNGENESS AND ROCK CRABS

These are both packaged in one grade, combining body and claw meat. The rock crab flesh is brownish. Dungeness is best in 2½ to 3 lb. size.

KING CRABS

These are pinkish in tone, and consist mainly of leg meat.

OYSTER CRABS AND HERMIT CRABS

There are two edible types of miniature crabs. Oyster crabs are crispy ½-inch pinkish "boarders," found living right in the shell with live oysters and may be eaten raw. They may also be sautéed or deep-fat fried, as is. When deep fried, several dozen may be served with several dozen fried whitebait as one portion. Tiny hermit crabs are found in vacated univalve shells and respond to deep-fat frying and sautéing, but not to being eaten raw.

Preheat deep fryer to 390°.

To deep fry either of these crabs or whitebait, keep them on ice until the last minute. Wash and dry carefully and put in a bag to dust with flour (II, 160), then in a sieve to bounce off as much flour as possible. Place a few at a time in a frying basket and cook only 2 to 3 seconds until crisp.

HARD-SHELL CRABS

These do not ship well. ‣ From a 5 oz. hard crab, you can expect about 1½ oz. of crab meat. ‣ Crabs must be alive and lively when cooked.

SOFT-SHELL OR EASTERN BLUE CRABS

These are crabs that have just molted and not yet hardened.

Their hardening up is a matter of only a few days. They ship very satisfactorily.

‣ Freshly cooked crab meat in partially aerated cans must be under constant refrigeration until used. It should have no ammonialike odor. The completely sealed canned crab meats, Japanese and Korean, are all nonperishable until the cans are opened.

‣ To prepare crab shells for restuffing, select large, perfect shells and scrub them well with a brush until clean. Place them in a large kettle, covered with hot water. Add one teaspoon baking soda. Cover the kettle closely. Bring to a boil and simmer for 20 minutes. Drain, wash and dry. They are then ready for refilling.

‣ For crab dishes made with cooked or canned crab, see page 231. In using canned meat, be sure to pick it over for small bits of shell and bone.

‣ To prepare soft-shell crabs, wash them in several waters. Place live crab face down on a board. Make an incision just back of the eyes and cut out the face. Lift the tapering points on each side of the back shell to remove sandbag and spongy gills, as shown in sketch. Turn crab on its back and with a pointed knife remove the small pointed apron at the lower part of the shell. These crabs, since the shell is edible, are usually broiled or breaded and sautéed, or are deep-fat fried as follows.

DEEP-FAT FRIED SOFT-SHELL CRABS

Preheat Deep Fryer to 375°.
▶ Please read About Deep-Fat Frying, pages 75–79. Dip:
        Cleaned soft-shell crabs
in:
        A Bound Breading (II, 160)
Fry from 3 to 5 minutes or until golden brown, in deep fat. Turn them once while they are frying. Drain on absorbent paper. Sprinkle well with:
        Salt and pepper
Serve at once with:
        Tartare Sauce, page 349
        Remoulade Sauce, page 349, with parsley

BROILED SOFT-SHELL CRABS

Preheat broiler.
Prepare for cooking:
        Soft-shell crabs
Combine:
        ¼ cup butter
        2 tablespoons lemon juice
        A few grains cayenne
        A few grains pepper
Roll the crabs in the butter mixture, then lightly in:
        Flour
Place them on the broiling rack, 2 inches from the heat. Broil for about 10 minutes. Turn once.

SAUTÉED SOFT-SHELL CRABS

Follow the above recipe for:
        Broiled Soft-Shell Crabs
Sauté them in butter or other fat over moderate heat. Place on a platter. Serve with:
        Fried Parsley, page 305

STEAMED HARD-SHELL CRABS

We are very grateful to a Maryland fan who put us wise to handling this type of crab. She says, "When I moved into this crab country, I began to boil hard crabs and threw the natives into fainting fits. They were right."

This is the way she describes the Maryland method: "Dump the crabs into a large vessel or deep sink and cover them with water a little hotter than the hand can bear. The crabs sometimes drop their claws at the contact with hot water—but it is no matter—just pile the claws on top when steaming.

"This hot water bath anesthetizes them quickly with 2 good results: first, you can handle them safely, like softshells; and second, they do not appear to suffer when they are placed over the steam. Otherwise they struggle woefully in the pot while the steam is rising. I scrub the muck from each crab with a vegetable brush. This is my own discovery—the natives do not bother. But somehow I like to suck a clean crab better. If you have a suitable rack, place it in a large pot with a close lid and put a little water in the bottom, but not nearly enough to touch the rack. If a rack is lacking, moisten the bottom of the vessel with 2 or 3 tablespoons of water. In any case, lay in the crabs and set upon the heat. Sprinkle well with:
        About 1 teaspoon red pepper
        2 tablespoons salt
        ½ cup vinegar or lemon juice
        (2 tablespoons Crab Boil)
        1 tablespoon monosodium glutamate
        ½ cup beer or what-have-you
Have no fear that the pot will get dry while steaming. It never does, for the crabs put out a lot of moisture. The problem, on the

contrary, is to keep them from getting sodden. Cover and steam until the aprons begin to rise, about 30 minutes or a little more. Eat hot or cold, preferably over newspapers, and dip each bit in melted butter. Some people use simple French dressing, but not me. If you pull off the apron and open the crab from that point with the fingers, it is easy.

"For the uninitiated we might interpolate: eat only the meat and discard the intestines and spongy gills. Otherwise, a knife is useful to pry off the shell. A mallet or hammer is better than crackers for opening the claws. And don't forget to pry in the points of the top shell for a bite of fat. Some crabs are lean, but some are not. Many crabs—followed by a general hand washing—and then green salad, French bread and dessert make a fine dinner for the fanciest guests."

ABOUT LOBSTERS

The Northern lobster or French "homard," with its great delicious claw meat, is sketched on page 438. It is caught from New England to the Carolinas and in North European waters.

The **spiny rock lobster**, or **langouste**, as it is called, is shipped from Florida, California, Australia, South Africa and the Mediterranean. It has extra-long antennae and most of the meat is in the heavy tail. These are also sometimes called crawfish, in contradistinction to the freshwater écrevisses or crayfish of both continents. The Northerns are reputed most delicious when served hot. The spinys, when frozen, especially if over 10 oz., may be tough. If fresh, they are often preferred in cold dishes. The Northerns, when caught, are a dark mottled blue green. The spinys vary

from tan to reddish orange and maroon with more or less light spotting and more or fewer spines. Both kinds require about the same cooking time and may be cut and cleaned as shown on page 438. But as lobster ritual is more complicated in the Northern type, we will discuss it in further detail below.

The female is considered finer in flavor. Look for the soft, leathery, finlike appendages on the underside, just where the body and tail meet. In the male, these appendages are bony. In opening the female lobster, you may find a delicious roe or coral that reddens in cooking. Use it as a garnish or to color a sauce. The flesh of the male stays firmer when boiled. The greenish substance in both of them is the liver or tomalley.

◗ Allow ½ large lobster or 1 small lobster per serving. Buy active live lobsters weighing from 1¼ to 2½ pounds. Lobsters weighing 3 pounds and over are apt to be coarse and tough. A 2½-pound lobster will yield about 2 cups of cooked meat.

◗ To store live lobsters until ready to use, place them in the refrigerator, but not directly on ice. The claws should be plugged with a small piece of wood and held together with rubber bands. Before cooking, test to make sure lobsters are lively and that, when picked up, if the tail is stretched out flat, it snaps back.

POACHED OR "BOILED" LOBSTER

I. To boil or poach lobster for hot family-type table service, put a folded towel on the bottom of a large, heavy pan. Place on it:

A 1½ to 2½ lb. live
    lobster

Cover with:

Cold sea or salted water

Bring the water to a boil and cook for 5 minutes. ♦ Reduce the heat and simmer for 15 minutes, slightly less if the lobsters have recently shed and are soft. Drain. Serve at once, leaving the head, body and tail intact, and surrounding this portion with the claws. Garnish with a small bowl of:

Drawn Butter, page 383
Lemon wedges

And provide each person with a finger bowl, a bib and abundant napkins. The uninitiated are sometimes balked by the ferocious appearance of a lobster at table. They may take comfort from the little cannibal who, threading his way through the jungle one day at his mother's side, saw a strange object roar overhead. "Ma, what's that?" he quavered. "Don't worry, sonny," said Ma. "It's an airplane. Airplanes are pretty much like lobsters. There's an awful lot you have to throw away, but the insides are delicious."

All the lobster components lie on your plate—the body, head and tail intact, arched shell up, surrounded by the large claws which, on removal before serving, have been cracked to allow excess moisture to drain off. Pick the lobster up in your fingers, turn it soft side up and arch it until the tail cracks off the body. Then break off and discard the tail flippers by bending them back. Pick up the tail piece, again upside down, and push the meat at the small flipper end of the tail with the oyster fork. The tail meat should emerge in one piece out of the large end. Unhinge the back from the back shell and crack open the back by pulling it open. Be sure to eat the greenish tomalley or liver and all the meat. At this point, we call

your attention to the finger bowl.

II. To boil lobster for salad, hors d'oeuvre or sauced dishes, prepare as for I, using:

A 2½ to 3 lb. lobster

Larger ones are apt to be tough. After the cooking period, drain and plunge into cold water to arrest further cooking. When cool ♦ to remove the meat from the shell, place the lobster on its back. With sharp scissors cut a lengthwise gash in the soft underside as sketched on page 439. Draw out the tail meat in one piece. Remove and discard the lady, or sandbag, and the intestinal vein, as well as the spongy lungs which, while harmless, are tough. Add the red coral, if any, and the green liver, or tomalley, to the lobster meat or reserve it for use in sauces.

If you buy pre-boiled lobster in the shell, see that the color is bright red and that it has a fresh seashore aroma. ♦ Most important of all, the tail should be curled and, when pulled, should roll back into place under the body. This means the lobster was alive, as it should have been, when cooked.

To remove lobster meat from the large claws, crack them with a nutcracker or a mallet. If you want them in a single piece for garnish, break the claw off at the first joint. Place it on a flat surface, the lighter underside up. Using a mallet, hit the shell at the inner hump. This will crack it, so that the meat in the entire larger pincer claw is released. Crack off the small pincer shell and its meat will slide out. For attractive service, you may want to keep the lobster shell to refill with the seasoned sauced meat or you may want to use it to make Lobster Butter, page 385.

☰ BROILED LOBSTER   [1]

Preheat broiler.
Prepare for broiling:

A 1¼ lb. live lobster

Sever the vein at the base of
the neck. Place the lobster on
his back. Hold him with your
left hand firmly over the head.
Be sure to protect your hand
with a towel. Draw the knife
from the head down through the
base of the abdomen, as shown
below, so the lobster will lie
flat with the meat evenly exposed to the heat. All the lobster meat is edible, except for
the stomach, or lady—a hard

sac near the head—and the intestinal vein that runs through
the middle of the underside of
the tail meat. Remove and discard these inedible parts. The
spongy substance to either side
of the body—the lungs—is
harmless. It may or may not be
removed when the lobster is
cooked in the half shell. Beyond a doubt edible are the delicious red coral and the greenish liver or tomalley. You may

prepare a stuffing by removing
and mixing together:

The coral
The tomalley
1 tablespoon toasted bread
crumbs
1 teaspoon of lemon juice
or
dry sherry

Replace in the cavity and brush
with:

Melted butter

Also brush with:

Melted butter

the exposed lobster meat. ◗ If
broiling stuffed, place shell side
down on the oven grill and broil
about 16 minutes. If broiling
unstuffed or grilling over charcoal, place shell side toward
heat for 7 to 8 minutes, turn and
broil, flesh side to heat, for
about 8 minutes more. In either
case serve with:

Lemon wedges and
Drawn Butter,
page 383

◗ To eat broiled lobster served
to you on the half-shell, begin
with the tail meat first, using
the small, sharp-pronged lobster
or oyster fork, see sketches
below. You may twist off bite-
size pieces with the fork. This
needs some skill, and we often
wish when dining out, for a
good European fish knife. Dip
the pieces in the sauce. You may
also squeeze lemon juice from
the garnish wedges over the lobster meat. Twist off a large claw
with the fingers and, if necessary, also use the cracker which
should always be provided.

Crack the claw, as shown, to release the delicate rich meat. You may then pull off the small side claws, one by one, with the fingers, and suck out the meat. As you empty the shells, place them on the bone tray or extra plate and make use of the finger bowl when needed. Continue to eat the contents of the shell: it is good to the last shred. Some people even suck the knuckle after releasing it from the grey gristle.

LOBSTER AMÉRICAINE [2] OR ARMORICAINE

Who really cares how it's spelled? This method of cooking lobster is good enough to credit regional inventiveness on both sides of the Atlantic. Have ready:

    ½ cup Fish Fumet (II, 143)

Place on a flat pan, so as to be able to reserve any juice that results from cutting:

    2 live 1½ lb. hen lobsters

With a sharp knife, sever the vein at the base of the neck. Cut off the claws. Divide the body at the tail and cut the tail in 3 or 4 pieces at the segmentations. Divide the shell in half, lengthwise. Remove and discard the sac. Reserve the coral, if any, and the tomalley, for the sauce.
Have ready 2 heavy skillets. In one, sauté:

    3 tablespoons butter
    1 cup Mirepoix (II, 221)
    ½ cup chopped shallots

Heat in the other, to the point of fragrance:

    ½ cup olive oil
    1 clove garlic

Sauté in the oil for about 4 minutes ▶ still in the shell, the cut-up lobster. Keep the pan moving. When the lobster shell is red and the flesh firm, add it to the mirepoix in the first skil-

let. Flambé, page 80, the lobster mixture in:

    1 oz. brandy

Place in the second skillet and simmer about 5 minutes:

    ½ cup tomato purée
    1 cup white wine
    3 peeled, seeded, chopped tomatoes

In winter use the small Italian-type canned tomatoes.
Add the sautéed lobster pieces still in the shell, the fumet and:

    1 teaspoon chopped fresh tarragon
    The juice or "blood" of lobster
    The coral and tomalley

to the tomato mixture. Heat the sauce.

    Correct the seasoning

Thicken the sauce slightly with:

    (Beurre Manié, page 357)

Serve the lobster with the hot sauce poured over it and garnish with:

    Chopped parsley

▤ GRILLED LOBSTER [4] TAILS

Preheat broiler or grill.
Marinate for several hours:

    4 spiny lobster tails

in a mixture of:

    ¼ cup lemon or lime juice
    ¼ cup salad oil
    1 teaspoon each salt and paprika
    ¼ cup minced shallots

Remove with scissors the soft under-cover of the lobster tails, as sketched above.

Slightly crack the hard upper shell with a cleaver so the tails will lie flat, and grease the meat lightly. Broil for about 5 minutes to a side, basting the exposed side well with the marinade. Hold about 4 inches above coals or under broiler. These make an attractive plate when served with:

Asparagus spears

placed to either side and garnished with:

Polonaise Sauce, page 386

▤ CHARCOAL-GRILLED BAHAMIAN LOBSTER TAILS WITH LIME BUTTER SAUCE

You can use fresh or frozen lobster tails for this recipe and grill them outdoors or in a broiler. Split:

Lobster tails

Do not remove meat from the shells. Several hours before cooking, marinate lobster tails in:

Melted butter or olive oil

or a mixture of the two, allowing 2 to 3 tablespoons of fat for each lobster, plus:

Freshly ground black pepper
1 teaspoon lime or lemon juice

Broil until top is crisp and golden brown, 10 to 15 minutes. Keep basting with the marinade. Serve hot, with the drippings or extra butter and cut limes or lemons, if desired.

BAKED STUFFED LOBSTER   [2]

Split in half, as for Broiled Lobster, page 438:

A freshly Boiled Lobster, page 437: about 2 lbs.

Remove the meat. Chop it. Melt:

¾ tablespoon butter

Stir in until blended:

¾ tablespoon flour

Stir in slowly:

½ cup Chicken Stock (II, 142), or Fumet (II, 143)

Season the sauce with:

1¼ teaspoons dry mustard
1 teaspoon chopped onion
Salt
Paprika

Melt in a separate saucepan:

2 tablespoons butter

Sauté the lobster meat in the butter until it is heated. Add the boiling sauce. Simmer these ingredients for about 2 minutes. Remove them from the heat. Preheat broiler.

Beat, then stir in:

1 tablespoon cream
2 egg yolks

Add:

(½ cup chopped Sautéed Mushrooms, page 296)

Fill the lobster shells with the mixture. Cover them with:

Buttered Crumbs (II, 159), or Au Gratin I or II, page 389

Broil the lobster until the crumbs are brown. Season it, as it is removed from the oven, by pouring over it:

(2 tablespoons sherry)

LOBSTER THERMIDOR   [2]

This calls for cream, as well as stock. Split in halves:

2 freshly Boiled Lobsters, page 436:
1 to 1½ lbs. each

Remove the meat, as directed. Dice the meat. Melt:

2 teaspoons butter

Stir in, until blended:

2 teaspoons flour

Add the lobster meat. Stir in slowly:

¼ cup rich cream
1 cup Stock (II, 141)

Simmer these ingredients for about 10 minutes. Stir them frequently. Season them lightly, if required, with:

Salt, paprika and celery
salt
A few grains cayenne
Preheat broiler.
Remove the lobster from the
pan. Add:

1 tablespoon dry sherry
Melt:

3 tablespoons butter
Add:

1½ cups shredded white
bread
Cook and stir these ingredients
until all the butter is absorbed.
Wash the lobster shells thoroughly. Fill them with the mixture. Spread the tops with the
bread crumbs. Brown them
under a broiler. Serve the lobster with:

Wilted Cucumbers,
page 43

ABOUT SHRIMP

Formerly our Southern shrimp
or crevette was the only one
available in most of our markets. Today we can buy many
members of this family. So let
us remind you of the tiny forms
from our West coast and from
Scandinavia—now widely used
as hors d'oeuvre; scampi, Dub-
lin prawns or langoustines—all
large—from Europe; and the
giants from India—shrimp so
large that 2 or 3 suffice for a
serving. In spite of slight differences in flavor and texture, all
can be substituted for one another if size is taken into consid-

eration for serving amounts and
cooking time. If poaching, cooking varies from 3 to 8 minutes.

◗ To test shrimp for freshness,
see that they are dry and firm.
Allow about 1 pound of shrimp
in the shell—these are called
"green" shrimp—½ pound of
cooked shrimp without shells
for 3 servings. In buying, remember, 2 to 2½ lbs. of shrimp
in the shell gives only about 1
lb. cooked, shelled shrimp, or
2 cups. While shrimp may be
cooked in the shell or unshelled,
the shells add considerable flavor. Shelling is easy—either before or after cooking. A slight
tug releases the body shell from
the tail.

Devein before or after cooking, using a small pointed knife
or the end of a toothpick, as
sketched. This is essential.

◗ If using canned shrimp, you
may rinse briefly in cold water
to remove excess salt. Large
shrimp may be made more
decorative by slicing lengthwise, as shown below. ◗ To

butterfly shrimp, peel the
shrimp down to the tail, leaving
it on. Devein. Hold so the underside is up. Slice down its
length, almost to the vein, to
form the hinge. Spread and flatten to form the butterfly shape.

◗ Never overcook shrimp. If
they are fresh, drop them into
boiling stock or water ◗ reduce
the heat at once and simmer 3
to 4 minutes. But be sure to re-

move them from the heat before they begin to curl up. ◗ Drain at once, to prevent curling and also overcooking. To cook frozen shrimp, peeled and deveined, and also the "green" types, start from the frozen state, drop into boiling stock or water and count the time when the stock comes to a boil again.

For other shrimp recipes, see Hors d'Oeuvre chapter (II, 82).

BUTTERFLY SHRIMP

◗ Please read About Deep-Fat Frying, pages 75–79. To cut for butterfly shape, see About Shrimp, page 441.
Preheat deep fryer to 370°.
Don't flour or crumb the tails, but do coat the body of the shrimp with:

> Bread crumbs or grated coconut or flour or egg or both; or in a batter

Fry 8 to 10 minutes or until golden. Drain on absorbent paper. Serve at once with:

> Soy Sauce, Tartare Sauce, page 349, or Chinese Sweet-Sour Sauce, page 371

POTTED SHRIMP OR LOBSTER

This terrine can be used as a luncheon or hors d'oeuvre spread. Cook:

> Raw shrimp or lobster

Drain and remove meat from shells. Chop coarsely. Reserve shells. Allow for every cup of seafood:

> 2 to 3 tablespoons butter

To ½ the butter, add the reserved shells to make:

> Shrimp or Lobster Butter, page 385

Season with:

> ⅛ teaspoon mustard or mace
> ⅛ teaspoon salt
> A few grains cayenne

Stir the seafood into the heated shrimp or lobster butter until well coated. Place it in a small terrine. Clarify the remaining butter. ◗ Do not let it color. Pour it while hot over the seafood, making sure the food is well covered. Refrigerate covered.

▤ SHRIMP TERIYAKI   [3]

Marinate:

> 1 lb. shelled, deveined "green" shrimp

for about 15 minutes, in:

> ½ cup pineapple juice
> 2 to 4 tablespoons soy sauce
> ½ cup bland cooking oil

Drain and broil or grill 3 or 4 minutes on each side, 4 inches from heat. Serve with:

> Rice, page 158

POACHED SHRIMP   [6]

Simmer for about 5 minutes:

> 8 cups water
> ¼ cup sliced onion
> 1 clove garlic
> 1 bay leaf
> 2 celery ribs with leaves
> 1½ tablespoons salt

Wash, drain and add:

> 2 lbs. "green" shrimp

Slice and add:

> ½ lemon

Simmer the shrimp for about 5 minutes or till pink. Drain immediately and chill. Serve very cold in their shells—to be shelled at table—with a bowl of:

> Russian Dressing, page 349, or Remoulade Sauce, page 349

or shell them, remove the intestinal vein and use them as desired.

SHRIMP CASSEROLE   [4]
WITH SNAIL BUTTER

Preheat oven to 400°.
Prepare:

1½ lbs. Poached Shrimp, see
    above
Have ready in refrigerator:
    Colbert or Snail Butter,
    page 384
Put a ¼-inch layer of the butter
in the bottom of a shallow casserole. Lay shrimp in rows and
press into the butter. Cover the
shrimp with the remaining butter and bake about 10 minutes. Broil for a few minutes
to let top brown. Serve at
once.

DEEP-FAT FRIED [3]
SHRIMP

Shell:
    1 lb. raw shrimp
Remove the intestinal vein.
Combine:
    ⅔ cup milk
    ⅛ teaspoon paprika
    ¼ teaspoon salt
Soak the shrimp in the milk for
30 minutes.
Preheat deep fryer to 375°.
Drain the shrimp well. Sprinkle
with:
    Lemon juice
    Salt
Roll in:
    Corn meal
Fry in deep fat until golden
brown. Drain on absorbent
paper. Serve hot with:
    Lemon juice or
    mayonnaise seasoned
    with puréed chutney

DEEP-FAT FRIED
STUFFED SHRIMP

[2 Dozen Shrimp]
Shell and devein:
    10 jumbo-size shrimp
Chop them into a pulp and add:
    6 water chestnuts
which have been smashed with
a cleaver and finely chopped.
Shell, leaving the tails intact,
and devein:
    14 jumbo-size shrimp
Split lengthwise along the deveined edge ♦ but not far

enough to separate. Spread
them flat and lay along each
crevice:
    A thin julienne of
    Prosciutto or
    Westphalian ham
Spread the shrimp and chestnut mixture in the crevices
above the ham and mold it into
the form of a wide beveled edge
when you partially reclose the
shrimp for breading. Dip into:
    Beaten egg
then into:
    Flour
Allow to dry on a rack 15 to 20
minutes.
♦ Please read About Deep-Fat
Frying, pages 75–79.
Preheat deep fryer to 370°.
Lift the shrimp by the tails and
slide them gently into the
heated fat. Fry for about 5 minutes or until golden. Drain on
absorbent paper. Serve at once
with:
    Chinese Sweet-Sour
    Sauce, page 371
adding some:
    Plum jam

SHRIMP FRIED IN [3]
BATTER

Preheat deep fryer to 370°.
Shell and clean, page 441:
    1 lb. "green" shrimp
You may leave the tails on.
Prepare:
    Fritter Batter for Fish
    (II, 125)
Dip a few shrimp at a time in
the batter, holding them by the
tail. ♦ Do not cover the tail with
batter. Fry in deep fat until
golden brown. Drain on absorbent paper. Serve with:
    Lemon wedges or
    mayonnaise
    seasoned with catsup and
    mustard

SHRIMP TEMPURA

♦ Please read About Deep-Fat
Frying, pages 75–79.

Preheat deep fat fryer to 350°.
Prepare:

> Butterfly Shrimp, page
> 442

Dip them in:

> Fritter Batter for Fish
> (II, 125)

Fry until golden.
Serve with:

> Hot Mustard Sauce,
> page 363, soy sauce,
> Chinese Sweet-Sour
> Sauce, page 371

NEW ORLEANS SHRIMP [4 to 6]

Poach:

> 2 lbs. fresh shrimp, page
> 442

Shell and clean them. Serve well
chilled on:

> Lettuce

Prepare the following sauce.
Rub a bowl with:

> Garlic

Add:

> ½ cup finely chopped celery
> 1 stalk finely chopped
>   green onion
> 1 tablespoon chopped
>   chives
> 6 tablespoons olive oil
> 3 tablespoons lemon juice
> ¼ teaspoon hot pepper
>   sauce
> 5 tablespoons horseradish
> 2 tablespoons prepared
>   mustard
> ¼ teaspoon paprika
> ¾ teaspoon salt
> ½ teaspoon white pepper

You may marinate the shrimp
in this sauce for 12 hours, or the
time may be much shorter. A
clove of garlic may be added
to the mixture for 2 hours.

SHRIMP NEWBURG [3 to 4]

Prepare, page 442:

> 1 lb. Poached Shrimp

Serve with:

> Newburg Sauce, page
> 361

using 1 to 1½ cups of sauce.
Serve in a:

> Rice Ring, page 162

or over:

> Baked Green Rice, page
> 159

ABOUT CRAYFISH, CRAWFISH, OR ÉCREVISSES

[♦ Allow about one dozen
per serving]
One of the thrills of our grand-
parents was to find in Missouri
streams the crayfish they had so
relished in Europe. These crustaceans, looking like miniature
lobsters, were brought to the
table in great steaming crimson
mounds, garnished with dill or
swimming in their own juices,
that is, "à la nage."
To cook, wash well in several
waters:

> Crayfish

If they have been kept in fresh
running water for several days,
they need not be eviscerated. If
they have not, they are cleaned
while still alive. Grasp the middle tail fin, as sketched, give a
long firm twist and pull to remove the stomach and intestinal
vein. Have ready a large pot of:

> Boiling water

seasoned with:

> A leek—white part only
> Parsley
> 1 chopped carrot

Drop the crayfish one by one
into the boiling water at a rate
which will not disturb the boiling. Cook not longer than 5 to
7 minutes. Serve in the shell.
Have on the side plenty of:

> Melted butter

seasoned with:

> Fresh dill

They are eaten with the fingers.
Separate tail from body. Crack
open tail by holding between
thumb and finger of both hands
and force it back against the
curve of the shell. Be sure to

serve with finger bowls. If you are preparing them for hors d'oeuvre, cook only until the water is boiling well after they are all immersed. Then remove

from heat. Let them cool in the liquid. Shelled, they lend themselves to all kinds of combinations and sauces, but the connoisseur usually wants them for themselves alone.

ABOUT SNAILS

The Romans, who were addicted to snails, grew them on ranches where they were fed special foods like bay, wine and spicy soups to preseason them. Only snail types that are sealed in their opercula before hibernating are edible. If your snails are less privileged than the Roman ones, be sure to ♦ let them fast for about 10 days to get rid of any possible poisons they may have imbibed from foliage inimical to humans. After the fast, they may be fattened for the feast before cooking. ♦ Allow about 1 dozen snails per serving.

Before cooking, scrub and remove the membrane which closes them. Place in water to cover and add ½ cup salt or ¼ cup vinegar for every 50 snails. Change the water several times during this 3 to 4 hour soaking. Then rinse in several waters until the slime is removed. Blanch à blanc (II, 147), 8 minutes. After draining from the cold water, place the snails in a court bouillon to cover, made with:

½ water or stock and ½ white wine
seasoned with:
    A Bouquet Garni (II, 220)
    An onion stuck with cloves
    2 cloves garlic

♦ Simmer gently for 3 to 4 hours, depending on the size of the snails. After cooling in the court bouillon, drain.
I. Remove snails from shells. Cut off and discard the black end. Dry the snails and shells in a cloth. Place a dab of Snail Butter, page 384, in each shell. Replace the snails. Pack them firmly in the shell, so generously covered that only the lovely green herbed butter is visible at the opening. You may chill the snails for later use or bake them at once on a pan lightly sprinkled with water in a 425° oven just long enough to get them piping hot—a matter of a few minutes only. Have ready heated, grooved, snail dishes. The shell holder has a spring in the handle which allows you to regulate its viselike end to the size of the snail. The long, closely tined fork is used with a slight twist to remove the snail. See sketch above.

II. For those of us who have to rely on canned snails, the following is a snail rejuvenation. Prepare enough to fill 48 snails:
    Snail Butter, page 384

Reduce to 1 cup over high heat:
>   1 cup consommé
>   1 cup dry white wine
cooked with:
>   ½ bay leaf
>   1 clove garlic
Put in a colander:
>   48 canned snails
Pour over them:
>   1 quart warm water
Drain well. Simmer the snails
briefly in the hot reduced consommé and wine. Wash the snail
shells well and drain. Pack, as
above, with:
>   Snail Butter, page 384
Heat and serve as for I.

III. Or, replace the shells with:
>   Sautéed Mushroom Caps,
>   page 296
Fill the mushrooms with one or
more snails, depending on size.
Coat the snails with:
>   Snail Butter, page 384
and run under a broiler briefly
until heated.

ABOUT FROG LEGS

Frog legs resemble chicken in
texture and flavor. They are
usually bought skinned and
ready to use. Allow 2 large or
6 small frog legs per person. If
the frogs are not prepared, cut
off the hind legs—the only part
of the frog used—close to the
body. Separate and wash them
in cold water. Begin at the top
and strip off the skin like a
glove. Through an experiment
with a twitching frog leg, Gal-
vani discovered the electric current that bears his name. Should
you prefer keeping your kitchen
and your scientific activities
separate and distinct, chill the
frog legs before skinning.

BRAISED FROG LEGS   [4]

Clean:
>   8 large frog legs
Roll them in:
>   Seasoned flour
Melt in a skillet:

>   6 tablespoons clarified
>   butter
Add to it:
>   ½ cup chopped onions
Brown the frog legs in the butter. Reduce the heat and add:
>   ¾ cup boiling Stock (II,
>   141)
Cover the skillet closely and
cook the frog legs until they are
tender, for about 10 minutes.
Melt:
>   6 tablespoons butter
Sauté in the butter:
>   1¼ cups seasoned bread
>   crumbs
>   ¾ cup finely chopped
>   hazelnuts
Add:
>   1 teaspoon lemon juice
Roll the frog legs in the bread
crumbs and serve them garnished with:
>   Fennel
or, if you have used the hazel-
nuts, with:
>   Parsley

DEEP-FAT FRIED FROG LEGS

▶ Please read About Deep-Fat
Frying, pages 75–79.
Preheat deep fryer to 375°.
Clean:
>   Frog legs
Dip them in:
>   A Bound Breading (II,
>   160)
Let dry for 1 hour. Fry the frog
legs until golden. Drain. Serve
with:
>   Tartare Sauce, page 349

FROG LEGS IN   [3]
MUSHROOM SAUCE

Clean:
>   6 large frog legs
Cut the meat into 3 or 4 pieces.
Place in a saucepan. Cover with:
>   Boiling water or Light
>   Stock (II, 142)
Add:
>   2 thin slices lemon
>   ⅛ teaspoon white pepper
>   (Celery, parsley, onion or

vegetables suitable for
soup)
Simmer the frog meat, covered,
until it is tender. Drain well.
Melt in a saucepan:

3 tablespoons butter

Add to it and sauté until light
brown:

1 cup sliced mushrooms

Stir in:

1½ tablespoons flour

Stir in slowly:

1½ cups chicken stock or
stock in which the frog
legs were cooked
Correct the seasoning

When the sauce is hot, add the
frog meat. Reduce the heat to
low. Beat well:

3 egg yolks
3 tablespoons rich cream

Stir these ingredients into the
sauce. Let them thicken off the
heat. Add:

1½ teaspoons lemon juice or
2 teaspoons dry sherry

Serve the meat at once, covered with the sauce.

FROG LEGS FORESTIÈRE

[Allow 5 Per Serving]
Sprinkle small frog legs with:

Brandy

Let stand about 2 hours and
wipe dry. Sauté them in:

Clarified Butter, page 383

During the last few minutes of
cooking when the frog legs become firm to the touch, sauté
with the meat for each portion:

2 thinly sliced mushrooms
(1 tablespoon very finely
sliced fresh sweet red
pepper)
1 tablespoon chopped
parsley
1 teaspoon lemon juice
Correct the seasoning

ABOUT TURTLES AND
TERRAPIN

Sea turtles attain huge size and
their habits are nowhere more
fascinatingly described than in
"The Windward Road" by
Archie Carr.

Handling and cooking these
monsters, some of which weigh
over 100 pounds, is not a usual
household procedure. Therefore
most of us are content to enjoy
their highly prized, highly
priced, gelatinous meat ready-
diced and in cans. The greenish
meat from the top shell is considered the best—that taken
from the bottom is whitish.

The terrapin is a freshwater
snapping turtle: our children
bring them home from the creeks
in our neighborhood, as yours
may, too. If you cannot use them
at once or wish to keep them at
least long enough to make certain that they are rid of waste or
pollution, you may put them in
a deep open box—and don't forget a wire screening on top—
give them a dish of water and
feed them for a week or so on
3 or 4 small handouts of ground
meat.

♦ To cook, place in a pan of
cold water:

A 7-inch terrapin

Bring water slowly to a boil and
parblanch for at least 10 minutes. Drain. Plunge into cold
water and leave until cool
enough to handle. Scrub the
terrapin well. Place it in rapidly
boiling water, and add:

(A Bouquet Garni (II,
220))
(An onion stuck with
cloves)
(3 stalks celery)

♦ Reduce the heat at once and
simmer 35 to 45 minutes or until
the claws can be removed by
pulling. Drain, reserving the
stock. Allow the terrapin to cool
on its back in order to trap the
juices as it cools. When cool,
pry the flat plastron free from
the curved carapace—easier said
than done. Near the head you
will find the liver. ♦ Free it
carefully from the gall. Discard

the gall. Slice the liver thin and reserve it, as well as the eggs, if any. You may or may not want to reserve the small intestines, which may be chopped and added to the meat or sauce. Remove the meat both from the carapace and the skinned legs. When ready to serve, you may toss the meat, including the ground liver and intestines, in:

> 6 tablespoons melted butter

until heated. Garnish with parsley and serve with:

> Sherry, as a drink

or you may heat the meat briefly over very low heat or in the top of a double boiler ◗ over—not in—hot water in a sauce made by combining:

> 1 cup Brown Sauce, page 365
> The chopped, cooked eggs, if any
> 1 teaspoon mixed herbs: including basil, sweet marjoram, thyme, with a touch of rosemary, bay and sage
> 3 tablespoons Madeira or dry sherry

MEAT

ABOUT MEATS

When a novice approaches the meat counter, she may also approach a state of panic. The friendly informative butcher of a generation ago has often been succeeded by an automaton, mysteriously cutting, grinding, and packaging behind a glass partition. The meats he so impersonally presents in transparent film look bafflingly similar and equally attractive. As a result, they often react in the pan or on the palate in a totally unexpected way. We hope, if you are a rank amateur, that the charts in this chapter will give you the skill of an expert in choosing the right cut for the right dish. For each animal, the charts show you first the general layout of the bone structure; next, the relation of bone to common commercial cuts.

Tender cuts, you will note, lie in those sections where the least body movement and stress occurs and respond to dry heat cooking: roasting, broiling, panbroiling and sautéing.

Meats with more connective tissue will need very slow cooking with moisture: braising, stewing, fricasseeing, pot roasting or poaching. ◊ In these processes, the liquid should never go above the simmering point, 185°. For this reason, we do not recommend the pressure cooking of meats, although expediency sometimes overcomes our better judgment. If you pressure cook meat, follow the directions given by the manufacturer of your appliance.

The third chart shows how these commercial cuts are further subdivided into the meat shapes we are familiar with at table. Listed nearby are the recipes appropriate for each cut. Meat cuts and their names vary not only from country to country but even from region to region in the United States. This makes us wish that there were, as in plants, a sound Linnaean classification. We hope that the charts will not only identify the names most commonly used, but correlate for you the meat and bone relationships involved and—along with the government grading—give you some relative ideas of fat and lean content.

But there is much about meat that must be learned the hard way. How the animal was fed—on grass or corn—and how it was aged, are important factors. Also important are the temperatures at which meat has been held; whether it is watered, or whether treated with preservatives, page 515; how long it has been packaged; and whether it is fairly priced. These are all factors in which you must rely partly on experience and mostly on ◊ the integrity of the butcher.

ABOUT THE GRADING OF MEAT

Before you plunge into purchasing, a word about ◊ grades and prices. The U.S. Government gives you grade protection by stamping all meat sold in interstate commerce. And some states and cities have their own inspection laws. Federal standards of sanitation are rigid, but do be critical of any uninspected locally butchered meats. U.S. grading falls into six classes.

PRIME

This is not commonly available in neighborhood markets. Lean portions, unless the meat is aged, are bright red and well-marbled with fat. Because it comes from young, specially fed cattle, "prime" is well-flavored, fine-textured, tender and encased in white fat. It is very expensive because you pay for the excess fat, much of which is rendered out in cooking.

CHOICE

This grade has less fat than "prime" in its marbling of the lean portions. And, in its coloring, it has a slightly darker tone in both of these portions, but retains high, tender, juicy eating quality.

GOOD

This is still a relatively tender grade, but has a higher ratio of lean to fat meat than either of the above. The lean meat is darker, with little fat marbling, the encasing fat is yellowish and thin.

STANDARD

This grade is cut from young low-quality animals with a very thin fat covering and virtually no marbling in the lean portions. The youth of the animals gives this meat a bland flavor. Tenderness cannot be counted on.

COMMERCIAL AND UTILITY

These are very lean grades and come from old animals. While they are by reason of maturity better in flavor than those in "standard," such meats are coarse in flesh texture and tough, even when carefully cooked, because of their great proportion of connective tissue and their lack of fat.

Although we are always being assured that ◗ the food value of the meat from older animals is comparable to that from younger, more tender ones, we know that they rarely match them in eating quality. One definite exception applies to stocks and soups (II, 138). Both are enhanced by extractives from more mature animals. Whatever grade or cut of meat you buy, there is a great deal that you as a cook can do to make less tender cuts pleasanter to eat.

But before we discuss the cook's role, let's consider ◗ how much to purchase per serving. ◗ While price may go down for bonier cut., the amount you need per serving goes up. So that ◗ for highly processed and canned meats you need less poundage per person. Another thing to watch is the weight of meat, trimmed and untrimmed. In buying trimmed meats, allow: ◗ for boneless cuts, ¼ to ⅓ lb. per serving. This category includes ground beef, lamb and veal, boneless stew, boned roasts and steaks, flank tenderloin and most variety meats. ◗ For meat with some bone, allow ⅓ to ½ lb. per serving. These cuts include rib roasts, unboned steaks, chops and ham. ◗ For bony cuts, allow ¾ to 1 lb. per serving. In this bracket are short ribs, spareribs, lamb shanks, shoulder, breast and plate cuts, brisket and hock.

ABOUT STORING MEAT BEFORE COOKING

We assume that the meat you buy is properly aged (II, 561). ♦ Raw meat should be stored at once at 42° loosely wrapped; or, if encased in fat, uncovered. You will see a typical butcher wrap illustrated on (II, 551). If you simply pull out the ends of the paper and loosen them, adequate protection and proper ventilation are usually ensured. As a general rule, the larger the piece of meat the longer it will store.

Ground meat, fresh sausage and variety meats are among the most perishable kinds—both as to flavor-retention and safety. Use them within 24 hours of purchase; and, if the ground meat is in amounts over a pound, make sure it is stored, loosely covered, in a container not more than 2½ inches thick in depth, so that the chill of the refrigerator penetrates it quickly. Uncooked diced and cubed meats should be used within 48 hours or so. Roasts will hold 3 to 5 days, steaks 2 to 4.

Pork, lamb and veal are slightly less stable than beef. Prepackaged cured or smoked meat and sausages may be stored refrigerated in the original wrapper. Tenderized hams can be kept much longer in the refrigerator—about 2 weeks—provided the seal of the original wrapper is not broken; only one week otherwise. Once opened, the cut surfaces should be protected. The only exception to an invariable rule is so-called "dry sausage," which need not be refrigerated.

ABOUT SEASONING MEAT

Early salting brings the juices of meat to the surface and into the pan. These juices, which are themselves quite salty, are retained if the meat is seared before seasoning. If meat is breaded or dredged (II, 160), or if it is browned before stewing and the pan drippings or liquors used in gravy, salt may be added when cooking begins. In cooking ground meat, allow ¾ teaspoon salt to 1 pound, but do not apply it to patties until the first side is seared and turned. Allow 1 teaspoon to 2 pounds of solid meat with bone.

There are other ways to accent flavor. About half an hour before cooking, either rub meat with garlic, onion, herbs or spices or insert slivers of garlic or onion near the bone of a roast or else distribute them over a cut surface of steak or roast. Remove any exposed garlic before cooking, as its scorched flavor is not attractive.

Delicacy of flavor may be preserved in meat heavy with fat by pouring off any excess grease after the first half hour of cooking.

ABOUT COOKING TOUGH MEATS

Tenderness in raw meats depends not only on the comparative youth of the animal, but on the strain of cattle to which it belongs and the way it was fed. ♦ Toughness is due to the presence of connective tissues and lack of fat in the muscle. Larding and Barding, page 453, can help to make up somewhat for the lack of fat. The best way to convert stringy to tenderer tissue is by very long and ♦ very slow covered cooking in the presence of moisture. See Braising, Pot-Roasting and Stewing, page 493. Grinding and mincing make chewing easier. But the texture of the meat, if basically tough, remains so and it should never be used in luxury dishes like galantines or, for that matter, even in those as humdrum as hamburger.

Any meat can be made more palatable by seasonings and by added fats or dressings. Pounding and scoring are a help in cuts that are normally treated by dry heat methods, like sautéing and pan-frying. Another favorite technique is marinating, although it involves nutritive losses, some of which can be recaptured if the marinade itself is subsequently used in making up the dish.

Chemical tenderizing is a modern development. One controversial innovation of this type is beyond the control of the consumer. The live animal is given an injection of vegetable enzyme, the tenderizing effects of which are carried throughout the body before butchering. Special aging and storing techniques must accompany this method. The enzyme is reactivated at 130° and reduces the cooking time. A 22-lb. piece of beef will cook at 400° in about 1 hour.

Unfortunately all meat tissues —those which need it and those which do not—are affected by enzyme injection. As a result, the prime portions are usually flabby and somewhat tasteless and the meat generally has a jellied consistency which we find unpleasant. Nor can we say much for the older methods of injecting or dusting the meat with papain, a derivative of papaya, which also tenderizes. We feel that both the flavor and the texture of the meat itself are adversely affected. Meat may be tenderized with a papain derivative of the household type. Usually it is sprinkled on both sides, allowing 1 teaspoon of tenderizer per lb. Prick the meat all over with a fork after applying the tenderizer. Recent studies indicate that papain enzymes seem to tenderize meat as it warms

up to between 140° and 176°, so apply the tenderizer as the meat is put in the oven.

ABOUT MINCING, GRINDING AND POUNDING MEAT

The effect of the first two processes is quite different. Particles of minced meat remain separate in further preparation; but ground meat, especially if ground 2 or 3 times, tends to pack. ◗ Always handle ground meat lightly to avoid a dense finished texture.

Pounding, which breaks down the tough fibers of the meat, may be done with a wooden mallet or the flat side of a cleaver. Shown below is a Chinese cleaver which can also be used for chopping, just like a French knife, page 250. ◗ If you are inexperienced, hold the cleaver in both hands and be sure the handle projects beyond the board or table surface—so that you don't pound your fingers.

If you strike with a glancing motion or if you slightly moisten the cleaver, the meat is not so apt to stick. If you are pounding something delicate, like capon breasts, and don't want the fillets to separate, put them in a fold of oiled parchment paper. This allows a sliding and slipping comparable to the glancing action the professional achieves and keeps the meat intact, even when it is pounded paper thin. A chef friend has suggested that if you find the appearance of a very thin piece of meat disappointing, it can be pounded and then folded over for the cooking —to make it more presentable when served.

ABOUT LARDING AND BARDING MEAT

Lean meat is frequently "larded" to give it additional juiciness and flavor. ◗ Lardoons are thin strips of salted pork or bacon. They may be first blanched briefly, page 88, and dried before use. French cooks rub them with garlic and other herbs or dust them with cloves and cinnamon. They are cut into 2- or 3-inch strips ¼ inch thick for heavy meat cuts, ⅛ inch thick for small fowl. A larding needle may be used to draw lardoons through the surface of the meat or, as a stopgap measure, a thin knife or ice pick can be pressed into service. Insert lardoons about 1 inch apart. When larding a fowl, place the lardoons at right angles to the breast bone. Larger strips of salt pork may be forced through such meat cuts as chuck and round from surface to surface. After pulling the lardoons through, the ends may be cut off. Allow about 3 oz. of fat per pound of meat.

Lardoons are sometimes placed so their ends form rosettes or decorations. Larding needles are of 2 types. The one in use opposite is also shown, center left, before the lardoon is firmly tightened in it by pinching the pliable fringed ends together. The lower needle has a more than semicircular profile and can be used to form the lardoon itself by plunging it into the salt pork. Then turn the needle to cut the lardoon free. It is shown loaded and ready to run through the meat. To keep the lardoon in the meat, after forcing the needle in, place your thumb or forefinger at the base of the needle groove and slip the needle out with an even, steady pressure. If salt pork is used to lard a meat, as in Galantine, page 529, the lardoons are placed with the grain of the meat, as sketched above. Then, in carving, the pork shows attractively in cross section.

LARDOONS

[Enough for 2½ Lbs. of Meat]
I. Rub:
    ¼ lb. salt pork or bacon
with a cut:
    Clove of garlic
Cut into small strips. Dip into:
    Freshly ground pepper
    Ground cloves
    Minced parsley or chives

II. Marinate:
    ¼ lb. salt pork lardoons
in:
    A few tablespoons of brandy
Just before using, sprinkle with:
    Nutmeg
    Chopped parsley

III. Lardoons or Cracklings
These are also called grattons.
Dice:
    Salt pork
Try it out (II, 174) in a skillet until brown and crisp or place the dice in a very slow oven

until golden brown. Use for garnishing.

Any lean meat or that of fowl, like guinea or partridge, which is low in fat content, or any fowl from which the skin has been removed can profit by barding before roasting. Meat cuts are simply covered with slices of salt pork, about ¼ inch thick, or fat bacon, as shown on the left in the sketch. For fowl, truss the bird. For each small bird, use 4 pieces of ¼-inch-thick salt pork or fat bacon about 3 x 3½ inches square. Slip one on either side between the leg and breast, see sketch above, left and center. Cover the bird—legs and all—with 2 other pieces and tie, as shown on the right, ◗ making sure that the high exposed surfaces of the bird are blanketed. After cooking, the salt pork or bacon which has served its protective purpose is discarded.

ABOUT MARINATING MEAT

Although you may gain tenderness through marination, you also stand to lose substantial nutritive value, since, by this method, a good many proteins and vitamins are leached away. Marinades are made of both raw and cooked materials and ◗ just to remind you of the importance of using them in making up the finished dish, you will find them in Sauces, page 380. ◗ Marinating for 12 hours or more cuts

the cooking time by approximately ⅓. Allow about ½ cup of marinade for every pound of food to be processed.

ABOUT RETAINING MEAT JUICES IN COOKING

When raw meat is put into a cold liquid, as in the making of stocks (II, 138), the meat juices are released into the liquid. But when we cook meat for the table, we want these juices to stay in the meat itself. ◗ Do not cook chilled meats or ✷ frozen meat unthawed. Temperature and cooking times in all of our recipes are given for meat at 70°. Of course, this method does not apply if the meat is salt, like ham and tongue, when it may first be blanched, page 88, or unless the broth is being used for stock. In a stew, one approved method of preparation is to drop the meat into boiling water—disturbing the boiling as little as possible— ◗ and as soon as the meat turns in color, to reduce the heat to a simmer. This method is effective with veal or poultry and is called cooking "à blanc."

But the proper browning, see below, of most meats not only does a sealing job but adds immeasurably to flavor.

ABOUT SEARING OR BROWNING MEAT

Before browning meat, be sure that it is wiped ◗ dry. It is best to use as little fat as possible in browning, but be sure it covers the entire bottom of the pan. If there is not enough fat to keep the meat from burning, the charring will give a bitter taste to the sauces or gravies which may be prepared from it later. Use fat that comes from the meat you are browning or one that complements it in flavor. The ♦ heavy pan should be thoroughly and slowly heated before the fat is added and the meat ♦ slowly browned. Turn it frequently. ♦ Be sure not to crowd the pan, because this lowers the heat and the meat becomes greyish rather than the desired brown. If necessary, until you learn to brown without burning, use a little more fat and pour it off after the searing. In fact, it is always wise to pour off most of the excess grease which may accumulate in the pan before adding a liquid for stewing. When browning a meat, it is often desirable to cook a few chopped onions or other vegetables with it. Since vegetables are apt to cook more rapidly, the meat may be partially browned before they are added. Keep the vegetables moving so they, too, cook without scorching. You may, if you prefer, brown them separately in order to control the heat more easily and then add them to the meat pan. If you are cooking the onion separately, sprinkle them with a very small amount of sugar. It caramelizes them attractively and gives good color to a stew. For vegetables used as meat flavoring, see Mirepoix (II, 221).

To braise, stew or pot-roast, see page 493.

ABOUT BROILING MEAT

♦ Please read About Broiling, page 74, then choose tender cuts, see Chart, pages 464–471, like beef steak and lamb chops. Flank is also handled this way, but should be cooked rare. See London Broil, page 475. The broiling of veal and fresh pork is not recommended. Sauté or pan-fry such cuts instead.

For broiling ♦ have the meat at room temperature. Score it about every 2 inches around the edge to keep it from curling. Cut off excess fat, if any.

Place the meat ♦ on a cold rack to keep it from sticking or, should your rack be hot, grease the meat or rack. Set the meat on the middle of the broiler rack, 3 inches from the heating unit.

Broil the meat until the top side is well browned. Turn, season and broil until the second side is browned. ♦ Only one turning is necessary for a 1-inch steak or chop. Turn frequently for thicker ones and lower the rack about 1 inch for each successive inch of meat thickness— although 2 inches is considered the limit for broiling. Season and serve the meat on a hot platter. Broiling time depends largely upon the thickness of the meat, the length of time it has been hung, its fat content and the degree of doneness desired. If you use a thermometer, rare steaks are broiled to an internal temperature of 130°; medium to 160°. Lamb chops are broiled to 155° for rare and to 170° if well done. Ham is cooked well done. The time for broiling bacon is influenced by personal preference as to crispness, but ♦ to keep it from curling, the heat should be low. Should your broiler be an infrared one, follow manufacturer's directions.

ABOUT PANBROILING MEAT

♦ Preheat a heavy skillet. Rub the pan with a small quantity of fat if the meat is not prime. Sear the meat on one side until the blood rises to the surface. Then turn at once and sear it on the other side. ♦ Reduce the heat and continue to process the meat uncovered. If cooked too long, it toughens badly and dries out. In the case of a steak about 1½ inches thick, cooking time may be 10 minutes or more if you want it medium to well done. During the cooking, pour excess fat from the pan for, if allowed to accumulate, the meat is "fried" rather than "broiled" in quality.

If meat is solid and well-marbled or if fat has been incorporated with it—as is often the case with ground meats, like hamburger—it can go directly into a preheated ungreased pan. Sometimes a salt base is suggested, allowing 1 teaspoon salt for each pound of meat. This rather surprising technique works but is, in our judgment, best avoided, since the salt extracts meat juices which, of course, are promptly discarded when broiling is over. If you are obliged to follow fat-free procedures, try oven broiling, a soapstone griddle or a pan whose surface has been specially treated for fat-free frying. With such treated pans, follow the manufacturer's directions.

ABOUT ROASTING MEAT

After trying out different methods of roasting meat over a long period of years, we are convinced that the quality of the meat is the decisive factor. We suggest you choose a method best suited to the meat at hand. ♦ To cook vegetables with a roast, see page 258.

I. If the meat is Prime or Choice, we get the best flav . by placing not less than 2 ribs at about 70° temperature ♦ on a rack in a pan greased with suet or oil, in a preheated 500° oven, fat side up. The rack allows proper circulation of air. As soon as the oven door is closed ♦ reduce the heat to 350° and time the cooking from that point, depending on the size of the roast and the degree of doneness wanted. Timings are given in the individual recipes.

No basting is necessary in this procedure, there being sufficient fat in the meat. You will get minimal, but very precious, juice in the pan. To make gravy from pan drippings, see page 358.

II. ♦ If meat is Good or Standard grade and its weight not under 4 lbs., place it when it has reached 70° ♦ uncovered in a preheated 325° oven—except for pork, for which we prefer an oven heated to 350°. Sometimes we first brown the roast, page 454. But usually we put a thermometer in it and simply place the meat, unbrowned, on a rack, in a pan directly in the preheated oven and forget about it until it is almost time to check for internal temperature. The method just described produces practically no fat or juice in the pan, and needs a gravy confected from precooked stocks, see (II, 138). In adopting either of the above methods, remember that if the roast is carved in the kitchen rather than at the table, the juices which run into the carving dish can and should be quickly defatted and incorporated into any gravy previously prepared—to give it a final authentic flavor. Meanwhile, keep the already sliced meat warm on a hot platter.

♦ Sometimes very low, slow roasting is suggested. ♦ It is important not to have the oven under 275°, for unwanted microorganisms may not be destroyed below this temperature, no matter how long the cooking. ◗ The insertion of metal pins in a roast cuts down cooking time somewhat and the meat will be juiːer but not quite as tender.

ABOUT BASTING MEAT

In roasting and broiling, everything is done to preserve the dry quality of the heat. If roasts are Prime grade, they are so heavy in fat that basting is not necessary. In fact, with prime meats, fat losses run as high as 40% of weight. Just brush a small amount of fat in the base of the pan to tide over until some from the meat is rendered. An exception is tenderloin, which may be simply rubbed with fat or oil or be larded or barded, page 453.

The leaner cuts profit by basting ◗ with melted fat. But the moment you baste with stocks or water, excess steam is created which lessens the dry heat quality that makes a roast so delicious. ◗ Baste preferably with fatty pan drippings by using a bulb-type baster, as sketched on the left, or with a spoon as shown on the right.

There are also 2 types of self-basting. One is with fat, in barding, page 454. The other is with steam, which takes place in a covered pan—when the steam rising from the food falls back from the lid onto the braising meat or stew. This kind of basting never goes on in roasting—where, to achieve the essential dry heat ◗ no cover is used.

ABOUT TIMING IN COOKING MEAT

Timing is given in each recipe, but it is most difficult to advise about this accurately without knowing the thickness of the meat, its quality, its shape and how much bone it contains. Ovens and broilers should always be preheated. All meat, we repeat, should be at about 70° throughout before roasting or broiling begins. If meat is chemically tenderized, the papain derivatives used in the household, see page 452, begin to take effect during cooking and greatly shorten its cooking period.

If meats have been ✳ frozen, bring them to 70° and time as for fresh meat. Thawing before cooking keeps to a minimum the amount of juices released. But there are times—occasional emergencies—when one must cook meat before thawing it.

In roasting unthawed frozen meat, preheat the oven to about 25° less than indicated in the recipes and allow about ½ again as much time for the cooking period.

In broiling unthawed meat, regardless of its thickness, place it at least 5 to 6 inches below the heat source. Again allow at least ½ again as much time as normally indicated. For further comments on timing, see page 97. ◗ To test for doneness, see below.

▲ In high altitudes, roasted and baked meats require no adjustment up to 7000 ft. After that a longer cooking period may be needed. We recommend the pressure cooking of meats only in cases of emergency. Tests show that these have less shrinkage and more flavor if cooked at 10 rather than at 15 pounds pressure.

ABOUT DONENESS IN MEAT

Rare, medium, or well done—these are such personal preferences that set rules become difficult to prescribe. What you should realize is that ◗ in cooking any meats, heat should at some point be high enough to destroy unwanted and harmful organisms. We give these necessary internal temperatures for various meats in our individual recipes and elsewhere in this chapter. But we ask you to realize that meat roasted for as long as 12 hours and to as high a temperature as 200° may still be insufficiently cooked to ensure safety—since roasting is merely a reflected heat; whereas stewing at a simmering temperature of 180° over a comparably long period will be sufficient—this heat being moist, and a more penetrating one. ◗ Reaching the proper temperature is especially vital for safety in cooking pork, page 484. We suggest in recipes for roasts, steaks and stews a certain timing—usually minutes to the pound at a given temperature. But with this rough and ready formula you may not get the result you expected. The reasons are many: if you have not allowed the meat to reach 70°, if its shape is very thick or if it is not well aged, it will require longer cooking. Or the meat may have much fat, which will allow the heat to be transmitted more rapidly.

Since it requires a trained eye to judge the doneness of meat

from its external appearance ◗ use a meat thermometer for accurate results. Before broiling meat over 3 inches thick or before roasting it, insert the thermometer in the center and fleshy portion of the meat, away from bony or fatty sections. Unless the glass of the thermometer is metal-shielded, make a gash with a pointed sharp knife to ease the insertion of the thermometer. Place the top so that it is as far away from the source of heat as possible.

If you have no thermometer, there are two ways to judge doneness. In the touch method, firm meat is well done. If it responds as a cake does (II, 336)—is soft yet resilient—the meat is medium rare. You can also detect the degree of doneness by pricking roasted or broiled meats, but when you do you lose valuable juices. If the juice runs red, the meat is rare; pink, medium rare; colorless, well done.

◗ Pork and fowl with light meat must be cooked until the juice is colorless. Most other meats are overdone at this point.

To test for braised meats, use a sharply pointed knife near the bone. The juice should run clear.

ABOUT COOKING MEAT EN CROÛTE

Meat in a crust, or en croûte, lends itself particularly to buffet service. If served hot, the meat remains "à point," page 72, for at least half an hour. Hot or cold, the finished dish is beautiful to behold. The crust is not eaten. It serves only as a medium for retaining aromas. You may encase ham, fowl, lamb or beef roast when cooked to within ½ to ¾ of an hour of doneness. Starting with uncooked fowl or roast is described later.

Cool the meat while you prepare the following crust, heavy in egg, which lends the tensile strength necessary to keep large or heavy meats covered. Have all ingredients at 70°. Mix together, to the consistency of coarse corn meal:

4 cups all-purpose flour
1 cup shortening
1½ teaspoons salt

Make a well (II, 301) of these ingredients and work in one at a time:

3 to 4 eggs
½ cup water

Knead the dough until well bound. Roll into a ball and rest covered for several hours at 70°. Preheat the oven to 450°. Roll the dough into a large sheet, about ⅜ inch thick. Place the meat you want to cover so that the top surface is down on the dough. Then fold the dough over it, as neatly as possible, pressing it to take the form of the meat. Be careful to keep the covering intact. Then turn the covered meat right side up. Brush any excess flour off the dough with a dry brush.

Now the fun begins. From the pastry scraps that remain, cut rounds, flowers and leaves or any decorations that suit your mood. If you like, score them with a fork to give their surfaces a variation that will show up markedly after baking. You may even use Puff Paste (II, 300) for such trimmings. Space them out on the dough up to three thicknesses by applying French Egg Wash (II, 433) to each, as a glue. When you are satisfied with your design—and don't make it too cluttered—brush the surfaces with egg wash again. Cut a series of decorative gashes in the dough casing, as for a covered pie, to let the steam escape and to keep the crust from buckling. Put the covered meat in the hot oven, and ▶ reduce the heat at once to 350°.

Allow the crust to bake until it is delicately browned. Repeat the egg glazing at the end of baking, for an even effect. You may also brush the crust with butter on removal from the oven.

Another way to bake en croûte is to use, instead of the dough indicated above, a stiff bread dough. Punch it down once before rolling it out and cover as previously described.

▶ To cook uncooked meat en croûte, prepare the dough described previously. Coat the meat to be covered with Egg Wash (II, 433). Fold the pastry around the meat and decorate as described above.

Bake the meat in a preheated 280° to 300° oven, 2 to 3 hours, depending on size. Hams and legs of lamb may be boned and stuffed before wrapping. If a stuffing is used, be sure the food it is made of is precooked, as the heat may not penetrate it sufficiently otherwise to cook it through.

ABOUT STORING COOKED MEAT

It is much safer to ▶ put meat into the refrigerator while still fairly hot and this is only a slightly more expensive way to refrigerate. ▶ Cover it.

If you prefer, you may also leave meat that has been cooked to cool ▶ covered for 2 hours before refrigerating.

Do not store ▶ meat in hot gravy in quantities larger than 1 quart. Drain off the gravy and allow it to cool separately if the amounts are larger. If meats are ▶ stuffed, unstuff them and store the stuffing separately.

ABOUT REHEATING MEAT

It is a great temptation to try to prepare large joints of meat in advance and reheat them just before serving. This is not good practice. For the heat to penetrate on reheating, a very long period is necessary and the meat tends to dry out.

With hash or sauced meats, be sure the sauce is ♦ just to the point of boiling before the meat is added. ♦ Reduce the heat at once and allow the meat to heat thoroughly. Serve at once. An even better way to reheat thin sliced meats is described on page 98.

ABOUT CARVING MEAT

The convenient ready-to-serve platter, or so-called Russian service, has almost displaced carving. Fortunately, a few hosts still delight in practicing this gracious skill. And, given a very sharp knife, a large platter and the most rudimentary knowledge of animal anatomy, almost anyone can learn to carve.

Illustrations throughout this chapter show the general direction taken in approaching major cuts. Most meats are cut against the grain, although a leg of lamb or mutton may also be cut with it. If you are trying out in the kitchen, use a board until you become worthy of the art and can carve on a platter without scratching it. Ply the knife with

a long, light, pulling and pushing, sawlike action. Always try to keep your fork-hand behind, not in front of, the blade. Protect yourself further by using a fork with a thumb piece.

Slicing knives for ham, roast beef, big turkeys and pot roasts have a very flexible 10-inch blade, about 1¼ inches wide. Carving knives for game, loin of pork, rack of lamb or lobster are about a foot in length. Their 8½-inch pointed, rigidly firm blades, about 1¾ inches wide, are so shaped that at the blade edge they come to a fine V. ♦ Keeping the knife blade sharp and under easy control is important. But of equal importance to the successful carver is keeping the V-edge true by the use of a steel. And the following procedure should precede the use of the knife before each carving period. The steel, which must be kept magnetized, realigns the molecular structure of the blade.

♦ To true a blade, hold the steel firmly in the left hand, thumb on top of handle. Hold the knife in the right hand, point upward, and the hand slightly away from the body. Place the heel of the blade against the far side of the tip of the steel, as illustrated. The steel and blade should meet at about a 15° to 25° angle.

◗ Draw the blade across the steel, bringing it down toward the left hand, with a quick swinging motion of the right wrist. ◗ The entire blade should pass lightly over the steel. To start the second stroke, bring the knife into the same position as in the first, but this time the steel should lie behind the blade, away from you, as shown on the right. About twelve strokes are enough to true the edge.

Some carvers feel the results are better if they allow a roast to set—that is rest outside the oven on a hot platter. With very large joints which retain their heat well, this setting period may be from 30 to 45 minutes.

ABOUT ECONOMICAL USE OF LARGE CUTS OF MEAT

If shopping for a household of two, there are times when you may look longingly at the "weekly special" on meat. How tempting the standing rib roast of beef, the rump of beef, the leg of spring lamb, the loin of pork, the round of veal or the half or whole ham! But unless you are planning to have guests, it looks as if it is far more meat than you care to buy for two. But by taking advantage of special sales prices and planning ahead to freeze a part of the cut for future use, it is an economy to buy the larger piece. You can have your delicious roast for just two—or steaks from the ham or veal, chops from lamb or pork, short ribs from beef. Then the remainder may be used in many interesting leftover dishes.

2 RIBS OF BEEF—5 lbs.

Have butcher cut off:
Short Ribs, page 500; Roast Beef, page 463. The leftover beef can be reheated in: Cum-

GUIDE TO APPROXIMATE YIELD OR CUTS FROM 250 LB. SIDE OF BEEF, CUT FROM AN 800 LB. STEER

Please read About Steaks, page 472, and Fillet of Beef, page 472. FROM 26 LBS. OF SHORTLOIN You have a choice of club, sirloin and porterhouse steaks—which are a combination of T-bone, sirloin and fillet. But, if you want 5 lbs. of fillet from the shortloin, you must forego the porterhouse steaks, which will leave you 21 lbs. of shortloin for sirloin steaks, T-bone and club steaks. If you choose to have the fillet, see page 472 to utilize it to the best advantage.

FROM	CHOICE OF
21 lbs. of loin end	Butt steaks and roasts
2 lbs. of flank steak	Ground beef—flank steak
45 lbs. of boneless round	Top and bottom, Swiss steak, pot roasts, hamburger, cubed steak
23 lbs. of rib	7-rib roast, rolled roast, rib steaks
42 lbs. of boneless chuck	Ground beef, stew, pot roast
10 lbs. of boneless brisket	For braising, stewing, ground, corned beef
17 lbs. of plate	Ground beef, stew
10 lbs. of shank	Soup meat, marrow bones
49 lbs. of fat, bone and waste	Also, tripe, tongue, liver, heart,
5 lbs. loss in trimming	sweetbreads, brains, kidneys, oxtail and head

berland Sauce, page 372. Or
used in Hot Roast Beef Sand-
wich with Olive Sauce, page
242; Shepherd's Pie, page 225;
Leftover in Bacon, page 218;
Peppers filled with Meat and
Rice, page 308; Cold Roast Beef
and Tomato Sauce, page 376;
Acorn Squash Filled with
Creamed Food, page 331.

RUMP OF BEEF—4 to 5 lbs.

Have butcher cut off a piece
about 2 inches thick, dice into
1-inch cubes for:
Beef Stew with Wine, page 496.
Or use in one piece for Pot
Roast, page 498. Us the left-
overs as Cold Roast Beef and
Curry Sauce, page 363; or hot
as beef reheated in Cumberland
Sauce, page 372. Or use in Hot
Roast Beef Sandwich, page 242;
Turnovers filled with meat, page
210; or Leftover Timbales, page
202.

ROUND OF VEAL

Have butcher cut off 1 or 2 thin
slices of veal for:

Veal Birds	Page 505
Veal Scallopini	479
Mexican Veal Steak	506
Wiener Schnitzel	480

Have another slice cut off
to dice into 1-inch cubes
for:

| Blanquette de Veau | 504 |
| Cubed Veal Baked in Sour Cream | 506 |

Use the remainder for:

| Veal Roast | 478 |

Use leftovers in:

Curried Veal and Rice	217
Creamed Veal	217
Veal and Spinach	217
Veal Timbales	204
Meat Shortcakes	211

LEG OF LAMB—5 to 6 lbs.

Have butcher cut off:
4 chops for:

| Broiled II | Page 483 |

| Stuffed Lamb Chops | 483 |

Also a slice about 2 inches
thick, diced into 1-inch
cubes for:

| Curried Lamb | 509 |
| Lamb Stew | 508 |

Roast the remaining shank
end 482
Leftovers may be used in:

Veal or Lamb and Spinach Dish	217
Eggplant Filled with Leftover Food	291
Lamb Terrapin	318
Lamb Sandwich	246
Scotch Broth	116

LOIN OF PORK—9 to 10 lbs.

Have butcher cut off:
4 chops from center of loin for:

Pork Chops	Page 487
Deviled Pork Chops	512
Pork Chops Baked in Sour Cream	511

Use one end for:

| Pork Roast | 485 |

Freeze the other end for:

| Pork Roast with Sauerkraut | 487 |

Use leftovers in:

Meat Pie Roll	211
Chop Suey	218
Shepherd's Pie	225
Pizza	213
Scrapple or Goetta	533

HALF HAM—4 to 7 lbs.

Have butcher cut off 1 or 2
slices to use for:

Broiled Ham	Page 491
Stuffed Ham Rolls, III	219
Ham with Fruit	490

Use remainder as:

| Baked Ham | 488–490 |

Use leftovers for:

Ham and Corn Croquettes	(II, 122)
Ham à la King	220
Ham Rolls with Asparagus	219
Jellied Ham Mousse	60
Split Pea or Lentil Soup	120

Ham Cakes with
Pineapple and Sweet
Potatoes   220
Ham Loaf with Cooked
Ham   219
Lima Bean Casserole
with Ham   269
Ham Waffles with À la
King Sauce   375

TO MAKE A FRILL FOR A
SHANK BONE

To make a frill for a shank ham,
a lamb bone or drumsticks, fold
in half stiff paper dinner napkins, about 12 x 8 inches. Cut
through fold at ½-inch intervals to within 1 inch of open
edge. Reverse the fold, bringing the open edges together.
Begin to roll the uncut portion
of the newly folded paper, leaving an opening at the folded
open edge big enough to slip
over the bone. Fasten this roll
with scotch tape and slide the
frill over the bone.

ABOUT BEEF

Beef, its aging, grading and
general characteristics are described in About Meats, page
449. With the exception of
game, no meat profits more by
proper aging. Few households
are able to buy, not for lack of
money, but for lack of supply,
the kinds of beef purchased by
hotels and clubs. The scarce superior grades are almost always
reserved for these commercial
establishments.

The American woman, through
visual advertising, has been
made to feel that bright red
lean beef is the desirable grade,
but actually beef for best flavor
should be well aged to a purplish tone and show definite
evidence of mottling, as well as
heavy fat coverings.

ROAST BEEF

[3 to 4 Servings to the Pound]
Preheat oven to 550°.
When buying a standard rib of
beef, be sure to have your
butcher remove the spinal cord,
the shoulder bone and the
chine. Have him tie the chine
back on—to keep the contour
of the meat and to protect the
eye of the roast during the
cooking period. If the roast is
made oven-ready in this way,
the carving, illustrated, is very
simple. Remove the roast from
the refrigerator at least 3 hours
before preparing for cooking.
Trim off the excess fat and hard
edges of:
A rib roast of beef
Place the roast, fat side up, on
a rack in a pan in the oven.
◆ Reduce the heat immediately
to 350° and cook 18 to 20 minutes to the pound for medium
rare. To cook vegetables with
roast, see page 258.
A rolled roast will require 5 to
10 minutes longer to the pound.
To make gravy from pan drippings see page 258. Serve the
roast with:
Macaroni Loaf, page 171
Yorkshire Pudding, page
182, or Tomato Pudding,
page 335
To carve see below.

DIVISIONS OF COMMERCIAL CUTS AND RETAIL
CUTS OF BEEF

BEEF

RECIPES KEYED TO CHART

Roast of Beef, Page 463; Rib 12; Sirloin 6–7; Short Loin 8–9–10.

Pot Roasts, Page 495; Shoulder 18; Chuck 15; Rump 1; or Brisket 19.

Sauerbraten, and Boeuf à la Mode, Page 497; Shoulder 18.

Steaks: For details of beef cuts bearing this name, see Page 472. For Chart of Fillet Steaks, see Page 472; also see Broiled Steaks, Page 474 and Pan-Broiled Steaks, Page 474, for which you can use Shoulder 18; Rib Steak 12; Tip Steak 5; Ground Round 2.

Boeuf Fondu Bourguignonne, Page 475: Fillet 6–9; Sirloin 6–7.

Beef Stroganoff, Page 476: Fillets 6–9.

Beef Kebabs, Page 476: Round 2; Sirloin 6–7; Fillets 6–9.

Beef Rolls, Roulades or Paupiettes, Page 502: Round 2; Flank 11.

Burgoo, Page 503: Chuck 15; Neck 16; Shoulder 18; Foreshank 21–22.

Sukiyaki, Page 477: Tenderloin 6–9; Sirloin Tip 6; Eye of Round 2.

Beef Goulash, Page 500: Round 2; Shinbone 21–22.

Flank Steak With Dressing, Page 499: Flank 11.

Oxtail Stew, Page 501: Tailbones.

Corned Beef, Page 493: Brisket 19.

Ground Beef and Meat Loaves, Page 522, and Hamburgers, Page 516: Chuck 15; Flank 11; Neck 16; Round 2.

Heart, Page 546, Tongue, Page 544, and Tripe, Page 548, are the favored beef variety meats.

BONE STRUCTURE AND COMMERCIAL CUTS FROM A CARCASS OF BEEF

1 ROUND
2 SIRLOIN
3 SHORT LOIN
4 RIB
5 CHUCK
6 FORESHANK
7 SHORT END OF BRISKET
8 FLANK

DIVISIONS OF COMMERCIAL CUTS AND
RETAIL CUTS OF VEAL

VEAL

RECIPES KEYED TO CHART

Roast of Veal, Page 478: Rib 10.

Stuffed or Rolled Veal Roast, Page 478: Shoulder 11–12; Breast 9.

Veal Kidney Roast, Page 478: Loin 7.

Veal Post Roast, Page 505 or Veal Pot Roast In Red Wine, Page 503: Rump 4.

Veal Cutlet, Scaloppini or Schnitzel or Veal Parmigiana, Pages 479–481; Leg 3; Loin 5–6–7.

Veal Stew, or Veal Stew in Red Wine, Page 503: Breast 9; Neck 13.

Blanquette de Veau, Page 504: Shoulder 11–12.

Veal Porkolt, Page 500: Leg 3; Shoulder 11–12; Neck 13.

Mock Chicken Drumsticks or City Chicken, Page 505: Breast 9; Neck 13.

Osso Buco, Page 506: Shank 14.

Veal Patties, Page 518: Flank 8; Breast 9.

Terrine, Page 528: Leg 3.

Veal Birds or Paupiettes, Page 505: Leg 3.

All Veal Variety Meats are considered choice.

See Index for Liver, Sweetbreads, Brains, and Kidneys; Also Steak and Kidney Pie, Page 504, and Head Cheese and Brawn, Page 550.

BONE STRUCTURE AND COMMERCIAL CUTS FROM A CARCASS OF VEAL

1 SHANK
2 SHOULDER
3 RIB
4 LOIN
5 LEG
6 BREAST
7 FLANK

DIVISION OF COMMERCIAL CUTS AND RETAIL CUTS OF LAMB

LAMB

RECIPES KEYED TO CHART

Lamb or Mutton Roast, Page 482: Rib 3.

Broiled Lamb Chops, Page 483: Rib 3; Loin 2; Leg 1.

Broiled Lamb Kebabs, Page 483: Shoulder 6.

Lamburgers, Page 517: Shoulder 6.

Since lamb is a relatively tender meat, almost any cut, especially of young lamb, can be cooked by the dry heat methods above. Also see pages 482–483. Cuts from active areas where the muscle is firmer may be cooked according to the following moist heat methods on pages 506–510.

Braised Stuffed Shoulder or Farce of Lamb, Page 507: Shoulder 6.

Braised Lamb Shanks or Trotters, Page 508: Shank 7.

Irish Stew, Page 509: Shoulder 6; Breast 4.

Navarin Printanier, Page 508: Shoulder 6; Breast 4.

Try cooked lamb in Curry of Lamb, Page 501; Lamb and Eggplant Casserole, Page 509; Stuffed Eggplant, Page 291.

For Variety Meat Recipes, see Tongue in Creole Sauce, Page 546; Steak and Kidney Pie, Page 502.

BONE STRUCTURE AND COMMERCIAL CUTS FROM A CARCASS OF LAMB

1 LEG
2 LOIN
3 RACK OR RIB
4 BREAST
5 NECK
6 SHOULDER
7 SHANK

DIVISIONS OF COMMERCIAL CUTS AND RETAIL CUTS OF PORK

PORK

RECIPES KEYED TO CHART

Roast of Pork, Page 485: Loin 3.

Roast of Pork Stuffed with Sauerkraut, Page 487: Shoulder Butt 6.

Pork Tenderloin, Page 487: Loin 3.

Frenched Fruit Casserole, Page 487; Loin 3; with Mushrooms, Page 511: Loin 3.

Rib Pork Chops Broiled, Page 487: Loin 3.

Rib or Loin Chops, Page 511 or with Fruit, or Stuffed, Page 512: Loin 3.

Sweet and Sour Pork, Page 514: Boned Ribs 5.

Baked Spareribs, or Ribs With Sauerkraut, Page 514 or Barbecued Ribs, Page 97: Ribs 5.

Stewed Pork Hocks, Page 514: Hock 8.

Hams, Pages 489–491, or Ham En Croûte, Page 458, or Ham Slices Casseroled or with Fruit, Page 490: Ham 1.

Rolled Smoked Picnic Shoulder, Page 491: Picnic Shoulder 7.

Broiled or Sautéed Bacon, Page 491: Flank 4.

Broiled Sautéed or Baked Canadian Bacon, Page 492: Loin 3.

Parblanched Salt Pork, Page 551: Flank 4.

Pigs' Feet, Page 551: Forefoot 11.

Pork Scrapple or Goetta, Page 533: Shoulder Butt 6.

Pork Variety Meats are not choice with the exception of Suckling Pig's Livers, see Pâté En Croûte, Page 525; for Suckling Pig, see page 485.

BONE STRUCTURE AND COMMERCIAL CUTS FROM A CARCASS OF PORK

1 HAM
2 FAT BACK
3 PORK LOIN
4 BACON
5 SPARERIBS
6 SHOULDER BUTT
7 PICNIC SHOULDER
8 HOCK
9 SNOUT
10 JOWL
11 FORE FOOT
12 HIND FOOT

For ways to utilize leftover roasted meat, see Boeuf Miroton, page 217, and Luncheon Dishes, page 208.

ROAST STRIP SIRLOIN   [24 to 30]

Preheat oven to 550°.
Have the meat at 70° and trim excess top fat from:

>   An 18 to 22 lb. eye of the
>   strip sirloin

Place on a rack in a pan, fat side up, in the oven. ◗ Reduce heat at once to 350°. Roast uncovered 1½ hours for rare meat.

ABOUT FILLET OF BEEF

This choicest, most tender cut can be utilized in many ways; but trim off, first of all, the fat and sinew. Loosen fat at the small or tail end and tear this off as well as the clods of fat, near the wing-shaped portion of the fillet. Then, with a sharp pointed knife, remove the thin, tough, bluish sinew that lies underneath. To cook whole, either cut off about 6 inches of the tail end and save it for Stroganoff or Sukiyaki—or fold thin end under to equalize the thickness of the whole before roasting. To make the classic cuts, start at the upper end on the left and cut Filet Mignon, below, in slices 1½ to 2 inches thick. As you approach the center or Châteaubriand area, below, the small wing pieces will cut free. The Châteaubriand section is always cooked

whole, either roasted or broiled, and is sliced at the table before serving. The narrower portion can be cut into 1-inch-thick slices called Tournedos, to within about 4 inches of the end. Use the tail again for Stroganoff, page 476, or Steak Tartare (II, 78).

FILLET OR TENDERLOIN OF BEEF

[Allow ⅓ Pound per Serving]
Preheat oven to 500°.
Have the meat at room temperature. Remove the surplus fat and skin from:

>   At least a 5 lb. fillet of
>   beef

You may lard, page 453, with narrow strips of:

>   (Salt pork or country
>   bacon)

Fold over the thin ends of the fillet and secure them with string. If not larded, spread the meat generously with butter or tie strips of bacon over it. Do not cover or baste it. Place on a rack in a roasting pan in the oven. You may oil the pan. ◗ Reduce the heat immediately to 350° and bake from 18 to 30 minutes in all. A fillet is usually cooked rare when the internal temperature reaches 120°. Season when done. You may surround the fillet with:

>   Broiled Mushrooms, page
>   297

Garnish the platter with:

>   Sprigs of parsley
>   Soufflé Potatoes, page
>   316

Serve with:

>   Marchand de Vin Sauce,
>   page 367
>   Bordelaise Sauce, page
>   366
>   Béarnaise Sauce, page
>   370

ABOUT STEAKS

When in doubt, the stock answer to the menu problem is, "Let's have steak!" Steak—from ▣ charcoal grill to planked Châteaubriand, page 80—does duty for so many different occasions that we would like to discuss steak varieties below. Unless special recipes are given, they may all be broiled, page 455, or pan-broiled, page 455. The meat should of course ♦ be at least 70° and the ♦ grill should be hot and oiled ♦ the broiler preheated. ♦ Season at the end of cooking and not before.

Steak, hot or cold, is greatly enhanced by a sauce and the most usual accompaniments are one of the following:

> Colbert Butter, page 384
> Béarnaise Sauce, page 370
> Bordelaise Sauce, page 366
> Marchand de Vin Sauce, page 367
> Sour Cream Horseradish Sauce, page 351
> Mushroom Sauce, page 367

FLANK STEAK

This is considered the least choice cut, probably because so often poorly prepared. It is a treat if properly cooked, see London Broil, page 475.

HAMBURGER

This, too, can be a real treat, not just a stopgap, see page 516.

RUMP, SWISS AND ROUND STEAK

Made from the round, these are prized for their flavor but are never truly tender. Since they must be braised and do not respond to dry heat methods, they are steaks only in name, see Moist Heats, page 81. Scrape

and serve raw for Steak Tartare (II, 78).

CUBE STEAKS

These are top butt or round and macerated to tenderize for grilling. They are usually tough.

RIB OR SPENCER STEAKS

These are comparable in price but varying in flavor and texture and cut from a choice area of the eye of the rib.

CLUB OR MINUTE STEAK

This is cut from the end of the shortloin and makes a good individual serving.

T-BONE STEAK

This also is cut from the shortloin but near the middle. It combines the tail of fillet and the tail of the sirloin.

PORTERHOUSE STEAK

Another shortloin cut. It is very like T-bone—but a larger version—and includes the choice fillet and choice sirloin.

SIRLOIN

Cut from the shortloin, it is comparable to a French entrecôte. Its flavor is the one associated most often with the word steak.

SIRLOIN STRIP STEAK

This is the eye of the sirloin—the choice cut most often met with in hotels. In serving large groups, the eye of the sirloin, 18 to 22 lbs., from which these strip steaks come, is often roasted whole, page 472, and sliced.

TENDERLOIN OR FILLET STEAKS

These include Filet Mignon, Châteaubriand,   Tournedos,

Steak Tartare. They vary in name and size, depending on the portion of the fillet from which they are cut. For details, see the illustration on page 472. Prized for their tenderness, they are somewhat lacking in flavor and require an interesting sauce.

BROILED STEAK

Preheat broiler.
Prepare for cooking a 2-inch-thick:

> Sirloin, T-bone, strip or porterhouse steak

Have the meat at room temperature. You may rub the steak with:

> (A cut clove of garlic)

You may spread it an hour before it is cooked with:

> (Olive oil)

Add:

> (Grated onion and prepared mustard)

Or spread when ¾ cooked with:

> French Dressing

A very thick steak may be browned on both sides, then cooked until done, 4 inches from the heat. When done, spread with:

> Butter or the pan drippings, after removing most of the fat

Add:

> Chopped parsley or chives

If the drippings are meager, you may add:

> (1 to 2 tablespoons butter or wine)

Serve the steak garnished with:

> Sautéed Mushrooms, page 296
> French Fried Onions, page 303

Or serve with:

> Bordelaise Sauce, page 366
> Béarnaise Sauce, page 370
> Maître d'Hôtel Butter,

> page 384
> Marchand de Vin Sauce, page 367
> Garlic Butter, page 385
> Colbert Butter, page 384

PAN-BROILED STEAK

Prepare for cooking:

> A beefsteak

Heat a heavy frying pan over lively heat until very hot. If the meat is not prime, rub the pan very lightly with:

> A bit of beef fat

Put the steak in the pan and sear for 1 minute or until the blood rises on the uncooked surface. Turn and sear the other side.

◗ Reduce the heat and continue cooking the steak until done, about 10 minutes for a 1½-inch steak. Pour off any fat in the pan for, if it is allowed to remain, the steak will be "fried" and not "broiled." Season the steak with:

> Salt and freshly ground pepper

Make with the drippings:

> Pan Gravy, page 358

or use:

> Maître d'Hôtel Butter, page 384

For suggestions for steak sauces, see Broiled Steak, above.
Serve with:

> Franconia Potatoes, page 314

PAN-BROILED FILLET STEAK

Pan-broil, as above:

> Four 1-inch fillet steaks

using, to prevent sticking, a small amount of:

> Butter

When the meat is done—not more than 3 minutes to a side —deglaze the pan, page 358, with:

> ¼ cup dry red wine
> 2 tablespoons beef stock

1 teaspoon Meat Glaze
(II, 145)
Serve with:
Artichoke hearts, stuffed
with Creamed Spinach,
page 326

BROILED TOURNEDOS OR FILET MIGNON STEAK

Preheat broiler.
Upon request a butcher usually
will cut fillet steaks, shape them
and surround them with a strip
of bacon secured by a wooden
pick. Otherwise follow instructions and sketch on page 472,
to find from which portion of
the fillet these cuts come. The
thickness of the steaks may vary
from ¾ to 1 inch or more.
Prepare for cooking:
Fillet steaks: 1 to 2
inches thick
Spread with:
Butter
Broil as for:
Broiled Steak, page 474
When done, remove the bacon.
Serve on:
A fried or toasted
crouton, page 390
with:
Béarnaise Sauce, page
370
Lemon and parsley
Broiled Mushrooms, page
297
Potatoes Anna, page 315,
or
Duchess Potatoes, page
319

STEAK AU POIVRE OR PEPPERED STEAK

Use:
Trimmed 1-inch-thick
strip sirloin, club or filet
mignon steaks
Crush:
1 to 2 tablespoons
peppercorns
The pepper should not be
ground but crushed coarsely on
a board with a pressing, rolling
movement, using the bottom of
a pan. Press the steaks into the
crushed pepper and work it into
both sides of the meat with the
heel of your palm or with the
flat side of a cleaver. Sprinkle
the bottom of a skillet with:
2 teaspoons salt
When it begins to brown, put
the steaks into the pan and
brown ♦ uncovered over high
heat.
♦ Reduce to medium heat, turn
the steaks and cook to desired
degree of rareness. In a separate
pan, prepare:
¼ cup butter
1 teaspoon Worcestershire
sauce
2 tablespoons lemon juice
Remove the steaks from the pan
in which they have been cooked
and discard the pan drippings.
Pour the butter mixture over
steaks. Flambé steaks, page 80,
with:
(2 oz. cognac)

LONDON BROIL OR FLANK STEAK

Preheat broiler.
Place on a greased broiler rack:
A 2 to 3 lb. flank steak
Broil within 2 inches of source
of heat—the hotter the better—
about 5 minutes on each side ♦
making sure the meat is kept
rare. If a flank steak is cooked
medium or well done, it becomes extremely tough. ♦ Carve
by slicing against or across the
grain to make it more tender.
Serve with:
Bearnaise Sauce, page
370
Bordelaise Sauce, page
366

BOEUF FONDU BOURGUIGNONNE

This dish is cooked at table in
a special deep metal pot which
narrows at the top to keep the

butter from sputtering. It can be cooked in an electric skillet ▸ if the butter is sweet and clarified, which keeps it from popping. We love this dish inordinately. It gives the hostess an easy time, both from the cooking angle and from the entertaining one—as the guests quickly reveal their individual characteristics. They are all there—the hoarder, the cooperator, the kibitzer, the boss. ▸ Don't try to get more than 5 or 6 guests around one heat source. Allow for each person ⅓ to ½ lb. fillet of beef. Cut into ¾-inch dice:

About 3 lbs. fillet of beef

Have ready 2 to 4 sauces:

Mustard with capers
Thickened Tomato
Sauce, page 376
Mayonnaise with garlic
and herbs
Marchand de Vin with
Mushrooms, page 367
A curry sauce
A chutney-based sauce
A sweet-sour sauce

Melt in an electric skillet:

1 cup clarified butter

When butter is brownish, announce the rules of the game. Allow to each guest only one to two pieces of meat at a time, so as to keep the cooking heat constant. Impale the beef on long forks, worry it around in the butter until it is done to your liking. If rare is your choice, the time is very short. Arrange the sauces on your plate like oils on a palette. The plate can be a compartmented one, but this is not necessary. Dip the hot browned meat in the sauce of your choice. Serve with the beef crusty French bread or rolls and a tossed salad—with green grapes or avocado slices.

BEEF STROGANOFF [4]

This dish ✳ freezes well and is economical when made with fillet ends. See chart, page 472.

I. Cut into ½-inch slices:

1½ lbs. fillet of beef

Pound them with a mallet until thin. Cut into strips about 1 inch wide. Melt in a pan:

1 tablespoon butter

Sauté in the butter for about 2 minutes:

¾ tablespoon grated onion

Sauté the beef quickly in the butter for about 5 minutes. Turn so that it will be browned evenly. Remove and keep it hot. Add to the pan:

2 tablespoons butter

Stir and sauté in the butter:

¾ lb. sliced mushrooms

Add the beef. Season with:

Salt and pepper
A grating of nutmeg
(½ teaspoon basil)

Add and heat, but do not boil:

¼ cup white wine
1 cup warm sweet or
cultured sour cream

Serve with:

Green Noodles, page 149

II. Or have ready:

1¼ lbs. hot cooked fillet

Slice as described above, but omit the first sauté and add the grated onion to the mushrooms.

▤ BEEF KEBABS OR [4]
BEEF ON SKEWERS

▸ Please read About Skewer Cooking, page 75, and About Marinades, page 380.
Preheat broiler or grill.
Use:

1½ lbs. better or good grade round

Cut the marinated beef, page 380, into about 1½-inch cubes. You may alternate the cubes on skewers with:

Parboiled onion slices
Firm tomato chunks
Mushrooms
Bacon, etc.

Or put the vegetables on sep-

MEAT477

arate skewers to cook more slowly at the side of the grill. Roll the filled skewers in:

Melted butter

Broil or grill about 3 inches from the source of heat. Brush while cooking with the melted butter. Turn to cook evenly, about 18 minutes for rare, 25 for well done.

Correct the seasoning and serve hot. The meat may be presented flambé by igniting a brandy-soaked bit of cotton impaled on the sharp end of the skewer.

SUKIYAKI [4]

Known in Japan as a "friendship dish," this one-plate meal, which may be cooked in the kitchen in a heavy skillet, lends itself to pleasant preparation at table in an electric skillet. The cooking proceeds as an orderly ritual which lasts about 25 minutes, while the uniformly sliced ingredients are taken from a beautifully arranged platter. Have ready on the platter:

2 lbs. thinly sliced beef:
    sirloin tip, eye of the
    round or fillet of beef

The meat can be sliced most easily if put in the freezer about 20 minutes and then cut on a #5 slicer. When ready to cook, however, it should be ▶ at room temperature—as should all the other ingredients. Have ready:

2 strips beef suet, about 1 oz. each, or 3 tablespoons cooking oil

A small dish to hold:

½ cup thinly sliced onions
½ cup ¾-inch squares bean curd: Tofu

Arrange also on the platter in uniform diagonally cut sizes, see page 250:

6 scallions with 3 inches of green left on

6 ribs celery or Chinese cabbage
2 cups thinly sliced mushrooms
1 lb. spinach, cut in 1-inch strips after stem is removed, or water cress
2 cups bean sprouts or cooked, drained Shirataki

These last are spaghetti-shaped yam shreds. We find that if a single skillet is used for cooking, it is best to cook only half the amount on the platter at one time, sharing the first batch and then cooking the "seconds" later. Put the suet in the hot skillet over medium heat and, when it reaches the point of fragrance, remove the unmelted bits and add the thin beef slices. Cook ▶ without browning, turning frequently for about 3 minutes, then push the meat to one side of the skillet and sauté the vegetables. Add them in sequence, beginning with those that need longer cooking. First sauté the onions until almost golden, then as you incorporate the other vegetables, pour in a little at a time a mixture of:

½ cup soy sauce
½ cup stock

This procedure gives a quickly rising steam, but not enough moisture to waterlog the vegetables. Sprinkle over the vegetables while stirring them:

1 teaspoon sugar
½ teaspoon monosodium glutamate

From the sautéing of the onions through the rest of the vegetables cooking, count about 7 minutes. Then push the meat into the center of the skillet and combine with the sprouts or Shirataki, continuing to heat and stir for about 4 minutes more. The vegetables should retain their crispness and good color.

Correct the seasoning

Serve this mixture at once over:
　　Boiled Rice, page 158
As an authentic detail, you may
have at room temperature a raw
egg in a small dish into which
bits of the Sukiyaki can be
dipped before eating.

ABOUT VEAL

In America veal is a very mis-
understood meat—and the milk-
fed variety is hard to come by.
Veal should be tender, succulent and white. If it is not, there
are two ways to improve it. One
is to blanch briefly, starting in
cold water. The other is to soak
refrigerated in milk overnight
before using. Veal needs a careful cooking approach, as it is
lacking in fat and may toughen
quickly. Although abroad certain dishes—like Veal à la
Meunière or à la Crème—are
served both rosy and juicy, veal
here is generally served after
reaching an internal temperature of 175°. It is roasted 25 to
30 minutes per lb. until well
done. Although a leg of veal
may be roasted, most large
pieces of veal are pot-roasted.
The long round muscle of the
leg, when cut across the grain,
produces scallops.

VEAL ROAST STUFFED OR FARCI

The meat may be rubbed first
with garlic or gashes may be
cut in a shoulder roast, in which
fine slivers of garlic, marjoram,
peppercorns, anchovies or anchovy paste may be inserted.
Preheat oven to 450°.
Have a pocket cut in:
　　A breast or shoulder of
　　veal
Remove the meat from the refrigerator at least ½ hour before
preparing. Rub with:
　　Garlic
Dust the pocket lightly with:
　　Ginger

before filling with:
　　3 cups Dry Dressing, page
　　561, Bread Dressing,
　　page 560, with 2 slices
　　chopped salt pork added,
　　Oyster Dressing, page
　　561, or Green Rice, page
　　159, the cheese omitted
Sew the pocket up with a coarse
needle and thread. If the meat
is not fat, rub with:
　　Butter
Dredge with:
　　Seasoned flour
Place in the oven in a greased
roasting pan and ♦ reduce the
heat to 300°. Bake ♦ uncovered
about 20 to 30 minutes to the
pound until done. You may
place on the roast several strips
of:
　　(Bacon)
Make:
　　Pan gravy, page 358
When the gravy is done, you
may remove it from the heat
and add:
　　(¼ cup cultured sour cream)
　　(1 or 2 tablespoons dry
　　white wine)
Heat the gravy but ♦ do not let
it boil. To carve a stuffed veal
shoulder, see illustration. For
ways to utilize roasted meat, see
Luncheon Dishes, page 208.

VEAL ROAST, KIDNEY, LOIN, ETC., OR ROLLED ROAST

Follow the preceding recipe for
preparing and cooking breast or
shoulder—but allow 35 to 40
minutes to the pound for rolled

roast. Turn every ½ hour. You may add parboiled vegetables—potatoes, carrots, etc.—for the last ½ hour or so of cooking. If there are insufficient drippings, add a little fat to the pan. This roast is good served with:

> Dumplings, page 178
> Spatzen, page 179, and
> Pickled Prunes (II, 108)

ABOUT VEAL CUTLETS

From these thin flattened pieces of meat come collops, scallops, scallopini and Schnitzels—all of which may be cooked with or without breading.

So-called "natural" cutlets, unflavored or very lightly so, are one of the easiest, quickest and most delightful of all.

For any of these dishes a white veal is best, sometimes hard to obtain. You may soak the veal in milk overnight, as suggested previously, or in lemon juice for 1 hour. Dry well before flouring or breading.

All these cutlets should be cut as thin as possible and may be pounded. The pounding gives a very different texture. Watch your thumb during this process. ▶ To pound, see illustration, page 452.

In the following recipes use about 1½ lbs. of veal that has been carefully trimmed and from which the bone has been removed. There is often a thin membrane that holds the meat taut as it cooks. Be sure it is slashed in a number of places before cooking. This should serve 3 to 4 persons. If you are serving more and have to repeat your sautéing, keep the already finished cutlets ▶ uncovered in a 250° oven until all the rest are ready.

VEAL CUTLET OR SCALLOPINI

Please read About Veal Cutlets,

above. Dredge lightly with flour on one side only:

> Thin pounded veal
> scallops

Sauté them, floured-side first in:

> ¼ cup butter

heated until fragrant. In about 3 minutes, when the juices begin to emerge on the upper side, turn the meat and continue to sauté for about 3 minutes more. Shake the skillet vigorously from time to time, until the meat is done. Veal is never served rare. Remove from the skillet and keep warm.

Deglaze the pan juices with:

> ½ cup veal or chicken stock
> or ¼ cup stock and ¼
> cup Marsala or Madeira
> Correct the seasoning

You may swirl in, at the end:

> (1 tablespoon butter)

If you do not use the wine, you may add:

> (1 tablespoon lemon juice)

Pour the sauce over the cutlets and serve at once.

VEAL SCALLOPINI [3 to 4] WITH TOMATOES

Preheat oven to 325°.
Cut into 1-inch squares:

> 1½ lbs. veal cut thin,
> trimmed, boned and
> pounded

Dredge with:

> Flour

Brown in a mixture of:

> 1 tablespoon butter
> 1 tablespoon olive oil

Add:

> ½ lb. thinly sliced
> mushrooms
> ½ to 1 clove pressed garlic
> 2 tablespoons chopped
> parsley
> 2 tablespoons chopped
> fresh basil
> ½ cup peeled, seeded,
> diced, fresh tomatoes
> ½ cup Marsala
> 2 tablespoons Parmesan
> cheese

Cover and cook in a 325° oven for about 45 minutes.

VEAL PAPILLOTE

Veal lends itself very well to this method of cooking. See Papillote, page 87. Trim veal for cutlet. To season and cook, see Chicken Suprême Papillote, page 583.

VEAL PARMIGIANA

Slice a ¼-inch-thick:
        Veal cutlet
into 2 x 2-inch slices. Pound thin until they reach about 3 x 3 inches. Dip into a:
        Bound Breading (II, 160)
using equal parts bread crumbs and Parmesan cheese. Sauté the pieces until crisp in:
        Clarified Butter, page 383
about 2 minutes on each side. Serve with:
        Tomato Sauce, page 376

VEAL SCALLOP OR ESCALOPE DE VEAU ORLOFF

A good party dish, as it can be partially prepared in advance. Preheat oven to 350°.
Slice:
        A ¼-inch-thick veal cutlet
into 2 x 2-inch slices. Pound them until they reach about 3 x 3 inches. Sauté until barely frizzled on both sides in:
        Clarified Butter, page 383
Remove from pan and drain on absorbent paper. To make a Soubise, mix and grind in a food chopper:
        ½ cup cooked rice
        ½ cup white onions
        ½ cup mushrooms
Season with:
        Salt and pepper
Cover each scallop of veal with:
        1 tablespoon liver paste

Then press on firmly over each scallop the soubise mixture. Sprinkle over each:
        1 teaspoon brandy or sherry
Dust generously with:
        Grated Parmesan cheese
Place the scallop in an ovenproof serving platter and bake for about 15 minutes until the cheese is golden.

PAPRIKA SCHNITZEL OR CUTLET

◗ Please read About Veal Cutlets, page 479. Trim the edges and remove the bone from:
        A ¼- to ½-inch-thick slice of veal from the round
Dredge one side only in:
        Seasoned flour
Heat in a skillet:
        ¼ cup butter or bacon drippings
Sauté lightly in the fat:
        (½ cup or more sliced onions)
Sauté the meat, first on the seasoned side, in the hot fat, until lightly browned. Turn, then add until the fat becomes red:
        Paprika
Remove the pan from the heat and add:
        1 cup boiling vegetable or chicken stock
Cover the skillet and cook the veal ◗ over very low heat until it is almost tender, about 15 minutes. Add:
        ½ cup cultured sour cream
        Correct the seasoning
Serve garnished with:
        Parsley, capers, sardelles
        Applesauce (II, 95)
        Creamed Spinach, page 326

WIENER SCHNITZEL OR BREADED VEAL CUTLET   [3 to 4]

Viennese friends insist that the true Wiener Schnitzel is deep-fat fried—other authorities insist it is sautéed. But most typical Viennese recipes put up to ¾ cup of butter in the sauté pan which virtually gives a deep fat, rather than a sautéed result anyway, see page 79. Although there are many variations, we suggest the following. ◗ Please read About Veal Cutlets, page 479. Just before cooking, bread (II, 160):

>   1½ lbs. veal cutlet

Sauté over low heat for 2 minutes on one side in:

>   ½ to ¾ cup butter

Turn and cook 2 minutes on the other side. Turn again and cook until done—about 10 to 15 minutes in all. Garnish with:

>   Lemon slices and rolled anchovies

If you also cap the garnished cutlet above with a fried egg, you may call it Holstein.

VEAL SCALLOPS WITH HAM [4]

This recipe is also good using pounded chicken breasts.
Pound:

>   2 veal cutlets

and slice into about 12 three-inch squares. Sauté the pieces until barely frizzled on both sides in:

>   Clarified Butter, page 383

Remove from pan and drain on absorbent paper. Cut into 6 thin slices:

>   Prosciutto or smoked ham

Place the ham on 6 slices of veal. Top with a similar sized slice of:

>   Swiss cheese

Cover each piece with the remaining veal slices. Gently pat in:

>   Bound Breading (II, 160)

Sauté in:

>   Clarified Butter, page 383

until golden on each side, about 3 minutes. Or you may bake the meat on an ovenproof platter in a 350° oven about 15 minutes.

ABOUT LAMB AND MUTTON

Since lamb is shipped from different climates it is no longer referred to as spring lamb. When it is from 3 to 5 months old, lamb is now called baby or milk-finished lamb. From 5 months to a year and a half, it is simply called lamb, and from there on out—mutton. Mutton may be substituted for lamb, but the cooking time is usually increased from 5 to 10 minutes to the pound. Both lamb and mutton are covered with a whitish brittle fat, called the fell, which is usually removed before cooking, as it tends to make the flavor of the meat strong. Almost any cut of lamb may be cooked by the dry heat methods which follow. For ground lamb recipes, see page 514. For moist heat methods, see Braises and Pot Roasts, page 493, and for cooked meat recipes, see Luncheon Dishes, page 208.

LAMB OR MUTTON ROAST

[About 8 Servings]
▶ Please see Economical Use of Large Cuts, page 461.
Preheat oven to 450°.
Remove from the refrigerator at least ½ hour before cooking:

> A 5-lb. leg of lamb or mutton

Remove the fell or papery outer covering. Rub the meat with:

> (Cut garlic or lemon and rosemary)

Insert under the skin, using a pointed knife:

> (Slivers of garlic or herbs)

Place the meat fat side up on a rack in an uncovered pan. Immediately after putting it in the oven ▶ reduce the heat to 350°. Roast it 30 minutes to the pound if you want it well done or until the internal temperature is 175° to 180°. Most Europeans like lamb slightly rare or at an internal temperature of 160° to 165°. ▶ Do not cover or baste. Make:

> Pan Gravy, page 358, using cultured sour cream or milk

Or serve the roast with:

> Deglazed drippings, page 358

and:

> Mint Sauce, page 371

If the mint sauce is not desired, see:

> Cumberland Sauce, page 343

To carve a lamb roast, see the illustration, page 481, or carve it parallel to the bone. For ways of reusing roasted meat, see Leftover and Luncheon Dishes, page 208.

▤ BARBECUED LEG OF LAMB

Preheat grill.
Have butcher bone and flatten:

> A leg of lamb

At least 2 hours before cooking, cover the leg with:

> Fresh mint

Rub with:

> Dry mustard
> Pepper
> Onion juice

While the charcoal is burning down to embers, cook gently for about 5 minutes a sauce of:

> ¼ cup butter
> ½ clove garlic
> 1 tablespoon grated onion

Take out the garlic and add:

> ½ cup chopped fresh mint leaves
> ¼ cup butter

Put the lamb on the grill and brush often with the warm sauce. After about 20 minutes, salt and pepper and turn the meat. If you like lamb pink, it should be "à point" in 35 to 45 minutes, depending on the heat of the coals. Well-done lamb will take 15 minutes longer.

CROWN ROAST OF LAMB

[Allow 2 Ribs per Person]
Preheat oven to 450°.
Wipe with a cloth:

> A crown roast of lamb

Protect the ends of the bones by covering with aluminum foil. Immediately after putting the meat in the oven ▶ reduce the heat to 350°. Process as directed for Lamb Roast, above, but remove the roast before the last hour of cooking. Fill the center with:

> 3 cups Bread Dressing, page 560, or Dressing for Cornish Hen, page 564

Return to the oven and complete the cooking. Remove the covering from the bones. Garnish them with a paper frill, a slice of pickle or a stuffed olive and carve as shown, page 484. Make:

> Pan Gravy, page 358

An unfilled crown roast may be cooked upside down. Omit covering the bones. When done, fill the hollow of the roast with:

> Green Peas, page 305

or with:

> Baked Chestnuts, page 284

Garnish with:

> Parsley

Serve with the gravy and:

> Mint Sauce, page 371, or currant jelly

LAMB SHOULDER ROAST

[About 8 Servings]
Preheat oven to 450°.
Prepare or have prepared with one side left open for inserting dressing:

> A 4- to 5-lb. cushion shoulder of lamb

Rub the meat with:

> A cut clove of garlic

Fill the cavity with:

> Bread or other dressing, page 560

Sew or skewer up the open side. Place the roast uncovered on a rack in a pan in the oven. ◗ Reduce the heat immediately to 350° until done, about 30 minutes to the pound. Serve with:

> Pan Gravy, page 358

☰ BROILED LAMB KEBABS [4]

Take:

> 1 lb. lamb shoulder

Cut the meat into 2-inch squares. Marinate if you like for 3 hours in Marinade I, page 380, turning several times.
Preheat broiler.
Place the meat on skewers, alternately with:

> Pineapple slices
> Blanched Bermuda onion slices
> Tomatoes
> Stuffed olives

Place 4 inches from the heat source and broil. Turn frequently. Baste while cooking with:

> Butter or olive oil

and cook about 15 minutes or until done. Serve on a shallow bed of:

> Cooked Green Rice, page 159

LAMB CHOPS

[2 Chops per Person]
◗ Trim the outer skin, which is strong in flavor, from:

> Lamb chops

I. Pan-boiled
Sear the chops in a hot dry skillet. ◗ Reduce the heat and cook slowly until done. Allow for well-done 2-inch chops about 20 minutes, for 1½-inch chops about 16 minutes. Pour off the fat as it accumulates in the pan. Season the chops with:

> Salt and freshly ground pepper

Serve very hot. Garnish with:

> Parsley

II. Broiled
Follow directions for:

> Broiled Steak, page 474

allowing a shorter time for cooking, according to the thickness of the chops.

STUFFED LAMB CHOPS [6]

I.
Preheat broiler.
To prepare for stuffing, see:

> Braised Stuffed Pork Chops Cockaigne, page 512

Substitute:

> 6 double lamb chops

The chops may be wrapped before cooking with:

> Strips of bacon

Use toothpicks to hold it in place.

II. Or cut out the bone from:

> Lamb chops

Wrap the tail around:

> 1-inch balls of sausage meat

Secure them with a toothpick. Broil or pan-broil the chops.

GARNISHED [1 to 2]
ENGLISH MIXED GRILL

While this is the classic serving for one, it does very well for 2 in our family.

Preheat broiler.

Grease the broiling rack. Arrange on it:

2 single lamb chops
2 small link sausages
2 chicken livers
½ blanched veal kidney
1 slice of bacon
½ small tomato seasoned with salt, pepper and butter
½ cup mushroom caps dipped in butter
3 to 4 small whole blanched onions

Place the broiler rack about 3 inches from the source of heat. During the cooking process, turn the meats and mushrooms. Baste if necessary with clarified butter. The cooking time is dependent on the thickness of the chops and the degree of doneness desired. Arrange ingredients on hot plates or a platter and serve with:

Sauce Béarnaise, page 370

ABOUT PORK

Someone has observed that a pig resembles a saint in that he is more honored after death than during his lifetime. Speaking further of his social standing, we have noticed that, when smoked, he is allowed to appear at quite fashionable functions; but that only one's best friends will confess to anything more than a bowing acquaintance with pork and sauerkraut or pickled pigs' feet.

High-grade pork is fine-grained and firm—the shoulder cuts finely marbled, the fat white. Because of the heavy fat content, all parts of pork can be roasted. Because of the pervasive fat, too, the meat is virtually self-basting. ◗ Pork demands thorough cooking. Otherwise the very harmful trichinae or parasites which often exist in it may be transmitted to the eater. Rules of thumb for judging doneness are to cook the meat until the juices run clear when the flesh is pricked and to make sure, when cut into, that the meat is white or greyish ◗ never pink. Slow cooking is desirable, allowing 30 to 45 minutes to the pound, 5 to 10 minutes longer per pound for rolled or stuffed roasts. Internal temperature should register 185°. The choice roasts are rib, loin and shoulder. The lower half of the foreleg—also called picnic—may be boned, rolled or flattened or rolled and stuffed. Fresh hams or legs of pork are good either roasted or braised. For details about cuts, consult the charts and compare them with the recipes listed. Also read Economical Use of Large Cuts, page 461.

For uses of cooked pork, see Luncheon Dishes, page 208.

ROAST OF PORK

Preheat oven to 450°.
Use for a fine, juicy roast:

A rib end of loin

Or roll or stuff a shoulder or loin, which will need about 10 minutes more cooking to the lb. than recommended here, even when the meat is at 70° before cooking. Rub the roast well with:

A cut clove of garlic,
fresh sage, dried rose-
mary, tarragon or thyme

Dredge with:

Seasoned Flour (II, 160)

Place fat side up on a rack in a pan in the oven. ♦ Reduce the heat at once to 350°. Cook ♦ un-covered 30 to 35 minutes to the pound. The internal tempera-ture should be 185°. Make:

Pan Gravy, page 358

You may roast alongside the meat for the last 35 minutes of cooking:

Peeled and parboiled
sweet potatoes or
parsnips

or on top of the roast:

Prunes and apricots

or serve the roast with:

Applesauce (II, 95),
seasoned with 2 table-
spoons horseradish and
a grating of nutmeg
Sweet Potatoes and
Apples, page 324
Apples with Sauerkraut
(II, 95), or other
sauerkraut variations
Apple and Onion Dish,
page 304
Turnips and Apples, page
338
Puree of Lentils or Peas,
page 306

♦ Please read about the Eco-nomical Use of Large Cuts, page 461; and for other ways of using

leftover roasted meats, see Luncheon Dishes, page 208.

CROWN ROAST OF PORK

[Allow 2 Ribs per Person]
Preheat oven to 450°.
Wipe with a cloth:

A crown roast of pork

Protect the ends of the bones by covering with aluminum foil. Immediately after putting the roast in the oven ♦ reduce the heat to 350°, allowing 30 to 45 minutes to the pound. If the crown is not to be filled with dressing, omit covering the bones and cook the roast upside down. Serve filled with a cooked vegetable; or, if the roast is to be stuffed, remove it 1 hour be-fore it is done and fill the center with:

Sausage Dressing, page
562
Apple and Onion
Dressing, page 563
or fruit dressing

Return the roast to the oven and complete the cooking. Make

Pan Gravy, page 358

To garnish and to carve, see il-lustration, page 484. Serve with:

Glazed Onions, page 302
Cinnamon Apples (II,
94)
Water cress, or broiled
canned apricots and
crystallized ginger slices

ROAST SUCKLING PIG

We never think of suckling pig without thinking of our friend Amy, an American, long a resi-dent of Mexico but determined to reconstruct in alien surround-ings the traditional Christmas dinners of her youth. Describing the preparation of roast pig to her skilled Indian cook, she wound up with the announce-ment, "The pig is brought to table on plenty of greenery, with an apple in the mouth." The cook looked first baffled, then resentful and finally burst out with a succession of "no's." Her employer persisted patiently, but with increasing firmness. When the pig was served, she discovered that her cook could effect an entrée which surpassed her wildest expectations. There was plenty of greenery and a distinct air of martyrdom; but the apple was clenched, not in the pig's mouth, but in that of the desperate cook!

[10]

Preheat oven to 450°.
Dress, by drawing, scraping and cleaning:

> A suckling pig

Remove eyeballs and lower the lids. The dressed pig should weigh about 12 pounds. Fill it with:

> Onion Dressing, page 562, or
>
> Forcemeat, page 564

It takes 2½ quarts of dressing to stuff a pig of this size. Multiply all your ingredients, but not the seasonings. Use these sparingly until the dressing is combined, then taste it and add what is lacking. Sew up the pig. Put a block of wood in its mouth to hold it open. Skewer the legs into position, pulling the forelegs forward and bending the hindlegs into a crouching stance. Rub the pig with:

> Oil or soft butter
> (A cut clove of garlic)

Dredge it with:

> Flour

Cover the ears and the tail with aluminum foil. Place the pig in a pan ♦ uncovered, in the oven for 15 minutes. ♦ Reduce the heat to 325° and roast until tender, allowing 30 minutes to the pound. Baste every 15 minutes with:

> About 2 cups boiling stock and the pan drippings

Remove the foil from ears and tail before serving. Place the pig on a platter. Remove the wood from the mouth. Replace it with a small:

> Apple, lemon or carrot

Place in the eyes:

> Raisins or cranberries

Drape around the neck a wreath of:

> Small green leaves

or garnish the platter or board with:

> Water cress

The pig may be surrounded with:

> Cinnamon Apples (II, 94), Apples Stuffed with Sweet Potatoes, page 324, Apples Stuffed with Mincemeat (II, 315), Tomatoes Florentine, page 336, etc.

Make:

> Pan Gravy, page 358

To carve, place head to left of carver. Remove forelegs and hams. Divide meat down center of back. Separate the ribs. Serve a section of crackling skin to each person.

FRESH HAM

I. You may place a fresh leg of pork called:

> A fresh ham

in a marinade, page 380, and refrigerate covered for 24 to 48 hours.
Preheat oven to 450°.
Remove the ham from the marinade. Wipe dry. Cook as for:

> Pork Roast, page 485

basting every ½ hour with part of the marinade or with the traditional:

> (Beer)

Make:

> Pan Gravy, page 358

Serve with any of the accompaniments suggested in Pork Roast.

II. Or cook a:

> Boned fresh ham

as for:

> Veal Pot Roast, page 505

PORK ROAST STUFFED WITH SAUERKRAUT

Preheat oven to 350°.
Have the butcher remove the bones from:
> A pork shoulder

Fill it with:
> Drained sauerkraut

Dredge with:
> Flour

Prepare and cook as for:
> Roast Shoulder of Lamb, page 483

PORK TENDERLOIN

Preheat oven to 350°.
Split lengthwise:
> A pork tenderloin

Flatten it out. Rub lightly with:
> Butter
> (Garlic)

Spread with:
> Bread Dressing, page 560, using ¼ the amount given or with Apple and Sweet Potato Dressing, page 565, using about ⅓ the amount given, or with stewed, drained, pitted prunes

Sew or tie it up. Dredge with:
> Seasoned flour

or brush with an unsalted fat.
Place the tenderloin on a rack.
Bake 30 to 45 minutes to the pound. Make:
> Pan Gravy, page 358

You may add to the gravy:
> (Cultured sour cream and cooked mushrooms or sweet cream and currant jelly)

FRENCHED PORK TENDERLOIN

Cut crosswise into ¾-inch slices:
> Pork tenderloin

Flatten the slices slightly with a cleaver, as shown on page 452. Dredge with:
> (Flour)

Sauté as for:
> Pork Chops, below

Add to the pan juices or the gravy you serve with the meat:
> ½ teaspoon grated lemon rind

PORK CHOPS

I. Sear in a hot pan:
> Pork chops

in just enough cooking oil or rendered pork fat to keep them from sticking. Before searing, they may be rubbed with:
> (Garlic or powdered rosemary)

After searing ♦ reduce the heat.
Cook the chops slowly, covered or uncovered, until done. Pour off the excess grease as they cook. Season with:
> Salt and pepper

Make:
> Pan Gravy, page 358

II. Preheat oven to 350°.
A good way to do thick chops.
After searing them as above, bake covered for about 1 hour:
> 4 pork chops

During the last half hour, you may add for seasoning:
> 3 tablespoons minced green pepper and celery
> 1 clove garlic
> 1 piece ginger root mashed in 1 tablespoon vinegar
> 3 slices orange
> ½ cup orange juice

PORK TENDERLOIN   [6]
FRUIT CASSEROLE

♦ Please read About Deep-Fat Frying, pages 75–79.
Preheat deep fryer to 375°.
Cut into ½-inch cubes:
> 1 lb. pork tenderloin

Dip the pieces into:
> 2 beaten eggs

then roll in:
> 2 tablespoons cornstarch

Deep fry for about 10 minutes.
Drain. In a large, deep skillet, melt:

2 tablespoons cooking oil
Add the pork and:
2 tablespoons wine vinegar
2 tablespoons sugar
1 cup chicken stock
1 tablespoon catsup
1 cup canned pineapple
pieces
1 chopped green pepper
½ cup thinly sliced carrots
1 teaspoon salt
A grating of fresh black
pepper

Mix and cook over high heat for about 5 minutes, stirring constantly. Serve at once.

BREADED PORK CHOPS [4]

Rub with garlic:
4 half-inch-thick pork
chops

Bread them (II, 160). Brown lightly, using a heavy hot pan, in:

2 to 3 tablespoons rendered
pork fat or cooking oil

Reduce the heat. Cook uncovered for about 20 minutes longer or until done. Make:

Pan Gravy, page 358

SWEET AND SOUR   [6]
PORK

◗ Please read About Deep-Fat Frying, pages 75–79.
Preheat deep fryer to 375°.
Cut into ½-inch squares:
2 lbs. boned pork loin
Toss with:
3 teaspoons soy sauce
3 tablespoons flour

Fry in deep fat until the squares come to the surface and float. When crisp and golden brown, drain on absorbent paper. Have ready and ◗ simmering the following sauce. Mix:

2 tablespoons water
1½ teaspoons cornstarch
Heat:
2 tablespoons lard
Sauté until golden:

1 very small chopped
onion
Add:
6 tablespoons sugar
½ cup water
¼ finely chopped garlic
clove
1 tablespoon soy sauce
¼ cup vinegar
½ cup chopped sweet and
sour pickle
(6 pieces of red haw)

and the cornstarch mixture. Cook and stir for 1 minute. Add the meat and heat. Serve with:
Rice, page 158

ABOUT SALTED MEATS

Because of the prevalence of refrigeration, Ham (II, 543), Tongue, page 544, Corned Beef, page 492, and Salt Pork (II, 545), today are subjected to much weaker brining than formerly. Therefore a preliminary soaking or blanching in the kitchen, see Blanching II, page 88, can often be skipped. ◗ But all of these salted meats, of course, like brined vegetables, still are less valuable nutritionally than fresh meats. They are particularly enjoyed because of their "cured" flavors. If the meats were ◗ given heavy brines or aged like "old" hams, page 490, be sure to soak 12 hours—allowing 1 quart of water to 1 lb. of ham. Or ◗ parblanch them before cooking. After blanching, put the meat into rapidly boiling water, bring to a boil again and ◗ at once reduce the heat to a simmer. Salted meats are always cooked à blanc, see (II, 147). Cook ◗ uncovered until tender. Time indications are given in the recipes.

UNPROCESSED BAKED
HAM

◗ Please read About Ham (II, 543).

If it has not been processed, scrub well:

A smoked ham

Place it in a kettle of ♦ simmering:

Water, cider, beer or ginger ale

Add:

Vegetables suitable for soup
1 bay leaf
8 peppercorns
(6 allspice)

Simmer 20 to 30 minutes per lb. Allow a longer time per lb. for a small ham than for a large one. The thermometer will register 165° when the meat is done. This takes care of the actual cooking, but to make it look attractive at table proceed as follows.

Let it partially cool in the liquid in which it was cooked. Drain. Strip off skin.

Preheat oven to 425°.

Cover the top of the ham with:

Brown sugar
(A little dry mustard)

Stud with:

Whole cloves

Place in the oven and ♦ lower heat at once to 325° for about 20 minutes. Baste with a choice of:

1 cup cider, pineapple or orange juice, the juice of pickled peaches, cooked prunes or apricots, wine, ginger ale, molasses or beer

Cook for 30 minutes longer, without basting, after dredging with:

Brown sugar

sprinkling with:

Grated orange rind

and garnishing the top with:

Pineapple slices
Maraschino cherries

Serve with:

Raisin Cider Sauce, page 373, Sour Cream and Horseradish Sauce, page 362, Barbecue Sauce, page 374, Hot Cumberland Sauce, page 331, or horseradish

And:

Scalloped Potatoes, page 312, or a barquette of Puréed Chestnuts, page 283

To carve see sketch above.

PROCESSED BAKED HAM

♦ Please read About Ham (II, 543).

Preheat oven to 325°.

Unwrap and wipe with a damp cloth:

A processed ham

Bake on a rack, uncovered. Allow 30 minutes to the pound for ½ a ham, 25 minutes for a whole ham. The meat is done when the thermometer registers 160°. Take the ham from the oven about 1 hour before it is done. Remove the rind, all but a collar around the shank bone. Cut diagonal gashes across the fat side of the ham, in diamond shapes. Combine and glaze the top fat side of the ham with:

1⅓ cups brown sugar
2 teaspoons dry mustard

⅓ cup fine bread crumbs

Moisten these ingredients with:

3 tablespoons cider
vinegar, prune juice,
wine or ham drippings

Stud the fat at the intersections or center of each diamond with:

Whole cloves

Return the ham to the oven for about 45 minutes. ♦ Increase the heat to 425°. Bake 15 minutes longer. Place on a platter. Garnish with:

Cranberries and Orange
Slices (II, 102), or
Pineapple slices

heated in the pan for the last 15 minutes. Or with already cooked:

Apple Cups filled with
sweet potatoes (II, 95)

The ham may be served with:

Marchand de Vin Sauce,
page 367

or some other sauce for ham.

COUNTRY HAMS: VIRGINIA, SMITHFIELD, KENTUCKY, ETC.

It is the custom in some parts of the U.S. to hang hams, after special processing, for several years, after which time, of course, they develop a heavy exterior mold. ♦ To prepare one of these old hams, soak it in cold water to cover for 24 to 36 hours. Then scrub it well, using a brush and yellow soap, if necessary, to remove the mold. Rinse thoroughly and place in a kettle of simmering water, skin side down. Allow 20 minutes to the pound until the meat reaches an internal heat of 150°. Add to the water before last ¼ of cooking time:

1 quart cider
¼ cup brown sugar

Drain when the cooking time has elapsed. Remove the skin while the ham is still warm, being careful not to tear the fat.

Trim the fat partially. Dust the ham with a mixture of:

Black pepper
Corn meal
Brown sugar

Put it in a 425° oven long enough to glaze it. If you want more of a baked quality, allow the ham to reach an internal heat of 160° to 165°. Serve hot or cold. Be sure to slice very, very thin.

CASSEROLED HAM [2 to 3] SLICES

Good dishes variously flavored are easily made from raw ham slices.

Preheat oven to 350°.

Place in a casserole:

A slice of smoked ham,
about 1 inch thick

Pour over the ham:

Barbecue Sauce I or II,
page 374
or Hot Cumberland
Sauce, page 372

Bake ♦ covered, until tender, about 1 hour.

HAM BAKED WITH [2 to 3] FRUIT

Preheat oven to 325°.

Ham lends itself to combination with fruit—almost better than any other meat. You may arrange the fruit either between layers and on top of several ham slices or just on top of a single slice. If the ham is not fat, grease the bottom of a casserole lightly. Place in it:

A slice of ham, about 1
inch thick

Cover the ham with fruit seasoned to taste.

Sliced apples, oranges or
cranberries

Sprinkled with:

Brown sugar or honey

Or cover with drained:

Slices of canned
pineapple, apricots,
peaches, red plums,

prunes, cherries or
raisins

These may be sprinkled with:
Cinnamon, cloves or
curry powder

♦ Cover the casserole with a
lid. Baste several times with the
pot juices or additional:
Fruit juice, sherry or
cider

Bake about 45 minutes or until
done. Uncover for the last 10
minutes of cooking.

HAM BAKED WITH [2 to 3] TOMATOES AND CHEESE

Preheat oven to 350°.
Place in a baking dish:
A slice of smoked ham,
about 1 inch thick
Pour over it:
1 cup seeded, chopped,
canned tomatoes

♦ Cover the dish. Bake the ham
until tender, about ¾ hour. Uncover for the last 15 minutes of
cooking. When you uncover,
sprinkle over the ham:
¼ cup grated Parmesan
cheese

BROILED HAM

[Allow ⅓ lb. per person]
Preheat broiler.
Slash in several places the fat
edge of:
A piece of smoked ham,
about 1 inch thick

Place it on a broiler rack, 3
inches below the heating unit.
Broil 10 to 12 minutes to a
side. A processed ham slice will
require from 8 to 10 minutes to
a side. You may brush the ham
after cooking it on one side and
turning it for final broiling with
a mixture of:
1 teaspoon mustard
1 tablespoon lemon juice
¼ cup grape jelly

If you do not use the glaze, a
traditional accompaniment is:
Corn Fritters, page 286
Tomato Slices, page 333

SAUTÉED HAM AND EGGS

Trim the edges of:
A thin slice of smoked
ham

Rub a skillet with ham fat. Heat
it. Brown the ham on one side,
reverse it and brown on the
other. Remove to a hot platter.
Keep hot. Reduce the heat.
Sauté gently in the tried-out
ham fat:
Eggs, page 183

HAM BUTT, SHANK OR PICNIC HAM

Use these comparatively small
cuts of ham as for:
New England Boiled
Dinner, page 493

Cook the ham until nearly tender or until the internal temperature is 170°. Add the vegetables the last ½ hour of cooking.

SMOKED SHOULDER BUTT OR COTTAGE ROLL

This cut may be boned. You
may cut slices from this piece
for broiling or sautéing or you
may roast or "boil" it.

ABOUT BACON

Crisp, thin, properly cured
breakfast bacon is attainable,
but sometimes the search is
long. Bacon should have a good
proportion of lean meat and not
taste too salty. It cannot take
much heat. Broil it or start it in
a cold pan to keep it from curling. We have found this a better
method than the use of pressure
or of specialized gadgets. In
pan-broiling, keep pouring off
accumulated grease and watch
carefully. Bacon burns in seconds and old bacon burns twice
as fast as fresh.

Canadian bacon is from the
eye of a pork loin, which accounts for its leanness and high
cost. It should be treated more
like ham. In England a side of

salted smoked or dried bacon is called a gammon and a slice or portion is a rasher.

◗ Allow about 2 slices per person.

BROILED BACON

Preheat broiler.
Place on a fine wire broiler or rack in a dripping pan:
Strips of bacon
Keep the bacon about 5 inches from source of heat and broil until crisp. Drain on absorbent paper.

SAUTÉED BACON

◗ Please read About Bacon, page 491.
Place in a cold skillet:
Strips of bacon
Sauté slowly until done. You may pour off the drippings while cooking. Turn frequently. Place it between paper towels to drain.

CANADIAN BACON

If you are a twosome with a craving for ham but don't want leftovers, try this smoked substitute.
I. Place in boiling water to cover:
1 lb. or more Canadian bacon
◗ Simmer until tender, about 1 hour.

II. [8]
Preheat oven to 325°.
Combine and have ready:
**½ cup brown sugar
½ teaspoon dry mustard
2 tablespoons fine bread crumbs
1 tablespoon cider vinegar**
Bake uncovered for 1 hour. Baste every 15 minutes for 45 minutes with:
½ cup pineapple or other acid fruit juice, dry sherry, cider, ginger ale or a cola drink

Then spread the brown sugar mixture over it. Bake for about 15 minutes more or until the sugar has glazed.

III. Place in a heavy skillet:
**⅛-to-¼-inch slices
Canadian bacon**
Cook them over low heat for 3 to 5 minutes. Turn frequently. When done, the lean part is a red brown and the fat a light golden brown. Serve with:
**Hot Cumberland Sauce, page 372
Raisin Cider Sauce, page 373**

ABOUT CORNED BEEF

At this printing, for want of a better substance the government still allows the use of sodium nitrate or saltpeter in commercial meat packing to prevent botulism. Packers also like the color it gives their meats.
To corn, combine:
**4 quarts hot water
2 cups coarse salt
¼ cup sugar
2 tablespoons mixed whole spice
(1½ teaspoons saltpeter, for color)**
When cool, pour over:
A 5 lb. piece of beef: brisket or tongue
which has been placed in a large enameled pot or stone jar. Add:
3 cloves garlic
Weight the meat to keep it submerged and cover the jar. Cure in the refrigerator for 3 weeks, turning the meat every 5 days.
◗ To cook corned beef, wash under running water to remove surface brine. Cover with boiling water and simmer 4 hours until a fork can penetrate to the center.
Serve hot with:
Horseradish Sauce, page 362

Boiled Potatoes, page
310
Gnocchi with Farina,
page 157
Serve cold with:
Horseradish
♦ To press for slicing cold, when
cool force into a deep pan.
Cover and refrigerate weighted.
The moisture pressed from the
meat should form a jellied coat-
ing.

CORNED BEEF AND CABBAGE OR NEW ENGLAND BOILED DINNER

I. [10 to 12]
This is a delicious dinner using
only corned beef, onions and
cabbage, but it is customary to
cook and serve separately:

10 to 12 beets

Skin and serve them with the
rest of the dinner, garnished
with:

Parsley

Prepare and cook:

Corned Beef, above

You may add about:

½ lb. salt pork

for the last 2 hours. Remove the
meat from the pot. Peel, quarter
and simmer in the stock for 30
minutes:

3 small parsnips
6 large carrots
3 large yellow turnips

Skin and add:

8 small onions

Peel, quarter and simmer in the
stock for 15 minutes longer:

6 medium-sized potatoes

Cut into wedges, add and simmer until tender, for about 10 to
15 minutes:

A head of cabbage

Reheat the meat in the stock.
Serve it on a platter, surrounded
by the vegetables.

II. If using a ✪ pressure cooker,
use the ingredients above but
cook for 10 minutes before adding the salt pork. Reduce heat.
Add the salt pork. Bring up to
pressure and cook 10 minutes
more. Reduce pressure. Add the
vegetables, except for beets.
Bring up to pressure. Cook for
2 minutes more. Reduce pressure and serve at once, using
the separately cooked beets as a
garnish.

ABOUT BRAISING, POT-ROASTING AND STEWING

Escoffier believed that braising
was a process which warranted
the use of choice meats and the
exercise of all his immense skill
and patience. We concur. However, we wish to point out that
quite inexpensive meat cuts can
also be made to respond well
not only to braising, but to
other kinds of moist heat, like
stewing and pot-roasting. Time,
with most of them, is of the essence: relax and resign yourself
to cooking ♦ very, very slowly
and ♦ very, very long.

More exact directions will be
given in each recipe. You can of
course shortcut by using a ✪
pressure cooker, but the necessarily high heat of this process
will give you a less desirable
result and a "canned" taste.
Instead—and preferably—find
yourself a ♦ heavy, covered pot
or casserole, slightly bigger than
the piece or quantity of meat
you customarily cook. ♦ Do not
use this process for a piece of
meat over 4 to 5 pounds. If it is
larger, cut it into pieces and
make a stew of it, following the
same method described for
braising.

♦ If the meat is lean, you may
want to lard it with seasoned
Lardoons, page 453. If salt pork
is called for and if it is very
fat or salty, you may parblanch
it, page 88, before rendering
or before cooking it in a stew.

▶ Do not worry if the meat comes from an older animal. Maturity will add to its flavor. So will a good browning, page 494, in rendered fat of the same type, unless you are cooking veal or fowl. These are usually cooked "à blanc"—the term in this instance meaning that the meat is not seared before stewing. You may want to ▶ tenderize the meat by marinating, page 453; and you may dredge the meat with flour or not, as you like. ▶ If you do not dredge, be sure that the meat is wiped dry. When you have browned it on one side and are browning it on the other, you may add finely chopped onions. After it is seared, pour off all but 1 or 2 tablespoons of the fat which may have been rendered out of it. Then set the meat on a bed of about 1 cup Mirepoix (II, 221), on a rack, or on a rind of pork. Have ready enough ▶ boiling stock to cover the bottom of the pan, at least 1 to 2 inches. In any case, if you use more, barely cover the meat. ▶ Cover the pan tightly. As soon as the liquid reaches a boil, reduce the heat at once to ▶ maintain a simmer. Do not allow the liquid to get too low during the cooking. Replenish it with boiling stock or water, if necessary. Turn the meat over occasionally to keep it moist.

Vegetables may be cooked entirely in the pot-roasting pan. ▶ Allow about ¼ lb. vegetables to ¾ lb. meat. If cooking on top of the stove and if the vegetables are of medium size, add them during the last ¾ hour of cooking. But if they are very mature—especially carrots, onions, turnips, parsnips and the outer ribs of celery—they may profit by a brief blanching, see Blanching II, page 88. Or you may cook vegetables partially and separately before adding

them toward the end of the pot-roasting. Should the stew or braise be cooked in the oven, the vegetables may need as long as 1½ hours. When the stew is served, the sauce will not be thick, but should have good body—what the French call "du corps."

▶ Always allow a stew to stand for at least 5 minutes off the heat so that grease rises and can be skimmed, page 109. To reheat leftover stews, see page 460. Also note recipes for cooked meats in Luncheon Dishes, page 208.

ABOUT MEAT PIES AND PIE TOPPING

To make meat pies taste and look well, be sure to have ▶ sufficient tastily seasoned gravy to almost cover the meat. There are several ways to top meat pies, but the trick in each instance is to assure the escape of steam, so that the under part of the crust will not be soggy. We find that unless the crusts are prebaked, it is difficult not to end up with some soggy surface. If you do not prebake, do brush the under surfaces exposed to moisture or steam with white of egg. ▶ Vent the crust well.

Prepare:
Any unsweetened Pie Dough (II, 293)
I. For a surefire method, cut and bake separately on a baking tin a piece, or pieces, of dough to cover the large or individual dishes in which you will serve the meat pie. To bake the dough, see (II, 295). Remember that pie dough shrinks in baking, so cut it slightly larger than the dish. Don't forget that this separate baking means you will have to cover your stew in some other way during the heating—such as

with a tight-fitting lid. Just before serving, when the casserole has been heated through, place the prebaked crust on top and serve at once.

II. If you want to put the topping on before heating, preheat the oven to 350°. Fill the baking dish to be covered to within 1 inch of the top.
Place the dough on rather generously—to allow for shrinkage. Brush with Egg Wash (II, 433). Be sure to vent it well. Heat the dish for 45 minutes to 1 hour, when the stew should be thoroughly heated and the crust golden. You may brush the crust with butter before serving. When the stew is done, the sauce should not be thick, but should have good body.

BOILED BEEF OR BOEUF BOUILLI   [4 to 6]

In his witty book about Viennese gourmandising, "Blue Trout and Black Truffles," Joseph Wechsberg describes no less than 24 different kinds of boiled beef specialties and announces categorically that in Imperial days only the best beef was "boiled." Viennese beef owes its special flavor to a special feed of sugar beet mash. Special feeding is the reason that the French, as well as the Viennese, consider this dish a treat rather than the boardinghouse stopgap it has come to be considered here. If you add Spaetzle, page 179, Noodles, page 172, or Dampfnudeln (II, 322), the result can become quite extraordinary.
Bring to a boil, in a heavy pot:
        6 cups water
Put in:
        3 lbs. lean, first cut brisket, bottom round or plate beef
Bring to a boil and skim the pot. Add:

        1 onion stuck with 3 cloves
        ½ cup sliced carrots
        ½ cup sliced celery with leaves
        1 teaspoon salt
        (1 sliced turnip)
◗ Cover the pot closely and simmer the meat until tender, about 3 to 4 hours. Drain and reserve the stock. Melt:
        ¼ cup butter
Brown lightly in the butter:
        ¼ cup chopped onions
Stir until blended:
        2 tablespoons flour
Stir in slowly 2 cups of the degreased stock. Season the sauce with:
        2 tablespoons freshly grated horseradish
        Salt
        Vinegar or lemon juice
        (Sugar)
Prepared horseradish contains vinegar and it is difficult to give exact proportions. So:
        Correct the seasoning
Cut the meat into thin slices against the grain and reheat ◗ very briefly in the boiling gravy. Garnish with:
        Chopped parsley
Serve with:
        Boiled New Potatoes in their jackets, page 310
        Sauerkraut, page 278
        Dumplings, page 147

BEEF POT ROAST   [6]

Please read About Pot Roasts, Braises and Stews, page 493.
Preheat oven to 300°.
Prepare for cooking:
        3 to 4 lbs. beef shoulder, chuck, blade, boneless neck, rump or brisket
If the meat is lean, you may lard it, page 453. Rub the meat with:
        (Garlic)
Dredge it in:
        (Flour)
Heat in a heavy pan over lively heat:

2 tablespoons rendered suet
    or cooking oil
Brown the meat on all sides in
the fat. ◗ Do not let it scorch.
Add to the pot when the meat is
half browned:

> 1 chopped carrot
> 1 rib diced celery
> (1 small diced white turnip)
> (2 tablespoons chopped
>   green pepper)

When the meat is browned, pour
off excess fat. Add to the pot:

> 1 small onion stuck with
>   3 cloves
> 2 cups boiling meat or
>   vegetable stock or part
>   stock and part dry wine

Cover and bake 2 to 3 hours.
During this time turn the meat
several times and, if necessary,
add additional:

> Hot stock

When the meat is firm,

> Correct the seasoning

Pour off excess fat and serve
with the pot liquor as it is or
slightly thickened with:

> Kneaded Butter, page
> 357

You may, if you wish, add to
the pot roast drained boiled
vegetables. Serve with:

> Potato Pancakes, page
> 316, Kasha, page 157, or
> Green Noodles, page 173
> Blue Plum Compote
> (II, 88)

BEEF POT ROAST IN
SOUR CREAM AND WINE

Prepare:

> Beef Pot Roast, above

Add to the liquid for gravy:

> 1 cup dry wine, preferably
>   red
> ½ cup water

Pour it around the roast and
cook until done. Heat over hot
water and stir in just before
serving:

> ¾ cup warm cultured sour
>   cream

GASTON BEEF STEW   [6]

This one-dish meal seems to
taste better when cooked a day
ahead.
Cut into small pieces and, if
very salty, parblanch, page 88,
briefly:

> ½ lb. salt pork

Dry the pork and sauté it slowly
in a large skillet. Cut into pieces
suitable for stewing:

> 2 lbs. beef

Brown the beef in the hot drippings over high heat. Pour off
most of the accumulated fat.
Sprinkle the meat with:

> Seasoned flour

Combine and heat until boiling:

> 1½ chopped cloves garlic
> 1 large chopped onion
> 1 cup bouillon
> 1 cup canned tomato sauce
> 12 peppercorns
> 3 whole cloves
> ¼ cup chopped parsley
> ⅓ bay leaf

Place the meat in a heavy saucepan. Pour the above ingredients
over it. Simmer closely covered
for about 2 to 3 hours or until
the meat can be easily pierced
with a fork. During the last hour
of cooking, add:

> ½ cup dry sherry or dry
>   white wine

Cook separately until nearly
tender:

> 6 medium-sized pared
>   quartered potatoes
> 6 pared quartered carrots
> 1 stalk chopped celery

Add these vegetables for the last
15 minutes of cooking.

BEEF STEW WITH   [4 to 6]
WINE OR BOEUF
BOURGUIGNONNE

For an added bouquet, you may
marinate the diced meat overnight in wine. Drain the wine
for later use in cooking. Preheat
oven to 300°.
Try out:

> ½ lb. thinly sliced salt pork

or use 3 tablespoons
butter
Peel, add and sauté lightly:
    12 small onions or 4 shallots
Remove pork and onions from
the pan. Cut into 1-inch dice
and sauté in the hot fat until
light brown:
    2 lbs. lean beef
Sprinkle the meat with:
    (1½ tablespoons flour)
Place it in an ovenproof dish
with:
    1 teaspoon salt
    4 peppercorns
    ½ bay leaf
    (½ teaspoon thyme or
    marjoram)
Cover the meat with:
    Dry red wine and
    water—¾ part wine
    to ¼ part water
Cook ▶ covered in oven for 1
hour. Place the pork and onions
on top and continue to cook for
another hour or until the beef is
tender. Or simmer the beef covered on top of the stove for
about 1½ hours in all. You may
add:
    (1 cup sautéed mushrooms)
    Correct the seasoning
and serve the stew sprinkled
with:
    Chopped parsley
Flambé at the last minute with:
    (¼ cup brandy)

BEEF BRISKET WITH [6]
SAUERKRAUT

Tie into a compact shape:
    3 lbs. beef brisket
Melt in a deep kettle:
    3 tablespoons bacon or
    other fat
Add, stir about and brown
lightly:
    (¼ cup chopped onions)
Add the meat and place over it:
    2 lbs. sauerkraut
which then acts as a marinade.
We prefer to add the sauerkraut
after the meat has cooked about
an hour. Add:

    2 cups boiling water
Simmer the meat covered for
about 2½ hours or until tender.
Season with:
    Salt and pepper
    Dry white wine
    (Caraway seed)
Serve with:
    Boiled Potatoes, page 319
Pour over them:
    Cultured sour cream
    Chopped parsley or
    chives

SOUP MEAT

Sometimes, for reasons of economy, soup meat is served at
table, but by and large it has,
by this time, been deprived of
most nutrients and flavor. Therefore, it must be presented with
a self-assertive sauce. Brisket or
other soup meat may be taken
from the kettle before the vegetables are added. Serve it with:
    Horseradish Sauce,
    page 362
    Mustard Sauce, page 363,
    Thickened Tomato
    Sauce, page 376, or
    Brown Onion Sauce,
    page 366

SAUERBRATEN [6]

Prepare for cooking:
    3 lbs. beef shoulder
Lard it, page 453, with:
    18 seasoned lardoons,
    ¼ inch thick
or choose a fat cut of meat. Rub
with:
    Pepper
    (Garlic)
Place in a deep crock or glass
bowl. Heat but do not boil:
    Equal parts mild vinegar
    or dry wine and water
Use in all about:
    1 quart of liquid
    ½ cup sliced onion
    2 bay leaves
    1 teaspoon peppercorns
    ¼ cup sugar
Pour this mixture while hot over

the beef, so that it is more than ½ covered. Place a lid over the crock and refrigerate 24 hours to a week. The longer you leave it, the sourer the meat will get. Drain it, saving the marinade, and cook like:

Pot Roast, page 496

Use the vinegar mixture in place of stock. When the meat is tender, remove from the pot. Thicken the stock with:

Flour, see Pan Gravy, page 358

Add:

1 cup sweet or cultured sour cream

We like the gravy "straight." Some cooks add:

(Raisins, catsup and gingersnaps)

Serve the roast with:

Potato Dumplings, page 179, or

Potato Pancakes, page 316

and you will have a treat. ▶ This dish does not freeze successfully.

BOEUF À LA MODE

A pot roast de luxe, because so elegantly presented. The meat is sliced very thin and even, covered with a sauce, and the platter garnished with beautifully arranged vegetables. Prepare the beef as for:

Sauerbraten, above

larding it but marinating only for 4 to 5 hours in a mixture of:

1½ to 2 cups dry red wine
¼ cup brandy

When ready to cook, add:

2 boned blanched calf feet

Use Blanch II, page 88, simmering for 10 minutes. ▶ Simmer covered for 3½ to 4 hours. You may, toward the last hour of cooking, add to the degreased sauce and cook with the meat:

1 cup parboiled, lightly sautéed carrots

1 cup parboiled, lightly sautéed onions

Just before serving, heat with the dish:

1 cup sautéed mushrooms

Serve the meat cut as described above, garnished with the vegetables and with the calf feet cut in one-inch squares.

SPICED BEEF   [8]

Good served hot. Fine for a cold meat platter. Cover:

4 to 5 lbs. chuck roast

with:

Cider vinegar, dry wine or cider
2 sliced onions
½ bay leaf
1 teaspoon each cinnamon, allspice and cloves
1½ teaspoons salt
1 teaspoon pepper

Let the roast stand refrigerated in this marinade for 12 hours or more. Drain it and reserve the liquor.

Preheat oven to 275°.

Place the meat in a roasting pan. Heat to the boiling point and pour over it ½ the vinegar and:

2 cups water

Cover closely and roast for about 3 hours. Put through a grinder or mince, then sauté in butter until a golden brown:

2 onions
4 large carrots
1 medium yellow turnip
1 stalk celery

Add these ingredients to the roast for the last ½ hour of cooking. Add, if needed:

Salt

The stock may be thickened with:

Flour, see Gravy, page 358

CHUCK ROAST IN   [12]
FOIL

Foil-cooked meats often have a pasty look about them, but the use in this recipe of dehydrated onion soup gives great vigor of color and flavor, in spite of the fact that the meat is not browned first. Try this for informal company.

Preheat oven to 300°.

Have ready 2 or 3 large pieces of heavy-duty foil. You may wipe the top of a:

> 7 lb. chuck roast

with:

> Cooking oil

Sprinkle with:

> ½ to 1 package dehydrated onion soup

Place the center of the foil over it and turn the meat and foil over. Sprinkle the other side with:

> ½ to 1 package dehydrated onion soup

Now wrap the roast very carefully with the pieces of foil, so that no juices can escape. Place the package in a pan and bake for 3½ to 4 hours. If your company is informal, do not cut the foil until you are at table and ready to carve. The sudden burst of fragrance adds to the anticipation. Serve with:

> Spaetzle, page 179
> A rice ring with mushrooms filled with Parslied Peas, page 306

SWISS STEAK [6]

Preheat oven to 300°.

Trim the edges of a ¾-inch-thick:

> 2-lb. round steak

Rub with:

> ½ clove garlic

Pound into both sides of the steak, with the edge of a heavy plate or a mallet:

> As much seasoned flour as the steak will hold

Cut it into pieces or leave it whole. If left whole, gash the edges to prevent curling. Heat in a large heavy casserole:

> ¼ cup bacon or ham drippings

Sear the steak on one side until brown. After you turn it over, add:

> ½ cup finely chopped onions
> 1 cup mixed finely chopped carrots, peppers and celery

Do not allow them to brown.

> Correct the seasoning

Add:

> (½ cup strained boiling tomatoes)
> 1 cup stock

Cover the casserole closely and place in the oven for 2 hours or more. Remove the steak to a hot platter. Strain the drippings. Degrease the drippings and make:

> Pan Gravy, page 358

Pour the gravy over the steak. Serve with:

> Mashed Potatoes, page 311

FLANK STEAK WITH DRESSING [4]

If you use sharp seasonings this gives a deviled effect.

Have ready:

> A 2-lb. flank steak, page 473

Trim the edges. Season with and pound in:

> 1 teaspoon salt
> ⅛ teaspoon paprika
> ¼ teaspoon mustard
> (⅛ teaspoon ginger)
> (1 teaspoon Worcestershire sauce)

Melt:

> ¼ cup butter or bacon drippings

Add and sauté until brown:

> 2 tablespoons chopped onion

Add:

> 1 cup bread crumbs
> ¼ teaspoon salt
> A few grains paprika
> 2 tablespoons chopped parsley
> 3 tablespoons chopped celery
> 1 slightly beaten egg

Spread this dressing over the flank steak, roll it loosely and tie it. For variety, try Sausage Dressing and apples, page 562. Heat in a skillet:

    3 tablespoons cooking oil

Sear the steak in the hot oil on all sides.

Preheat oven to 325°.

Place the steak in a casserole or closely covered dish. Stir into the oil in the skillet:

    2 tablespoons flour

Add:

    1 cup water or stock
    1 cup tomato juice or dry
        wine
    ¼ teaspoon salt

Pour this mixture over the steak. Bake closely covered for about 1½ hours. Add seasoning if required. Serve the steak with a:

    Green vegetable

SHORT RIBS OF BEEF   [2]

Cut into about 3-inch pieces:

    2 lbs. lean short ribs of
        beef

Place in a heavy pot with a lid:

    5 cups water
    1 small sliced onion
    1 small sliced carrot
    4 or more ribs celery with
        leaves

Bring these ingredients to the boiling point. Add the short ribs. Simmer ◗ covered until nearly tender, about 2 hours. Take out the meat. Strain and degrease the stock. Make about 3 cups of thin gravy, page 358, using:

    ¼ cup fat
    ¼ cup flour
    3 cups stock

Season the gravy mildly with:

    Salt and pepper
    A few drops brown
        coloring

Preheat oven to 325°.

Heat in a heavy skillet:

    ¼ cup fat

Slice, add and stir about until light brown:

    1 small onion

Brown the meat in the hot fat. Pour over it ½ the gravy. Bake ◗ uncovered for about 45 minutes and let it get brown and crisp. It may be basted occasionally with the drippings. Reheat the remaining gravy. Add:

    1 teaspoon fresh marjoram
    Correct the seasoning

Place the meat on a hot platter. Garnish with:

    Mashed potatoes

Serve piping hot with gravy.

ABOUT GOULASH, GULYAS OR PÖRKOLT

This Hungarian specialty is cooked in many ways, but its most distinguishing seasoning is usually sweet paprika (II, 214). In Beef Goulash, the meat is browned. In the variations that follow it is cooked à blanc—that is, without even browning at all. Beef, veal, and other meats are used separately and in combination. If lamb and pork are included in some of the following recipes, the dish may be called Pörkolt. Vegetables are sometimes added for the last hour of cooking. Goulash is always highly spiced. Some epicures insist that freshly ground peppercorns are a requisite, others prefer the imported Rosen paprika. Some cooks use water as the liquid, others prefer stock or dry red wine.

BEEF GOULASH   [6]

Cut into 1-inch cubes:

    2 lbs. beef: round steak,
        shinbone or 1 lb. beef
        and 1 lb. lean veal

Melt in a heavy pot:

    ¼ cup butter or cooking oil

Brown the meat on both sides in the hot oil. Add and sauté:

    1½ cups chopped onion

Add:

    1 cup boiling Stock (II,
        141), or tomato juice
    1 teaspoon salt

½ teaspoon paprika

Use just enough stock to keep the meat from scorching and add more gradually during the cooking, as necessary. Cover the pot closely and simmer the meat for 1½ hours. Six small peeled potatoes may be added for the last ½ hour of cooking, but they do soak up the gravy which is apt to be the best part of the goulash. Remove the meat from the pot and thicken the stock for:

Gravy, page 358

It may be necessary to add stock or tomato juice.

Correct the seasoning

If potatoes have not been made an ingredient, serve the goulash with:

Polenta, page 156,
Spaetzle, page 179, or
Noodles, page 172

LAMB OR PORK GOULASH AU BLANC

Sauté in:
¾ cup butter
1½ to 2 cups chopped
onions
Mash in a mortar and add:
1 teaspoon caraway
2 teaspoons marjoram
A grating of lemon rind
1 clove garlic
1 tablespoon sweet paprika
Add and bring to a boil:
1 cup water or stock
Add:
2 lbs. pork or lamb in
1½-inch cubes
Simmer covered for 1½ hours.
Garnish with:
Slivered red or green
peppers

VEAL AND PORK GOULASH [4]

Sauté until light brown:
6 tablespoons chopped
onions
in:
2 tablespoons butter

Add:
½ lb. one-inch veal cubes
½ lb. one-inch lean pork
cubes
Heat and add:
1 lb. sauerkraut
1 teaspoon caraway seed
Simmer these ingredients covered for about 1 hour. Heat and add:
1 cup cultured sour cream
A generous grating of
freshly ground pepper
Serve at once.

BELGIAN BEEF STEW [4] OR CARBONNADE FLAMANDE

Cut into 1½-inch cubes and coat in seasoned flour:
2 lbs. boneless beef: chuck,
etc.
Sauté lightly in:
1 tablespoon butter
¼ cup thinly sliced onions
Put them to one side. Add:
1 tablespoon butter
and brown the floured meat. Drain off any excess fat. Combine and bring to a boil:
1 cup dark beer
1 pressed clove garlic
½ teaspoon sugar
Pour over the meat and onion mixture. Cover and simmer 2 to 2½ hours. After straining the sauce, you may add:
(½ teaspoon vinegar)
To serve, garnish meat with:
Parsley or dill new
potatoes
Use sauce as gravy.

OXTAIL STEW [6]

Preheat oven to 350°.
Brown, page 454, in a heavy-lidded pan:
3 oxtails with separated
joints
in:
3 tablespoons beef fat
with:
¼ cup diced onion
Add:

¼ cup Mirepoix (II, 221)
4 cups hot stock or ½ stock
    and ½ tomato juice or
    water
1 teaspoon salt
2 peppercorns

Simmer 3½ to 4 hours. During
the last 35 minutes of cooking
you may add:

½ cup diced celery
½ cup diced carrots
(¼ cup tomato paste)

When the meat is tender
the stew degreased, page 109
    Correct the seasoning
Thicken the liquid with:

2 tablespoons of Beurre
    Manié, page 357

Add:

2 tablespoons chopped
    parsley

ABOUT BEEF ROLLS, ROULADES OR PAUPIETTES

Thin strips of meat or fish rolled
around vegetables or other stuffing are known also as Roulades
or Paupiettes. They may be further wrapped in salt pork or
bacon.
To make them with beef, use:

Thin strips of round or
    flank steak, 3 x 4 inches

Season with:

Salt and pepper

You may pound the meat. Place
on each strip about 2 tablespoons of one of the following
fillings:

I. A well-seasoned smoked or
cooked sausage, 1 teaspoon
chopped parsley or 1 sliver of
dill pickle.

II. A thick julienned carrot, a
rib of celery, 2 teaspoons minced
ham.

III. 2 tablespoons seasoned
cooked rice, 2 chopped stuffed
olives.

Roll the meat and tie with string
near both ends or wrap as for
cabbage leaves, sketched on
page 86. Dredge in:

Flour

Brown in bacon grease or rendered salt pork. Place in a casserole and use for every 6 rolls:

1½ cups stock or dry red
    wine
1½ to 2 tablespoons tomato
    paste

♦ Cover and cook slowly in a
preheated 325° oven or on direct
low heat for about 1 hour and
15 minutes.

STEAK AND KIDNEY PIE   [4]

Preheat oven to 350°.
Classic recipes for this dish often
call for beef kidneys. If they are
used, they must be blanched,
page 88, and the cooking time
must be increased to assure
tenderness. If a crust lines and
covers the baker—a process we
do not recommend, see below—
the top should be protected until
the final browning with a foil
lightly placed over it. Cut into
small, ½-inch-thick slices:

1½ lbs. round or other beef
    steak

Wash, skin and slice thin:

¾ lb. veal or lamb kidneys

Melt in a skillet:

3 tablespoons butter or
    beef fat

Sauté the kidneys in this over
high heat for 1 to 2 minutes.
Shake constantly. Shake the beef
in a bag of:

Seasoned flour

Lightly grease an ovenproof
baker. Place in it a layer of
meat, then a layer of kidneys.
Or you may reserve the kidneys
and add them the last 15 minutes before placing the pastry
cover. Add:

2 cups Brown Stock (II,
    141)
1 cup dry red wine or beer

Cover the dish and bake for 1½
to 2 hours. Cool slightly. Raise

oven heat to 400°. Cover the meat with:

Pâte Brisée (II, 297)

Bake about 12 to 15 minutes.

▤ BURGOO [10–12]

One of those mixtures not unlike Mulligan and Brunswick Stews —a combination of meats, fowl and gleanings from the garden patch. Addicts—and there are many in Kentucky—claim this stew is best if served the day after it is made. Put in a heavy-lidded kettle with:

3 qts. water or stock
¾ lb. lean inch-diced stewing beef
¾ lb. inch-diced pork shoulder

Bring slowly to a boil. ♦ Reduce heat at once and simmer about 2½ hours. In another heavy kettle put:

1 disjointed 3½ lb. chicken

with:

Enough water to just cover

Bring these ingredients to a boil. ♦ Reduce the heat at once and simmer about 1 hour or until the meat can easily be removed from the bones. Put the chicken meat and the water in which it was cooked into the first kettle with the other meat after it has simmered the 2½ hours as directed. At this time, also add:

2½ cups quartered ripe, peeled and seeded tomatoes
1 cup fresh Lima beans
½ diced red pepper
4 diced green peppers
¾ cup diced onions
1 cup diced carrots
2 cups diced potatoes
1 bay leaf
1 tablespoon Worcestershire sauce

Simmer this whole mixture ½ hour or more before adding:

2 cups corn, cut freshly from the cob

Cook about 15 minutes more or until all the vegetables are soft.

Correct the seasoning.

Serve hot in deep bowls with:

Chunks of French bread

on the side, to be used—you know how! It's that kind of a dish.

VEAL STEW [4]

Select:

1½ lbs. veal with little bone or 2 lbs. neck or shanks

The meat may be cooked in one piece, cut into 3-inch pieces or into 1½-inch cubes. Melt in a heavy pot or saucepan over moderate heat:

3 tablespoons butter or drippings

Brown the meat in the hot drippings. Reduce the heat. Cover the bottom of the pot ½ inch with boiling:

Vegetable Stock (II, 145)

Cover the pot closely and ♦ simmer the meat until tender, 45 minutes or more. Remove it from the pot. Strain the stock. Thicken it with:

Flour, see Pan Gravy, page 358

The browning of the meat in the fat is optional. For a pleasant change drop it directly into boiling vegetable stock and cook as directed. Serve the stew with:

Chopped parsley
Noodles, page 172
Farina Balls, page 147, or Rice Ring, page 162, and Fried Apples (II, 94)

or serve it in:

A Hominy Grits Ring, page 155

Veal stew is also good with a baked top crust. Follow the recipe for Quick Chicken Pot Pie, page 212.

VEAL STEW WITH RED WINE [4]

Cut into 12 chunks:

1½ lbs. boneless veal or beef
Roll each piece in:
    ½ slice bacon: 6 slices in all
Dredge the meat lightly with:
    Flour
Melt in a heavy skillet:
    2 tablespoons bacon or
      other fat
Add the meat and:
    12 small peeled onions
Stir these ingredients about and
permit them to brown on all
sides. Remove them from the
pan. Pour off all but 1 tablespoon of fat. Stir in:
    1 tablespoon flour
Add and stir until smooth:
    1½ cups consommé or stock
    ½ cup dry red wine
Add the meat and onions. Simmer closely covered 1½ to 2
hours until the meat is very
tender. Season and serve with
some baked dish like:
    Crusty or Soft-Centered
    Spoon Bread (II, 279)

BLANQUETTE DE [6]
VEAU OR ELABORATE
VEAL STEW

Cut into 1-inch pieces:
    1½ lbs. veal shoulder
    1½ lbs. veal breast
Parblanch, page 88, the pieces
of veal about 2 minutes in salted
water. Drain and wash well
under cold running water, removing all the scum. Put the
meat in a heavy pan and add:
    5 cups chicken or veal
      stock
    1 large onion studded with
      1 clove
    1 peeled carrot
    1 stalk chopped white
      celery
    A Bouquet Garni (II,
      220)
Simmer uncovered for about 1¼
to 1½ hours until the veal is
tender and may be pierced with
a fork. Now skim out the vegetables and the bouquet. Add:

    24 small blanched white
      onions
    2 cups fresh button mush-
      room caps
Simmer for about 10 minutes.
Combine:
    ¼ cup flour
    ¼ cup butter
Add this thickener to the veal
and simmer for another 10 min-
utes. Remove pan from heat.
Mix together:
    3 beaten egg yolks
    ½ cup whipping cream
Stir about 2 tablespoons of the
hot veal stock into the egg mix-
ture and return it to the pan.
Add:
    2 to 3 tablespoons lemon
      juice
    Correct the seasoning
Serve with:
    Noodles or rice
Garnished with:
    Chopped parsley

VEAL AND PORK PIE [4]

Cut into 1-inch pieces:
    ½ lb. veal
    ½ lb. lean pork
Stir and brown the meat lightly
in:
    2 tablespoons butter or
      cooking oil
Add and simmer covered for
about 15 minutes:
    3 cups boiling water
    1 teaspoon salt
    ½ teaspoon paprika
    ½ bay leaf
    2 whole cloves
Remove spices. Add:
    ¼ cup diced carrots
    ¾ cup diced celery
    1 cup diced potatoes
Bring the stew to the boiling
point ◗ reduce the heat and sim-
mer covered until the meat is
tender, about 30 minutes longer.
    Correct the seasoning
Make:
    Pan Gravy, page 358
Preheat oven to 450°.

Place the stew in a baking dish. Top it while hot with:

> Pie Crust (II, 293)

Bake for about 20 minutes.

MOCK CHICKEN DRUMSTICKS OR CITY CHICKEN [6]

Preheat oven to 325°.
Cut into 1 x 1½-inch pieces:

> 1 lb. veal steak
> 1 lb. pork steak

Arrange the veal and pork cubes alternately on 6 skewers. Press the pieces close together into the shape of a drumstick. Roll the meat in:

> Seasoned flour

Beat:

> 1 egg
> 2 tablespoons water

Dip the sticks in the diluted egg, then roll in:

> Bread crumbs

Melt in a skillet:

> ¼ cup butter

Brown the meat partially in the fat. Add:

> 1 tablespoon grated onion

Continue to brown the meat. Cover the bottom of the skillet with:

> Boiling Stock (II, 141)

Cover the skillet and place in oven, about 50 minutes or until the meat is tender.
Make:

> Pan Gravy, page 358

VEAL BIRDS OR PAUPIETTES

For other stuffings, see About Beef Rolls, page 502.
Trim the edges from ⅓-inch-thick:

> Slices of veal from the round

Pound the meat with a cleaver and cut into pieces about 2 x 4 inches. Make the following dressing. Chop the meat trimmings and combine them with an equal amount of chopped:

> Salt pork

Measure the salt pork and trimmings and add to them ½ the amount of:

> Bread crumbs

Add:

> Chopped onion, chopped raisins or seedless grapes
> Chopped celery
> (A grating of lemon rind)

Moisten these ingredients with sufficient:

> Cream or stock

to hold them together. Spread the meat lightly with the dressing and roll it. Secure with skewers or thread. Roll the birds in:

> Flour

Sauté them in hot:

> Butter or cooking oil

until golden in color. Reduce the heat and add:

> Hot cream, milk, stock or dry wine

until the meat is half covered.
◗ Cover the pot closely and simmer until tender, about 20 minutes.

> Correct the seasoning

Add:

> (½ lb. Sautéed Mushrooms, page 296)

Make:

> Pan Gravy, page 358

VEAL POT ROAST

Please read About Pot Roasts, page 493.
Prepare by boning and rolling:

> A rump roast of veal

Cook as for any unbrowned Stew, see à blanc, page 494. Classically, veal is not browned —but we've eaten some mighty good browned veal pot roasts!
Use:

> ½ cup water for every lb. of meat

Or prepare:

> Pot Roast in Sour Cream and Wine, page 496

omitting the browning. Add to the finished gravy:

> (Capers, basil or thyme)

MEXICAN VEAL [6]
STEAK WITH NOODLES

Cut into small slices:
    1 lb. thin veal steak
Dredge with:
    ¼ cup flour
Heat:
    3 teaspoons butter or olive
        oil
Sauté the meat quickly on both
sides until brown. ◗ Reduce the
heat. Cover the meat with:
    1½ cups sliced onions
    6 tablespoons chili sauce
    1¼ cups boiling stock
◗ Simmer closely covered about
½ hour.
Meanwhile, cook and drain:
    2 cups Noodles, page 172
Toss them in:
    ¾ cup cream of chicken
        soup
Serve the noodles mounded,
covered with:
    ¼ cup buttered crumbs
    2 tablespoons grated
        Parmesan cheese
Surround the noodles with the
steak. Garnish with:
    (Parsley)

CUBED VEAL BAKED [4]
IN SOUR CREAM

Preheat oven to 300°.
Cut into cubes:
    1½ lbs. boneless veal
Brown lightly in:
    1½ tablespoons butter
Remove the meat to an oven-
proof baking dish. Add to the
butter, stir and sauté lightly:
    1 tablespoon chopped
        onion
    ½ lb. sliced mushrooms
Remove from the heat. Stir in
slowly:
    1 tablespoon flour
    ⅓ cup stock
    ¾ cup cultured sour cream
    ½ teaspoon salt
    ⅛ teaspoon pepper
Pour sauce over the meat. Cover
the dish. Bake for about 1 hour.

BAKED MARROW [3]
BONES OR OSSO BUCO

Preheat oven to 300°.
◗ To make this dish really delectable, the animal should not
be more than 2 months old. Saw
into 2½ to 3 inch pieces:
    2 lbs. shin bone of veal
Dip the bones first in:
    Olive oil
Then in:
    Seasoned flour
Heat in the pan:
    ¼ cup olive oil
To keep the marrow intact, set
the bones upright. To conserve
stock, place them as close as
possible on the base of a heavy
pan just large enough to hold
them. Brown the bones very
slowly for about 15 minutes.
Pour over them:
    ½ cup white wine
    (½ cup skinned, diced,
        seeded, fresh tomatoes)
    Seasoned stock—enough
        to come at least ⅓ up
        the bones
Cover and bake for 1 to 1½
hours until the meat falls from
them. Before serving, sprinkle
the tops with:
    Gremolata (II, 222)
Serve garnished with:
    Fried Chipolata sausage
        and Boiled Chestnuts,
        page 283, or Risotto,
        page 165

BRAISED SHOULDER [6]
OF LAMB

Melt in a heavy pot:
    ¼ cup cooking oil or butter
Sear on all sides in the hot fat:
    A rolled shoulder of lamb
Remove it from the pot. Cook
slowly in the fat for 10 minutes:
    ½ cup chopped onion
    ¼ cup chopped carrots
    ¼ cup chopped turnips
    ½ cup chopped celery with
        leaves
    (1 sliced clove garlic)

Return the meat to the pot. Add:

> ½ bay leaf
> 4 whole peppercorns
> 1 teaspoon salt
> 4 cups boiling vegetable stock or 3 cups stock and 1 cup tomato pulp

◗ Cover the pot closely. ◗ Simmer the meat until tender, about 2 hours. When the meat is done, degrease the stew and thicken the stock slightly with:

> Kneaded Butter, page 357

Serve the roast surrounded by the vegetables.

BRAISED STUFFED SHOULDER OR FARCE OF LAMB [6]

This cut is hard to carve unless boned. Its flavor is highly prized.
Preheat oven to 325°.
Bone:

> A shoulder of lamb

You may rub it with:

> (Garlic)

or insert slivers of garlic under the skin.
Prepare about:

> 3 cups Bread Dressing, page 561

Spread it on the meat. Roll like a jelly roll. Secure with string, or fasten with spiral skewers, page 572. Brown in:

> 3 tablespoons cooking oil or butter

Place in a roasting pan:

> 1 cup Vegetable Stock (II, 145)

Put the browned roast in it and cook ◗ covered, allowing about 40 minutes to the pound. You may put some of the bones in the pan. Meanwhile, prepare for cooking:

> 3 cups diced vegetables: celery, carrots, onions, potatoes

After the meat has cooked about 45 minutes, place the vegetables in the pan with:

> 1 cup vegetable stock

Cover and continue to cook the meat about 1 hour after adding the vegetables or until the internal temperature of the meat is 175° to 180°. Pour off, but reserve most of the liquid and allow the meat and vegetables to glaze by cooking them ◗ uncovered for about 10 minutes longer. Meanwhile, to make the sauce, degrease the reserved liquid and reduce it somewhat.

Correct the seasoning before serving.

LAMB FORESTIÈRE OR MOCK VENISON

Wipe with a damp cloth:

> A leg of lamb or mutton

Cover it with:

> Buttermilk

Soak it refrigerated for 24 hours or more.
Preheat oven to 450°.
Drain, wipe dry and lard the meat, page 453, with:

> Salt pork or bacon

Dot it with:

> Butter

Dredge with:

> Flour

Put the roast on a rack in a pan in the oven and bake for 15 minutes. Add:

> ½ cup hot Vegetable Stock (II, 145)

Cover closely. ◗ Reduce heat at once to 325°. When the roast is nearly done, allowing 35 minutes to the pound, remove the cover and add:

> 1 cup Sautéed Mushrooms, page 296

Pour over the roast:

> 1 cup cultured sour cream

Cook ◗ uncovered for 10 minutes.

Correct the seasoning
Make:

> Pan Gravy, page 358

Serve the roast surrounded by:

Browned Potatoes, page
314
Garnish with:
    Parsley

BRAISED LEG OF MUTTON OR LAMB

[About 8 Servings]
If cooked this way, the flavor is
almost like venison.
Remove the fell from:
    A 5 lb. leg of mutton or
    lamb
You may place the meat for
several hours in a marinade,
page 380, or you may rub it all
over with:
    (A cut clove of garlic)
Rub the meat with:
    Butter
Melt in a heavy pan:
    ¼ cup fat or drippings
Brown the meat in it on all
sides. Add:
    4 cups boiling stock
Cover the pot. ◗ Simmer the
meat until tender, allowing 30
minutes to the pound. Add boiling water, if necessary. After
the meat has cooked for 1 hour,
add:
    2 small whole onions
    3 peppercorns
    3 cloves
    A sprig of thyme or ½
    teaspoon dried thyme
    ½ bay leaf
When the meat is tender, remove from the pot. Season
with:
    Salt
Place the meat where it will remain hot.
Serve with:
    Caper Sauce, page 263
and
    Puréed Turnips, page
    338

BRAISED LAMB   [4] SHANKS OR TROTTERS

Rub:

    4 lamb shanks: 3¾ to
    4 lbs.
with:
    Garlic
Roll in:
    Seasoned flour
Melt until fragrant:
    2 tablespoons cooking oil
Partially sear the shanks and
add:
    2 tablespoons diced onion
Continue to cook the meat until
browned on all sides. Pour off
the fat. Place the meat on a
rack in a lidded pan. Add:
    1½ cups boiling stock
    ⅓ teaspoon pepper
    1½ teaspoons salt
    ½ bay leaf
Cover the pan closely. ◗ Simmer
the meat or bake covered in a
325° oven for about 1½ hours
or until tender. You may add
for the last ½ hour of cooking:
    3 cups diced vegetables
    ½ cup boiling stock or
    water
The vegetables may be onions,
carrots, celery, peppers, turnips,
tomatoes and/or potatoes—a
matter of choice and expediency. Strain, degrease and reduce the stock. Serve as it is or
make:
    Pan Gravy, page 358
If you have not added the vegetables, you may serve the shanks
with:
    Creole Sauce, page 380

LAMB STEW OR   [8] NAVARIN PRINTANIER

Cut into about 1½-inch pieces:
    1 lb. shoulder of lamb
    1 lb. breast of lamb
Brown the meat in a heavy
skillet in:
    2 tablespoons fat
Remove the meat to a casserole.
Pour off the fat and deglaze the
pan with:
    2 cups light stock

to which you may add:

> 2 tablespoons tomato paste

Bring to a boil and pour over the meat. ◗ Simmer covered. Meanwhile, peel and shape into ovals about 1½ inches long:

> 2 cups new potatoes
> 6 carrots
> 3 white turnips

Add:

> 18 small onions: about
> 1 inch

After the lamb has cooked about 1 hour, skim off the fat, add the vegetables to the casserole and ◗ simmer covered for about 1 hour longer or until the vegetables are tender. Have ready to add:

> 1 cup cooked fresh peas
> 1 cup cooked fresh green
>   beans, cut in 1-inch
>   lengths

When the lamb and vegetables in the casserole are tender, skim any fat from the casserole and gently fold in the cooked peas and beans. Serve at once, sprinkled with ½ cup finely chopped parsley.

IRISH STEW [4 to 6]

This famous stew is not browned.

Cut into 1½-inch cubes:

> 1½ lbs. lamb or mutton

Peel and slice to ⅛-inch thickness:

> ¾ cup onions
> 2½ lbs. potatoes

Put in the bottom of a heavy pan a layer of potatoes, a layer of meat, a few slices of onion. Repeat this twice, ending with potatoes on top. Season each layer with:

> Salt and pepper

Add to the pot:

> 1 bay leaf

Pour over the layers:

> 2 cups boiling water or
>   stock

> 2 tablespoons finely
>   chopped parsley

Bring to a boil. ◗ Cover closely. Simmer gently over very low heat for about 2½ hours or until done. Shake the pot periodically so that the potatoes do not stick. When done, all the moisture should have been absorbed by the potatoes.

CURRY OF LAMB [4] WITH RICE

Remove the gristle and fat from:

> A 2 lb. lamb shoulder

Cut the meat into 1-inch cubes. Heat:

> 3 tablespoons fat or
>   cooking oil

Brown the meat in the hot fat with:

> 1 tablespoon chopped
>   onion
> ⅔ teaspoon curry powder

Add:

> 1 cup light Stock (II, 142)
> ¼ cup or more chopped
>   celery
> 2 tablespoons chopped
>   parsley
> (1 tablespoon chopped
>   pimiento)
> (¼ cup peeled, seeded,
>   diced cucumbers)

Cover the meat and simmer until done, about ½ hour. Stir frequently.

> Correct the seasoning

Make:

> Pan Gravy, page 358

Place on a platter a mound of:

> Rice, page 158

Arrange the meat and gravy around it. Garnish the platter with:

> Parsley

CASSOULET

[About 12 Servings]
With a thicker texture than a pot au feu, this controversial dish from the South of France

has one solid pivot—white beans. They are cooked usually with fresh pork and sausage: but often with mutton and "confit d'oie"—potted goose, page 589—or with duck, partridge or bacon. Goose fat is a frequent component, also an onion stuck with cloves. Vegetables vary seasonally. Garlic is essential. For this recipe you almost need a routing sheet. The beans soak overnight and are cooked the next day with meat and other trimmings. The pork roasts for a while before the lamb joins it. Then the meats that have been cooking with the beans are taken from the bone and sliced before they are returned to the beans. This way the flavors unite in a single casserole and make a final triumphant appearance under a golden crust of crumbs.

Soak overnight in cold water:

> 1 lb. white beans: haricots, marrow-fat or broad beans

Roast in a 350° oven for about 2½ hours or until tender:

> 3 lbs. Loin of Pork, page 485

Blanch, page 88, by placing in cold water and just bringing to a boil:

> 1 ham shank
> 1 lb. salt pork

Drain the beans. Heat the water in which they soaked, adding:

> Enough water to make 4 quarts

Bring to a boil and skim the pot. Add the drained, blanched ham shank and salt pork and:

> A Bouquet Garni (II, 220)
> 3 cloves garlic

Simmer covered for about 1½ hours. Add:

> 6 small white onions
> ½ lb. hard Italian sausage, like Salcisetta

◆ Simmer about 1 hour longer, until the beans are tender but

still intact. Brown, page 454, in a heavy skillet:

> 3 lbs. rolled lamb shoulder

in:

> 1 tablespoon butter

Drain off any excess fat. Roast the meat and the bones from the lamb with the pork ◆ uncovered. ◆ After about 1½ hours, pour over it:

> Thickened Tomato Sauce, page 376

and roast for about ½ hour more. ◆ Lower oven heat to 300°, then drain off and reserve the sauce and drippings. Remove and slice the meat of both the lamb and the pork roast. Drain the beans, adding the juice to the drained tomato sauce. Trim and slice the ham, the sausage and the salt pork in bite-sized pieces. Layer these meats with the beans in a casserole and skim excess fat from the combined tomato and bean juices before adding them to the other ingredients. Top with:

> 1 cup buttered dry bread crumbs

Bake about 1 hour longer in the oven, when the crumbs should have turned a golden color.

COUSCOUS   [6]

As with most basic native dishes, variations of this North African specialty abound. The following version comes from friends in Libya.

Soak overnight and cook the following day until about half tender:

> 1 cup Chick Peas, page 264

Drain them. Cut into about 10 pieces:

> 2 lbs. lamb, mutton or beef

Brown lightly in:

> 1 tablespoon olive oil
> 2 tablespoons butter

While browning slowly for about 10 minutes, add:

> ¾ cup minced onion

When the onion is translucent, add:

    2 teaspoons salt
    ½ teaspoon freshly ground
      pepper
    ⅛ teaspoon red pepper
    ½ teaspoon turmeric
    2 tablespoons tomato paste
◗ Reduce heat and barely simmer this thick mixture for about 10 minutes more. Place in a heavy pot with:

    2 knuckle bones
and enough:

    Water to cover
◗ Simmer covered until the meat can be pierced with a fork, but still offers slight resistance. Add:

    3 cups potatoes, cut
      Parisienne, page 250
    2 cups coarsely diced
      yellow or white squash
    2 cups coarsely diced
      zucchini
and the drained cooked chick peas. Add, if necessary:

    Stock (II, 141)
◗ Simmer covered until the meat and vegetables are tender, about ¾ of an hour longer. Remove from heat and reserve this meat and vegetable mixture. When the fat rises to the top, skim and reserve 2 tablespoons of it. Rinse briefly and place in the top of a perforated steamer or a couscous pot:

    1 lb. semolina, cracked
      millet, cracked wheat or
      kasha
Steam the cereal ◗ uncovered for 15 minutes, timing after you see steam rising from the top. Meanwhile reheat the meat and vegetable mixture. Drain the liquid and reserve it. Now ◗ working quickly so everything stays warm, remove the cereal from the steamer and add:

    2 tablespoons orange
      flower water
    ¼ teaspoon cinnamon
    ¼ teaspoon cloves
Toss the seasoned couscous

lightly in the 2 tablespoons of fat, reserved from the meat mixture, and put it in a serving dish. Pour over it 1 cup of the drained liquid. Put the meat, vegetables and chick peas on top of the couscous. Use the remaining liquid as a separate sauce. Serve at once.

PORK TENDERLOIN [4]
WITH MUSHROOMS
AND OLIVES

Cut into 1-inch crosswise slices:

    1 lb. or more pork
      tenderloin
Roll in:

    Seasoned flour
Sauté until golden in:

    2 tablespoons butter
with:

    A sliced onion
Bring just to the boiling point:

    ½ cup dry white wine
Pour over the meat. Add at this time:

    ½ lb. sliced mushrooms
    (⅛ teaspoon fresh rosemary)
Cover the skillet closely. ◗ Simmer the rounds until they are done, about 30 minutes. Add:

    6 sliced green olives,
      stuffed with almonds
    (2 tablespoons lemon juice)
Serve the pork garnished with:

    2 tablespoons chopped
      parsley

PORK CHOPS BAKED [4]
IN SOUR CREAM

Preheat oven to 350°.
Dredge:

    4 loin pork chops: ½ inch
      thick
with:

    Seasoned flour or bread
      crumbs
Insert in each chop:

    1 clove
Brown lightly in a little hot pork fat or lard. Place in a baking dish. Combine, heat and pour over the meat:

½ cup water or stock
½ bay leaf
2 tablespoons vinegar
1 tablespoon sugar
½ cup cultured sour cream
(¼ teaspoon summer savory)

Bake the chops ◆ covered for about 1 hour.

BRAISED PORK   [6]
CHOPS CREOLE

Preheat oven to 350°.
Dredge:
6 pork chops, ½ inch or
more thick
with:
Flour
Brown them in:
Hot fat or cooking oil
Place in a baking dish. Combine, heat and pour around them:
1 can condensed tomato
soup: 10½ oz.
1 can water or stock
½ cup chopped celery
1 chopped green pepper—
seeds and membrane
removed
¾ cup minced onions
¾ teaspoon salt
¼ teaspoon paprika
Bake ◆ covered for about 1¼ hours. ◆ Remove the cover for the last 15 minutes. Cover the top for this last period with:
Crushed cornflakes

BRAISED DEVILED   [4]
PORK CHOPS

Preheat oven to 325°.
Place in a dish:
4 pork chops, 1 inch thick
Marinate them for 3 to 6 hours covered and refrigerated in:
Pork Marinade, page 382
Drain the chops, reserving the marinade. Wipe them dry. Brown in a hot greased skillet. Heat the marinade and:
½ cup water or stock
Pour it around the chops. Bake ◆ covered until tender, about 1 hour.

BRAISED PORK CHOPS
WITH FRUIT

[Allow 1 Chop per Person]
Preheat oven to 350°.
Sear in a hot, lightly greased skillet:
Trimmed pork chops, ¾
inch thick or more
Season lightly. Place on the chops, skin side down:
Halved, cored apples,
pitted apricots, prunes
or pineapple slices
Fill the centers of the fruit with:
Brown sugar
Cover the bottom of the skillet to ½ inch with:
Chicken stock and/or
some of the fruit juice
◆ Cover the pan closely. Bake for about 50 minutes. Remove the chops from the pan carefully, so as not to disturb the fruit. Keep warm. Partially degrease and add to the pan juices:
¾ to 1 cup sweet or
cultured sour cream
Serve this sauce with the chops and fruit.

BRAISED STUFFED   [6]
PORK CHOPS COCKAIGNE

Preheat oven to 350°.
Cut from the bone:
6 rib pork chops, ¾ to 1
inch thick
Cut the bone from the meat. Trim off the excess fat and cut a large gash or pocket into the side of each chop. Prepare a dressing of:
1 cup bread crumbs
¼ cup chopped celery
¼ cup chopped onions
2 tablespoons chopped
parsley
Milk to moisten the
dressing
¼ teaspoon salt
⅛ teaspoon paprika
These proportions and ingredients may be varied. Fill the pockets with the dressing. Skewer them. Sear the chops in

a hot skillet and place in a pan with a little:

Milk or stock

♦ Cover the pan and bake about 1 hour and 15 minutes or until tender. Make:

Pan Gravy, page 358

PORK BIRDS [6]

Pound to the thickness of ¼ inch:

2 lbs. pork steaks which have been cut from the shoulder

Cut them into 6 oblong pieces. Spread them with half the recipe for:

Apricot or Prune Dressing, page 565

Roll them. Secure the rolls with string or toothpicks. Dredge in:

2 tablespoons flour

Brown in:

2 tablespoons fat

Add:

1 cup boiling water or Stock (II, 141)

Simmer covered for about 50 minutes or until tender. Serve with the liquor in the pan, degreased and thickened as:

Pan Gravy, page 358

or just reduced.

☰ ABOUT SPARERIBS

[♦ Allow at Least 1 lb. per Person]

These gloriously messy old favorites can simply be baked in a 325° oven about 1½ hours; but there are a good many more lively things to do with them. We find parboiling, page 88, the ribs for about 3 or 4 minutes not only removes unwanted fat, but makes the end result very palatable. After parboiling, try one of the following recipes or barbecue them, page 97.

BAKED SPARERIBS [4] WITH DRESSING

Preheat oven to 500°.

As there is much bone and little

meat to spareribs—we love the self-explanatory name—it is well to allow 1 pound of them to a person. Parboil for 2 minutes.

4 lbs. spareribs

Cut into 2 pieces. Spread 1 piece with:

Apple Onion Dressing, page 563

Cover the dressing with the other piece of meat. Tie the 2 pieces together. Rub the outside of the meat with:

2 tablespoons flour
⅛ teaspoon salt
A few grains pepper

Place on a rack in an uncovered roasting pan and ♦ reduce the heat at once to 325°. Bake for about 1 hour. Baste the meat every 10 minutes with the fat in the pan.

BAKED SPARERIBS [4] WITH SAUERKRAUT

Preheat oven to 400°.

Place in a mound, in the center of a small roasting pan:

1½ quarts Sauerkraut, page 278

Season:

4 lbs. parboiled spareribs, see above

lightly with:

Salt and pepper

Fold the ribs in half. Place between them:

Slices of onion

Cover the kraut with the folded spareribs. Bake ♦ uncovered in a hot oven until nicely browned. Baste frequently with kraut juice. Turn the ribs and brown the other side. Add water, if necessary. ♦ Cover the pan. ♦ Reduce the temperature to 350°. Parboil until nearly tender:

6 peeled medium-sized potatoes

When the meat is nearly done, after about 1¼ hours' cooking in all, uncover it and place the whole potatoes around it, turn-

ing them frequently to permit
them to brown. Serve the ribs
and vegetables when the meat is
tender.

BOILED SPARERIBS

Place:

Spareribs

in:

Boiling water to cover

Add:

Salt and pepper
Chopped onion, celery,
parsley and carrots
(1 teaspoon caraway seed)

◗ Simmer the meat covered until
tender, from 1½ to 2 hours.
Drain and serve on a mound of
hot:

Sauerkraut or Red
Cabbage, page 278

surrounded by:

Mashed Potatoes, page
211

SWEET-SOUR SPARERIBS

Preheat oven to 350°.
Cut into 2-inch pieces:

2 lbs. spareribs

Parboil, page 88, 3 to 4 minutes. Drain and dry. Brush with:

Soy sauce

Bake ◗ uncovered on a rack in
a pan in the oven for 1 hour.
Have ready the following sauce.
Boil briefly:

½ cup vinegar
½ cup sugar
¼ cup sherry
1 tablespoon soy sauce
1 teaspoon fresh ginger

Mix together and add:

2 teaspoons cornstarch
1 tablespoon water

Cook until cornstarch is transparent. Pour the sauce over the
cooked spareribs and serve at
once with:

Baked Green Rice, page
159

STEWED PORK
NECK BONES

Partly cover with seasoned boiling water:

Pork neck bones

◗ Simmer covered until tender,
about 1½ hours. Vegetables may
be added to the stew for the
last ½ hour or so of cooking.

STEWED PORK HOCKS

Cover with seasoned boiling
water:

Pork hocks

Simmer covered from 1½ to 3
hours. You may add potatoes for
the last ½ hour of cooking or
greens or cabbage for the last
20 minutes.

SALT PORK AND MILK   [4]
GRAVY

Dip thin slices of:

1 lb. salt pork

in:

Boiling water

Drain and dip in:

Corn meal

Brown slowly in a skillet, turning frequently. Thicken:

2 tablespoons drippings

With:

2 tablespoons flour, see
Gravy, page 358

Pour in slowly:

1 cup milk

Serve with:

Boiled or baked potatoes

ABOUT GROUND MEAT
VARIATIONS

When emergencies demand all
our ingenuity to make meat
stretch graciously or otherwise,
we have discovered the incon-
trovertible fact that by grinding
meat it can be made to seem in
much more ample supply than
it really is. This does not mean
that all the variations listed in
this section are economical—
although some are definitely so.
But many provide interesting
blends, seasoning and combinations that give a much-sought
variety in menu building. No

one needs an introduction to hamburger, although many people should be alerted to the best actual handling of the meat and the best ways to retain its tenderness, and flavor during cooking. Meat loaves, pâtés and galantines, meat balls, croquettes, timbales, farces and mousses—all have their own individuality, which we hope you will discover and exploit.

Many other dishes using already cooked, diced, slivered and minced meats—which are rather different in texture—will be found in Luncheon and Supper Dishes, page 208. While grinding does, of course, help with tough and old meats, remember that ◗ the distinctive succulence of pâtés and galantines depends on a base of moist young meat. ◗ Do not store any uncooked ground meat longer than 24 hours. ◗ Be sure the mass is not more than 2 inches thick, so the cold can penetrate it quickly and thoroughly.

ABOUT HAMBURGER

A mother we know has made the disheartening discovery that her children will eat nothing but hamburger. She calls it "The Daily Grind." At home and abroad, indoors and out, the dispensing and downing of these meat patties is so nearly universal that it is worth considering for a moment from just what beef the commercial variety is built. So all-embracing did some butchers find the term "hamburger" that the law saw fit to define any beef sold under this term as at least 70% meat, 30% fat. Federal statute further forbids the use of sodium sulphite, an additive which keeps the meat rosy. Recent surveys, however, indicate that the practice is far from dead. Should you find the color of ground meat

too persistently red—expose a sample to bright sunlight. Untreated meat will darken.

If, as many people do, you have lean beef ground specially for hamburgers, use chuck, flank, shank, neck, heel, round or hanging tenderloin. ◗ Twice-ground meat will compact more than once-ground. You may be surprised at the apparently large amount of fat you didn't see go into the grinder. Grinders are so constructed that often as much as a fourth of every pound of meat that goes in stays in; and the unexpected fat may come from the grinding of the previous order.

✴ To freeze beef for hamburgers, see (II, 552 and 561).

Good quality beef, freshly ground and used at once, needs only ◗ light shaping. You may want to incorporate into it some onion juice or finely chopped chives. ◗ If the beef has to be kept ground for 12 to 18 hours, it profits by having worked into it with a fork about 2 tablespoons beef stock for each pound of meat. This is done before shaping.

◗ If beef is to be "stretched," you may add to each pound about ½ cup soft bread crumbs (II, 159), soaking them briefly in about ½ cup seasoned milk or stock. Or you may use ½ cup finely grated raw carrots, potatoes or ground and cooked soy beans, page 265, or 1 cup dry processed cereal. ◗ Incorporate these ingredients into the meat lightly with a fork and, with a light touch, shape the mixture into patties. Always decide before you put the meat into the pan how thick you want the finished hamburger. ◗ Never compact it in the pan by pressing down on it with a spatula.

◗ To cook hamburger, consider your grind. The degree of fattiness is important in helping

determine how you will treat the
pan for sautéing or whether you
will brush the patties with butter
during broiling.

If you use ◆ ready-ground hamburger, preheat an ungreased
skillet slowly, to the point where
a small sample of meat when
added will sizzle, not hiss
sharply. Drop the patties in the
pan and leave them, cooking
over medium heat ◆ uncovered,
for 3 or 4 minutes. During this
time sufficient fat should be
available from the patty itself
to permit the hamburger to be
turned without sticking. Turn
and cook on the other side another 3 minutes or even longer,
depending on the thickness of
the patty and the whims of your
diners.

Another prevalent, if flavor-
destroying, way of preparing a
fat-free pan is to preheat it
slowly and scatter over the surface of it about 1 teaspoon salt
for each pound of meat. The
salt will keep quite lean meat
from sticking—and for a very
good reason. It draws the juices
from the meat, see (II, 195).
Because of this, too, we prefer
◆ withholding seasoning from
hamburgers until after at least
one side of the meat is seared.
If you use ◆ very lean beef, you
will need at least 1 tablespoon
butter or suet added to the preheated skillet. Heat the fat to
the point of fragrance before
you add the meat, and proceed
to cook as for ready-ground
hamburger.

SAUTÉED   [4]
HAMBURGERS

◆ Please read About Hamburger,
page 515. Shape lightly into
patties, allowing 2 for each
serving:

> 1 lb. ground beef

You may mix in lightly with a
fork any one of the following.
To stretch, add:

> ½ cup soft bread crumbs
> (II, 159)

soaked briefly in:

> ⅓ to ½ cup milk or stock

or add:

> ½ cup finely grated raw
> carrots or potatoes

moistened with:

> 2 tablespoons beef stock,
> cream, tomato paste or
> lemon juice

To flavor, use:

> 2 teaspoons chili sauce, 1
> teaspoon ground anchovy
> or anchovy paste, 3
> tablespoons sautéed
> mushrooms, 1 tablespoon
> finely diced stuffed olives
> or 1 teaspoon capers

or:

> ¼ teaspoon thyme
> 1 squeeze garlic clove
> 1 teaspoon Worcestershire
> sauce

or:

> 2 tablespoons fresh
> chopped parsley and
> chives or 1 tablespoon
> sautéed chopped shallots
> or onions

After turning to complete the
cooking, season with about:

> 1 teaspoon salt
> ⅛ teaspoon pepper
> (1 teaspoon monosodium
> glutamate)

Defat the pan drippings. Deglaze them with:

> Stock

Reduce the juices slightly and
pour over the patties before
serving. Or mix with the pan
juices a little:

> Barbecue, chili sauce,
> tomato catsup, horse-
> radish, a few chopped
> olives or sautéed onions
> or mushrooms

Or spread over them:

> Herb butters or mustard,
> page 383
> A slice of Swiss cheese,
> crumbled blue cheese

or grated cheddar or
Parmesan

Run the patties briefly under a
broiler. You may garnish the
tops with one of the following:

Very thin, sweet, raw or
sautéed onion slice
A slice of tomato or
cucumber

BROILED HAMBURGERS [4]

Preheat broiler.
♦ Please read About Hamburger,
page 515. Shape lightly into
¾-inch-thick patties:

1 lb. ground beef

Place them on a broiler pan, 4
inches from the heat, or place
them so they cover the untoasted
side of:

A piece of bread toasted
on one side only

If on the bread broil about 10
minutes. If not broil 6 minutes
on one side, turn and broil about
4 minutes on the other. If the
meat is very lean, you may brush
it during broiling with:

Butter

◙ GRILLED HAMBURGERS

We have watched with agony
as good juices fed the flames of
barbecues and the guests were
dealt dry chips. If you must grill
ground meat, please see page
89.
Prepare previous recipe for:

Hamburgers

To make the meat adhere well
during handling, you may add
to it:

1 beaten egg for each
pound

Proceed as for:

Broiled Hamburgers,
above

◙ SLOPPY JOES

[8 Sandwiches]
Sauté in:

2 tablespoons butter

½ cup minced onions
½ cup chopped green
pepper, seeds and
membrane removed

When these are translucent,
add:

1½ lbs. ground beef

Cook and stir until meat is
slightly browned. Add:

½ cup chopped mushrooms
2 to 4 tablespoons chili
sauce
Correct the seasoning

Cook, uncovered, over low heat
until the mushrooms are done.
Fill with this hot mixture:

8 slightly toasted sandwich
buns

◙ FILLED BEEF OR LAMBURGERS [6]

Preheat broiler.
Vary the fillings by using
chopped celery, pickles, chili
sauce, bread dressing, chopped
leftover vegetables.
♦ Please read About Hamburger,
page 515. Sauté lightly:

(6 slices bacon)

Divide into 12 portions:

1½ lbs. ground beef or lamb

Shape into flat cakes and fill
with:

I.

6 tablespoons chopped nut
meats
3 tablespoons chopped
parsley
2 tablespoons grated onion

II.

Anchovy and a few
capers for each patty

III.

Slice of Roquefort or
cheddar cheese or
liverwurst

Spread it on 6 of the cakes. Top
them with those remaining. Bind
the edges with the partially
sautéed bacon strips and fasten
with a toothpick. Broil for 10
to 15 minutes, turning them
once.

LIVER PATTIES [6]

Preheat oven to 350°.
Combine:

    1 lb. ground liver
    1 slice chopped bacon
    ½ cup dry bread crumbs
    ¼ cup evaporated milk or
      cream
    ½ teaspoon salt
    ⅛ teaspoon pepper
    2 teaspoons grated onion
    2 tablespoons chopped
      parsley

Shape these ingredients into 6
flat cakes. Wrap around them:

    6 slices bacon

Secure the bacon with toothpicks. Place the cakes in a lightly
greased pan. Bake until well
browned, about 6 minutes. Turn
to insure even baking.

CHICKEN, VEAL [12 to 14] OR LAMB PATTIES

Preheat broiler.
The French make many attractive dishes by grinding uncooked
meat or fish, shaping it with
other ingredients and poaching,
broiling or sautéing the patties.
Cut the meat from:

    A 4½ lb. chicken or use
    3½ lbs. veal or lamb

Pick over the carcass for all
edible bits of meat. Put the meat
through a grinder, using a coarse
knife. Save the juices, if any.
Combine the ground meat, the
juices and:

    ¾ cup whipping cream
    1½ cups soft bread crumbs
    1 teaspoon salt
    1 teaspoon dried basel or
    1 tablespoon chopped
      parsley
      A grating of lemon rind
    ¼ teaspoon paprika
      A grating of nutmeg

Shape the mixture into 10
patties. Roll them in a:

    Bound Breading (II,
    160)

Place them in a ♦ shallow
greased pan. Broil under mod-

erate heat about 10 minutes to
a side or until lightly browned.
The patties may be left unbreaded and poached in a pan
in the oven in a small amount
of milk or stock, enough to cover
the bottom of the skillet, until
done. This means very low heat.
Serve with:

    Béarnaise Sauce, page
    370, or
    Soubise Sauce, page 363

GERMAN MEATBALLS OR KOENIGSBERGER KLOPS

[6 Servings—About Ten
2-Inch Balls]
A good buffet dish.
Soak in water, milk or stock to
cover:

    1 slice of bread, 1 inch
      thick

Put through a meat grinder
twice:

    1½ lbs. meat: ½ lb. beef,
      ½ lb. veal, ½ lb. pork
      or liver

Beat well and add:

    2 eggs

Melt:

    1 tablespoon butter

Sauté in it until golden:

    ¼ cup finely minced onion

Add them to the meat. Wring
the liquid from the bread. Add
the bread to the meat and:

    3 tablespoons chopped
      parsley
    1¼ teaspoons salt
    ¼ teaspoon paprika
    ½ teaspoon grated lemon
      rind
    1 teaspoon lemon juice
    1 teaspoon Worcestershire
      sauce or a grating of
      nutmeg

A few minced sardelles or ¼
herring may be added to the
meatballs at this time or they
may be added later to the gravy.
Combine these ingredients well.
Do this lightly with the hands—
a better method than using a

fork or spoon. Shape lightly in 2-inch balls. Drop into:

>   5 cups boiling Vegetable
>   Stock (II, 142)

◗ Simmer covered for about 15 minutes. Remove from the stock. Measure the stock. Make Gravy of it, page 358, by using, for every cup stock:

>   2 tablespoons butter
>   2 tablespoons flour
>   Correct the seasoning

Cook and stir until smooth and hot. Add:

>   2 tablespoons capers, or 2
>   tablespoons chopped
>   pickles, lemon juice or
>   cultured sour cream
>   2 tablespoons chopped
>   parsley

Reheat the meatballs in the gravy. Serve with a platter of:

>   Boiled Noodles, page
>   172, or
>   Spaetzle, page 179

Cover generously with:

>   Buttered Crumbs, page
>   389

ITALIAN MEATBALLS

Preheat oven to 350°.
Follow the preceding rule for:

>   German Meatballs

Omit the Worcestershire sauce. Add to the meat mixture:

>   ½ chopped clove garlic
>   3 tablespoons grated
>   Parmesan cheese
>   ¼ teaspoon orégano

Mix and form into balls. Brown lightly in:

>   2 tablespoons butter

Place in a casserole. Half cover with:

>   Unthickened Tomato
>   Sauce, page 376, or
>   Marinara Sauce, page
>   379

Bake covered for about 30 minutes.

SWEDISH MEATBALLS

[6 Servings of About Eighteen 1½-Inch Balls]

There are many recipes for this dish, all similar to and, in our opinion, none superior to:

>   German Meatballs, page
>   518

Shape the meat into 1½-inch balls. Brown in:

>   1 tablespoon butter or
>   drippings

Simmer closely covered until done, about 15 minutes, in:

>   2 cups consommé or other
>   stock

Make:

>   Pan Gravy, page 358

Season it with:

>   Sherry

Reheat the balls in the gravy. This is attractive served in a chafing dish, garnished with:

>   Potato Dumplings, page
>   180

CHINESE MEATBALLS   [6]

Shape into 18 balls:

>   1½ lbs. ground beef

Season with:

>   1½ teaspoons salt
>   1 teaspoon monosodium
>   glutamate
>   1 tablespoon finely chopped
>   parsley

Coat the balls with:

>   Fritter Batter for Meat
>   (II, 125)

Let them dry on a rack for 30 minutes. Deep-fat fry, pages 75–79, at 375°, until golden brown. Serve at once, covered with a:

>   Chinese Sweet-Sour
>   Sauce, page 371

PORK BALLS IN   [4]
TOMATO SAUCE

Soak in water to cover:

>   A slice of bread, 1½
>   inches thick

Wring the water from it. Add to the bread:

>   1 lb. ground pork
>   ⅓ cup chopped onion
>   1 beaten egg

¾ teaspoon salt
¼ teaspoon paprika

Combine these ingredients lightly with the hands until well blended. Shape into 2-inch balls. Combine the contents of:

  1 can tomato soup: 10½ oz.
  An equal amount of water

Bring the liquid to the boiling point. Drop the balls into it. ◗ Reduce the heat at once. Cover the pan and simmer until done, about ½ hour.

SAUERKRAUT BALLS

[4 Dozen 1¼-Inch Balls]

The sauerkraut helps tenderize as well as flavor these meatballs. ◗ Please read About Deep-Fat Frying, pages 75–79.

Preheat deep fryer to 375°.
Grind with a medium blade:

  ½ lb. each ham, corned beef and lean pork

Sauté the meat in:

  3 tablespoons butter or fat

with:

  ⅓ cup finely chopped onion

Mix, stir in and ◗ simmer until thick, stirring constantly:

  2 cups flour
  ½ to 1 teaspoon dry mustard
  1 teaspoon salt
  2 cups milk

When this mixture has cooked, combine it with:

  2 lbs. cooked, drained sauerkraut

Then regrind the entire mixture. Form into 1¼-inch balls. Roll them in:

  Bound Breading (II, 160)

Deep fry until golden brown. Drain on absorbent paper and serve at once.

CHILI CON CARNE   [8]

Melt:

  2 to 3 tablespoons bacon drippings or butter

Sauté in the fat:

  ½ cup chopped onion or
  ½ chopped clove garlic

Add:

  1 to 2 lbs. ground beef or lamb

Stir and sauté the beef until well done.
Add:

  1¼ cups canned tomatoes
  4 cups canned kidney beans
  ¾ teaspoon or more salt
  ½ bay leaf
  (1 teaspoon sugar)
  2 teaspoons to 2 tablespoons chili powder

depending on your taste and the strength of the chili powder. Cover and cook slowly for about 1 hour. Serve with:

  Tortillas or crackers

PORCUPINES   [6]

Combine:

  1 lb. ground beef
  ½ cup bread crumbs
  1 egg
  ¾ teaspoon salt
  ¼ teaspoon paprika
  (2 tablespoons chopped green peppers)

Roll these ingredients ◗ lightly into balls. Press into flat cakes. Roll in:

  ¼ cup raw rice

Heat in a heavy pot:

  Thickened Tomato Sauce, page 376

Add:

  (1 teaspoon chili powder)

Add the meat cakes. Cover the pot. Simmer the meat for about 45 minutes.

  Correct the seasoning and serve.

SPANISH CASSEROLE   [6]
WITH RICE

This is a one-dish meal.
Preheat oven to 350°.
Steam:

  ⅔ cup rice

Prepare:

  1 cup chopped celery

¼ cup chopped green
pepper
Melt in a saucepan:
      2 tablespoons butter or
      other fat
Peel, chop and sauté in the butter until golden:
      1 medium-sized onion
Add and sear:
      1 lb. ground round steak
Season with:
      ¾ teaspoon salt
      ¼ teaspoon paprika
Place in a greased baking dish
⅓ of the rice and ½ of the
meat. Sprinkle over it ½ of the
celery and pepper. Repeat this
process. Place the last of the rice
on top. Pour over these ingredients:
      1 can condensed tomato
      soup: 10½ oz.
      Seasonings
Cover the dish and bake about
½ hour.

LAMB AND EGGPLANT [4]
CASSEROLE

Preheat oven to 350°.
Pare and chop until fine:
      1 medium-sized eggplant
Combine with:
      2 cups ground lamb: 1 lb.
      ½ cup chopped onion
      3 tablespoons chopped
      parsley
      1 teaspoon salt
      ¼ teaspoon paprika
      (½ teaspoon curry powder)
      1 cup canned chopped
      tomatoes
Butter a casserole. Fill it with
the lamb mixture. Bake covered
for about ¾ hour. Remove the
cover and let the top brown.

HAMBURGER [4]
CASSEROLE

Preheat oven to 400°.
Melt in a skillet:
      ¼ cup butter
Sauté in it until the meat loses
its ruddiness:
      1 lb. ground steak or veal

      1 cup minced celery
      1 medium-sized cubed
      onion
      ½ lb. mushrooms
Add:
      1 teaspoon salt
Place the ingredients in a casse-
role. Cover with:
      1 cup condensed tomato
      soup
Bake for about 45 minutes. Serve
with:

      Fried Noodles, page 172

STUFFED CABBAGE OR [6]
GEFUELLTER KRAUTKOPF

Separate and prepare by blanching for about 5 minutes, page
88:
      The leaves from a head
      of cabbage
Reserve the liquor. Place the
leaves at once on towels to drain.
Prepare one of the following
meat dressings.
I.
Soak in water for 2 minutes:
      1 slice of bread, 1 inch
      thick
Press the water from it. Combine the bread with:
      ½ lb. ground pork
      ½ lb. ground beef
      ½ lb. ground veal
      3 beaten eggs
      ¾ teaspoon salt
      ¼ teaspoon paprika

II.
Or use a filling of:
      1 lb. fresh pork sausage
      meat
      3 half-inch slices of bread
      1 beaten egg
Line a bowl with a large napkin
or cloth and fill it with alternate
layers of the leaves and the meat
dressing. Cover the top with 1
or 2 large leaves, gather up the
cloth and tie it with a string.
Place the bag in boiling water—
the water in which the cabbage
was boiled and as much fresh
boiling water as needed to cover

well. ◆ Simmer the cabbage gently for 2 hours if you are old-fashioned, but 45 minutes should be ample time. Drain it in a colander, untie the bag and place the cabbage in a hot serving dish. Serve with the following onion sauce. Brown in the top of a double boiler:

> ¼ cup butter

Add and stir until brown:

> 2 tablespoons flour

Have ready:

> 2 cups Stock (II, 141)
> or cabbage water

Stir ½ cup of this into the butter mixture. Add:

> ½ cup or more chopped onion

If required,

> Correct the seasoning

Cook the onions covered ◆ over —not in—hot water, until they are very tender. Add the remainder of the stock gradually. The gravy is best when it is thick with onions.

GROUND BEEF IN   [4]
CABBAGE LEAVES

Preheat oven to 375°.
Wash and parblanch, page 88:

> 8 large cabbage leaves

Drain and dry them on a towel. Combine:

> 1 lb. ground beef or a
>   mixture of beef, veal,
>   pork and liver
> 3 tablespoons finely
>   chopped onions
> 2 tablespoons finely
>   chopped parsley
> ¾ teaspoon salt
> ½ teaspoon thyme
> ½ mashed clove garlic
>   A few grains cayenne

If you want a sweet-sour effect, add:

> 2 tablespoons vinegar
> 3 tablespoons brown sugar
> 1 teaspoon capers

Divide the meat mixture into 8 parts. Put one part on each cabbage leaf. Roll the leaves, as shown on page 86. Tie or secure them with toothpicks. Place them close together in a buttered baking dish. Dot each roll with:

> ½ teaspoon butter

Pour into the dish:

> ½ cup boiling Stock
>   (II, 141)

or you may use:

> ½ cup water, tomato juice
>   or cultured sour cream
>   and paprika

Bake the rolls, covered, until the cabbage leaves are very tender, about 50 minutes.

STUFFED GRAPE LEAVES
OR DOLMAS

[30 Dolmas or 9 to 10 Portions]
Prepare for stuffing:

> 30 tender Grape Leaves,
>   page 86

Fill each one with a tablespoon of the following mixture:

> 2 cups finely chopped
>   onions
> ½ cup rice
> ⅓ cup olive oil
> 2 tablespoons finely
>   chopped parsley
> 2 tablespoons finely
>   chopped dill
> ¼ cup pine nuts
> ¼ cup currants
>   (1 cup finely minced lamb)

Do not roll the leaves too tightly, as the rice will swell. Cook as directed, page 86, weighted, over low heat about 1½ hours. Serve chilled.

ABOUT MEAT LOAF

Although proportions of beef, veal and pork are specified in the following recipes, they may be varied, provided the total amount of meat remains the same. Be sure to ◆ cook thoroughly if pork is used. Handle ingredients for meat loaf ◆ lightly, mixing with a two-tined fork. To stretch, see About Hamburger, page 515.

Meat loaf may be mounded

on a flat greased pan or put into a greased ring mold or loaf pan. Also, it may be baked in 2 layers with a good stuffing between. You may pour about ½ cup of catsup in the bottom of the mold or pan before you fill it with the meat; or you may pour about 2 tablespoons of chili sauce over the meat loaf when it is half baked. This gives it a good flavor and a light crust.

For more rapid cooking, individual meat loaves take only about 15 minutes and—for attractive service—may be baked in greased muffin tins and glazed. Bake the loaf and baste it, as directed in the following recipes. You may cover it with a piece of foil. Remove the foil for the last ¼ hour of the baking period. If using chili sauce on top or covering the loaf with foil, do not baste it. Invert the mold.

Serve a ring hot, filled with green peas or some other vegetable and surrounded by browned potatoes. Or serve cold, filled with potato or some other vegetable salad.

MEAT LOAF [4]
I.

Preheat oven to 350°.
Combine and shape into a loaf:

    1 lb. ground beef: ¼ this
        amount may be pork
    (1 egg yolk)
    2 tablespoons chopped
        parsley
    1 tablespoon soft butter
    1 tablespoon bread crumbs
    1 teaspoon lemon juice
    1 teaspoon salt
    ¼ teaspoon pepper
    ½ teaspoon onion juice

Place the loaf in a lightly greased pan. Bake it for 1 hour. Pour some over the top and baste at intervals with the remainder of:

    ¼ cup butter
    1 cup Vegetable Stock

    (II, 142), or 1 cup boiling
        water plus ½ package
        dried soup mix
Serve the loaf with:
    Sweet Potato Puffs,
        page 323

II. [4]
Preheat oven to 350°.
Place in a bowl:

    1 lb. ground round steak
    1 to 2 tablespoons
        horseradish
    2 tablespoons catsup
    1 teaspoon salt
    ¼ teaspoon pepper
    ½ cup cream
Grind in a food chopper then add:

    6 slices bacon
    2 medium-sized onions
    1 cup broken-up crackers
Mix with a fork. Mold into a loaf. Roll it in:

    ¼ cup cracker crumbs
Place the loaf in a shallow baking pan. Pour into the pan:

    ½ cup stock
Bake the loaf for about 1½ hours. Baste occasionally, adding more liquid, if necessary. Make:
    Pan Gravy, page 358

MEAT LOAF [6]
COCKAIGNE

Preheat oven to 350°.
Mix lightly with:

    1½ lbs. lean ground beef—
        be sure beef has only
        been ground once
    1 can condensed cream
        of chicken or mushroom
        soup
    ¾ cup dry bread crumbs
    ¼ cup mixed fresh tarragon,
        parsley, basil or chives
    1 teaspoon salt
    1 pressed clove garlic
    10 or more chopped stuffed
        olives or ¼ cup chopped
        water chestnuts
Place the mixture in a 4 x 8 x 4-inch pan. Bake about 45 minutes. Serve hot with:
    (Thickened Tomato
        Sauce, page 376)

VEAL LOAF [8 to 10]

Preheat oven to 350°.
Grind:

    2 lbs. veal
    1 lb. smoked ham or
        sausage

Add and ◆ mix together very
lightly:

    1 tablespoon minced onion
    ¼ cup seeded chopped
        green pepper
    2 beaten eggs
    ½ teaspoon salt
    ⅛ teaspoon paprika
    ¾ cup dry bread crumbs
    1 cup condensed
        mushroom soup

Place ½ to ⅓ of this mixture
in a 4 x 8 x 4-inch loaf pan. You
may then press whole mushrooms or hard-cooked eggs,
stuffed olives or pistachio nuts
into the meat in a pattern. Cover
wi.h another third of meat and
repeat the pattern or cover with
half the meat. Bake for about 1
hour. Serve hot or cold.

LIVER LOAF [6 to 8]

This makes a most appetizing
everyday liver spread.
Preheat oven to 350°.
Boil for 5 minutes:

    1 cup water
    1 medium-sized chopped
        onion
    ၁ ribs celery with leaves

Prepare for cooking, page 535,
slice, add and simmer for 2
minutes:

    1 lb. liver: beef, lamb or
        pork

Drain, reserving liquid. Put liver
and vegetables through a meat
chopper with:

    2 slices bacon or a 1½-inch
        cube salt pork

Add and blend well:

    1 or 2 beaten eggs
    ¾ teaspoon salt
    ⅛ teaspoon pepper
    1 cup cracker or dry bread
        crumbs

    ½ teaspoon dried marjoram
        or thyme
    1 cup liquid: liver stock,
        milk, tomato juice, etc.

Pour into a greased loaf pan:
    (½ cup catsup)
Place the meat in the pan. Bake
for about 40 minutes.

RAW SMOKED [4 to 6]
HAM LOAF

You may dress this up or down.
Preheat oven to 350°.
Try using:

    ½ cup crushed pineapple
    ½ teaspoon dry mustard

in the bottom of the pan or end
up with the glazes suggested
below. Grind:

    1 lb. raw smoked ham
    ½ lb. lean pork
    (½ onion)

Add and mix together with the
hands:

    2 well-beaten eggs
    ½ to 1 cup cracker or dry
        bread crumbs
    An equal amount of milk
    ⅛ teaspoon pepper
    3 tablespoons mixed fresh
        herbs

Shape into a loaf, place in a
greased bread pan and bake for
about 2 hours, basting frequently
with:

    Honey Glaze, page 387,
    or Spirit Glaze for Ham,
    page 387

ABOUT PÂTÉ DE FOIE

The famed foie gras of Europe
is produced by the forced feeding of geese, which causes their
livers to become marbled in appearance and ɔo increase their
bulk that they often account for
¼ the bird's weight. In this
country the law forbids this
practice, although unfatted
goose liver is available. As a
matter of fact, the liver of
which American pâtés are usually composed—that of chickens

—makes a more than merely acceptable substitute.

⅄✳ PÂTÉ DE FOIE DE VOLAILLE OR CHICKEN LIVER PÂTÉ

I. [About Twenty ½-Inch Slices]

Divide into 3 parts:

1½ lbs. chicken livers

Blend one part with:

2 eggs

Blend the second part briefly with:

¼ cup whipping cream

Blend the third part with:

4 slices chopped bacon
1 egg
3 tablespoons cognac
2 tablespoons port wine
¼ cup flour

Mix these three blends together
♦ very lightly with:

1 teaspoon ginger
2 teaspoons salt
½ teaspoon black pepper
1 teaspoon allspice or nutmeg

Line a loaf pan with dough for a pâté, see this page.

Preheat oven to 325°.

Put ½ the above mixture in the loaf pan. You may add:

1 to 2 sliced truffles

Cover with the remaining mixture. Top with:

Thin-sliced salt pork

Cover tightly with foil. Bake the pâté in a pan of hot water for 1½ to 2 hours. Test for doneness, as for poultry.

II. ✳ [About 40 Slices, ½-Inch Thick]

Should the veal be red, as it is so often in our markets, marinate it overnight covered with milk and refrigerated.

♦ Please read About Pâté En Croûte below. Preheat oven to 325°.

Pound:

1 lb. white veal

Add to it and ♦ grind 3 times:

1½ lbs. chicken livers

¼ lb. salt pork
2 anchovy fillets

Mix in lightly until very smooth:

4 beaten eggs
½ cup whipping cream
3 tablespoons grated onion
2 tablespoons chopped parsley or chervil
⅛ teaspoon freshly ground black pepper
¼ cup cognac
1 tablespoon Madeira
2 tablespoons chopped truffles

You may put this mixture in a loaf pan lined with dough for pâté, page 527, or directly into a greased loaf pan. If you do not use the pastry liner on page 527, set the pan in a larger one of hot water. Bake for about 1½ hours or to an internal temperature of 180°. To test for doneness, see (II, 336). The pâté should still be pink in color when done. After cooling, you may glaze the pastry case with:

Aspic, page 387

if you do not plan freezing it.

ABOUT PÂTÉ EN CROÛTE

The term alone evokes an instant image of glamorous dining. But for those of us who know pâtés only in canned form—

where the heat necessary to preserve them destroys their bloom —a good pâté maison is a revelation. And it makes us want at once to develop our own pâté ménagère. Basically this isn't any harder than making a meat pie. Pâté en croûte is beautiful to see in its glazed case. And it is even lovelier when sliced, revealing first the crusty edge and, within, the nugget-filled farce, with its clear gelatin top —see illustration. The novice does not realize that the crust is not really meant to be eaten, but is the protection the pâté needs to develop flavor to the fullest and to retain the juices.

Our friend, Chef Pierre Adrian, worried so about his American diners' insistence on consuming this tough protective coating that he now customarily uses a more appetizing, if harder to handle, pâte brisée (II, 297), to line his molds. He also suggests that the conventional hinged pâté molds nearly always leak and, should the pâté crust break in any way, the delicious juices run into the oven. If, instead, you use a loaf pan, 9 x 4½ x 4½ inches, you will still retain the characteristic shape, and the juices, if released, are trapped for later use. Also your oven does not become a mess.

First choose one of the Fillings or Farces on page 525, for your pâté. Endless combinations and textures are possible. Some people—if the materials are beef, veal and pork—prefer a coarse grind, some a fine one. Chicken is nearly always ground fine. Calf liver and chicken liver, diced or ground, are sometimes used for reasons of economy. Suckling pigs' livers are a real treat.

♦ Cut into dice only the tenderest, choicest parts of young meat—free from all connective tissue or sinew. Marinate these and any liver in white wine refrigerated for 24 hours. Foie gras is often marinated in cognac. Mix with at least ½, up to twice, as much fat as meat. Then grind both meat and fat together 3 times, with the finest meat grinder blade. You may be tempted to use a blender, but we find the texture that results is both stringy and pasty. The ground meat is then folded into the yolks, spices, cream and the other ingredients to form the pâté.

Now it's time to prepare the pâte or crust, which for easier handling should rest covered for several hours. Have ready the tenderloins, livers, truffles, tongue or other choice bits which will form the eventual mosaiclike pattern in cross section when the pâté is cut. Now, line the pâté mold with the crust. You may roll and fit it in by making a ⅓-inch-thick circular shape of ¾ of the dough. Reserve the other fourth for the lid. We find it easier to form ¾ of the dough into a thick oval approximately the size of the base of the mold and line the bottom. With the sides of the hands, used in chopping motions, gradually work the dough from the base so that it thins out and creeps up the sides. Then, with the fingers patting it thin, form the rest of the crust to lap over the top, page 525. Do not stretch the dough or tear it. Next, line the mold with thin strips of fat bacon in parallel U shapes, as sketched. Allow them to rest, temporarily, over the side. When the pâté is built up to the top, fold the bacon ends over to encase it completely. Now back to the lining. First spread on it a ¾-inch layer of farce. Begin then to imbed the choice solids called for in the recipe, separating and surrounding them with more of the farce, so that the pâté when cut shows a pattern in cross section, as sketched. When the mold is filled and the bacon placed over the top of the filling, crimp the edge of the dough and cut off the excess.

From the remaining ¼ amount of dough, roll a ³⁄₁₆-inch-thick section of crust for the lid. Brush the edges of the mold with Egg Wash (II, 433). In applying the top, pinch it onto the already crimped top edges. Do not stretch the dough, but leave it lax enough so that it will not crack or become distorted during baking. Cut from the scraps small geometric or floral shapes to ornament the top. Work your pattern around 2 or 3 circles which can hold pastry vents, as shown in the drawing. These will later form a guide for the funnel when the aspic is carefully poured between the pâté and the upper crust. Apply the ornaments with egg wash and brush the top with it before baking. Vent the top crust with a few fancy cuts, as you would for a pie. Preheat the oven to 400°. To avoid too rapid browning of the crust, you may have ready a piece of foil to put loosely over the top. This will protect it in the early stages of baking. As soon as you put the pâté in the oven ◗ lower the heat to 325°. Pâtés are usually cooked about 1½ hours. Test for doneness as for cake (II, 336).

Allow the pâté, still in the pan, to cool on a rack. When cold, fill the space which will have formed at the top between the filling and the crust by pouring through the vents enough flavorful aspic which—when it solidifies—will support the crust. Use a firm gelatin, allowing 1 tablespoon of gelatin for each cup of meat stock. Hold a funnel in one of the vents and pour the mixture—being careful not to moisten the crust on the outside. Allow the pâté to remain in the pan refrigerated until the aspic is set. To unmold the pâté, proceed as for unmolding a gelatin (II, 186). Use a rack, however, on which to reverse it—to facilitate turning the pâté right side up onto a serving platter.

Pâtés should, of course, be stored refrigerated and most pâtés profit by ◗ resting refrigerated for at least 48 hours before serving—so that the flavors blend and the contents are firm enough for even slicing.

When served, the whole pâté may be garnished with a border of chopped aspic jelly, parsley and lemon wedges. When serving, cut it with a warm knife. An individual serving should be at least ⅜ to ½ of an inch thick and garnished with parsley and a lemon wedge.

For the size described here, you can produce 40 servings this way: slice about ½ inch thick, then cut each slice in half on the diagonal.

CRUST OR PÂTE FOR PÂTÉ

Work together with your fingers until you have achieved the consistency of coarse corn meal:

> 6 cups sifted all-purpose flour
> 2 teaspoons salt
> 1½ cups lard or shortening

Make a well (II, 301) of these ingredients and break into the center, one at a time:

> 2 eggs

working them into the flour mixture from the inside and adding gradually:

> About 3 cups water

You may need a little more water to make a dough that can be worked into a smooth mass and rolled into a ball. The mold is easier to form if you rest it covered at about 70° for several hours. To mold, see About Pâté en Croûte, page 525.

LIVER PÂTÉ

A less luxurious version of this dish may be made more quickly by omitting the gelatin and consommé.
Blend with a fork:

  1½ cups liver sausage
   ½ can condensed cream of
      tomato soup

Dissolve:

  1 tablespoon gelatin

in:

  ¼ cup cold water

Bring to a boil:

  1 can condensed consommé

and combine with the dissolved gelatin. Reserve ¾ cup of this mixture to line a pint mold. Add to the remainder:

  1 teaspoon Worcestershire
     sauce
  ¼ teaspoon salt
  (1 pressed clove garlic)
  (1 tablespoon finely chopped
     parsley)

and the blended liver mixture. Fold into the mold. Let set. Reverse to serve.

SOUFFLÉED LIVER PÂTÉ

Preheat oven to 350°.
I. Have ready two 9-inch bread pans, one rinsed in cold water, the other prepared as for a soufflé baker, page 196. Into the rinsed pan, pour ½ inch of the following gelatin mixture and place it in the refrigerator.
Soak for 3 minutes:

  2 teaspoons gelatin

in:

  ¼ cup cold water

Combine it with:

  2 cups well-seasoned
    Double Consommé,
    page 109

Reserve the rest of the gelatin mixture and keep it at room temperature. Grind:

  1 lb. raw chicken livers

◗ Or if you use ⅄ a blender put the liver and the following ingredients into it and blend briefly. Beat in:

  2 eggs
  2 egg yolks
  2 teaspoons onion juice
  2 tablespoons chopped
    parsley

Fold in:

  2 cups whipping cream
  2 stiffly beaten egg whites

Bake this mixture in the greased pan at 350° until set, about 1 hour. Before placing it in the oven, you may set the pan in a larger one of warm water. When the loaf is thoroughly cold, remove from the pan and place on top of the chilled and set gelatin. Pour the reserved gelatin over the reversed bottom of the loaf, letting it run down the sides so that it is entirely enclosed in the gelatin. Let the added gelatin set and the loaf become thoroughly chilled before serving. Unmold and decorate the top with:

  Thinly sliced limes

Garnish the platter with:

  Parsley

II. An alternate suggestion for glazing this loaf is to replace the consommé with a combination of 1 cup water or stock and 1 cup port wine. Jell and mold it in 2 steps, as described previously.

ABOUT TERRINES

Terrines are the poor relations of the pâté. They are often made from leftovers, game or rabbit. Like pâté, the meat must be succulent and is often in the form of medallions or scallops. ◗ There should be about ⅛ fresh veal to jelly the whole when it cools. Terrines are baked without a crust in lidded earthenware dishes. Set them in a pan of water. For an 11½ x 9 x 4½-inch size, allow about 2 hours of baking in a 300° oven. Use the following method or make up your own meat mixture which you may reinforce with liver. The meat may, if you like, be placed in a wine marinade before cooking.

✳ VEAL OR CHICKEN TERRINE

Line the bottom and sides of a mold with strips of bacon, overlapping them ever so slightly. Strew with:

> 1 tablespoon chopped
> parsley
> 1 tablespoon chopped
> onion

Pound very thin:

> 2 lbs. veal scallops, cut in
> ¼-inch-thick slices

In pounding veal, use your mallet with a glancing action, as sketched, page 452, and the meat will not stick to it. Have ready:

> 2 lbs. finely sliced ham,
> chicken or pork

Overlay the bacon with a layer of the thin pounded veal. Season it with:

> A grind of pepper
> A pinch of thyme
> A pinch of powdered
> bay leaf

Put down a layer of the thin-sliced ham. Continue to build layers of parsley and onion and veal, seasoning and ham. Cover the top with overlapping bacon strips. Pour about:

> A cup of white wine
> A dash of brandy

over the meat layers until all the crevices are filled with liquid. Set the pan in a larger pan of hot water. Bake at 300° about 2 hours or until done. As soon as you remove the meat from the oven, cover with heavy aluminum foil and weight the layers with a brick. When the meat has cooled, a grease-covered jelly will have formed, which keeps the meat in prime condi-

tion. To serve, slice very thin. Use for hors d'oeuvre or as a main informal luncheon dish. Store refrigerated any that remains, covered with:

> Clarified butter

ABOUT GALANTINES

When galantines appear in all their truffled chaud-froid splendor, it is hard to believe that they started out with the boning of a bird, page 570. Begin with a slit down the spine but it is vital that during the rest of the boning the skin be kept intact. If cut, as around the leg and wing joints, it must be patched by sewing.

GALANTINE OF TURKEY

[If Served Hot, 12 to 15 Servings —if Served Cold, 30 Servings]
Bone, page 570:

> A 12- to 15-lb. turkey

Reserve the meat, including that cut from the drumsticks and the breast. Make a Stock (II, 143) of the bones. Reserve ½ the breast meat for decorations and cut it into ½-inch strips. Grind 3 times and put into a large bowl:

> 1 lb. lean white veal
> 1 lb. lean pork

as well as all the turkey meat, except the reserved portion. Season the mixture with:

> ¼ cup cognac, dry sherry or
> Madeira
> 1 teaspoon freshly grated
> nutmeg
> Ground black pepper
> 2 teaspoons Worcestershire
> sauce
> 1 tablespoon salt
> A dash hot pepper sauce
> 2 teaspoons monosodium
> glutamate

Add:

> 8 eggs
> ½ cup finely chopped
> parsley

Mix these ingredients into a smooth paste.

Correct the seasoning

Spread a large piece of clean linen or cheesecloth on the table. Place in the center of the cloth the turkey skin, outer side down, as shown in the center below. Carefully follow the instructions under Boned Chicken, page 585, about arranging the skin. Pat the meat mixture onto it in an even rectangular shape, extending it all the way to the edges. Arrange in neat alternating rows down the center, as shown:

Strips of cooked ham or tongue

and the reserved strips of turkey breast. Arrange a center row of:

Small whole truffles, page 300

Over the whole, sprinkle:

¾ cup pistachio nuts
¼ cup finely chopped parsley

Starting at the long side farthest away from you, pull the cloth toward you gently—rolling the filled turkey skin into a sausage-like shape. You do not want the cloth to be inside the turkey roll, but keep manipulating it until it forms an outside casing. You may need help. Tie the cloth securely at both ends. The roll should be smooth and even. Also tie it lengthwise, as sketched. Place it on a rack, seam side down, in a large poaching kettle. Add:

Mirepoix (II, 221)
Enough turkey or chicken Stock to cover (II, 142)

Cover the kettle and bring to a boil then ♦ reduce the heat and simmer very gently for 1½ to 2 hours until the roll is firm to the touch. Carefully remove it from the broth. You may serve it hot, sliced, with buttered toast. Or let it cool—wrapped—on a large platter. You may weight it if you wish. When it has reached at least room temperature, remove the outside wrapping and refrigerate thoroughly. To decorate, either use:

Chaud-Froid, page 388

or cover with a savory:

Aspic Glaze, page 388

made from the poaching broth. Serve thinly sliced with:

Buttered toast

as an hors d'oeuvre or an entrée.

ABOUT SAUSAGE

One of our early European memories was the rapt stance of the citizenry as they gazed at window displays of sausage. It made us aware for the first time of their wealth of choice and, on a considerably more limited scale, of our own. There is freshly ground sausage meat or Country Sausage, page 531, which must be used at once. There are smoked sausages: frankfurters, wieners or Vienna sausage, Bologna and Mettwurst

—all of which may be eaten as bought, but may also be simmered, baked or broiled for serving with pasta, hot vegetables and fruit garnish. See Stewed Fruits (II, 88). ◆ To make Smoked Sausages, see (II, 545).

If you broil or pan-fry these cased sausages ◆ prick them to keep the skins from bursting. This is not necessary if you have added a small quantity of water to the pan at the beginning of cooking or have first blanched, dried and floured them lightly before frying. Even then, if they swell quickly, prick them lightly before they burst, to give greater protection to the meat.

◆ For 4 servings, allow about 1 lb. of freshly ground sausage meat or the smoked types, slightly less for the more aged and drier types.

Dry sausages are also available: hard and soft cervelat, salami, saucison de Lyon, mortadella, pepperoni and chorizo. They are delicious as hors d'oeuvre, in sandwiches and for seasoning bland dishes.

Be sure that any kind of sausage you buy or make involves good quality meats. Cereal "stretchers" are almost certainly present in commercial sausages unless they are marked "pure" or "all meat." When properly made and if the casing is intact, dry sausages may be kept indefinitely in a cool place. For this reason, they have become known as "summer sausages"— although they are available the year round. Dry types are particularly prized when refrigeration is lacking. Available, too— although they need constant refrigeration—are spiced meats like liver loaf or Braunschweiger, blood sausage, deviled minced ham and veal loaves. ◆ Once the sausage casing is cut open, smoked or cooked sausage can be stored refrigerated about 1 week; semidry and dry types, 2 weeks or more.

COUNTRY SAUSAGE

At butchering time in our valley, the popular man is the one who knows how to flavor the sausage —not too much pepper or sage and just enough coriander. This process has to be played by ear, for ◆ uncooked meat cannot be tasted to correct the seasoning and the strength of spices is so variable. The best way to learn is to mix a small batch and cook up a sample for the always hungry helpers to test.

I. To each part:
>   Firm diced lard

Use:
>   2 parts lean ground pork

Season the lard with a mixture of:

>   Thyme
>   Summer savory
>   Coriander
>   Sweet marjoram
>   Pulverized bay leaf
>   Freshly ground pepper

◆ To cook fresh sausage patties, start them in a ◆ cold ungreased pan over moderate heat and cook until medium brown on both sides and done throughout.

II.
[6 Medium Patties]
If you have a sudden hankering for one of these small-scale recipes, grind ◆ twice with the finest grinder knives:
>   ½ lb. lean pork
>   ½ lb. pork fat
>   ½ lb. lean veal

Mix in a large bowl:
>   1 cup bread crumbs
>   Grated rind of 1 lemon
>   ¼ teaspoon each sage, sweet marjoram and thyme
>   ⅛ teaspoon summer savory
>   ½ teaspoon freshly ground black pepper
>   2 teaspoons salt

A grating of fresh nutmeg
Add the ground meat and form
this mixture into a 1½-inch
layer. Store overnight refrigerated and covered to blend the
seasoning. ◗ To cook, see I,
above.

SAUTÉED SAUSAGE [4]
MEAT PATTIES

Combine:
   1 lb. sausage meat
   2 tablespoons flour
   (¼ cup drained crushed
      pineapple or grated
      fresh apple)
Shape the meat into cakes ½
inch thick. Sprinkle with:
   Flour
Heat a skillet. No fat is required. Brown the cakes quickly
on both sides. Cover with a lid.
◗ Reduce the heat and cook
about 10 minutes on one side.
Pour off excess fat. Turn and
cook 10 minutes on the other
side or until done. Serve with:
   Sautéed Onions, page
      302
   Applesauce (II, 95)

▤ PAN-BROILED [4]
SAUSAGE

◗ Please read About Sausage,
page 530. Cut apart and place
in a skillet:
   8 sausages
Add:
   ½ cup boiling water
Cover the pan. Simmer gently,
not over 190°, for 8 to 10 minutes or until almost done. Pour
off the liquid. Return the sausages to the pan. Cook them
over low heat, shaking the pan
constantly until they are an even
brown. Drain. Serve with:
   Prepared mustard
For picnics, serve between:
   Rolls

BROILED SAUSAGE [2]
PATTIES

Preheat broiler.

Shape into 4 flat cakes:
   ½ lb. sausage meat
Roll the cakes in:
   1 tablespoon flour
Broil under moderate heat for 8
to 10 minutes or until done.
Arrange on a hot platter:
   Apple Rings (II, 94)
Place the sausage cakes on them.
Serve garnished with:
   Parsley

BOILED SAUSAGE

Place in a kettle:
   Smoked sausage
Cover with:
   Boiling water
Simmer for about 10 minutes.
Drain, skin, slice and serve with:
   Sauerkraut, page 278

BAKED SAUSAGE [6]
MEAT RING

Preheat oven to 350°.
Grease lightly a 7-inch ring
mold. Press onto the bottom:
   3 tablespoons cornflakes
Combine well:
   1 lb. sausage meat
   1 tablespoon minced onion
   ¾ cup fine bread crumbs
   2 tablespoons chopped
      parsley
   1 beaten egg
Place these ingredients in the
mold. Bake the ring 15 minutes.
Drain the fat from it. Bake 15
minutes longer or until done.
Invert the ring onto a hot platter
and fill the center with:
   8 Scrambled Eggs, page
      191
Garnish the top with:
   Chopped parsley or
      paprika

BAKED SAUSAGE [4]
MEAT, SWEET POTATOES
AND FRUIT

Preheat oven to 350°.
This is a good dish for large
groups.
Cook:
   4 large sweet potatoes

Peel and cut them into thin slices. Grease a baking dish. Cover the bottom with ½ the sweet potatoes. Shape into 4 flat cakes:

> 1 lb. sausage meat

Brown the cakes lightly in a greased pan, to which you may add:

> 1 tablespoon minced bacon

Peel and cut into thick slices:

> 4 large apples or pineapple slices

Place the drained meat cakes on the sweet potatoes and cover with apple slices. Sprinkle lightly with:

> Salt and brown sugar

Place the remaining sweet potatoes over the fruit. Brush the potatoes with:

> Milk

and sprinkle with:

> Brown sugar

Bake for about ¾ hour.

PORK SCRAPPLE OR GOETTA

[About 6 Servings]

If you use corn meal, call it scrapple. If you use oats, call it goetta. This may also be made with ¾ cup cooked pork. Use stock from the pork bones in cooking the cereal. Place in a pan:

> 2 lbs. pork neck bones or other bony pieces

Add:

> 1½ quarts boiling water
> 1 sliced onion
> 6 peppercorns
> (1 small bay leaf)

Simmer the pork until the meat falls from the bones. Strain, reserving the liquor. There should be about 4 cups. Add water or light stock if necessary to make this amount. Prepare, using this liquid in place of boiling water:

> Corn Meal Mush, page 157

You may substitute 1 cup oatmeal for the corn meal. In cook-

ing oatmeal, you may want to reduce the liquid by one cup. Remove all meat from the pork bones and chop or grind it fine. Add it to the cooked mush. Season with:

> Salt, if required
> 1 teaspoon or more grated onion
> (½ teaspoon dried thyme or sage)
> A grating of fresh nutmeg
> A little cayenne

Pour the scrapple into a bread pan that has been rinsed with cold water. Let it stand until cold and firm. Slice it. To serve, sauté slowly in:

> Melted butter or drippings

BLOOD SAUSAGE, BOUDIN NOIR OR BLACK PUDDING

Have the sausage casings ready. Cook gently without browning:

> ¾ cup finely chopped onions

in:

> 2 tablespoons lard

Dice into ½-inch cubes and half melt:

> 1 lb. fresh pork fat

Cool slightly and mix in a bowl with:

> ⅓ cup whipping cream
> 2 beaten eggs
> A grind of fresh pepper
> ⅛ teaspoon fresh thyme
> ½ pulverized bay leaf

When these ingredients have been gently combined, mix in:

> 2 cups fresh pork blood

Fill casings about ⅘ full, as this mixture will swell during the poaching period. Without overcrowding, put the sealed casings into a wire basket. Plunge them into boiling water. ▶ Reduce heat at once to 200° to 203° and continue to cook at this temperature for about 20 minutes. Should any of the sausages rise to the surface of the simmering liquid, pierce them to release the air that might burst the skins. To serve, split and grill them very gently.

ABOUT VARIETY MEATS

Variety, we know, is the spice of life. And variety meats provide welcome relief from the weekly round of beef, pork, veal, chicken and fish. Variety meats include organ meats like sweetbreads, brains, liver and kidney; muscle meats like heart, tongue and tripe; and very bony-structured meats like tails, knucklebones and their delicious marrow centers. Time was when most of these tidbits were ours almost for the asking. Today, hospital authorities—aware of the special virtues of organ meats—purchase them in large quantity. And the remainder are increasingly used in meat processing. As a result, the American housewife is apt to find variety meats of all types scarcer and considerably more expensive than they were a decade ago. ♦ It is essential that these meats be very, very fresh. Even when they are, the pan drippings from kidney and liver may sometimes be strong, and some cooks prefer to discard them. If in doubt, taste the drippings before serving.

ABOUT LIVER

Chicken and calf livers are the tenderest and most desirable unless, of course, you can secure extra-fat goose livers—the kind which in Europe almost invariably find their way into Pâtés, page 524. Baby beef liver comes next for quality. It should be handled like that of lamb, sheep, pork and older beef livers—that is, soaked for about 30 minutes in a marinade, page 380, or in milk. Before cooking, all these stronger types of liver should be dried and the liquids in which they have been soaked discarded.
♦ To prepare any liver for cooking, wipe it first with a damp cloth, then remove the thin outer skin and veining. Except for the timing noted in individual recipes, the cooking method for liver generally is the same. ♦ Never toughen it by cooking it too long or over excessive heat. ♦ Never cook it beyond the point of tenderness. Sometimes the drippings in which liver has been cooked are bitter. Test them by tasting before you use them as sauce. Allow 1 pound liver for 4 servings.

CALF OR CHICKEN [2] LIVER LYONNAISE

♦ Please read About Liver, above.
Have sliced to a ⅛-inch even thickness:
    ½ lb. calf liver or 12
        chicken livers cut in half
Season with:
    Salt and pepper
Coat on both sides with:
    Flour
♦ patting well between your hands to make the flour adhere and to remove the excess. Sauté until golden brown in:
    2 tablespoons butter
    ¼ cup sliced onions
    (¼ cup sliced mushrooms)
and set aside nearby. Now melt over high heat in a heavy skillet:
    1 tablespoon butter
Heat it until it starts making slight crackling noises. Put the floured liver into the skillet, allowing 1 minute to each side. Remove the liver and discard the butter it was cooked in, which may be bitter. Put the liver on a hot plate, cover with the onion butter and:
    Chopped parsley
Serve at once. We hate to add this, because we feel liver should

be rare—but if you don't like it this way, cook it over medium heat 2 minutes to the side for medium doneness.

GOOSE LIVER

Goose liver is considered a great delicacy. Remove the gall bladder. Soak in cold salted water for 2 hours:

A goose liver

Dry it with a cloth.

I. Sprinkle it with:
⅛ teaspoon paprika
½ teaspoon sugar
⅛ teaspoon ginger

Sauté it in hot goose fat until it is tender. Excellent served with sautéed onions and apples and with a little dry sherry.

II. Prepare and soak as directed previously:

A goose liver

Place it in an ovenproof dish. Cover it with:
1 cup brown sugar
¼ teaspoon salt
1 cup dry sherry

Broil it slowly for ½ hour. Watch it so that it does not burn. Baste it frequently to prevent a crust from forming. Cook sliced apples in a thick sirup until well glazed. Place them around the liver. Continue to baste with apple sirup until the liver is tender.

🖩 BROILED LIVER

◗ Please read About Liver, page 534.

I. Preheat broiler.

Some epicures have a preference for liver prepared in the following way—doctors have, too. We lean toward sautéed liver, but must acknowledge the good qualities of this recipe which accents liver—pure and simple.

Place on a broiler rack, about 3 inches from the source of heat:

Slices of calf liver, ⅛ inch thick

You may brush them with:
(Butter or cooking oil)

Leave the door of the broiling oven open. Broil the liver exactly 1 minute on each side.

Correct the seasoning

It is remarkably good as it is.

II. Preheat broiler.

Allowing 2 to 3 slices of bacon and onion for each slice of liver, broil:

Slices of lean thin bacon
Thin slices of Bermuda onion

Prepare:
Broiled Liver I, page 534

Serve the liver, bacon and onions on a hot platter garnished with:
Parsley
A lemon cut into quarters

BRAISED LIVER WITH [6] VEGETABLES

◗ Please read About Liver, page 534.

Cut into 1-inch slices:
1½ lbs. beef or calf liver

If you substitute beef liver, you may lard it, page 453. Dredge with:

Seasoned flour

Brown the liver in:
¼ cup hot bacon drippings

Combine and heap on the slices:
2 diced carrots
2 seeded chopped green peppers
6 small onions
1 cup sliced celery

Add to the pan:
1 cup boiling water or stock

Cover and simmer until the liver is tender. Add, if necessary, more boiling stock. Calf liver will be tender in about 15 minutes, beef liver in about 30.

BRAISED LIVER   [8]
COCKAIGNE WITH WINE

◗ Please read About Liver, page
534.
Place:

      2½ lbs. calf liver in 1 piece
in the following marinade for 1
hour or more:

      ⅓ cup salad oil
      1½ tablespoons lemon juice
      ¼ teaspoon salt
      ⅛ teaspoon paprika
      ¼ bay leaf
Turn it from time to time.
Preheat oven to 325°.
Melt in an ovenproof baking
dish:

      3 tablespoons butter
Add and stir about until lightly
cooked:

      1 small chopped onion or
        leek
      1 diced carrot
      2 or 3 diced ribs celery
      2 or 3 sprigs minced parsley
      1 tablespoon fresh basil or
        tarragon
Place the liver, marinade and all,
in the ovenproof dish. Cover
closely and bake until nearly
tender, for about 50 minutes.
Baste from time to time. If you
wish to serve the liver without
further additions, continue cooking it until very tender. The following ingredients are optional,
but they complement the dish.
While the liver is cooking, place
in a heavy skillet:

      4 slices diced bacon
Cook over very slow heat until
the bacon is clear. Add and stir
until well glazed:

      18 small peeled shallots or
         onions
      6 large or 8 small sliced
         carrots
      3 ribs sliced celery
Add:

      1 cup Stock (II, 141), or
        canned consommé
Cover the skillet and cook the
vegetables over direct low heat
for 15 minutes. Add them to the

liver in the baking dish, cover
and cook for 15 minutes longer.
Drain the contents of the baking
dish, reserving the liquor. Place
the liver on a hot platter. Add to
the liquor:

      ½ cup dry white wine, or
      ¼ cup dry sherry
      (2 beaten egg yolks)
Cook and stir the sauce over low
heat until hot. If you have added
the eggs, do not permit it to boil.
Pour the sauce over the liver.
Serve with:

      Small new browned
        potatoes
garnished with:

      Parsley

BEEF LIVER CREOLE   [4]

◗ Please read About Liver, page
534.
Cut into thin slices:

      1 lb. beef liver
Dust the slices lightly with:

      Flour
Melt, then brown the liver in:

      3 tablespoons hot butter
        or drippings
Add:

      1¼ cups sliced onions
      1½ cups heated canned
         tomatoes
      ½ cup diced celery
      1 thinly sliced green
        pepper
      ½ teaspoon salt
      A few grains cayenne
Cover the pan and simmer these
ingredients for about 20 minutes. Drain them. Thicken the
liquid with:

      Flour, see Pan Gravy,
        page 534
Add the liver and vegetables.
Simmer 2 minutes longer. Serve
with:

      Boiled Rice, page 158, or
        Noodles, page 192

▤ LIVER, PEPPER,   [4]
ONIONS AND OLIVES
ON SKEWERS

Preheat broiler.

Simmer covered in a little boiling water until nearly tender:

¾ lb. calf liver

Drain the liver. Cut it into 1-inch cubes. Cut into quarters:

4 medium-sized onions

Place them in water to separate the sections. Cut into 1-inch pieces:

6 strips bacon

Cut into 1-inch pieces:

2 green peppers, seeds and membrane removed

Alternate on skewers pieces of liver, onion, green pepper, bacon and:

Stuffed olives

Heat in a skillet over low heat a few bacon scraps or butter. Add the filled skewers. Move them about and cook them for about 3 minutes. Place them under a broiler until the bacon is crisp and the liver is tender.

CHICKEN LIVERS À LA KING

Prepare:

1 cup or more Chicken Liver Lyonnaise, page 534

Serve in:

1 cup à la King Sauce, page 375

CHICKEN LIVERS IN BATTER

Preheat deep fryer to 375°.

Wipe with a cloth:

Chicken livers

Season them lightly with:

Salt and pepper

Dip them into:

Fritter Batter for Meat (II, 125)

Fry them in deep fat, pages 75–79, until well browned. Serve with:

Herb Omelet, page 187

or as a garnish for a hot vegetable plate.

ABOUT SWEETBREADS

To paraphrase Puck: "What foods these morsels bel" Veal sweetbreads are those most favored. But beef sweetbreads are sometimes incorporated into mixtures like meat pies, pâté and terrines. Sweetbreads, properly so-called, are the rounded more desirable "heart" or "kernel" types, the pancreas. Also sold as sweetbread is the less desirable "throat," which is the thymus gland of the animal.

♦ Like all organ meats, sweetbreads are highly perishable and should be prepared for use as soon as purchased. First soak them at least 1 hour in a large quantity of cold water to release any blood. You may change the water several times during this period. Next they must be blanched. This is done by putting them into cold acidulated water to cover (II, 148). Bring them slowly to a boil and simmer uncovered from 2 to 5 minutes depending on their size. Drain. Firm them by plunging them at once into cold water. When they have cooled, drain again and trim them by removing cartilage, tubes, connective tissue and tougher membrane. Weight them refrigerated for several hours if you plan using them whole. If you are not using them in one piece, break them into smaller sections with your hands, being careful not to disturb the very fine membrane that surrounds the smaller units. Allow 1 pair for 2 servings.

After these preliminary processes, to which all sweetbreads must be subjected, you may poach, braise, broil or sauce them.

SAUCED POACHED [2] SWEETBREADS

♦ Please read About Sweetbreads, above. Soak, blanch, firm, drain and trim:

1 pair calf sweetbreads

Bring to the boiling point:
    Enoug': water to cover
to which you may add:
    ¼ cup chopped onions
    3 ribs celery with yellow
        leaves
    2 peppercorns
Drop the sweetbreads into the
liquid and ♦ lower the heat at
once. Simmer covered with a
parchment paper, page 83, for
about 15 to 20 minutes depending on size. ♦ Do not overcook.
Serve in a delicate sauce flavored with:
    1 tablespoon sherry,
        Madeira or brandy
Add a few:
    Toasted English walnuts
        and/or almonds
Allow about:
    1 cup Béchamel, Poulette,
        Mushroom or Wine Sauce
        for Light Meats
Sauced sweetbreads are often
served on:
    A thin slice of Virginia
        ham
or with a:
    Spinach Ring, page 205,
        a Vegetable Soufflé,
        page 198, or Wild Rice,
        page 160.

SAUTÉED   [2]
SWEETBREADS

♦ Please read About Sweet-
breads, page 537.
Blanch, firm, dry, trim and
poach for about 25 minutes:
    1 pair calf sweetbreads
Bread with a:
    Seasoned Bound
        Breading (II, 160)
Sauté them in:
    Hot butter
until they are a rich brown.
Serve them with:
    Cream sauce of sweet-
        bread stock and cream
Season the stock with:
    Sherry or lemon juice
    Chopped parsley
Serve the sweetbreads with:

New potatoes and green
    peas
garnished with:
    Watercress

BROILED   [2]
SWEETBREADS

♦ Please read About Sweetbreads, page 537.
Soak, blanch, firm, drain, trim
and poach for about 25 minutes:
    1 pair calf sweetbreads
Preheat broiler.
Place the broiling rack about 6
inches from the heat source.
Break the sweetbreads into large
pieces. Roll them in:
    Seasoned flour
Surround them with:
    Strips of bacon
Secure it with toothpicks. While
broiling them, baste frequently
with the juices that drip and, if
they are rather dry, use additional:
    Butter
Add to the drippings a small
amount of:
    (Sherry or lemon juice)
Serve with:
    Madeira Sauce, Poulette
        Sauce or broiled
        tomatoes
or on a bed of:
    Spinach

BRAISED   [2]
SWEETBREADS

Make this as simple or as fancy
as you like. ♦ Please read About
Sweetbreads, page 537.
Soak, blanch for 5 minutes, firm,
drain and trim:
    1 pair calf sweetbreads
You may press them between 2
plates under a weight if you
want them to have uniform
thickness and to mellow.
Preheat oven to 375°.
Break sweetbread into several
large pieces. You may lard, page
453, the pieces or surround each
one with:
    (Strips of lean bacon,

very thin pieces of
Virginia ham or
smoked tongue)
Sauté in a casserole in:

2 tablespoons melted butter

for about 10 minutes or until the
onions are transparent:

⅓ cup finely chopped
onions
2 tablespoons finely minced
carrot
⅓ cup chopped celery

Add:

½ cup dry white wine and
¾ cup light stock, or
1¼ cups stock
½ teaspoon salt
¼ teaspoon freshly ground
white pepper

Arrange the sweetbreads on this
bed of sautéed vegetables.
◗ Cover and bake for about 30
minutes.
This is an added touch, particularly good if you have used the
ham or bacon. In a skillet, sauté
for about 5 minutes:

(½ cup sliced mushrooms)
(¾ cup chopped cooked
chestnuts, page 283)

in:

2 tablespoons butter

GLAZED [2] SWEETBREADS

◗ Please read About Sweetbreads, page 537.
Soak, blanch, firm, drain and
trim:

1 pair calf sweetbreads

Melt in a casserole and sauté
for about 10 minutes or until the
onions are transparent:

3 tablespoons butter
2 tablespoons finely
julienned carrots
2 tablespoons finely
chopped shallots or
onions

Add:

1½ cups veal stock

Simmer closely covered for
about 20 minutes. ◗ Make sure
that the vegetables do not

brown. Add more stock, if
necessary. When the sweetbreads are cooked, help to deglaze the pan by the addition
of.

½ cup dry white wine
Correct the seasoning

Preheat oven to 400° for glazing.
Now, remove the sweetbreads
from the pan, but keep warm in
an ovenproof dish on which they
can be served. Reduce the pan
liquors to a demi-glaze. Cover
the sweetbreads, allowing about
2 tablespoons of glaze for each
one, and place the dish in the
oven, basting often for about 10
minutes. Serve at once, garnished with:

Chervil or parsley

Serve with:

Fresh young peas
Soufflé Potatoes, page
316

RAGOÛT FIN [4]

A delicate and far-reaching dish.
◗ Please read About Sweet-
breads, page 537.
Prepare and drain:

1 pair poached sweetbreads

Drain and cut in two:

2 cups cooked asparagus
tips

Reserve the liquid. Melt in a
heavy skillet:

¼ cup butter

Sauté in the butter for about 3
minutes:

½ lb. mushrooms
(¼ cup chopped shallots)

Remove them from the skillet.
Add to the fat in it:

6 tablespoons butter

Add and stir until blended:

6 tablespoons flour

Stir in slowly:

3 cups liquid: milk or
cream, asparagus water
or Stock (II, 141)

When the sauce is smooth and
boiling, add gradually the
asparagus tips, the mushrooms

and the sweetbreads. ◆ Reduce
the heat. Put a small amount of
sauce in a separate pan and
beat in:

2 egg yolks

Combine the sauces and ◆ without letting them boil, stir for
about 1 minute very gently, so
as not to mash the asparagus.
Season with:

Salt and paprika
Freshly grated nutmeg

Just before serving, add:

(2 tablespoons dry sherry or
1 teaspoon Worcester-
shire sauce)

Serve the ragoût at once in:

Hot patty shells, on hot
buttered toast, in Bread
Cases, page 208, in a
baked Noodle Ring, page
173, or on hot Waffles
(II, 119)

☰ SWEETBREADS ON   [2]
SKEWERS

Preheat oven to 400°.
◆ Please read About Sweetbreads, page 537.
Soak, blanch for about 10 minutes, firm and trim:

1 pair calf sweetbreads

Break them into 1-inch chunks.
Partially cook:

Thin slices of lean bacon

enough to surround the pieces
of sweetbread. Spread:

Mushroom caps

lightly with:

Butter

Place the sweetbreads and the
mushrooms alternately on skewers. Put them over the edge of
a pan and bake for about 10
minutes or grill over charcoal
until the bacon is crisp.

ABOUT BRAINS

Calf, sheep, lamb, pork and beef
brains are listed in order of
preference. Brains may be used
in all recipes calling for sweetbreads but in both cases they
must be very fresh.

◆ To prepare them, give them
a preliminary soaking of about
3 hours in cold acidulated water
(II, 148). After skinning, soak
them in lukewarm water to free
them from all traces of blood.
Then, as they are rather mushy
in texture, firm them by again
blanching in acidulated water
to cover for about 20 minutes
for calf brains, 25 for the others.
◆ Be sure the water does not
boil. Allow 1 pound of brains
for 4 servings or 1 set for 2
servings.

Brains are often combined
with eggs or in ragoût and soufflés with sweetbreads. Because
they are bland, be sure to give
the dish in which they are used
a piquant flavoring, as suggested
below.

SAUTÉED BRAINS   [4]

◆ Please read About Brains,
above.
Prepare:

2 sets cooked brains

Cut in two, lengthwise. Dry
them between towels. Season
them with:

Salt and paprika

Roll them in:

Corn meal or flour

Melt in a skillet rubbed with:

Garlic
⅓ cup butter or bacon
grease

When the fat reaches the point
of fragrance, cook the brains on
each side for about 2 minutes.
Cover them, reduce the heat
and complete the cooking, about
10 minutes in all. Serve them
with:

Lemon wedges
Thickened Tomato
Sauce, page 376, or
Worcestershire sauce
Beurre Noir, page 383

with a few:

Capers or black olives

BAKED BRAINS [3]

♦ Please read About Brains, page 540.
Preheat oven to 400°.
Chop coarsely:

> 1 set cooked brains

Combine them with:

> ½ cup bread crumbs
> 2 chopped hard-cooked eggs
> 6 tablespoons cream
> 1 tablespoon catsup
> 2 peeled chopped green chilis
> ½ tablespoon lemon juice

Correct the seasoning
Place in a greased baking dish or in individual dishes. Sprinkle the top with:

> Au Gratin II, page 389

Bake for about 15 minutes.

BAKED BRAINS AND [4] EGGS

♦ Please read About Brains, page 540.
Preheat oven to 350°.
Cut into 1-inch dice:

> 2 sets cooked brains

Place them in 4 small greased casseroles.
Peel, seed and dice:

> 4 tomatoes

Combine them with:

> 1½ tablespoons hot olive oil
> 1 teaspoon chopped parsley
> 1 teaspoon chopped onion or chives
> Salt and paprika
> 1 teaspoon brown sugar

Pour these ingredients into the casseroles.
Break into each one:

> 1 egg

Bake for about 5 minutes until the eggs are firm. Melt and brown lightly:

> ¼ cup butter

Add:

> 2 teaspoons lemon juice

Pour this over the eggs. Garnish with:

> Parsley

Serve at once.

BROILED BRAINS

♦ Please read About Brains, page 540.
Preheat broiler.
Brush:

> Cooked brains

with:

> Oil or melted butter

Dust with:

> Paprika

Place the broiler about 6 inches from the source of heat and broil the brains for about 8 minutes on each side or until done. Baste with oil or butter. Serve piping hot with:

> Broiled Bacon, page 492
> Chopped parsley and lemon wedges

or

> Grilled Tomato Slices, page 333
> Water Cress

ABOUT KIDNEYS

Veal kidneys are the most delicious. Those of lamb are somewhat soft and flat in flavor, but especially suitable for grilling. Large beef kidneys tend to be hard and strong in flavor. Soak them first for 2 hours in cold salted water. Off-flavors may be withdrawn either by blanching, page 88, in acidulated water or by drying after soaking and sautéing briefly over brisk heat, after which the kidneys are allowed to cool partially before cooking.

Beef, mutton and pork kidneys, which are prepared as for beef, are most often used in terrines, braises and stews where very slow cooking helps make them tender.

The white membrane should be snipped from all kidneys before they are washed. Curved scissors makes the job easier. Another way to remove the membrane conveniently is to sauté the kidneys first for about 1 minute in fat. Discard the fat.

◗ To prepare for broiling, almost halve them and keep from curling during cooking by skewering them open. Expose the cut side first to the heat.

Veal and lamb kidneys should be cooked for as short a time as possible over medium heat. ◗ Do not overcook. The center should be slightly pink. If kidneys are of the best quality, pan juices may be used. If not, discard the juices and use freshly melted butter or wine sauce. In any case, ◗ never allow kidneys to boil in a sauce, as this only hardens them. Pour the hot sauce over them or toss them in it for a moment or two.

Beef, mutton and pork kidneys need slow, moist cooking which is described in some of the following recipes. Allow 1 medium veal, 2 or 3 lamb, 1½ to 2 mutton, ½ beef or 1 small pork kidney per person. The veal kidney is surrounded by delicious delicate fat which you can use for seasoning or render for deep-fat frying, pages 75–79. If kidneys are to be ◗ flambéed, never do it for more than 1 minute. Longer exposure to this high heat will toughen them.

BAKED VEAL KIDNEYS

◗ Please read About Kidneys, page 541.
Preheat oven to 300°.
Note for the lone housekeeper: 1 kidney makes a fine little roast for 1 person. Prepare and bake kidneys, leaving the fat on.
Place in a pan, fat side up:
    Veal kidneys
Bake them uncovered until tender, about 1 hour.

KIDNEY NUGGETS   [2]

◗ Please read About Kidneys, page 541.
Preheat oven to 375°.

Prepare for cooking and slice in half:
    4 lamb kidneys
Prepare:
    Dressing for Stuffed
    Pork Chops, page 512
adding:
    1 beaten egg
Spread the dressing on:
    8 slices of thin lean bacon
Wrap the spread bacon around the kidney halves and fasten it with a toothpick. Bake about 20 minutes.

SAUTÉED KIDNEYS   [3]

This could be called Kidneys Bercy because it has both shallots and dry white wine.
◗ Please read About Kidneys, page 541.
Remove some of the fat from:
    3 veal kidneys
Cut them crosswise into slices, removing all the white tissue.
Rub a pan with:
    (Garlic)
Melt in it:
    ¼ cup butter
Sauté in the butter until golden:
    ½ cup sliced onions or
    shallots
Remove the onions and keep hot. Then sauté the kidneys in the hot fat, a quick process, about 5 minutes. Add the onions and season with:
    Salt and paprika
    1 tablespoon lemon juice
    or ¼ cup dry white wine
You may serve this flambé, page 80, with:
    Mushrooms on toast

SAUTÉED KIDNEYS   [4]
WITH CELERY AND
MUSHROOMS

If you can get very young fresh kidneys and follow this recipe closely, you may imagine yourself—for a mealtime—in France.
◗ Please read About Kidneys, page 541.
Prepare:

8 lamb kidneys

Skin and quarter them. Sprinkle them with:

Lemon juice

Heat:

3 tablespoons butter or drippings

Sauté lightly in this:

1 cup chopped celery
¼ cup chopped onion

Add the kidneys. ◗ Simmer them covered for about 5 minutes. Stir in:

1 tablespoon flour
1 cup hot Stock (II, 141)

When these ingredients are blended, add:

½ lb. chopped mushrooms

Season the kidneys lightly with:

Paprika
Worcestershire sauce

Simmer them covered for about 15 minutes. Add:

2 tablespoons dry sherry
1 tablespoon chopped parsley
Correct the seasoning

and serve.

▤ BROILED KIDNEYS

[Allow 1 Kidney per Person]
◗ Please read About Kidneys, page 541.

Preheat broiler.

Remove most of the fat from:

Veal kidneys

Cut them crosswise into slices. Broil them for about 5 minutes or until done. Turn them, baste with:

Melted butter

and broil for about 5 minutes longer. Season with:

Lemon juice
Salt and paprika

BROILED BEEF   [2]
KIDNEYS, TOMATOES AND ONIONS

◗ Please read About Kidneys, page 541.

Soak and blanch, page 88, in acidulated water for about 20 minutes or until tender:

A beef kidney

Cut it into ⅛-inch slices.

Preheat broiler.

Meanwhile, simmer until nearly tender:

Sliced onions

in:

Milk or water

Drain these ingredients. Dry them between towels. Grease an ovenproof dish. Arrange the kidneys and onions upon it with:

Thick slices tomato

Season the vegetables with:

Salt and pepper

Dot them and the meat with:

Butter

Place the broiler pan about 6 inches from the heat source and broil until the tomatoes are done. Dust with:

Finely chopped parsley

▤ KIDNEYS EN BROCHETTE

[Individual Serving]
◗ Please read About Kidneys, page 541.

Prepare for cooking, allowing per serving:

1 veal or 3 lamb kidneys

Blanch in:

Milk or cold water and lemon juice

about 2 to 3 minutes or until tender. Dry. Cut in quarters. Wrap in:

Bacon

Arrange on skewers and broil 3 inches from the heat source, about 3 minutes. Turn and broil 3 minutes more. Serve at once.

VEAL KIDNEY   [4]
CASSEROLE

◗ Please read About Kidneys, page 541.

Preheat oven to 350°.

Wash and core:

4 veal kidneys

Skin and dice after heating them for about 1 minute in:

2 tablespoons fat

Discard the fat. Put the kidneys in a heated ovenproof dish. Then heat in a skillet:

1 tablespoon butter

Sauté in the butter:

¼ to ½ lb. sliced mushrooms
2 tablespoons minced onion or ¼ clove garlic
1 tablespoon minced parsley

Stir and cook these ingredients for about 2 minutes. Stir in:

3 tablespoons flour

Stir in:

1 cup boiling veal or light stock

Bring these ingredients to the boiling point. Add:

¼ cup dry white wine or ½ cup orange juice
Correct the seasoning

Pour these ingredients into the casserole. Cover it closely. Bake for about 20 minutes or until tender. If you want to reduce the juices slightly, remove the kidneys and keep warm, then pour the thickened hot gravy over them. Have ready, by cutting into triangles:

4 thick slices bread

Sprinkle them with:

Grated cheese

Place them on top of the kidneys. Broil them until the cheese is melted.

KIDNEY STEW   [4]

A favorite for Sunday breakfast. ♦ Please read About Kidneys, page 541.
Cut away all the white tissue from:

2 small beef kidneys

Drop them into acidulated water to cover and blanch, page 88, for 30 minutes or until tender. Remove the kidneys from the liquid and cool them. For easier slicing, you may place them in a covered dish in the refrigerator. When cold, cut the meat into wafer-thin slices. Melt:

1 or 2 tablespoons butter

Sauté the kidneys lightly in the hot butter. Remove the kidneys and keep them warm. Stir into the drippings:

1½ to 2 tablespoons flour

Pour in:

1 cup stock or ½ cup stock and ½ cup beer

Stir until the gravy is smooth and boiling. Flavor by adding:

1 slice lemon or 2 tablespoons tomato paste
Salt and paprika, as needed

Toss the kidneys in the hot sauce and serve on:

Noodles, page 192, toast or Corn Meal Waffles (II, 121)

Garnished with:

Chopped parsley

ABOUT TONGUE

No matter from which source—beef, calf, lamb or pork—the smaller-size tongues are usually preferable. The most commonly used and best flavored, whether fresh, smoked or pickled, is beef tongue. For prime texture, it should be under 3 pounds. ♦ Scrub the tongue well. If it is smoked or pickled, you may wish to blanch it first, page 88, simmering for about 10 minutes. Immerse the tongue in cold water. After draining, put it into seasoned boiling water to cover. ♦ Reduce the heat immediately and simmer uncovered 2 to 3 hours or until tender.

If the tongue is to be served hot, drain it from the hot water, plunge it into cold water for a moment so you can handle it, skin it and trim it by removing the roots, small bones and gristle and return it very briefly to the hot cooking water to reheat before serving.

If the tongue is to be served cold, take the pot from the heat when the tongue is tender, remove the tongue and allow it to cool just enough to handle comfortably. It skins easily at this point ◗ but not if you let it get cold. Trim it and return it to the pot to cool completely in the cooking liquor. It is attractive served with Chaud-Froid Sauce, page 388, or in the Aspic, page 546.

◗ To carve tongue, cut nearly through at the hump parallel to the base. But toward the tip, better-looking slices can be made if the cut is diagonal.

BOILED FRESH BEEF TONGUE [6 to 8]

◗ Please read About Tongue, page 544.
Place in a kettle:
    A fresh beef or calf
    tongue: about 2 lbs.
Peel and add:
    2 medium-sized onions
    1 large carrot
    3 or more ribs celery with
    leaves
    6 sprigs parsley
    8 peppercorns
Barely cover these ingredients with boiling water. Simmer the tongue uncovered until it is tender, about 3 hours for beef, about 2 hours for calf. Drain it. Skin and trim the tongue. Serve it with:
    Mustard Sauce, page 363
    Piquant Sauce, page 367
    Hot Vinaigrette Sauce,
    page 341
    Harvard Beets, page 270
    Horseradish, capers or
    chopped pickle

BEEF TONGUE WITH RAISIN SAUCE

An undemanding dish to prepare while working on other things in the kitchen.

◗ Please read About Tongue, page 544.
Cook, as in previous recipe:
    A fresh beef tongue,
    boiled
After it has been skinned and trimmed, place it where it will keep hot.
Sauce:
Blanch, page 88, and split:
    ½ cup almonds
Place them in:
    2 cups water
and simmer for 20 minutes. Add and simmer for ½ hour longer:
    ⅔ cup seedless raisins
Drain the sauce. Reserve the liquid. Melt:
    6 tablespoons fat from the
    tongue stock or butter
Stir in until blended:
    3 tablespoons flour
Stir in gradually:
    The raisins, almond
    liquid and tongue stock
    to make 3 cups liquid
    in all
    ¼ cup crushed ginger snaps
    (2 teaspoons Caramel II
    (II, 169))
Add the almonds, raisins and:
    1 teaspoon grated lemon
    rind
    Correct the seasoning
Serve the tongue with:
    A Rice or Noodle Ring,
    pages 173, and 174, filled
    with green peas

BOILED CORNED OR PICKLED TONGUE

Keeps better in a refrigerator than ham and is a less usual emergency dish.
◗ Please read About Tongue, page 544. If the tongue is very salty, soak it or blanch it, page 88, in cold water to cover for several hours. Prepare as for Fresh Beef Tongue, Boiled, above, using:
    A corned or pickled
    beef tongue

BOILED SMOKED TONGUE [6 to 8]

◗ Please read About Tongue, page 544.

Cover with cold water and soak in a cool place for 12 hours or blanch, page 88:

> A 2-lb. smoked beef tongue

Drain, then cover the tongue with:

> Fresh water

Add:

> 1 sliced or whole onion stuck with 3 cloves
> ½ cup chopped celery with leaves
> 3 bay leaves
> 1 teaspoon peppercorns

Simmer it uncovered until it is tender, from 2 to 4 hours. Skin and trim, as directed. Slice and serve hot with:

> Creamed Spinach, page 326
> Horseradish Sauce, page 362

or cold in:

> Aspic, page 546

TONGUE BAKED IN CREOLE SAUCE [6]

◗ Please read About Tongue, page 544.

Cook:

> A fresh or smoked tongue, about 1½ lbs., or 2 veal or 8 lamb tongues

Skin and trim as directed.
Preheat oven to 375°.
Prepare:

> Creole Sauce, page 380

Place the drained tongue, sliced or unsliced, in a casserole. Pour the sauce over it. Bake it covered for ½ hour. Serve it with:

> Chopped parsley

TONGUE IN ASPIC [8]

A fine-looking dish.
Cook:

> A Smoked Beef Tongue, above

Leave it in the stock until it is cool, then prepare it as directed. Make the following aspic. Soak:

> 1½ tablespoons gelatin

in:

> ½ cup cold beef stock

Dissolve it in:

> 2½ cups boiling beef stock
> ½ cup dry white wine or the juice of 2 lemons
> 1 tablespoon sugar
> Salt, if required
> A few drops Caramel II (II, 169), or commercial coloring
> 1 teaspoon Worcestershire sauce

Chill the aspic and, when it is about to set, add:

> ½ cup chopped sweet-sour pickles
> 1 cup chopped celery
> ½ cup chopped green peppers

Have ready a mold or bread pan moistened with cold water. Place a small amount of aspic in the bottom of the mold. If desired, mold into this carrots, cooked beets, canned mushrooms, etc. Put the tongue into the mold and pour the remaining aspic around and over it. When well chilled, unmold the aspic on a platter. Garnish it with:

> Lettuce leaves
> Deviled eggs
> Parsley
> Slices of lemon

Serve it with:

> Mayonnaise or see Mayonnaise Collée, page 387

ABOUT HEART

Heart, which is firm and rather dry, is best prepared by slow cooking. In texture, it more nearly resembles muscle than organ meat and so may be used in many recipes calling for ground meat. An especially good way to prepare heart is to stuff it with a savory dressing. Before cooking, wash it well, removing fat, arteries, veins and blood and dry carefully. A 4- to 5-lb. beef heart will serve 6, a veal heart will serve 1.

BAKED STUFFED HEART [3]

◗ Please read About Heart, page 546.
Preheat oven to 325°.
Prepare:

A small beef heart or
3 veal hearts

Tie with a string to hold its shape if necessary. Place on a rack in an ovenproof dish and pour over it:

2 cups stock or diluted tomato soup

Place over the heart:

4 slices bacon

Cover the dish closely and bake until tender—if beef, a matter of 3 to 4 hours, if veal, about 2 hours. Remove the heart to a plate and cool it slightly. Heat in a double boiler, then fill the heart cavity with:

Apple and Onion
Dressing, page 563, or
Olive and Celery
Dressing, page 562

You will need about 1 cup for a veal heart, about 3 cups for a beef heart. ◗ To allow for expansion, do not pack the dressing tightly. Sprinkle the heart with:

Paprika

Return it to a 400° oven long enough to heat quickly before serving. The drippings may be thickened with:

Flour, see Pan Gravy,
page 358

HEART EN PAPILLOTE [3]

Preheat oven to 400°.
Prepare:

Baked Stuffed Heart,
this page

using a small beef heart. Before cooking wrap it in greased parchment paper, as shown on page 83. Put the wrapped heart on a rack in the oven. ◗ Reduce the heat at once to 300° and continue to bake for 2½ to 3 hours. About 15 minutes before serving, remove the paper and discard it. Baste the heart for about 10 minutes, allowing it to glaze in the drippings. Thicken the drippings with:

Flour, see Pan Gravy,
page 358

and serve.

BRAISED HEART SLICES IN SOUR SAUCE [6]

A homey treat.
◗ Please read About Heart, page 546.
Prepare:

A 4 to 5 lb. beef heart
or 6 veal hearts

If veal, you may halve the heart, if beef, cut it across the fiber into ¼-inch slices. Pour into a saucepan or ovenproof dish to the depth of ¾ inch:

Boiling water

Add:

¼ cup diced carrots
¼ cup chopped celery with leaves
¼ cup sliced onion
½ teaspoon salt
(¼ cup diced green pepper)

Place the heart slices on a rack in the pan, well above the water. Cover closely. Steam the meat until tender for about 1½ hours. Strain the stock. Chill and degrease it. Save the fat. Reserve the stock. Melt:

3 tablespoons butter or fat
from the stock

Stir in:

3 tablespoons flour

Then add:

1½ cups stock

When it reaches a boil, add the meat and vegetables and ◗ reduce the heat. You may add:

2 tablespoons lemon juice
or dry wine
½ teaspoon sweet marjoram
or 2 tablespoons chopped
parsley or olives
Correct the seasoning

Good with Spoon Bread (II,
279), rice or Potato Dumplings,
page 180.

ABOUT TRIPE

If you start from scratch, cooking tripe is a long-drawn-out
affair—as you will see by the
following description. But today
you will find almost everywhere
that you can buy it partially
precooked, so that your job is
just the final seasoning and heating. Using the following recipes,
you need only cook it about ½
hour, as in Spanish Tripe.

Tripe is the muscular lining
of beef stomach. There are 4
kinds, all of which, as you will
note, are used in at least one
classic recipe. The fat part of
the belly, called in France "gras
double," usually comes already
cooked. Then there are 3 different sections of honeycomb tripe
which comes from the second
stomach of beef—the extremity
of the belly, which is only partially honeycombed, the dark
and the light.

Fresh whole tripe calls for a
minimum of 12 hours of cooking,
some time-honored recipes demanding as much as 24. Sometimes tripe is pickled after cooking and served hot or cold in a
marinade.

▶ To prepare fresh tripe, trim
if necessary. ▶ Wash it thoroughly, soaking overnight, and
blanch it, page 88, for ½ hour
in salted water. Wash well again,
drain and cut for cooking. When
cooked, the texture of tripe
should be like that of soft gristle.
More often, alas, because the
heat has not been kept low

enough, it has the consistency of
wet shoe leather.

COOKED TRIPE   [4 to 5]

▶ Please read About Tripe,
opposite.
Trim, wash, soak, blanch, wash
again and drain:
2 lbs. fresh honeycomb
tripe
Cut it into 1½- to 2-inch squares.
Have ready a heavy pot that
you can lid tightly later. Add to:
Enough water to cover
¼ teaspoon salt
¼ teaspoon sugar
1 clove garlic
⅔ cup chopped onion
1 cup chopped mixed celery
and parsley
4 peppercorns
Bring to a boil and add the tripe.
▶ Reduce the heat at once. Seal
the lid with a strip of pastry
or tape (II, 293), and simmer
for 12 hours. When the tripe is
tender, you may serve it with:
Pan Gravy, page 358
seasoned with:
Salt
½ teaspoon mustard
1 teaspoon Worcestershire
sauce

TRIPE À LA MODE DE   [8]
CAEN

This famous Normandy dish demands a deep earthenware casserole and the inclusion of all 4
types of beef tripe.
▶ Please read About Tripe, this
page.
Preheat oven to 250°.
Trim, wash, soak, blanch, wash
again, drain and cut into 1½-
inch squares:
3 lbs. fresh tripe
Wash and blanch:
A split calf's foot
Peel and slice:
2 lbs. onions
Dice:
¼ lb. beef suet
Line the bottom of the casserole

with a layer of onions, then a layer of tripe and a sprinkling of the beef suet. Continue to build successive layers, topping with the split calf's foot and:

> An onion stuck with
> 3 cloves
> A bay leaf
> A Bouquet Garni
> (II, 220)

Pour over this:

> ¼ cup brandy

or, if you can get it:

> ¼ cup Calvados

and enough:

> Cider or water

t cover all the ingredients. Bring just to a boil. Seal the casserole with a strip of Pastry Dough (II, 293). Bake in the oven at least 12 hours. When ready to serve, break the seal on the casserole, remove the bouquet garni, the bay leaf and the whole onion. Degrease the sauce and pick the meat from the calf's foot. Return the meat to the casserole to heat through and serve the tripe in individual hot covered casseroles, garnished with:

> Boiled parsley potatoes

FRIED TRIPE

◗ Please read About Tripe, page 548.

Cut into squares or strips:

> Cooked Tripe, page 548, or precooked tripe

Sprinkle with:

> Salt and paprika

Dip it into:

> Fritter Batter for Meat
> (II, 125)

Fry in deep fat, pages 75–79. Serve with:

> Tartare Sauce, page 349

SPANISH TRIPE

◗ Please read About Tripe, page 548.

Wash partially precooked:

> Tripe

Follow the directions for Cooked Tripe, page 548, and add to the vegetables:

> 1 cup more or less tomato
> purée
> A few grains cayenne
> 1 teaspoon Worcestershire
> sauce

Simmer at least ½ hour and add for the last 15 minutes:

> ½ cup cooked minced ham
> ½ cup sliced mushrooms

Good served with:

> Boiled Rice, page 158

LAMB FRIES   [2]

Skin, cut into quarters:

> 4 medium lamb fries

You may marinate them for about 1 hour in:

> (¼ cup olive oil)
> (2 tablespoons lemon juice)

If you marinated them, dry them before rolling them in:

> Bounding Bread
> (II, 160)

Sauté until golden brown in:

> ¼ cup butter

Garnish with:

> Fried Parsley, page 305

and serve with:

> Tomato sauce

CALF OR LAMB HEAD

[4 Servings for a Calf Head—
2 Servings for Lamb]

It is always so easy to say, "Let the butcher prepare, etc." In this case, it is assumed that the head is skinned and the eyes removed. The head is split the long way, so the brains can be removed. We prefer to cook the Brains, page 540, and the Tongue, page 345, separately. Scrape away any clots. Soak overnight in salted cold water to cover:

> 1 calf or lamb head

Wash again in cold water. You may dry the head and brown it in butter or put in a large kettle and bring to a boil:

Enough water to cover
the head

with:

    1 carrot
    1 onion
    ½ sliced lemon
    1 bay leaf
    4 cloves
    1 tablespoon salt
    ¼ teaspoon pepper

In actuality you may also add,
to keep the bones white:

    (½ cup veal kidney fat or
    suet)

When this reaches a boil, add
the head. ♦ Reduce the heat at
once and simmer uncovered until
the meat is tender, about 1 hour
for lamb, about 2 hours for calf.
If you have included the tongue,
it may take a little longer. When
the meat is tender, drain and
remove it from the bones and
dice it. Keep the meat warm.
Skin, trim and slice the tongue.
Meanwhile prepare a double
portion of:

    Rosemary Wine Sauce,
    page 369

using as stock the liquid in
which the calf head was cooked.

    Correct the seasoning

You may want to spice the sauce
with:

    Mild white wine vinegar,
    lemon juice or wine

Reheat the meat, the tongue and
the cooked brains in the sauce.
♦ Do not boil. Serve this dish
garnished with:

    Chopped parsley

It is sometimes served with the
addition at the last moment
of:

    ½ cup scalded cream

Or part of the sauce is drained
off into:

    2 beaten egg yolks

Return this mixture to the pot.
Heat, but do not boil, the sauce
after adding the yolks. But ♦ if
you add cream or egg yolks, to
avoid curdling do not add lemon,
vinegar or wine until the last
moment.

HEAD CHEESE   [4]
OR BRAWN

A well-liked old-fashioned dish.
Quarter:

    A calf head

Clean teeth with a stiff brush,
remove ears, brains, eyes, snout
and most of the fat. Soak the
quarters about 6 hours in cold
water to extract the blood. Wash
them. Cover with cold water, to
which you may add:

    2 onions
    5 celery stalks

Simmer until the meat is ready
to fall from the bones, about 2
to 3 hours. Drain but reserve
stock. Chip the meat off the
bones. Dice it. Cover it well with
the stock. Reserve the brains.
Now add:

    Salt
    Pepper
    Herbs

Cook for ½ hour. Pour into a
mold and cover with a cloth.
Put a weight on top. Chill. Serve,
cut into slices, with:

    Vinaigrette Sauce,
    page 341

to which you have added the
diced cooked brains.

CALF LUNGS   [6]
OR LIGHTS

Cut into julienne strips, wash
well and simmer in stock until
just tender, about 1½ hours:

    3 lbs. calf lungs

Remove lungs and keep warm.
Reduce the stock by ½, adding:

    A Bouquet Garni (II,
    220), of bayleaf, thyme
    and lemon rind

Brown in a heavy skillet:

    ½ cup flour
    1 teaspoon sugar

Add:

    ½ cup butter

Stir until smooth and add:

    ½ cup finely minced onion

Strain the reduced stock and add
it gradually to the flour mixture.
Cook and stir until thickened.

Add:

> 1 tablespoon anchovy paste

Preheat oven to 325°.

Put the cooked lungs in a casserole. Cover with the sauce. Cover the whole tightly with a lid. Bake for about ½ hour. Before serving

> Correct the seasoning

and stir in gently:

> 1 cup cream or cultured
>   sour cream
> 1 tablespoon capers

Continue to bake until cream is heated through.

CHITTERLINGS [6 to 7]

We were well along in years before we discovered that the name of this dish had an "e," an "r," a "g"—and 3 syllables. Just after slaughtering, empty the large intestines of a young pig while still warm by turning them inside out and scraping as clean as possible. Soak 24 hours in cold salted water to cover. Then wash in 5 or 6 waters. Remove excess fat, but leave some for flavor. To:

> 10 lbs. chitterlings

allow:

> 1 garlic clove
> ½ sliced lemon
> ½ teaspoon salt
> ½ teaspoon pepper
> ½ teaspoon each thyme,
>   clove, mace and allspice
> 1 bay leaf
> ¼ cup sliced onions
> (3 red pepper pods)
> 2 tablespoons fresh parsley
> 2 tablespoons white wine
>   vinegar
> Enough cold water to
>   cover

Add:

> Chitterlings, cut up in
>   2-inch lengths

Bring slowly to a boil. ◆ Reduce the heat at once and simmer for about 3 hours. During the last 30 minutes of cooking, you may add:

> (¼ cup tomato catsup)
> Correct the seasoning

and serve with:

> Corn Bread (II, 277)
> Cole Slaw, page 36

SAUTÉED CHITTERLINGS

Prepare previous recipe for:

> Chitterlings

omitting the vinegar and catsup. Drain and dry well. Dip in:

> Seasoned flour

Sauté them gently in:

> Butter

until a delicate brown.

STEWED PIGS' FEET [4]

Wash, leave whole or split in halves and blanch, page 88:

> 4 pigs' or calves' feet

You may wrap them in cheesecloth to retain their shape. Cover them with water. Bring just to a boil. ◆ Reduce the heat at once and simmer for about 4 hours uncovered. During the last 30 minutes of simmering, add:

> 1½ to 2 lbs. green beans,
>   cabbage or sauerkraut

Cook the vegetables until they are tender.

> Correct the seasoning

and serve hot.

JELLIED PIGS' OR [6]
CALVES' FEET

Wash, leave whole or split in halves and blanch, page 88:

> 6 pigs' or calves' feet

You may wrap them in cheesecloth to retain their shape. Cover them with water. Add:

> 1 large sliced onion
> 1 cut clove garlic
> 1 sliced lemon
> 2 bay leaves
> 3 or 4 whole black
>   peppercorns
> 6 or 8 whole cloves

Bring this mixture to the boiling point. ◆ Reduce the heat and simmer uncovered for about 4 hours. Add boiling water, if

needed. Strain the stock through
a sieve and reserve it. Remove
the skin and the bones from the
pigs' feet. Place the meat in the
stock. Season to taste with:

>　White vinegar or
>　　dry wine

and

>　Correct the seasoning

Chop and add:

>　(1 pimiento, decorative but
>　　optional)

Pour the pigs' or calves' feet
into a mold and chill until the
stock is firm.

BAKED PIGS' FEET

Prepare:

>　Stewed Pigs' Feet, page
>　551

Preheat oven to 375°.
Cut the pigs' feet in two, lengthwise. Roll them in:

>　Melted butter

then in:

>　Corn meal or cracker
>　crumbs

Bake them about 20 to 30 minutes or until tender. Serve with:

>　Sweet-sour Beets, page
>　270, or lemon wedges

BRAISED OXTAILS　　[5 to 6]

Preheat oven to 350°.
Cut into joints:

>　2 oxtails

Melt in a skillet:

>　¼ cup butter or beef
>　drippings

Sauté the oxtail sections until
they are browned. Season them
with:

>　Salt and paprika

Add:

>　2 cups boiling Brown
>　Stock I (II, 141), or
>　tomato juice

Bring these ingredients to the
boiling point. Place them in a
casserole. Cover it closely. Bake
until the oxtails are tender, 3 to
5 hours. Add additional stock,
as needed. For the last 45 minutes of cooking, add:

>　8 small peeled onions
>　½ cup diced celery
>　¼ cup peeled diced carrots

When the oxtails are tender,
strain the stock from them. Skim
off most of the fat. Thicken the
stock with:

>　Flour, see Pan Gravy,
>　page 358
>　Correct the seasoning

Return the meat, the vegetables
and the gravy to the casserole.
Serve with a platter of:

>　Noodles, page 172

Cover the noodles with:

>　Au Gratin II, page 389

VARIETY MEAT　　　　[4]
PATTIES

◆ Please read About Kidneys,
page 541, About Liver, page
534, or About Brains, page 540.
Prepare one of the following for
cooking and then chop until fine:

>　2 pairs steamed brains,
>　½ lb. raw liver or 1 beef,
>　2 pork or veal or 5 lamb
>　kidneys

Sprinkle them with:

>　1 tablespoon lemon juice

Rub a skillet with:

>　Garlic

Heat in it:

>　2 tablespoons butter

Sauté in this lightly:

>　1 chopped onion or leek
>　½ cup minced celery
>　2 tablespoons minced
>　green pepper

Remove from heat. Add the
chopped variety meat and:

>　¼ cup dry bread crumbs
>　¼ cup milk
>　1 egg
>　¼ teaspoon salt
>　¼ teaspoon freshly ground
>　pepper
>　4 drops Worcestershire
>　sauce
>　(¼ teaspoon caraway or dill
>　seed)

Drop this mixture by the tablespoon into a hot pan, in which
you have:

2 tablespoons hot bacon
drippings
Brown the patties lightly on
both sides. Serve them with:
  Tomato sauce, slaw or
  Vegetables à la Grecque,
  page 257

CHICKEN GIBLETS

Dice, put in boiling water or
stock, then ♦ reduce the heat at
once and simmer until tender,
about 1 hour:
  Chicken giblets: gizzards
  and hearts
You may add, for the last 15
minutes of cooking:
  Chopped green pepper
  Chopped celery
Drain these ingredients, reserving the stock. Make:
  Gravy, page 358
using:
  2 tablespoons butter
  2 tablespoons flour to 1 cup
  stock or stock and
  dry wine
  Correct the seasoning
Add the giblets and vegetables
and simmer ♦ but do not boil.
Serve on:
  Toast

COCKSCOMBS

These have been used since the
time of Apicius as a garnish.
Blanch:
  Cockscombs
Peel off the outer skin. ♦ Steam,
covered, on a:
  Mirepoix (II, 221)
moistened with:
  1 cup Mushroom Stock
  (II, 145)
until tender, about 45 to 50
minutes.

Preheat deep fryer to 375°.
Drain well, cut an incision and
stuff with:
  Duxelles (II, 220)
  Chicken Farce, page 564
Cover with:
  Allemande Sauce,
  page 362
Dip in crumbs and deep-fat fry
till crumbs color.

ABOUT MARROW

Spinal marrow, which is really
a continuation of the brain, may
be substituted in any of the
recipes for brains. Bone marrow
may be removed from split large
bones. ♦ It must not be overcooked, as it is very fat and
simply disintegrates under too
high heat. Bone marrow may be
cut into ½-inch slices and softened in the top of a double
boiler or gently and briefly
poached in a little stock, for
about 1½ to 2 minutes. You
may serve it this way for hors
d'oeuvre. It may also be gently
poached in the bone in water
barely to cover or roasted in a
300° oven for about 1 hour. See
also Marrow Balls, page 150, for
soup and Osso Buco, page 506.

MARROW

I. Cut into ¼-inch rounds:
  Marrow
Poach it gently in:
  Stock (II, 141)
for a few minutes. Drain and
serve at once on:
  Toast rounds

II. Or use raw in a:
  Sauce Bordelaise,
  page 366

GAME

ABOUT SMALL GAME

Small game such as rabbit, squirrel and muskrat may be substituted in most recipes calling for chicken. But following are some classic, and not so classic, recipes which take the special characteristics of these small animals into account. If you are a novice, the most important things to remember is ♦ never handle rabbit or any wild meat without using gloves, because of the danger of tularemia infection. ♦ Always make sure the meat of wild animals is sufficiently cooked. Be guided in your choice of recipe by the age of the animal. ♦ Use a moist heat process, page 81, for older animals.

ABOUT RABBITS AND HARES

When rabbit or hare is young and fresh, the cleft in the lip is narrow, the claws smooth and sharp. Test for the youth of the animal, also, by turning the claws sideways to see if they crack. The ears should be soft and bend easily. A young hare has a stumpy neck and long legs. To ensure tender meat, hang the animals by the feet from 1 to 4 days. They will, however, be tender without hanging if used before they have time to stiffen. Once stiffened, they are edible as long as the hind legs are rigid. Some of the most delicious game sauces use blood as a thickener. To trap and preserve the blood, see (II, 540). To incorporate it in a

sauce, see page 357. Hares may weigh up to 10 to 14 pounds. European hare is all dark meat, while American domestic hare is all white.

♦ To dress rabbit or hare, sever the front legs at the joint, as shown (page 555) by the dotted line. Cut through the skin around the hind legs, as shown again by a dotted line. Tie the feet together securely. Hang the rabbit on a hook where tied. Pull the skin down off the legs, stripping it inside out like a glove, and over the body and forelegs. Sever the head and discard it with the skin. Slit the rabbit down the front. Remove the entrails and discard them, except for the heart and liver. Wash the carcass inside and out with acidulated water—water to which 1 or 2 tablespoons of vinegar are added. Rinse and dry carefully.

RABBIT OR HARE À LA MODE, HASENPFEFFER OR CIVET

Skin:
A rabbit
Cut into pieces by severing the legs at the joints and cutting the back in 3 sections. Place the pieces in a crock or jar. Marinate refrigerated for 24 to 48 hours in:
Cooked Marinade for Game, page 380
Drain and reserve the marinade. Dry the pieces of rabbit. Dip them in:
Flour
Brown until golden in:

3 tablespoons bacon
   drippings

Remove the browned rabbit to
an ovenproof casserole.
Preheat oven to 350°.
Sauté in the pan the rabbit was
browned in:

1 cup finely sliced onions
2 tablespoons butter

Add the sauté to the casserole
with the warmed marinade and
bring to a boil on top of the
stove. ◗ Cover and remove to
oven for about 1½ hours or
until tender. Correct the seasoning. Place rabbit on a serving
dish. Pour sauce over it. Serve
with:

Noodles, page 172

SAUTÉED RABBIT

If rabbit is very young, prepare
as for:

Sautéed Chicken,
   page 577

Serve with:

Elderberry preserves

SMOTHERED RABBIT OR HARE WITH ONIONS

Skin, clean and cut into pieces:

A rabbit

Dredge with:

Seasoned flour

Melt in a pot or skillet:

3 tablespoons drippings or
   butter

Sauté the rabbit in the drippings
until browned. Cover thickly
with:

Sliced onions

Pour over them:

1 cup cultured sour cream

Cover the pot closely and simmer for 1 hour or place the pot
in a slow oven—300°—and
bake the rabbit until tender, 1
hour or more.

ROAST RABBIT OR HARE

Preheat oven to 450°.
Skin and clean:

A rabbit or hare

Stuff it with any recipe suitable
for fowl, using the sautéed
chopped liver. Close the opening and truss it. Brush the rabbit
all over with:

Melted butter or cooking
   oil

Dredge with:

Seasoned flour

Place on a rack on its side in a
roasting pan in the oven. ◗ Reduce the heat to 350°. Baste
every 15 minutes with the
drippings in the pan or, if necessary, with:

(Additional butter)

Turn the rabbit when cooking
time is about ½ over. Cook until
tender, about 1½ hours. Make:

Pan Gravy, page 358

FRICASSEE OF RABBIT OR HARE

Skin, clean and cut into pieces:

A rabbit

Dredge with:

Seasoned flour

Melt in a skillet:

    ¼ cup butter

or you may use:

    (¼ lb. diced, lightly
    rendered salt pork—a
    wonderful substitution)

Add:

    ¼ cup chopped shallots or
    onions

    (1 cup cut-up mushrooms)

Remove the shallots and mushrooms before sautéing the meat in the drippings until lightly browned. To flambé the rabbit pour over it:

    (2 oz. brandy)

Add:

    1½ cups stock or dry wine

and, in a cloth bag:

    A piece of lemon rind
    10 peppercorns
    2 sprigs parsley
    2 ribs celery with leaves

Cover the pot closely. Simmer the meat until done, 1 hour or more, or put it in a 300° oven covered for about 2 hours—but do not let it boil at any time. Ten minutes before you remove the rabbit from the pot, take out the seasoning bag and add the mushrooms and shallots. Place the rabbit on a hot serving dish. Remove the sauce from the heat and thicken with:

    Beurre Manié, page 357

ABOUT SQUIRREL

Gray squirrels are the preferred ones; red squirrels are small and quite gamey in flavor. There are, proverbially, many ways to skin a squirrel, but some hunters claim the following one is the quickest and cleanest. It needs a sharp knife.

▶ To skin, cut the tail bone through from beneath, but take care not to cut through the skin of the tail. Hold the tail as shown on the left and then cut the skin the width of the back, as shown in the dotted lines. Turn the squirrel over on its back and step on the base of the tail. Hold the hind legs in one hand and pull steadily and slowly, as shown in the center sketch, until the skin has worked itself over the front legs and head. While holding the squirrel in the same position, pull the remaining skin from the hind legs. Proceed then as for Rabbit, page 555, cutting off the head and feet and removing the internal organs, plus two small glands found in the small of the back and under each foreleg, between the ribs and the shoulders.

Stuff and roast squirrels as for Pigeons, page 590, barding them, or use them in Brunswick Stew, page 582, or prepare as for Braised Chicken, page 578. Season the gravy with:

    Walnut catsup

and serve with:

    Polenta, page 157

OPOSSUM

If possible, trap 'possum and feed it on milk and cereals for 10 days before killing. Clean, but do not skin. Treat as for pig by immersing the unskinned animal in water just below the boiling point. Test frequently by plucking at the hair. When it slips out readily, remove the 'possum from the water and scrape. While scraping repeatedly, pour cool water over the surface of the animal. Remove small red glands in small of back and under each foreleg between the shoulder and rib. Parboil, page 88, 1 hour. Roast as for pork, page 485. Serve with:

> Turnip greens

BEAR

Remove all fat from bear meat at once, as it turns rancid very quickly.

If marinated at least 24 hours in an oil-based marinade, all bear, except black bear, is edible. Cook after marination, as for any recipe for Beef Pot Roast or Stew, pages 493–505. Bear cub will need about 2½ hours' cooking; for an older animal, allow 3½ to 4 hours. Bear, like pork, can carry trichinosis, so be sure the meat is always well cooked through.

RACCOON

Skin, clean and soak overnight:

> 1 raccoon

in:

> Salt water

Scrape off all fat inside and out. Blanch, page 88, for 45 minutes. Add:

> 2 tablespoons baking soda

and continue to cook uncovered for 5 minutes. Drain and wash in warm water. Put in cold water and bring to a boil. ◗ Reduce heat and simmer 15 minutes.

Preheat oven to 350°.

Stuff the raccoon with:

> Bread Dressing, page 560

Bake covered, about 45 minutes
◗ uncover and bake 15 minutes longer before serving.

MUSKRAT [2]

Skin and remove all fat from hams of:

> 6 muskrats

Poach, page 83, for 45 minutes. Sauté until golden:

> ½ cup minced onions

in:

> 2 tablespoons butter

Add the drained, dried muskrat hams and cook until brown. Serve with:

> Creamed Celery, page 282

WOODCHUCK

Dress woodchuck as for rabbit, but watch for and remove 7 to 9 small sacs or kernels in the small of the back and under the forearm. Soak overnight in salted water. Drain and wipe dry. Cook by any recipe for rabbit or chicken.

BEAVER

Use young animals only.

Remove kernels in small of back and under forelegs, between rib and shoulder. Hang in the cold for several days. Poach in salted water for 1 hour. Braise as for beef, page 493, until tender.

BEAVER TAIL

Hold over open flame until rough skin blisters. Remove from heat. When cool, peel off skin. Roast over coals or simmer until tender.

PECCARY

Immediately after killing, remove the musk glands in the

middle of the back. This meat needs marinating before cooking. After this, you may prepare it as in any pork recipe in the section on Pot Roasts and Stews, page 493.

WILD BOAR

If very young, prepare as for:
> Suckling Pig, page 486

If older, prepare by a moist heat process for:
> Pork, page 512

ABOUT VENISON

This romantic word can cover any of the edible animals taken in the chase, but we are discussing here only antlered types. A famous sportsman called venison a gift of joy to some, a matter of secret interment to others.

Today, when hunters are so aware of the need to treat their booty with care from the moment it is shot, joy can prevail. No matter what the method of handling, certain preparations are basic. Game shot in an unsuspecting moment is more tender than game that is chased and will also deteriorate less quickly. Avoid buying any trapped animals for food. Immediate and careful gutting (II, 540), immediate removal of all hair near exposed flesh and prompt skinning are essential.

Some authorities recommend only a week of hanging, some as long as 4 weeks in 40° temperature in a cool, airy place, away from sun, screened against insects and protected from predators. Venison is lean and needs barding, page 454, or larding, page 453.

◗ Care must be taken, though, to remove all fat from any of these game animals themselves, as it grows rancid rapidly. ◗ Do not use it to grease pans or for sautéing or browning. The livers and heart are often eaten and

should be marinated under refrigeration or soaked in salt water for 12 hours or longer. As with all game, the lushness of the season and the age of the animal contribute to the decision as to how to cook it.

Moose meat, which is relatively fat, calls for cooking like pork and can also have the same sweet and sweet-sour garnishes and sauces. Elk is more like beef than any other game. Calf elk sours rapidly. Cook it as for veal.

The choice cuts of very young deer or goat and fat old bucks can be roasted or broiled as for beef. Other cuts should be marinated, drained, dried and prepared as for any moist-processed beef, see pages 494–499.

For sauces for game, see page 366. Cabbage, turnips, chestnuts and mushrooms are often suggested as classic game accompaniments, as are brandied fruits.

SADDLE OF DEER,   [8]
MOOSE OR ELK

Preheat oven to 550°.
Lard, page 453.
> A 6 to 7 lb. saddle of venison

Rub it with:
> A cut clove of garlic
> Butter

Place the roast, fat side up, uncovered on a rack in the oven.
◗ Reduce the heat to 350° and cook, allowing in all 20 minutes to the pound. Make:
> Pan Gravy, page 358

Serve with:
> Hot Cumberland Sauce, page 372
> Wild Rice, page 160

ROAST LEG OF VENISON

Bard the roast. Cook as for Beef Roast, page 453.

VENISON STEAKS

I. Have ready:
> ½-inch young venison steaks

Before frying, rub with:
> Garlic

To keep them crisp and brown on the outside, rare and juicy within, sauté them, page 79, in:
> 1 tablespoon butter
> 2 tablespoons cooking oil

5 to 6 minutes to the side. Serve with:
> Hot Cumberland Sauce, page 372

or with:
> Maître d'Hôtel Butter, page 384

or with:
> Puréed celery with croutons and Sauce Poivrade, page 368

II. Soak for 24 hours refrigerated:
> ¾-inch venison steaks

in:
> Lamb or Game Marinade, page 381

Drain and dry. Sauté and serve as for Venison Steaks I, above.

BRAISED VENISON

For this process, use the less tender cuts of meat either in 1 large piece or cut into small ones, but be sure to remove all fat. Place the meat in a marinade, page 380, from 12 to 48 hours in the refrigerator. Turn it from time to time. Dry it. Prepare as for Pot Roast, page 493. If you have marinated, use the marinade in the stock. Cook until tender—depending on the age of the animal.

VENISON HAMBURGER

To make this lean meat more interesting in ground form, combine:
> 2 parts ground venison

with:
> 1 part fresh sausage meat

Cook as for Hamburger, page 515, but allow extra time ♦ to be sure the meat is no longer pink.

VENISON MEAT LOAF

Prepare:
> Meat Loaf I, page 523

using:
> ¾ lb. ground venison
> ¼ lb. ground sausage

STUFFINGS, DRESSINGS, FARCES OR FORCEMEAT

When you get that desperate feeling that you simply must find a new species of meat—try instead combining meats or variety meats with some unusual dressing or farce. Don't save stuffings just for heavy festive meals; make them part of your daily fare.

Many foreign and old-fashioned stuffing recipes call for bread soaked in a liquid and then pressed before using. We find that most American bakery breads are already so soft in texture that soaking produces too pasty a dressing.

The quality of the crumbs is very important, so check (II, 159) to differentiate between fresh or dry. ◖ Never grind bread, as the stuffing will be too compact. It is important ◖ to stuff food just before cooking; ◖ to handle stuffings lightly so as not to compact them; and ◖ to allow space when stuffing, so the mixture can swell and stay light. Should there be extra dressing that does not fit the cavity of fish, fowl or roast, cook it separately in a greased baking dish.

A useful rule of thumb in judging the amount of stuffing needed is ◖ to allow ½ cup of stuffing for each pound of bird or fish.

◖ Never use raw pork in dressings. Dressings are done when they reach an internal temperature of 165° to 170°.

For stuffings for vegetables, see individual stuffed vegetable recipes and page 256.

BREAD DRESSING WITH MUSHROOMS, OYSTERS, NUTS, GIBLETS, ETC.

[About 5 Cups]

There is no set rule for the proportions of ingredients in bread dressing. It should be palatable, light and slightly moist, well flavored but bland. Chopped green peppers, nut meats, sautéed mushrooms and drained or slightly sautéed oysters may be added to it. Stock or oyster liquor may be substituted for milk.

Chop:
    Giblets
Melt:
    ¼ cup butter
Add and sauté for about 2 minutes:
    (2 tablespoons or more chopped onion)
and the chopped giblets. Combine these ingredients with:
    4 cups crustless day-old or slightly toasted, diced white, whole wheat or corn bread crumbs
    ¼ cup chopped parsley
    ¼ to 1 cup chopped celery
    1 teaspoon dried tarragon or basil
    ¾ teaspoon salt
    ½ teaspoon paprika
    ⅛ teaspoon nutmeg
    Milk, stock or melted butter to moisten the dressing very lightly
    (2 or 3 eggs)

You may add:

   1½ cups nut meats: Brazil,
      pine, pecans, walnuts
and one of the following:
   1 cup browned sausage
      meat
   1 cup or more sliced
      mushrooms, sautéed with
      onion
   1 cup chopped or whole
      drained oysters
   1 cup chopped or whole
      soft-shell clams
   1 cup cooked chopped
      shrimp

DRY DRESSING

This name is given by our cook, Sarah Brown, to a dressing she frequently makes, which is by no means dry when served. Proportions seem to be of little importance here, as the ingredients are never measured and the dressing always turns out light and good. Chopped pecans, oysters, olives, etc., may be added to it.
Make of day-old white, graham or whole wheat bread:

      Soft bread crumbs, as
      sketched on (II, 159)
Combine with:
      Chopped celery
      Chopped onion
Season with:
      Salt and paprika
Partly fill chicken, quail or turkey with the dressing. Melt:
   ¾ to 1 cup butter
Pour ½ of it onto the dressing in the cavity. Fill it lightly with the remaining dressing and pour the remaining butter on it. Sew up the opening.

SHERRY BREAD DRESSING

[1½ Cups]
Soak for 10 minutes:
   1 cup bread crumbs
in:
   ½ cup dry sherry
Wring the wine from the bread. Stir and sauté for 3 minutes:

   ¼ cup finely chopped green
      pepper
   ½ cup finely chopped onion
in:
   3 tablespoons butter
Add the bread crumbs and:
   2 teaspoons chili sauce
   ½ cup canned or Sautéed
      Mushrooms, page 296
   2 tablespoons chopped
      parsley

OYSTER BREAD DRESSING

[2½ Cups]
Enough for a 4-lb. fish or the crop of a turkey.
Melt:
   6 tablespoons butter
Sauté in the butter until brown:
   ¼ cup chopped onion
Add:
   1 tablespoon chopped
      parsley
   2 cups bread crumbs
   1 cup drained whole or
      chopped oysters: ½ pint
   ¾ teaspoon salt
   ¼ teaspoon paprika
   2 tablespoons capers
   (½ cup drained chopped
      spinach)

BREAD DRESSING FOR FISH

[2 Cups]
A fine but plain, unsophisticated dressing. Combine:
   1½ cups bread crumbs
   2 tablespoons chopped
      onion
   ½ cup chopped celery
   2 tablespoons chopped
      parsley
   1 or 2 beaten eggs
Season these ingredients well with:
   ½ teaspoon salt
   ⅛ teaspoon paprika
   ½ teaspoon dried tarragon
      or dill seed
   2 tablespoons capers
   (¼ teaspoon nutmeg)
Use enough:

Milk, melted butter or
soup stock

to make a loose dressing.

GREEN DRESSING FOR FISH OR FOWL

[About 1½ Cups]

This has a tempting pistachio green color. Sauté until transparent:

    2 tablespoons chopped
      shallots

in:

    2 tablespoons butter

Cool slightly. Place this in a blender and ⋏ blend to a paste with:

    1 egg
    ½ cup tender celery with
      leaves
    ½ cup parsley tops
    ½ cup water cress tops
    ½ cup crumbled crustless
      bread
    ½ teaspoon salt
    ⅛ teaspoon dried basil

Blend in with a fork:

    ½ cup pulled crustless
      bread crumbs (II, 159)
    ¼ cup pistachio nuts or
      sliced water chestnuts

SAUSAGE DRESSING

[About 2½ Cups]

Heat and stir in a skillet:

    ½ cup sausage meat

Drain off the surplus fat. Add:

    ½ cup chopped celery
    2 cups cracker crumbs
    ¼ teaspoon minced onion
    ¼ teaspoon salt
    ⅛ teaspoon paprika
    (½ cup chopped tart apples)

Moisten the dressing with:

    ½ cup stock

CHESTNUT DRESSING FOR GAME

[About 4 Cups]

Rice:

    2½ cups cooked chestnuts,
      page 283

Combine them with:

    ½ cup melted butter
    1 teaspoon salt
    ⅛ teaspoon pepper
    ¼ cup cream
    1 cup dry bread or cracker
      crumbs
    2 tablespoons chopped
      parsley
    ½ cup chopped celery
    (1 tablespoon grated onion
      or ¼ cup seedless
      raisins)

You may add, but remember this will increase the amount:

    ½ cup liver sausage, ¼ cup
      chopped Chipolata
      sausage or 2 cups raw
      or creamed oysters

ONION DRESSING

[About 4 Cups]

Prepare:

    2 cups chopped onions

Drop them in:

    4 cups boiling salted water

Simmer for 10 minutes. Drain. Mix the onions and:

    3 cups dry bread crumbs
    1 beaten egg
    ½ cup melted butter
    ¾ teaspoon salt
    ⅛ teaspoon paprika
    ½ teaspoon poultry
      seasoning
    (1 cup chopped tart apple
      or ½ cup sliced olives)

Moisten the mixture slightly with:

    Stock

FENNEL DRESSING

[About 1 Cup]

Brown:

    1 cup bread crumbs

in:

    1 tablespoon butter
    1 teaspoon Meat Glaze
      (II, 145)

Cut into julienned strips:

    1 carrot
    1 white base of leek
    2 stalks celery

Add the above to the butter mixture. Add:

2 drops garlic juice

and simmer until coated. Add:

A sprig of chopped fresh fennel

1 small pinch thyme and bay leaf

¼ teaspoon salt

Mix with the crumbs:

Freshly ground pepper

APPLE AND PRUNE DRESSING

[About 4½ Cups]

Combine lightly:

3 cups diced crustless bread

½ cup melted butter or drippings

1 cup cubed apples

¾ cup chopped cooked prunes

½ cup chopped nut meats

1 teaspoon salt

½ teaspoon paprika

1 tablespoon lemon juice

APPLE AND ONION DRESSING

[About 12 Cups]

Place in boiling water for 5 minutes:

1 cup raisins

Drain well. Add them to:

7 cups soft bread crumbs

Melt:

¾ cup butter

Sauté in it for 3 minutes:

1 cup chopped onion

1 chopped clove garlic

1 cup chopped celery

Add these ingredients to the bread crumbs with:

3 cups tart diced apples

¼ cup finely chopped parsley

1½ teaspoons salt

¼ teaspoon paprika

HAM DRESSING FOR TURKEY

[About 7 Cups]

Combine:

1 to 1½ cups ground cooked ham

4 cups soft bread crumbs (II, 159)

1 cup crushed pineapple

1 cup plumped white raisins

1 cup walnuts

¼ to ½ cup honey

LIVER DRESSING

[About 4 Cups]

Chop:

½ lb. calf or baby beef liver

Sauté it lightly in:

1½ tablespoons butter

(1 tablespoon grated onion)

Combine these ingredients with:

2 cups soft bread crumbs

¾ cup chopped nut meats

2 beaten eggs

½ cup rich milk or cream and stock

1 teaspoon salt

½ teaspoon paprika

1½ tablespoons mixed minced chives and parsley

1 teaspoon chopped fresh tarragon

½ teaspoon lemon juice

(2 tablespoons dry sherry)

RICE DRESSING

[About 5 Cups]

Mince:

6 slices bacon

Sauté lightly for 5 minutes with:

3 tablespoons chopped onion

Pour off all but 2 tablespoons of the fat. Combine the contents of the skillet with:

4 cups cooked rice

1 cup dry bread crumbs (II, 159)

1 cup chopped celery

¾ teaspoon salt

¼ teaspoon pepper

⅛ teaspoon sage or nutmeg

½ cup milk

½ cup cream

WILD RICE DRESSING FOR GAME

[About 3 Cups]
Chop:
> Giblets

Bring to the boiling point:
> 4 cups water, stock or
> tomato juice
> 1 teaspoon salt

Drop the giblets into the water and simmer for about 15 minutes. Remove from the water, bring it to a rolling boil and stir into it:
> 1 cup wild rice, page 160

▶ Simmer until nearly tender, about 30 minutes. Melt in a skillet:
> ¼ cup butter

Sauté in it for about 3 minutes:
> 2 tablespoons chopped
> shallots
> 1 tablespoon chopped
> green pepper
> ¼ cup chopped celery

Add the hot drained rice and the chopped giblets. You may also use one or two of the following ingredients, but remember the quantity of dressing will be increased:
> 1 cup sautéed mushrooms
> ½ cup chopped ripe or
> green olives
> ¼ cup tomato paste
> ½ cup chopped nuts
> ½ cup sliced water
> chestnuts

DRESSING FOR CORNISH HEN OR PIGEON

Soak for 10 minutes:
> ½ cup white raisins

in:
> ¼ cup cognac

Sauté them in:
> 6 tablespoons butter

Add:
> ¼ cup chopped shallots

Combine with the above and toss lightly:
> ½ teaspoon salt
> 1½ cups Boiled Rice, page
> 158

> ¼ cup chopped pistachio
> nuts

CHICKEN FARCE OR FORCEMEAT

[Enough for 3 Six-Pound Chickens]
A gala stuffing for boned chicken, squabs or galantines.
Grind 3 times:
> About 3½ lbs. raw
> chicken meat
> 3 cups mushrooms

Add to this mixture:
> 2 cups pistachio nuts
> 1⅓ cups dry sherry
> ¼ cup sliced truffles
> 1 teaspoon grated onion
> 8 or 9 slightly beaten eggs
> 1½ cups butter, cut in small
> dice
> 1½ tablespoons salt
> ¼ teaspoon freshly ground
> pepper
> Grating of fresh nutmeg

Moisten until just softened:
> 2 cups soft bread crumbs

in:
> 1½ to 2 cups milk

Add the bread crumbs to this mixture with:
> ¼ cup cognac, brandy,
> Madeira or lemon juice

SEAFOOD DRESSING

For filling fish or for use in Vegetable Cases, page 256.
Add to:
> 1 cup flaked crab meat,
> drained oysters or
> mussels
> 2 slightly beaten eggs

Melt:
> 2 tablespoons butter

Sauté in it:
> ½ cup chopped onion
> ¾ cup chopped celery
> 2 slices minced bacon
> 1 cup fresh bread crumbs

Combine with the seafood.
> Correct the seasoning

Add:
> (1 teaspoon Worcestershire
> sauce, 1 tablespoon dry

sherry, ⅛ teaspoon
ginger or ½ teaspoon
grated lemon rind)

TANGERINE OR PINEAPPLE RICE DRESSING

[2 Cups]
Try this for chicken and squab.
Combine:

6 ribs pascal celery, leaves
and stems cut up
¼ cup chopped parsley
1 cup dry cooked rice,
lightly sautéed in
chicken fat or butter
Sections and julienned
strips of 1 tangerine
and its rind or 1 cup
drained crushed
pineapple
⅓ cup lightly sautéed
shallots
⅓ cup lightly sautéed
mushrooms
(⅓ cup pine nuts)

APRICOT OR PRUNE DRESSING

[About 5 Cups]
Cut into strips:

1½ cups cooked apricots or
seeded prunes
Combine with:

4 cups dry bread crumbs
or
3 cups Boiled Rice, page
158
¼ cup melted butter
½ teaspoon salt
⅛ teaspoon pepper
½ cup chopped green
pepper or celery
Moisten lightly with:

Stock or apricot water

POTATO DRESSING

[About 6 Cups]
Beat:

2 eggs
Add:

2 cups milk
and pour over:

4 cups soft bread crumbs

Fold in:

1½ cups freshly mashed
potatoes
Sauté until golden:

½ cup finely chopped onion
½ cup finely chopped celery
in:

¼ cup butter
Add:

2 tablespoons chopped
parsley
Combine with the potato mixture.

SWEET POTATO AND SAUSAGE STUFFING

[About 7 Cups]
Sufficient for a 10 lb. turkey.
Prepare:

4 cups Mashed Sweet
Potatoes, page 322
Sauté until light brown:

½ lb. sausage meat: 1 cup
Break it up with a fork. Remove
it from the pan. Add to the pan
and sauté for 3 minutes:

3 tablespoons chopped
onion
1 cup chopped celery
Add the sausage meat, the sweet
potatoes and:

2 cups dry bread crumbs
(3 tablespoons chopped
parsley)
Correct the seasoning
Mix these ingredients well.

SWEET POTATO AND APPLE DRESSING

[About 5 Cups]
Prepare:

Sweet Potatoes and
Apples, page 324
replacing the apple water with
light or dark stock.

APPLE DRESSING

[About 4 Cups]
Peel and slice:

6 cups tart cooking apples
Combine them with:

1 cup currants or raisins
(2 tablespoons lemon juice)
You may steam the currants or

raisins in 2 tablespoons of water in the top of a double boiler for 15 minutes before combining with the apples.

SAUERKRAUT DRESSING FOR GAME

Mix:

    1 quart chopped drained sauerkraut

with:

    1 clove garlic
    ¼ cup chopped onion
    1 tart peeled and chopped apple
    (2 tablespoons brown sugar)
    (¼ cup dried currants)
    (1 cup chopped water chestnuts)
    (⅛ teaspoon thyme)
    Correct the seasoning

POULTRY AND GAME BIRDS

The chicken is a world-citizen; duck and geese cosmopolites. Along with a number of the game birds which migrate from continent to continent, they are international favorites. And each nation has learned to cook them in a manner distinctively its own. The worldly-wise cook will not be content with chicken dumplings, roast turkey or quail on toast. But he will welcome into the kitchen some of the specialties—chicken cacciatore, duck bigarade, turkey mole, pheasant smitane—all of which have enlivened a global cuisine.

The principles of cooking poultry and game birds are just sufficiently different to warrant separate treatment; wild fowl having its own peculiarities in handling before cooking. There is the length of hanging time and the method of determining age—the results of which, in turn, establish the specific method of cooking. ♦ Wild fowl also demands extra fat during the cooking process. Preliminaries are identical. Bleeding the bird, plucking, singeing, drawing, removing tendons, trussing, stuffing, cutting it up—even boning, if you need this information—these steps are alike for all fowl, wild or domestic, as described later.

Whether you shoot your bird, catch it or buy it, you will always have to assess its quality and potential, sizing it up for the application of those cooking techniques which will be most individually suitable and re-warding. ♦ See, for example, under the dry heat processes, page 73, ways to cook young birds. Consult the moist heat processes, page 81, for those of questionable age or cook them in milk or marinate to tenderize.

ABOUT POULTRY

Poultry cooks and tastes best if used within 8 to 24 hours after slaughter. Cut-up poultry is more perishable than whole birds and turkey more perishable than chicken. All poultry is difficult to keep well in home refrigerators and, if you have to hold it more than a day or two, cook it and reheat it in a sauce before serving. Should you have bought chicken in airtight wrappings, loosen the wrapping before refrigerating.

For amounts of bird to allow per serving, see individual recipes, but if a large number of people are to be fed, turkey meat is the least expensive and turkey breast yields the greatest amount of protein per pound—duck, the least. The net amount of edible meat, minus fat or skin, is about 46% for turkeys, 41% for chicken and 22% for duckling.

Although a federal inspection stamp for poultry is authorized, its use is voluntary and applies only to already slaughtered birds in interstate commerce. It is well worth looking for, as its presence insures certain sanitary and grading standards.

Young chickens of either sex are called broilers if they weigh about 2½ lbs. and fryers if they weigh 2½ to 3½ lbs. Roasters, also of either sex, are under 8 months old and weigh 3½ to 5 lbs. and are very good for rotisseries or for use in Suprêmes, page 583. Capons, or castrated males, weigh 6 to 8 lbs. "Fowl" is a broadly polite "nom de plume" for hens aged 10 months or more and "stag" and "cock" for males that are too old to roast, but are well-flavored adjuncts for the stock pot.

♦ To size up a chicken, look for moist skin, soft legs and feet, bright eyes, a red comb, a wing tip that yields readily if pressed back and, most importantly ♦ a flexible breastbone. If the tip of the bone bends easily, the bird is young; if it is stiff, the bird is past its prime. For prepackaged chicken, the last test is the only one applicable. ♦ Beware of skin which is dry, hard, purplish, broken, bruised or scaly or that has long hairs sprouting from it.

On any bird that is frozen, watch for brownish areas called freezer burn, which indicate dehydration or long and improper storage. ♦ Commercially frozen birds may have been watered before freezing and the loss of this water on thawing may make them more expensive and less flavorful than those freshly killed.

In some households, arguments rage every Thanksgiving as to whether a cock or a hen turkey is to grace the board. The butcher might settle most of these disputes, since he invariably charges more for the latter.

ABOUT PLUCKING AND SINGEING POULTRY

Poultry is usually plucked and drawn when purchased. Buy dry-picked poultry whenever possible. If it is not plucked, do so at once—except for those game birds which must hang and are easier to pluck later. It is much easier to pluck and draw a bird that is thoroughly chilled. ♦ To pluck, pick the feathers from a bird. Remove all pin feathers—use a pair of tweezers or grasp each pin feather between forefinger and the tip of a knife, then pull.

After removing the coarser feathers, if those remaining are downy or small, you may use the paraffin method. Make up a mixture of ⅜ lb. melted paraffin and 7 quarts boiling water. Brush enough of this mixture over the bird to cover. Allow it to harden. Pull against the paraffin coating and it will carry the feathers with it.

♦ TO SINGE A BIRD

Hold it by the legs and singe the pin feathers over a gas flame or a candle. Turn it, so that all parts of the skin are exposed to the heat. ♦ But do not singe a bird that is to be frozen until you are just ready to use it. The heat of singeing breaks down the fat and hastens rancidity.

ABOUT PREPARING AN UNDRAWN BIRD FOR SAUTÉ OR FRICASSEE

First remove the wings and legs as shown on page 569 and on left at the top of page 570. Then be careful in making the diagonal incision—shown in the center illustration, page 569, by a dotted line—not to cut so deeply as to pierce the innards. Now reach in with the palm down and loosen the entrails at the top of the cavity. Place the bird on its back as on the right and crack the backbone by bending it sharply. Cut around the vent and remove the entrails. Discard the lungs and kidneys and save the giblets. Remove the oil sac, as described on page 571.

ABOUT PREPARING GIBLETS

◗ Among the entrails of a fowl the most valuable are the giblets, the heart, the liver and the gizzard. Remove veins, arteries, thin membrane and blood from around the heart and discard them. Cut the green sac or gall bladder away from the liver very carefully. It is better to leave a small piece of liver attached to the sac than to cut the sac so close to the liver as to risk puncturing it, for the bitterness of its fluid will ruin whatever it touches. Discard the gall bladder. Cut away any portion of the liver which may be discolored. ◗ If the liver of a fryer is yellow, it should very definitely be discarded. However, it may be normal to find a yellow liver in a stewer. Sever the intestines from the gizzard and remove membrane and fat from it. Then cut a shallow slit along the indented curve of the gizzard, being careful not to cut so deeply as to pierce the lining of the inner sac. Push against the outside of the opened gizzard with the thumbs to force out the sac. Discard it. Wash and dry giblets. Keep them well refrigerated and use or cook them as soon as possible. See Variety Meats, page 552, for the many ways to use giblets as meat and for stuffing, as well as in Gravies and Sauces, page 358.

ABOUT CUTTING UP A DRAWN BIRD

If the bird has been drawn, hold it up by a wing, letting its weight tug against the skin at the wing joint, see below. Clip through the skin, flesh and joint, severing the wing from the body. Use the same method to sever the second wing. For easier eating, you may want to transform the wings into mock legs. Just cut off the wing tips and straighten the two remaining joints with the hands. You may have to cut through the skin to do this. Pull them into a straight line to look like a small double leg. Silly, but the wings seem to taste better this way.

To cut off the legs, press them outward and down. If the bird is young the joint will break easily under this pressure. You will have to make a longer gash into the skin of the legs and continue the cut until it nearly meets in the back. Now cut the body apart in two pieces, separating the breast from the back. Cut, as sketched —below—along the dotted line. With a young chicken, it is possible to make a gash toward the back on either side of the opening previously used to eviscerate the chicken and to pry the body apart until the back cracks, as shown on the right. Leave the breast in 1 piece or cut it into from 2 to 4 pieces.

▶ TO REMOVE TENDONS

In large domestic fowl and in game birds the leg tendons are apt to be tough and should be removed. Most butchers use a clever gadget that breaks the foot, holds the carcass securely and draws the tendons as the foot separates from the body. Amateurs have a somewhat harder time. It is easier to get the tendons out if the feet have not been cut off. Cut through the skin 1½ inches above the knee joint. Be careful not to cut the tendons. Lay the fowl down at the edge of a table or board, with the cut in the skin occurring just on the board and the rest of the leg projecting beyond it. Press the foot and ankle down, sharply, to snap the bone at the knee joint. Pull steadily. The tendons should come away with the foot and lower leg bone. If they do not, remove them by forcing a skewer under each and pulling them out one by one, as shown above.

ABOUT BONING FOWL

Chicken breasts are easy to bone either in a butterfly double or in singles. The two singles break down into a large upper and small lower fillet and are sometimes separated for quicker cooking. It is almost impossible to bone a bird that is already dressed and to restuff it to look like its original self. This is due to the careless way in which the cavity opening and neck are usually cut. A dressed fowl can, however, be made into a Galatine, page 529, but be sure to ▶ choose a bird in which the cavity opening is as small as possible.

In these instructions, we are assuming that the bird you are boning is not dressed. The procedure for boning a dressed one is very similar, except that you must provide protection against possible leakage from the entrails. Singe the bird, page 568. Cut off the feet and the first two joints of the wings. Cut off the head, so that the neck is as long as possible and at once catch and bind the two tubes that come from the craw, so that nothing from it can leak out. During the entire boning job—and it is not too difficult once you have tried it—▶ be careful not to pierce the skin except for the initial slits. All through the cooking period, the skin acts as protection, encasement and insulation.

▶ Always keep the tip of the knife toward the skeleton and stay close to the bone at all times. When all the bones are out, the result, when held up, should look like a small romper with wing and leg sleeves pulled into the lining.

Begin the boning by placing the bird breast down on the board. Make an incision the entire length of the spine, through both skin and flesh. Using a short, sharp-pointed boning knife, follow as close to the frame as you can cut, pushing the skin and flesh back as you cut. Work the skin of the neck down, so you can get the neck bone to extend way beyond it. Chop the neck off short, protecting the skin and being careful ◗ not to cut through the craw tubes. Work first toward the ball-and-socket joint of the shoulder, cutting it free and boning the shoulder blade. Pull the wing bone through from the inside, bringing the skin with it. Bone the meat from the wing and reserve it. Then strike for the ball-and-socket joint of the leg and pull the bone through. Reserve the meat. After you have freed and reserved both wings and legs, continue to work the meat free, first from one side of the body, then from the other, until the center front of the breast-bone is reached. ◗ Here great care is needed to free the skin without piercing it, as it is very thin at this point. You should now be able to get the whole skeleton out with its contents all in one piece. Leave the severing of the opening into the intestine to the last. When the skeleton is removed, wash the skin and flesh in cold running water and pat with a towel ◗ until it is very dry. For a farce for boned chicken, see page 564.

ABOUT PREPARING AN UNDRAWN BIRD FOR ROASTING

Cut off the head, so that the neck is as long as possible and at once catch hold of and bind the 2 tubes attached to the craw, to prevent leakage. Draw down the neck skin. Cut or twist off the neck, close to the body ◗ being careful not to tear or cut through the tubes or the neck skin. The skin should then be loose enough to allow you to reach in at the base of the neck and draw out the bound tubes and the crop.

Now make an incision through the skin below the breastbone, large enough to admit the hand, as sketched above. Insert the hand, palm down, into the cavity between the organs and the breast bone. Feel for the gizzard, which is firm and roundish and pull it out steadily. It will bring most of the other entrails with it. Keep giblets for gravies or stuffings. Remove the kidneys in the hollows near the base of the backbone and the spongy red lungs to either side of the spine between the ribs. Explore carefully to ensure the removal of every bit of the viscera from the cavity, as well as surplus fat, as it may be too strong in flavor. Turn the chicken over and cut out the oil sac at the base of the tail, as shown on the right, by making a small oyster-shaped scoop above the heart-shaped area called the croupion or—by the irreverent—the pope's nose.

▶ Do not soak the bird in water at any time. Wipe it well with a damp cloth after drawing. Should it be necessary to wash the bird, hold it briefly under running water to cleanse the inside and ▶ dry it well with a cloth.

ABOUT STUFFING AND TRUSSING A BIRD

Always wait to stuff a bird until just before roasting. This may not be convenient, but it is much the safest procedure. Contamination is frequent in pre-stuffed fowl, for even when the dressing is refrigerated, the cold may not fully penetrate it.

Fill the bird only three-fourths full, as the dressing will expand. Stuff it loosely, as sketched below, left. Your task will be easier if you place the bird in a large pan. The crop cavity may be stuffed, too. You may also loosen the breast skin with a spoon and fill out the breast between the skin and the flesh. Close the openings with small skewers and a crisscrossed string. Or use a spiral skewer as shown in the center drawing, or sew them with the old-fashioned needle and thread. Fasten the legs so they will be close to the body by tying the ends of the drumsticks together, as shown in the center. Tie a piece of string around the skin of the neck. Leave two long ends. Turn the wings back, as shown on the right, and pass the string around them and secure it.

ABOUT ROASTING CHICKEN, CAPON, CORNISH HEN OR TURKEY

You may want to salt both the outside and inside of the poultry before roasting. We prefer to salt, if at all, after the browning and never salt the interior. If the bird is lean, rub it well with melted unsalted shortening. Place it on a greased rack ▶ uncovered, in a roasting pan, breast side up with the oven preheated to 450°. Reduce the heat immediately to 350°, baste frequently with pan drippings or additional fat and cook until tender. Some people like to use an even, slow heat throughout the cooking period, placing the bird in a preheated 325° oven and not basting at all. This method has gained popularity because it is carefree and because it was, until recently, reputed to entail less meat shrinkage. It has now been conclusively proved that even-heat roasting does not reduce shrinkage. And we are quite convinced, on the basis of the old reliable taste-test, that the flavor of meat sealed at the onset of roasting by high heat is markedly superior.

◗ In timing meat, remember that many factors are involved: the age of the bird and its fat content, whether it was frozen or not and, of course, its size. If it is a large bird, the total cooking time required will be longer, but it will require less time per pound than a smaller one. ◗ Have fowl at 70° before putting it in the oven. If using a thermometer, insert it between the thigh and the body of the bird, taking care that the tip is not in contact with the bone. Cook to an internal temperature of 190°. If not using a thermometer, allow about 20 minutes to the pound for birds up to 6 pounds. For larger birds, allow about 15 minutes per pound. In either case, add about five minutes to the pound if the bird you are cooking is stuffed. Other popular tests for doneness are to prick the skin of the thigh to see if the juice runs clear or to jiggle the drumstick to see if the hip joint is loose. This latter response, we find, usually means that the bird is not done but overdone. As a matter of fact, in cooking any bird, you are faced with a real and built-in problem. Putting it simply, the flesh of a fowl is of two quite different kinds: the tender breast meat and the tougher, relatively fatty, legs. The breasts are usually just right—as the French say, "à point"—an appreciable time before the legs have reached doneness. To correct this imbalance, especially in cooking larger birds, cover the breast after the first hour of cooking with a cloth that has been dipped in melted unsalted shortening.

There are several ways to glaze a bird toward the end of cooking. You may remove the cloth and dust the bird with flour or coat it with a thin roux during the last half hour or so of cooking. When the flour or roux sets, baste frequently with pan drippings. If the flavor is compatible with your dressing, or if the bird is unstuffed, you may baste by brushing it with a combination of peach or apricot preserves or currant jelly mixed with melted butter.

ABOUT ROASTING DUCK OR GOOSE

Pluck, singe, draw and truss, as described on page 568. Since these birds are fat, it is wise, especially with mature ducks and geese, to ◗ preroast them for about 15 minutes before stuffing. We often prefer to prepare a separate stuffing in a baker, so that the dressing will not be overpowered by the flavor and slickness of the fat. But, whether these birds are preroasted or not ◗ they must be pricked frequently, if lightly, all over to allow excess fat to escape. If they are not stuffed, you can place a cored and peeled apple, a carrot, an onion, celery stalks or a potato in the body cavity to attract off-flavors. Discard these vegetables before serving. You may also hasten the cooking with the old Chinese trick of placing several heated metal forks in the cavity to intensify the heat at that point. After preroasting in a 400° preheated oven or after placing the bird in a 450° preheated oven, proceed as for chicken, allowing about 20 minutes to the pound.

ABOUT ROASTING FOWL IN FOIL

Today, "roasting" fowl in aluminum foil has become fashionable. But calling this process roasting is a misnomer, for true roasting can only go on under ventilation. The foil, which causes steam to form and entraps it, gives the bird a stewed taste. It also insulates against heat and when you cook in it you will need a hotter oven. A further caution: if you remove the foil during the last half hour or so of cooking in an attempt at browning, you will simply dry out the meat.

ABOUT CARVING FOWL

If a bird is to be carved at table ▶ be sure the heated platter is large enough and garnish it lightly with parsley or watercress. There is a subtle art to carving, which is not easily mastered. But a sharp, long-bladed knife and a two-tined fork with a guard are helpful for the amateur.

Place the bird, breast side up, on a platter. Insert the fork firmly into the knee joint, as sketched below. This will act as a lever to pull the leg away from the body of the bird. Slice the thigh flesh away from the body until the ball-and-socket hip joint is exposed. A twisting movement with the knife will disengage the tendons if the fork holds the tension against the knee. Have an extra platter close at hand, on which to place the leg. Cut the joint between the thigh and drumstick, as shown. Repeat the above, cutting off the other leg. Begin to arrange the pieces on the extra platter, so they will look attractive when it is passed. If a large bird is being carved, some slices of meat may be cut from the thigh and the drumstick at this time. Proceed to remove the wings in a similar manner and, if the bird is large, divide the wings at the major joint. To slice the breast, begin at the area nearest the neck and slice thinly across the grain—the entire length of the breast. If the bird is very large, such as a turkey, carve only one side, unless more is needed at the first serving. This way, the meat can be kept from drying out.

In carving a duck, you will find the leg joint is more difficult to sever because it is attached much farther under the bird and is somewhat recessed at the joint. Here, as in general, for the inexperienced carver or the impatient one, poultry shears are an inspired addition to his weaponry.

ROAST CHICKEN [6]

Preheat oven to 450°.

◗ Draw, singe, stuff and truss, pages 568–572:

>A 4 to 5 lb. chicken or capon

Use for the stuffing ½ the recipe for:

>Rice Dressing, page 563,
>Bread Dressing with Oysters, Nuts and Giblets, page 560, or Chestnut Dressing, page 562

or make:

>2 cups Dry Dressing, page 561

replacing the onion with:

>½ cup chopped leeks—white part only

and using:

>French bread

Put the bird on a rack, uncovered, in the oven and ◗ reduce the heat at once to 350°. Roast about 20 minutes per pound. Serve with gravy, page 358.

ROAST STUFFED TURKEY [12]

Preheat oven to 450°.
◗ Draw, singe, stuff and truss, pages 568–572.

>A 10 to 16 lb. turkey

5 cups of one of the following stuffings should fill a 10-lb. bird:

>Dry Dressing, page 561
>Potato Dressing, page 565, or ½ the recipe for Apple Onion Dressing, page 563

Or you may want to use two kinds of dressing, a richer one like:

>Sausage or Oyster Dressing

in the crop and:

>Celery or Bread Dressing

in the cavity. Put the bird on a rack, uncovered, in the oven and ◗ reduce the heat at once to 350°, allowing about 20 minutes to the pound for an unstuffed bird and 25 minutes for a stuffed one. Baste frequently or after first half hour cover the bird with a cloth soaked in melted butter. Baste frequently with pan drippings. Remove the cloth the last half hour of roasting so the bird may brown. If using a smaller turkey allow 20 to 25 minutes per lb. For a bird weighing 18 to 25 lbs., reduce the oven to 300° and allow 13 to 15 minutes per lb.
Make:

>Pan Gravy, page 358

adding:

>Sautéed Mushrooms, page 296

or flavoring it with the finely chopped giblets if they were not used in the stuffing.

CHICKEN AND TURKEY BAKED IN FOIL

Preheat oven to 450°.
If you don't have time to baste, an accepted way of cooking halves or parts of chicken or turkey is in a wrap of aluminum foil. But before roasting see Foil Cooking, page 86. Season it well, and add a little butter and fresh herbs, such as tarragon or rosemary. Or use one of the barbecue sauces on page 374.
Cook a 5 lb. stuffed chicken about 2½ to 3 hours; parts or halves about 45 minutes.

BROILED SPRING CHICKEN

[Allow ¾ Pound per Person]
Preheat broiler.
Clean and cut into halves:

>Broilers

Rub them on both sides with:

>Butter

Place them in a pan, skin side down. The skin side will brown quicker than the under side. Broil the chickens until brown, about 15 to 20 minutes, turning them occasionally. There are so many good basting sauces for broilers. We suggest that, during the cooking, you baste occasionally for excellent flavor with:

2 tablespoons butter to 1
tablespoon lemon juice
A grind of fresh pepper
(Fresh or dry herbs)

Or, for an accent on beautiful color:

2 tablespoons butter
¼ teaspoon paprika

Allow the above amounts for each ½ broiler. Or when the broilers are ready, flambé them, page 80, with:

1 oz. warmed brandy

for each broiler.
Or make:

A thickened Pan Gravy,
page 358, using tarragon,
or an unthickened one—
deglazing with dry white
wine

STUFFED BROILER

A convenient party dish, as all but the final heating may be done in advance. Broil each:

½ broiler, as above

until ¾ done. Remove from heat and cool. Stuff each broiler cavity with:

½ cup of any stuffing, page
560

Preheat oven to 350°.
Place the stuffed broilers on a baking tray and brush top of stuffing with:

Melted butter

Bake for 15 to 20 minutes or until both broiler and stuffing are heated through.

BROILED TURKEY

Prepare for cooking:

Turkeys weighing from
3 to 4 lbs.

Cut them into 4 pieces. Prepare as for:

Broiled Chicken, above

allowing about 45 minutes cooking time.

☰ BARBECUED CHICKEN

◗ Please read About Outdoor Cooking, page 93. Prepare:

Broiled Chicken, above

placing the broiler 5 inches from the heat. Cook in all about 30 minutes, turning often and brushing the birds the last 10 minutes with:

A Barbecue Sauce, page
374

If preparing outdoors, place on a grill, cavity side down, for 15 minutes at moderate heat before turning and cooking until tender, about 10 minutes more.

OVEN-FRIED CHICKEN   [2]

I.
Preheat oven to 350°.
Disjoint:

A broiler

Wipe dry. Dredge it in:

Seasoned flour

Heat to the point of fragrance in a heavy skillet:

¼ cup butter

Sauté the chicken lightly. Remove from the skillet to a rack in a baking pan. Baste with the skillet pan drippings. Let it bake until tender, about 30 to 35 minutes, basting with added fat if necessary and turning occasionally.

II.   [2]
Preheat oven to 400°.
This is a simpler but not quite as tasty a version as I.
Disjoint:

A broiler

Use neck, wing tips for Stock (II, 142). Wipe the remaining pieces with a damp cloth and ◗ dry carefully. In a shallow 9 x 12 baking pan, melt in the preheated oven:

½ cup butter

Dredge the broiler in:

Seasoned flour

Remove the butter from the oven when melted and hot. Place the chicken in it ◗ skin side down. Baste the upper surface with melted butter from the pan. Put the uncovered pan back in the preheated oven and bake the chicken 20 to 30 minutes. Turn it skin side up. Put it back in the oven. ◗ Reduce the heat to 350° and bake until tender, about 30 to 35 minutes. ◗ Do not overcook or the chicken will be dry. While baking, baste the chicken several times with the drippings. You may also wish to remove the white meat portions and keep them warm, uncovered, while you continue to cook the dark meat slightly longer. Serve at once. For gravy and other suggestions, see page 358.

PAN-FRIED OR SAUTÉED CHICKEN

[Allow ¾ Pound per Person]
Please read About Sautéing, page 79.
Do not attempt to saute chicken in this way unless it is young and tender. Clean and cut into pieces:

Young chickens
Dredge them lightly with:
(Seasoned flour or corn meal)
Melt in a skillet:
A mixture of butter and oil
allowing for each half chicken 2 or more tablespoons of fat. When the fat has reached the point of fragrance, add the chicken. Cook and turn it in the hot fat until brown. Reduce the heat and continue cooking the chicken, turning frequently until done, from 20 to 30 minutes, according to size. ◗ Cook only until tender, as further cooking will dry and toughen the meat. Remove the chicken from the pan and make:
Pan Gravy, page 358
Add:
Cream or stock
Correct the seasoning
Serve at once, garnished with:
Parsley

I.
CHICKEN IN BATTER   [4]

Preheat deep fryer to 350°.

◗ Please read About Deep-Fat Frying, pages 75–79.
Some cooks prepare this dish with raw chicken, as in the recipe. Others prefer to use a partially cooked fowl. Cut into pieces:

A young 3 lb. roasting chicken
Dip into:
Fritter Batter for Meat (II, 125)
Place the dipped pieces on a rack and let them dry for 15 to 30 minutes. Immerse them in the hot fat and cook for 15 to 17 minutes. Drain on paper towels. Serve hot or cold.

II.
[Allow ¾ Pound per Person]
Prepare:
A young 3 lb. roasting chicken
using the recipe for:
Chicken Stew, below
Remove the meat from the liquid. Cool thoroughly. Dry well. Preheat deep fryer to 375°. Dip the chicken into:
Fritter Batter for Meat (II, 125)
and cook in deep fat until golden. Serve at once.

CHICKEN OR TURKEY   [5]
STEW OR FRICASSEE

I.
Clean and cut into pieces:
A 5 lb. stewing chicken
Place the chicken in a stewing pan and bring to the boiling point with:
3 cups water
1 sliced carrot
2 ribs celery with leaves
1 small sliced onion
Simmer the chicken about 15 minutes and remove scum. Continue to ◗ simmer uncovered until the chicken is tender, 2 hours or more. ◗ Do not boil at any time. At the end of the first hour of cooking, add:
3 or 4 peppercorns

Remove the chicken and strain the stock. If a very concentrated gravy is desired, boil the stock before thickening until it is reduced to 1½ cups. Thicken it with:

> Flour, see Gravy, page 358

Pour the gravy over the chicken. Garnish it with:

> Parsley

Serve it with:

> Noodles, page 172
> Dumplings, page 178 or
> Boiled Rice, page 158

II. This can be a stew like Blanquette de Veau, page 504, cooking the meat for 45 minutes.

III.   [4 to 5]
Have ready about:

> 1 dozen mushrooms
> 1 dozen small onions

cooked à Blanc, page 504, until tender. Cut into pieces:

> A 5 lb. stewing chicken

reserving the neck and back for stock. Dust the meat with:

> Flour

Melt in a heavy pan:

> 2 tablespoons butter

When the butter reaches the point of fragrance, add the floured chicken. Cook long enough so the flour crusts but does not color. Add just enough to cover:

> Water or chicken stock
> An onion stuck with 3 cloves
> 1 teaspoon salt

Bring the liquid to a boil. ◗ Reduce the heat at once. ◗ Simmer, uncovered, for about 45 minutes. Remove the meat and the clove-studded onion from the liquid. Discard the onion. Keep the meat warm. Melt in the top of a double boiler:

> 3 tablespoons butter

Add:

> 3 tablespoons all-purpose flour

Make a sauce by adding to above roux the liquid from the meat. Simmer, stirring, about 5 minutes. Have everything else ready to serve, because the sauce does not hold well once the eggs are added. Add ◗ off the heat:

> 3 beaten egg yolks
> ¾ cup cream

Place the sauce ◗ over—not in—hot water, stirring until the eggs thicken. Add the mushrooms and onions. Place the chicken on a hot platter, inside a:

> Rice Ring, page 162

Pour the garnished sauce over the meat. You may decorate the platter with small bunches of:

> Cooked carrots
> Parsley

so arranged as to look like fresh carrots with tops.

BRAISED BROILERS

[Allow ¾ Pound per Person]
If you like your chicken falling from the bone, this is your recipe.
Preheat oven to 350°.
Clean and cut into quarters:

> Young chickens

Heat in a skillet:

> Butter

Add the chickens and sauté them until brown. Place in a baking dish. Pour over them, to the depth of 1 inch:

> ½ cup boiling Chicken Stock (II, 142), or milk

Before covering the dish, add:

> (1 teaspoon sautéed chopped onions)
> (1 teaspoon honey)

for each piece of chicken and for the pot a:

> (Tiny pinch of rosemary)

Bake ◗ covered, about 40 minutes. When tender, remove them from the dish.
Make:

> Pan Gravy, page 358

Add to the stock, if required:

> Chicken Stock (II, 142)
> Cream
> Salt and pepper

MARYLAND CHICKEN [4 to 5]

Cut into pieces for serving:
> A young frying chicken, about 3½ lbs.

Bread it by dipping each piece in:
> Milk

and rolling it in:
> Flour

Let dry for 1 hour. Heat in a heavy skillet:
> ½ to 1 inch fat, a combination of cooking oils or bacon drippings

Heat the fat until it reaches the point of fragrance. Add the chicken. Brown it on all sides. Preheat oven to 375°.
Place the brown chicken in a fresh pan and bake, covered, until steamed through, about ½ hour. This Border dish is usually served with a cream gravy made from the drippings, that is, some of the fat thickened with:
> Flour

to which milk is added, see Pan Gravy, page 358. You may further enrich the gravy with:
> (Egg Yolks, page 356)

Serve with:
> Ham and Corn Fritters (II, 128)

SMOTHERED CHICKEN [6 to 7]

Preheat oven to 350°.
Prepare for cooking:
> A 4-lb. roasting chicken

Disjoint it. Place the chicken in a paper bag with:
> ¼ cup Seasoned Flour (II, 160)

Close the bag and shake vigorously.
Brown the chicken in:
> ¼ cup olive or salad oil

Place it in a casserole. Cook in the fat for 10 minutes:
> 1 small sliced onion
> 1 sliced clove garlic
> 3 or 4 chopped celery stalks

> 1 medium-sized carrot

Put the vegetables in the casserole. Pour over the mixture:
> 1½ cups hot chicken stock

Bake ▶ covered, for about 1½ hours or until tender. Add to the dish, 5 minutes before it is done:
> (1 cup sliced sautéed mushrooms)
> (12 stuffed sliced olives)

CHICKEN PAPRIKA [3]

Cut up as for frying:
> A young chicken: about 2½ lbs.

Melt in a heavy pot:
> 1½ tablespoons butter
> 1½ tablespoons cooking oil

Add and simmer until golden:
> 1 cup chopped onions
> 2 teaspoons to 2 tablespoons mild paprika

Add:
> ½ teaspoon salt
> 2 cups well-seasoned stock

As soon as these ingredients have reached boiling point, add the chicken. ▶ Simmer it, covered, until tender, about 1 hour. Stir:
> 1 teaspoon flour

into:
> 1 cup cultured sour cream

Stir it slowly into the pot. Heat the chicken 5 minutes longer but ▶ do not boil. Serve at once. Good with noodles or rice.

CHICKEN BRAISED IN WINE OR COQ AU VIN

We are often asked why this recipe turns out a rich medium brown rather than the very dark brown sometimes served in restaurants. Abroad, in country places where chickens are locally butchered, the blood is often kept and added to the gravy at the last minute as a thickener, see page 357. After this addition, it is not allowed to boil. Here in America, this effect is often imitated by adding caramel coloring. Recipe I is best with a youngish chicken.

If you have an old one, use II below.

I.   [4]
Disjoint:

A broiler or roasting chicken

Use the back and neck for the stock pot. Melt:

3 tablespoons butter or olive oil

Add and brown lightly:

¼ lb. minced salt pork
¾ cup chopped mild onions or ½ cup pearl onions
1 sliced carrot
3 minced shallots
1 peeled clove garlic

Push the vegetables aside. Brown the chicken in the fat. Add and stir:

2 tablespoons flour
2 tablespoons minced parsley
1 tablespoon fresh chervil or marjoram
½ bay leaf
½ teaspoon thyme
1 teaspoon salt
⅛ teaspoon freshly ground pepper
(1 tablespoon brandy)

Stir in:

1½ cups dry red wine or sherry

Simmer the chicken over low heat until done, about 1 hour. Keep it covered. Add for the last 5 minutes of cooking:

½ lb. sliced mushrooms

Skim off excess fat.

Correct the seasoning

Serve the chicken on a hot platter, the sauce and vegetables poured over it.

II. To tenderize an old chicken before braising, place it in ♦ a closely lidded heavy casserole on a piece of bacon rind or a few strips of bacon. Put the casserole in a 250° oven for about 45 minutes or until the flesh of the bird becomes white and has a pleasant aroma. The chicken is then ready to use for braising, as in I above.

CHICKEN TARRAGON   [4]
WITH WINE

Disjoint:

2 broilers

Marinate the pieces for about 1 hour in:

¼ cup fresh or 2 tablespoons dried tarragon leaves
4 finely minced shallots
1 cup dry white wine

Preheat broiler.
Broil the chicken for about 20 minutes or until tender.
Baste it with:

Melted butter

and the strained marinade. Save some of the marinade to deglaze the broiler pan.

Correct the seasoning

and serve the chicken on a hot platter with the drippings poured over it.

HUNTER'S CHICKEN,   [4]
CHICKEN CACCIATORE
OR CHASSEUR

Hunters always seem to have tomatoes and mushrooms handy. Cut into individual pieces:

A 4 lb. chicken

Dredge with:

2 to 3 tablespoons flour

Sauté until golden brown in:

¼ cup olive oil

with:

2 tablespoons chopped shallots
(1 minced clove garlic)

Add:

¼ cup Italian tomato paste
½ cup dry white wine
1 teaspoon salt
¼ teaspoon white pepper
¾ cup chicken stock
½ bay leaf
⅛ teaspoon thyme
⅛ teaspoon sweet marjoram
½ to 1 cup sliced mushrooms

(2 tablespoons brandy or
¼ cup Muscatel)
Simmer the chicken ♦ covered,
for 1 hour or until tender. Serve
with:

Boiled Spaghetti

CHICKEN MARENGO   [8]

A good buffet casserole which
profits by a day's aging, refrigerated.
Cut into quarters:
2 frying chickens
Sauté until delicately colored:
1 thinly sliced onion
in:
½ cup olive oil
then remove. Add the chicken
pieces and brown on all sides.
Add:
½ cup dry white wine
2 crushed cloves garlic
½ teaspoon thyme
1 bay leaf
Sprigs of parsley
1 cup chicken stock
2 cups Italian style
tomatoes
Correct the seasoning
Cover the pot and simmer for
about 1 hour, until tender. When
meat is done, remove it to a
platter. Strain the sauce and reduce it for about 5 minutes.
Now sauté:
16 to 20 small white onions
1 lb. sliced mushrooms
in:
¼ cup butter
Juice of 1 lemon
Arrange chicken quarters, mushrooms, onions and:
1 cup pitted black olives
in a deep earthenware casserole.
Sprinkle over all:
1 jigger cognac
Add the sauce and reheat in a
350° oven. Garnish with:
Chopped parsley
Serve with:
Rice

SPANISH CHICKEN   [4]

Preheat oven to 350°.

Also see Paella, page 105.
Cut into pieces:
A 4 lb. frying chicken
Dredge them with:
Seasoned Flour (II, 160)
Heat in a skillet:
¼ cup olive oil
Brown the chicken in it. Place
in a casserole. Sauté in the oil
in the skillet:
¼ cup chopped onion
3 tablespoons chopped
green pepper
1 minced clove garlic
Add:
½ cup chopped carrots
½ cup chopped celery
1 cup chopped, peeled,
seeded tomatoes
¾ cup tomato juice
Pour these ingredients over the
chicken in the casserole. Bake
♦ covered, for about 1 hour or
until tender. Add, if needed:
Boiling stock
Five minutes before the chicken
is done, add:
¾ cup Sautéed Mushrooms,
page 296
⅓ cup sliced stuffed olives
Make:
Pan Gravy, page 358

FRENCH CASSEROLE   [5]
CHICKEN

Whenever we see one of our
contemporaries trying to regain
her youthful allure with gaudy
sartorial trappings, we think of
a dish we found in a collection of
college alumnae recipes, called:
"Suprême of Old Hen." We all
know that "Suprême," in chef's
parlance simply means a breast
of fowl. But, in this case, it
really lives up to its billing and
makes such a good dish out of
a poorish bird that the old girl
is still an acceptable morsel.
Prepare for cooking and disjoint:
A 5 lb. fowl
Sear the pieces in:
¼ cup hot butter
Add:

¼ cup dry white wine

Remove the chicken from the pot. Place in the pot:

2 pared, cored, sliced tart apples
6 chopped celery ribs with leaves
1 minced or grated onion
3 sprigs parsley
½ teaspoon salt
¼ teaspoon paprika

Cover and cook these ingredients gently until tender. Stir in:

2½ tablespoons flour
2 cups Stock (II, 141)

Cook and stir the sauce until it boils. Add the chicken. Cover and simmer until it is tender, 1 hour or more. Remove the chicken to a hot ovenproof serving dish. Strain the sauce. Warm over hot water and add to the strained sauce:

⅓ cup sweet or cultured sour cream
Correct the seasoning

Add:

1 tablespoon fresh tarragon or basil

Pour the sauce over the chicken. Sprinkle it generously with:

Parmesan cheese

Place it under a broiler until the cheese is melted.

BRUNSWICK STEW   [8]

Disjoint for cooking:

A 5 lb. chicken

Sauté it slowly until light brown in:

¼ cup butter or drippings

Remove from the pan. Brown in the fat:

½ cup chopped onions

Place in a large stewing pan the chicken, onions and:

1½ to 2 cups peeled, seeded, quartered tomatoes
3 cups fresh lima beans
1 cup boiling water
A few grains cayenne
(2 cloves)

◗ Simmer these ingredients, cov-

ered, until the chicken is nearly tender. Add:

3 cups corn, cut from the cob

Simmer the chicken and vegetable mixture, covered, until tender. The chicken meat may be removed from the bones.

Correct the seasoning

Add:

2 teaspoons Worcestershire sauce

Stir in:

(1 cup toasted bread crumbs)

CHICKEN KIEV   [8]

Preheat deep fryer to 325°.

Bone, skin, page 570, cut in halves and pound, page 452, to a ¼-inch thickness:

4 chicken breasts

Form into 8 balls:

½ lb. butter

Roll butter balls lightly in a mixture of:

2 tablespoons chopped chives
2 tablespoons chopped parsley
(1 minced clove garlic)
¼ teaspoon white pepper

Place one of the seasoned butter balls in the center of each half breast and roll so that the butter is completely enclosed. Secure with a toothpick, if necessary. Dust with:

Flour

Brush with:

Beaten egg

Roll in:

Dry bread crumbs

Fry in deep fat, page 75, until golden brown, about 5 to 7 minutes.

BRANDIED CHICKEN   [4]
BREASTS

Remove the breasts from:

4 young chickens

Skin, bone and divide into halves, and rub with:

Brandy

Let them stand about 10 minutes. Season with:

> Salt, pepper and
> marjoram

Heat to the point of fragrance:

> 6 tablespoons sweet butter

Sauté the fillets over medium heat, 6 to 8 minutes on each side. Remove to a heated ovenproof platter and keep warm. To the remaining butter in the pan, add:

> ½ cup dry sherry

Simmer over ◗ low heat until the liquid is reduced to half. Add, stirring constantly:

> 2 cups cream

beaten with:

> 4 egg yolks

Season with:

> Salt, pepper and nutmeg

Stir and cook until slightly thickened. Pour the sauce over the chicken breasts. Sprinkle with:

> Grated Swiss cheese

mixed with equal parts of:

> Fine buttered crumbs

Glaze under the broiler.

BREAST OF CHICKEN COCKAIGNE

[Allow a Single Breast per Serving]
This delicate recipe does not work with frozen chicken. Cook up a flavorful stock (II, 142), from the skin and bones of the chicken you are using. Skin, bone, divide in halves:

> Chicken breasts

When ready to cook, dust the chicken breasts, which should be 70°, lightly with:

> Flour

For each breast, heat to the point of fragrance, in a heavy skillet:

> ½ tablespoon butter
> ½ tablespoon cooking oil

Put the floured pieces of chicken in the hot oil. Shake the pan constantly so the flour crusts but does not color. Cover and poach in the butter over very low heat, turning occasionally, for 10 to 15 minutes, depending on the thickness of the meat. Remove from heat and allow to stand covered for about 10 minutes more. This rather unorthodox procedure makes breasts puff up, so the meat is both tender and moist. Remove from the pan and keep warm. Make a gravy of the pan drippings and the stock made from the bones and skins.

CHICKEN SUPRÊME PAPILLOTE

Preheat oven to 400°.
Prepare:

> Breast of Chicken
> Cockaigne

allowing it to cook until ½ done. Place it on a parchment heart for Papillote, page 88. Before folding, place:

> 1 tablespoon Colbert
> Butter, page 384

on each ½ breast. Seal the paper and bake on a baking sheet for about 15 minutes. Serve with:

> Pilaf, page 166

STUFFED CHICKEN BREASTS

[Individual Serving]
These are quickly prepared in a chafing dish or electric skillet. Have ready:

> A boned, skinned breast
> of chicken

beaten with a cleaver until very thin. Heat to the point of fragrance.

> 1½ to 2 tablespoons butter

Quickly move the chicken about in this hot fat until it is no longer pink, about 2 to 3 minutes in all. Fold this thin piece over once to hold:

> 1 thin slice Virginia ham
> 1 very thin small piece
> Swiss cheese

Remove the chicken from the

pan and keep it warm. Sauté
with pan drippings:

> 1 tablespoon finely minced
> shallots
> 3 mushroom caps

When mushrooms have cooked
for about 3 minutes, add:

> ¼ cup dry white wine
> 2 tablespoons freshly
> chopped, peeled, seeded
> tomato

Simmer about 3 minutes again.
Add to this sauce:

> 2 tablespoons cream

Heat the chicken breasts in the
sauce slowly, but ♦ do not let
them boil. Turn them once or
twice. When heated through,
about 3 minutes, add:

> 1 tablespoon chopped
> parsley
> Correct the seasoning

Serve at once, over:

> Saffron rice or fine
> buttered noodles

CHICKEN BREASTS IN QUANTITY FOR CREAMING OR SALAD

This recipe is particularly useful in preparing large quantities
of chicken meat for such dishes
as Chicken à la King, page 226,
or Chicken Pot Pies, page 212.
Many knowledgeable cooks consider poaching an ideal approach, but we should like to
suggest this method which we
find more flavorful. After the
chicken is baked, save the pan
juices and make a stock of the
skins and bones. Combine these
two defatted by-products in
making sauce if the chicken is
to be served hot or in an aspic.
Or use the juices and defatted
stock for broth or other cooking
if the chicken is served as salad.
Preheat oven to 300°.
Place on a rack in a large shallow pan, skin side up:

> Chicken breasts

Brush them, allowing for each
whole breast:

> 1½ tablespoons butter

Bake for about 1 hour. When
slightly cooled, remove the skins
and bone the breasts. Cover and
refrigerate the meat until ready
to use.

STUFFED CHICKEN LEGS

[Allow 1 or 2 Legs per Person]
I. Preheat oven to 350°.
Remove bone and tendons, page
570, from:

> Large chicken legs

Stuff the cavities with:

> Bread or other dressing,
> page 560

Close the opening with poultry
pins. Brown the legs lightly in:

> Butter or other fat

to which you may add:

> A slice of onion

Place the stuffed legs in a casserole. Cover the bottom of the
dish with:

> ⅓ inch boiling Chicken
> Stock (II, 142)

Bake the meat, covered, until
tender, about 45 minutes. Make:

> Pan Gravy, page 358

II. Bone:

> 4 chicken legs

Replace the bone with:

> 4 pineapple spears

Dredge the stuffed legs in:

> A Bound Breading
> (II, 160)

Melt in a skillet, to the point of
fragrance:

> 2 tablespoons butter
> 2 tablespoons cooking oil

Sauté the chicken legs, uncovered, until golden brown. Cover
them with:

> ½ cup shredded fresh
> coconut

Cover the skillet and ♦ simmer
the chicken until tender. Meanwhile, make up a mixture of:

> ½ cup pineapple sirup
> ½ cup chicken stock
> 2 slices fresh gingerroot
> 1 to 2 teaspoons cornstarch

and cook until the cornstarch is

clear. Pour this sauce over the chicken and heat through again. Serve with:

> Rice and Orange and Avocado Salad

BONED CHICKEN

See About Boning Fowl, page 570.

This recipe, which we have enjoyed on many holiday occasions with Clara Kupferschmid, is one she has brought close to perfection over the years. Choose a very fresh, dry-picked, undressed:

> 6 lb. chicken

Be sure the skin is intact. Bone it, page 570. Allow for filling ⅓ of the recipe for:

> Chicken Farce, page 564

Before stuffing the chicken, tie it off securely at the neck, wing ends and legs. Sew shut the vent under the tail. Be sure not to pack the farce or fill the skin too tightly or it may burst during the cooking as the stuffing swells. In filling, pretend you are a taxidermist or a frustrated sculptor and try to shape the stuffing so that, when you have sewed the seam down the back, the bird will resemble its former self. Preheat oven to 450°.

Bard, page 454, the chicken with:

> ⅛ inch thick salt pork

If you do not like a salt pork flavor, brush the bird generously all over with:

> Clarified Butter, page 383

Allow, for this and for subsequent basting, about ½ lb. butter. Prick the chicken all over with a darning needle and repeat this operation after every basting. Place the bird on a rack in a pan in the hot oven and ♦ reduce the heat at once to 350°. If the chicken was not barded, baste it at 10-minute intervals after 40 minutes of

cooking and continue until it is done, about 2 hours in all. If the bird was barded with salt pork, remove the barding about 20 minutes before the end of the cooking time in order to give the bird a better color. Boned stuffed chickens may be served hot, but are unusually delicious when chilled for at least 24 hours to allow the seasonings to develop.

Slice very thin with hot serrated knife when serving.

COUNTRY CAPTAIN [4] OR EAST INDIA CHICKEN CURRY

This dish has become a favorite in America, although it probably got its name not from the sea-captain who brought the recipe back to our shores, but from the Indian officer who first made him acquainted with it. So says Cecily Brownstone, a great friend; and this is her time-tested formula. For still another Oriental chicken curry, see Rijsttafel, page 166.

Preheat oven to 350°.

Cut into 10 pieces:

> A fryer

Coat them with:

> Seasoned Flour (II, 160)

Brown the chicken in:

> ¼ cup butter

Remove, drain and place in a casserole.

♦ Simmer gently in the pan drippings until golden:

> ¼ cup finely diced onions
> ½ cup finely diced green pepper
> 1 clove minced garlic
> 1½ teaspoons curry powder
> ½ teaspoon thyme

Add:

> 2 cups stewed tomatoes

and ♦ simmer until the pan is deglazed. Pour this sauce over the chicken and bake ♦ uncovered, for about 30 minutes or until the chicken is tender. During the last 5 minutes of cooking, add:

 3 tablespoons currants

Serve with:

 Steamed Rice

garnished with:

 Toasted slivered almonds

CHICKEN OR TURKEY À LA CAMPAGNE [10 to 12]

Roast, uncovered, at 350° for 2 hours:

 A 5-lb. chicken

Remove meat from bones. Use bones, skin and any vegetable parings in your stock pot. Sauté, page 296:

 1 lb. small button mushrooms

Have ready:

 1 cup cooked green peas (3 cups canned artichoke hearts)

Prepare à la Parisienne, page 250:

 1 cup each cooked carrots and white turnips

Arrange these ingredients in a 3-quart casserole, alternating layers of chicken and vegetables until all are used, with chicken on the top layer. Make the sauce by putting into a saucepan:

 ½ cup melted butter

Add and stir until smooth over low heat about:

 ½ cup flour

Continue to stir over low heat and add:

 2 cups strong chicken stock
 1 cup dry white wine
 ½ cup dry sherry
 1 cup cream
 ½ cup chopped parsley

Season to taste with:

 Salt
 Monosodium glutamate
 Freshly ground white pepper

Continue to cook over low heat for 10 minutes. Pour the sauce over the food in the casserole. Shake it well, so the sauce penetrates all layers. You may cover the top with:

 Au Gratin, page 389

and heat for about 30 to 40 minutes.

If you ✳ freeze this mixture, cool uncovered before freezing. To reheat, remove from freezer 3 hours in advance. Bake, uncovered, at 350° for 1 to 1¼ hours.

TURKEY CASSEROLE MOLE

This Mexican recipe combines the native peppers and chocolate with a native bird. ◗ Please read About Deep-Fat Frying, pages 75–79.

Preheat deep fryer to 370°.

Cut up:

 A 12- to 14-lb. turkey

Dip the pieces first in:

 Milk

then in:

 Flour

and put them on a rack to dry. Prepare:

 6 Chimayo peppers
 6 broad peppers
 3 chili peppers

If the chilies are dry, drop them into hot water for about 10 minutes before removing seeds and veins. Deep-fat fry all 3 kinds of peppers for about 5 minutes. Drain and reserve them.

Preheat oven to 325°.

When the turkey pieces have dried about 15 minutes, slide them gently into the 370° pepper-flavored fat and deep fry them for about 5 minutes. Drain the pieces and put them in a large casserole. Cover them with:

 Turkey or game stock

◗ Cover the casserole and bake the turkey about 1 hour. Toast in a dry pan, over gentle heat:

 1 tablespoon sesame seeds
 ½ cup pine nuts
 ½ cup blanched almonds

Grind together with the browned peppers:

2 tortillas

Cook:

3 minced cloves garlic

in

2 tablespoons oil

Add:

2 cups peeled, seeded
tomatoes
1 bay leaf
½ teaspoon coriander
3 cloves
1 teaspoon cinnamon

Combine the above ingredients
with the nuts and pepper mixture and ◗ simmer for 15 minutes. Put this thick sauce with
about 2 cups of turkey stock
over the cut up turkey and simmer, covered, for about 2½
hours more. This dish may be
made a day or two before serving, but its most characteristic
ingredient is reserved for the
very last. Just before serving,
add:

1 to 2 oz. grated chocolate

mixing it well into the heated
sauce.

ROAST DOMESTIC   [3]
DUCK

Most duck on the American
market is not descended from
the wild native variety, but from
a type bred in China where, of
course, this bird is held in high
esteem. As duck has both a
heavy frame and a high fat
content, allow 1⅓ to 1½ lbs.
per serving.

Preheat oven to 450°.

Pick, clean and singe, page 568,
if necessary:

A 5 to 6 lb. duckling

Rub it with:

(Garlic)

Place it on a rack in a roasting
pan. Stuff with:

Celery stalks and sliced
onions or a quartered
apple, which you remove
before serving, or with
an apple stuffing, page
565

Put the bird in the oven and
◗ reduce the heat at once to
350°. Cook until tender, allowing about 20 minutes to the lb.

Make:

Pan Gravy, page 358

Serve with:

Polenta, page 156

or, if the duck has not been
stuffed, with:

Crushed pineapple,
Orange Sauce for Duck,
page 365, Sauce
Rouennaise, page 587,
or any other suitable
sauce

APRICOT HONEY   [2 to 3]
GLAZED DUCK

Preheat oven to 450°.

For those who like sweet with
meat.

Prepare and roast as for Roast
Duck:

3½ to 4 lb. domestic duck

Remove from oven just before
done.

Make a thick glaze to pour over
the duck. Combine and mix well:

1 cup apricot preserves
½ cup clover honey
1 tablespoon brandy
1 tablespoon cointreau or
other orange-flavored
liqueur

Coat the duck with this glaze
and return to the oven for 10 to
15 minutes until the glaze caramelizes.

DUCKLING ROUENNAISE

Unless you choke your duck,
pluck the down on its breast immediately afterward and cook it
within 24 hours, you cannot lay
claim to having produced an
authentic Rouen duck. The first
two steps assure the dark red
flesh and the special flavor of
this dish. If, as is likely, duck-
strangling will bring you into
local disrepute, you may waive
the sturdy peasant preliminaries
and serve a modified version,

garnished with quotation marks.
Clean:

A duckling

reserving the liver. Free it from
the gall. Tuck the liver into the
body cavity. Use a spit or rotisserie to roast the duck only 20
to 22 minutes in all. Only the
breast and legs, if tender, are
reserved and kept warm. The
rest of the carcass is pressed,
see About Salmi, page 592.
Meanwhile melt:

2 tablespoons butter

When the fat reaches the point
of fragrance, add and simmer:

1 finely minced onion
¾ cup Burgundy

When the duckling is done, remove and crush the liver and
add to the reduced wine mixture. Poach it gently in the wine
with the drippings from the
pressed carcass. Add several
tablespoons of:

(Pâté de Foie, page 524)
Correct the seasoning

Slice the breast lengthwise into
about 20 thin strips and put
them in a chafing dish. Should
you want to serve the legs, they
must at this point be removed
and grilled, as they are too raw
without further cooking. We
prefer to utilize them later in
some other dish, so the breast
can be served "à point."

▶ Cover the sliced meat
quickly with the hot liver sauce,
and serve ▶ immediately from
the chafing dish at table.

ROAST DUCK BIGARADE

This famous recipe depends for
its flavor on the Seville or bitter
orange, known also as "bigarade."
Prepare:

Roast Duck, page 587

When it is done, remove it from
the roasting pan and keep warm.
Degrease the pan juices and deglaze the pan, as described in

Orange Sauce for Duck or
Goose, page 365, omitting the
lemon juice. The curaçao is optional.

★ ROAST GOSLING   [6]
OR GOOSE

Economy-minded farmers raise
geese because it takes only
about ⅕ as much cereal feed to
fatten them as it does for other
fowl. Economy-minded housewives know that they get more
protein value from turkey, page
567. There is, of course, the advantage of having goose liver,
which is superior, page 524.
Preroasting of goose or pricking
to release fat is imperative, page
573. Unless goose is under ten
months old, it is apt to be
tough. Braise rather than roast
any bird you suspect of being
over this age limit.
Preheat oven to 450°.
Prepare for cooking, page 571:

An 8 lb. gosling or a
12 to 14 lb. goose

Fill the cavities with:

Apple, Prune, Chestnut
or other dressing, page
560
(Sauerkraut made with
wine)

Allow 1 cup dressing to each
pound of bird. Place the goose
on a rack in an uncovered pan,
allowing 25 minutes to the
pound. ▶ Reduce the heat at
once to 350° and pour off the
fat as it accumulates. Make:

Pan Gravy, page 358

Season it with:

Ginger and pearl onions

Or serve with:

Prunes in Wine (II,
108), Gooseberry
Preserves (II, 581),
Red Cabbage, page 277,
Curried Fruit, or
Chestnut Purée, page
283, and Cucumber
Salad, page 43

BRAISED PARTS OF GOOSE OR GAENSEKLEIN

Rub with garlic:

Goose back, neck, gizzard, wings and heart

Let them stand for several hours. Place in a heavy pot. Add:

Mirepoix (II, 221)

Half cover with boiling water. Simmer ♦ closely covered, until nearly tender, about 1½ hours.

Correct the seasoning

and add:

(A pinch of ginger)

Cover and simmer the meat until tender, about ½ hour longer. Remove from the pot. Strain the stock, removing the grease. Make:

Pan Gravy, page 358

Pour it over the meat. Serve with:

Apples Stuffed with Sauerkraut

Also good with:

Chopped parsley
Dumplings and applesauce

POTTED GOOSE OR CONFIT D'OIE

Draw, pluck, singe, page 568, and cut as for fricassee:

A 10 lb. goose

Cut off, reserve and refrigerate the heavy fat. Salt the pieces of goose well on all sides. Place in an earthenware crock and weight with a nonresinous hardwood board. Cover and leave in a cool, dry place 6 to 8 days. When ready to cook, place the refrigerated fat in the bottom of a large heavy pan. Put on top of it:

A Bouquet Garni (II, 220)

Wipe the salt from the meat and put the pieces on the fat layer. ♦ Simmer slowly for about 2 to 4 hours. ♦ Be sure, as the fat melts, that there is enough to cover the meat completely. If not, add, as needed:

Lard

Use at once or store in a cool place, again, making sure that the meat is ♦ well covered with the fat. This dish will keep for months and can be served cold or reheated in the fat. If hot, a good accompaniment is:

Franconia Potatoes, page 314

which are cooked in the goose fat. Or use in:

Cassoulet, page 509

GUINEA FOWL, ROAST PIGEONS, SQUABS OR CORNISH HENS

[Allow 1 Small Bird Per Person]

Preheat oven to 450°.

Pick and draw:

Small guinea fowl, pigeons, squabs or Cornish hens

It is best to coat them with a Roux, page 355. They may be stuffed with:

Cooked Wild Rice, page 160, or Bread Dressing, etc., pages 560–566

or:

A Fruit Dressing, page 565

Bard, page 454, or brush with:

Melted butter

Dredge with flour. Place the birds, uncovered, in the oven. ♦ Reduce the heat at once to 350° and roast until tender, 45 minutes or more if stuffed, about 30 if not. They may be basted while cooking. If barded, remove the bacon and allow to brown. Make:

Pan Gravy, page 358 with mushrooms

or serve with:

Bar le Duc Jam (II, 576)

BREASTS OF GUINEA HEN

[Allow 1 Breast per Person]

Preheat oven to 425°.

Bard, page 454, each:

Breast of guinea hen

Put in oven and ♦ reduce the

heat at once to 350°. Baste the breasts frequently. Cook them for about 45 minutes or until they are tender. Serve "sous cloche," or under a glass bell, with:

> Colbert Butter, page 384

POTTED PIGEONS [6]
OR SQUABS

Preheat oven to 350°.
Cut into pieces or leave whole:

> 4 large pigeons or 6 squabs

Dredge them with:

> Seasoned Flour (II, 160)

Melt:

> ¼ cup butter

Sauté the birds slowly in the butter until they are just seared. Place them in a casserole. Add to the fat in the pan:

> ¼ chopped onion
> 1 diced carrot
> ¼ cup chopped celery

Stir these ingredients for about 3 minutes. Add:

> 1 cup boiling chicken
> stock or water

Pour this over the birds. Cover them closely. Roast them until they are tender, about 45 to 60 minutes. You may add for the last ½ hour:

> 1 cup sliced mushrooms

Do not permit the birds to become dry. If they do, add more stock or water. Make:

> Pan Gravy, page 358

to which you may add:

> Cultured sour or sweet
> cream
> (Chopped olives)

Serve the squabs in a border of:

> Rice

Sprinkle them with:

> Chopped parsley or
> chives

BROILED PIGEONS
OR SQUABS

Preheat broiler.
Pick, then split down the back and remove entrails from:

> Squabs

Flatten them. You may cut out the back bone with shears. Put them on a greased broiler, skin side up. Brush well with:

> Melted butter

Place the birds 4 inches from the heat. Broil from 15 to 30 minutes, turning once. Season when you turn them with:

> Salt and paprika

Serve on:

> Buttered toast

Pour the drippings over them. Good with:

> Chopped parsley
> Cranberry jelly
> Crusty Spoon Bread
> (II, 279)

ABOUT WILD BIRDS

The opening of the season for grouse—that very British bird which dwells in and feeds on heather—stirs up a degree of knowledgeable excitement equalled only by a vendange in the Côte d'Or. All over Southern Europe, each autumn, small birds, spicy with berries, are netted by the hundreds. And along the shores of Chesapeake Bay, the canvasback duck—which in October feeds on the wild celery of the shoreline—is preferred above all others.

We lived for years under one of the major flyways of the world and looked forward to the days when the males in our family sought out the bird-blinds in the surrounding marshes and rich fields. On their return, dinner parties were held in profusion. The children usually clamored for the plump little quail, leaving the rare, well-hung ducks to their more sophisticated elders.

To a large extent, proper care, immediately after shooting, determines the ultimate excellence of flavor in wild birds. While the bird is still warm, the neck is split and the carcass bled. To keep the blood for use in sauces, see page 357. Check the neck for any undigested food and remove.

Some birds—snipe, woodcock and plover—are cooked with the trail still inside, see page 598. Quail and a few other smaller birds should be plucked, drawn and cooked within 24 hours of killing. But do not pluck or draw any wild fowl until you are ready to cook it, since the added surface exposure of the carcass to air will induce spoilage before the necessary tenderization can be accomplished.

To tenderize and improve flavor, it is necessary to hang many wild birds, specifically partridge, prairie fowl, ducks and plover, grouse and hazel hen—unless they are to be roasted. How long to hang depends first on age. Old birds can be held longer than young ones. A second consideration is the weather. In muggy periods ripening is accelerated. The third—and perhaps the most important—is personal preference. Some hunters go to extremes, holding a bird until the legs stiffen, even until head and body part company. A more moderate and acceptable state of maturity is reached when the feathers just above the tail can be drawn out easily or when a slight bluish green tinge appears on the thin skin of the abdomen. However long birds are to be hung ♦ suspend them, undrawn, by the feet ♦ in a cool, dry, airy place. If the weather is very warm, dust the feathers with charcoal. In any season, the birds should be protected with cheesecloth or screening.

♦ Dry pluck all fowl. Remember that this is easier to do if the bird is chilled. Scalding or soaking preparatory to plucking breaks down the fatty tissues in the skin too rapidly if they are subsequently to be held for even a short time or are to be frozen. ♦ To pluck, see page 588.

Before cooking, look the birds over carefully and remove any shot with a pointed utensil. Cut out meat that has discolored near the shot or any dog-damaged areas. Remove the oil sac, page 572. After plucking, wild fowl should never be washed before cooking, merely wiped with a damp cloth. Safe exceptions are fish-feeding ducks which, if they must be used, should be parblanched for ½ hour before cooking.

♦ Singe all fowl just before cooking, including those which have been frozen. ♦ All game should be at 70° before timing for cooking. The interior of the bird may first be salted or rinsed with 2 tablespoons of brandy or sherry. Should it be necessary to counteract a too gamey taste, we suggest cooking with sauerkraut or using a marinade. Never try to soak out the taste with water. If the bird is to be cooked unstuffed, the placement in it of an apple, an onion, a carrot, parsley, a few celery stalks or some juniper berries helps attract off-flavors. These fillers are, of course, discarded before serving.

♦ Age determines how wild fowl shall be cooked. To judge age refer to the individual recipes. If you are at all doubtful that a bird is young or prime, do not hesitate ♦ to use a moist heat method of cooking, page 81. Very old birds are fit only for the stock or soup pot or for making hash, forcemeat and sauces.

On many occasions only the breasts of wild fowl are served, as the legs are often tough and full of tendons. If you use the legs, remove the tendons, see page 570. Otherwise, simmer the legs with the wings, necks and giblets for game stock. This is most useful, for in no cooking is less gravy naturally produced as in that of game. Therefore, it is doubly important to increase the stock of the game you are cooking, in order to bring up the flavor of a sauce or aspic. If game stock is not available, veal is the most sympathetic substitute.

Before roasting or marinating wild fowl, break down the breast bone by a blow with the flat side of a cleaver. This not only makes carving easier, but reduces the amount of marinade needed. To prepare a wild fowl for broiling, split the back and spread the breasts flat, using poultry shears for small birds.

Whether roasted or broiled, wild birds are, without exception, leaner than domestic varieties and should usually be barded, page 454. Sometimes a flour and butter paste is used to coat them before the barding is applied. The barding may be removed halfway through the cooking process but, if so, basting with butter or pan drippings should continue until the bird is taken from the heat. If a paste has not been applied you may, after the removal of the barding, want to dust the bird with flour to hasten its browning.

◆ Most light-fleshed wild fowl is cooked well done and most dark fowl is cooked "vertcuit" or "saignant," that is roasted brown on the outside under high heat, but still rare and running with juice and blood within. With these differences in mind, you can cook most wild fowl by the recipes suggested for chicken, pages 574 to 586, but suggestions are given in individual game reci-

pes for those combinations which are classic with game.

Let us also recommend, as sympathetic accompaniments, a dressing of chestnuts or wild rice; a salad of chicory or cress; a dish of gooseberry or quince conserve; a sour cream or wine sauce—not too powerfully seasoned.

If you have more game than you can use immediately, you may consider freezing (II, 562), or smoking (II, 545). ◆ To cook smoked game, parsteam it (II, 545) a few minutes to remove excess salt. Then cook as for ham.

ABOUT SALMI OF WILD BIRDS

A true salmi has two major characteristics. The meat is roasted—barely so, if the game is dark. And the meat from the breasts and from the legs, if they are choice, is sliced and put to one side and kept warm. Preparation is concluded at table, much as in Duck Rouennaise, page 587, where the skin and the chopped carcass are pressed in a duck press. The pressed juices are combined with the flambéed livers, the sauce reduced with a Mirepoix and then strained. Reinforce the sauce by a Demi-glaze Sauce, page 365, or Sauce Espagnole, page 365, based on the same kind of game as that being served. If the game is a waterbird, the skin may be too oily to use. Salmis may also be enriched with mushrooms or truffles. The meat is just heated through at table in a chafing dish with this very rich sauce, given a swirl of butter, page 357, and served at once.

Obviously, a classic salmi, fully accoutered, is only for the skilled cook whose husband is a Nimrod and has presented her with more than a single bird. If she is less well endowed, she will have to base her sauce on the backs, wings and necks of the bird that is being presented and eke out her Espagnole Sauce with veal stock. Needless to say, the dish is rarely presented in its original form. And the salmis that appear on menus are usually made from reheated meat, with sauces which have been previously confected. They can still be delicious, especially if care is taken ♦ not to boil the sauce and thereby toughen the meat. Another simpler way to serve precooked game is to make up a mixture similar to Pheasant in Game Sauce, page 595, which lends itself even to ✱ freezing.

MARINATED [2]
WILD BIRDS

♦ Please read About Wild Birds, page 590. Clean and disjoint a:
> Pheasant, partridge or
> grouse

Place in a casserole and cover with a marinade of:
> 1 small quartered onion
> 1 small bay leaf
> 1 clove garlic
> 2 cups port wine
> 1½ teaspoons salt
> ½ teaspoon pepper

Be sure the wine covers the pieces. Let stand in the refrigerator for 3 days. Remove the bird from the marinade, dry with a towel. Save the marinade. Preheat oven to 375°.
Put:
> 2 tablespoons butter

in a casserole. Brown and roast the pieces for about 45 minutes, turning several times. Strain the marinade and pour it over the pieces. Return to the oven for another 30 minutes or until tender. Take the pieces from the casserole. Keep warm. Reduce the sauce and:

> Correct the seasoning

Serve with:
> Wild rice or noodles

ABOUT WILD DUCKS

Flavor depends so much on the way ducks have been feeding. The shallow water types may have been feeding in nearby grain fields and may be very succulent. These include mallard, black duck, pintail, baldpate, gadwall and teal. The deepwater or sea ducks thrive on aquatic vegetation. They include canvasback, redhead, the golden eyes, scaup and ring neck. The mergansers or fish eaters should be used only in emergencies.

Wild ducks are usually not stuffed, but their insides may be greased to help retain juices. If too gamey, they may be rubbed with ginger or lemon. Also celery, grapes or sliced apple in the cavity help minimize a too pronounced taste. Discard before serving.

Cooking times vary with types. They may be as long as 20 minutes for canvasback or just 12 minutes for teal.

ROAST WILD DUCK [4]

To draw, pluck, singe and truss ♦ please read About Wild Birds, page 590. This method seems to be the hunter's ideal. The juices are red and flow freely when the duck is carved.
Preheat oven to 500°.
Prepare:
> 2 wild ducks

Have them at room temperature. Dry them thoroughly inside and out. Rub the insides with:
> Butter

Fill the cavities loosely with:
> A few skinned onions or
> peeled, cored and
> chopped apples or
> drained sauerkraut

Bard, page 454. Place the ducks on a rack in a roasting pan. ♦

Reduce heat to 350° and roast, uncovered, for 18 to 20 minutes. Degrease the drippings, and add:

Wine and stock

Reduce, then remove from heat and add:

Cultured sour cream

Reheat, but ◗ do not boil. Serve at once with:

Braised Celery, page 282

▤ BROILED OR BARBECUED WILD DUCK

Preheat broiler.
A good way to cook wild duck and an easy fashion of serving it is to split it down the back, clean it well and wipe until dry. Rub with:

(Garlic)

Spread with:

Unsalted butter

Season with:

Paprika

Broil about 4 inches under the broiler or 4 inches above charcoal. Baste frequently with:

An unsalted fat or oil
and wine

Cook until tender. Remove to a hot platter.

Correct the seasoning

Make a sauce with the drippings, page 358. Serve with:

Poached Oranges or
Kumquats (II, 101)

Fried hominy is a well-known accompaniment to wild ducks. So are grilled sweet potatoes or apples stuffed with sweet potatoes.

BRAISED WILD DUCK

◗ To draw, pluck, singe and truss:

A wild duck

please read About Wild Birds, page 590. Melt in a heavy casserole:

4 tablespoons butter

When it reaches the point of fragrance, put in the duck and brown on all sides. Add, when browned:

1 leek—white part only or
6 button onions
4 tender turnips
1 Bouquet Garni (II,
220)

◗ Simmer, covered, 25 to 35 minutes or until the duck is tender. Degrease the drippings and garnish the casserole with:

Cooked tender green
peas

Serve at once.

ABOUT PHEASANT

◗ Please read About Wild Birds, page 590. We hope your pheasant is young, with a flexible breast bone, grey legs and a pointed, large terminal feather in its wings. If it is a cock, it should have rounded, not sharp or long, spurs. Then you may roast or broil it even without hanging. Barding is advisable.

Otherwise, to give it both flavor and tenderness, about a 3 day hanging period is advised, during which the color of the breast will change somewhat and there will be a slight odor.

An old bird should be barded and either braised or used in a moist heat recipe, see page 81.

ROAST PHEASANT   [3]

Preheat oven to 400°.
◗ Please read About Wild Birds, page 590, and About Pheasant, above.

Bard, page 454:

A young pheasant

You may stuff it with:

A Chestnut and Sausage
Dressing

Place in oven. ◗ Reduce heat at once to 350°. Cook about 25 minutes to the lb. or until tender. If unstuffed, serve with:

Fried Croutons, page
390, Bread Sauce, page
364, Currant Jelly and

Braised Celery or Rice
Pilaf, page 166, and
Gooseberry Preserves
(II, 581)

or, classically, with:

Sauce Smitane, page 364

BRAISED PHEASANT

This recipe comes from a hunting fan:

◆ Please read About Wild Birds, page 590, and About Pheasant, page 594.

Preheat oven to 400°.

Prepare:

A pheasant

Pound:

A thin slice salt pork

Separate the skin from the breast flesh of the pheasant and insert the salt pork. Place in the body cavity the pheasant liver and:

A small peeled tangerine

Lace the opening tightly. Truss the pheasant. Melt in a heavy pan:

¼ cup lard

Brown the pheasant, turning it and basting until it is golden all over. Place in a casserole. Add and turn in the fat:

12 sliced mushroom caps

Pour these over the pheasant. Melt in a saucepan:

¼ cup butter

Stir in, cook, but do not permit to brown:

3 shallots or 1 small
minced onion

2 teaspoons flour

Stir in gradually:

¼ to ⅓ cup Marsala or
Madeira

½ teaspoon salt and freshly
ground pepper

Pour this into the casserole. Our correspondent adds a sprig of fresh fennel and 2 crushed juniper berries. ◆ Cover the casserole and bake the pheasant for about ½ hour. Serve it from the casserole with:

Fried hominy and
currant jelly
A green salad

✻ PHEASANT   [10 to 12]
IN GAME SAUCE

Preheat oven to 400°.

Prepare for roasting:

5 or 6 pheasants

Bard, page 454, with:

Bacon or salt pork

Fill the cavity, if you wish to reduce the game taste, with:

Apple or onion slices

Discard them after birds are roasted. Roast at 400° for 20 minutes. Remove meat from bones. Keep the meat in as large pieces as possible. Cook for 2 hours or until reduced about ⅓, a stock made from the bones, skins, drippings and barding, using:

2 large chopped onions

2 cloves garlic

2 bay leaves

1 tablespoon black
peppercorns

1 teaspoon thyme

1 small pinch rosemary

1 cup chopped parsley

(6 juniper berries)

¼ lb. ham trimmings

1 quart dry red wine

2 quarts water or chicken
stock

Stems from 2 lbs.
mushrooms

3 fresh tomatoes

Strain the stock and add it to:

¾ cup Cream Sauce, page
359

Add to this sauce:

Caps of 2 lbs. mushrooms

¾ cup red wine

Simmer about 25 minutes.

Correct the seasoning

Reduce by ⅓, strain and add:

¼ cup cognac

Simmer another 10 minutes. Arrange meat in 3-quart casserole. You may put it on a bed of:

(Cooked wild rice)

Pour sauce over it. To serve, reheat, uncovered, in a 350° oven, 45 to 55 minutes. If frozen, thaw and bring to room temperature before reheating.

PHEASANT SMITANE [3]

Bard, page 454:
> A 3½ to 4 pound pheasant

with:
> Sliced salt pork or bacon

Brown the pheasant in:
> Butter

in a heavy pan. Then place in a deep casserole with the drippings. Cover tightly and let simmer over low heat until tender, about 45 minutes. Add:
> 4 cups diced tart apples
> 2 tablespoons cognac or Calvados
> 2 cups cultured sour cream
> Correct the seasoning

and cook over low heat until the apples are tender. ◗ Do not boil. Serve with:
> Wild rice, page 160

ABOUT PARTRIDGE

Beware of an old bird, which must be braised or marinated, even if it is hung to the maximum of seven days. You will recognize an old bird in its feathers—by a conspicuous red ring on the eye circle, its yellow beak, its dark legs and, in a restaurant, by the French term "perdrix." For, by some strange convention, old partridges—regardless of sex—are ungraciously designated as female. If a partridge is under six months old, it still has its pointed first-flight feather and, on the menu, is gallantly referred to as perdreau or male—sex discrimination again actually being ignored. The red-legged French partridges are larger and not considered as delicate as the English. There is some confusion in America about the very name of partridge. No true partridge is native, but the name is given in the north to the ruffed grouse and in the south to quail.

If the bird is fresh, it has a rigid vent. ◗ A true partridge can be cooked by any recipe for chicken if larded; or, if barded, as for pheasant. But, if it is old, a longer cooking period may be necessary. It may be served in a Salmi, page 592, as for duck. Some people like it braised with Sauerkraut, page 278, allowing 2 lbs. of the sauerkraut to three 3-lb. birds. Add the sauerkraut the last ½ hour of cooking. Others shudder at so strongly flavored an accompaniment. A more delicate one is Braised Endive, page 292—and stuff it before cooking with marrow. Or wrap the partridge in grape leaves, simmer it in wine and stock for 35 minutes. Then roast it in a 350° oven for 25 minutes. Allow 1 lb. per person. Make Pan Gravy, page 358, and serve the partridge with Boiled New Potatoes, page 310, and water cress.

GROUSE, PTARMIGAN OR PRAIRIE CHICKEN

[Allow 1 lb. per Person]
Preheat oven to 300°.
Young grouse which feeds on the tender shoots of the heather is one of the more coveted of all game. To test for youth, hold the bird aloft by the lower mandible. If this breaks, failing to support the weight of the bird, you have a young specimen. Roast or broil if young. Braise if old. The same treatments apply to Canadian Grouse or Black Game, also known as Black Grouse or Coq de Bruyère. Resinous in flavor, this is not quite as good as true grouse. However, it is cooked in the same way.
Prepare for cooking as you would a chicken:

Young grouse

You may lard the breast, page 453, with thin strips of:

> Salt pork

or bard it, page 454. You may stuff it with:

> A small apple, a skinned onion or ribs of celery

Grouse is served rare, to a pale pink tone. Allow about 30 to 45 minutes cooking in all. Baste it frequently with:

> Melted butter or drippings

Remove the bacon. Brush the bird with:

> Butter

Dredge it lightly with:

> Flour

Place it in a hot 500° oven, until brown. Make:

> Pan Gravy, page 358

Serve with:

> Rowanberries or Cranberry Sauce

BROILED GROUSE

The bird must be young, see above. Bard, page 454, and broil only the:

> Breast of young grouse

Prepare it by splitting down the back and flattening the breast without separating it. Brush with:

> Cooking oil

Broil about 7 minutes to each side, heating the bony side first. It is classic to serve it with:

> Bread Sauce, page 364, or
> Sauce Périgueux, page 367

WILD GOOSE AND WILD TURKEY

[1 lb. per Person]

If you talk to someone who has eaten only an old goose—and they do live to a great old age—he will claim it is abominable. Indeed, these birds are worth bothering with only if they are less than a year old. Hang from 24 hours to a week and cook with moist heat, page 81, whether the goose is old or young. Weights fluctuate, depending on variety and age, from about 4 to 9 lbs.

◗ To draw, pluck, singe and truss, see pages 568–572.

For young goose and wild turkey proceed as for turkey, page 574, or cut as for fricassee, page 568:

> A 5 to 6 lb. wild goose

In a heavy casserole heat to the point of fragrance:

> ⅓ cup butter
> 1½ cups small, white, whole onions

Add:

> ¼ lb. finely diced salt pork

and continue to cook until onions are golden. Lift out onions and pork and discard. In the remaining fat, brown the cut up bird. Add:

> Juice of ½ lemon
> ½ teaspoon allspice
> (A few slivers gingerroot)

◗ Simmer, covered, about 30 minutes. Stir if necessary. Add:

> 2 cups dry red wine

◗ Simmer, covered, at least 45 minutes longer or until tender. Thicken the pan gravy slightly with:

> Toasted dry bread crumbs

Serve with:

> Noodles
> Spiced apricots or crabapples

POTTED WILD FOWL

[Allow 1 lb. per Person]

A good way to preserve any extra wild fowl.

◗ Please read about Wild Goose, above.

Draw, pluck, singe and cut for fricassee:

> A young wild goose or other wild fowl

Prepare as for:
> Potted Goose, page 589

Serve either hot or cold.

HAZEL HEN

[Allow 1 lb. per Person]

Since this bird is quite resinous, it is best to poach it first in milk for 15 minutes. Bone and grill for about 12 minutes in all.

ABOUT SMALL GAME BIRDS

Birds here discussed are of many kinds: ortolans, figpickers, coot, doves, woodcock, snipe, rails, curlew, plover, quail, larks, reed birds, thrush, moorhen and gallinule. They are bracketed on the basis of similar treatment and the fact that they are served one or more to a person. ♦ Small birds are usually used as fresh as possible, although they remain edible as long as the legs are flexible. Quail, which is about the largest discussed here, should not be hung longer than 24 hours. ♦ All small birds should be dry plucked. In fact, some, like snipe, plover, ring dove and woodcock may be cooked undrawn, although the eyes and crop are discarded before roasting. To use the entrails after cooking, sieve or chop the intestines and flambé them, page 80, briefly, in cognac. Mix with pan drippings and spread on a crouton or over the bird as a glaze before serving. Or, if you draw the bird before cooking, reserve the intestines, chop them, sauté them briefly in butter, then proceed as above.

Small birds should be barded, page 88, or you may wrap them first in fig or grape leaves. All these birds lend themselves to roasting and skewering or broiling from 3 to 10 minutes. Blackbirds and crows, if eaten as a matter of necessity, must be parblanched first, page 88.

All these small birds produce very little pan dripping. Pour what there is on a Crouton, page 390, or a piece of crisp scrapple. Or combine the drippings with a Demiglaze Sauce and wine or lemon, page 365, with Smitane Sauce or Sauce Veneur or use any recipe for braised chicken—allowing in the timing for difference in size. Any peculiarities or classic combinations are listed in individual recipes.

ROASTED SMALL GAME BIRDS

♦ Please read About Small Birds, above.

Preheat oven to 450°.

Bard, page 454:
> 6 small birds

It is not necessary to stuff them, although a few peeled grapes or bits of celery or parsley may be tucked inside and discarded later. Place in the pan:
> 1 tablespoon butter

Bake the birds for about 5 minutes ♦ reduce the heat to 350° and bake them from 5 to 15 minutes longer, according to their size.

Quail—unstuffed	
	10 to 15 minutes
—stuffed	
	15 to 18 minutes
Woodcock	8 to 10 minutes

BROILED SMALL GAME BIRDS

Preheat broiler.

Bard, page 454:
> 6 small game birds

Place them on a broiler. Cook them from 12 to 20 minutes, according to size. Turn frequently. The barding may be removed toward the end of the cooking period and the birds browned briefly by further broiling. Add the juice of:
> 1 lemon

to:
> Stock or wine

if there is an insufficient amount of drippings.

Correct the seasoning
Serve the birds on:

Fried toast

Pour the gravy over them. Garnish them with:

Parsley

Permit the sauce to soak into the toast.

BRAISED SMALL GAME BIRDS

◗ Please read About Small Game Birds, page 598.
Preheat oven to 350°.
Prepare for cooking:

6 birds

Melt in a saucepan:

2 tablespoons butter

Add and sauté for 1 minute:

A Mirepoix (II, 221)

Add the birds and sauté them until they are lightly browned. Add:

½ cup boiling stock or wine

Cover the birds with a poaching paper, page 83, and bake them for 15 to 20 minutes. Make:

Pan Gravy, page 358

Add to the gravy:

(2 tablespoons lemon juice or cultured sour cream or brandy)

Serve on:

Croutons, page 390

garnished with:

Parsley

▤ SKEWERED SMALL BIRDS

◗ Please read About Small Game Birds, page 598.
Wrap in buttered grape or fig leaves:

Small birds

and then bard in very thin slices of:

Salt pork

Roast skewered over coals 10 to 15 minutes. To finish for serving, you may remove the bard-ing, roll the birds in bread crumbs, baste with drippings and heat in a moderate oven 5 minutes longer.

DOVE OR WOOD [1 to 2] PIGEONS

◗ Please read About Small Game Birds, page 598.
A dark meat with a fine flavor. The brain may be mixed with the trail. To prepare these parts, see page 598. Unless the birds are very young, prepare as for:

Braised Small Game Birds, this page

Serve the sauce garnished with:

Almond stuffed olives

or with a compote of:

Red Sour Cherries (II, 88)

QUAIL

[1 per Person]

Sometimes called partridge in our deep South. ◗ Please read About Small Game Birds, page 598. This bird has a delicious white meat. If the fat of the bird is hard rather than firm before cooking, the flesh will be tough and must be prepared by a moist heat method. If the bird is young, roast or broil.
◗ Never overcook. Serve with:

Quince preserves and curried rice or water cress and lemon wedges

or serve with:

Sauce Smitane, page 364, and green grapes or a baked pear, the core stuffed with a pimiento

If you have broiled the quail, brush it with:

(Anchovy Butter, page 384)

SNIPE OR WOODCOCK

[Allow 1 to 2 Birds per Person]

Known in France as bécassine and bécasse, respectively, these birds are highly prized by some epicures, in the fall, when they are fat and meaty. But de Pomiane claims that it takes man's snobbishness to elevate to one of life's great moments the woodcock flambé, with its long beak, meager body and prominent eyes. He claims that even dogs scorn this status symbol and that the entrail-soaked crouton alone deserves attention.

▶ Please read About Small Game Birds, page 598.

Prepare and cook as for:

Small Game Birds, page 598

or use the recipe for Grouse, page 596. You may use the trail, see page 598. Skin the head, but leave it on. Remove the eyes and crop. Bring the long, curved beak down to pierce and hold the legs in place. Bard, page 454, and roast 10 to 15 minutes.

INDEX

"Knowledge," said Dr. Johnson, "is of two kinds. We know a subject as our own, or we know where we can find information on it." Below we put into your hands the second kind of knowledge—a kitchen-door key which will help to open up the first.

If you want information on a certain food you will find that the initial listing is often an "About"; giving characteristics, peculiarities of handling, tests for doneness, storage needs and serving quantities. The titles which follow usually indicate how that particular food may be cooked: Sweetbreads, braised, or Fish, broiled.

In using the Index look for a noun rather than an adjective: Torte, almond, not Almond Torte: unless the modifying term is a foreign one, in which case it will be listed and lead you to an explanation. Foreign terms are frequently translated in an alternate title, thus: Pickled Fish or Escabèche, revealing a process; or, as in Senegalese or Chicken Curry Soup, showing the ingredients mainly responsible for the term. Or the recipe itself will clear your doubts—for "à la mode" used with a savory food like beef will describe a stew, whereas with a sweet one, like pie or cake, it will indicate the expected scoop of ice cream. Since cooking terms, both foreign and domestic, are dealt with at the point of use, as described above, we have dispensed with a separate glossary.

Remember, too, that the book as a whole divides into three sections: The Foods We Eat, The Foods We Heat and the Foods We Keep, with Know Your Ingredients at the center of things. And that many "convenience" recipes are grouped under Lunch, Brunch and Supper Dishes. Within chapters, too, initial text or recipes often cover basic methods of preparation, and are followed, as in Fruits, Fish and Vegetables by alphabetical listings of varieties—from Apples to Rhubarb, Carp to Whale, Artichokes to Water Chestnuts. Under Meats you will find in the Index general comments and processes, with further references to Beef, Veal, Lamb, Pork, Ham, Ground and Variety Meats and Game. In this chapter a further differentiation is made between those cuts cooked by dry heat—often a quick process—and those cooked by moist heat which, to be effective, is always slower. Note, too, that in the listings below, illustrations can be found immediately by looking up the boldfaced numerals.

As you familiarize yourself with the "Joy" you will need the Index less and less and will become, in Dr. Johnson's fullest sense, a know-it-all. Meanwhile, happy hunting!

À Blanc, to cook, 454
À la King Sauce, Quick, 375
À la Mode, as savory, 498, 548, 554
À l'Étouffée, to cook, 85
À Point, to cook, 72
Abalone, Sautéed, 433
Accessory Factors In Food, 4
Additives, 2
Agrodulce, defined, 353
Aioli Sauce, 347
Albert Sauce, 362
Allemande Sauce, 362
Allumette, 251
Almonds, blanching, 88
    butter, 383
    garnish or Amandine, 390
Amandine Garnish, 390
Anchovy, butter, 384
    dressings, 342, 343
    sauce for fish, 361
    stuffing for tomatoes, 337
Andalouse Sauce, 347
Anise, or fennel, to cook, 292
    tisane, 20
Anna, potatoes, 315
Apple, also see individual names
    baked, with sausage, 221
    beets, sweet-sour, 270
    casserole, onion and, 304
    dressings, 563, 565
    salad, 53; molded, 67, 70
    sweet potatoes, and, 324
Arrowroot Flour or Starch, as
    thickener, 356
Artichokes, globe; cored, 259, 259
    hearts, 260
    Jerusalem, 260
    salads, 40
    stuffed, baked, 260
    to eat, 259
    to wash, 259
Asparagus, 260, 261
    creamed eggs Cockaigne, and,
    194
    salads, 41, 58
    sandwich, and ham, 243
    soup, cream of, 126; quick, 139
    timbales, 203
Aspic, about, 57; additions to, 58
    chicken, 60
    eggs in, Cockaigne, 63
    fish in, Cockaigne, 405
    garnish, 59
    glaze, 387
    layered, 57
    salads, 57–70
    to make, 58
    tomato, 65, 66
    tongue in, 546
    vegetable juice, 66
    wine or liquor in, 58
Attereaux, defined, 75
Au Gratin, defined, 389
Aubergine, see Eggplant, 289
Aurore Sauce, 362
Avocados, cups, to prepare, 53, 54
    dressing, 342
    salads, 53, 54, 66
    soup, cream, chilled, quick, 140

Bacon, about; broiled, 492; sautéed,
    492

Canadian, 492
    rice custard, and, 163
    rings, eggs baked in, 193
    sandwiches, 240–247
    sauce, sweet-sour, 371
Baking, altitude, see High Altitude
    defined, 73
Bamboo Shoots, 261
Banana, salad, and nut, 54
Barbecue, also see Meat, Poultry,
    Outdoor symbol 🍴
    cole slaw, 37
    defined, 73
    sauces, 374, 375
Barding, 453, 454
Barley, soup, 115
Basting, 457, 457
Baumwollsuppe, 146
BEANS, about, see Dried or Fresh,
    below
    baked; with fruit, 266
    baked and bacon or frankfurters,
    267
    boiled, 266
    broad, 261
    butter, 268
    campfire, 266
    dinner in one dish, 265
    dried, see Dried Legumes, 264
    dried, patties, 265; salad, 41
    dried, soup, 119
    dried, to soften, quick, 264
    fava, 261
    fresh, about, 261
    garbanzo or flageolets, 264
    green, 261
    green, additions to, 262
    green, casserole, 262
    green, potatoes and smoked
    meat, 263
    green, sweet-sour, 263
    haricot, 262, 264
    kidney, canned, and tomatoes,
    267
    Lima, about, 268, 268
    Lima, chili; casserole, 269
    Lima, dried, 264
    Lima, French, 269
    Lima, mushrooms, and, 270
    Lima, puréed, 263
    Lima, with cheese, 269; with
    sauce, 269
    Mung, 264
    navy; substitute for chestnuts,
    264
    pinto, and rice, 267
    preprocessed, 264
    puréed, 263
    salads, 41, 42
    snap, 262
    soups, 118–120
    soy, see Soybeans, 265
    string, 261
    to keep from toughening, 262
    white, 264
Bean Sprout, salad, 36; cooked, 264
Bear, 557
Béarnaise Sauce, 370
Beaver, 557; tail, 557
Béchamel Sauces, 359
BEEF, 463–477, 495–502; also see
    Meat

BEEF (*cont.*)
à la mode, 498
balls, *see* Meatballs, 518
Boeuf Bourguignonne, 496
Boeuf Fondu Bourguignonne, 475
Boeuf Miroton, 217
boiled or Boeuf Bouilli, 495
brisket with sauerkraut, 497
burgers, filled, 517
Chili Con Carne, 520
chipped, *see* Chipped Beef; 222
chuck roast in foil, 498
commercial and retail cuts, 461, 465
consommé, jellied, 114
corned, *see* Corned Beef
dried, *see* Chipped Beef, 222, 223
fillet, or tenderloin, 472, 472
fillet, Tournedos, 472, 473
Goulash, 500
ground, 514, *also see* Hamburger
ground, in cabbage leaves, 521, 522
Gumbo, 118
hash, and ham, 223
juice, 111
Kebabs or on skewers, 475
kidneys, broiled, tomatoes and onions, 543
liver Creole, 536
loaf Cockaigne, 523
New England boiled dinner, 493
oxtail, braised, 552
pot pie, quick, 212
pot roast; sour cream and wine, 496
roast, 463; chuck, 498
roast in sauce, 216
roast, sirloin strip, 472
rolls, Roulades or Paupiettes, 502
salad, 52
sandwiches, 242
Sauerbraten, 497
short ribs, 500
Spanish casserole with rice, 520
spiced, 498
steak, about, 472
steak and kidney pie, 502
steak au Poivre or peppered, 475
steak, broiled, pan-broiled, 474
steak, club or minute, 473
steak, cube, 473
steak, Filet Mignon, broiled, 472, 475
steak, fillet, Chateaubriand, 472, 472, 473
steak, fillet, pan-broiled, 474
steak, flank, 473; with dressing, 499
steak, London Broil or flank, 475
steak, porterhouse, 473
steak, rib or Spencer, 473
steak, round, 473
steak, rump, 473
steak, sauces for, 473, 475
steak, sirloin; strip, 473
steak, Swiss, 473, 499
steak, t-bone, 473
steak, tenderloin or fillet, 473

steak, Tournedos, broiled, 472, 473
stew, Belgian or Carbonnade Flamande, 501
stew, Gaston, 496
stew, oxtail, 501
stew with wine, 496
Stroganoff, 476
Sukiyaki, 477
tea, 111
tenderloin, 472, 472
to carve, 401, 460, 463
tongue boiled, fresh, 545; with raisin sauce, 545
yield from side of beef, chart, 461
Beer, in soup, 107
sauce, raisin, 373; marinade, 382
Beet, cooked, 270; baked, 271
boiled, in sour cream, 271
casseroled, 270
consommé, jellied, 114
cups, cold, 42
dressing, and anchovy, 342
greens, 271
Harvard or sweet-sour, 270; and apples, 271
salad, gelatin, 63
salad, pickled, 42; and chicory, 35
soup or Borsch, 117; blender, 140
young, and leaves, 271
Belgian Stew or Carbonnade Flamande, 501
Benne Seed, wafers, 152
Bercy Butter, 384; sauce, 373
Beurre de Provence, *see* Aïoli Sauce, 347
Manié, 357
Noir, 383
Noisette, 383
Bigarade, Duck, 588
Birds, *see* Game Birds, Poultry
BISCUIT, hot, with filling, 241
Bisques, *see* Soups
Black Game, 596
Blanching, 188–189
vegetables, 252
Blanquette de Veau, 504
Blender, look for blender symbol
Bleu Cheese French Dressing, 343
Bloaters, grilled or baked, 412
Blood, as thickener, 357
sausage, 533
Blowfish, about, 416
Boar, wild, 558
Boiling, 181
Bolognese Sauce, 379
Bonito, fresh, 420
Bordelaise Sauce, 366
Borsch, 117; blender, 140
Bouchées, à la Reine, 228
Boudin Noir or Blood Sausage, 533
Bouillabaisse, 135
Bouillon, 111
chicken with egg, 110
jellied, 114
tomato, 111
Boula Boula, 122
Bracken, young or fern shoots, 293

Brains, about, **540**; broiled, **541**
    baked, and eggs, **541**
    sautéed, **540**
Braising pot, classic, **90–91, 91**
Bran, *also see* Bread, Rolls
Braunschweiger Sandwich, toasted,
    244
Brawn, 550
BREAD, blocks, puffed, **151**
    cases, 209
    crumbs, *see* Crumbs
    cubes, cheese, 152
    dressings, 560–565
    fancy for soup, about, **151**
    loaf with cheese and nuts, **238**
    puddings, *see* Puddings
    rolls, *see* Rolls
    sauce, 364
    to serve with soups, 151–152
Breadfruit, seeds, 272
Broccoli, 272; braised, 273
    creamed, quick, 273
    deep-fat fried, 273
    ring mold, 205; timbales, **202**
Brochette, 75; *see* Skewer
Broiling, 74, 455; outdoor, 93
    heat, to lower, 74
    infra-red, 99
Broiler Rack, preparation of, **74,**
    455
Broths, *see* Soups
Brown Sauce, quick, 366
BRUNCH DISHES, 208–248
Brunoise, consommé, 109
Brunswick Stew, 582
Brussels Sprouts, baked, 274
Buckwheat Cakes, groats, 156
Burgoo, 503
Burgundy Sauce, 372
Burners, gas, heat-pot relations,
    100–101
Burns and Burning, about, 104
BUTTER, *also see* Seasoned Butter
    drawn or clarified, 383
    kneaded or Beurre Manié, 357
    sauces, *see* Sauce
    swirls, 357
BUTTER, SEASONED, 383–386
    almond, 384
    anchovy, 384
    Bercy, 384
    black or Beurre Noir, 383
    brown or Beurre Noisette, 383
    caviar, 384
    Colbert, 384
    deviled for seafood, 385
    garlic, 385
    green or Ravigote, 385
    lemon or Meunière, 384
    Maître d'Hôtel, 384
    shrimp or lobster, 385
    snail, 384
    white, 385
Butterkloesse or Butter Dumplings,
    149

Cabbage, about, 274
    baked, 275
    celery, 31, 42, 282
    creamed, hash in, 224
    dish, and rice, 276
    French fried, 275

    leaves, ground beef in, 522
    leaves for wrap cooking, 85, **86**
    potatoes and ham, 275
    red, 277; and chestnuts, 278
    rolls, stuffed with rice, cheese,
      277
    salads, *see* Cole Slaw, 36–37
    sauerkraut, 278, 279
    sautéed, 275
    scalloped, 276
    soup, 117
    Strudel, savory, 276
    stuffed or Gefuellter Krautkopf,
      521
    stuffed with corned beef, 277;
      with ham, 277
    with tomatoes; and cheese, 277
Caesar Salad, 35
Café, Caffè, *see* Coffees, **14–19**
Caffeine, sources of, 15
Calf, feet, jellied, 551
    head, 549
    liver, 534, 537; *also see* Liver
    lungs or lights, 550
    sweetbreads, 537
Cali, see Cabbage and Ham, 275
Calico Salad, 50
Calories, about, 2; values, **5–12**
    defined, 2
    dressing, low, 345
    recommended daily allowances,
      13
Camp Cooking, 89–93, 89
Campfire Beans, 266
Canadian Bacon, 492
Canned Goods, opened, storage,
    255
Canneloni or Manicotti, 176
CANNING, *see individual names of*
    Fruits, Vegetables, Meat, Poultry,
    and Game
Capers, sauce, 363
Capon, roasting, about, 572
Carbohydrates, about, 3; values, **2**
Carbonnade Flamande, 501
Cardoons, 279
Carp, 407
Carrots; baked, 280
    caramelized, 281
    in bunches, 280
    mashed or carrot ring, 280
    peas and, 306
    salad with raisins and nuts, 42
    Vichy, 280
    waterless, 280
Carving, 460, 460, 463, 574
Cases, food, 208–211
CASSEROLES, *also see* Stews, Fish,
    and Shellfish
    bacon and rice custard, 163
    bean dinner in one dish, 265
    bean, Lima, chili, 269
    beans, canned, baked with fruit,
      266
    beans, green, 262, 263
    cabbage, tomato and cheese dish,
      277
    Cassoulet, 509
    cheese, 238
    chicken and turkey, 577–583,
      585, 586
    Chili Con Carne, 520

CASSEROLES (*cont.*)
corn bread tamale pie, 212
crab meat custard, 232
defined: true, mock, 84
egg, creamed, and asparagus,
　　Cockaigne, 194
egg, hard-cooked, and vegetable,
　　193
eggplant or Ratatouille
　　Provençale, 291
equipment, 84
fruit, nut and rice, 166
ham noodles, 174
ham slices, 490
hamburger, 521
hominy, scalloped, and ham,
　　156
Jambalaya, 164
Kedgeree of lobster, 230
kidney, veal, 543
lamb and eggplant, 521
lamb shanks, braised, 508
lentil and sausage, 221
liver, braised with wine, 536
macaroni with shellfish, 172
meatballs in sauce, 518–520
noodle and cheese loaf, quantity,
　　175
noodle and pork, Rumanian, 175
noodle dish, leftover, 175
onion and apple, 304
oxtails, braised, 552
Paella, 165
pheasant, 594–596
pigeons or squabs, potted, 590
Pilaf, 166
pork chops Creole, braised, 512
pork chops with fruit, 512
pork tenderloin, fruit, 487
pottery, to season, 84–85
rabbit or hare à la mode, 554
Ragoût Fin, 539
rice loaf or casserole, 161
sauerkraut and tomato, 279
seafood in Creole sauce, 230
seafood Tetrazzini, 170
spaghetti, quick, 169
Spanish, with rice, 520
sweetbreads, braised, 538
to glaze a sauce, 386
to reheat, 99
tomato olive, 334
tripe à la mode de Caen, 548
tuna, noodle and mushroom
　　soup, 175
turkey or chicken with
　　vegetables, 227
veal and spinach dish, 217
veal, cubed, baked in sour
　　cream, 506
veal with red wine, 503
Cassoulet, 509
Catfish, 407
Cauliflower; deep fried, 281
mushroom and, in sauce, 282
sautéed, 281
soup, cream of, 126; quick, 141
timbales, 202
Caviar, butter, 384
molded egg salad, and, 49
sauce, 352
Celeriac or Celeri-Rave, 283

Remoulade, 43
salad, 43; ring mild, 205
Celery; braised or glazed, 282
dressing, 561, 562
salads for, 31; cooked for, 43
seed dressing, 352
soup, cream of, 126
Celery Cabbage, cooked, 282
salad, 31, 43
Celery Root, 283; ring mold, 205
CEREALS, about; cooking, 153; *also
see individual names*
finely and coarsely milled, 154–
　　155
to thicken soups with, 108
whole, 155
Chantilly, mayonnaise, 348
potatoes, 311
Chapon, 33
Charcoal Fire, to prepare, 95
Chard, Swiss, 283
Chasseur Sauce, 366
Chateaubriand, 472, 473
Chaud-Froid, defined; decorations,
　　388
Chayotes, 283
CHEESE, balls for soup, 151
bread, nut loaf, 238
casserole, 238
cottage, *see* Cottage Cheese
cream, *see* Cream Cheese
dressings, 364
dumplings; quick, 177
Fondue, 239–240
Head or brawn, 550
pastas and, 168–177
pie, 214
Quiches, 214
Rarebits, 237
rice ring, 160, 162
rounds, Melba, 152
sandwiches, 240–248
sauces, *see* Sauces
soufflés, 197–198
soup, quick, 141
timbales, 203
Cherries, salad, 54; aspic, 67
Chestnut, baked, 284; boiled, 283;
　　Brussels sprouts, 274; red cabbage,
　　278
dressing for game, 562
ring mold, 205
soup, 127
Water, 339
CHICKEN, 567–586; *also see* Poultry
à la Campagne, 586
à la King, 226
aspic, 60
baked in foil, 575; barbecued,
　　576
boned, 585
braised in wine or Coq au Vin,
　　579
breasts, brandied, 582;
　　Cockaigne, 583; in quantity,
　　584; stuffed, 583
broilers, defined, 567; braised,
　　578; broiled, 576; stuffed,
　　576
broth, 110; and clam, quick,
　　143
Brunswick stew, 582

Cacciatore, Chasseur or Hunter's, 580
casserole, French, 581
casserole with vegetables, 227
Country Captain or East India curry, 585
creamed, 226
Creole, quick, 227
curry, 585; soup, 117
Divan, 228
farce or forcemeat, 564
giblets, 553
gravy, pan, 358
Gumbo, 118
hash, 220
in batter, 577
in patty shells, and sweetbreads, 228
Jambalaya, 164
Kiev, 582
legs, stuffed, 584; City Chicken, 505
livers à la King, 537; in batter, 537
livers, Lyonnaise, 534; pâté, 525
liver timbales, 203
liver topping for pasta, 391
loaf, cooked; quantity, 228
Marengo, 581
marinade for, 383
Maryland, 579
mousse, jellied, 60
oven-fried, 576
pan-fried or sautéed, 577
Paprika, 579
patties, 518
pot pie, quick, 212
roast, 574; roasting, about, 572
salad; variations, 52; hot, 52
sandwiches, 246–247
smothered, 579
soufflés, 200
soup, cream of, 127; quick, 140
soup, curry or Senegalese, 117
Spanish, 581
stew or fricassee, 577–578, 569
Suprême Papillote, 583
Tarragon with wine, 580
terrine, 528
Tetrazzini, 170
timbales, 203
to cut up a drawn bird, 569, 569
to size up, 567
Chicory, 284; Witloof, 31
salad, beetroot and, 35
Chiffonade, dressing, 344
of fresh herbs, for soup, 151
Chili Con Carne, 520
Chinese or Celery Cabbage, 31, 42, 282
egg rolls, 212
Chipped Beef, creamed, 222; in canned soup, 223
in sauce, cheese, 222; Creole, 222
sweet potatoes, and, 222
Chips, fish and, 401
potato or Saratoga, 319
Chitterlings, sautéed, 551
CHOCOLATE, beverages, about, 20
Brazilian or Russian, 21

hot, 22
iced, 22
malt sirups, 22
shake sirups, 22
Chop Suey, 218
Choux Paste, garnish, 148
Chow Mein, 218
Chowder, defined, 107; see Soups
Christmas, watch for symbol ★
Chutney, dressing, 344
Cider, hot or mulled, 25
sauce, raisin, 373
City Chicken, 505
Civet, 554
CLAMS, about, 427–428; to open, 427–428
bisque, and mushroom, 134
broiled on the half shell, 430
broth or soup, 132, 431; and chicken, quick, 143
cakes, 234
clambakes, 428
chowder: Manhattan, 137; New England, 137
fried, 430
hard-shell, 428, 428; steamed, broth, 431
juice, 24; ring, jellied, 61
mushrooms, stuffed with, 297
razor, 428
sauce for pasta, quick, 379
soft or longneck, 427, 427; baked, 430
soft-shelled, steamed with broth, 430
surf, 428
Club Sandwich, 246
Cockaigne, see Foreword
Cock-a-leekie Soup, 123
Cockscombs, 553
COCKTAILS, sauce, 344
COCOA, beverages, about, 20
hot, 21, 22
malt or shake sirup, 22
Cocozelle, 327–328, 328
Cod, about, 407
balls or cakes, 408
fresh, à la Portugaise, 408
fresh, Boulangère, 409
salt or Morue à la Provençale, 408
scalloped, 407
scrod, fresh, broiled, 409
sounds and tongues, 408
COFFEE, 14–18; also see Mocha
about, 14
amount per cup, 15
Café au Lait, 17
Café Brûlot, Diable or Royal, 17, 18
Capuccino, 17
chicory in, 15
cream in, 15
drip or Café Filtré, 15
equipment, 14–15, 14
Espresso, 16
filters, care of, 15
frozen, blender, 18
iced, 18; Viennoise, 18
in quantity, 16
instant, 16
Irish, 18

COFFEE (*cont.*)
  percolated, 16
  steeped, 16
  Turkish, 17
  vacuum method, 15
  water for, 15
Colbert Butter, 384
Cole Slaw, 36; Roquefort, 36
  de luxe, 36; for barbecue, 37
Color in Food, about, 251
  in sauces, 353
  in soups, 107
Conch Chowder, 137
Confit d'Oie or potted goose, 589
Consommé, Brunoise, 109
  canned, quick variations, 139
  jellied beet, 114; Madrilène, 110
Cooking, equipment, 99
  outdoor, 89
Coot, 598
Coq au Vin, 579
Coq de Bruyère, 596
Coquina Broth, 132
Corn, about, 284
  à la King, peppers stuffed with, 309
  breads or cakes, *see* Corn Meal
  chowder, 127, 141
  Creole, 286
  fritters or corn oysters, 286, 287
  grilled or roasted, 285
  husks, for wrap cooking, 86, 86
  off the cob, cooked, 285
  on the cob, 284
  pudding, Cockaigne, 285
  salad, or field, 30
  scalloped, 286
  soufflé, 199
  soup, cream of, 127
  succotash, 286
  Tamales, 287
  timbales, egg and cheese, 202
Corn Meal, bread, Tamale pie, 212
  dumplings, 178
  mush, 156
  Polenta, 156
Corned Beef, about, 492; baked, 222
  cabbage and, 493
  hash, cabbage stuffed with, 277
  hash patties, 226; and potatoes, 225
  in canned soup, 223
  salad, 52
  sandwiches, 242
Cornish Hen, dressing for, 564
  roasted, 589; about roasting, 572
Cornstarch, thickener for sauces, 356
Cottage Cheese, salad, 37; grape and, 55
Country, ham, 490
  sausage, 531
Couscous, 510
CRAB, 433–434
  about types, 433–434
  cakes, 234
  Gumbo, 135
  Louis, 50
  hard-shell, 444; steamed, 435
  meat, cheese toasted rolls, 247
  meat custard, 232
  meat, deviled, 232

  meat Mongole, 231; soup, 143
  meat, salad, 50
  soft-shell, deep-fat fried, **434, 435**
  soft-shell, sautéed, 435; broiled, 435
Cracker, for soups, 151–152
  meal dumplings, 147
  seeded, 152
Cracklings, 453
Cranberry, juice, 25; hot, 25
  glaze for fowl, 387
  salads, molded, 67
Crane Cooking, 90, 90
Crayfish, Crawfish or **Écrevisses**, about, 444, 445
CREAM, *also see* Sour Cream.
  cheese, *see* Cream Cheese
  dressing, sweet-sour, 371
  mayonnaise, 348
  sauces or Béchamel, 359–360
  soups, 125–131; *also see* Soups
Cream Cheese, dressings, 342; for fruit salad, 352
  sandwich, and chicken, 246
Creole Sauce, 380; quick, 376
Cress, garden, 31; winter, 32
Croutons, 390; in salad, 34; soup, 151
Crumb, buttered, 389
  sauce, browned, 386
Crustaceans, about, 421
Cucumber, about, 288; to score, 43
  boats, 38, 39
  casserole, Creole, 289
  casserole, or mock-oyster, 289
  jelly on tomato slices, 64
  mousse, 65; sour-cream, 65
  mulled, 288
  salad, 43; tomato and, 49
  sauce, 351
  soup, Bulgarian, cold, 128
  soup, Cockaigne, quick, 140
  soup, cold, quick, 141
  soup, herb, chilled cream, 128
  stuffed, cold, 44
  wilted, 43
Cumberland Sauce, 343; hot, 372
Curlew, 598
Currant, jellies, sauces, 372
Curry, chicken, 585
  dressing for fruit salad, 352
  lobster or seafood, 230
  sauce, 363
CUSTARD, cheese pie, 214
  crab meat, 232
  for vegetable timbales, 201
  rice, and bacon, 163
  soup, or Royale, 146
  tomato, 335
Cymling, 327, 328

Daikon, *see* Radishes, 325
Dandelion, 32
Darnes, 394, 394
Dasheen, 289
Dauphine Potatoes, 320
Deep-fat Frying, about, 75–79
  coatings for, 79
  equipment, 76, 77
  fats for, 78
  frozen foods, 79

high altitude, 79
temperature test, 76–77
Deer, 559; *also see* Venison
Deglazing, sauces, 358
Demi-glaze Sauce, 365
Devil Sauce, Soyer's Universal, 374
Deviled, butter for seafood, 385
crab, 232
eggs, 195, 196
ham sandwiches, and cheese, 244
Diet, 1–5; daily allowance chart, 13
dressings, 340, 345
Divans, 228, 231
Dolmas, 522
Double Boiler Cooking, 132
Doughnuts, to fry, 75–79
Dove, 598
Dresden Sauce, 351
DRESSING, 560–566; *also see* Salad
Dressings
apple, 565; prune or onion and, 563
apricot, 565
bread for, crumbs for, 560
bread with mushrooms, oysters, nuts, giblets, etc., 560
chestnut, for game, 562
chicken farce or forcemeat, 564
dry, 561
fennel, 562
for Cornish hen or pigeon, 564
for fish, 561
green for fish or fowl, 562
ham for turkey, 563
liver, 563
onion, 562; and apple, 563
oyster bread, 561
potato, 565
prune, 565
rice, pineapple, 565
rice, tangerine, 565
rice, 563; wild for game, 564
ring filled with hash, 225
sauerkraut for game, 566
sausage, 562
seafood, 564
sherry bread, 561
sweet potato and apple, 565; sausage, 565
Dried Beef Sandwich, 242; *also see* Chipped Beef
DRINKS, Alcoholic, Irish coffee, 18
Duchess Potatoes, 319
Duck, duckling Rouennaise, 587
glazed, apricot honey, 587
orange sauce for, 365
Pilaf, 229
roast, 587; Bigarade, 588
roasting, about, 573
stuffed or unstuffed, 573
wild, about; gaminess, 593
wild, braised, 594
wild, broiled or barbecued, 594
wild, roast, 593
Dumplings, 178–180
about, 146, 147
butter or Butterkloesse, 149
cheese, quick, 178
corn meal, 178
farina Cockaigne, 179; balls, 147

German egg, Spatzen or Spaetzle, 179
liver, or Leberkloesse, 148
liver sausage, 150
Matzo or cracker meal, 147
potato or Kartoffelkloesse, 180
to test for doneness, 146–147

Earthenware, 101
Écrevisses or Crayfish, 444, **445**
Eel, about, 409
EGG AND EGG DISHES, 183–207
about, 183
aspic, in; Cockaigne, 63
baked, additions to, 192
baked in bacon rings, 193
baked on toast, 192
baked or shirred, 192
Benedict, 186
beverages, 22
Blackstone, poached, 186
coddled, 184
cream sauce, 360
creamed, and asparagus, Cockaigne, 194
creamed au gratin, 194
curried, 193
deviled or stuffed, 195; in sauce, 196
dishes, about, 183
drops, hard-cooked, 146; for soup, 145, **145**
Foo Yoong, with shrimp, 190
fried or sautéed, 184; additions, 184
Frittata, 190
garnishes for soups, about, 144
gratin, and cheese, 390
ham cakes, and, 193
hard-cooked, 183
hard-cooked, vegetable casserole, 193
Huevos Rancheros or Cowboy, 186
in a nest, 193
masked, 194
omelets, 187–190; *see* Omelets
pickled, 195
poached; additions to, 185
poached in soup, 185; in wine, 186
rolls, Chinese, 212
salad, asparagus and, 41
salad, molded, and caviar, 49
sandwiches, 243, 244
sauce thickeners, 356, 368
sauces for, *see* Sauces
Scotch, 194; Woodcock, 192
scrambled; additions to, 191
scrambled, with cream cheese, 191
shirred or en Cocotte, 192
smoked salmon and, 186
soft-cooked, 183
soufflés and timbales, 196–207
stuffed or deviled, 195
stuffed on Rosettes with sauce, 195
timbales and ring molds, 202–207
to glaze, *see* Masked, 194
to serve, 183

EGG AND EGG DISHES (*cont.*)
yolk as sauce thickener, 356
yolk, hard-cooked; as emulsifier, 357
yolk, to add to hot liquid, 356
Eggnog, milk, 22
pineapple or orange, 26
Eggplant, about, 289
casserole or Ratatouille, 291
casserole, and lamb, 521
halves, baked, 290
scalloped, 291
slices, baked, 290; deep-fried, 291; and sautéed, 291
soufflé, 199
stuffed or Farcie, 292, 292; Creole 292
to avoid discoloration, 290
to rid of excess moisture, 289
Elderberry, in tisanes, 20
Elk, *see* Venison, 558
En Croûte Cookery, 85; meat, 525
En Papillote Cooking, 87, 87
Enchiladas, 214
Enamelware, 101
Endive, Belgian, French or Witloof, 31, 31
braised or glazed, 292
curly or chicory, 30, 31
salad, cooked, 43
Enzymes, 4; action, to retard, 89
Equipment, cooking, about, 99–104
Escabèche, 406
Escarole or Chicory Escarole, 30, 31
Espagnole Sauce, 365

Farces, 560–566; *see* Dressings
Farina, balls, Cockaigne, 147
dumplings, Cockaigne, 179
FATS AND OILS, about, 3
absorption in frying, 75
all-purpose, 78
for deep-fat frying, 78
hydrogenation of, 78
kidney, 542
liquid, similarity of, 78
smoking of, 77
unsaturated, 3
Fecula, thickener, 356
Fennel, 292
dressing, 562; tisane, 20
Fern Shoots or Young Bracken, 293
Fettuccini or Noodle Dough, 149, 150
Figaro Sauce, 370
Figpeckers, 598
Filet Mignon, 472, 473
Fillets, *see* Beef, Fish
Fillings, *see* names of
Finnan Haddie, baked, 410; creamed, 410
Fireless Cooking, 89
FISH, *also see* Seafood, Shellfish
about, 392; cooking, 395
au Bleu cooking, about, 399
aspic, in, Cockaigne, 405
baked in a covered dish, 404
baked in foil, 405
baked, stuffed, 404; unstuffed, 402
baked with sour cream, 404
balls or cakes, 233, 234, 408

blowfish, 416
bonito, fresh, 420
braising, about, 398, 398
broiling, about, 399, 400
cakes, emergency, 234
carp, about, 407
catfish, Southern-fried, 407
chips, and, 401
cleaning and preparing, 393–395, 393, 394, 395
cod, about, 407; fresh, Boulangère, 409
cod, fresh, à la Portugaise, 408
cod, salt or Morue à la Provençale, 408
cod, scalloped, 408
cod sounds and tongues, 408
codfish balls or cakes, 408
creamed, molded, 62
cured, 397
dishes for lunch, supper, 229–237
dressings, 561, 562
eel, about, 409
fillets à la Bonne Femme, 402
fillets, baked in wine, 404; quick, 403
fillets, fresh, sautéed Palm Beach, 402
fillets, Marguéry, baked in sauce, 403
fillets, molded filled or Paupiettes, 405
fillets on spinach with shrimp and mushrooms, 403
fillets, oven-fried, 401
fillets, sautéed Amandine, 401
fillets, sole Ambassador, 418; Florentine, 418
Finnan Haddie, baked, 410; creamed, 410
flat, 395
flounder fillets, marinated, 409
freshwater, 393
fried, 400; deep-fat, 401; marinated, 401
frozen, 397
Gefüllte, 406
haddock, about, 410; baked, stuffed, 410
haddock, fillets baked in sauce, 411
herring, about, 411
herring, baked and potatoes, 411
herring, marinated, 411; sour cream, 412
herring, Scotch fried, 412; salad, 50
kebabs, 400
kippers or bloaters, grilled or baked, 412
loaf, quick, 233, 235
mackerel, fresh, broiled, 413
mackerel, salt, boiled, 413; broiled, 414
marinades, 381
mousse or timbales, 204
muskellunge, about, 414
octopus, about, 412; casseroled, 413
Paupiettes, 405

pickerel, about, 414
pickled or Escabèche, 406
pike, about, 414
planked, 405
poaching, about, 398, 398
pompano en Papillote, 414
Quenelles in lobster sauce, 181,
181
red snapper baked with sauce,
418
roe and milt, about, 416
roe, canned; in ramekins, 237
salads, 50–51, 61–62
salmon, about, 414; cold, glazed,
415
salmon steaks or darnes, boiled,
414
sardines, about, 415
sauces, *see* Sauces
scrod, fresh, broiled, 409
sea, 392
sea squab or blowfish, 416
shad, baked with creamed roe,
417
shad, carving, 417
shad roe, baked, 416; broiled,
417; parboiled, 416; sautéed,
416; canned, 236; salad, 51,
61
shark, about, 417
smelts, 417
soufflé, 200, 201
squid, about, 412
soups, *see* Soups
steaks Marguéry, baked in sauce,
403
steaks, poached, 402
steaming, about, 398, 398
stews, about, 135
sticks, oven-fried, 401
swordfish steaks, 419
timbales, 204
to fillet, 394, 394, 395
to glaze, 386
to grill, 399, 400
to remove odors, 396
to serve, 396, 398, 399
trout, blue or Truite au Bleu,
419
trout, brook, Meunière, 419
trout, lake, broiled, 419
tuna, fresh, 420
turbot, poached, 420
whale, 420
whitefish, 419
Flambéing, hints, 80
Florentine Sauce, 360
Flounder Fillets, marinated, 409
FLOUR, browned, thickening power,
355–356
paste, sauce thickener, 356
Foie Gras, 524
Foil Cookery, 86
Fondue, cheese, 239–240; beef, 475;
vegetable, 256
Foo Yoong, 190
FOODS WE EAT, 1–13
biologic values, 2
energy values, 1–3
seasonal, 4
FOODS WE HEAT, 72–103
about; dry, 73–81; moist, 81–89

destruction of micro-organisms,
72
nutritive value of, 72
temperatures for holding, 98
to grill, 93–94, 94
to reheat, 98
Forcemeat, 564
Fowl, 567–600; *also see* Poultry
and Game Birds
cranberry glaze for, 387
Franconia or Browned Potatoes, 314
Frankfurter, baked beans and, 267
barbecued, 220; kebabs, 220
in sauces, 221
French, chicken casserole, 581
dressings, 341, 342, 343
fried potatoes, 318
onions, fried, 303
parsnips, 305
omelet, 188, 188
salad, tomato slices, 47
toast, cheese, 244; tomato, 245
toast, sandwich, ham and pineapple, 243
Fries, Lamb, 549
Frijoles, 264
Frittata, 190
FRITTER, corn, 286, 287
garnish, for soup, 148
Fritto Misto, 258
Frog Legs, braised, 446
deep-fat fried, 446
Forestière, 447
in mushroom sauce, 446
FRUIT, *see* individual names of
beverages, about, 23
casserole, nut and rice, 166
juices, 23–28
juice twosomes, 25
punch, 26–28
salad dressings, *see* Salad Dressings
salads, 53–57, 64, 66–71
shake, milk, 23
shrubs or vinegars, 25
soups, about, 114
sticks, 246
stuffed, molded for salads, 69
sweet potatoes with, 324
Frying or Sautéing, 79–80, *also see*
Deep-fat Frying
basket, 76, 77
stir-frying, 253

Gaenseklein, 589
Galantines, about, 529, 530
Gallinule, 598
GAME BIRDS, 590–600; *see names*
of
marinated, 593
Salmi of, about, 592
small: broiled, braised, roasted,
skewered, 598–599
wild, about, 590; potted, 597
wild, gaminess, 591; barding,
592
wild, to hang, 591; shot removal,
591
GAME, 554–559; *see individual*
names
dressings, 560–566
marinades for, 380–382

GAME (*cont.*)
    salad for, orange, 55
    saddles of, 558
    sauces for, *see* Sauces
    small, about, 554
    vegetable accompaniments, 558
Garbure or Bean Soup, 119
Garlic or Ail, butter, 385
    for salads, 33
    sauce or Aïoli, 347
    to press, 33, 340, **341**
Garnishes, almond or Amandine, 390
    aspic, 58
    au gratin, 389
    Choux paste, 148
    croutons, buttered crumbs, 389–
        390
    for beverages and drinks, 23, 27
    for pasta, 390
    for salad, 38–39, 39
    for soup, 144–152
    fritters, for soup, 148
    truffle, 300; and pimiento, 300
    vegetable shapes, to cut, 39, 39
Gaston Beef Stew, 496
Gazpacho Soup, 113; blender, 139
Gefüllter Krautkopf, 521
GELATIN, for salads, basic, 58
    for salads, fruit, basic, 66
    fruit, for salads, 66–71
    mayonnaise, 387
    salads, 57–71
German, meat balls, 518
Giblets, about, 569; chicken, 553
Ginger, ale salad, 67
Gingham Salad, 37
Glaçages, about, 386–387
Glass, heatproof utensils, 101
GLAZE, 386–389
    about, 386
    aspic, 387
    casserole, on, 386
    Chaud-Froid sauce, 388
    cranberry, for fowl, 387
    demi, sauce for meats, 365
    for vegetables, 258, 386
    honey for meat or onions, 387
    Mayonnaise Collée or gelatin,
        387
    spirit for ham, 387
Gnocchi, with farina or flour, 157
    with potatoes, 157, **157**
Goetta, 533
Goose, braised parts, 589
    gosling, roast, 588; about, 573
    liver, 534
    orange sauce for, 365
    pâté de foie, 524–528
    potted or Confit d'Oie, 589
    roast, 588; about roasting, 573
    wild, 597
Goulash, 500–501
Grape, leaves stuffed, or Dolmas, 522
    salads, 54, 64, 69
Grapefruit, juices, 25, 28
    salads, 55, 68
Grater, rotary, 341
Gravies, 358; *also see* Sauces
    pan, 358; chicken pan, 359
    quick, 366; canned soup, 375
Grease, to remove from soup, 109,
    109

Green Goddess Dressing, 348
Greens, about, 293; for salad, 29–32
    beet, 271
    wild, about, 32, 293
    wilted, salad, 35
Grenache, mayonnaise, 348
Gribiche Sauce, 348
Grill, brazier types, 93, 94
    meat, mixed, English, 484
    vegetable, mixed, 216
Grits, *see* Hominy, 155
Groats, Buckwheat, 156
Grouse, broiled, 597; roasted, 596
Guinea Hen, breasts of; roasted, 589
Gulyas, 500
Gumbo Soups, 118, 135

Haddock, fillets, baked in sauce, 411
    Finnan Haddie, baked or
        creamed, 410
    fresh, baked, stuffed, 410
Halibut Ring Mold, 206
HAM, 488–491
    à la King, 220
    aged, to prepare, 488, 490
        baked, processed, 489; un-
        processed, 488
    baked with tomatoes, cheese,
        491
    broiled, 491
    butt, shank or picnic, 491
    cabbage, potatoes and, 275
    cakes and eggs, 193
    cakes with potato, 220
    country, 490
    deviled, sandwich, 244
    dressing for turkey, 563
    fresh, 486
    glaze, spirit for, 387
    ground on pineapple slices, 219
    hash, and beef, 223
    hominy and, 156
    loaf, raw smoked, 524; cooked
        ham, 219
    mousse, jellied, 60
    noodles, 174
    rolls, stuffed, 219
    salad, 52
    sandwiches, 240–244
    sautéed and eggs, 491
    slices, casseroled, 490
    slices with fruit, 490
    smoked shoulder butt or cottage
        roll, 491
    timbales, 203
    to carve, 489
    to decorate, 489, 490
    with veal scallops, 481
HAMBURGER, 514–522
    broiled, 517; grilled, 517;
        sautéed, 516
    filled beef or lamburgers, 517
    Sloppy Joes, 517
    venison, 559
Hare, *see* Rabbit, 554
Haricots Verts, Beans, 262, 264
Hasenpfeffer, 554
Hash, about, 223; browned or
    sautéed, 224
    beef and ham with vegetables,
        223
    chicken or turkey, 226

corned beef and potatoes, 225
in bread dressing ring, 225
in creamed cabbage, 224
patties, canned corned beef, 226
potatoes stuffed with, 314
quick, 224
Shepherd's pie, 225
to reheat, 223
with vegetables, 224
Hazel Hen, 598
Head Cheese or Brawn, 550
Heart, about, 546
braised in sour sauce, 547
en Papillote, 547
stuffed, baked, 547
HEAT, deep-fat frying, 75–79, 77
dry, about, 73–81
equipment, outdoor, 89–97, 89,
91, 92, 93
hunter's fire, 89
moist, about, 81–89
placement of oven racks, 99,
100
poaching paper, to prepare, 87,
87
spit and rotisserie cooking, 97,
97
HERBS, see individual names
à Tortue, see Rosemary Sauce,
368
butters, 384–386
chiffonade of, for soups, 151
for tisanes, 20
to garnish beverages, 23
to soften for decorations, 88
Herring, baked, and potatoes, 411
marinated, 411
marinated with sour cream,
412
salad, 50; and potato, 46
Scotch fried, 412
Hibachi Grill, 93, 94
HIGH ALTITUDE COOKING,
watch for symbol ▲
deep-fat frying, 72, 79
elevation chart, 73
meats, 457
pressure cooking, 83
soups, 107
vegetables, 254
Himmel und Erde, 338
Holding Food at Serving Temperatures, 98
Hollandaise Sauces, 368, 369, 370
Hominy, cakes, 155
scalloped and ham, 156
Honey, dressing for fruit, 352
glaze for meat, 387
HORS D'OEUVRE, to glaze, 386
Horseradish, dressing, 343; cream,
351
dressing, sour cream, 351
sauce, 362; frozen, 343
Household Needs, 103–104
Huevos Rancheros, or Cowboy eggs,
186
Hungarian, goulash, 500; sauce, 362
Hunter's Sauce, 366
Hydrogenated Fats, 78

Ice, cubes, flavored, 23
ICES, tomato, see Avocado Cup, 54

INGREDIENTS, see individual
names;
optional, watch for symbol, ( )
Iron Utensils, 101
Italian, meat sauce, 378
meatballs, 519
omelet, Frittata, 190
rice or Risotto, 165
salad, 40
spaghetti with sauce, 168
tomato paste, 377

Jambalaya, chicken; meat; fish;
vegetable, 164
Juices, about, 23
blended, about, 25
fruit, 23–28
vegetable, 23

Kale, 293; sea, 31
Kartoffelkloesse, 180
Kasha, 156
Kebabs, 74, 75; also see Skewer
Cooking
beef, 476; frankfurters, 220
fish, 400; scallops, 432
Kedgeree of Lobster, etc., 230
Kettle, Campfire, 90
Kidney, about, 541
baked, 542; casserole, 543
beef, broiled, 543; tomatoes,
onions, broiled, 543
en Brochette, 543
fat, 542
nuggets, 542
pie, steak and, 502
sautéed, 542; celery and mush-
room, 542
stew, 544
Kippers, grilled or baked, 412
Kitchen, accessories, 103–104
Knives, to sharpen, 460, 460
Koenigsberger Klops, 518
Kohlrabi, 293
Kreplach Soup, 111

LAMB, 481–484, 507–510
about, 481
barbecued, leg of, 482
burgers or patties, 517
casserole, and eggplant, 521
Cassoulet, 509
chops, broiled and pan-broiled,
483
chops, stuffed, 483
crown roast, 482
curried with rice, 509; cooked,
217
cuts, commercial and retail,
468–469
farce of, 507
Forestière or mock venison, 507
fries, 549
Goulash à Blanc, 501
grape leaves stuffed with, 522
grill, English mixed, 484
head, 549
Kebabs, broiled, 483
leg, braised, 508
marinades, 381
mint sauce for, 371
patties, 517
roast leg, 482

LAMB (*cont.*)
    sandwich, 246
    shanks or trotters, braised, 508
    shoulder, braised, 506; stuffed,
       507
    shoulder roast, 483
    stew, Irish, 509
    stew or Navarin Printanier, 508
    Terrapin, 218
    to carve, 481
Larding and Lardoons, 453, 453
Lark, 598
Lasagne, 176
Leaf Wrappings, 85, 86
Leberkloesse or Liver Dumplings,
    148
Leeks, about, 294
    pie, 215
    purée of, 294
    soup, potato, 130
LEFTOVERS, in bacon, 218
    meat, deviled, 217
    potatoes, 320
    veal, creamed, 217
Legumes, dried, about, 264; purée,
    265
    danger of pressure cooking, 265
    soups, about, 118
Lemon, butter, 384
    dressing, and sherry, 352
    tisane, 20
Lemonade, sirup for, 27; quantity,
    26, 27
Lentils, about, 267; and prunes, 268
    casserole, and sausage, 221
    purée of, 265
    soups, 118, 120, 121
Lettuce, green peas and, 306
    leaves for wrap cooking, 86, 86
    rice dish, 276
    rolls, cheese stuffed, 49
    soup, 131
    to prepare, 32, 32, 33; cooked,
      294
    varieties, 30, 31
Lights, Calf, 550
Lima Beans, *see* Beans
Lime, juice and orange, 24
Liquid, reducing, 80; sauces, 357
Liver, *also see* Beef, Calf, etc.
    about, 534
    beef, Creole, 536
    braised, 535; with wine, 536
    broiled, 534
    calf or chicken Lyonnaise, 534
    chicken, à la King, 537
    chicken, in batter, 537
    dressing, 563
    dumplings or Leberkloesse, 148
    goose, 534
    loaf, 524
    pâté, 528; chicken, 525
    pâté, souffléed, 528
    patties, 518
    pepper, onions, on skewers, 536
    sausage dumplings, 150
    spaghetti sauce with, 378
Lobster, about, 436; to eat, 436,
    438
    Américaine or Amoricaine, 439
    bisque, 133
    broiled, 438, 438

    butter, 385
    chowder, quick, 143
    curry, 230
    kedgeree, 230
    mold, 51
    Mongole, 231; soup, 143
    mousse, 62
    Newburg, 231
    parfait, 232
    poached or "boiled," 436
    potted, 442
    ring, hot, 233
    salad, 50
    sandwiches, 247
    stew, 135
    stuffed, baked, 440
    Supreme, quick, 143
    tails, grilled, 439, 439
    Thermidor, 440
Long Rice or Harusame, 167
London Broil Steak, 475
Lorenzo Dressing, 342
Lotus Root Salad, 44
Louis Sauce, 350
Lungs, Calf, 550
Lyonnaise, sauce, 366; potatoes, 314

Macaroni, about, 167
    baked, 170; with sour cream,
      171
    boiled with cheese, 170
    loaf, 171
    Mostaccioli, 172
    salad, 50
    with shellfish, 172
    with tomatoes, livers, mushrooms,
      and cheese, 171
Mâche, 31, 31
Mackerel, boiled, 413; broiled, 414
Madeira Sauce, 366
Madrilène, consommé, 110
    ring with shad roe, 61
Maître d'Hôtel Butter, 384
Malt, 22
Maltaise Sauce, 370
Manhattan, chowder, 137
Manicotti or Canneloni, 176
Marchand de Vin Sauce, 367
Marinades, 380–383
Marinara Sauce, 379
Marmite, Petite, 110
Marrow, about, 553; poaching, 553
    balls, for soup, 150
    bones, baked, or Osso Buco, 506
Matelote, defined, 136
Matzo Dumplings, 147
Mayonnaise, 345–347
    Collée or gelatin, 387
    dressings, cold, 347–350; hot,
      370
    fat content, 340
    jelly or Grenache, 348
    storage of, 346
MEAT, 449–559; *also see* Beef, Ham,
    Lamb, Pork, Veal, etc.
    about, 449
    altitude cooking, 457
    amount to buy and serve, 450
    balls, Chinese, 519
    balls for soup, 150
    balls, German, or Koenigsberger
      Klops, 518

balls, Italian, 519
balls, Porcupines, 520
balls, pork in tomato sauce, **519**
balls, sauerkraut, 520
balls, Swedish, 519
barding, 453, 454
basting, 457, **457**
braising, about, **493**
broiling, 455
Burgoo, 503
carving, 460, **460**
Couscous, 510
cracklings or lardoons, 453
crust, or Pâte for Pâté, 527
cuts, charts, 461, 465–471
dressings and stuffings, 560–566
En Croûte cooking, 458
frill for a shank bone, 463
frozen, to thaw and cook, 457
Galantines, 529–530
game, *see names of*
glaze, demi-, 365
glaze, honey, 387
Goulash, Gulyas or Pörkolt,
    about, 500
grades, about, 449
gravies, 358–359, 366
grilling, 93, 94
grinding and mincing, about,
    452
ground, uncooked, to store, 451,
    515
ground variations, about, 514
inspection of, 450
juices, keeping in, 454
larding, about, 453, **453;**
    lardoons, 453
large-cut suggestions, 461
leftover, *see* Brunch, 208
leftover, deviled, 217
loaf, about, 522
marinades, 380–383
marinating, about, 454
moist heat processes, 81, 449
pan-broiling; fat free, 456
pastries, about, 210; for soup,
    149
Pâté, 525
patties, variety, 552
pie, roll or Pinwheels, 211
pies and topping, 210–212,
    494, 504
pot-roasting, about, 493
pounding, about, 452, **452**
pressure cooked, high altitude,
    457–458
reheating, 98, 459
roasting, 456
salad, 52
salted, about, 488
sauces for, *see* Sauces
sausage, about, 530
searing or browning, 454
seasoning, about, 451
shortcakes, 211
smoked, green beans, and
    potatoes, 263
soufflé, cooked, 200
soup, 109, 497
steaks, *see* Beef and Salmon
    Steaks
stewing, about, 493

storing raw, 451; cooked, 459
tenderizing of, 451–452
Terrines, 528
testing for doneness, 458
to glaze, defined, 386
to stretch, 515
tough, about cooking, 451
turnovers, Piroshki or rolls,
    filled, 210
variety, about, 534; patties,
    552

Melba, baskets, 209
Melons, salad, 55; frosted, 70
Meunière Butter, 384
Mexican, sauce, 378
MILK, *also see* Cream, Sour Cream
    beverages, 22
    eggnog, 22
    shake, fruit, 23
    toast or soup, 131
Milt, about, 416
Minerals, 4
Minestrone, 120
Mint, gelatin for fruit salads, 66
    sauce, 371
Miroton, Boeuf, 217
Mocha, punch, 28
Molds, broccoli ring, 205
    chestnut ring, 205
    fish and seafood, 51; jellied and
        creamed, 61–63
    gelatin, fruit, 63–71
    rice, 161–162
    salads, 49–50, 57–71
    timbale, 201–207
Mole, turkey, 586
Mollusks, about, 421
Mongole, crab or lobster, 231; soup,
    143
Moorhen, 598
Moose, *see* Venison, 558
Mornay Sauce, 361
Morue à la Provençale, 408
Mostaccioli, 172
Mousse, chicken, jellied, 60
    cucumber; sour cream, 65
    fish, 204
    ham, jellied, 60
    lobster, 62
    mushroom ring, 299
    seafood, 62
    veal, jellied, 60
Mousseline, of shellfish, 61
    sauce, 370
Mulled, cider, 25
Mulligatawny Soup, 122
Mush, corn meal, 156
Mushroom, about, 294, **294, 295**
    à la Schoener, 296
    bisque and clam, 134
    broiled, 297
    broth, 112
    cauliflower and, in cheese sauce,
        282
    creamed, 296
    Florentine, 298
    identification, 294–295, **294**
    Lima beans and, 270
    on toast, and puffed cheese, 245
    onions in wine, and, 298
    peas and, 307
    rice ring, 162

MUSHROOM (*cont.*)
 ring or mousse, 299
 ring mold with sweetbreads or
  chicken, 206
 sauce, 367
 sausages and, 221
 sautéed, 296
 slicing and channeling, 295, 295
 soup, cream of, 128; quick, 141
 steamed, 296
 stuffed, broiled, Cockaigne, 297
 stuffed with clams or oysters,
  297
 stuffed with seafood or snails,
  298
 timbales, 202
 under glass, 299
Muskellunge, about, 414
Muskrat, 557
Mussels, about, 426
 baked, buttered, 427
 steamed or Moules Marinère,
  427
 stew, 135
Mustard, sauce, cold, 344; hot, 363
 sauce, sweet-sour, 371
 white, 31
MUTTON, 481–484, 506–511; *also*
  see Lamb
 about, 481
 Couscous, 510
 leg, braised, 508
 roast, 482
 stew, Irish, 509

Nantua Sauce, 361
Navarin Printanier, 508
Nettle Soup, cream of, 129
New England Boiled Dinner, 493
 clam chowder, 137
New Year's Soups, 125
Newburg, lobster or seafood, 231
 sauce, 361
 shrimp, 444
Niçoise Salads, 46
Nockerln or Austrian Pancakes, for
  soup or stew, 147
NOODLES, *also see* Pastas
 baskets, 173
 boiled, 172
 buttered, 173
 dish, leftover, 175
 dough, green or white, 149
 dough, to make, 149, 150
 fried, 173
 ham, 174
 loaf and cheese, quantity, 175
 prunes, stewed, and croutons,
  174
 rarebit, 175
 ring and salmon in sauce, 236
 ring, baked, 173; whipped
  cream, 174
 Rumanian and pork casserole,
  175
 soup casserole, tuna mushroom,
  175
NUTS, *also see* individual names
 loaf, 161; cheese and bread, 238
NUTRITION, 1–13, 29, 72, 249–250

Octopus, 412; casseroled, 413

 pasta sauce, 380
Oeufs, en Gelée, 63
Oils, *also see* individual names
 dressing, 341
Okra, salad, 44
 sautéed, 301; stewed, 300
Omelet, about, 187, 188
 baked, 189
 firm, 190
 fluffy or soufflèd, 189
 French, 188, 188
 Frittata or Italian, 190
 pans, about, 188
 shrimp Foo Yoong, 190
 sweet, 190
 to fill, 187
 to glaze, 187
Onions, about, 301, 301
 baked, whole, 302
 braised, small, 302
 casserole, and apple, 304
 creamed, 301
 cups and rings, 38, 39
 dressings, 562, 563
 French fried or Shoestring, 303
 glazed, 302; honey, 387
 green, or scallions, 302
 mushrooms and, in wine, 298
 peppers and, 307
 pie, 215
 salad, orange, 55; tomato, 49
 sauce, brown, or Lyonnaise, 366
 sausage and, 221
 sauce, white or Soubise, 363
 sautéed, 302
 scalloped with cheese, 303
 shortcake, 215
 soufflé, 199
 soup, 113; quick, 141
 soup, cream of or Velouté, 129
 steamed, 301
 stuffed, 303; with sauerkraut,
  304
 to peel and chop, 301
Opossum, 557
Orange, eggnog, 26
 juice, and lime, 24; tomato, 24
 salads, 55
 sauce, for duck or goose, 365
Orangeade, 27
Ortolans, 598
Osso Buco, 506
**OUTDOOR COOKING AND
  EQUIPMENT**, 89; watch for
  symbol ⊟
Oven, heating and cooking, 99
 placement of racks, 99, 100
 thermostats, 100
Oxtail, braised, 552
 soup, 122; wine, quick, 142
 stew, 501
Oysters, about, 422
 baked, 424
 bisque, 134
 broiled, 423
 cakes, 234
 Casino, 426
 celery, 425
 creamed, 424; and mushrooms,
  425
 creamed, and seafood, baked,
  425

creamed, peppers stuffed with, 309
dressings, 560, 561, 564
fried, grilled and sautéed, 423
Gumbo, wtih crab and shrimp, 135
in mushrooms, 297; au gratin, 425
on the half shell, 423
rarebit, 425
Rockefeller, 425
sauce for fish, 361
scalloped, 424; in canned soup, 424
soufflé, 201
stews, 134
to open shells, 422, 422
Oyster Plant or Salsify, about, 304
à Blanc, 304; sautéed, 304

Paella, 165
Palm, hearts of, 305; salad, 45
Panade, 123
PANCAKES, potato, 316
spinach in, 327
Pan-frying, 80
Pans, about, 101–103; omelet, 188, 188
Papain, 452
Papaya, leaves, for wrap cooking, 86, 86
salad, molded, see Frosted Melon, 70
Papillote, to make, 87, 87
Paprika, sauce, 362
Parblanching, 88
Parboiling, 88
Parmigiana, Veal, 480
Parsley, deep-fat fried, 305
Parsnips, 305
Parsteaming, 89
Parties, Beverages, 14–28
Partridge, about, 596
Pasta, 167–178; sauces, 378–380
topping, chicken liver, 391
Pastate, see Tamales, 287
Paste, tomato, 377
PASTRIES, for meats, 210
meat, for soup, 149
Pâte, crust for pâté, 527
Pâté, about, de Foie, 524
de Foie de Volaille, or chicken liver, 525
de Foie, to test for doneness, 527
en Croûte, about, 525, 525
liver, souffléed, 528
mold, to line and fill, 526–527
to bake, 527
to store, 527
Patty, meat, see Hamburger, Chicken, Variety, etc.
Paysanne Soup, 116
Peas, 305
carrots, and, 306
green and lettuce, 306
mushrooms and, 307
podded, sugar, snow or Mange-tout, 307
purées, 306; dried, 264
soup, green, 121; quick, 140
soup, split, 120, 121
Peach, salad, 53; and cheese, 56

to peel by blanching, 88
Peanuts, butter sandwiches, 245
Pears, salads, 53, 56; molded, 68
Peccary, 557
Pepper, Pot Soup, 123
sauce or Poivrade, 368
Peppers, green, onions and, 307
green in sauce, 307
slices with fillings, 45
stuffed, 307–309
sweet or pimientos, about, 307
to peel, 307
to remove seeds and membranes, 307
vitamin C content, 307
Périgordine, defined, 300
Persimmon, salad, Japanese, 56
Petite Marmite, 110
Pheasant, about, 594
braised, 595
in game sauce, 595
roast, 594
Smitane, 596
Pickerel, 414
PICKLE AND RELISH, see Chutney
PIES, also see Pastries
cheese custard, 214
corn bread Tamale, 212
meat, quick, 212; topping, 494
onion or leek, 215
pans, 99–103
pizza, 213
pot, 212, 494
Shepherd's, 225
steak and kidney, 502
tuna, individual, 232
veal and pork, 504
Piémontaise, defined, 300
Pig, feet, baked, 552; jellied, 551; stewed, 551
roast suckling, 485
Pigeon, broiled, 590
dressing for, 564
potted, 590
roasted, 589
Pike, 414
Pilaf, 166; duck, 229
Pimiento, about, 307
garnish, see Truffle, 300
salad, filled, Christmas, 45
Pineapple, dressing, and rice, 565
effect on gelatins, 66
eggnog, 26
juice, fresh, 24; and blends, 25
punch, 27
rice, baked, 163
salads, 56, 67, 69
sandwich with ham, 243
Piquant Sauce, 367
Piroshki, 210
Pit Cooking, 90–92
Pizza, 213
Planking, to season, 80
Plantain, 309
Plastic Utensils, 102
Plover, 598
Poaching, defined, 83, 83
Poi, 289
Pointers to Success, watch for symbol ♦
Poireaux, see Leeks, 294
Poivrade Sauce, 368

Polenta, 156
Polonaise Sauce, 386
Pompano en Papillote, 414
Porcupine Meat Balls, 520
PORK, 484–492, 511–514
    about, 484
    bacon, see Bacon
    balls in tomato sauce, 519
    birds, 513
    casserole, and Rumanian
        noodles, 175
    Cassoulet, 509
    Chop Suey or Chow Mein, 218
    chops, baked in sour cream, 511
    chops, braised, Creole, 512;
        deviled, 512; with fruit, 512
    chops, breaded, 488
    chops, pan fried or baked, 487
    chops, stuffed, Cockaigne, 512
    crown roast, 484, 485
    cuts, commercial, 470, 471
    Goulash, and veal, 501
    Goulash à Blanc, 501
    ham, see Ham
    hocks, stewed, 514
    in meat loaf, about, 522
    marinade, 382
    neck bones, stewed, 514
    need for thorough cooking, 484,
        560
    pie, and veal, 504
    pigs' feet, 551, 552
    roast, 485
    roast stuffed with sauerkraut,
        487
    roast suckling pig, 485
    salt, and milk gravy, 514
    sausage, see Sausage
    scrapple or Goetta, 533
    spareribs, about, 512; to grill,
        96–97, 97
    spareribs, baked with dressing,
        512
    spareribs, baked with sauerkraut,
        512
    spareribs, boiled, 514; sweet-
        sour, 514
    sweet and sour, 488
    tenderloin, 487; with mushrooms
        and olives, 511
    tenderloin, frenched, 487
    tenderloin fruit casserole, 487
    trichinae in, 484
Pörkölt, 500
Pot Liquor, see Vegetable Waters
Pot Pies, 212, 235, 494
Pot Roast, 495–499, 505
Potage, defined, 115; St. Germain,
    121
    Germiny, 130
POTATO, 309–324
    about, 309
    Anna, 315
    baked, 313; French-fried, 318
    baked, wafers, 319
    balls, baked, mashed, 311
    balls, fried, 320
    baskets, 319
    boiled, 310
    browned, Franconia, 314
    cabbage and ham, 275
    cakes, and ham, 220

cakes, leftover, 321
cakes, salmon, 234
Chantilly, 311
chip loaf, tuna, 232
chips, Saratoga, 319
creamed, 312; casserole, 312
cups, stuffed, 314
Dauphine or Lorette, 320
dressing, 565
Duchess, 319
dumplings, 180
French-fried, never-fail, 318
grated, pan-broiled, 316
green beans, smoked meat, and,
    263
hashed brown, 315
leftover, about, 320, 321
leftover, au gratin, 321; baked,
    320
leftover, German-fried, 321
leftover, mashed, 320
leftover, O'Brien, 321
Lyonnaise, 314
mashed, 311; cheese puffs, 311
mashed, to keep warm, 311
pancakes, 316
pigs in, 221
puffs, 318
riced, 310
salad and herring, 46
salad, 45; hot German, 46
salad, Niçoise, 46
sautéed, tiny new, 314
scalloped, 312; in butter, 312
Shoestring, 318
soufflé or puffed, 316, 317
soups, 129, 130
starch as sauce thickener, 356
stuffed, 313
stuffed, with hash, baked, 314
stuffed, with vegetables, baked,
    313
sweet, or yams, about, 322
sweet, and apples, 324
sweet, and orange juice, 324
sweet, baked, 322
sweet, boiled, 322
sweet, cakes with ham and
    pineapple, 220
sweet, candied, 323; caramelized,
    323
sweet, chipped beef and, 222
sweet, deep-fried, 323
sweet, dressing, and apple, 565
sweet, mashed, 322
sweet, puffs, 323
sweet, sautéed, 323
sweet, soufflé, and pineapple or
    applesauce, 199
sweet, stuffed, 322
sweet, stuffing and sausage, 565
sweet, with fruits, 324
Pot-au-Feu, 110
Poule-au-Pot, 110
Poulette Sauce, 362
POULTRY, 567–600; see Chicken,
    Turkey, Duck, etc.
    about, 567
    boning, about, 570
    carving, about, 574, 574
    cutting a drawn bird, 569, 569
    dressings, 560–566

Federal stamp, 567
frozen, buying, 568
giblets, about preparing, 569
plucking, about, 568
relative cost of, 568
roasting, about, 572, 574
roasting in foil, about, 574
sauces, see Sauces
singeing, about, 568
stuffing and trussing, about, 572, 572
tendons, to remove, 570, 570
to draw for roasting, 571
to draw for sauté or fricassee, 568
to glaze, 573
to grill out of doors, 97
to test for doneness, 573
Prairie Chicken, roasted, 596
Pressure Cooking, about, 81; also watch for symbol ⊙
as sterilizer, 82
high altitude, 83, 458
meat, 458
vegetables, 252
Printanier, 508
Proteins, about, 2
Prune, dressings, 563, 565
lentils and, 268
with noodles and croutons, 174
Ptarmigan, roasted, 596
PUDDING, SAVORY, corn, 285
corn, Cockaigne, 285
tomato Cockaigne, 335
Yorkshire, 182
Puff, balls, mushroom, 294, 294
potato, 318; mashed, 311
sweet potato, 323
Pumpkin, about, 311
soup, 130
Punch, fruit; in quantity, 28
mocha, 28
pineapple, 27
strawberry fruit, 28
tomato, gala, 26
Purée, defined, 106
Purslane, 324; soup, 131

Quail, 599
Quenelle, about, 180, 180, 181; for soup, 150
fish, in lobster sauce, 182
poached, or baked, 181
Quiche, about, 214
crustless, 203
Lorraine; Alsacienne, 214

Rabbit, about, 554; to skin, 554, 555, 556
à la mode, Hasenpfeffer or Civet, 554
fricassee of, 555
roast, 555
sautéed, 555
smothered with onions, 555
Raccoon, 557
Radish, cooked, 325
Ragoût Fin, 539
Rails, 598
Raisin, sauce, 545; cider or beer, 373
Rarebit, noodle, 175
oyster, 425

tomato or Woodchuck, 237
Welsh, 237
Ratatouille Provençale, 291
Ravigote, butter, 385
sauce, 342; hot, 364
Ravioli, 177; dough for, 150
Red Snapper, baked, 418
Reduction, liquids, 80
roux-based sauces, 357
Reed Birds, 598
Reheating Food, 98, 255, 459
Remoulade, celeriac, 43
sauce, 349
Rhubarb, salad molds, and strawberry, 70
RICE, 158–167
about, 158
baked, 159; pineapple, 163
beans, Pinto, and, 267
boiled, 158
casserole and onion, 163
casserole, fruit and nut, 166
cheese, 160
Chinese fried, 160
cooked in chicken stock, 159
curried, 159; and veal or lamb, 217
custard and bacon, 163
dish, cabbage or lettuce, 276
dish, Rombauer, 163
dressings, 563, 564, 565
green, baked, 159
Italian or Risotto, 165
Jambalaya, chicken; vegetable; with meat or fish, 164
loaf or casserole, 161
long or Harusame, 167
nut loaf, 161
Paella, 165
peppers stuffed with, 308; and meat, 308
Pilaf, 166; duck, 229
ring, cheese and, 162
ring, ham and, 162
ring, mushroom and, 162
ring, salmon and, 236
rings or molds, 162
salad, 47
spanish, 161; casserole, 520
table or Rijsttafel, 166
timbales, 203
wild, ring, 160
with spinach and chestnuts, 163
Rijsttafel or Rice Table, 166
Risotto or Italian Rice, 165
Roast, also see Beef, Lamb, etc.
vegetables for, 258
Robert Sauce, 367
Rockefeller, Oysters, 425
Roe, about, 416
canned, in ramekins, 237
ROLLS AND BUNS, cases for food, 208
egg, Chinese, 212
fillings, savory, 210, 240
meat-filled, 210–212
meat pie or Pinwheels, 211
toasted with crab meat, 247
Romaine, 30, 31
Romanian Noodle and Pork Casserole, 175

Roquefort, dressing, and anchovy, 343
   dressing, French, 343
   salad, cole slaw, 36
Rose Hips, for tisanes, 20
Rosemary, sauce, wine, 368
Rosettes, 209, 209
Rotisserie Cooking, 97, 97
Rouennaise Duckling, 587
Rouille Sauce, 347
Roulades, 502
Roux, about, 355
Russian, dressing, 349
   salad, 40
Rutabaga or Swedes, 300

Safflower Oil, 33
Sage, in tisanes, 20
SALAD, 29–71
   apple, 53
   artichoke hearts, 41; stuffed, 40
   asparagus; tip, 41; and egg, 41
   aspic, about, 57; basic, 58
   aspic, luncheon, 59; garnish, 59
   aspic, tomato or vegetable juice, 66
   avocado, 53; cups, 54; molded, 66
   banana and nut, 54
   bean, dried, 41
   bean, snap, hot and cold, 42
   bean sprout, Oriental, 36
   beef, 52
   beet cups, cold, 42
   beet, pickled, 42; gelatin, 64
   beetroot and chicory, 35
   Black-eyed Susan, 55
   bowls, wooden, 34
   Caesar, 35
   carrot with raisins and nuts, 42
   cases, to make, 39, 39
   celeriac or Celeri-rave Remoulade, 43
   celery cabbage, 42
   celery, cooked, 43
   celery root or celeriac, 43
   cherry and hazelnut, 54
   cherry, black, and almond aspic, 67
   chicken, 51; hot, 52
   chicken aspic, 60
   chicken, jellied mousse, 60
   chicory and beetroot, 35
   Christmas, 45
   clam juice ring, jellied, 61
   cole slaw, 36; deluxe, 36
   cole slaw, blender, 37
   cole slaw for barbecue, 37
   cole slaw, Roquefort, 36
   combination, 38
   corn or field, 30, 31
   corned beef, 52
   crab Louis, 50
   crab meat, 50
   cranberry, molded, 67; and apple, 67
   cucumber, 43, 43; wilted, 43
   cucumber gelatin on tomato, 64
   cucumber mousse, 65; sour cream, 65
   cucumber, stuffed, cold, 44
   defined, 29

   dressings for, 34; also see Salad Dressing
   egg, molded, and caviar, 49
   eggs in aspic, and Cockaigne, 63
   endive, cooked, 43
   field, 30, 31
   fish, 51; creamed, molded, 62
   fruit, 53–57; gelatin for, 66–71
   fruit, soufflé, 70
   fruits, stuffed, molded, 69
   fruit with cream, 24-hour, 70
   garnishes for, 38; cutting, 38, 39, 39
   gelatin, basic, 58; for fruit, 66
   gelatin, Golden Glow, 63
   gelatin, mint for fruit, 66
   ginger ale, 67
   Gingham with cottage cheese, 37
   grape; and cottage cheese, 55
   grape, aspic, and asparagus, 64
   grape and celery ring, 69
   grapefruit, 55; orange, 55
   grapefruit jelly with sherry, 68
   greens, cultivated, 30–32, 31;
     also see individual names
   greens, to dry, 33, 33
   greens, wild, 32
   greens, wilted, 35
   ham, 52; mousse, jellied, 60
   herring, Christmas, 50; and potato, 46
   in fish mold, 51
   Italian, 40
   lettuce rolls, stuffed, 49
   lobster, 50, 51; mold, 51
   lobster mousse, 62
   lotus root, 44
   macaroni, spaghetti or Calico, 50
   meat, 51, 52
   melon, 55; frosted, 70
   molded, 51, 57–71
   Mousseline of shellfish, 61
   mousses, 60, 61, 62
   Niçoise, 47
   oils, 33
   okra, 44
   onion, 55
   orange, 55; for game, 55
   palm, hearts of, 45
   papaya, frosted, 70
   peach, 53; fresh and cheese, 56
   pear, 53, 56; molded, 68
   pear and grape, 56
   pepper slices with fillings, 45
   persimmon, Japanese, 56
   pimientos, filled, 45
   pineapple, 56; ring, molded, 69
   potato, 45; and herring, 46
   potato, German, hot, 46
   potato, Niçoise, 46
   rice, 47
   rings, 51, 57–71
   Russian, 40
   seafood, jellied ring or mold, 61
   seafood mousse, 62
   shad roe, 51; jellied Madrilène ring, 61
   shrimp; mold, 51
   slaw, hot with apple, 37
   strawberry and rhubarb molds, 70
   to serve, 29

tomato, about, 47
tomato and cucumber or onion, 48, 49
tomato aspic, 65, 66
tomato, canned, 48
tomato, French, 47, 49
tomatoes, stuffed, and fillings, 48–49, 48
tossed, about, 32; for picnic, 33
tossed, additions to, 33–34; combinations, 38–39
tossed, dressings for, 34
tuna fish, 51
veal, 52; mousse, jellied, 60
veal stock, jellied, 59
vegetables for, about, 39
vegetable gelatin, molded, quick, 63
vegetable platter, cooked, 40
Waldorf, 53
Western, 35
SALAD DRESSING, 340–352; also see Sauces
about, 29, 33, 340
anchovy; and beet, 342
anchovy and Roquefort, blender, 343
avocado, 342
boiled, 350
celery seed, 352
Chantilly or cream, 348
chiffonade, 344
Chinese low calorie, 345
chutney, 344
cold, about, 340
commercial, about, 340
cream cheese for fruit, 352
curry for fruit, 352
diet, 340, 345
Dresden, 351
French or sauce Vinaigrette, 341
French fruit-salad, 341
French, Roquefort or Bleu cheese, 343
French with cream cheese, 342
garlic seasoning for, or Chapon, 33
half and half, 350
honey, 352
horseradish, 343
lemon and sherry for fruit, 352
Lorenzo, 342
low calorie, 345
mayonnaise, 345; for fruit, 348
mayonnaise, cream or Chantilly, 348
mayonnaise, curry, 348
oil, 341; without oil, 345
Roquefort or Bleu cheese, 343
Russian, 349
Salsa Verde, 342
sour cream for vegetable, 351
sweet-sour low calorie, 345
Thousand Island, 349; low calorie, 345
tossed, for, 33, 34
Vinaigrette, or sauce, 341
vinegars, for, 33
water cress, 343; blender, 343
yogurt, 351
Salmi, about, 592
Salmon, about, 414

cakes; with potatoes, 234
casserole, 235
glazed, cold, 415
in rice or noodle ring, 236
loaf with cheese sauce, 235
pot pie, 235
puffs, 234
scallop, tomato, 236
smoked with eggs, 186
steaks or Darnes, broiled, 414
Salpicon, 251
Salsa Verde, 342
Salsify or Oyster Plant, 304
SALT, as egg toughener, 187
in fat-free frying, 516
SANDWICH, 240–248
about, 240
bacon and cheese, 244
biscuits with fillings, 241
Braunschweiger, toasted, 244
cheese puffed, with mushrooms on toast, 245
cheese with mushroom sauce, 245
chicken, 246; and cream cheese, 246
chicken, hot, 246
club, 246
corned beef, 242
deviled ham and cheese, toasted, 244
dried beef and cheese, 242
egg and cheese with sauce, 244
fillings, finger roll, 241
French toast, cheese, 244; tomato, 245
French toast, ham and pineapple, 243
fruit sticks, 246
grilled or sautéed, 240
ham or tongue salad, 242
ham, tomato and egg, 243
Hawaiian toast with bacon, 243
lamb or chicken, 246
lobster, 247
meal-in-one, 241
open-faced seafood salad and tomato, 247
peanut butter and bacon, 245
peanut butter and tomato, 245
Poor Boy, Submarine or Hero, 244
roast beef, hot, 242
Savoyarde, 242
shrimp with cheese sauce, 248
toasted, 240
toasted rolls with crab meat and cheese, 247
toast rolls with ham and asparagus, 243
waffle or toasted, 241
Saratoga Chips, 319
Sardine, about, 415
Sassaties Sauce, 382
SAUCE, 340–391; also see Salad Dressings
à la King, quick, 375
Aïoli or garlic, 347
Allemande or thickened Velouté, 362
almond butter, 384

SAUCE (cont.)

almond or Amandine garnish, 390
anchovy butter, 384
anchovy, for fish, 361
Andalouse, 347
arrowroot thickener, 356
aspic glaze, 387
au gratin, 389
Aurore, 362
barbecue, 374–375
Béarnaise, 370
Béchamel, 359–360
Bercy, 373; butter, 384
black butter, or Beurre Noir, 383
blood thickener, 357
Bolognese, 379
Bordelaise, 366
bread, 364
brown or Sauce Espagnole, 365
brown butter or Beurre Noisette, 383
brown, quick, or gravy, 366
Burgundy or Bourguignonne, 372
butter, drawn or clarified, 383
butter for canned or boiled vegetables, 386
butter, kneaded or Beurre Manié, 357
butter, seasoned, 383–386
butter swirls, 357
butter, to serve, 383
caper, 363
caviar, 352; butter, 384
Chaud-Froid, 388
cheese, 364
Chinese for vegetables, 372
chutney, 344
cider or beer, and raisins, 373
cocktail, 344
Colbert butter, 384
cold, about, 340
color in, about, 353; from aluminum pans, 362; see Velouté
cornstarch thickener, 356
cranberry glaze for fowl, 387
cream, I, or Béchamel, 359
cream, II, or heavy Béchamel, 359
cream, III, or binding Béchamel, 359
cream, IV, or enriched Béchamel, 360
cream, egg, 360
cream, mix, 360
Creole, 380; quick, 376
crumbs, buttered, 389
cucumber, 351
Cumberland, 343; hot, 372
currant jelly, 372
curry: I, for fish; II, 363
deglazing, 358
demi-glaze, 365
Devil, Soyer's Universal, 374
deviled butter, for seafood, 385
Dresden, 351
egg and cheese gratin, 390

egg-thickened, about, 368
egg yolks as thickener, 356
Figaro, 370
Florentine, 360
flour, browned, thickener, 355
flour paste thickener, 356
for light meat game, 373
freezing, 354
garlic butter, 385
glazes and Glaçage, 386–388
gravy, chicken, pan, 359
gravy, pan, 358
gravy, quick, 366
green butter or Ravigote, 385
Green Goddess, 348
Gribiche, 348
Hollandaise, about, 368, 369; blender, 369
Hollandaise, mock, 370
Hollandaise, never-fail, 369
honey glaze for meat or onions, 387
horseradish or Albert, 362
horseradish dressing, cream and sour cream, 351
horseradish, frozen, 343
hunter's or Chausseur, 366
ingredients, about, 354
Italian meat, 378
Italian tomato paste, 377
kneaded butter or Beurre Manié, 357
lemon butter or Meunière, 384
lobster butter, 385
Louis, 350
Lyonnaise or brown onion, 366
Madeira, 366
Maître d'Hôtel butter, 384
Maltaise, 370
Marchand de Vin, 367
marinades, 380–383
Marinara, 379
mayonnaise, 345–347
mayonnaise Collée or gelatin, 387
mayonnaise, cream or Chantilly, 348
mayonnaise, curry, 348
mayonnaise, egg, hard-cooked, 348
mayonnaise, green, 348
mayonnaise, hot, 370
mayonnaise jelly or Grenache, 348
mayonnaise, souffléd for fish, 371
Mères, defined, 352
Meunière, 384
Mexican, 378
mint, 371
Mornay, 361
Mousseline, 370
mushroom, 367
mustard, hot, 363; cold, 344
mustard, sweet-sour, 371
Nantua, 361
Newburg, 361
octopus pasta, 380
onion, brown or Lyonnaise, 366
onion, white or Soubise, 363
orange for duck or goose, 365

overbeating, effects of, 353
oyster, for fish, 361
paprika or Hungarian, 362
pasta, 378, 379, 380
pasta, chicken liver topping, 391
pepper or Poivrade, 368
Périgueux, 367
piquant, 367
Polonaise or browned crumb, 386
potato starch or fecula thickener, 356
Poulette, 362
raisin cider or beer, 373
Ravigote, cold, 342; hot, 364
reduction, to thicken by, 357
Remoulade, 349
Robert, 367
rosemary wine, 368
Rouille, 347
Roux, thickeners for, 355
Roux, to keep, 355
Salsa Verde, 342
Sassaties or marinade, 382
shrimp and clam, quick, for pasta, 379
shrimp butter, 385
shrimp, for fish, 377
Skordalia, 347
Smitane, 364
smoked food, for, 347
snail butter, 384
Soubise or white onion, 363
soup, canned, quick, 375
soup, dried, 375
sour cream, for baked potatoes, 351
Soyer's Devil, 374
spaghetti, 378-380
spaghetti meat, 378
spaghetti seafood, 379
spaghetti, with liver, 378
stocks in, 354
Supreme, 363
sweet-sour bacon, 371
sweet-sour, Chinese, 371
sweet-sour cream dressing, 371
Tartare, 349
thickeners for, about, 355-358
to avoid thinning, 353, 355
to hold heated, 99
to serve attractively, 358
to store, 354
tomato paste or Velvet, 377
tomato, quick, 376; cheese, 376
tomato, thickened and unthickened, 376
tools, about, 340-341, 341
topping, elaborate or gratin, 390
types, about, 352
vegetable, blender, 344
Velouté or Blanche, 362
Verte, 348
Vinaigrette, 341
water cress, or au Cresson, 349
white, quick, 360
white butter, 385
wine, white for fish, 373
wine, white for light meats, 373
Sauerbraten, 497

Sauerkraut, 278
beef brisket with, 497
casserole, and tomato, 279
dressing for game, 566
juice, 24
meat balls, 520
onions stuffed with, 304
soup, 124
spareribs with, 512
SAUSAGE, 530-534
about, 530
baked, sweet potatoes and fruit, 532
baked with apples, 221
balls for soup, 151
blood or Boudin Noir, 533
boiled, 532
broiled, 532
casserole and lentils, 221
country, 531
dressing, 562, 565
in sauces, 221
liver, see Liver
mushrooms, and, 221
onions, and, 221
pan-broiled, 532
patties, broiled and sautéed, 532
Pigs in Potatoes, 221
ring, baked, 532
scrapple or Goetta, 533
stuffing, and sweet potato, 565
"summer," 531
Sautéing, 79
Savoyarde Sandwich, 242
Scalding, 83
Scallions, 302
Scallopini, veal, 479; with tomatoes, 479
Scallops, about, 431
bay, Fondu Bourguignonne, 432
creamed, and mushrooms, 432
deep-fat fried, 432
in wine, 432
Kebabs, 432
Meunière, 431
scalloped or Mornay, 433
veal, defined, 478
Schnitzel, 480
Scorzonera or Salsify, 304
Scotch, eggs, 194
herring, fried, 412
Woodcock, 192
Scrapple, 533
Scrod, 409
Sea Kale, 31
Sea Squab or Blowfish, 416
SEAFOOD, also see Fish and Shellfish
à la King, 229
butter, 385
casserole, quick, 229; in Creole sauce, 230
color and flavor, to add, 421
creamed, and vegetables, 230
creamed au gratin, 229
curry, 230
Divan, quick, 231
dressings and stuffings, 560-562
mousse, 62
mushrooms stuffed with, 297

SEAFOOD (*cont.*)
Newburg, 231
ring or mold, jellied, 61
salads, 50–51, 61–63
sandwiches, 247, 248
sauces, *see* Sauces
spaghetti sauce, 379
Tetrazzini, 170
tureen, quick, 143
Searing, 454, grilling, 96
Seasonings, *also see* individual
names
soup, about, 107
Seed, breadfruit, 272
Shad, baked with creamed roe, 417
carving, 417
Shad Roe, baked, 416; broiled, 417;
par-boiled, 416; sautéed, 416
canned: broiled, 236; creamed,
236
salads, 51; jellied, 61
soufflé, 201
Shark, 417
SHELLFISH, 421–448; *also see*
individual names
abalone, sautéed, 433
color and flavor, to add, 421
bisques, to prepare for, 132
clams, 427–431
cocktails, 421
crabs, 433–436
crayfish, crawfish or Écrevisses,
444
crustaceans, about, 421
lobsters, 436–441
macaroni and, 421
mollusks, about, 421
Mousseline of, 61
mussels, 426–427
oysters, 422–426
scallops, 431–433
shrimps, 441–445
snails, 445–446
Sherry, dressing for fruit salad, 352
Shoestring Potatoes, 318
Shortcake, meat, 211
onion, 215
Shortening, for frying, 78
Shrimp, about, 441
bisque, 133
butter, 385
butterfly, 442
casserole with snail butter, 442
deep-fat fried, 443; stuffed, 443
eggs Foo Yoong, 190
fried in batter, 443
Gumbo, 135
mold, 51
New Orleans, 444
Newburg, 444
poached, 442
potted, 442
sandwich with cheese sauce, 248
sauce for fish, 377
sauce for pasta, 379
Tempura, 443
Teriyaki, 442
to prepare, 441, 441
tomatoes stuffed with, 337
with cheese and sauce, 230
Shrubs, Fruit, or vinegars, 25

Sicilian Spinach, 326
Simmering, 83
Skewer Cooking, about, 74, 75; *also
see* Kebabs and Outdoor symbol ▤
Skirret, 325
Skordalia Sauce, 347
Slaw, 36–37
Sloppy Joes, 517
Smelts, 417
Smitane Sauce, 364
Smoke Cookery, 92–93
can for smoking, 92, 92, 93
Chinese oven, 93
Snails, about, 445–446, 445
butter, 384
canned, 445
mushrooms stuffed with, 298
Snipe, 598, 599
Sole, Ambassador, 418; Florentine,
418
Sorrel, about, 325; for salad, 32
soup, cream of, 130
Soubise, *also see* Veal Scallop, 480
sauce, 363
SOUFFLÉ, 196–201; *also see*
Timbales
about, 196
cheese, additions to, 198
cheese Cockaigne, 198; blender,
198
cheese, made-in-advance, 197
chicken, 200; leftover, 200
corn, 199
eggplant, 199
fish, cooked, 200
meat, 200
onion, 201
oven placement of, 99, 100
oyster, 201
shad roe, 201
sweet potato and pineapple or
applesauce, 199
to make a crown, 197
to prepare baking dish, 197
vegetable, 198
SOUP, 106–152; (*also see* Stock)
asparagus, cream of, 126; quick,
139
avocado, cream of, chilled, 140
barley, 115
bean, black, 119
bean, dried; U.S. Senate, 119
bean with vegetables, 119
beef Gumbo, 118
beef tea, 111
beet consommé, jellied, 114
beet or Borsch, 117; blender,
140
bisque, 133–134; defined, 107
Bouillabaisse, 135
bouillon, 110, 111; jellied, 114
Boula-Boula, 122
breads to serve with, 145, 151–
152
broth, chicken, 110; and clam,
143
broth, clam, 132
broth, Coquina, 132
broth, mushroom, 112
broth on the rocks, 114
broth, vegetable, 112

cabbage, 117
canned for quick sauces, 375
cauliflower, cream of, 126; quick, 141
celery, cream of, 126
cheese, quick, 141
cheese balls for, 151
chestnut, 127
chicken, cream of, 127; quick, 140
chicken curry or Senegalese, 117
chicken Gumbo, 118
chiffonade of herbs for, 151
Choux paste, garnish for, 148
chowder, clam, Manhattan, 137
chowder, clam, New England, 137
chowder, conch, 137
chowder, corn, 127
chowder, lobster, quick, 143
chowder, tomato corn, quick, 141
chowder, vegetable, 116
clear, about, 109; jellied, 113
Cock-a-leekie, 123
cold, to prepare quickly, 107
coloring, about, 107
consommé, 109; canned variations, 139
consommé Brunoise, 109; Tropical, 139
consommé Madrilène, 110
corn, cream of, 127
crab Mongole, quick, 143
crackers, fancy, for, 151–152
crawfish bisque, 133
cream, about, 125; defined, 106
croutons for, 151, 390
cucumber, Bulgarian, cold, 128
cucumber Cockaigne, quick, 140
cucumber, cold, quick, 141
cucumber, cream of, herb, chilled, 128
custard or Royale, 146
dried, for sauces, 375
dumplings, about, 146, 147
dumplings, butter, 149
dumplings, liver, or Leber-kloesse, 148
dumplings, liver sausage, 150
dumplings, Matzo or cracker meal, 147
egg drops, hard-cooked, 145, 146
egg garnishes for, 145
farina balls, Cockaigne for, 147
fish, about, 132
fisherman's stews, about, 135
fritter garnish for, 148
fruit, 114
Garbure, 119
garnishes for, 144–152
Gazpacho, 113; blender, 139
green kern, 116
Gumbos, 118, 135
high altitude, 107
jellied, clear, 113
Kreplach, 111
leek potato, 130
legume, about, 118; to bind, 119
lentil, 120; or split pea, 120, 121

lettuce, cream of, 131
lobster bisque, 133; Mongole, 143
lobster stew, 135
lobster Supreme, quick, 143
marrow balls for, 150
Matelote, 136
meat, about, 109
meat balls for, 150
meat pastries for, 149
milk toast, 131
Minestrone, 120
Mulligatawny, 122
mushroom broth, 112
mushroom, cream of, 128; quick, 141
mushroom and clam bisque, 134
mussel stew, 135
nettle, cream of, 129
New Year's, 125
Nockerln for, 147
noodle dough, white or green, 149, 150
onion, 113; quick, 141
onion, cream of, or Velouté, 129
oxtail, 122; quick, 142
oyster stews and bisques, 134
Panades, 123
Paysanne, 116
pea, quick, 140
pea, green or Potage St. Germain, 121
pea, split, 120, 121
Pepper Pot, 123
Petite Marmite, 123
potato, 129; with tomatoes, 129
Pot-au-Feu or Poule-au-Pot, 110
pumpkin, 130
purslane, 131
Quenelles for, 150
quick, about, 138
sauerkraut, 124
sausage balls for, 151
Scotch broth, 116
seafood tureen, 143
seasoning, 107
Senegalese, 117
shrimp bisque, 134
shrimp Gumbo, 135
sorrel, cream of, 130
Spatzen for, 150
spinach, 124; quick, 142
spinach, cream of, 131
split pea, 120; au Maigre, 121
split pea, blender, 121
thick, about, 115
thickenings for, 108
to reheat, 99
to remove grease from, 109, 109
to serve, 107
tomato, cold or Gazpacho, 113
tomato cream, chilled, quick, 143
tomato, cream of, 131
tomato, quick, 142
turkey, 110
turtle, green, 124; mock, 125
types, 106
vegetable, 116; quick, 139
vegetable, blender, 117

SOUP (cont.)
  vegetable, cream of, blender, 139
  Vichyssoise, 130
  water cress, clear, 113; cream of, 131
  wine in, 107
  Won Ton, 112
Sour Cream, beets boiled in, 271
  dressings, 351; horseradish, 351
  sauce for baked pottaoes, 351
Sous Cloche, see Guinea Hen, 590
Soybean, green, 265
Soyer's Devil Sauce, 374
Spaetzle or German Egg Dumplings, 179
Spaghetti, about, 167; to cook, 167, 167
  boiled, 168; and baked, 168
  Italian with sauce, 168
  meat pie, quick, 169
  salad, or Calico, 50
  sauces, 378–380
  Tetrazzini, 170
  topping for, chicken liver, 391
  with egg and cheese, 168
  with soup and bacon, quick, 169
  with tuna, salmon or beef, quick, 169
Spanish, casserole wtih rice, 520
  chicken, 581
  rice, 160
  tripe, 549
Spareribs, 512–514; see Pork
  grilled, 97
Spatzen, 179; for soup, 150
Spice, see individual names
Spinach, about, 325
  boiled, 325; blender, 327
  creamed, 326
  ground, 327
  loaf, tomato and cheese, 326
  panned or Sicilian, 326
  pancakes, in, 327
  ring mold, 205
  salads, for, 32
  soup, 124; cream of, 131; quick, 142
  timbales, 202
  tomatoes, and, 326
  veal dish, 217
  with rice and chestnuts, 163
Spit Cooking, 138, 138
Squab, broiled, 590; potted, 590; roasted, 589
Squash, about, 327
  blossoms, stuffed, 329
  summer, about, 327, 328
  summer, baked, 329
  summer, casserole Cockaigne, 330
  summer, Creole, 330
  summer, sautéed, 329
  summer, steamed, 328
  summer, stuffed, 329; raw, 330
  winter, about, 328, 328
  winter, baked, 331; mashed, 331
  winter, stuffed, 331
Squid, 412

Squirrel, about, 453; to skin, 556, 556
Stainless Steel Utensils, 101
Steak, see Beef, Salmon, Venison, etc.
Steaming, 88
  fish, 398
  vegetable, 252; blanching, 88
STEWS, MEAT, also see Fish and Shellfish
  about, 493
  beef, Belgian, or Carbonnade Flamande, 501
  beef Gaston, 496
  beef, with wine or Boeuf Bourguignonne, 496
  Brunswick, 582
  Burgoo, 503
  Cassoulet, 509
  chicken, 577–582
  corned beef and cabbage, 493
  Couscous, 510
  fisherman's, about, 135
  Goulash, beef, 500
  Goulash, lamb or pork à Blanc, 501
  Irish, 509
  kidney, 544
  lamb or Navarin Printanier, 508
  lamb shanks or trotters, braised, 508
  oxtail, 501
  pigs' feet, 551
  pork hocks, 514
  pork neck bones, 514
  rabbit fricassee, 555
  Rombauer rice dish, 163
  turkey, 577
  veal, 503
  veal, or Blanquette de Veau, 504
  veal, with red wine, 503
STOCK, also see Soup
  homemade, about, 106
  veal, jellied, for salads, 59
Stove, camp, gas or gasoline, 93; wood, 92, 92, 93
  household, 74, 99–101
  oven rack placement, 99, 100
  solar heat, 93
Strawberry, punch, fruit, 28
  salad molds, and rhubarb, 70
Stroganoff, Beef, 476
Strudel, savory, 276
Stuffings, 560–565; see Dressings
Succotash, 286
Sukiyaki, 477
Supper Dish Suggestions, 208–248
Supreme Sauce, 363
Swedes or Rutabagas, 325
Swedish, meatballs, 519
Sweet Potatoes, 322–324; see Potatoes
Sweetbreads, about, 537
  braised, 538; glazed, 539
  broiled, 538
  creamed, tomatoes stuffed with, 337
  in patty shells, and chicken, 228
  on skewers, 540
  poached, sauced, 537

Ragoût Fin, 539
sautéed, 538
Sweet-Sour, dressing, 345; sauces, 371
Swiss Chard, 283
Swiss Steak, 499; about, 473
Swordfish Steaks, 419
Symbols, *see* Foreword

Tamale, 86, 86, 287; pie, 212
Tangerine Rice Dressing, 565
Taro, 289
Tarragon, chicken with wine, 580
Tart, tomato, 335; quick, 216
Tartare, sauce, 349
TEA, 18-20
about, 18
beef, 111
flavoring for, 20
iced, 20
spiced, 19
Tempura, shrimp, 443; vegetables, 258
Tenderloin, *see* Beef, Pork
Teriyaki, Shrimp, 442
Terrapin, about, 447
lamb, 218
Terrines, 528
Tetrazzini, chicken; turkey; seafood, 170
Thermidor, Lobster, 440
Thermometer, deep-fat, 76
meat, 458
Thickenings, for sauces, 355-358; soups, 108
Thousand Island Dressing, 349
low calorie, 345
Thrush, 598
Thyme, for tisanes, 20
TIMBALE, 201-207
about, 196, 201
asparagus, 203
broccoli or cauliflower, 202
cases for food, 209; irons, 209
celery root ring mold, 205
cheese, or crustless Quiche, 203
chestnut ring mold, 205
chicken or ham, 203
corn, egg and cheese, 202
custard for vegetable, 201
fish, or mousse, 204
halibut ring mold, 206
leftover, 202
mushroom, 202; ring mold, 206
rice, 203
ring molds, 205-207
spinach, 202; or broccoli ring mold, 205
veal, 204; mold, steamed, 206
Tinware, 101
Tisanes and Infusions, 20
Toast, French, tomato, 245; or cheese, 244
Hawaiian, with bacon, 243
Melba, baskets, 209
milk, 131
sandwiches, 240
TOMATO, 331-338
aspics, 65, 66
baked, 333; grilled, 333
bouillon, 111; jellied, 114

broiled breaded, 334
candied, 334
casserole, olive, 334; sauerkraut, 279
cheese dish, cabbage and, 277
creamed, canned, 333
Creole, 334
custard, 335
ice, *see* Avocado Cup, 54
juice, canned, 23
juice, fresh, 23; combination, 24
kidney beans and, 267
loaf, cheese and spinach, 326
pastes, 377
Provençale, 333
pudding Cockaigne, 335
punch, gala, 26
Rarebit or Woodchuck, 237
salads, 47, 48, 48, 49, 49, 64, 65, 66
sandwiches, 240-248
sauce, cheese, quick, 376
sauce, quick, 376
sauce, thickened, 376; unthickened, 376
sautéed, seasoned, 332
scallop, salmon, 236
soup, corn chowder, quick, 141
soup, cream of, 131; chilled, quick, 143
soup, quick, 142; cold, 113
spinach and, 326
stewed 332; green, 332
stuffed, cold; fillings for, 48, 48, 49
stuffed, hot, 335-338
tart, 335; quick, 216
to cut for salad, 34, 47, 48, 48, 49
to peel, 48
to press moisture from, 332
Tongue, about, 544
baked, in Creole sauce, 546
beef, fresh, boiled, 545; raisin sauce, 545
corned or pickled, boiled, 545
in aspic, 546
salad sandwich, 242
smoked, boiled, 546
Topepo, *see* About Tomatoes, 47
TOPPINGS, *also see* Garnishes
Tournedos, 472, 472, 473
Tripe, about, 548
à la Mode de Caen, 548
cooked, 548; fried, 549
Spanish, 549
Trotters or Lamb Shanks, 508
Trout, blue or Truite au Bleu, 419
brook, Meunière, 419
lake, broiled or whitefish, 419
Truffles, about, 299; freezing, 300
Tuna Fish, balls, 233
casseroles, 175, 229
fresh or Bonito, 420
loaf and potato chips, 232
pies, individual, 232
salad, 51
Turbot, poached, 420
TURKEY, à la Campagne, 586
baked in foil, 575

TURKEY (*cont.*)
broiled, 576
broth, 110
casseroles, 227, 586
Divan, 228
dressings, 560–566
Galantine of, 529
hash, 226; loaf, cooked, 227
roasting, about, 572; stuffed, 575
stew or fricassee, 577
Tetrazzini, 170
to carve, 574, **574**
wild, 597
Turnips, about, 338
cooked, 338; glazed, 338
cups, stuffed, 339
to pare, 338, **338**
scalloped, 338
Turnovers, 210
Turtle, about, 447; soup, 124

Utensils, 101–103

Variety Meats, 534–553; about, 534
VEAL, 478–481, 503–506
about, 478
baked in sour cream, cubed, 506
Birds or Paupiettes, 505
Blanquette of, 504
chart of cuts, 466–467
City Chicken, 505
creamed, 226
curried, and rice, 217
cutlets, about, 479; Scallopini, 479
cutlet, breaded, 480
cutlet or Schnitzel, paprika, 480
Goulash, 500; and pork, 501
kidneys, baked, 444, 542; casserole, 543
leftover, creamed, 217
loaf, 524; cooked, 227
mold, steamed, or timbale, 206
mousse, jellied, 60
Osso Buco, 506
Papillote, 480
Parmigiana, 480
patties, 518
pie, and pork, 504
pot roast, 505
roast: kidney, loin, rolled, 478
roast, stuffed or Farci, 478, **478**
salad, 52
scallop or Escalope de Veau Orloff, 480
scallops with ham, 481
Scallopini; with tomatoes, 479
spinach dish, and, 217
steak, Mexican with noodles, 506
stew; elaborate, 504; with wine, 503
stock, jellied for salad, 59
Terrine, 529
timbales, 204
to blanch, 478
Wiener Schnitzel, 480; Holstein, 481
VEGETABLE, 249–339; *also see* individual names
à la Grecque, about, 257

altitude cooking, about, 254
baked, unpeeled, about, 258
braised or panned, about, 252
broth, 112
campfire, about, 254
cases, to cut, 39, 39
casserole, eggs and, 193
Chinese style, 254
chowder, 116
cleaning and preparing, 250
color retention, 251
creamed, and seafood, 230
creamed, buttered and sauced, about, 255
deep-fat fried, about, 258
Fondues, about, 256
for a roast, 258
Fritto Misto, 258
frozen, cooking, about, 254
garnishes, to cut, 83, 39, 39
glazed root, about, 258
grill, mixed, 216
juices, 23, 24; aspic, 65
marinades, 380
nutritional values, to keep, 249–251
panning, 252
podded, braised, 253
potatoes stuffed with, 313
pressure cooked, 254
pressure steaming, 252
puréed, blended, about, 254
reheated, 98, 255
salads, for, 39; gelatin, 63
sauce for canned, 386; *also see* Sauces
slicing and chopping, 250, **251**
soufflé, 198
soup, 116; blender, 117
soup, cream of, blender, 139
soup, quick, about, 138
steamed, about, 252, **253**
stir-fried, 253
stuffed, about, 256
Tempura, about, 258
timbales, custard for, 201
to glaze, 386
to store, 249
waters or pot liquors, 252
when to salt, 249
with hash, 224
Velouté, onion, or soup, 129
sauces, 362
Venison, about, to clean and hang, 558
braised, 559
hamburger, 559
marinades, 381
meat loaf, 559
roast: leg of, 558; saddle of, **558**
steaks, 559
Verte Sauce, 348
Vichyssoise, 130
Vinaigrette Sauce, 341
Vinegar, fruit shrubs, 25
Vitamins, fat soluble, 3, 4
water soluble, 4

Waldorf Salad, 53
Water, daily intake, 4
Water Chestnuts, 339

Water Cress, about, 31, 31, 339
    dressings, 343; sauce, 349
    soup, 113; cream of, 131
Welsh Rarebit, 237
Western Salad, 35
Whale, 420
White Sauces, 359, 360
Whitefish, 419
Wiener, barbecue or roast, 220
    Schnitzel, 480
Wild Birds or Fowl, *see* Game Birds
Wild Rice, 160; dressing, 564
Wines, in soup, 107
    sauce, Marchand de Vin, 367
Winter Cress, 32

Wintergreen for Tisanes, 20
Witloof Endive, 31
Won Ton, dough for, 149; soup, 112
Wood Pigeon, 599
Woodchuck, 557
Woodchuck or tomato Rarebit, 237
Woodcock, 599
Wrap Cookery, 85–87, 86

Yam, 322–324; *see* Potatoes, Sweet
Yogurt, dressing, 351
Yorkshire Pudding, 182

Zucchini, deep-fat fried, 328, 330
    see Squash, Summer, 327–330